Mastering Object-oriented Python

Grasp the intricacies of object-oriented programming in Python in order to efficiently build powerful real-world applications

Steven F. Lott

BIRMINGHAM - MUMBAI

Mastering Object-oriented Python

First published: April 2014

Production Reference: 1150414

Published by Packt Publishing Ltd.
Livery Place
35 Livery Street
Birmingham B3 2PB, UK

ISBN 978-1-78328-097-1

`www.packtpub.com`

Cover Image by Duraid Fatouhi (`duraidfatouhi@yahoo.com`)

Credits

Author
Steven F. Lott

Reviewers
Mike Driscoll
Róman Joost
Sakis Kasampalis
Albert Lukaszewski, Ph.D
Hugo Solis

Commissioning Editor
Usha Iyer

Acquisition Editor
Gregory Wild

Content Development Editor
Shaon Basu

Technical Editors
Kapil Hemnani
Monica John
Akashdeep Kundu

Copy Editors
Insiya Morbiwala
Kirti Pai
Stuti Srivastava

Project Coordinator
Akash Poojary

Proofreaders
Stephen Copestake
Clyde Jenkins
Linda Morris
Jonathan Todd

Indexer
Mariammal Chettiyar

Graphics
Abhinash Sahu

Production Coordinator
Alwin Roy

Cover Work
Alwin Roy

About the Author

Steven F. Lott has been programming since the 70s, when computers were large, expensive, and rare. As a contract software developer and architect, he has worked on hundreds of projects from very small to very large. He's been using Python to solve business problems for over 10 years.

Steven is currently a technomad who lives in various places on the east coast of the US. His technology blog is: `http://slott-softwarearchitect.blogspot.com`

I owe deep gratitude to Floating Leaf for all her support and guidance.

About the Reviewers

Mike Driscoll has been programming in Python since 2006. He enjoys writing about Python on his blog at `http://www.blog.pythonlibrary.org/`. He has co-authored *Core Python refcard* for *DZone*. Mike has also been a technical reviewer for various books of Packt Publishing, such as *Python 3 Object Oriented Programming, Python 2.6 Graphics Cookbook*, and *Tkinter GUI Application Development Hotshot*. Mike recently wrote the book *Python 101*.

I would like to thank my beautiful wife, Evangeline, for always supporting me. I would also like to thank my friends and family for all that they do to help me. I would also like to thank Jesus Christ for saving me.

Róman Joost first learned about open source software in 1997. He is the project manager of GIMP's user documentation. He has contributed to GIMP and Python/Zope open source projects for eight years. Róman works for Red Hat in Brisbane, Australia.

Sakis Kasampalis is based in the Netherlands, where he currently works as a Software Engineer for a location-based B2B provider. He is not dogmatic about particular programming languages and tools; his principle is that the right tool should be used for the right job. One of his favorite tools is Python because he finds it very productive.

Among the FOSS activities of Kasampalis is maintaining a GitHub repository that is related to implementing design patterns in Python, which are available at `https://github.com/faif/python-patterns`. He was also a technical reviewer of the book *Learning Python Design Patterns, Packt Publishing*.

Albert Lukaszewski, Ph.D, is principal consultant for Lukaszewski Consulting Services in southeast Scotland. Having programmed computers for over 30 years, he consults on the system design and implementation. Previously, he served as Chief Engineer for ACCESS Europe GmbH. Much of his experience is related to text processing, database systems, and **Natural Language Processing (NLP)**. In addition to *MySQL for Python, Packt Publishing,* he previously wrote a column on Python for the New York Times subsidiary, `About.com`.

Hugo Solis is an assistant professor in the Physics department at the University of Costa Rica. His current research interests are computational cosmology, complexity, and the influence of hydrogen on material properties. He has wide experience with languages including C/C++ and Python for scientific programming and visualization. He is a member of the Free Software Foundation and has contributed code to some free software projects. Currently, he is in charge of the IFT, a Costa Rican scientific, non-profit organization for the multidisciplinary practice of physics (`http://iftucr.org`).

I'd like to thank Katty Sanchez, my beloved mother, for her support and vanguard thoughts.

www.PacktPub.com

Support files, eBooks, discount offers and more

You might want to visit www.PacktPub.com for support files and downloads related to your book.

Did you know that Packt offers eBook versions of every book published, with PDF and ePub files available? You can upgrade to the eBook version at www.PacktPub.com and as a print book customer, you are entitled to a discount on the eBook copy. Get in touch with us at service@packtpub.com for more details.

At www.PacktPub.com, you can also read a collection of free technical articles, sign up for a range of free newsletters and receive exclusive discounts and offers on Packt books and eBooks.

http://PacktLib.PacktPub.com

Do you need instant solutions to your IT questions? PacktLib is Packt's online digital book library. Here, you can access, read and search across Packt's entire library of books.

Why Subscribe?

- Fully searchable across every book published by Packt
- Copy and paste, print and bookmark content
- On demand and accessible via web browser

Free Access for Packt account holders

If you have an account with Packt at www.PacktPub.com, you can use this to access PacktLib today and view nine entirely free books. Simply use your login credentials for immediate access.

Table of Contents

Part 2: Persistence and Serialization

Preface

This book will introduce you to more advanced features of the Python programming language. The focus is on creating the highest quality Python programs possible. This often means creating programs that have the highest performance or are the most maintainable. This means exploring design alternatives and determining which design offers the best performance while still being a good fit with the problem that is being solved.

Most of the book will look at a number of alternatives for a given design. Some will have better performance. Some will seem simpler or be a better solution for the problem domain. It's essential to locate the best algorithms and optimal data structures to create the most value with the least computer processing. Time is money, and programs that save time will create more value for their users.

Python makes a number of internal features directly available to our application programs. This means that our programs can be very tightly integrated with existing Python features. We can leverage numerous Python features by ensuring that our OO designs integrate well.

We'll often focus on a specific problem and examine several variant solutions to the problem. As we look at different algorithms and data structures, we'll see different memory and performance alternatives. It's an important OO design skill to work through alternate solutions in order to properly optimize the final application.

One of the more important themes of this book is that there's no single *best* approach to any problem. There are a number of alternative approaches with different attributes.

On programming *style*, the subject of style generates a surprising amount of interest. The astute reader will note that the examples do not meticulously conform to PEP-8 in every single particular detail of the name choice or punctuation.

As we move towards achieving mastery over object-oriented Python, we'll spend a great deal of time reading Python code from a variety of sources. We'll observe wide variability even within the Python Standard Library modules. Rather than presenting examples that are all perfectly consistent, we've opted for some inconsistency, the lack of consistency will better confirm with code as seen in the various open source projects encountered in the wild.

What this book covers

We'll cover three advanced Python topics in a series of chapters that dig into the details.

- *Some Preliminaries*, covers some preliminary topics, such as unittest, doctest, docstrings, and some special method names.

Part 1, Pythonic Classes via Special Methods: This part looks more deeply at object-oriented programming techniques and how we can more tightly integrate the class definitions of our applications with Python's built-in features. It consists of nine chapters, which are as follows:

- *Chapter 1, The _init_() Method*, provides us with a detailed description and implementation of the `_init_()` method. We will look at different forms of initialization for simple objects. From this, we can look into more complex objects that involve collections and containers.
- *Chapter 2, Integrating Seamlessly with Python – Basic Special Methods*, will explain in detail as to how we can expand a simple class definition to add special methods. We'll need to take a look at the default behavior inherited from the object so that we can understand what overrides are needed and when they're actually needed.
- *Chapter 3, Attribute Access, Properties, and Descriptors*, shows us how the default processing works in some detail. We need to decide where and when to override the default behavior. We will also explore descriptors and gain a much deeper understanding on how Python's internals work.
- *Chapter 4, The ABCs of Consistent Design*, looks at the abstract base classes in the `collections.abc` module in general. We'll look at the general concepts behind the various containers and collections that we might want to revise or extend. Similarly, we'll look at the concepts behind the numbers that we might want to implement.

- *Chapter 5, Using Callables and Contexts*, looks at several ways to create context managers using the tools in `contextlib`. We'll show you a number of variant designs for callable objects. This will show you why a stateful callable object is sometimes more useful than a simple function. We'll also take a look at how to use some of the existing Python context managers before we dive in and write our own context manager.
- *Chapter 6, Creating Containers and Collections*, focuses on the basics of container classes. We'll review the variety of special methods that are involved in being a container and offering the various features that containers offer. We'll address extending built-in containers to add features. We'll also look at wrapping built-in containers and delegating methods through the wrapper to the underlying container.
- *Chapter 7, Creating Numbers*, covers these essential arithmetic operators: `+`, `-`, `*`, `/`, `//`, `%`, and `**`. We'll also take a look at these comparison operators: `<`, `>`, `<=`, `>=`, `==`, and `!=`. We'll finish by summarizing some of the design considerations that go into extending or creating new numbers.
- *Chapter 8, Decorators and Mixins – Cross-cutting Aspects*, covers simple function decorators, function decorators with arguments, class decorators, and method decorators.

Part 2, Persistence and Serialization: A persistent object has been serialized to a storage medium. Perhaps it's transformed to JSON and written to the filesystem. An ORM layer can store the object in a database. This part will take a look at the alternatives to handle persistence. This section contains five chapters, which are as follows:

- *Chapter 9, Serializing and Saving – JSON, YAML, Pickle, CSV, and XML*, covers simple persistence using libraries focused on various data representations such as JSON, YAML, pickle, XML, and CSV.
- *Chapter 10, Storing and Retrieving Objects via Shelve*, explains basic database operations with Python modules, such as `shelve` (and `dbm`).
- *Chapter 11, Storing and Retrieving Objects via SQLite*, moves to the more complex world of SQL and the relational database. Because SQL features don't match object-oriented programming features well, we have an **impedance mismatch** problem. A common solution is to use ORM to allow us to persist a large domain of objects.
- *Chapter 12, Transmitting and Sharing Objects*, takes a look at the HTTP protocol, JSON, YAML, and XML representation to transmit an object.
- *Chapter 13, Configuration Files and Persistence*, covers various ways in which a Python application can work with a configuration file.

Part 3, Testing, Debugging, Deploying, and Maintaining: We'll show you how to gather data to support and debug high-performance programs. This will include information on creating the best possible documentation in order to reduce the confusion and complexity of the support. This section contains the final five chapters, which are as follows:

- *Chapter 14, The Logging and Warning Modules*, takes a look at using the `logging` and `warning` modules to create audit information, as well as debug. We'll take a significant step beyond using the `print()` function.
- *Chapter 15, Designing for Testability*, covers designing for testability and how we use `unittest` and `doctest`.
- *Chapter 16, Coping with the Command Line*, takes a look at using the `argparse` module to parse options and arguments. We'll take this a step further and use the command design pattern to create program components that can be combined and expanded without resorting to writing shell scripts.
- *Chapter 17, The Module and Package Design*, covers module and package design. This is a higher-level set of considerations. We will take a look at related classes in a module and related modules in a package.
- *Chapter 18, Quality and Documentation*, covers how we can document our design to create trust that our software is correct and has been properly implemented.

What you need for this book

In order to compile and run the examples mentioned in this book, you require the following software:

- Python Version 3.2 or higher with the standard suite of libraries. We'll focus on Python 3.3, but the differences from 3.2 are minor.
- We'll take a look at some additional packages. These include PyYaml, SQLAlchemy, and Jinja2.
    - `http://pyyaml.org`
    - `http://www.sqlalchemy.org`. When building this, check the installation guide, `http://docs.sqlalchemy.org/en/rel_0_9/intro.html#installation`. Using the `--without-cextensions` option can simplify installation.
    - `http://jinja.pocoo.org/`

- Optionally, you might want to add Sphinx or Docutils to your environment, as we'll cover them as well.
    - `http://sphinx-doc.org`
    - `http://docutils.sourceforge.net`

Who this book is for

This is advanced Python. You'll need to be quite familiar with Python 3. You'll also benefit from having fairly large or complex problems to solve.

If you are a skilled programmer with the other languages, you may find this book helpful if you want to switch to Python. This book doesn't introduce syntax or other foundational concepts.

Advanced Python 2 programmers may find this helpful when they switch to Python 3. We won't cover any of the conversion utilities (such as from Version 2 to 3) or any of the coexistence libraries (such as six.) This book is focused on new development that has happened entirely in Python 3.

Conventions

In this book, you will find a number of styles of text that distinguish between different kinds of information. Here are some examples of these styles, and an explanation of their meaning.

Code words in text are shown as follows: "We can access other Python modules through the use of the `import` statement."

A block of code is set as follows:

```
class Friend(Contact):
    def __init__(self, name, email, phone):
        self.name = name
        self.email = email
        self.phone = phone
```

When we wish to draw your attention to a particular part of a code block, the relevant lines or items are set in bold:

```
class Friend(Contact):
    def __init__(self, name, email, phone):
        self.name = name
        self.email = email
        self.phone = phone
```

Any command-line input or output is written as follows:

```
>>> e = EmailableContact("John Smith", "jsmith@example.net")
>>> Contact.all_contacts
```

New terms and **important words** are shown in bold. Words that you see on the screen, in menus or dialog boxes for example, appear in the text like this: "We use this feature to update the label to a new random value every time we click on the **Roll!** button".

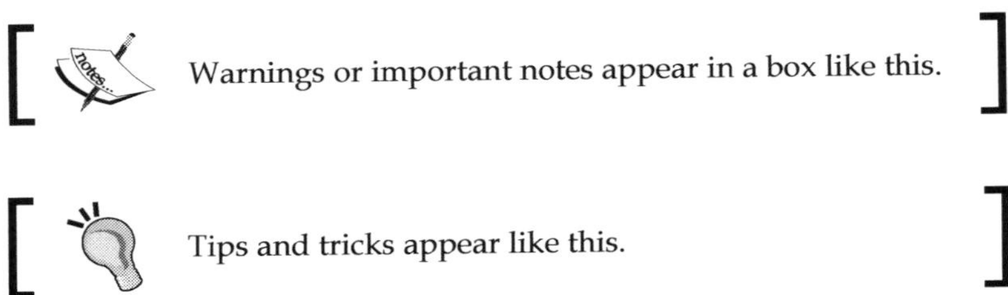

Warnings or important notes appear in a box like this.

Tips and tricks appear like this.

Reader feedback

Feedback from our readers is always welcome. Let us know what you think about this book—what you liked or may have disliked. Reader feedback is important for us to develop titles that you really get the most out of.

To send us general feedback, simply send an e-mail to `feedback@packtpub.com`, and mention the book title via the subject of your message.

If there is a book that you need and would like to see us publish, please send us a note in the **SUGGEST A TITLE** form on `www.packtpub.com` or e-mail `suggest@packtpub.com`.

If there is a topic that you have expertise in and you are interested in either writing or contributing to a book, see our author guide on `www.packtpub.com/authors`.

Customer support

Now that you are the proud owner of a Packt book, we have a number of things to help you get the most from your purchase.

Downloading the example code for this book

You can download the example code files for all Packt books you have purchased from your account at `http://www.PacktPub.com`. If you purchased this book elsewhere, you can visit `http://www.PacktPub. com/support` and register to have the files e-mailed directly to you.

Errata

Although we have taken every care to ensure the accuracy of our content, mistakes do happen. If you find a mistake in one of our books—maybe a mistake in the text or the code—we would be grateful if you would report this to us. By doing so, you can save other readers from frustration and help us improve subsequent versions of this book. If you find any errata, please report them by visiting `http://www.packtpub.com/support`, selecting your book, clicking on the let us know link, and entering the details of your errata. Once your errata are verified, your submission will be accepted and the errata will be uploaded on our website, or added to any list of existing errata, under the Errata section of that title. Any existing errata can be viewed by selecting your title from `http://www.packtpub.com/support`.

Piracy

Piracy of copyright material on the Internet is an ongoing problem across all media. At Packt, we take the protection of our copyright and licenses very seriously. If you come across any illegal copies of our works, in any form, on the Internet, please provide us with the location address or website name immediately so that we can pursue a remedy.

Please contact us at `copyright@packtpub.com` with a link to the suspected pirated material.

We appreciate your help in protecting our authors, and our ability to bring you valuable content.

Questions

You can contact us at `questions@packtpub.com` if you are having a problem with any aspect of the book, and we will do our best to address it.

Some Preliminaries

To make the design issues in the rest of the book clearer, we need to look at some of our motivational problems. One of these is the game of Blackjack. Specifically, we're interested in simulating strategies for playing Blackjack. We don't want to endorse gambling. Indeed, a bit of study will show that the game is stacked heavily against the player. This should reveal that most casino gambling is little more than a tax on the innumerate.

Simulation, however, was one of the early problem domains for object-oriented programming. This is an area where object-oriented programming works out particularly elegantly. For more information, see `http://en.wikipedia.org/wiki/Simula`. Also see *An Introduction to Programming* in Simula by *Rob Pooley*.

This chapter will provide some background in tools that are essential for writing complete Python programs and packages. We'll use these tools in later chapters.

We'll make use of the `timeit` module to compare various object-oriented designs to see which has better performance. It's important to weigh objective evidence along with the more subjective consideration of how well the code seems to reflect the problem domain.

We'll look at the object-oriented use of the `unittest` and `doctest` modules. These are essential ingredients in writing software that are known to actually work.

A good object-oriented design should be clear and understandable. In order to assure that it is understood and used as well as maintained properly, writing Pythonic documentation is essential. Docstrings in modules, classes, and methods are very important. We'll touch on RST markup here and cover it in depth in *Chapter 18, Quality and Documentation*.

Apart from this, we'll address the **Integrated Development Environment** (IDE) question. A common question regards the *best* IDE for Python development.

Finally, we'll introduce the concepts behind Python's special method names. The subject of special methods fills the first seven chapters. Here, we'll provide some background that may be of help in understanding *Part 1, Pythonic Classes via Special Methods*.

We will try to avoid digressing into the foundations of Python object-oriented programming. We're assuming that you've already read the *Python 3 Object Oriented Programming* book by *Packt Publishing*. We don't want to repeat things that have been thoroughly stated elsewhere. In this book, we will focus solely on Python 3.

We'll refer to a number of common, object-oriented design patterns. We'll try to avoid repeating the presentation in Packt's *Learning Python Design Patterns*.

About casino Blackjack

If you're unfamiliar with the casino game of Blackjack, here's an overview.

The objective is to accept cards from the dealer to create a hand that has a point total that is between the dealer's total and 21.

The number cards (2 to 10) have point values equal to the number. The face cards (jack, queen, and king) are worth 10 points. The ace is worth either 11 points or one point. When using an ace as 11 points, the value of the hand is *soft*. When using an ace as one point, the value is *hard*.

A hand with an ace and seven, therefore, has a hard total of 8 and a soft total of 18.

There are four two-card combinations that total twenty-one. These are all called *blackjack* even though only one of the four combinations involves a jack.

Playing the game

The game of Blackjack can vary from casino to casino, but the outline is similar. The mechanics of play work as follows:

- First, the player and dealer each get two cards. The player, of course, knows the value of both of their cards. They're dealt face up in a casino.
- One of the dealer's cards is face up and the other is face down. The player therefore knows a little bit about the dealer's hand, but not everything.
- If the dealer has an ace showing, there's a 4:13 chance that the hidden card is worth 10 and the dealer has 21. The player can elect to make an additional insurance bet.

- Next, the player can elect to either receive cards or stop receiving cards. These two most common choices are called **hit** or **stand**.
- There are some additional choices too. If the player's cards match, the hand can be split. This is an additional bet, and the two hands are played separately.
- Finally, the players can double their bet before taking one last card. This is called **doubling down**. If the player's cards total 10 or 11, this is a common bet to make.

The final evaluation of the hand works as follows:

- If the player went over 21, the hand is a bust, the player loses, and the dealer's facedown card is irrelevant.
- If the player's total is 21 or under, then the dealer takes cards according to a simple, fixed rule. The dealer must hit a hand that totals less than 18. The dealer must stand on a hand that totals 18 or more. There are some small variations here that we can ignore for the moment.
- If the dealer goes bust, the player wins.
- If both the dealer and player are 21 or under, the hands are compared to see if the player has won or lost.

The amounts of the final payoffs aren't too relevant for now. For a more accurate simulation of various play and betting strategies, the payoffs will matter quite a bit.

Blackjack player strategies

In the case of Blackjack (which is different from a game such as Roulette), there are actually two kinds of strategies that the player must use, as follows:

- A strategy to decide what game play to make: take insurance, hit, stand, split, or double down.
- A strategy to decide what amount to bet. A common statistical fallacy leads players to raise and lower their bets in an attempt to preserve their winnings and minimize their losses. Any software to emulate casino games must also emulate these more complex betting strategies. These are interesting algorithms that are often stateful and lead to the learning of some advanced Python programming techniques.

These two sets of strategies are the prime examples of the **STRATEGY** design pattern.

Object design for simulating Blackjack

We'll use elements of the game like the player hand and card as examples of object modeling. However, we won't design the entire simulation. We'll focus on elements of this game because they have some nuance but aren't terribly complex.

We have a simple container: one hand object will contain zero or more card objects.

We'll take a look at the subclasses of `Card` for `NumberCard`, `FaceCard`, and `Ace`. We'll take a look at a wide variety of ways to define this simple class hierarchy. Because the hierarchy is so small (and simple), we can easily try a number of implementation alternatives.

We'll take a look at a variety of ways to implement the player's hand. This is a simple collection of cards with some additional features.

We also need to look at the player as a whole. A player will have a sequence of hands as well as a betting strategy and a Blackjack play strategy. This is a rather complex composite object.

We'll also take a quick look at the deck of cards that cards are shuffled and dealt from.

Performance – the timeit module

We'll make use of the `timeit` module to compare the actual performance of different object-oriented designs and Python constructs. The `timeit` module contains a number of functions. The one we'll focus on is named `timeit`. This function creates a `Timer` object for some statement. It can also include some setup code that prepares the environment. It then calls the `timeit()` method of `Timer` to execute the setup just once and the target statement repeatedly. The return value is the time required to run the statement.

The default count is 100,000. This provides a meaningful time that averages out other OS-level activity on the computer that is performing the measurement. For complex or long-running statements, a lower count may be prudent.

The following is a simple interaction with `timeit`:

```
>>> timeit.timeit( "obj.method()", """
... class SomeClass:
...     def method(self):
...        pass
... obj= SomeClass()
""")
0.1980541350058047
```

> **Downloading the example code**
>
> You can download the example code files for all Packt Publishing books you have purchased from your account at `http://www.packtpub.com`. If you have purchased this book elsewhere, you can visit `http://www.packtpub.com/support` and register to have the files e-mailed directly to you.

The statement `obj.method()` is provided to `timeit()` as a string. The setup is the class definition and is provided as a string as well. It's important to note that everything required by the statement must be in the setup. This includes all imports as well as all variable definitions and object creation. Everything.

It can take a few tries to get the setup complete. When using interactive Python, we often lose track of global variables and imports that have scrolled off the top of the terminal window. This example showed that 100,000 method calls that do nothing take 0.198 seconds.

The following is another example of using `timeit`:

```
>>> timeit.timeit( "f()","""
... def f():
...     pass
... """ )
0.13721893899491988
```

This shows us that a do-nothing function call is slightly less expensive than a do-nothing method invocation. The overhead in this case is almost 44 percent.

In some cases, OS overheads may be a measurable component of the performance. These tend to vary based on factors that are hard to control. We can use the `repeat()` function instead of the `timeit()` function in this module. It will collect multiple samples of the basic timing to allow further analysis of OS effects on performance.

For our purposes, the `timeit()` function will provide all the feedback we need to measure the various object-oriented design considerations objectively.

Testing – unittest and doctest

Unit testing is absolutely essential. If there's no automated test to show a particular element functionality, then the feature doesn't really exist. Put another way, it's not done until there's a test that shows that it's done.

We'll touch, tangentially, on testing. If we were to delve into testing each object-oriented design feature, the book would be twice as big as it is. Omitting the details of testing has the disadvantage that it makes good unit tests seem optional. They're emphatically not optional.

Unit testing is essential

When in doubt, design the tests first. Fit the code to the test cases.

Python offers two built-in testing frameworks. Most applications and libraries will make use of both. The general wrapper for all testing is the `unittest` module. In addition, many public API docstrings will have examples that can be found and used by the `doctest` module. Also, `unittest` can incorporate modules of `doctest`.

One lofty ideal is that every class and function has at least a unit test. More importantly, visible classes, functions, and modules will have `doctest` too. There are other lofty ideals: 100 percent code coverage, 100 percent logic path coverage, and so on.

Pragmatically, some classes don't need testing. A class created by `namedtuple()`, for example, doesn't really need a unit test, unless you don't trust the `namedtuple()` implementation in the first place. If you don't trust your Python implementation, you can't really write applications with it.

Generally, we want to develop the test cases first and then write code that fits these test cases. The test cases formalize the API for the code. This book will reveal numerous ways to write code that has the same interface. This is important. Once we've defined an interface, there are still numerous candidate implementations that fit the interface. One set of tests should apply to several different object-oriented designs.

One general approach to using the `unittest` tools is to create at least three parallel directories for your project as follows:

- `myproject`: This directory is the final package that will be installed in `lib/site-packages` for your package or application. It has an `__init__.py` package, and we'll put our files in here for each module.
- `test`: This directory has the test scripts. In some cases, the scripts will parallel the modules. In some cases, the scripts may be larger and more complex than the modules themselves.
- `doc`: This directory has other documentation. We'll touch on this in the next section as well as in *Chapter 18, Quality and Documentation*.

In some cases, we'll want to run the same test suite on multiple candidate classes so that we can be sure that each candidate works. There's no point in doing `timeit` comparisons on code that doesn't actually work.

Unit testing and technology spikes

As part of object-oriented design, we'll often create technology spike modules that look like the code shown in this section. We'll break it down into three sections. First, we have the overall abstract test as follows:

```
import types
import unittest

class TestAccess( unittest.TestCase ):
    def test_should_add_and_get_attribute( self ):
        self.object.new_attribute= True
        self.assertTrue( self.object.new_attribute )
    def test_should_fail_on_missing( self ):
        self.assertRaises( AttributeError, lambda: self.object.
undefined )
```

This abstract `TestCase` subclass defines a few tests that we're expecting a class to pass. The actual object being tested is omitted. It's referenced as `self.object`, but no definition is provided, making this `TestCase` subclass abstract. A `setUp()` method is required by each concrete subclass.

The following are three concrete `TestAccess` subclasses that will exercise three different kinds of objects:

```
class SomeClass:
    pass
class Test_EmptyClass( TestAccess ):
    def setUp( self ):
       self.object= SomeClass()
class Test_Namespace( TestAccess ):
    def setUp( self ):
       self.object= types.SimpleNamespace()
class Test_Object( TestAccess ):
    def setUp( self ):
       self.object= object()
```

The subclasses of the `TestAccess` classes each provide the required `setUp()` method. Each method builds a different kind of object for testing. One is an instance of an otherwise empty class. The second is an instance of `types.SimpleNamespace`. The third is an instance of `object`.

In order to run these tests, we'll need to build a suite that doesn't allow us to run the `TestAccess` abstract test.

The following is the rest of the spike:

```
def suite():
    s= unittest.TestSuite()
    s.addTests( unittest.defaultTestLoader.loadTestsFromTestCase(Test_
EmptyClass) )
    s.addTests( unittest.defaultTestLoader.loadTestsFromTestCase(Test_
Namespace) )
    s.addTests( unittest.defaultTestLoader.loadTestsFromTestCase(Test_
Object) )
    return s

if __name__ == "__main__":
    t= unittest.TextTestRunner()
    t.run( suite() )
```

We now have concrete evidence that the `object` class can't be used the same way the `types.SimpleNamespace` class can be used. Further, we have a simple test class that we can use to demonstrate other designs that work (or don't work.) The tests, for example, demonstrate that `types.SimpleNamespace` behaves like an otherwise empty class.

We have omitted numerous details of potential unit test cases. We'll look at testing in depth in *Chapter 15, Designing for Testability*.

Docstrings – RST markup and documentation tools

All Python code should have docstrings at the module, class, and method levels. Not every single method requires a docstring. Some method names are really well chosen, and little more needs to be said about them. Most times, however, documentation is essential for clarity.

Python documentation is often written using **ReStructured Text** (**RST**) markup.

Throughout the code examples in the book, however, we'll omit docstrings. It keeps the book to a reasonable size. This gap has the disadvantage that it makes docstrings seem optional. They're emphatically not optional.

We'll emphasize this again. *Docstrings are essential.*

The docstring material is used by Python in the following three ways:

- The internal `help()` function displays the docstrings
- The `doctest` tool can find examples in docstrings and run them as test cases
- External tools such as **Sphinx** and **epydoc** can produce elegant documentation extracts

Because of the relative simplicity of RST, it's quite easy to write good docstrings. We'll take a look at documentation and the expected markup in detail in *Chapter 18, Quality and Documentation*. For now, however, we'll provide a quick example of what a docstring might look like:

```
def factorial( n ):
    """Compute n! recursively.

    :param n: an integer >= 0
    :returns: n!

    Because of Python's stack limitation, this won't
    compute a value larger than about 1000!.

    >>> factorial(5)
    120
    """
    if n == 0: return 1
    return n*factorial(n-1)
```

This shows RST markup for parameters and return values. It includes an additional note about a profound limitation. It also includes the `doctest` output that can be used to validate the implementation using the `doctest` tool. There are numerous markup features that can be used to provide additional structure and semantic information.

The IDE question

A common question regards the *best* IDE for Python development. The short answer is that the IDE choice doesn't matter at all. The number of development environments that support Python is vast.

All the examples in this book show interactive examples from the Python `>>>` prompt. Running examples interactively makes a profound statement. Well-written Python should be simple enough to run from the command line.

We should be able to demonstrate a design at the >>> prompt.

Exercising code from the `>>>` prompt is an important quality test for Python design complexity. If the classes or functions are too complex, then there's no easy way to exercise it from the `>>>` prompt. For some complex classes, we may need to provide appropriate mock objects to permit easy, interactive use.

About special method names

Python has multiple layers of implementation. We're interested in just two of them.

On the surface, we have Python's source text. This source text is a mixture of a traditional object-oriented notation and procedural function call notation. The postfix object-oriented notation includes `object.method()` or `object.attribute` constructs. The prefix notation involves `function(object)` constructs that are more typical of procedural programming languages. We also have an infix notation such as `object+other`. Plus, of course, some statements such as `for` and `with` invoke object methods.

The presence of `function(object)` prefix constructs leads some programmers to question the "purity" of Python's object orientation. It's not clear that a fastidiously strict adherence to the `object.method()` notation is necessary or even helpful. Python uses a mixture of prefix and suffix notations. The prefix notations are stand-ins for special method suffix notations. The presence of the prefix, infix, and postfix notations is based on choices of expressiveness and esthetics. One goal of well-written Python is that it should read more or less like English. Underneath the hood, the syntax variations are implemented consistently by Python's special methods.

Everything in Python is an object. This is unlike Java or C++ where there are "primitive" types that avoid the object paradigm. Every Python object offers an array of special methods that provide implementation details for the surface features of the language. We might, for example, write `str(x)` in an application program. This prefix surface notation is implemented as `x.__str__()` under the hood.

A construct such as `a+b` may be implemented as `a.__add__(b)` or `b.__radd__(a)` depending on the type of compatibility rules that were built into the class definitions for objects `a` and `b`.

The mapping between surface syntax and the implementation of special methods is emphatically not a trivial rewrite from `function(x)` to `x.__function__()`. There are numerous language features that have interesting special methods to support that feature. Some special methods have default implementations inherited from the base class, `object`, while other special methods have no default implementation and will raise an exception.

Throughout *Part 1, Pythonic Classes via Special Methods*, we'll introduce the special methods and show how we can implement these special methods to provide seamless integration between Python and our class definitions.

Summary

We've looked at one of our sample problem domains: the casino game of Blackjack. We like it because it has some algorithmic complexity, but isn't too sophisticated or esoteric. We've also introduced three important modules that we'll be using throughout the book:

- The `timeit` module is something we'll use to compare performance of alternative implementations
- The `unittest` and `doctest` modules will be used to confirm that our software works correctly

We've also looked at some of the ways we'll add documentation to our Python programs. We'll be using docstrings in modules, classes, and functions. To save space, not every example will show the docstrings. In spite of this, they should be considered as essential.

The use of an **integrated development environment** (**IDE**) isn't essential. Any IDE or text editor that works for you will be fine for advanced Python development.

The eight chapters which follow will address different subsets of the special method names. These are about how we'll create our own Python programming that integrates seamlessly with the built-in library modules.

In the next chapter, we'll focus on the `__init__()` method and the various ways we can use it. The `__init__()` method is profound because initialization is the first big step in an object's life; every object must be initialized properly to work properly. More important than that, the argument values for `__init__()` can take on many forms. We'll look at a variety of ways to design `__init__()`.

Part 1

Pythonic Classes via Special Methods

Pythonic Classes via Special Methods

Python exposes a great deal of its internal mechanisms through its special method names. The idea is pervasive throughout Python. A function such as `len()` will exploit the `__len__()` special method of a class.

What this means is that we have a tidy, universal public interface (`len(x)`) that works on any kind of class. Python's polymorphism is based in part on the way any class can implement a `__len__()` method; objects of any such class will respond to the `len()` function.

When we define a class, we can (and should) include these special methods to improve the integration between our class and the rest of Python. *Part 1, Pythonic Classes via Special Methods*, will extend basic object-oriented programming techniques to create classes that are more *Pythonic*. Any class should be able to integrate seamlessly with other parts of Python. A close fit with other parts of Python will allow us to use many language and standard library features, and the clients of our packages and modules will be more confident about using them and more successful in maintaining and extending them.

In a way, our classes can appear as extensions of Python. We want our classes to be so much like native Python classes that distinctions between language, standard library, and our application are minimized.

The Python language uses a large number of special method names. They fall into the following few discrete categories:

- **Attribute Access**: These special methods implement what we see as `object.attribute` in an expression, `object.attribute` on the left-hand side of an assignment, and `object.attribute` in a `del` statement.

- **Callables**: This special method implements what we see as a function that is applied to arguments, much like the built-in `len()` function.
- **Collections**: These special methods implement the numerous features of collections. This involves methods such as `sequence[index]`, `mapping[key]`, and `some_set|another_set`.
- **Numbers**: These special methods provide arithmetic operators and comparison operators. We can use these methods to expand the domain of numbers that Python works with.
- **Contexts**: There are two special methods we'll use to implement a context manager that works with the `with` statement.
- **Iterators**: There are special methods that define an iterator. This isn't essential since generator functions handle this feature so elegantly. However, we'll take a look at how we can design our own iterators.

A few of these special method names have been introduced in *Python 3 Object Oriented Programming*. We'll review these topics and introduce some additional special method names that fit into a kind of *basic* category.

Even within this basic category, we've got deeper topics to discover. We'll start with the truly basic special methods. There are some rather advanced special methods that are thrown into the basic category because they don't seem to belong anywhere else.

The `__init__()` method permits a great deal of latitude in providing the initial values for an object. In the case of an immutable object, this is the essential definition of the instance, and clarity becomes very important. In the first chapter, we'll review the numerous design alternatives for this method.

1

The __init__() Method

The `__init__()` method is profound for two reasons. Initialization is the first big step in an object's life; every object must be initialized properly to work properly. The second reason is that the argument values for `__init__()` can take on many forms.

Because there are so many ways to provide argument values to `__init__()`, there is a vast array of use cases for object creation. We take a look at several of them. We want to maximize clarity, so we need to define an initialization that properly characterizes the problem domain.

Before we can get to the `__init__()` method, however, we need to take a look at the implicit class hierarchy in Python, glancing, briefly, at the class named `object`. This will set the stage for comparing default behavior with the different kinds of behavior we want from our own classes.

In this chapter, we take a look at different forms of initialization for simple objects (for example, playing cards). After this, we can take a look at more complex objects, such as hands that involve collections and players that involve strategies and states.

The implicit superclass – object

Each Python class definition has an implicit superclass: `object`. It's a very simple class definition that does almost nothing. We can create instances of `object`, but we can't do much with them because many of the special methods simply raise exceptions.

When we define our own class, `object` is the superclass. The following is an example class definition that simply extends `object` with a new name:

```
class X:
    pass
```

The following are some interactions with our class:

```
>>> X.__class__
<class 'type'>
>>> X.__class__.__base__
<class 'object'>
```

We can see that a class is an object of the class named `type` and that the base class for our new class is the class named `object`.

As we look at each method, we also take a look at the default behavior inherited from `object`. In some cases, the superclass special method behavior will be exactly what we want. In other cases, we'll need to override the special method.

The base class object __init__() method

Fundamental to the life cycle of an object are its creation, initialization, and destruction. We'll defer creation and destruction to a later chapter on more advanced special methods and only focus on initialization for now.

The superclass of all classes, `object`, has a default implementation of `__init__()` that amounts to `pass`. We aren't required to implement `__init__()`. If we don't implement it, then no instance variables will be created when the object is created. In some cases, this default behavior is acceptable.

We can always add attributes to an object that's a subclass of the foundational base class, `object`. Consider the following class that requires two instance variables but doesn't initialize them:

```
class Rectangle:
    def area( self ):
        return self.length * self.width
```

The `Rectangle` class has a method that uses two attributes to return a value. The attributes have not been initialized anywhere. This is legal Python. It's a little strange to avoid specifically setting attributes, but it's valid.

The following is an interaction with the `Rectangle` class:

```
>>> r= Rectangle()
>>> r.length, r.width = 13, 8
>>> r.area()
104
```

While this is legal, it's a potential source of deep confusion, which is a good reason to avoid it.

However, this kind of design grants flexibility, so there could be times when we needn't set all of the attributes in the `__init__()` method. We walk a fine line here. An optional attribute is a kind of subclass that's not formally declared as a proper subclass. We're creating polymorphism in a way that could lead to confusing and inappropriate use of convoluted `if` statements. While uninitialized attributes may be useful, they could be the symptom of a bad design.

The *Zen of Python* poem (`import this`) offers the following advice:

> "*Explicit is better than implicit.*"

An `__init__()` method should make the instance variables explicit.

Pretty Poor Polymorphism

There's a fine line between flexibility and foolishness.

We may have stepped over the edge off *flexible* into *foolish* as soon as we feel the need to write:

```
if 'x' in self.__dict__:
```

Or:

```
try:
    self.x
except AttributeError:
```

It's time to reconsider the API and add a common method or attribute. Refactoring is better than adding `if` statements.

Implementing __init__() in a superclass

We initialize an object by implementing the `__init__()` method. When an object is created, Python first creates an empty object and then calls the `__init__()` method for that new object. This method function generally creates the object's instance variables and performs any other one-time processing.

The following are some example definitions of a `Card` class hierarchy. We'll define a `Card` superclass and three subclasses that are variations of the basic theme of `Card`. We have two instance variables that have been set directly from argument values and two variables that have been calculated by an initialization method:

```
class Card:
    def  __init__( self, rank, suit ):
        self.suit= suit
        self.rank= rank
        self.hard, self.soft = self._points()
class NumberCard( Card ):
```

```
        def _points( self ):
            return int(self.rank), int(self.rank)
    class AceCard( Card ):
        def _points( self ):
            return 1, 11
    class FaceCard( Card ):
        def _points( self ):
            return 10, 10
```

In this example, we factored the `__init__()` method into the superclass so that a common initialization in the superclass, `Card`, applies to all the three subclasses `NumberCard`, `AceCard`, and `FaceCard`.

This shows a common polymorphic design. Each subclass provides a unique implementation of the `_points()` method. All the subclasses have identical signatures: they have the same methods and attributes. Objects of these three subclasses can be used interchangeably in an application.

If we simply use characters for suits, we will be able to create `Card` instances as shown in the following code snippet:

```
cards = [ AceCard('A', '♠'), NumberCard('2','♠'), NumberCard('3','♠'),
]
```

We enumerated the class, rank, and suit for several cards in a list. In the long run, we need a much smarter factory function to build `Card` instances; enumerating all 52 cards this way is tedious and error prone. Before we get to the factory functions, we take a look at a number of other issues.

Using __init__() to create manifest constants

We can define a class for the suits of our cards. In blackjack, the suits don't matter, and a simple character string could work.

We use suit construction as an example of creating constant objects. In many cases, our application will have a small domain of objects that can be defined by a collection of constants. A small domain of static objects may be part of implementing a **Strategy** or **State** design pattern.

In some cases, we may have a pool of constant objects created in an initialization or configuration file, or we might create constant objects based on command-line parameters. We'll return to the details of initialization design and startup design in *Chapter 16, Coping with the Command Line*.

Python has no simple formal mechanism for defining an object as immutable. We'll look at techniques to assure immutability in *Chapter 3, Attribute Access, Properties, and Descriptors*. In this example, it might make sense for the attributes of a suit to be immutable.

The following is a class that we'll use to build four manifest constants:

```
class Suit:
    def __init__( self, name, symbol ):
        self.name= name
        self.symbol= symbol
```

The following is the domain of "constants" built around this class:

```
Club, Diamond, Heart, Spade = Suit('Club','♣'), Suit('Diamond','♦'),
Suit('Heart','♥'), Suit('Spade','♠')
```

We can now create `cards` as shown in the following code snippet:

```
cards = [ AceCard('A', Spade), NumberCard('2', Spade), NumberCard('3',
Spade), ]
```

For an example this small, this method isn't a huge improvement over single character suit codes. In more complex cases, there may be a short list of Strategy or State objects that can be created like this. This can make the Strategy or State design patterns work efficiently by reusing objects from a small, static pool of constants.

We do have to acknowledge that in Python these objects aren't technically constant; they are mutable. There may be some benefit in doing the extra coding to make these objects truly immutable.

The irrelevance of immutability

Immutability can become an attractive nuisance. It's sometimes justified by the mythical "malicious programmer" who modifies the constant value in their application. As a design consideration, this is silly. This mythical, malicious programmer can't be stopped this way. There's no easy way to "idiot-proof" code in Python. The malicious programmer has access to the source and can tweak it just as easily as they can write code to modify a constant.

It's better not to struggle too long to define the classes of immutable objects. In *Chapter 3, Attribute Access, Properties, and Descriptors*, we'll show ways to implement immutability that provides suitable diagnostic information for a buggy program.

Leveraging __init__() via a factory function

We can build a complete deck of cards via a factory function. This beats enumerating all 52 cards. In Python, we have two common approaches to factories as follows:

- We define a function that creates objects of the required classes.
- We define a class that has methods for creating objects. This is the full factory design pattern, as described in books on design patterns. In languages such as Java, a factory class hierarchy is required because the language doesn't support standalone functions.

In Python, a class isn't *required*. It's merely a good idea when there are related factories that are complex. One of the strengths of Python is that we're not forced to use a class hierarchy when a simple function might do just as well.

> While this is a book about object-oriented programming, a function really is fine. It's common, idiomatic Python.

We can always rewrite a function to be a proper callable object if the need arises. From a callable object, we can refactor it into a class hierarchy for our factories. We'll look at callable objects in *Chapter 5, Using Callables and Contexts*.

The advantage of class definitions in general is to achieve code reuse via inheritance. The function of a factory class is to wrap some target class hierarchy and the complexities of object construction. If we have a factory class, we can add subclasses to the factory class when extending the target class hierarchy. This gives us polymorphic factory classes; the different factory class definitions have the same method signatures and can be used interchangeably.

This class-level polymorphism can be very helpful with statically compiled languages such as Java or C++. The compiler can resolve the details of the class and methods when generating code.

If the alternative factory definitions don't actually reuse any code, then a class hierarchy won't be helpful in Python. We can simply use functions that have the same signatures.

The following is a factory function for our various `Card` subclasses:

```
def card( rank, suit ):
    if rank == 1: return AceCard( 'A', suit )
    elif 2 <= rank < 11: return NumberCard( str(rank), suit )
```

```
    elif 11 <= rank < 14:
        name = { 11: 'J', 12: 'Q', 13: 'K' }[rank]
        return FaceCard( name, suit )
    else:
        raise Exception( "Rank out of range" )
```

This function builds a `Card` class from a numeric `rank` number and a `suit` object. We can now build cards more simply. We've encapsulated the construction issues into a single factory function, allowing an application to be built without knowing precisely how the class hierarchy and polymorphic design works.

The following is an example of how we can build a deck with this factory function:

```
deck = [card(rank, suit)
    for rank in range(1,14)
        for suit in (Club, Diamond, Heart, Spade)]
```

This enumerates all the ranks and suits to create a complete deck of 52 cards.

Faulty factory design and the vague else clause

Note the structure of the `if` statement in the `card()` function. We did not use a catch-all `else` clause to do any processing; we merely raised an exception. The use of a catch-all `else` clause is subject to a tiny scrap of debate.

On the one hand, it can be argued that the condition that belongs on an `else` clause should never be left unstated because it may hide subtle design errors. On the other hand, some `else` clause conditions are truly obvious.

It's important to avoid the vague `else` clause.

Consider the following variant on this factory function definition:

```
def card2( rank, suit ):
    if rank == 1: return AceCard( 'A', suit )
    elif 2 <= rank < 11: return NumberCard( str(rank), suit )
    else:
        name = { 11: 'J', 12: 'Q', 13: 'K' }[rank]
        return FaceCard( name, suit )
```

The following is what will happen when we try to build a deck:

```
deck2 = [card2(rank, suit) for rank in range(13) for suit in (Club,
Diamond, Heart, Spade)]
```

Does it work? What if the `if` conditions were more complex?

Some programmers can understand this `if` statement at a glance. Others will struggle to determine if all of the cases are properly exclusive.

For advanced Python programming, we should not leave it to the reader to deduce the conditions that apply to an `else` clause. Either the condition should be obvious to the newest of n00bz, or it should be explicit.

> **When to use catch-all else**
>
> Rarely. Use it only when the condition is obvious. When in doubt, be explicit and use `else` to raise an exception.
>
> Avoid the vague `else` clause.

Simplicity and consistency using elif sequences

Our factory function, `card()`, is a mixture of two very common factory design patterns:

- An `if-elif` sequence
- A mapping

For the sake of simplicity, it's better to focus on just one of these techniques rather than on both.

We can always replace a mapping with `elif` conditions. (Yes, always. The reverse is not true though; transforming `elif` conditions to a mapping can be challenging.)

The following is a `Card` factory without the mapping:

```
def card3( rank, suit ):
    if rank == 1: return AceCard( 'A', suit )
    elif 2 <= rank < 11: return NumberCard( str(rank), suit )
    elif rank == 11:
        return FaceCard( 'J', suit )
    elif rank == 12:
        return FaceCard( 'Q', suit )
    elif rank == 13:
        return FaceCard( 'K', suit )
    else:
        raise Exception( "Rank out of range" )
```

We rewrote the `card()` factory function. The mapping was transformed into additional `elif` clauses. This function has the advantage that it is more consistent than the previous version.

Simplicity using mapping and class objects

In some cases, we can use a mapping instead of a chain of `elif` conditions. It's possible to find conditions that are so complex that a chain of `elif` conditions is the only sensible way to express them. For simple cases, however, a mapping often works better and can be easy to read.

Since `class` is a first-class object, we can easily map from the `rank` parameter to the class that must be constructed.

The following is a `Card` factory that uses only a mapping:

```
def card4( rank, suit ):
    class_= {1: AceCard, 11: FaceCard, 12: FaceCard,
        13: FaceCard}.get(rank, NumberCard)
    return class_( rank, suit )
```

We've mapped the `rank` object to a class. Then, we applied the class to the `rank` and `suit` values to build the final `Card` instance.

We can use a `defaultdict` class as well. However, it's no simpler for a trivial static mapping. It looks like the following code snippet:

```
defaultdict( lambda: NumberCard, {1: AceCard, 11: FaceCard, 12:
FaceCard, 12: FaceCard} )
```

Note that the *default* of a `defaultdict` class must be a function of zero arguments. We've used a `lambda` construct to create the necessary function wrapper around a constant. This function, however, has a serious deficiency. It lacks the translation from `1` to `A` and `13` to `K` that we had in previous versions. When we try to add that feature, we run into a problem.

We need to change the mapping to provide both a `Card` subclass as well as the string version of the `rank` object. What can we do for this two-part mapping? There are four common solutions:

- We can do two parallel mappings. We don't suggest this, but we'll show it to emphasize what's undesirable about it.
- We can map to a two-tuple. This also has some disadvantages.
- We can map to a `partial()` function. The `partial()` function is a feature of the `functools` module.
- We can also consider modifying our class definition to fit more readily with this kind of mapping. We'll look at this alternative in the next section on pushing `__init__()` into the subclass definitions.

We'll look at each of these with a concrete example.

Two parallel mappings

The following is the essence of the two parallel mappings solution:

```
class_= {1: AceCard, 11: FaceCard, 12: FaceCard, 13: FaceCard
}.get(rank, NumberCard)
rank_str= {1:'A', 11:'J', 12:'Q', 13:'K'}.get(rank,str(rank))
return class_( rank_str, suit )
```

This is not desirable. It involves a repetition of the sequence of the mapping keys `1`, `11`, `12`, and `13`. Repetition is bad because parallel structures never seem to stay that way after the software has been updated.

Don't use parallel structures

Two parallel structures should be replaced with tuples or some kind of proper collection.

Mapping to a tuple of values

The following is the essence of how mapping is done to a two-tuple:

```
class_, rank_str= {
    1:  (AceCard,'A'),
    11: (FaceCard,'J'),
    12: (FaceCard,'Q'),
    13: (FaceCard,'K'),
    }.get(rank, (NumberCard, str(rank)))
return class_( rank_str, suit )
```

This is reasonably pleasant. It's not much code to sort out the special cases of playing cards. We will see how it could be modified or expanded if we need to alter the `Card` class hierarchy to add additional subclasses of `Card`.

It does feel odd to map a `rank` value to a `class` object and just one of the two arguments to that class initializer. It seems more sensible to map the rank to a simple class or function object without the clutter of providing some (but not all) of the arguments.

The partial function solution

Rather than map to a two-tuple of function and one of the arguments, we can create a `partial()` function. This is a function that already has some (but not all) of its arguments provided. We'll use the `partial()` function from the `functools` library to create a partial of a class with the `rank` argument.

The following is a mapping from `rank` to a `partial()` function that can be used for object construction:

```
from functools import partial
part_class= {
    1:  partial(AceCard,'A'),
    11: partial(FaceCard,'J'),
    12: partial(FaceCard,'Q'),
    13: partial(FaceCard,'K'),
    }.get(rank, partial(NumberCard, str(rank)))
return part_class( suit )
```

The mapping associates a `rank` object with a `partial()` function that is assigned to `part_class`. This `partial()` function can then be applied to the `suit` object to create the final object. The use of `partial()` functions is a common technique for functional programming. It works in this specific situation where we have a function instead of an object method.

In general, however, `partial()` functions aren't helpful for most object-oriented programming. Rather than create `partial()` functions, we can simply update the methods of a class to accept the arguments in different combinations. A `partial()` function is similar to creating a fluent interface for object construction.

Fluent APIs for factories

In some cases, we design a class where there's a defined order for method usage. Evaluating methods sequentially is very much like creating a `partial()` function.

We might have `x.a().b()` in an object notation. We can think of it as $x(a,b)$. The `x.a()` function is a kind of `partial()` function that's waiting for `b()`. We can think of this as if it were $x(a)(b)$.

The idea here is that Python offers us two alternatives for managing a state. We can either update an object or create a `partial()` function that is (in a way) stateful. Because of this equivalence, we can rewrite a `partial()` function into a fluent factory object. We make the setting of the `rank` object a fluent method that returns `self`. Setting the `suit` object will actually create the `Card` instance.

The following is a fluent `Card` factory class with two method functions that must be used in a specific order:

```
class CardFactory:
    def rank( self, rank ):
        self.class_, self.rank_str= {
            1:(AceCard,'A'),
```

```
            11:(FaceCard,'J'),
            12:(FaceCard,'Q'),
            13:(FaceCard,'K'),
            }.get(rank, (NumberCard, str(rank)))
        return self
    def suit( self, suit ):
        return self.class_( self.rank_str, suit )
```

The `rank()` method updates the state of the constructor, and the `suit()` method actually creates the final `Card` object.

This factory class can be used as follows:

```
card8 = CardFactory()
deck8 = [card8.rank(r+1).suit(s) for r in range(13) for s in (Club, 
Diamond, Heart, Spade)]
```

First, we create a factory instance, then we use that instance to create `Card` instances. This doesn't materially change how `__init__()` itself works in the `Card` class hierarchy. It does, however, change the way that our client application creates objects.

Implementing __init__() in each subclass

As we look at the factory functions for creating `Card` objects, we see some alternative designs for the `Card` class. We might want to refactor the conversion of the rank number so that it is the responsibility of the `Card` class itself. This pushes the initialization down into each subclass.

This often requires some common initialization of a superclass as well as subclass-specific initialization. We need to follow the **Don't Repeat Yourself** (**DRY**) principle to keep the code from getting cloned into each of the subclasses.

The following is an example where the initialization is the responsibility of each subclass:

```
class Card:
    pass
class NumberCard( Card ):
    def  __init__( self, rank, suit ):
        self.suit= suit
        self.rank= str(rank)
        self.hard = self.soft = rank
class AceCard( Card ):
    def  __init__( self, rank, suit ):
        self.suit= suit
```

```
        self.rank= "A"
        self.hard, self.soft =  1, 11
class FaceCard( Card ):
    def  __init__( self, rank, suit ):
        self.suit= suit
        self.rank= {11: 'J', 12: 'Q', 13: 'K' }[rank]
        self.hard = self.soft = 10
```

This is still clearly polymorphic. The lack of a truly common initialization, however, leads to some unpleasant redundancy. What's unpleasant here is the repeated initialization of `suit`. This must be *pulled up* into the superclass. We can have each `__init__()` subclass make an explicit reference to the superclass.

This version of the `Card` class has an initializer at the superclass level that is used by each subclass, as shown in the following code snippet:

```
class Card:
    def __init__( self, rank, suit, hard, soft ):
        self.rank= rank
        self.suit= suit
        self.hard= hard
        self.soft= soft
class NumberCard( Card ):
    def  __init__( self, rank, suit ):
        super().__init__( str(rank), suit, rank, rank )
class AceCard( Card ):
    def  __init__( self, rank, suit ):
        super().__init__( "A", suit, 1, 11 )
class FaceCard( Card ):
    def  __init__( self, rank, suit ):
        super().__init__( {11: 'J', 12: 'Q', 13: 'K' }[rank], suit,
10, 10 )
```

We've provided `__init__()` at both the subclass and superclass level. This has the small advantage that it simplifies our factory function, as shown in the following code snippet:

```
def card10( rank, suit ):
    if rank == 1: return AceCard( rank, suit )
    elif 2 <= rank < 11: return NumberCard( rank, suit )
    elif 11 <= rank < 14: return FaceCard( rank, suit )
    else:
        raise Exception( "Rank out of range" )
```

Simplifying a factory function should not be our focus. We can see from this variation that we've created rather complex `__init__()` methods for a relatively minor improvement in a factory function. This is a common trade-off.

Factory functions encapsulate complexity

There's a trade-off that occurs between sophisticated `__init__()` methods and factory functions. It's often better to stick with more direct but less programmer-friendly `__init__()` methods and push the complexity into factory functions. A factory function works well if you wish to wrap and encapsulate the construction complexities.

Simple composite objects

A composite object can also be called a **container**. We'll look at a simple composite object: a deck of individual cards. This is a basic collection. Indeed, it's so basic that we can, without too much struggle, use a simple `list` as a deck.

Before designing a new class, we need to ask this question: is using a simple `list` appropriate?

We can use `random.shuffle()` to shuffle the deck and `deck.pop()` to deal cards into a player's `Hand`.

Some programmers rush to define new classes as if using a built-in class violates some object-oriented design principle. Avoiding a new class leaves us with something as shown in the following code snippet:

```
d= [card6(r+1,s) for r in range(13) for s in (Club, Diamond, Heart, 
Spade)]
random.shuffle(d)
hand= [ d.pop(), d.pop() ]
```

If it's that simple, why write a new class?

The answer isn't perfectly clear. One advantage is that a class offer a simplified, implementation-free interface to the object. As we noted previously, when discussing factories, a class isn't a requirement in Python.

In the preceding code, the deck only has two simple use cases and a class definition doesn't seem to simplify things very much. It does have the advantage of concealing the implementation's details. But the details are so trivial that exposing them seems to have little cost. We're focused primarily on the `__init__()` method in this chapter, so we'll look at some designs to create and initialize a collection.

To design a collection of objects, we have the following three general design strategies:

- **Wrap**: This design pattern is an existing collection definition. This might be an example of the **Facade** design pattern.
- **Extend**: This design pattern is an existing collection class. This is ordinary subclass definition.
- **Invent**: This is designed from scratch. We'll look at this in *Chapter 6, Creating Containers and Collections*.

These three concepts are central to object-oriented design. We must always make this choice when designing a class.

Wrapping a collection class

The following is a wrapper design that contains an internal collection:

```
class Deck:
    def __init__( self ):
        self._cards = [card6(r+1,s) for r in range(13) for s in (Club,
Diamond, Heart, Spade)]
        random.shuffle( self._cards )
    def pop( self ):
        return self._cards.pop()
```

We've defined `Deck` so that the internal collection is a `list` object. The `pop()` method of `Deck` simply delegates to the wrapped `list` object.

We can then create a `Hand` instance with the following kind of code:

```
d= Deck()
hand= [ d.pop(), d.pop() ]
```

Generally, a Facade design pattern or wrapper class contains methods that are simply delegated to the underlying implementation class. This delegation can become wordy. For a sophisticated collection, we may wind up delegating a large number of methods to the wrapped object.

Extending a collection class

An alternative to wrapping is to extend a built-in class. By doing this, we have the advantage of not having to reimplement the `pop()` method; we can simply inherit it.

The `pop()` method has the advantage that it creates a class without writing too much code. In this example, extending the `list` class has the disadvantage that this provides many more functions than we truly need.

The following is a definition of `Deck` that extends the built-in `list`:

```
class Deck2( list ):
    def __init__( self ):
        super().__init__( card6(r+1,s) for r in range(13) for s in
(Club, Diamond, Heart, Spade) )
        random.shuffle( self )
```

In some cases, our methods will have to explicitly use the superclass methods in order to have proper class behavior. We'll see other examples of this in the following sections.

We leverage the superclass's `__init__()` method to populate our `list` object with an initial single deck of cards. Then we shuffle the cards. The `pop()` method is simply inherited from `list` and works perfectly. Other methods inherited from the `list` also work.

More requirements and another design

In a casino, the cards are often dealt from a shoe that has half a dozen decks of cards all mingled together. This consideration makes it necessary for us to build our own version of `Deck` and not simply use an unadorned `list` object.

Additionally, a casino shoe is not dealt fully. Instead, a marker card is inserted. Because of the marker, some cards are effectively set aside and not used for play.

The following is `Deck` definition that contains multiple sets of 52-card decks:

```
class Deck3(list):
    def __init__(self, decks=1):
        super().__init__()
        for i in range(decks):
            self.extend( card6(r+1,s) for r in range(13) for s in
(Club, Diamond, Heart, Spade) )
        random.shuffle( self )
        burn= random.randint(1,52)
        for i in range(burn): self.pop()
```

Here, we used the `__init__()` superclass to build an empty collection. Then, we used `self.extend()` to append multiple 52-card decks to the shoe. We could also use `super().extend()` since we did not provide an overriding implementation in this class.

We could also carry out the entire task via `super().__init__()` using a more deeply nested generator expression, as shown in the following code snippet:

```
( card6(r+1,s) for r in range(13) for s in (Club, Diamond, Heart,
Spade) for d in range(decks) )
```

This class provides us with a collection of `Card` instances that we can use to emulate casino blackjack as dealt from a shoe.

There's a peculiar ritual in a casino where they reveal the burned card. If we're going to design a card-counting player strategy, we might want to emulate this nuance too.

Complex composite objects

The following is an example of a blackjack `Hand` description that might be suitable for emulating play strategies:

```
class Hand:
    def __init__( self, dealer_card ):
        self.dealer_card= dealer_card
        self.cards= []
    def hard_total(self ):
        return sum(c.hard for c in self.cards)
    def soft_total(self ):
        return sum(c.soft for c in self.cards)
```

In this example, we have an instance variable `self.dealer_card` based on a parameter of the `__init__()` method. The `self.cards` instance variable, however, is not based on any parameter. This kind of initialization creates an empty collection.

To create an instance of `Hand`, we can use the following code:

```
d = Deck()
h = Hand( d.pop() )
h.cards.append( d.pop() )
h.cards.append( d.pop() )
```

This has the disadvantage that a long-winded sequence of statements is used to build an instance of a `Hand` object. It can become difficult to serialize the `Hand` object and rebuild it with an initialization such as this one. Even if we were to create an explicit `append()` method in this class, it would still take multiple steps to initialize the collection.

We could try to create a fluent interface, but that doesn't really simplify things; it's merely a change in the syntax of the way that a `Hand` object is built. A fluent interface still leads to multiple method evaluations. When we take a look at the serialization of objects in *Part 2, Persistence and Serialization* we'd like an interface that's a single class-level function, ideally the class constructor. We'll look at this in depth in *Chapter 9, Serializing and Saving - JSON, YAML, Pickle, CSV, and XML.*

Note also that the hard total and soft total method functions shown here don't fully follow the rules of blackjack. We return to this issue in *Chapter 2, Integrating Seamlessly with Python – Basic Special Methods.*

Complete composite object initialization

Ideally, the `__init__()` initializer method will create a complete instance of an object. This is a bit more complex when creating a complete instance of a container that contains an internal collection of other objects. It'll be helpful if we can build this composite in a single step.

It's common to have both a method to incrementally accrete items as well as the initializer special method that can load all of the items in one step.

For example, we might have a class such as the following code snippet:

```
class Hand2:
    def __init__( self, dealer_card, *cards ):
        self.dealer_card= dealer_card
        self.cards = list(cards)
    def hard_total(self ):
        return sum(c.hard for c in self.cards)
    def soft_total(self ):
        return sum(c.soft for c in self.cards)
```

This initialization sets all of the instance variables in a single step. The other methods are simply copies of the previous class definition. We can build a `Hand2` object in two ways. This first example loads one card at a time into a `Hand2` object:

```
d = Deck()
P = Hand2( d.pop() )
p.cards.append( d.pop() )
p.cards.append( d.pop() )
```

This second example uses the `*cards` parameter to load a sequence of `Cards` class in a single step:

```
d = Deck()
h = Hand2( d.pop(), d.pop(), d.pop() )
```

For unit testing, it's often helpful to build a composite object in a single statement in this way. More importantly, some of the serialization techniques from the next part will benefit from a way of building a composite object in a single, simple evaluation.

Stateless objects without __init__()

The following is an example of a degenerate class that doesn't need an `__init__()` method. It's a common design pattern for **Strategy** objects. A Strategy object is plugged into a Master object to implement an algorithm or decision. It may rely on data in the master object; the Strategy object may not have any data of its own. We often design strategy classes to follow the **Flyweight** design pattern: we avoid internal storage in the `Strategy` object. All values are provided to `Strategy` as method argument values. The `Strategy` object itself can be stateless. It's more a collection of method functions than anything else.

In this case, we're providing the game play decisions for a `Player` instance. The following is an example of a (dumb) strategy to pick cards and decline the other bets:

```
class GameStrategy:
    def insurance( self, hand ):
        return False
    def split( self, hand ):
        return False
    def double( self, hand ):
        return False
    def hit( self, hand ):
        return sum(c.hard for c in hand.cards) <= 17
```

Each method requires the current `Hand` as an argument value. The decisions are based on the available information; that is, on the dealer's cards and the player's cards.

We can build a single instance of this strategy for use by various `Player` instances as shown in the following code snippet:

```
dumb = GameStrategy()
```

We can imagine creating a family of related strategy classes, each one using different rules for the various decisions a player is offered in blackjack.

Some additional class definitions

As noted previously, a player has two strategies: one for betting and one for playing their hand. Each `Player` instance has a sequence of interactions with a larger simulation engine. We'll call the larger engine the `Table` class.

The `Table` class requires the following sequence of events by the `Player` instances:

- The player must place an initial bet based on the betting strategy.
- The player will then receive a hand.
- If the hand is splittable, the player must decide to split or not based on the play strategy. This can create additional `Hand` instances. In some casinos, the additional hands are also splittable.
- For each `Hand` instance, the player must decide to hit, double, or stand based on the play strategy.
- The player will then receive payouts, and they must update their betting strategy based on their wins and losses.

From this, we can see that the `Table` class has a number of API methods to receive a bet, create a `Hand` object, offer a split, resolve each hand, and pay off the bets. This is a large object that tracks the state of play with a collection of `Players`.

The following is the beginning of a `Table` class that handles the bets and cards:

```
class Table:
    def __init__( self ):
        self.deck = Deck()
    def place_bet( self, amount ):
        print( "Bet", amount )
    def get_hand( self ):
        try:
            self.hand= Hand2( d.pop(), d.pop(), d.pop() )
            self.hole_card= d.pop()
        except IndexError:
            # Out of cards: need to shuffle.
            self.deck= Deck()
            return self.get_hand()
        print( "Deal", self.hand )
        return self.hand
    def can_insure( self, hand ):
        return hand.dealer_card.insure
```

The `Table` class is used by the `Player` class to accept a bet, create a `Hand` object, and determine if theinsurance bet is in play for this hand. Additional methods can be used by the `Player` class to get cards and determine the payout.

The exception handling shown in `get_hand()` is not a precise model of casino play. This may lead to minor statistical inaccuracies. A more accurate simulation requires developing a deck that reshuffles itself when empty instead of raising an exception.

In order to interact properly and simulate realistic play, the `Player` class needs a betting strategy. The betting strategy is a stateful object that determines the level of the initial bet. The various betting strategies generally change the bet based on whether the game was a win or a loss.

Ideally, we'd like to have a family of betting strategy objects. Python has a module with decorators that allows us to create an abstract superclass. An informal approach to creating Strategy objects is to raise an exception for methods that *must* be implemented by a subclass.

We've defined an abstract superclass as well as a specific subclass as follows to define a flat betting strategy:

```
class BettingStrategy:
    def bet( self ):
        raise NotImplementedError( "No bet method" )
    def record_win( self ):
        pass
    def record_loss( self ):
        pass

class Flat(BettingStrategy):
    def bet( self ):
        return 1
```

The superclass defines the methods with handy default values. The basic `bet()` method in the abstract superclass raises an exception. The subclass must override the `bet()` method. The other methods can be left to provide the default values. Given the game strategy in the previous section plus the betting strategy here, we can look at more complex `__init__()` techniques surrounding the `Player` class.

We can make use of the `abc` module to formalize an abstract superclass definition. It would look like the following code snippet:

```
import abc
class BettingStrategy2(metaclass=abc.ABCMeta):
    @abstractmethod
    def bet( self ):
        return 1
    def record_win( self ):
        pass
    def record_loss( self ):
        pass
```

This has the advantage that it makes the creation of an instance of `BettingStrategy2`, or any subclass that failed to implement `bet()`, impossible. If we try to create an instance of this class with an unimplemented abstract method, it will raise an exception instead of creating an object.

And yes, the abstract method has an implementation. It can be accessed via `super().bet()`.

Multi-strategy __init__()

We may have objects that are created from a variety of sources. For example, we might need to clone an object as part of creating a memento, or freeze an object so that it can be used as the key of a dictionary or placed into a set; this is the idea behind the `set` and `frozenset` built-in classes.

There are several overall design patterns that have multiple ways to build an object. One design pattern is complex `__init__()` that is called multi-strategy initialization. Also, there are multiple class-level (static) constructor methods.

These are incompatible approaches. They have radically different interfaces.

Avoid clone methods

A clone method that unnecessarily duplicates an object is rarely needed in Python. Using cloning may be an indication of failure to understand the object-oriented design principles available in Python.

A clone method encapsulates the knowledge of object creation in the wrong place. The source object that's being cloned cannot know about the structure of the target object that was built from the clone. However, the reverse (targets having knowledge about a source) is acceptable if the source provides a reasonably well-encapsulated interface.

The examples we have shown here are effectively cloning because they're so simple. We'll expand on them in the next chapter. However, to show ways in which these fundamental techniques are used to do more than trivial cloning, we'll look at turning a mutable `Hand` object into a frozen, immutable `Hand` object.

The following is an example of a `Hand` object that can be built in either of the two ways:

```
class Hand3:
    def __init__( self, *args, **kw ):
        if len(args) == 1 and isinstance(args[0],Hand3):
            # Clone an existing hand; often a bad idea
```

```
            other= args[0]
            self.dealer_card= other.dealer_card
            self.cards= other.cards
        else:
            # Build a fresh, new hand.
            dealer_card, *cards = args
            self.dealer_card=  dealer_card
            self.cards= list(cards)
```

In the first case, a `Hand3` instance has been built from an existing `Hand3` object. In the second case, a `Hand3` object has been built from individual `Card` instances.

This parallels the way a `frozenset` object can be built from individual items or an existing `set` object. We look more at creating immutable objects in the next chapter. Creating a new `Hand` from an existing `Hand` allows us to create a memento of a `Hand` object using a construct like the following code snippet:

```
h = Hand( deck.pop(), deck.pop(), deck.pop() )
memento= Hand( h )
```

We saved the `Hand` object in the `memento` variable. This can be used to compare the final with the original hand that was dealt, or we can *freeze* it for use in a set or mapping too.

More complex initialization alternatives

In order to write a multi-strategy initialization, we're often forced to give up on specific named parameters. This design has the advantage that it is flexible, but the disadvantage that it has opaque, meaningless parameter names. It requires a great deal of documentation explaining the variant use cases.

We can expand our initialization to also split a `Hand` object. The result of splitting a `Hand` object is simply another constructor. The following code snippet shows how the splitting of a `Hand` object might look:

```
class Hand4:
    def __init__( self, *args, **kw ):
        if len(args) == 1 and isinstance(args[0],Hand4):
            # Clone an existing handl often a bad idea
            other= args[0]
            self.dealer_card= other.dealer_card
            self.cards= other.cards
        elif len(args) == 2 and isinstance(args[0],Hand4) and 'split'
in kw:
            # Split an existing hand
            other, card= args
```

```
            self.dealer_card= other.dealer_card
            self.cards= [other.cards[kw['split']], card]
        elif len(args) == 3:
            # Build a fresh, new hand.
            dealer_card, *cards = args
            self.dealer_card=  dealer_card
            self.cards= list(cards)
        else:
            raise TypeError( "Invalid constructor args={0!r}
kw={1!r}".format(args, kw) )
    def __str__( self ):
        return ", ".join( map(str, self.cards) )
```

This design involves getting extra cards to build proper, split hands. When we create one `Hand4` object from another `Hand4` object, we provide a split keyword argument that uses the index of the `Card` class from the original `Hand4` object.

The following code snippet shows how we'd use this to split a hand:

```
d = Deck()
h = Hand4( d.pop(), d.pop(), d.pop() )
s1 = Hand4( h, d.pop(), split=0 )
s2 = Hand4( h, d.pop(), split=1 )
```

We created an initial `h` instance of `Hand4` and split it into two other `Hand4` instances, `s1` and `s2`, and dealt an additional `Card` class into each. The rules of blackjack only allow this when the initial hand has two cards of equal rank.

While this `__init__()` method is rather complex, it has the advantage that it can parallel the way in which `fronzenset` is created from an existing set. The disadvantage is that it needs a large docstring to explain all these variations.

Initializing static methods

When we have multiple ways to create an object, it's sometimes more clear to use static methods to create and return instances rather than complex `__init__()` methods.

It's also possible to use class methods as alternate initializers, but there's little tangible advantage to receiving the class as an argument to the method. In the case of freezing or splitting a `Hand` object, we might want to create two new static methods to freeze or split a `Hand` object. Using static methods as surrogate constructors is a tiny syntax change in construction, but it has huge advantages when organizing the code.

The following is a version of `Hand` with static methods that can be used to build new instances of `Hand` from an existing `Hand` instance:

```
class Hand5:
    def __init__( self, dealer_card, *cards ):
        self.dealer_card= dealer_card
        self.cards = list(cards)
    @staticmethod
    def freeze( other ):
        hand= Hand5( other.dealer_card, *other.cards )
        return hand
    @staticmethod
    def split( other, card0, card1 ):
        hand0= Hand5( other.dealer_card, other.cards[0], card0 )
        hand1= Hand5( other.dealer_card, other.cards[1], card1 )
        return hand0, hand1
    def __str__( self ):
        return ", ".join( map(str, self.cards) )
```

One method freezes or creates a memento version. The other method splits a `Hand5` instance to create two new child instances of `Hand5`.

This is considerably more readable and preserves the use of the parameter names to explain the interface.

The following code snippet shows how we can split a `Hand5` instance with this version of the class:

```
d = Deck()
h = Hand5( d.pop(), d.pop(), d.pop() )
s1, s2 = Hand5.split( h, d.pop(), d.pop() )
```

We created an initial `h` instance of `Hand5`, split it into two other hands, `s1` and `s2`, and dealt an additional `Card` class into each. The `split()` static method is much simpler than the equivalent functionality implemented via `__init__()`. However, it doesn't follow the pattern of creating a `fronzenset` object from an existing `set` object.

Yet more __init__() techniques

We'll take a look at a few other, more advanced `__init__()` techniques. These aren't quite so universally useful as the techniques in the previous sections.

The following is a definition for the `Player` class that uses two strategy objects and a `table` object. This shows an unpleasant-looking `__init__()` method:

```
class Player:
```

```
    def __init__( self, table, bet_strategy, game_strategy ):
        self.bet_strategy = bet_strategy
        self.game_strategy = game_strategy
        self.table= table
    def game( self ):
        self.table.place_bet( self.bet_strategy.bet() )
        self.hand= self.table.get_hand()
        if self.table.can_insure( self.hand ):
            if self.game_strategy.insurance( self.hand ):
                self.table.insure( self.bet_strategy.bet() )
        # Yet more... Elided for now
```

The `__init__()` method for `Player` seems to do little more than bookkeeping. We're simply transferring named parameters to same-named instance variables. If we have numerous parameters, simply transferring the parameters into the internal variables will amount to a lot of redundant-looking code.

We can use this `Player` class (and related objects) as follows:

```
table = Table()
flat_bet = Flat()
dumb = GameStrategy()
p = Player( table, flat_bet, dumb )
p.game()
```

We can provide a very short and very flexible initialization by simply transferring keyword argument values directly into the internal instance variables.

The following is a way to build a `Player` class using keyword argument values:

```
class Player2:
    def __init__( self, **kw ):
        """Must provide table, bet_strategy, game_strategy."""
        self.__dict__.update( kw )
    def game( self ):
        self.table.place_bet( self.bet_strategy.bet() )
        self.hand= self.table.get_hand()
        if self.table.can_insure( self.hand ):
            if self.game_strategy.insurance( self.hand ):
                self.table.insure( self.bet_strategy.bet() )
        # etc.
```

This sacrifices a great deal of readability for succinctness. It crosses over into a realm of potential obscurity.

Since the `__init__()` method is reduced to one line, it removes a certain level of "wordiness" from the method. This wordiness, however, is transferred to each individual object constructor expression. We have to add the keywords to the object initialization expression since we're no longer using positional parameters, as shown in the following code snippet:

```
p2 = Player2( table=table, bet_strategy=flat_bet, game_strategy=dumb )
```

Why do this?

It does have a *potential* advantage. A class defined like this is quite open to extension. We can, with only a few specific worries, supply additional keyword parameters to a constructor.

The following is the expected use case:

```
>>> p1= Player2( table=table, bet_strategy=flat_bet, game_
strategy=dumb)
>>> p1.game()
```

The following is a bonus use case:

```
>>> p2= Player2( table=table, bet_strategy=flat_bet, game_
strategy=dumb, log_name="Flat/Dumb" )
>>> p2.game()
```

We've added a `log_name` attribute without touching the class definition. This can be used, perhaps, as part of a larger statistical analysis. The `Player2.log_name` attribute can be used to annotate logs or other collected data.

We are limited in what we can add; we can only add parameters that fail to conflict with the names already in use within the class. Some knowledge of the class implementation is required to create a subclass that doesn't abuse the set of keywords already in use. Since the `**kw` parameter provides little information, we need to read carefully. In most cases, we'd rather trust the class to work than review the implementation details.

This kind of keyword-based initialization can be done in a superclass definition to make it slightly simpler for the superclass to implement subclasses. We can avoiding writing an additional `__init__()` method in each subclass when the unique feature of the subclass involves simple new instance variables.

The disadvantage of this is that we have obscure instance variables that aren't formally documented via a subclass definition. If it's only one small variable, an entire subclass might be too much programming overhead to add a single variable to a class. However, one small variable often leads to a second and a third. Before long, we'll realize that a subclass would have been smarter than an extremely flexible superclass.

We can (and should) hybridize this with a mixed positional and keyword implementation as shown in the following code snippet:

```
class Player3( Player ):
    def __init__( self, table, bet_strategy, game_strategy, **extras
):
        self.bet_strategy = bet_strategy
        self.game_strategy = game_strategy
        self.table= table
        self.__dict__.update( extras )
```

This is more sensible than a completely open definition. We've made the required parameters positional parameters. We've left any nonrequired parameters as keywords. This clarifies the use of any extra keyword arguments given to the `__init__()` method.

This kind of flexible, keyword-based initialization depends on whether we have relatively transparent class definitions. This openness to change requires some care to avoid debugging name clashes because the keyword parameter names are open-ended.

Initialization with type validation

Type validation is rarely a sensible requirement. In a way, this might be a failure to fully understand Python. The notional objective is to validate that all of the arguments are of a *proper* type. The issue with trying to do this is that the definition of *proper* is often far too narrow to be truly useful.

This is different from validating that objects meet other criteria. Numeric range checking, for example, may be essential to prevent infinite loops.

What can create problems is trying to do something like the following in an `__init__()` method:

```
class ValidPlayer:
    def __init__( self, table, bet_strategy, game_strategy ):
        assert isinstance( table, Table )
        assert isinstance( bet_strategy, BettingStrategy )
        assert isinstance( game_strategy, GameStrategy )

        self.bet_strategy = bet_strategy
        self.game_strategy = game_strategy
        self.table= table
```

The `isinstance()` method checks circumvent Python's normal **duck typing**.

We write a casino game simulation in order to experiment with endless variations on `GameStrategy`. These are so simple (merely four methods) that there's little real benefit from inheritance from the superclass. We could define the classes independently, lacking an overall superclass.

The initialization error-checking shown in this example would force us to create subclasses merely to pass the error check. No usable code is inherited from the abstract superclass.

One of the biggest duck typing issues surrounds numeric types. Different numeric types will work in different contexts. Attempts to validate the types of arguments may prevent a perfectly sensible numeric type from working properly. When attempting validation, we have the following two choices in Python:

- We write validation so that a relatively narrow collection of types is permitted, and someday the code will break because a new type that would have worked sensibly is prohibited
- We eschew validation so that a broad collection of types is permitted, and someday the code will break because a type that would not work sensibly was used

Note that both are essentially the same. The code could perhaps break someday. It either breaks because a type was prevented from being used even though it's sensible or a type that's not really sensible was used.

> **Just allow it**
>
> Generally, it's considered better Python style to simply permit any type of data to be used.
>
> We'll return to this in *Chapter 4, The ABCs of Consistent Design*.

The question is this: why restrict potential future use cases?

And the usual answer is that there's no good reason to restrict potential future use cases.

Rather than prevent a sensible, but possibly unforeseen, use case, we can provide documentation, testing, and debug logging to help other programmers understand any restrictions on the types that can be processed. We have to provide the documentation, logging, and test cases anyway, so there's minimal additional work involved.

The following is an example docstring that provides the expectations of the class:

```
class Player:
    def __init__( self, table, bet_strategy, game_strategy ):
```

```
"""Creates a new player associated with a table,
  and configured with proper betting and play strategies

:param table: an instance of :class:`Table`
:param bet_strategy: an instance of :class:`BettingStrategy`
:param  game_strategy: an instance of :class:`GameStrategy`
"""
self.bet_strategy = bet_strategy
self.game_strategy = game_strategy
self.table= table
```

The programmer using this class has been warned about what the type restrictions are. The use of other types is permitted. If the type isn't compatible with the expected type, then things will break. Ideally, we'll use too like `unittest` or `doctest` to uncover the breakage.

Initialization, encapsulation, and privacy

The general Python policy regarding privacy can be summed up as follows: *we're all adults here*.

Object-oriented design makes an explicit distinction between interface and implementation. This is a consequence of the idea of encapsulation. A class encapsulates a data structure, an algorithm, an external interface, or something meaningful. The idea is to have the capsule separate the class-based interface from the implementation details.

However, no programming language reflects every design nuance. Python, typically, doesn't implement all design considerations as explicit code.

One aspect of a class design that is not fully carried into code is the distinction between the *private* (implementation) and *public* (interface) methods or attributes of an object. The notion of privacy in languages that support it (C++ or Java are two examples) is already quite complex. These languages include settings such as private, protected, and public as well as "not specified", which is a kind of semiprivate. The private keyword is often used incorrectly, making subclass definition needlessly difficult.

Python's notion of privacy is simple, as follows:

- It's all *essentially* public. The source code is available. We're all adults. Nothing can be truly hidden.

- Conventionally, we'll treat some names in a way that's less public. They're generally implementation details that are subject to change without notice, but there's no formal notion of private.

Names that begin with _ are honored as less public by some parts of Python. The `help()` function generally ignores these methods. Tools such as Sphinx can conceal these names from documentation.

Python's internal names begin (and end) with __. This is how Python internals are kept from colliding with application features above the internals. The collection of these internal names is fully defined by the language reference. Further, there's no benefit to trying to use __ to attempt to create a "super private" attribute or method in our code. All that happens is that we create a potential future problem if a release of Python ever starts using a name we chose for internal purposes. Also, we're likely to run afoul of the internal name mangling that is applied to these names.

The rules for the visibility of Python names are as follows:

- Most names are public.
- Names that start with _ are somewhat less public. Use them for implementation details that are truly subject to change.
- Names that begin and end with __ are internal to Python. We never make these up; we use the names defined by the language reference.

Generally, the Python approach is to register the intent of a method (or attribute) using documentation and a well-chosen name. Often, the interface methods will have elaborate documentation, possibly including `doctest` examples, while the implementation methods will have more abbreviated documentation and may not have `doctest` examples.

For programmers new to Python, it's sometimes surprising that privacy is not more widely used. For programmers experienced in Python, it's surprising how many brain calories get burned sorting out private and public declarations that aren't really very helpful because the intent is obvious from the method names and the documentation.

Summary

In this chapter, we have reviewed the various design alternatives of the `__init__()` method. In the next chapter, we will take a look at the special methods, along with a few advanced ones as well.

2
Integrating Seamlessly with Python – Basic Special Methods

There are a number of special methods that permit close integration between our classes and Python. *Standard Library Reference* calls them **basic**. A better term might be *foundational* or *essential*. These special methods form a foundation for building classes that seamlessly integrate with other Python features.

For example, we need string representations of a given object's value. The base class, `object`, has a default implementation of `__repr__()` and `__str__()` that provides string representations of an object. Sadly, these default representations are remarkably uninformative. We'll almost always want to override one or both of these default definitions. We'll also look at `__format__()`, which is a bit more sophisticated but serves the same purpose.

We'll also look at other conversions, specifically `__hash__()`, `__bool__()`, and `__bytes__()`. These methods will convert an object into a number, a true/false value, or a string of bytes. When we implement `__bool__()`, for example, we can use our object in an `if` statement as follows: `if someobject:`.

Then, we can look at the special methods that implement the comparison operators `__lt__()`, `__le__()`, `__eq__()`, `__ne__()`, `__gt__()`, and `__ge__()`.

These basic special methods are almost always needed in class definitions.

We'll look at `__new__()` and `__del__()` last because the use cases for these methods are rather complex. We don't need these as often as we need the other basic special methods.

We'll look in detail at how we can expand a simple class definition to add these special methods. We'll need to look at both the default behaviors inherited from object so that we can understand what overrides are needed and when they're actually needed.

The __repr__() and __str__() methods

Python has two string representations of an object. These are closely aligned with the built-in functions `repr()`, `str()`, `print()`, and the `string.format()` method.

- Generally, the `str()` method representation of an object is commonly expected to be more friendly to humans. This is built by an object's `__str__()` method.
- The `repr()` method representation is often going to be more technical, perhaps even a complete Python expression to rebuild the object. The documentation says:

  > *For many types, this function makes an attempt to return a string that would yield an object with the same value when passed to* `eval()`.

  This is built by an object's `__repr__()` method.
- The `print()` function will use `str()` to prepare an object for printing.
- The `format()` method of a string can also access these methods. When we use `{!r}` or `{!s}` formatting, we're requesting `__repr__()` or `__str__()`, respectively.

Let's look at the default implementations first.

The following is a simple class hierarchy:

```
class Card:
    insure= False
    def  __init__( self, rank, suit ):
        self.suit= suit
        self.rank= rank
        self.hard, self.soft = self._points()
class NumberCard( Card ):
    def _points( self ):
        return int(self.rank), int(self.rank)
```

We've defined two simple classes with four attributes in each class.

The following is an interaction with an object of one of these classes:

```
>>> x=NumberCard( '2', '♣')
>>> str(x)
'<__main__.NumberCard object at 0x1013ea610>'
>>> repr(x)
'<__main__.NumberCard object at 0x1013ea610>'
>>> print(x)
<__main__.NumberCard object at 0x1013ea610>
```

We can see from this output that the default implementations of `__str__()` and `__repr__()` are not very informative.

There are two broad design cases that we consider when overriding `__str__()` and `__repr__()`:

- **Non-collection objects**: A "simple" object doesn't contain a collection of other objects and generally doesn't involve very complex formatting of that collection
- **Collection objects**: An object that contains a collection involves somewhat more complex formatting

Non collection __str__() and __repr__()

As we saw previously, the output from `__str__()` and `__repr__()` are not very informative. We'll almost always need to override them. The following is an approach to override `__str__()` and `__repr__()` when there's no collection involved. These methods belong to the `Card` class, defined previously:

```
    def __repr__( self ):
        return "{__class__.__name__}(suit={suit!r}, rank={rank!r})".
format(
            __class__=self.__class__, **self.__dict__)
    def __str__( self ):
        return "{rank}{suit}".format(**self.__dict__)
```

These two methods rely on passing the object's internal instance variable dictionary, `__dict__`, to the `format()` function. This isn't appropriate for objects that use `__slots__`; often, these are immutable objects. The use of names in the format specifications makes the formatting more explicit. It also makes the format template longer. In the case of `__repr__()`, we passed in the internal `__dict__` plus the object's `__class__` as keyword argument values to the `format()` function.

The template string uses two kinds of format specifications:

- The `{__class__.__name__}` template that could also be written as `{__class__.__name__!s}` to be more explicit about providing a simple string version of the class name
- The `{suit!r}` and `{rank!r}` template both use the `!r` format specification to produce the `repr()` method of the attribute values

In the case of `__str__()`, we've only passed the object's internal `__dict__`. The formatting uses implicit `{!s}` format specifications to produce the `str()` method of the attribute values.

Collection __str__() and __repr__()

When there's a collection involved, we need to format each individual item in the collection as well as the overall container for those items. The following is a simple collection with both `__str__()` and `__repr__()` methods:

```
class Hand:
    def __init__( self, dealer_card, *cards ):
        self.dealer_card= dealer_card
        self.cards= list(cards)
    def __str__( self ):
        return ", ".join( map(str, self.cards) )
    def __repr__( self ):
        return "{__class__.__name__}({dealer_card!r}, {_cards_str})".
format(
        __class__=self.__class__,
        _cards_str=", ".join( map(repr, self.cards) ),
        **self.__dict__ )
```

The `__str__()` method is a simple recipe, as follows:

1. Map `str()` to each item in the collection. This will create an iterator over the resulting string values.
2. Use `", ".join()` to merge all the item strings into a single, long string.

The `__repr__()` method is a multiple-part recipe, as follows:

1. Map `repr()` to each item in the collection. This will create an iterator over the resulting string values.
2. Use `", ".join()` to merge all the item strings.

3. Create a set of keywords with `__class__`, the collection string, and the various attributes from `__dict__`. We've named the collection string `_cards_str` so that it doesn't conflict with an existing attribute.
4. Use `"{__class__.__name__}({dealer_card!r}, {_cards_str})".format()` to combine the class name and the long string of item values. We use the `!r` formatting to ensure that the attribute uses the `repr()` conversion too.

In some cases, this can be optimized and made somewhat simpler. Use of positional arguments for the formatting can somewhat shorten the template string.

The __format__() method

The `__format__()` method is used by `string.format()` as well as the `format()` built-in function. Both of these interfaces are used to get presentable string versions of a given object.

The following are the two ways in which arguments will be presented to `__format__()`:

- `someobject.__format__("")`: This happens when the application does `format(someobject)` or something equivalent to `"{0}".format(someobject)`. In these cases, a zero-length string specification was provided. This should produce a default format.
- `someobject.__format__(specification)`: This happens when the application does `format(someobject, specification)` or something equivalent to `"{0:specification}".format(someobject)`.

Note that something equivalent to `"{0!r}".format()` or `"{0!s}".format()` doesn't use the `__format__()` method. These use `__repr__()` or `__str__()` directly.

With a specification of `""`, a sensible response is `return str(self)`. This provides an obvious consistency between the various string representations of an object.

The format specification will be all the text after the `":"` in a format string. When we write `"{0:06.4f}"`, the `06.4f` is the format specification that applies to item `0` of the argument list to be formatted.

Section 6.1.3.1 of the *Python Standard Library* documentation defines a sophisticated numeric specification as a nine-part string. This is the format specification mini-language. It has the following syntax:

```
[[fill]align][sign][#][0][width][,][.precision][type]
```

We can parse these standard specifications with a **regular expression (RE)** as shown in the following code snippet:

```
re.compile(
r"(?P<fill_align>.?[\<\>=\^])?"
"(?P<sign>[-+ ])?"
"(?P<alt>#)?"
"(?P<padding>0)?"
"(?P<width>\d*)"
"(?P<comma>,)?"
"(?P<precision>\.\d*)?"
"(?P<type>[bcdeEfFgGnosxX%])?" )
```

This RE will break the specification into eight groups. The first group will have both the `fill` and `alignment` fields from the original specification. We can use these groups to work out the formatting for the numeric data of the classes that we've defined.

However, Python's format specification mini-language might not apply very well to the classes that we've defined. Therefore, we might need to define our own specification mini-language and process it in our class `__format__()` method. If we're defining numeric types, we should stick to the predefined mini-language. For other types, however, there's no reason to stick to the predefined language.

As an example, here's a trivial language that uses the character `%r` to show us the rank and the character `%s` to show us the suit. The `%%` character becomes `%` in the resulting string. All other characters are repeated literally.

We could extend our `Card` class with formatting as shown in the following code snippet:

```
    def __format__( self, format_spec ):
        if format_spec == "":
            return str(self)
        rs= format_spec.replace("%r",self.rank).replace("%s",self.
suit)
        rs= rs.replace("%%","%")
        return rs
```

This definition checks for a format specification. If there's no specification, then the `str()` function is used. If a specification was provided, a series of replacements is done to fold rank, suit, and any `%` characters into the format specification, turning it into the output string.

This allows us to format cards as follows:

```
print( "Dealer Has {0:%r of %s}".format( hand.dealer_card) )
```

The format specification ("%r of %s") is passed to our `__format__()` method as the `format` parameter. Using this, we're able to provide a consistent interface for the presentation of the objects of the classes that we've defined.

Alternatively, we can define things as follows:

```
    default_format= "some specification"
    def __str__( self ):
        return self.__format__( self.default_format )
    def __format__( self, format_spec ):
        if format_spec == "":  format_spec = self.default_format
       # process the format specification.
```

This has the advantage of putting all string presentations into the `__format__()` method instead of spreading it between `__format__()` and `__str__()`. This has a disadvantage because we don't always need to implement `__format__()`, but we almost always need to implement `__str__()`.

Nested formatting specifications

The `string.format()` method can handle nested instances of `{}` to perform simple keyword substitution into the format specification. This replacement is done to create the final format string that's passed to our class `__format__()` method. This kind of nested substitution simplifies some kinds of relatively complex numeric formatting by parameterizing an otherwise generic specification.

The following is an example where we've made `width` easy to change in the `format` parameter:

```
width=6
for hand,count in statistics.items():
    print( "{hand} {count:{width}d}".format(hand=hand,count=count,wid
th=width) )
```

We've defined a generic format, `"{hand:%r%s} {count:{width}d}"`, which requires a `width` parameter to make it into a proper format specification.

The value provided with the `width=` parameter to the `format()` method is used to replace the `{width}` nested specification. Once this is replaced, the final format as a whole is provided to the `__format__()` method.

Collections and delegating format specifications

When formatting a complex object that includes a collection, we have two formatting issues: how to format the overall object and how to format the items in the collection. When we look at `Hand`, for example, we see that we have a collection of individual `Cards` class. We'd like to have `Hand` delegate some formatting details to the individual `Card` instances in the `Hand` collection.

The following is a `__format__()` method that applies to `Hand`:

```
    def __format__( self, format_specification ):
        if format_specification == "":
            return str(self)
        return ", ".join( "{0:{fs}}".format(c, fs=format_
specification)
            for c in self.cards )
```

The `format_specification` parameter will be used for each individual `Card` instance within the `Hand` collection. The format specification of `"{0:{fs}}"` uses the nested format specification technique to push the `format_specification` string to create a format that applies to each `Card` instance. Given this method, we can format a `Hand` object, `player_hand`, as follows:

```
"Player: {hand:%r%s}".format(hand=player_hand)
```

This will apply the `%r%s` format specification to each `Card` instance of the `Hand` object.

The __hash__() method

The built-in `hash()` function invokes the `__hash__()` method of a given object. This hash is a calculation which reduces a (potentially complex) value to a small integer value. Ideally, a hash reflects all the bits of the source value. Other hash calculations—often used for cryptographic purposes—can produce very large values.

Python includes two hash libraries. The cryptographic-quality hash functions are in `hashlib`. The `zlib` module has two high-speed hash functions: `adler32()` and `crc32()`. For relatively simple values, we don't use either of these. For large, complex values, these algorithms can be of help.

The `hash()` function (and the associated `__hash__()` method) is used to create a small integer key that is used to work with collections such as `set`, `frozenset`, and `dict`. These collections use the hash value of an **immutable** object to rapidly locate the object in the collection.

Immutability is important here; we'll mention it many times. Immutable objects don't change their state. The number `3`, for example, doesn't change state. It's always `3`. More complex objects, similarly, can have an immutable state. Python strings are immutable so that they can be used as keys to mappings and sets.

The default `__hash__()` implementation inherited from an object returns a value based on the object's internal ID value. This value can be seen with the `id()` function as follows:

```
>>> x = object()
>>> hash(x)
269741571
>>> id(x)
4315865136
>>> id(x) / 16
269741571.0
```

From this, we can see that on the author's particular system, the hash value is the object's `id//16`. This detail might vary from platform to platform. CPython, for example, uses portable `C` libraries where Jython relies on the Java JVM.

What's essential is that there is a strong correlation between the internal ID and the default `__hash__()` method. This means that the default behavior is for each object to be hashable as well as utterly distinct, even if it appears to have the same value.

We'll need to modify this if we want to coalesce different objects with the same value into a single hashable object. We'll look at an example in the next section, where we would like two instances of a single `Card` instance to be treated as if they were the same object.

Deciding what to hash

Not every object should provide a hash value. Specifically, if we're creating a class of stateful, mutable objects, the class should *never* return a hash value. The definition of `__hash__` should be `None`.

Immutable objects, on the other hand, might sensibly return a hash value so that the object can be used as the key in a dictionary or a member of a set. In this case, the hash value needs to parallel the way the test for equality works. It's bad to have objects that claim to be equal and have different hash values. The reverse—objects with the same hash that are actually not equal—is acceptable.

The `__eq__()` method, which we'll also look at in the section on comparison operators, is intimately tied up with hashing.

There are three tiers of equality comparison:

- **Same Hash Value**: This means that two objects could be equal. The hash value provides us with a quick check for likely equality. If the hash value is different, the two objects cannot possibly be equal, nor can they be the same object.
- **Compare As Equal**: This means that the hash values must also have been equal. This is the definition of the `==` operator. The objects may be the same object.
- **Same IDD**: This means that they are the same object. They also compare as equal and will have the same hash value. This is the definition of the `is` operator.

The **Fundamental Law of Hash** (**FLH**) is this: objects that compare as equal have the same hash value.

We can think of a hash comparison as being the first step in an equality test.

The inverse, however, is not true. Objects can have the same hash value but compare as not equal. This is valid and leads to some expected processing overhead when creating sets or dictionaries. We can't reliably create distinct 64 bit hash values from much larger data structures. There will be unequal objects that are reduced to coincidentally equal hash values.

Coincidentally, equal hash values are an expected overhead when working with `sets` and `dicts`. These collections have internal algorithms to use alternate locations in the event of hash collisions.

There are three use cases for defining equality tests and hash values via the `__eq__()` and `__hash__()` method functions:

- **Immutable objects**: These are stateless objects of types such as tuples, namedtuples, and frozensets that cannot be updated. We have two choices:
    - Define neither `__hash__()` nor `__eq__()`. This means doing nothing and using the inherited definitions. In this case, `__hash__()` returns a trivial function of the ID value for the object, and `__eq__()` compares the ID values. The default equality test may sometimes be counterintuitive. Our application might require two instances of `Card( 1, Clubs )` to test as equal and compute the same hash; this won't happen by default.
    - Define both `__hash__()` and `__eq__()`. Note that we're expected to define both for an immutable object.

- **Mutable objects**: These are stateful objects that can be modified internally. We have one design choice:
    - Define `__eq__()` but set `__hash__` to `None`. These cannot be used as `dict` keys or items in `sets`.

Note that there's an additional possible combination: defining `__hash__()` but using a default definition for `__eq__()`. This is simply a waste of code, as the default `__eq__()` method is the same as the `is` operator. The default `__hash__()` method would have involved writing less code for the same behavior.

We'll look at each of the three situations in detail.

Inheriting definitions for immutable objects

Let's see how the default definitions operate. The following is a simple class hierarchy that uses the default definitions of `__hash__()` and `__eq__()`:

```
class Card:
    insure= False
    def  __init__( self, rank, suit, hard, soft ):
        self.rank= rank
        self.suit= suit
        self.hard= hard
        self.soft= soft
    def  __repr__( self ):
        return "{__class__.__name__}(suit={suit!r}, rank={rank!r})".
format(__class__=self.__class__, **self.__dict__)
    def  __str__( self ):
        return "{rank}{suit}".format(**self.__dict__)

class NumberCard( Card ):
    def   __init__( self, rank, suit ):
        super().__init__( str(rank), suit, rank, rank )

class AceCard( Card ):
    def   __init__( self, rank, suit ):
        super().__init__( "A", suit, 1, 11 )

class FaceCard( Card ):
    def   __init__( self, rank, suit ):
        super().__init__( {11: 'J', 12: 'Q', 13: 'K' }[rank], suit,
10, 10 )
```

This is a class hierarchy for *philosophically* immutable objects. We haven't taken care to implement the special methods that prevent the attributes from getting updated. We'll look at attribute access in the next chapter.

Let's see what happens when we use this class hierarchy:

```
>>> c1 = AceCard( 1, '♣' )
>>> c2 = AceCard( 1, '♣' )
```

We defined two instances of what appear to be the same `Card` instance. We can check the `id()` values as shown in the following code snippet:

```
>>> print( id(c1), id(c2) )
4302577232 4302576976
```

They have different `id()` numbers; they're distinct objects. This meets our expectations.

We can check to see if they're the same using the `is` operator as shown in the following code snippet:

```
>>> c1 is c2
False
```

The "is test" is based on the `id()` numbers; it shows us that they are indeed separate objects.

We can see that their hash values are different from each other:

```
>>> print( hash(c1), hash(c2) )
268911077 268911061
```

These hash values come directly from the `id()` values. This is our expectation for the inherited methods. In this implementation, we can compute the hash from the `id()` function as shown in the following code snippet:

```
>>> id(c1) / 16
268911077.0
>>> id(c2) / 16
268911061.0
```

As the hash values are different, they must not compare as equal. This fits the definitions of hash and equality. However, this violates our expectations for this class. The following is an equality check:

```
>>> print( c1 == c2 )
False
```

We created them with the same arguments. They didn't compare as equal. In some applications, this might not be good. For example, when accumulating statistical counts around dealer cards, we don't want to have six counts for one card because the simulation used a 6-deck shoe.

We can see that they're proper immutable objects as we can put them into a set:

```
>>> print( set( [c1, c2] ) )
{AceCard(suit='♣', rank=1), AceCard(suit='♣', rank=1)}
```

This is the documented behavior from the *Standard Library Reference* documentation. By default, we'll get a `__hash__()` method based on the ID of the object so that each instance appears unique. However, this isn't always what we want.

Overriding definitions for immutable objects

The following is a simple class hierarchy that provides us with definitions of `__hash__()` and `__eq__()`:

```
class Card2:
    insure= False
    def __init__( self, rank, suit, hard, soft ):
        self.rank= rank
        self.suit= suit
        self.hard= hard
        self.soft= soft
    def __repr__( self ):
        return "{__class__.__name__}(suit={suit!r}, rank={rank!r})".
format(__class__=self.__class__, **self.__dict__)
    def __str__( self ):
        return "{rank}{suit}".format(**self.__dict__)
    def __eq__( self, other ):
        return self.suit == other.suit and self.rank == other.rank
    def __hash__( self ):
        return hash(self.suit) ^ hash(self.rank)
class AceCard2( Card2 ):
    insure= True
    def  __init__( self, rank, suit ):
        super().__init__( "A", suit, 1, 11 )
```

This object is immutable in principle. There's no formal mechanism to make it immutable. We'll look at how to prevent the attribute value changes in *Chapter 3, Attribute Access, Properties, and Descriptors*.

Also, note that the preceding code omits two of the subclasses that didn't change significantly from the previous example.

The `__eq__()` method function compares these two essential values: `suit` and `rank`. It doesn't compare the hard and soft values; they're derived from `rank`.

The rules for Blackjack make this definition a bit suspicious. Suit doesn't actually matter in Blackjack. Should we merely compare rank? Should we define an additional method that compares rank only? Or, should we rely on the application to compare ranks properly? There's no best answer to these questions; these are just trade-offs.

The `__hash__()` method function computes a bit pattern from the two essential values using an exclusive OR of the bits that comprise each value. Using the ^ operator is a quick-and-dirty hash method that often works pretty well. For larger and more complex objects, a more sophisticated hash might be appropriate. Start with `ziplib` before inventing something that has bugs.

Let's see how objects of these classes behave. We expect them to compare as equal and behave properly with sets and dictionaries. Here are two objects:

```
>>> c1 = AceCard2( 1, '♣' )
>>> c2 = AceCard2( 1, '♣' )
```

We defined two instances of what appear to be the same card. We can check the ID values to be sure that they're distinct objects:

```
>>> print( id(c1), id(c2) )
4302577040 4302577296
>>> print( c1 is c2 )
False
```

These have different `id()` numbers. When we test with the `is` operator, we see that they're distinct.

Let's compare the hash values:

```
>>> print( hash(c1), hash(c2) )
1259258073890 1259258073890
```

The hash values are identical. This means that they could be equal.

The equality operator shows us that they properly compare as equal:

```
>>> print( c1 == c2 )
True
```

As they're immutable, we can put them into a set as follows:

```
>>> print( set( [c1, c2] ) )
{AceCard2(suit='♣', rank='A')}
```

This meets our expectations for complex immutable objects. We had to override both special methods to get consistent, meaningful results.

Overriding definitions for mutable objects

This example will continue using the `Cards` class. The idea of mutable cards is strange, perhaps even wrong. However, we'd like to apply just one small tweak to the previous examples.

The following is a class hierarchy that provides us with the definitions of `__hash__()` and `__eq__()`, appropriate for mutable objects:

```
class Card3:
    insure= False
    def __init__( self, rank, suit, hard, soft ):
        self.rank= rank
        self.suit= suit
        self.hard= hard
        self.soft= soft
    def __repr__( self ):
        return "{__class__.__name__}(suit={suit!r}, rank={rank!r})".
format(__class__=self.__class__, **self.__dict__)
    def __str__( self ):
        return "{rank}{suit}".format(**self.__dict__)
    def __eq__( self, other ):
        return self.suit == other.suit and self.rank == other.rank
        # and self.hard == other.hard and self.soft == other.soft
    __hash__ = None
class AceCard3( Card3 ):
    insure= True
    def  __init__( self, rank, suit ):
        super().__init__( "A", suit, 1, 11 )
```

Let's see how objects of these classes behave. We expect them to compare as equal but not work at all with sets or dictionaries. We'll create two objects as follows:

```
>>> c1 = AceCard3( 1, '♣' )
>>> c2 = AceCard3( 1, '♣' )
```

We've defined two instances of what appear to be the same card.

We'll look at their ID values to ensure they really are distinct:

```
>>> print( id(c1), id(c2) )
4302577040 4302577296
```

No surprise here. We'll see if we can get hash values:

```
>>> print( hash(c1), hash(c2) )
Traceback (most recent call last):
  File "<stdin>", line 1, in <module>
TypeError: unhashable type: 'AceCard3'
```

As `__hash__` is set to `None`, these `Card3` objects can't be hashed and can't provide a value for the `hash()` function. This is the expected behavior.

We can perform equality comparisons, though, as shown in the following code snippet:

```
>>> print( c1 == c2 )
True
```

The equality test works properly, allowing us to compare cards. They just can't be inserted into sets or used as a key to a dictionary.

The following is what happens when we try:

```
>>> print( set( [c1, c2] ) )
Traceback (most recent call last):
  File "<stdin>", line 1, in <module>
TypeError: unhashable type: 'AceCard3'
```

We get a proper exception when trying to put these into a set.

Clearly, this is not a proper definition for something that—in real life—is immutable like a card. This style of definition is more appropriate for stateful objects such as `Hand`, where the content of the hand is always changing. We'll provide you with a second example of stateful objects in the following section.

Making a frozen hand from a mutable hand

If we want to perform statistical analysis of specific `Hand` instances, we might want to create a dictionary that maps a `Hand` instance to a count. We can't use a mutable `Hand` class as the key in a mapping. We can, however, parallel the design of `set` and `frozenset` and create two classes: `Hand` and `FrozenHand`. This allows us to "freeze" a `Hand` class via `FrozenHand`; the frozen version is immutable and can be used as a key in a dictionary.

The following is a simple `Hand` definition:

```
class Hand:
     def __init__( self, dealer_card, *cards ):
        self.dealer_card= dealer_card
        self.cards= list(cards)
    def __str__( self ):
        return ", ".join( map(str, self.cards) )
    def __repr__( self ):
        return "{__class__.__name__}({dealer_card!r}, {_cards_str})".
format(
        __class__=self.__class__,
        _cards_str=", ".join( map(repr, self.cards) ),
        **self.__dict__ )
    def __eq__( self, other ):
        return self.cards == other.cards and self.dealer_card ==
other.dealer_card
    __hash__ = None
```

This is a mutable object (`__hash__` is `None`) that has a proper equality test that compares two hands.

The following is a frozen version of `Hand`:

```
import sys
class FrozenHand( Hand ):
    def __init__( self, *args, **kw ):
        if len(args) == 1 and isinstance(args[0], Hand):
            # Clone a hand
            other= args[0]
            self.dealer_card= other.dealer_card
            self.cards= other.cards
        else:
            # Build a fresh hand
            super().__init__( *args, **kw )
    def __hash__( self ):
        h= 0
        for c in self.cards:
            h = (h + hash(c)) % sys.hash_info.modulus
        return h
```

The frozen version has a constructor that will build one `Hand` class from another `Hand` class. It defines a `__hash__()` method that sums the card's hash value that is limited to the `sys.hash_info.modulus` value. For the most part, this kind of modulus-based calculation works out reasonably well for computing hashes of composite objects.

We can now use these classes for operations such as the following code snippet:

```
stats = defaultdict(int)

d= Deck()
h = Hand( d.pop(), d.pop(), d.pop() )
h_f = FrozenHand( h )
stats[h_f] += 1
```

We've initialized a statistics dictionary, `stats`, as a `defaultdict` dictionary that can collect integer counts. We could also use a `collections.Counter` object for this.

By freezing a `Hand` class, we can use it as a key in a dictionary, collecting counts of each hand that actually gets dealt.

The __bool__() method

Python has a pleasant definition of falsity. The reference manual lists a large number of values that will test as equivalent to `False`. This includes things such as `False`, `0`, `''`, `()`, `[]`, and `{}`. Most other objects will test as equivalent to `True`.

Often, we'll want to check for an object being "not empty" with a simple statement as follows:

```
if some_object:
    process( some_object )
```

Under the hood, this is the job of the `bool()` built-in function. This function depends on the `__bool__()` method of a given object.

The default `__bool__()` method returns `True`. We can see this with the following code:

```
>>> x = object()
>>> bool(x)
True
```

For most classes, this is perfectly valid. Most objects are not expected to be `False`. For collections, however, this is not appropriate. An empty collection should be equivalent to `False`. A nonempty collection can return `True`. We might want to add a method like this to our `Deck` objects.

If we're wrapping a list, we might have something as shown in the following code snippet:

```
def __bool__( self ):
    return bool( self._cards )
```

This delegates the Boolean function to the internal `_cards` collection.

If we're extending a list, we might have something as follows:

```
def __bool__( self ):
    return super().__bool__( self )
```

This delegates to the superclass definition of the `__bool__()` function.

In both cases, we're specifically delegating the Boolean test. In the wrap case, we're delegating to the collection. In the extend case, we're delegating to the superclass. Either way, wrap or extend, an empty collection will be `False`. This will give us a way to see whether the `Deck` object has been entirely dealt and is empty.

We can do things as shown in the following code snippet:

```
d = Deck()
while d:
    card= d.pop()
    # process the card
```

This loop will deal all the cards without getting an `IndexError` exception when the deck has been exhausted.

The __bytes__() method

There are relatively few occasions to transform an object into bytes. We'll look at this in detail in *Part 2, Persistence and Serialization*.

In the most common situation, an application can create a string representation, and the built-in encoding capabilities of the Python IO classes will be used to transform the string into bytes. This works perfectly for almost all situations. The main exception would be when we're defining a new kind of string. In that case, we'd need to define the encoding of that string.

The `bytes()` function does a variety of things, depending on the arguments:

- `bytes(integer)`: This returns an immutable bytes object with the given number of `0x00` values.
- `bytes(string)`: This will encode the given string into bytes. Additional parameters for encoding and error handling will define the details of the encoding process.
- `bytes(something)`: This will invoke `something.__bytes__()` to create a bytes object. The encoding or error arguments will not be used here.

The base `object` class does not define `__bytes__()`. This means our classes don't provide a `__bytes__()` method by default.

There are some exceptional cases where we might have an object that will need to be encoded directly into bytes before being written to a file. It's often simpler to work with strings and allow the `str` type to produce bytes for us. When working with bytes, it's important to note that there's no *trivial* way to decode bytes from a file or interface. The built-in `bytes` class will only decode strings, not our unique, new objects. We might need to parse the strings that are decoded from the bytes. Or, we might need to explicitly parse the bytes using the `struct` module and create our unique objects from the parsed values.

We'll look at encoding and decoding `Card` to bytes. As there are only 52 card values, each card could be packed into a single byte. However, we've elected to use a character to represent `suit` and a character to represent `rank`. Further, we'll need to properly reconstruct the subclass of `Card`, so we have to encode several things:

- The subclass of `Card` (`AceCard`, `NumberCard`, `FaceCard`)
- The parameters to the subclass-defined `__init__()`

Note that some of our alternative `__init__()` methods will transform a numeric rank into a string, losing the original numeric value. For the purposes of a reversible byte encoding, we need to reconstruct this original numeric rank value.

The following is an implementation of `__bytes__()`, which returns a **UTF-8** encoding of the `Cards` class, `rank`, and `suit`:

```
    def __bytes__( self ):
        class_code= self.__class__.__name__[0]
        rank_number_str = {'A': '1', 'J': '11', 'Q': '12', 'K': '13'}.
get( self.rank, self.rank )
        string= "("+" ".join([class_code, rank_number_str, self.suit,]
) + ")"
        return bytes(string,encoding="utf8")
```

This works by creating a string representation of the `Card` object and then encoding the string into bytes. This is often the simplest and most flexible approach.

When we are given a pile of bytes, we can decode the string and then parse the string into a new `Card` object. The following is a method that can be used to create a `Card` object from bytes:

```
def card_from_bytes( buffer ):
    string = buffer.decode("utf8")
    assert string[0 ]=="(" and string[-1] == ")"
    code, rank_number, suit = string[1:-1].split()
    class_ = { 'A': AceCard, 'N': NumberCard, 'F': FaceCard }[code]
    return class_( int(rank_number), suit )
```

In the preceding code, we've decoded the bytes into a string. Then we've parsed the string into individual values. From those values, we can locate the class and build the original `Card` object.

We can build a bytes representation of a `Card` object as follows:

```
b= bytes(someCard)
```

We can reconstruct the `Card` object from the bytes as follows:

```
someCard = card_from_bytes(b)
```

It's important to note that the external bytes representation is often challenging to design. We're creating a representation of the state of an object. Python already has a number of representations that work well for our class definitions.

It's often better to use the `pickle` or `json` modules than to invent a low-level bytes representation of an object. This is the subject of *Chapter 9, Serializing and Saving – JSON, YAML, Pickle, CSV, and XML*.

The comparison operator methods

Python has six comparison operators. These operators have special method implementations. According to the documentation, the mapping works as follows:

- `x<y` calls `x.__lt__(y)`
- `x<=y` calls `x.__le__(y)`
- `x==y` calls `x.__eq__(y)`
- `x!=y` calls `x.__ne__(y)`
- `x>y` calls `x.__gt__(y)`
- `x>=y` calls `x.__ge__(y)`

We'll return to comparison operators again when looking at numbers in *Chapter 7, Creating Numbers*.

There's an additional rule regarding what operators are actually implemented that's relevant here. These rules are based on the idea that the object's class on the left defines the required special method. If it doesn't, Python can try an alternative operation by changing the order.

Here are the two basic rules

First, the operand on the left is checked for an operator implementation: `A<B` means `A.__lt__(B)`.

Second, the operand on the right is checked for a reversed operator implementation: `A<B` means `B.__gt__(A)`.

The rare exception to this occurs when the right operand is a subclass of the left operand; then, the right operand is checked first to allow a subclass to override a superclass.

We can see how this works by defining a class with only one of the operators defined and then using it for other operations.

The following is a partial class that we can use:

```
class BlackJackCard_p:
    def __init__( self, rank, suit ):
        self.rank= rank
        self.suit= suit
    def __lt__( self, other ):
        print( "Compare {0} < {1}".format( self, other ) )
        return self.rank < other.rank
    def __str__( self ):
        return "{rank}{suit}".format( **self.__dict__ )
```

This follows the Blackjack comparison rules where suits don't matter. We've omitted comparison methods to see how Python will fallback when an operator is missing. This class will allow us to perform the `<` comparisons. Interestingly, Python can also use this to perform the `>` comparisons by switching the argument order. In other words, $x<y \equiv y>x$. This is the mirror reflection rule; we'll see it again in *Chapter 7, Creating Numbers*.

We see this when we try to evaluate different comparison operations. We'll create two `Cards` classes and compare them in various ways as shown in the following code snippet:

```
>>> two = BlackJackCard_p( 2, '♠' )
>>> three = BlackJackCard_p( 3, '♠' )
>>> two < three
Compare 2♠ < 3♠
True
>>> two > three
Compare 3♠ < 2♠
False
>>> two == three
False
>>> two <= three
Traceback (most recent call last):
  File "<stdin>", line 1, in <module>
TypeError: unorderable types: BlackJackCard_p() <= BlackJackCard_p()
```

From this, we can see where `two < three` maps to `two.__lt__(three)`.

However, for `two > three`, there's no `__gt__()` method defined; Python uses `three.__lt__(two)` as a fallback plan.

By default, the `__eq__()` method is inherited from `object`; it compares the object IDs; the objects participate in `==` and `!=` tests as follows:

```
>>> two_c = BlackJackCard_p( 2, '♣' )
>>> two == two_c
False
```

We can see that the results aren't quite what we expect. We'll often need to override the default implementation of `__eq__()`.

Also, there's no logical connection among the operators. Mathematically, we can derive all the necessary comparisons from just two. Python doesn't do this automatically. Instead, Python handles the following four simple reflection pairs by default:

$$x < y \equiv y > x$$

$$x \leq y \equiv y \geq x$$

$$x = y \equiv y = x$$

$$x \neq y \equiv y \neq x$$

This means that we must, at the minimum, provide one from each of the four pairs. For example, we could provide `__eq__()`, `__ne__()`, `__lt__()`, and `__le__()`.

The `@functools.total_ordering` decorator overcomes the default limitation and deduces the rest of the comparisons from just `__eq__()` and one of these: `__lt__()`, `__le__()`, `__gt__()`, or `__ge__()`. We'll revisit this in *Chapter 7, Creating Numbers*.

Designing comparisons

There are two considerations when defining the comparison operators:

- The obvious question of how to compare two objects of the same class
- The less obvious question of how to compare objects of different classes

For a class with multiple attributes, we often have a profound ambiguity when looking at the comparison operators. It might not be perfectly clear what we're going to compare.

Consider the humble playing card (again!). An expression such as `card1 == card2` is clearly intended to compare `rank` and `suit`. Right? Or is that always true? After all, `suit` doesn't matter in Blackjack.

If we want to decide whether a `Hand` object can be split, we have to see which of the two code snippets is better. The following is the first code snippet:

```
if hand.cards[0] == hand.cards[1]
```

The following is the second code snippet:

```
if hand.cards[0].rank == hand.cards[1].rank
```

While one is shorter, brevity is not always best. If we define equality to only consider `rank`, we will have trouble defining unit tests because a simple `TestCase.assertEqual()` method will tolerate a wide variety of cards when a unit test should be focused on exactly correct cards.

An expression such as `card1 <= 7` is clearly intended to compare `rank`.

Do we want some comparisons to compare all attributes of a card and other comparisons to compare just `rank`? What do we do to order cards by `suit`? Furthermore, equality comparison must parallel the hash calculation. If we've included multiple attributes in the hash, we need to include them in the equality comparison. In this case, it appears that equality (and inequality) between cards must be full `Card` comparisons because we're hashing the `Card` values to include `rank` and `suit`.

The ordering comparisons between `Card`, however, should be `rank` only. Comparisons against integers, similarly, should be `rank` only. For the special case of detecting a split, `hand.cards[0].rank == hand.cards[1].rank` will do nicely because it's explicit on the rule for a split.

Implementation of comparison for objects of the same class

We'll look at a simple same-class comparison by looking at a more complete `BlackJackCard` class:

```
class BlackJackCard:
    def __init__( self, rank, suit, hard, soft ):
        self.rank= rank
        self.suit= suit
        self.hard= hard
        self.soft= soft
    def __lt__( self, other ):
        if not isinstance( other, BlackJackCard ): return
NotImplemented
        return self.rank < other.rank

    def __le__( self, other ):
        try:
            return self.rank <= other.rank
        except AttributeError:
            return NotImplemented
    def __gt__( self, other ):
        if not isinstance( other, BlackJackCard ): return
NotImplemented
        return self.rank > other.rank
    def __ge__( self, other ):
        if not isinstance( other, BlackJackCard ): return
NotImplemented
        return self.rank >= other.rank
    def __eq__( self, other ):
        if not isinstance( other, BlackJackCard ): return
NotImplemented
        return self.rank == other.rank and self.suit == other.suit
    def __ne__( self, other ):
        if not isinstance( other, BlackJackCard ): return
NotImplemented
```

```
            return self.rank != other.rank and self.suit != other.suit
        def __str__( self ):
            return "{rank}{suit}".format( **self.__dict__ )
```

We've now defined all six comparison operators.

We've shown you two kinds of type checking: **explicit** and **implicit**. The explicit type checking uses `isinstance()`. The implicit type checking uses a `try:` block. There's a tiny conceptual advantage to using the `try:` block: it avoids repeating the name of a class. It's entirely possible that someone might want to invent a variation on a card that's compatible with this definition of `BlackJackCard` but not defined as a proper subclass. Using `isinstance()` might prevent an otherwise valid class from working correctly.

The `try:` block might allow a class that coincidentally happens to have a `rank` attribute to work. The risk of this turning into a difficult-to-solve problem is nil, as the class would likely fail everywhere else it was used in this application. Also, who compares an instance of `Card` with a class from a financial modeling application that happens to have a rank-ordering attribute?

In future examples, we'll focus on the `try:` block. The `isinstance()` method check is idiomatic Python and is widely used. We explicitly return `NotImplemented` to inform Python that this operator isn't implemented for this type of data. Python can try reversing the argument order to see if the other operand provides an implementation. If no valid operator can be found, then a `TypeError` exception will be raised.

We omitted the three subclass definitions and the factory function, `card21()`. They're left as an exercise.

We also omitted intraclass comparisons; we'll save that for the next section. With this class, we can compare cards successfully. The following is an example where we create and compare three cards:

```
>>> two = card21( 2, '♠' )
>>> three = card21( 3, '♠' )
>>> two_c = card21( 2, '♣' )
```

Given those `Cards` classes, we can perform a number of comparisons as shown in the following code snippet:

```
>>> two == two_c
False
>>> two.rank == two_c.rank
True
```

```
>>> two < three
True
>>> two_c < three
True
```

The definitions seem to work as expected.

Implementation of comparison for objects of mixed classes

We'll use the `BlackJackCard` class as an example to see what happens when we attempt comparisons where the two operands are from different classes.

The following is a `Card` instance that we can compare against the `int` values:

```
>>> two = card21( 2, '♣' )
>>> two < 2
Traceback (most recent call last):
  File "<stdin>", line 1, in <module>
TypeError: unorderable types: Number21Card() < int()
>>> two > 2
Traceback (most recent call last):
  File "<stdin>", line 1, in <module>
TypeError: unorderable types: Number21Card() > int()
```

This is what we expected: the subclass of `BlackJackCard`, `Number21Card` doesn't provide the required special methods, so there's a `TypeError` exception.

However, consider the following two examples:

```
>>> two == 2
False
>>> two == 3
False
```

Why do these provide responses? When confronted with a `NotImplemented` value, Python will reverse the operands. In this case, the integer values define an `int.__eq__()` method that tolerates objects of an unexpected class.

Hard totals, soft totals, and polymorphism

Let's define `Hand` so that it will perform a meaningful mixed-class comparison. As with other comparisons, we have to determine precisely what we're going to compare.

For equality comparisons between `Hands`, we should compare all cards.

For ordering comparisons between `Hands`, we need to compare an attribute of each `Hand` object. For comparisons against an `int` literal, we should compare the `Hand` object's total against the literal. In order to have a total, we have to sort out the subtlety of hard totals and soft totals in the game of Blackjack.

When there's an ace in a hand, then the following are two candidate totals:

- The **soft total** treats an ace as 11. If the soft total is over 21, then this version of the ace has to be ignored.
- The **hard total** treats an ace as 1.

This means that the hand's total isn't a simple sum of the cards.

We have to determine if there's an ace in the hand first. Given that information, we can determine if there's a valid (less than or equal to 21) soft total. Otherwise, we'll fall back on the hard total.

One symptom of **Pretty Poor Polymorphism** is relying on `isinstance()` to determine the subclass membership. Generally, this is a violation of the basic encapsulation. A good set of polymorphic subclass definitions should be completely equivalent with the same method signatures. Ideally, the class definitions are opaque; we don't need to look inside the class definition. A poor set of polymorphic classes uses extensive `isinstance()` testing. In some cases, `isinstance()` is necessary. This can arise when using a built-in class. We can't retroactively add method functions to built-in classes, and it might not be worth the effort of subclassing them to add a polymorphism helper method.

In some of the special methods, it's necessary to see `isinstance()` used to implement operations that work across multiple classes of objects where there's no simple inheritance hierarchy. We'll show you an idiomatic use of `isinstance()` for unrelated classes in the next section.

For our cards class hierarchy, we want a method (or an attribute) that identifies an ace without having to use `isinstance()`. This is a polymorphism helper method. It ensures we can tell otherwise equivalent classes apart.

We have two choices:

- Add a class-level attribute
- Add a method

Because of the way the insurance bet works, we have two reasons to check for aces. If the dealer's card is an ace, it triggers an insurance bet. If the dealer's hand (or the player's hand) has an ace, there will be a soft total versus hard total calculation.

The hard total and soft total always differ by the `card.soft-card.hard` value for the card that's an ace. We can look inside the definition of `AceCard` to see that this value is 10. However, looking at the implementation breaks encapsulation by looking deeply at a class implementation.

We can treat `BlackjackCard` as opaque and check to see whether `card.soft-card.hard!=0` is true. If this is true, it is sufficient information to work out the hard total versus soft total of the hand.

The following is a version of the `total` method that makes use of the soft versus hard delta value:

```
def total( self ):
    delta_soft = max( c.soft-c.hard for c in self.cards )
    hard = sum( c.hard for c in self.cards )
    if hard+delta_soft <= 21: return hard+delta_soft
    return hard
```

We'll compute the largest difference between the hard and soft total as `delta_soft`. For most cards, the difference is zero. For an ace, the difference will be nonzero.

Given the hard total and `delta_soft`, we can determine which total to return. If `hard+delta_soft` is less than or equal to 21, the value is the soft total. If the soft total is greater than 21, then revert to a hard total.

We can consider making the value 21 a manifest constant in the class. A meaningful name is sometimes more helpful than a literal. Because of the rules of Blackjack, it's unlikely that 21 would ever change to a different value. It's difficult to find a more meaningful name than the literal 21.

A mixed class comparison example

Given a definition of a total for a `Hand` object, we can meaningfully define comparisons between the `Hand` instances and comparisons between `Hand` and `int`. In order to determine which kind of comparison we're doing, we're forced to use `isinstance()`.

The following is a partial definition of `Hand` with comparisons:

```
class Hand:
    def __init__( self, dealer_card, *cards ):
        self.dealer_card= dealer_card
        self.cards= list(cards)
    def __str__( self ):
```

```
            return ", ".join( map(str, self.cards) )
        def __repr__( self ):
            return "{__class__.__name__}({dealer_card!r}, {_cards_str})".
format(
            __class__=self.__class__,
            _cards_str=", ".join( map(repr, self.cards) ),
            **self.__dict__ )

        def __eq__( self, other ):
            if isinstance(other,int):
                return self.total() == other
            try:
                return (self.cards == other.cards
                    and self.dealer_card == other.dealer_card)
            except AttributeError:
                return NotImplemented
        def __lt__( self, other ):
            if isinstance(other,int):
                return self.total() < other
            try:
                return self.total() < other.total()
            except AttributeError:
                return NotImplemented
        def __le__( self, other ):
            if isinstance(other,int):
                return self.total() <= other
            try:
                return self.total() <= other.total()
            except AttributeError:
                return NotImplemented
        __hash__ = None
        def total( self ):
            delta_soft = max( c.soft-c.hard for c in self.cards )
            hard = sum( c.hard for c in self.cards )
            if hard+delta_soft <= 21: return hard+delta_soft
            return hard
```

We've defined three of the comparisons, not all six.

In order to interact with `Hands`, we'll need a few `Card` objects:

```
>>> two = card21( 2, '♠' )
>>> three = card21( 3, '♠' )
>>> two_c = card21( 2, '♣' )
```

```
>>> ace = card21( 1, '♣' )
>>> cards = [ ace, two, two_c, three ]
```

We'll use this sequence of cards to see two different `hand` instances.

This first `Hands` object has an irrelevant dealer's `Card` object and the set of four `Cards` created previously. One of the `Card` objects is an ace:

```
>>> h= Hand( card21(10,'♠'), *cards )
>>> print(h)
A♣, 2♠, 2♣, 3♠
>>> h.total()
18
```

The soft total is 18 and the hard total is 8.

The following is a second `Hand` object that has an additional `Card` object:

```
>>> h2= Hand( card21(10,'♠'), card21(5,'♠'), *cards )
>>> print(h2)
5♠, A♣, 2♠, 2♣, 3♠
>>> h2.total()
13
```

The hard total is 13. There's no soft total because it would be over 21.

The comparisons among `Hands` work very nicely, as shown in the following code snippet:

```
>>> h < h2
False
>>> h > h2
True
```

We can rank `Hands` based on the comparison operators.

We can also compare `Hands` with integers, as follows:

```
>>> h == 18
True
>>> h < 19
True
>>> h > 17
Traceback (most recent call last):
  File "<stdin>", line 1, in <module>
TypeError: unorderable types: Hand() > int()
```

The comparisons with integers work as long as Python isn't forced to try a fallback. The previous example shows us what happens when there's no `__gt__()` method. Python checks the reflected operands, and the integer 17 doesn't have a proper `__lt__()` method for `Hand` either.

We can add the necessary `__gt__()` and `__ge__()` functions to make `Hand` work properly with integers.

The __del__() method

The `__del__()` method has a rather obscure use case.

The intent is to give an object a chance to do any cleanup or finalization just before the object is removed from memory. This use case is handled much more cleanly by context manager objects and the `with` statement. This is the subject of *Chapter 5, Using Callables and Contexts*. Creating a context is much more predictable than dealing with `__del__()` and the Python garbage collection algorithm.

In the case where a Python object has a related OS resource, the `__del__()` method is a last chance to cleanly disentangle the resource from the Python application. As examples, a Python object that conceals an open file, a mounted device, or perhaps a child subprocess might all benefit from having the resource released as part of `__del__()` processing.

The `__del__()` method is not invoked at any easy-to-predict time. It's not always invoked when the object is deleted by a `del` statement, nor is it always invoked when an object is deleted because a namespace is being removed. The documentation on the `__del__()` method describes the circumstances as *precarious* and provides this additional note on exception processing: exceptions that occur during their execution are ignored, and a warning is printed to `sys.stderr` instead.

For these reasons, a context manager is often preferable to implementing `__del__()`.

The reference count and destruction

For the CPython implementation, objects have a reference count. The count is incremented when the object is assigned to a variable and decremented when the variable is removed. When the reference count is zero, the object is no longer needed and can be destroyed. For simple objects, `__del__()` will be invoked and the object will be removed.

For complex objects that have circular references among objects, the reference count might never go to zero and `__del__()` can't be invoked easily.

The following is a class that we can use to see what happens:

```
class Noisy:
    def __del__( self ):
        print( "Removing {0}".format(id(self)) )
```

We can create (and see the removal of) these objects as follows:

```
>>> x= Noisy()
>>> del x
Removing 4313946640
```

We created and removed a `Noisy` object, and almost immediately we saw the message from the `__del__()` method. This indicates that the reference count properly went to zero when the `x` variable was deleted. Once the variable is gone, there's no longer a reference to the instance of `Noisy` and it, too, can be cleaned up.

The following is a common situation that involves the shallow copies that are often created:

```
>>> ln = [ Noisy(), Noisy() ]
>>> ln2= ln[:]
>>> del ln
```

There's no response to this `del` statement. The `Noisy` objects have not had their reference counts go to zero yet; they're still being referenced somewhere, as shown in the following code snippet:

```
>>> del ln2
Removing 4313920336
Removing 4313920208
```

The `ln2` variable was a shallow copy of the `ln` list. The `Noisy` objects were referenced in two lists. They could not be destroyed until both lists were removed, reducing the reference counts to zero.

There are numerous other ways to create shallow copies. The following are a few ways to create shallow copies of objects:

```
a = b = Noisy()
c = [ Noisy() ] * 2
```

The point here is that we can often be confused by the number of references to an object that can exist because shallow copies are prevalent in Python.

Circular references and garbage collection

Here's a common situation that involves circularity. One class, `Parent`, contains a collection of children. Each `Child` instance contains a reference to the `Parent` class.

We'll use these two classes to examine circular references:

```
class Parent:
    def __init__( self, *children ):
        self.children= list(children)
        for child in self.children:
            child.parent= self
    def __del__( self ):
        print( "Removing {__class__.__name__} {id:d}".
format( __class__=self.__class__, id=id(self)) )

class Child:
    def __del__( self ):
        print( "Removing {__class__.__name__} {id:d}".
format( __class__=self.__class__, id=id(self)) )
```

A `Parent` instance has a collection of children as a simple `list`.

Each `Child` instance has a reference to the `Parent` class that contains it. The reference is created during initialization when the children are inserted into the parent's internal collection.

We've made both classes rather noisy so we can see when the objects are removed. The following is what happens:

```
>>>> p = Parent( Child(), Child() )
>>> id(p)
4313921808
>>> del p
```

The `Parent` and two initial `Child` instances cannot be removed. They both contain references to each other.

We can create a childless `Parent` instance, as shown in the following code snippet:

```
>>> p= Parent()
>>> id(p)
4313921744
>>> del p
Removing Parent 4313921744
```

This is deleted, as expected.

Because of the mutual or circular references, a `Parent` instance and its list of `Child` instances cannot be removed from the memory. If we import the garbage collector interface, `gc`, we can collect and display these nonremovable objects.

We'll use the `gc.collect()` method to collect all the nonremovable objects that have a `__del__()` method, as shown in the following code snippet:

```
>>> import gc
>>> gc.collect()
174
>>> gc.garbage
[<__main__.Parent object at 0x101213910>, <__main__.Child object at 
0x101213890>, <__main__.Child object at 0x101213650>, <__main__.
Parent object at 0x101213850>, <__main__.Child object at 0x1012130d0>, 
<__main__.Child object at 0x101219a10>, <__main__.Parent object at 
0x101213250>, <__main__.Child object at 0x101213090>, <__main__.
Child object at 0x101219810>, <__main__.Parent object at 0x101213050>, 
<__main__.Child object at 0x101213210>, <__main__.Child object at 
0x101219f90>, <__main__.Parent object at 0x101213810>, <__main__.Child 
object at 0x1012137d0>, <__main__.Child object at 0x101213790>]
```

We can see that our `Parent` objects (for example, ID of `4313921808 = 0x101213910`) are prominent on the list of nonremovable garbage. To reduce the reference counts to zero, we would need to either update each `Parent` instance on the garbage list to remove the children, or update each `Child` instance on the list to remove the reference to the `Parent` instance.

Note that we can't break the circularity by putting code in the `__del__()` method. The `__del__()` method is called *after* the circularity has been broken and the reference counts are already zero. When we have circular references, we can no longer rely on simple Python reference counting to clear out the memory of unused objects. We must either explicitly break the circularity or use a `weakref` reference, which permits garbage collection.

Circular references and the weakref module

In the cases where we need circular references but also want `__del__()` to work nicely, we can use **weak references**. One common use case for circular references are mutual references: a parent with a collection of children; each child has a reference back to the parent. If a `Player` class has multiple hands, it might be helpful for a `Hand` object to contain a reference to the owning `Player` class.

The default object references could be called **strong references**; however, direct references is a better term. They're used by the reference-counting mechanism in Python and can be discovered by the garbage collector if reference counting can't remove the objects. They cannot be ignored.

A strong reference to an object is followed directly. Consider the following statement:

When we say:

```
a= B()
```

The `a` variable has a direct reference to the object of the `B` class that was created. The reference count to the instance of `B` is at least 1 because the `a` variable has a reference.

A weak reference involves a two-step process to find the associated object. A weak reference will use `x.parent()`, invoking the weak reference as a callable object to track down the actual parent object. This two-step process allows the reference counting or garbage collection to remove the referenced object, leaving the weak reference dangling.

The `weakref` module defines a number of collections that use weak references instead of strong references. This allows us to create dictionaries that, for example, permit the garbage collection of otherwise unused objects.

We can modify our `Parent` and `Child` classes to use weak references from `Child` to `Parent`, permitting a simpler destruction of unused objects.

The following is a modified class that uses weak references from `Child` to `Parent`:

```
import weakref
class Parent2:
    def __init__( self, *children ):
        self.children= list(children)
        for child in self.children:
            child.parent= weakref.ref(self)
    def __del__( self ):
        print( "Removing {__class__.__name__} {id:d}".format( __
class__=self.__class__, id=id(self)) )
```

We've changed the child to parent reference to be a `weakref` object reference.

From within a `Child` class, we must locate the `parent` object via a two-step operation:

```
p = self.parent()
if p is not None:
```

```
        # process p, the Parent instance
    else:
        # the parent instance was garbage collected.
```

We can explicitly check to be sure the referenced object was found. There's a possibility that the reference was left dangling.

When we use this new `Parent2` class, we see that reference counting goes to zero and the object is removed:

```
>>> p = Parent2( Child(), Child() )
>>> del p
Removing Parent2 4303253584
Removing Child 4303256464
Removing Child 4303043344
```

When a `weakref` reference is dead (because the referent was destroyed), we have three potential responses:

- Recreate the referent. Reload it from a database, perhaps.
- Use the `warnings` module to write the debugging information on low-memory situations where the garbage collector removed objects unexpectedly.
- Ignore the problem.

Generally, the `weakref` references are dead because objects have been removed: variables have gone out of scope, a namespace is no longer in use, the application is shutting down. For this reason, the third response is quite common. The object trying to create the reference is probably about to be removed as well.

The __del__() and close() methods

The most common use for `__del__()` is to ensure files are closed.

Generally, class definitions that open files will have something like what's shown in the following code:

```
__del__ = close
```

This will ensure the `__del__()` method is also the `close()` method.

Anything more complex than this is better done with a context manager. See *Chapter 5, Using Callables and Contexts*, for more information on context managers.

The __new__() method and immutable objects

One use case for the `__new__()` method is to initialize objects that are otherwise immutable. The `__new__()` method is where our code can build an uninitialized object. This allows processing before the `__init__()` method is called to set the attribute values of the object.

The `__new__()` method is used to extend the immutable classes where the `__init__()` method can't easily be overridden.

The following is a class that does not work. We'll define a version of `float` that carries around information on units:

```
class Float_Fail( float ):
    def __init__( self, value, unit ):
        super().__init__( value )
        self.unit = unit
```

We're trying (improperly) to initialize an immutable object.

The following is what happens when we try to use this class definition:

```
>>> s2 = Float_Fail( 6.5, "knots" )
Traceback (most recent call last):
  File "<stdin>", line 1, in <module>
TypeError: float() takes at most 1 argument (2 given)
```

From this, we see that we can't easily override the `__init__()` method for the built-in immutable `float` class. We'd have similar problems with all other immutable classes. We can't set the attribute values on the immutable object, `self`, because that's the definition of immutability. We can only set attribute values during the object construction. Enter the `__new__()` method after this.

The `__new__()` method is auto-magically a static method. This is true without using the `@staticmethod` decorator. It doesn't use a `self` variable, as its job is to create the object that will eventually be assigned to the `self` variable.

For this use case, the method signature is `__new__( cls, *args, **kw )`. The `cls` parameter is the class for which an instance must be created. For the metaclass use case in the next section, the `args` sequence of values are more complex than shown here.

The default implementation of `__new__()` simply does this: `return super().__new__( cls )`. It delegates the operation to the superclass. The work winds up getting delegated to `object.__new__()`, which builds a simple, empty object of the required class. The arguments and keywords to `__new__()`, with the exception of the `cls` argument, will be passed to `__init__()` as part of the standard Python behavior.

With two notable exceptions, this is exactly what we want. The following are the exceptions:

- When we want to subclass an immutable class definition. We'll dig into that later.
- When we need to create a metaclass. That's the subject of the next section, as it's fundamentally different from creating immutable objects.

Instead of overriding `__init__()` when creating a subclass of a built-in immutable type, we have to tweak the object at the time of the creation by overriding `__new__()`. The following is an example class definition that shows us the proper way to extend `float`:

```
class Float_Units( float ):
    def __new__( cls, value, unit ):
       obj= super().__new__( cls, value )
       obj.unit= unit
       return obj
```

In the preceding code, we set the value of an attribute during the creation of an object.

The following code snippet gives us a floating-point value with attached units information:

```
>>> speed= Float_Units( 6.5, "knots" )
>>> speed
6.5
>>> speed * 10
65.0
>>> speed.unit
'knots'
```

Note that an expression such as `speed * 10` does not create a `Float_Units` object. This class definition inherits all the operator special methods from `float`; the `float` arithmetic special methods all create `float` objects. Creating `Float_Units` objects is the subject of *Chapter 7, Creating Numbers*.

The __new__() method and metaclasses

The other use case for the `__new__()` method as a part of a metaclass is to control how a class definition is built. This is distinct from how `__new__()` controls building an immutable object, shown previously.

A metaclass builds a class. Once a class object has been built, the class object is used to build instances. The metaclass of all class definitions is `type`. The `type()` function is used to create class objects.

Additionally, the `type()` function can be used as a function to reveal the class of an object.

The following is a silly example of building a new, nearly useless class directly with `type()` as a constructor:

```
Useless= type("Useless",(),{})
```

Once we've created this class, we can create objects of this `Useless` class. However, they won't do much because they have no methods or attributes.

We can use this newly-minted `Useless` class to create objects, for what little it's worth. The following is an example:

```
>>> Useless()
<__main__.Useless object at 0x101001910>
>>> u=_
>>> u.attr= 1
>>> dir(u)
['__class__', '__delattr__', '__dict__', '__dir__', '__doc__',
'__eq__', '__format__', '__ge__', '__getattribute__', '__gt__',
'__hash__', '__init__', '__le__', '__lt__', '__module__', '__ne__',
'__new__', '__reduce__', '__reduce_ex__', '__repr__', '__setattr__',
'__sizeof__', '__str__', '__subclasshook__', '__weakref__', 'attr']
```

We can add attributes to the objects of this class. It does work, minimally, as an object.

This is almost equivalent to using `types.SimpleNamespace` or defining a class as follows:

```
class Useless:
    pass
```

This brings up the important question: why would we mess with the way classes are defined in the first place?

The answer is that some of the default features of a class aren't *perfectly* applicable to some edge cases. We'll talk about four situations where we might want to introduce a metaclass:

- We can use a metaclass to preserve some information about the source text for a class. A class built by the built-in `type` uses `dict` to store the various methods and class-level attributes. As `dict` is inherently unordered, the attributes and methods appear in no particular order. It's extremely unlikely that they would appear in the order originally presented in the source. We'll show this in our first example.
- Metaclasses are used to create **Abstract Base Classes** (**ABC**) that we'll look at from Chapters 4 through 7. An ABC relies on a metaclass `__new__()` method to confirm that the concrete subclass is complete. We'll introduce this in *Chapter 4, The ABCs of Consistent Design*.
- Metaclasses can be used to simplify some aspects of object serialization. We'll look at this in *Chapter 9, Serializing and Saving – JSON, YAML, Pickle, CSV, and XML*.
- As a final and rather easy example, we'll look at a self-reference within a class. We'll design classes that reference a *master* class. This isn't a superclass-subclass relationship. It's a bunch of subclasses that are peer subclasses but have an association with one of its peer group as being the master. To be consistent with its peers, the master needs a reference to itself, something that's impossible without a metaclass. This will be our second example.

Metaclass example 1 – ordered attributes

This is the canonical example in section 3.3.3, *Customizing Class Creation*, of *Python Language Reference*. This metaclass will record the order in which the attributes and method functions are defined.

The recipe has the following three parts:

1. Create a metaclass. The `__prepare__()` and `__new__()` functions of that metaclass will change the way a target class is built, replacing a plain-old `dict` class with the `OrderedDict` class.
2. Create an abstract superclass that is based on the metaclass. This abstract class simplifies the inheritance for other classes.
3. Create subclasses of the abstract superclass that benefit from the metaclass.

The following is the example metaclass that will retain the order of the creation of the attribute:

```
import collections
class Ordered_Attributes(type):
    @classmethod
    def __prepare__(metacls, name, bases, **kwds):
        return collections.OrderedDict()
    def __new__(cls, name, bases, namespace, **kwds):
        result = super().__new__(cls, name, bases, namespace)
        result._order = tuple(n for n in namespace if not
n.startswith('__'))
        return result
```

This class extends the built-in default metaclass, `type`, with a new version of `__prepare__()` and `__new__()`.

The `__prepare__()` method is executed prior to the creation of the class; its job is to create the initial namespace object into which the definitions will be added. This method could work on any other preparation prior to the execution of the class body that is being processed.

The `__new__()` static method is executed after the class body elements have been added to the namespace. It is given the class object, the class name, the superclass tuple, and the fully built namespace mapping object. This example is typical: it delegates the real work of `__new__()` to the superclass; the superclass of a metaclass is the built-in `type`; we use `type.__new__()` to create the default class object that can be tweaked.

The `__new__()` method in this example adds an attribute, `_order`, into the class definition that shows us the original order of the attributes.

We can use this metaclass instead of `type` when defining a new abstract superclass, as follows:

```
class Order_Preserved( metaclass=Ordered_Attributes ):
    pass
```

We can then use this new abstract class as the superclass for any new classes that we define, as follows:

```
class Something( Order_Preserved ):
    this= 'text'
    def z( self ):
```

```
            return False
        b= 'order is preserved'
        a= 'more text'
```

When we look at the `Something` class, we see the following code snippet:

```
>>> Something._order
>>> ('this', 'z', 'b', 'a')
```

We can consider exploiting this information to properly serialize the object or provide debugging information that is tied to the original source definitions.

Metaclass example 2 – self-reference

We'll look at an example that involves unit conversion. For example, units of length include meters, centimeters, inches, feet, and numerous other units. Managing unit conversions can be challenging. Superficially, we need a matrix of all possible conversion factors among all the various units. Feet to meters, feet to inches, feet to yards, meters to inches, meters to yards, and so on—every combination.

Practically, however, we can do better than this if we define a standard unit for length. We can convert any unit to the standard and the standard to any other unit. By doing this, we can easily perform any possible conversion as a two-step operation, eliminating the complex matrix of all possible conversions: feet to standard, inches to standard, yards to standard, meters to standard.

In the following example, we're not going to subclass `float` or `numbers.Number` in any way. Rather than binding the unit to the value, we'll allow each value to remain a simple number. This is an example of a **Flyweight** design pattern. The class doesn't define objects that contain the relevant value. The objects only contain the conversion factors.

The alternative (binding units to values) leads to rather complex dimensional analysis. While interesting, it's rather complex.

We'll define two classes: `Unit` and `Standard_Unit`. We can easily be sure that each `Unit` class has a reference to its appropriate `Standard_Unit`. How can we ensure that each `Standard_Unit` class has a reference to itself? Self-referencing within a class definition is impossible because the class hasn't been defined yet.

The following is our `Unit` class definition:

```
class Unit:
    """Full name for the unit."""
    factor= 1.0
```

```
    standard= None # Reference to the appropriate StandardUnit
    name= "" # Abbreviation of the unit's name.
    @classmethod
    def value( class_, value ):
        if value is None: return None
        return value/class_.factor
    @classmethod
    def convert( class_, value ):
        if value is None: return None
        return value*class_.factor
```

The intent is that `Unit.value()` will convert a value in the given unit to the standard unit. The `Unit.convert()` method will convert a standard value to the given unit.

This allows us to work with units, as shown in the following code snippet:

```
>>> m_f= FOOT.value(4)
>>> METER.convert(m_f)
1.2191999999999998
```

The values created are built-in `float` values. For temperatures, the `value()` and `convert()` methods need to be overridden, as a simple multiplication doesn't work.

For `Standard_Unit`, we'd like to do something as follows:

```
class INCH:
    standard= INCH
```

However, that won't work. `INCH` hasn't been defined within the body of `INCH`. The class doesn't exist until after the definition.

We could, as a fallback, do this:

```
class INCH:
    pass
INCH.standard= INCH
```

However, that's rather ugly.

We could define a decorator as follows:

```
@standard
class INCH:
    pass
```

This decorator function could tweak the class definition to add an attribute. We'll return to this in *Chapter 8, Decorators and Mixins – Cross-cutting Aspects*.

Instead, we'll define a metaclass that can insert a circular reference into the class definition, as follows:

```
class UnitMeta(type):
    def __new__(cls, name, bases, dict):
        new_class= super().__new__(cls, name, bases, dict)
        new_class.standard = new_class
        return new_class
```

This forces the class variable standard into the class definition.

For most units, `SomeUnit.standard` references `TheStandardUnit` class. In parallel with that we'll also have `TheStandardUnit.standard` referencing `TheStandardUnit` class, also. This consistent structure among the `Unit` and `Standard_Unit` subclasses can help with writing the documentation and automating the unit conversions.

The following is the `Standard_Unit` class:

```
class Standard_Unit( Unit, metaclass=UnitMeta ):
    pass
```

The unit conversion factor inherited from `Unit` is 1.0, so this class does nothing to the supplied values. It includes the special metaclass definition so that it will have a self-reference that clarifies that this class is the standard for this particular dimension of measurement.

As an optimization, we could override the `value()` and `convert()` methods to avoid the multiplication and division.

The following are some sample class definitions for units:

```
class INCH( Standard_Unit ):
    """Inches"""
    name= "in"

class FOOT( Unit ):
    """Feet"""
    name= "ft"
    standard= INCH
    factor= 1/12

class CENTIMETER( Unit ):
    """Centimeters"""
    name= "cm"
    standard= INCH
    factor= 2.54
```

```
class METER( Unit ):
    """Meters"""
    name= "m"
    standard= INCH
    factor= .0254
```

We defined `INCH` as the standard unit. The other units' definitions will convert to and from inches.

We've provided some documentation for each unit: the full name in the docstring and a short name in the `name` attribute. The conversion factor is automatically applied by the `convert()` and `value()` functions inherited from `Unit`.

These definitions allow the following kind of programming in our applications:

```
>>> x_std= INCH.value( 159.625 )
>>> FOOT.convert( x_std )
13.302083333333332
>>> METER.convert( x_std )
4.054475
>>> METER.factor
0.0254
```

We can set a particular measurement from a given value in inches and report that value in any other compatible unit.

What the metaclass does is allow us to make queries like this from the unit-definition classes:

```
>>> INCH.standard.__name__
'INCH'
>>> FOOT.standard.__name__
'INCH'
```

These kinds of references can allow us to track all the various units of a given dimension.

Summary

We've looked at a number of *basic* special methods, which are essential features of any class that we design. These methods are already part of every class, but the defaults we inherit from the object may not match our processing requirements.

We'll almost always have a need to override `__repr__()`, `__str__()`, and `__format__()`. The default implementations of these methods aren't very helpful at all.

We rarely need to override `__bool__()` unless we're writing our own collection. That's the subject of *Chapter 6, Creating Containers and Collections*.

We often need to override the comparison and `__hash__()` methods. The definitions are suitable for simple immutable objects but not at all appropriate for mutable objects. We may not need to write all the comparison operators; we'll look at the `@functools.total_ordering` decorator in *Chapter 8, Decorators and Mixins – Cross-cutting Aspects*.

The other two *basic* special method names, `__new__()` and `__del__()`, are for more specialized purposes. Using `__new__()` to extend an immutable class is the most common use case for this method function.

These basic special methods, along with `__init__()`, will appear in almost every class definition we write. The rest of the special methods are for more specialized purposes; they fall into six discrete categories:

- **Attribute Access**: These special methods implement what we see as `object.attribute` in an expression, `object.attribute` on the left-hand side of assignment, and `object.attribute` in a `del` statement.
- **Callables**: A special method implements what we see as a function applied to arguments, much like the built-in `len()` function.
- **Collections**: These special methods implement the numerous features of collections. This involves things such as `sequence[index]`, `mapping[key]`, and `set | set`.
- **Numbers**: These special methods provide the arithmetic operators and the comparison operators. We can use these methods to expand the domain of numbers that Python works with.
- **Contexts**: There are two special methods we'll use to implement a context manager that works with the `with` statement.
- **Iterators**: There are special methods that define an iterator. This isn't essential, as generator functions handle this feature so elegantly. However, we'll look at how we can design our own iterators.

In the next chapter, we will address attributes, properties, and descriptors.

3

Attribute Access, Properties, and Descriptors

An object is a collection of features, including methods and attributes. The default behavior of the `object` class involves setting, getting, and deleting named attributes. We often need to modify this behavior to change the attributes available in an object.

This chapter will focus on the following five tiers of attribute access:

- We'll look at built-in attribute processing, which is the simplest, but least sophisticated option.
- We'll review the `@property` decorator. A property extends the concept of an attribute to include the processing defined in method functions.
- We'll look at how to make use of the lower-level special methods that control attribute access: `__getattr__()`, `__setattr__()`, and `__delattr__()`. These special methods allow us to build more sophisticated attribute processing.
- We'll also take a look at the `__getattribute__()` method, which provides more granular control over attributes. This can allow us to write very unusual attribute handling.
- Finally, we'll take a look at descriptors. These are used to access an attribute, but they involve somewhat more complex design decisions. Descriptors are used heavily by Python under the hood to implement properties, static methods, and class methods.

In this chapter, we'll see how the default processing works in detail. We need to decide where and when to override the default behavior. In some cases, we want our attributes to do more than simply be instance variables. In other cases, we might want to prevent adding attributes. We may have attributes that have even more complex behaviors.

Also, as we explore descriptors, we'll come to a much deeper understanding of how Python's internals work. We don't often need to use descriptors explicitly. We often use them implicitly, however, because they're the mechanism that implements a number of Python features.

Basic attribute processing

By default, any class we create will permit the following four behaviors with respect to attributes:

- To create a new attribute by setting its value
- To set the value of an existing attribute
- To get the value of an attribute
- To delete an attribute

We can experiment with this using something as simple as the following code. We can create a simple, generic class and an object of that class:

```
>>> class Generic:
...     pass
...
>>> g= Generic()
```

The preceding code permits us to create, get, set, and delete attributes. We can easily create and get an attribute. The following are some examples:

```
>>> g.attribute= "value"
>>> g.attribute
'value'
>>> g.unset
Traceback (most recent call last):
  File "<stdin>", line 1, in <module>
AttributeError: 'Generic' object has no attribute 'unset'
>>> del g.attribute
>>> g.attribute
Traceback (most recent call last):
  File "<stdin>", line 1, in <module>
AttributeError: 'Generic' object has no attribute 'attribute'
```

We can add, change, and remove attributes. We will get exceptions if we try to get an otherwise unset attribute or delete an attribute that doesn't exist yet.

A slightly better way to do this is using an instance of the class `types.SimpleNamespace` class. The feature set is the same, but we don't need to create an extra class definition. We create an object of the `SimpleNamespace` class instead, as follows:

```
>>> import types
>>> n = types.SimpleNamespace()
```

In the following code, we can see that the same use cases work for a `SimpleNamespace` class:

```
>>> n.attribute= "value"
>>> n.attribute
'value'
>>> del n.attribute
>>> n.attribute
Traceback (most recent call last):
  File "<stdin>", line 1, in <module>
AttributeError: 'namespace' object has no attribute 'attribute'
```

We can create attributes for this object. Any attempt to use an undefined attribute raises an exception. A `SimpleNamespace` class has different behavior from what we saw when we created an instance of the object class.. A simple instance of the object class doesn't permit the creation of new attributes; it lacks the internal `__dict__` structure that Python stores attributes and values in.

Attributes and the __init__() method

Most of the time, we create an initial suite of attributes using the `__init__()` method of a class. Ideally, we provide default values for all the attributes in `__init__()`.

It's *not* required to provide all attributes in the `__init__()` method. Because of this, the presence or absence of an attribute can be used as part of an object's state.

An optional attribute pushes the edge of the envelope for class definition. It makes considerable sense for a class to have a well-defined set of attributes. Attributes can often be added (or removed) more clearly by creating a subclass or superclass.

Consequently, optional attributes imply a kind of informal subclass relationship. Therefore, we bump up against Pretty Poor Polymorphism when we use optional attributes.

Consider a Blackjack game in which only a single split is permitted. If a hand is split, it cannot be resplit. There are several ways that we can model this:

- We can create a subclass for `SplitHand` from the `Hand.split()` method. We won't show this in detail.
- We can create a status attribute on an object named `Hand`, which can be created from the `Hand.split()` method. Ideally, this is a Boolean value, but we can implement it as an optional attribute as well.

The following is a version of `Hand.split()` that can detect splittable versus unsplittable hands via an optional attribute:

```
def  split( self, deck ):
    assert self.cards[0].rank == self.cards[1].rank
    try:
        self.split_count
        raise CannotResplit
    except AttributeError:
        h0 = Hand( self.dealer_card, self.cards[0], deck.pop() )
        h1 = Hand( self.dealer_card, self.cards[1], deck.pop() )
        h0.split_count= h1.split_count= 1
        return h0, h1
```

In effect, the `split()` method tests to see if there's a `split_count` attribute. If this attribute exists, then this is a split hand and the method raises an exception. If the `split_count` attribute does not exist, this is an initial deal, and splitting is allowed.

An optional attribute has the advantage of leaving the `__init__()` method relatively uncluttered with status flags. It has the disadvantage of obscuring some aspects of object state. This use of a `try:` block to determine object state can be very confusing and should be avoided.

Creating properties

A property is a method function that appears (syntactically) to be a simple attribute. We can get, set, and delete property values similarly to how we can get, set, and delete attribute values. There's an important distinction here. A property is actually a method function and can process, rather than simply preserve, a reference to another object.

Besides the level of sophistication, one other difference between properties and attributes is that we can't attach new properties to an existing object easily; however, we can add attributes to an object easily, by default. A property is not identical to simple attributes in this one respect.

There are two ways to create properties. We can use the `@property` decorator or we can use the `property()` function. The differences are purely syntactic. We'll focus on the decorator.

We'll take a look at two basic design patterns for properties:

- **Eager calculation**: In this design pattern, when we set a value via a property, other attributes are also computed
- **Lazy calculation**: In this design pattern, calculations are deferred until requested via a property

In order to compare the preceding two approaches to properties, we'll split some common features of the `Hand` object into an abstract superclass, as follows:

```
class Hand:
    def __str__( self ):
        return ", ".join( map(str, self.card) )
    def __repr__( self ):
        return "{__class__.__name__}({dealer_card!r}, {_cards_str})".
format(
        __class__=self.__class__,
        _cards_str=", ".join( map(repr, self.card) ),
        **self.__dict__ )
```

In the preceding code, we defined just some string representation methods and nothing else.

The following is a subclass of `Hand`, where `total` is a lazy property that is computed only when needed:

```
class Hand_Lazy(Hand):
    def __init__( self, dealer_card, *cards ):
        self.dealer_card= dealer_card
        self._cards= list(cards)
    @property
    def total( self ):
        delta_soft = max(c.soft-c.hard for c in self._cards)
        hard_total = sum(c.hard for c in self._cards)
        if hard_total+delta_soft <= 21: return hard_total+delta_soft
        return hard_total
    @property
    def card( self ):
        return self._cards
    @card.setter
    def card( self, aCard ):
        self._cards.append( aCard )
```

```
    @card.deleter
    def card( self ):
        self._cards.pop(-1)
```

The `Hand_Lazy` class initializes a `Hand` object with a list of the `Cards` object. The `total` property is a method that computes the total only when requested. Additionally, we defined some other properties to update the collection of cards in the hand. The `card` property can get, set, or delete cards in the hand. We'll take a look at these properties in setter and deleter properties section.

We can create a `Hand` object, `total` appears to be a simple attribute:

```
>>> d= Deck()
>>> h= Hand_Lazy( d.pop(), d.pop(), d.pop() )
>>> h.total
19
>>> h.card= d.pop()
>>> h.total
29
```

The total is computed lazily by rescanning the cards in the hand each time the total is requested. This can be an expensive overhead.

Eagerly computed properties

The following is a subclass of `Hand`, where `total` is a simple attribute that's computed eagerly as each card is added:

```
class Hand_Eager(Hand):
    def __init__( self, dealer_card, *cards ):
        self.dealer_card= dealer_card
        self.total= 0
        self._delta_soft= 0
        self._hard_total= 0
        self._cards= list()
        for c in cards:
            self.card = c
    @property
    def card( self ):
        return self._cards
    @card.setter
    def card( self, aCard ):
        self._cards.append(aCard)
        self._delta_soft = max(aCard.soft-aCard.hard,
            self._delta_soft)
```

```
            self._hard_total += aCard.hard
            self._set_total()
        @card.deleter
        def card( self ):
            removed= self._cards.pop(-1)
            self._hard_total -= removed.hard
            # Issue: was this the only ace?
            self._delta_soft = max( c.soft-c.hard for c in self._cards
            )
            self._set_total()
        def _set_total( self ):
            if self._hard_total+self._delta_soft <= 21:
                self.total= self._hard_total+self._delta_soft
            else:
                self.total= self._hard_total
```

In this case, each time a card is added, the `total` attribute is updated.

The other `card` property—the deleter—eagerly updates the `total` attribute whenever a card is removed. We'll take a look at the deleter in detail in the next section.

A client sees the same syntax between these two subclasses (`Hand_Lazy()` and `Hand_Eager()`) of `Hand`:

```
d= Deck()
h1= Hand_Lazy( d.pop(), d.pop(), d.pop() )
print( h1.total )
h2= Hand_Eager( d.pop(), d.pop(), d.pop() )
print( h2.total )
```

In both cases, the client software simply uses the `total` attribute.

The advantage of using properties is that the syntax doesn't have to change when the implementation changes. We can make a similar claim for getter/setter method functions. However, getter/setter method functions involve extra syntax that isn't very helpful nor informative. The following are two examples, one of which is using a setter method and the other that is using the assignment operator:

```
obj.set_something(value)
obj.something = value
```

The presence of the assignment operator (=) makes the intent very plain. Many programmers find it clearer to look for assignment statements than to look for setter method functions.

Setter and deleter properties

In the previous examples, we defined the `card` property to deal additional cards into an object of the `Hand` class.

Since setter (and deleter) properties are created from the getter property, we must always define a getter property first using the following code:

```
@property
def card( self ):
    return self._cards
@card.setter
def card( self, aCard ):
    self._cards.append( aCard )
@card.deleter
def card( self ):
    self._cards.pop(-1)
```

This allows us to add a card to the hand with a simple statement like the following:

```
h.card= d.pop()
```

The preceding assignment statement has a disadvantage because it looks like it replaces all the cards with a single card. On the other hand, it also has an advantage because it uses simple assignment to update the state of a mutable object. We can use the `__iadd__()` special method to do this a little more cleanly. But, we'll wait until *Chapter 7, Creating Numbers*, to introduce the other special methods.

For our current examples, there's no compelling reason to use a deleter property. Even without a compelling reason, there's still some use for a deleter. We could, however, make use of it to remove the last dealt card. This can be used as part of the process for splitting a hand.

We will consider a version of `split()` that works like the following code:

```
def split( self, deck ):
    """Updates this hand and also returns the new hand."""
    assert self._cards[0].rank == self._cards[1].rank
    c1= self._cards[-1]
    del self.card
    self.card= deck.pop()
    h_new= self.__class__( self.dealer_card, c1, deck.pop() )
    return h_new
```

The preceding method updates the given hand and returns a new hand. The following is an example of a hand being split:

```
>>> d= Deck()
>>> c= d.pop()
>>> h= Hand_Lazy( d.pop(), c, c ) # Force splittable hand
>>> h2= h.split(d)
>>> print(h)
2♠, 10♠
>>> print(h2)
2♠, A♠
```

Once we have two cards, we can use `split()` to produce the second hand. A card was removed from the initial hand.

This version of `split()` is certainly workable. However, it seems somewhat better to have the `split()` method return two fresh new `Hand` objects. That way, the old, presplit `Hand` instance can be used as a memento to gather statistics.

Using special methods for attribute access

We'll look at the three canonical special methods for attribute access: `__getattr__()`, `__setattr__()`, and `__delattr__()`. Additionally, we'll acknowledge the `__dir__()` method to reveal attribute names. We'll defer `__getattribute__()` to the next section.

The default behavior shown in the first section is as follows:

- The `__setattr__()` method will create and set attributes.
- The `__getattr__()` method will do two things. Firstly, if an attribute already has a value, `__getattr__()` is not used; the attribute value is simply returned. Secondly, if the attribute does not have a value, then `__getattr__()` is given a chance to return a meaningful value. If there is no attribute, it must raise an `AttributeError` exception.
- The `__delattr__()` method deletes an attribute.
- The `__dir__()` method returns a list of attribute names.

The `__getattr__()` method function is only one step in a larger process; it is only used if the attribute is otherwise unknown. If the attribute is a known attribute, this method is not used. The `__setattr__()` and `__delattr__()` methods do not have built-in processing. These methods don't interact with additional processing.

We have a number of design choices for controlling attribute access. These follow our three essential design choices to extend, wrap, or invent. The design choices are as follows:

- We can extend a class, making it almost immutable by overriding `__setattr__()` and `__delattr__()`. We can also replace the internal `__dict__` with `__slots__`.
- We can wrap a class and delegate attribute access to the object (or composite of objects) being wrapped. This may involve overriding all three of these methods.
- We can implement property-like behaviors in a class. Using these methods, we can assure that all property processing is centralized.
- We can create lazy attributes where the values aren't (or can't be) computed until they're needed. We may have an attribute that doesn't have a value until it's read from a file, database, or network. This is common use for `__getattr__()`.
- We can have eager attributes, where setting an attribute creates values in other attributes automagically. This is done via overrides to `__setattr__()`.

We won't look at all of these alternatives. Instead, we'll focus on the two most commonly used techniques: extending and wrapping. We'll create immutable objects and look at other ways to eagerly compute attribute values.

Creating immutable objects with __slots__

If we are not able to set an attribute or create a new one, then the object is immutable. The following is what we'd like to see in interactive Python:

```
>>> c= card21(1,'♠')
>>> c.rank= 12
Traceback (most recent call last):
  File "<stdin>", line 1, in <module>
  File "<stdin>", line 30, in __setattr__
TypeError: Cannot set rank
>>> c.hack= 13
Traceback (most recent call last):
  File "<stdin>", line 1, in <module>
  File "<stdin>", line 31, in __setattr__
AttributeError: 'Ace21Card' has no attribute 'hack'
```

The preceding code shows that we are not allowed to change an attribute or add one to this object.

We need to make two changes to a class definition for this to work. We'll omit much of the class and focus on just the three features that make an object immutable, as follows:

```
class BlackJackCard:
    """Abstract Superclass"""
    __slots__ = ( 'rank', 'suit', 'hard', 'soft' )
    def __init__( self, rank, suit, hard, soft ):
        super().__setattr__( 'rank', rank )
        super().__setattr__( 'suit', suit )
        super().__setattr__( 'hard', hard )
        super().__setattr__( 'soft', soft )
    def __str__( self ):
        return "{0.rank}{0.suit}".format( self )
    def __setattr__( self, name, value ):
        raise AttributeError( "'{__class__.__name__}' has no
attribute '{name}'".format( __class__= self.__class__, name= name
) )
```

We made three significant changes:

- We set `__slots__` to the names of only the allowed attributes. This turns off the internal `__dict__` feature of the object and limits us to just the attributes and no more.
- We defined `__setattr__()` to raise an exception rather than do anything useful.
- We defined `__init__()` to use the superclass version of `__setattr__()` so that values can be properly set in spite of the absence of a working `__setattr__()` method in this class.

With some care, we can bypass the immutability feature if we work at it.

```
object.__setattr__(c, 'bad', 5)
```

That brings us to a question. "How can we prevent an "evil" programmer from bypassing the immutability feature?" The question is silly. We can't stop the evil programmer. Another equally silly question is, "Why would some evil programmer write all that code to circumvent immutability?". We can't stop the evil programmer from doing evil things.

If this imaginary programmer doesn't like immutability in a class, they can modify the definition of the class to remove the redefinition of `__setattr__()`. The point of an immutable object like this is to guarantee `__hash__()` returning a consistent value and not to prevent people from writing rotten code.

Don't abuse __slots__

The `__slots__` feature is intended primarily to save memory by limiting the number of attributes.

Creating immutable objects as a tuple subclass

We can also create an immutable object by making our `Card` property a subclass of `tuple` and an override to `__getattr__()`. In this case, we'll translate `__getattr__(name)` requests to `self[index]` requests. As we'll see in *Chapter 6, Creating Containers and Collections*, `self[index]` is implemented by `__getitem__(index)`.

The following is a small extension to the built-in `tuple` class:

```
class BlackJackCard2( tuple ):
    def __new__( cls, rank, suit, hard, soft ):
        return super().__new__( cls, (rank, suit, hard, soft) )
    def __getattr__( self, name ):
        return self[{'rank':0, 'suit':1, 'hard':2 ,
'soft':3}[name]]
    def __setattr__( self, name, value ):
        raise AttributeError
```

In this example, we simply raised a simple `AttributeError` exception rather than providing detailed error messages.

When we use the preceding code, we see the following kinds of interaction:

```
>>> d = BlackJackCard2( 'A', '♠', 1, 11 )
>>> d.rank
'A'
>>> d.suit
'♠'
>>> d.bad= 2
Traceback (most recent call last):
  File "<stdin>", line 1, in <module>
  File "<stdin>", line 7, in __setattr__AttributeError
```

We can't change the value of a card easily. However, we can still tweak `d.__dict__` to introduce *additional* attributes.

Is this really necessary?

This is, perhaps, too much work to simply assure that an object isn't accidentally misused. Practically, we're more interested in the diagnostic information available from an exception and traceback than we are in a super-secure immutable class.

Eagerly computed attributes

We can define an object where attributes are computed eagerly as soon as possible after a value is set. This object optimizes access by doing a computation once and leaving the result to be used multiple times.

We're able to define a number of property setters to do this. However, a lot of property setters, each of which compute a number of attributes, can get wordy for a complex calculation.

We can centralize the attribute processing. In the following example, we'll use a few tweaks to extend Python's internal `dict` type. The advantage of extending `dict` is that it works well with the `format()` method of a string. Also, we don't have to worry much about setting extra attribute values that are otherwise ignored.

We'd like something that looks like the following code:

```
>>> RateTimeDistance( rate=5.2, time=9.5 )
{'distance': 49.4, 'time': 9.5, 'rate': 5.2}
>>> RateTimeDistance( distance=48.5, rate=6.1 )
{'distance': 48.5, 'time': 7.950819672131148, 'rate': 6.1}
```

We can set the values in this `RateTimeDistance` object. Additional attributes are computed as soon as sufficient data is present. We can do this either all at once, as shown earlier, or in stages, as shown in the following code:

```
>>> rtd= RateTimeDistance()
>>> rtd.time= 9.5
>>> rtd
{'time': 9.5}
>>> rtd.rate= 6.24
>>> rtd
{'distance': 59.28, 'time': 9.5, 'rate': 6.24}
```

The following is the extension to the built-in `dict` . We've extended the essential mapping that `dict` implements to compute a missing attribute:

```
class RateTimeDistance( dict ):
    def __init__( self, *args, **kw ):
        super().__init__( *args, **kw )
```

```
            self._solve()
        def __getattr__( self, name ):
            return self.get(name,None)
        def __setattr__( self, name, value ):
            self[name]= value
            self._solve()
        def __dir__( self ):
            return list(self.keys())
        def _solve(self):
            if self.rate is not None and self.time is not None:
                self['distance'] = self.rate*self.time
            elif self.rate is not None and self.distance is not None:
                self['time'] = self.distance / self.rate
            elif self.time is not None and self.distance is not None:
                self['rate'] = self.distance / self.time
```

The `dict` type uses `__init__()` to populate the internal dictionary, then tries to solve if enough data is present. It uses `__setattr__()` to add new items to the dictionary. It also attempts to solve the equation each time a value is set.

In `__getattr__()`, we use `None` to indicate a missing value from the equation. This allows us to set an attribute to `None` to indicate that it is a missing value, and this will force the solution to look for this value. For example, we might do this based on user inputs or a network request where all parameters were given a value but one variable was set to `None`.

We can use it as follows:

```
>>> rtd= RateTimeDistance( rate=6.3, time=8.25, distance=None )
>>> print( "Rate={rate}, Time={time}, Distance={distance}".format(
**rtd ) )
Rate=6.3, Time=8.25, Distance=51.975
```

Note that we can't set attribute values inside this class definition easily.

Let's consider the following line of code:

```
self.distance = self.rate*self.time
```

If we were to write the preceding code snippet, we'd have infinite recursions between `__setattr__()` and `_solve()`. When we used `self['distance']` in the example, we avoided the recursive call of `__setattr__()`.

It's also important to note that once all three values are set, this object can't be changed to provide new solutions easily.

We can't simply set a new value for `rate` and compute a new value for `time` while leaving `distance` unchanged. To tweak this model, we need to both clear one variable and set a new value for another variable:

```
>>> rtd.time= None
>>> rtd.rate= 6.1
>>> print( "Rate={rate}, Time={time}, Distance={distance}".format(
**rtd ) )
Rate=6.1, Time=8.25, Distance=50.324999999999996
```

Here, we cleared `time` and changed `rate` to get a new solution for `time` using the established value for `distance`.

We could design a model that tracked the order that the variables were set in; this model could save us from having to clear one variable before setting another to recompute a related result.

The __getattribute__() method

An even lower level attribute processing is the `__getattribute__()` method. The default implementation attempts to locate the value as an existing attribute in the internal `__dict__` (or `__slots__`). If the attribute is not found, it calls `__getattr__()` as a fallback. If the value located is a descriptor (see in the following *Creating descriptors* section), then it processes the descriptor. Otherwise, the value is simply returned.

By overriding this method, we can perform any of the following kinds of tasks:

- We can effectively prevent access to attributes. This method, by raising an exception instead of returning a value, can make an attribute more secret than if we were to merely use the leading underscore (_) to mark a name as private to the implementation.
- We can invent new attributes similarly to how `__getattr__()` can invent new attributes. In this case, however, we can bypass the default lookup done by the default version of `__getattribute__()`.
- We can make attributes perform unique and different tasks. This might make the program very difficult to understand or maintain. This could be a terrible idea, also.
- We can change the way descriptors behave. While technically possible, changing a descriptor's behavior sounds like a terrible idea.

When we implement the `__getattribute__()` method, it's important to note that there cannot be any internal attribute access in the method's body. If we attempt to get the value for `self.name`, it will lead to infinite recursions.

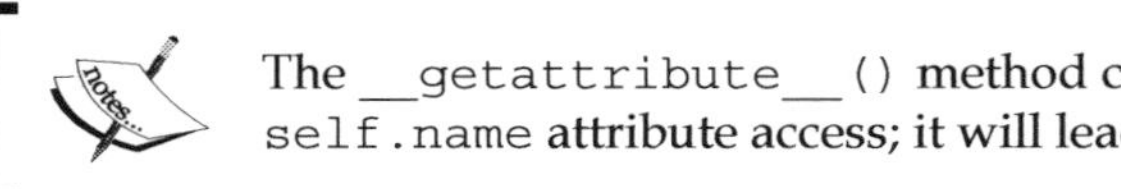

The `__getattribute__()` method cannot give any simple `self.name` attribute access; it will lead to infinite recursions.

In order to get attribute values within the `__getattribute__()` method, we must explicitly refer to the base method defined in `object`, as shown in the following declaration:

```
object.__getattribute__(self, name)
```

We could, for example, revise our immutable class to use `__getattribute__()` and prevent access to the internal `__dict__` attribute. The following is a class that conceals all the names beginning with the underscore character (_):

```
class BlackJackCard3:
    """Abstract Superclass"""
    def __init__( self, rank, suit, hard, soft ):
        super().__setattr__( 'rank', rank )
        super().__setattr__( 'suit', suit )
        super().__setattr__( 'hard', hard )
        super().__setattr__( 'soft', soft )
    def __setattr__( self, name, value ):
        if name in self.__dict__:
            raise AttributeError( "Cannot set {name}".
format(name=name) )
        raise AttributeError( "'{__class__.__name__}' has no attribute
'{name}'".format( __class__= self.__class__, name= name ) )
    def __getattribute__( self, name ):
        if name.startswith('_'): raise AttributeError
        return object.__getattribute__( self, name )
```

We've overridden `__getattribute__()` to raise an attribute error on private names as well as Python's internal names. This has a microscopic advantage over the previous example: we are not allowed to tweak the object at all. We'll see an example of an interaction with an instance of this class.

The following is an example of an object of this class being mutated:

```
>>> c = BlackJackCard3( 'A', '♠', 1, 11 )
>>> c.rank= 12
Traceback (most recent call last):
  File "<stdin>", line 1, in <module>
```

```
  File "<stdin>", line 9, in __setattr__
  File "<stdin>", line 13, in __getattribute__
AttributeError
>>> c.__dict__['rank']= 12
Traceback (most recent call last):
  File "<stdin>", line 1, in <module>
  File "<stdin>", line 13, in __getattribute__
AttributeError
```

As general advice, it's rarely a good idea to mess with `__getattribute__()`. The default method is quite sophisticated, and almost everything we need is available as a property or as a change to `__getattr__()`.

Creating descriptors

A descriptor is a class that mediates attribute access. The descriptor class can be used to get, set, or delete attribute values. Descriptor objects are built inside a class at class definition time.

The descriptor design pattern has two parts: an **owner class** and the **attribute descriptor** itself. The owner class uses one or more descriptors for its attributes. A descriptor class defines some combination of get, set, and delete methods. An instance of the descriptor class will be an attribute of the owner class.

Properties are based on the method functions of the owner class. A descriptor, unlike a property, is an instance of a class different from the owning class. Therefore, descriptors are often reusable, generic kinds of attributes. The owning class can have multiple instances of each descriptor class to manage attributes with similar behaviors.

Unlike other attributes, descriptors are created at the class level. They're not created within the `__init__()` initialization. While descriptor values can be set during initialization, descriptors are generally built as part of the class, outside any method functions.

Each descriptor object will be an instance of a descriptor class bound to a distinct class-level attribute name when the owner class is defined.

To be recognized as a descriptor, a class must implement any combination of the following three methods.

- `Descriptor.__get__( self, instance, owner ) → object`: In this method, the `instance` parameter is the `self` variable of the object being accessed. The `owner` parameter is the owning class object. If this descriptor is invoked in a class context, the `instance` parameter will get a `None` value. This must return the value of the descriptor.

- `Descriptor.__set__( self, instance, value )`: In this method, the `instance` parameter is the `self` variable of the object being accessed. The `value` parameter is the new value that the descriptor needs to be set to.
- `Descriptor.__delete__( self, instance )`: In this method, the `instance` parameter is the `self` variable of the object being accessed. This method of the descriptor must delete this attribute's value.

Sometimes, a descriptor class will also need an `__init__()` method function to initialize the descriptor's internal state.

There are two species of descriptors based on the methods defined, as follows:

- **A nondata descriptor**: This kind of descriptor defines `__set__()` or `__delete__()` or both. It cannot define `__get__()`. The nondata descriptor object will often be used as part of some larger expression. It might be a callable object, or it might have attributes or methods of its own. An immutable nondata descriptor must implement `__set__()` but may simply raise `AttributeError`. These descriptors are slightly simpler to design because the interface is more flexible.
- **A data descriptor**: This descriptor defines `__get__()` at a minimum. Usually, it defines both `__get__()` and `__set__()` to create a mutable object. The descriptor can't define any further attributes or methods of this object since the descriptor will largely be invisible. A reference to an attribute that has a value of a data descriptor is delegated to the `__get__()`, `__set__()`, or `__delete__()` methods of the descriptor. These can be tricky to design, so we'll look at them second.

There are a wide variety of use cases for descriptors. Internally, Python uses descriptors for several reasons:

- Under the hood, the methods of a class are implemented as descriptors. These are nondata descriptors that apply the method function to the object and the various parameter values.
- The `property()` function is implemented by creating a data descriptor for the named attribute.
- A class method or static method is implemented as a descriptor; this applies to the class instead of an instance of the class.

When we look at object-relational mapping in *Chapter 11, Storing and Retrieving Objects via SQLite*, we'll see that many of the ORM class definitions make heavy use of descriptors to map Python class definitions to SQL tables and columns.

As we think about the purposes of a descriptor, we must also examine the three common use cases for the data that a descriptor works with as follows:

- The **descriptor object** has, or acquires, the data. In this case, the descriptor object's `self` variable is relevant and the descriptor is stateful. With a data descriptor, the `__get__()` method returns this internal data. With a nondata descriptor, the descriptor has other methods or attributes to access this data.
- The **owner instance** contains the data. In this case, the descriptor object must use the `instance` parameter to reference a value in the owning object. With a data descriptor, the `__get__()` method fetches the data from the instance. With a nondata descriptor, the descriptor's other methods access the instance data.
- The **owner class** contains the relevant data. In this case, the descriptor object must use the `owner` parameter. This is commonly used when the descriptor implements a static method or class method that applies to the class as a whole.

We'll take a look at the first case in detail. We'll look at creating a data descriptor with `__get__()` and `__set__()` methods. We'll also look at creating a nondata descriptor without a `__get__()` method.

The second case (the data in the owning instance) shows what the `@property` decorator does. The possible advantage that a descriptor has over a conventional property is that it moves the calculations into the descriptor class from the owner class. This tends to fragment class design and is probably not the best approach. If the calculations are truly of epic complexity, then a strategy pattern might be better.

The third case shows how the `@staticmethod` and `@classmethod` decorators are implemented. We don't need to reinvent those wheels.

Using a nondata descriptor

We often have small objects with a few tightly bound attribute values. For this example, we'll take a look at numeric values that are bound up with units of measure.

The following is a simple nondata descriptor class that lacks a `__get__()` method:

```
class UnitValue_1:
    """Measure and Unit combined."""
    def __init__( self, unit ):
        self.value= None
        self.unit= unit
        self.default_format= "5.2f"
```

```
    def __set__( self, instance, value ):
        self.value= value
    def __str__( self ):
        return "{value:{spec}} {unit}".format( spec=self.default_
format, **self.__dict__)
    def __format__( self, spec="5.2f" ):
        #print( "formatting", spec )
        if spec == "": spec= self.default_format
        return "{value:{spec}} {unit}".format( spec=spec,
**self.__dict__)
```

This class defines a simple pair of values, one that is mutable (the value) and another that is effectively immutable (the unit).

When this descriptor is accessed, the descriptor object itself is made available, and other methods or attributes of the descriptor can then be used. We can use this descriptor to create classes that manage measurements and other numbers associated with physical units.

The following is a class that does rate-time-distance calculations eagerly:

```
class RTD_1:
    rate= UnitValue_1( "kt" )
    time= UnitValue_1( "hr" )
    distance= UnitValue_1( "nm" )
    def __init__( self, rate=None, time=None, distance=None ):
        if rate is None:
            self.time = time
            self.distance = distance
            self.rate = distance / time
        if time is None:
            self.rate = rate
            self.distance = distance
            self.time = distance / rate
        if distance is None:
            self.rate = rate
            self.time = time
            self.distance = rate * time
    def __str__( self ):
        return "rate: {0.rate} time: {0.time} distance:
{0.distance}".format(self)
```

As soon as the object is created and the attributes loaded, the missing value is computed. Once computed, the descriptor can be examined to get the value or the unit's name. Additionally, the descriptor has a handy response to `str()` and formatting requests.

The following is an interaction between a descriptor and the `RTD_1` class:

```
>>> m1 = RTD_1( rate=5.8, distance=12 )
>>> str(m1)
'rate:  5.80 kt time:  2.07 hr distance: 12.00 nm'
>>> print( "Time:", m1.time.value, m1.time.unit )
Time: 2.0689655172413794 hr
```

We created an instance of `RTD_1` with `rate` and `distance` arguments. These were used to evaluate the `__set__()` methods of the `rate` and `distance` descriptors.

When we asked for `str(m1)`, this evaluated the overall `__str__()` method of `RTD_1` that, in turn, used the `__format__()` method of the rate, time, and distance descriptors. This provided us with numbers with units attached to them.

We can also access the individual elements of a descriptor since nondata descriptors don't have `__get__()` and don't return their internal values.

Using a data descriptor

A data descriptor is somewhat trickier to design because it has such a limited interface. It must have a `__get__()` method and it can only have `__set__()` or `__delete__()`. This is the entire interface: from one to three of these methods and no other methods. Introducing an additional method means that Python will not recognize the class as being a proper data descriptor.

We'll design an overly simplistic unit conversion schema using descriptors that can do appropriate conversions in their `__get__()` and `__set__()` methods.

The following is a superclass of a descriptor of units that will do conversions to and from a standard unit:

```
class Unit:
    conversion= 1.0
    def __get__( self, instance, owner ):
        return instance.kph * self.conversion
    def __set__( self, instance, value ):
        instance.kph= value / self.conversion
```

This class does simple multiplications and divisions to convert standard units to other non-standard units and vice versa.

With this superclass, we can define some conversions from a standard unit. In the previous case, the standard unit is KPH (kilometers per hour).

The following are the two conversion descriptors:

```
class Knots( Unit ):
    conversion= 0.5399568

class MPH( Unit ):
    conversion= 0.62137119
```

The inherited methods are perfectly useful. The only thing that changes is the conversion factor. These classes can be used to work with values that involve unit conversion. We can work with MPH's or knots interchangeably. The following is a unit descriptor for a standard unit, kilometers per hour:

```
class KPH( Unit ):
    def __get__( self, instance, owner ):
        return instance._kph
    def __set__( self, instance, value ):
        instance._kph= value
```

This class represents a standard, so it doesn't do any conversion. It uses a private variable in the instance to save the standard value for speed in KPH. Avoiding any arithmetic conversion is simply a technique of optimization. Avoiding any reference to one of the public attributes is essential to avoiding infinite recursions.

The following is a class that provides a number of conversions for a given measurement:

```
class Measurement:
    kph= KPH()
    knots= Knots()
    mph= MPH()
    def __init__( self, kph=None, mph=None, knots=None ):
        if kph: self.kph= kph
        elif mph: self.mph= mph
        elif knots: self.knots= knots
        else:
            raise TypeError
    def __str__( self ):
        return "rate: {0.kph} kph = {0.mph} mph = {0.knots}
knots".format(self)
```

Each of the class-level attributes is a descriptor for a different unit. The get and set methods of the various descriptors will do appropriate conversions. We can use this class to convert speeds among a variety of units.

The following is an example of an interaction with the `Measurement` class:

```
>>> m2 = Measurement( knots=5.9 )
>>> str(m2)
'rate: 10.92680006993152 kph = 6.789598762345432 mph = 5.9 knots'
>>> m2.kph
10.92680006993152
>>> m2.mph
6.789598762345432
```

We created an object of the `Measurement` class by setting various descriptors. In the first case, we set the knots descriptor.

When we displayed the value as a large string, each of the descriptor's `__get__()` methods was used. These methods fetched the internal `kph` attribute value from the owning object, applied a conversion factor, and returned the resulting value.

The `kph` attribute also uses a descriptor. This descriptor does not do any conversion; however, it simply returns a private value cached in the owning object. The `KPH` and `Knots` descriptors require that the owning class implement a `kph` attribute.

Summary, design considerations, and trade-offs

In this chapter, we looked at several ways to work with an object's attributes. We can use the built-in features of the `object` class and get and set attribute values. We can define properties to modify how attributes behave.

If we want more sophistication, we can tweak the underlying special method implementations for `__getattr__()`, `__setattr__()`, `__delattr__()`, or `__getattribute__()`. These allow us very fine-grained control over attribute behaviors. We walk a fine line when we touch these methods because we can make fundamental (and confusing) changes to Python's behavior.

Internally, Python uses descriptors to implement features such as method functions, static method functions, and properties. Many of the cool use cases for descriptors are already first-class features of the language.

Programmers coming from other languages (particularly Java and C++) usually have the urge to try to make all attributes private and write extensive getter and setter functions. This kind of coding is necessary for languages where type definitions are statically compiled in.

In Python, it's considerably simpler to treat all attributes as public. This means the following:

- They should be well documented.
- They should properly reflect the state of the object; they shouldn't be temporary or transient values.
- In the rare case of an attribute that has a potentially confusing (or brittle) value, a single leading underscore character (_) marks the name as "not part of the defined interface." It's not really private.

It's important to think of private attributes as a nuisance. Encapsulation isn't broken by the lack of complex privacy mechanisms in the language; it is broken by bad design.

Properties versus attributes

In most cases, attributes can be set outside a class with no adverse consequences. Our example of the `Hand` class shows this. For many versions of the class, we can simply append to `hand.cards`, and the lazy computation of `total` via a property will work perfectly.

In cases where the changing of an attribute should lead to consequential changes in other attributes, some more sophisticated class design is required:

- A method function may clarify the state change. This will be necessary when multiple parameter values are required.
- A property setter may be clearer than a method function. This will be a sensible option when a single value is required.
- We can also use in-place operators. We'll defer this until *Chapter 7, Creating Numbers*.

There's no strict rule. In this case, where we need to set a single parameter value, the distinction between a method function and a property is entirely one of API syntax and how well that communicates the intent.

For computed values, a property allows lazy computation, while an attribute requires eager computation. This devolves to a performance question. The benefits of lazy versus eager computation are based on the expected use cases.

Designing with descriptors

Many examples of descriptors are already part of Python. We don't need to reinvent properties, class methods, or static methods.

The most compelling cases for creating new descriptors relate to mapping between Python and something non-Python. Object-relational database mapping, for example, requires a great deal of care to ensure that a Python class has the right attributes in the right order to match a SQL table and columns. Also, when mapping to something outside Python, a descriptor class can handle encoding and decoding data or fetching the data from external sources.

When building a web service client, we might consider using descriptors to make web service requests. The `__get__()` method, for example, might turn into an HTTP GET request, and the `__set__()` method might turn into an HTTP PUT request.

In some cases, a single request may populate the data of several descriptors. In this case, the `__get__()` method would check the instance cache and return that value before making an HTTP request.

Many data descriptor operations are more simply handled by properties. This provides us with a place to start: to write properties first. If the property processing becomes too expansive or complex, then we can switch to descriptors to refactor the class.

Looking forward

In the next chapter, we'll look closely at the **ABCs** (**Abstract Base Classes**) that we'll exploit in Chapters 5, 6, and 7. These ABCs will help us define classes that integrate nicely with existing Python features. They will also allow us to create class hierarchies that enforce consistent design and extension.

4 The ABCs of Consistent Design

The Python Standard Library provides abstract base classes for a number of features of containers. It provides a consistent framework for the built-in container classes, such as `list`, `map`, and `set`.

Additionally, the library provides abstract base classes for numbers. We can use these classes to extend the suite of numeric classes available in Python.

We'll look in general at the abstract base classes in the `collections.abc` module. From there, we can focus on a few use cases that will be the subject of detailed examination in future chapters.

We have three design strategies: Wrap, Extend, and Invent. We'll look at the general concepts behind the various containers and collections that we might want to wrap or extend. Similarly, we'll look at the concepts behind the numbers that we might want to implement.

Our goal is to assure that our application classes integrate seamlessly with existing Python features. If we create a collection, for example, it's appropriate to have that collection also create an iterator by implementing `__iter__()`. A collection that implements `__iter__()` will work seamlessly with a `for` statement.

Abstract base classes

The core of the **Abstract Base Class (ABC)** definition is defined in a module named `abc`. This contains the required decorators and metaclasses to create abstractions. Other classes rely on these definitions.

In Python 3.2, the abstract base classes for collections were buried in `collections`. In Python 3.3, however, the abstract base classes have been split into a separate submodule named `collections.abc`.

We'll also look at the `numbers` module, because it contains ABCs for numeric types. There are abstract base classes for I/O in the `io` module too.

We'll focus on Python Version 3.3. The definitions will work very similarly for Python 3.2, but the `import` statement will change slightly to reflect the flatter library structure.

An abstract base class has a number of features, as follows:

- Abstract means that these classes don't contain all of the method definitions required to work completely. For it to be a useful subclass, we will need to provide some method definitions.
- Base means that other classes will use it as a superclass.
- An abstract class provides some definitions for method functions. Most importantly, the abstract base classes provide the signatures for the missing method functions. A subclass must provide the right methods to create a concrete class that fits the interface defined by the abstract class.

The features of the abstract base classes include the following ideas:

- We can use them to define a consistent set of base classes for Python's internal classes and our customized application classes.
- We can use them to create some common, reusable abstractions that we can use in our applications.
- We can use them to support the proper inspection of a class to determine what it does. This allows better collaboration among library classes and new classes in our applications. In order to do an inspection properly, it helps to have the formal definition of concepts such as "container" and "number".

Without abstract base classes (that is, in the "bad old days") a container may, or may not, have provided all the features of a `Sequence` class consistently. This often leads to a class being almost a sequence or sequence-like. This, in turn, leads to odd inconsistencies and kludgy workarounds for a class that didn't quite provide all the features of a sequence.

With an abstract base class, you can assure that an application's given class will have the advertised features. If it lacks a feature, the presence of an undefined abstract method will make the class unusable for building object instances.

We'll use ABCs in several situations, as follows:

- We'll use ABC's as superclasses when defining our own classes
- We'll use ABC's within a method to confirm that an operation is possible
- We'll use ABC's within a diagnostic message or exception to indicate why an operation can't work

For the first use case, we may write modules with code that looks like the following:

```
import collections.abc
class SomeApplicationClass( collections.abc.Callable ):
    pass
```

Our `SomeApplicationClass` is defined to be a `Callable` class. It must then implement the specific methods required by `Callable`, or we will not be able to create an instance.

A function is a concrete example of a `Callable` class. The abstraction is a class that defines the `__call__()` method. We'll look at `Callables` classes in the following section and in *Chapter 5*, Using *Callables and Contexts*.

For the second use case, we may write methods with code that looks like the following:

```
def some_method( self, other ):
    assert isinstance(other, collections.abc.Iterator)
```

Our `some_method()` requires for the `other` argument to be a subclass of `Iterator`. If the `other` argument can't pass this test, we get an exception. A common alternative to `assert` is an `if` statement that raises `TypeError`, which may be more meaningful. We'll see this in the following section.

For the third use case, we might have something like the following:

```
try:
    some_obj.some_method( another )
except AttributeError:
    warnings.warn( "{0!r} not an Iterator, found {0.__class__.__
bases__!r}".format(another) )
    raise
```

In this case, we wrote a diagnostic warning that shows the base classes for a given object. This may help debug the problem with the application design.

Base classes and polymorphism

In this section, we'll flirt with the idea of **Pretty Poor Polymorphism**. Inspection of argument values is a Python programming practice that should be isolated to a few special cases.

Well-done polymorphism follows what is sometimes called the **Liskov Substitution Principle**. Polymorphic classes can be used interchangeably. Each polymorphic class has the same suite of properties. For more information, visit `http://en.wikipedia.org/wiki/Liskov_substitution_principle`.

Overusing `isinstance()` to distinguish between the types of arguments can lead to a needlessly complex (and slow) program. Instance comparisons are made all the time, but errors are generally only introduced through software maintenance. Unit testing is a far better way to find programming errors than verbose type-checking in the code.

Method functions with lots of `isinstance()` methods can be a symptom of a poor (or incomplete) design of polymorphic classes. Rather than having type-specific processing outside of a class definition, it's often better to extend or wrap classes to make them more properly polymorphic and encapsulate the type-specific processing within the class definition.

One good use of the `isinstance()` method is to create diagnostic messages. A simple approach is to use the `assert` statement:

```
assert isinstance( some_argument, collections.abc.Container ),
"{0!r} not a Container".format(some_argument)
```

This will raise an `AssertionError` exception to indicate that there's a problem. This has the advantage that it is short and to the point. However, it has two disadvantages: assertions can be silenced, and it would probably be better to raise a `TypeError` for this. The following example might be better:

```
if not isinstance(some_argument, collections.abc.Container):
    raise TypeError( "{0!r} not a Container".format(some_argument)
)
```

The preceding code has the advantage that it raises the correct error. However, it has the disadvantage that it is long winded.

The more Pythonic approach is summarized as follows:

> *"It's better to ask for forgiveness than to ask for permission."*

This is generally taken to mean that we should minimize the upfront testing of arguments (asking permission) to see if they're the correct type. Argument-type inspections are rarely of any tangible benefit. Instead, we should handle the exceptions appropriately (asking forgiveness).

What's best is to combine diagnostic information with the exception in the unlikely event that an inappropriate type is used and somehow passed through unit testing into operation.

The following is often what's done:

```
try:
    found = value in some_argument
except TypeError:
    if not isinstance(some_argument, collections.abc.Container):
        warnings.warn( "{0!r} not a Container".format(some_argument) )
    raise
```

The `isinstance()` method assumes that `some_argument` is a proper instance of a `collections.abc.Container` class and will respond to the `in` operator.

In the unlikely event that someone changes the application and `some_argument` is now of the wrong class, the application will write a diagnostic message and crash with a `TypeError` exception.

Callables

Python's definition of **callable object** includes the obvious function definitions created with the `def` statement.

It also includes, informally, any class with a `__call__()` method. We can see several examples of this in *Python 3 Object Oriented Programming, Dusty Phillips, Packt Publishing*. For it to be more formal, we should make every callable class definition a proper subclass of `collections.abc.Callable`.

When we look at any Python function, we see the following behavior:

```
>>> abs(3)
3
>>> isinstance(abs, collections.abc.Callable)
True
```

The built-in `abs()` function is a proper instance of `collections.abc.Callable`. This is also true for the functions we define. The following is an example:

```
>>> def test(n):
...     return n*n
...
>>> isinstance(test, collections.abc.Callable)
True
```

Every function reports itself as `Callable`. This simplifies the inspection of an argument value and helps write meaningful debugging messages.

We'll take a look at callables in detail in *Chapter 5, Using Callables and Contexts*.

Containers and collections

The `collections` module defines a number of collections above and beyond the built-in container classes. The container classes include `namedtuple()`, `deque`, `ChainMap`, `Counter`, `OrderedDict`, and `defaultdict`. All of these are examples of classes based on ABC definitions.

The following is a quick interaction to show how we can inspect collections to see the methods they will support:

```
>>> isinstance( {}, collections.abc.Mapping )
True
>>> isinstance( collections.defaultdict(int), collections.abc.Mapping
)
True
```

We can inspect the simple `dict` class to see that it follows the basic mapping protocol and will support the required methods.

We can inspect a `defaultdict` collection to confirm that it is also a mapping.

When creating a new kind of container, we can do it informally. We can create a class that has all of the right special methods. However, we aren't *required* to make a formal declaration that it's a certain kind of container.

It's more clear (and more reliable) to use a proper ABC as the base class for one of our application classes. The additional formality has the following two advantages:

- It advertises what our intention was to people reading (and possibly using or maintaining) our code. When we make a subclass of `collections.abc.Mapping`, we're making a very strong claim about how that class will be used.

- It creates some diagnostic support. If we somehow fail to implement all of the required methods properly, we can't create instances of the abstract base class. If we can't run the unit tests because we can't create instances of an object, then this indicates a serious problem that needs to be fixed.

The entire family tree of built-in containers is reflected in the abstract base classes. Lower-level features include `Container`, `Iterable`, and `Sized`. These are a part of higher-level constructs; they require a few specific methods, particularly `__contains__()`, `__iter__()`, and `__len__()`, respectively.

Higher-level features include the following characteristics:

- `Sequence` and `MutableSequence`: These are the abstractions of the concrete classes `list` and `tuple`. Concrete sequence implementations also include `bytes` and `str`.
- `MutableMapping`: This is the abstraction of `dict`. It extends `Mapping`, but there's no built-in concrete implementation of this.
- `Set` and `MutableSet`: These are the abstractions of the concrete classes, `frozenset` and `set`.

This allows us to build new classes or extend existing classes and maintain a clear and formal integration with the rest of Python's built-in features.

We'll look at containers and collections in detail in *Chapter 6, Creating Containers and Collections*.

Numbers

When creating new numbers (or extending existing numbers), we'll turn to the `numbers` module. This module contains the abstract definitions of Python's built-in numeric types. These types form a tall, narrow hierarchy, from the simplest to the most elaborate. In this case, simplicity (and elaboration) refers to the collection of methods available.

There's an abstract base class named `numbers.Number` that defines all of the numeric and number-like classes. We can see that this is true with interactions like the following one:

```
>>> import numbers
>>> isinstance( 42, numbers.Number )
True
>>> 355/113
3.1415929203539825
```

```
>>> isinstance( 355/113, numbers.Number )
True
```

Clearly, integer and float values are subclasses of the abstract `numbers.Number` class.

The subclasses include `numbers.Complex`, `numbers.Real`, `numbers.Rational`, and `numbers.Integral`. These definitions are roughly parallel mathematical thoughts on the various classes of numbers.

The `decimal.Decimal` class, however, doesn't fit this hierarchy extremely well. We can check the relationships using the `issubclass()` method as follows:

```
>>> issubclass( decimal.Decimal, numbers.Number )
True
>>> issubclass( decimal.Decimal, numbers.Integral )
False
>>> issubclass( decimal.Decimal, numbers.Real )
False
>>> issubclass( decimal.Decimal, numbers.Complex )
False
>>> issubclass( decimal.Decimal, numbers.Rational )
False
```

It shouldn't be too surprising that `Decimal` doesn't fit the established number types well. For a concrete implementation of `numbers.Rational`, look at the `fractions` module. We'll look at the various kinds of numbers in detail in *Chapter 7, Creating Numbers*.

Some additional abstractions

We'll look at some other interesting ABC classes that are less widely extended. It's not that these abstractions are less widely used. It's more that the concrete implementations rarely need extensions or revisions.

We'll look at the iterator, which is defined by `collections.abc.Iterator`. We'll also look at the unrelated idea of a context manager. This isn't defined with the same formality as other ABC classes. We'll look at this in detail in *Chapter 5, Using Callables and Contexts*.

The iterator abstraction

Iterators are created implicitly when we use an iterable container with a `for` statement. We rarely care about the iterator itself. And the few times we do care about the iterator, we rarely want to extend or revise the class definition.

We can expose the implicit iterators that Python uses via the `iter()` function. We can interact with an iterator in the following way:

```
>>> x = [ 1, 2, 3 ]
>>> iter(x)
<list_iterator object at 0x1006e3c50>
>>> x_iter = iter(x)
>>> next(x_iter)
1
>>> next(x_iter)
2
>>> next(x_iter)
3
>>> next(x_iter)
Traceback (most recent call last):
  File "<stdin>", line 1, in <module>
StopIteration
>>> isinstance( x_iter, collections.abc.Iterator )
True
```

We created an iterator over a list object and then stepped through the values in that iterator using the `next()` function.

The final `isinstance()` expression confirmed that this iterator object is an instance of `collections.abc.Iterator`.

Most of the time, we'll work with iterators that have been created by the collection classes themselves. However, when we branch out and build our own collection classes or extend a collection class, we may also need to build a unique iterator. We'll look at iterators in *Chapter 6, Creating Containers and Collections*.

Contexts and context managers

A context manager is used with the `with` statement. We're working with a context manager when we write something like the following:

```
with function(arg) as context:
    process( context )
```

In the preceding case, `function(arg)` creates the context manager.

One very commonly used context manager is a file. When we open a file, we should define a context that will also automatically close the file. Consequently, we should almost always use a file in the following way:

```
with open("some file") as the_file:
    process( the_file )
```

At the end of the with statement, we're assured that the file will be closed properly. The contextlib module provides several tools for building proper context managers. Rather than providing an abstract base class, this library offers decorators, which will transform simple functions into context managers, as well as a contextlib.ContextDecorator base class, which can be used extended to build a class that is a context manager.

We'll look at context managers in *Chapter 5, Using Callables and Contexts*.

The abc module

The core method of creating ABCs is defined in the abc module. This module includes the ABCMeta class that provides several features.

First, the ABCMeta class assures that abstract classes can't be instantiated. A subclass that provides all of the required definitions, however, can be instantiated. The metaclass will invoke the abstract class's special method, __subclasshook__(), as a part of processing __new__(). If that method returns NotImplemented, then an exception will be raised to show that the class didn't define all the required methods.

Second, it provides definitions for __instancecheck__() and __subclasscheck__(). These special methods implement the isinstance() and issubclass() built-in functions. They provide the checks to confirm that an object (or a class) belongs to the proper ABC. This includes a cache of subclasses to speed up the testing.

The abc module also includes a number of decorators for creating abstract method functions that must be provided by a concrete implementation of the abstract base class. The most important of these is the @abstractmethod decorator.

If we wanted to create a new abstract base class, we would use something like the following:

```
from abc import ABCMeta, abstractmethod
class AbstractBettingStrategy(metaclass=ABCMeta):
    __slots__ = ()
    @abstractmethod
    def bet(self, hand):
        return 1
    @abstractmethod
    def record_win(self, hand):
        pass
    @abstractmethod
    def record_loss(self, hand):
        pass
    @classmethod
```

```
    def __subclasshook__(cls, subclass):
        if cls is Hand:
            if (any("bet" in B.__dict__ for B in subclass.__mro__)
            and any("record_win" in B.__dict__ for B in
subclass.__mro__)
            and any("record_loss" in B.__dict__ for B in
subclass.__mro__)
            ):
                return True
        return NotImplemented
```

This class includes `ABCMeta` as its metaclass; it also uses the `__subclasshook__()` method, which checks for completeness. These provide the core features of an abstract class.

This abstraction uses the `abstractmethod` decorator to define three abstract methods. Any concrete subclass must define these in order to be a complete implementation of the abstract base class.

The `__subclasshook__` method requires that all of the three abstract methods be provided by a subclass. This is, perhaps, heavy-handed, since a super-simple betting strategy shouldn't have to provide methods for counting wins and losses.

The subclass hook relies on two internal features of a Python class definition: the `__dict__` attribute and the `__mro__` attribute. The `__dict__` attribute is where the method names and attribute names are recorded for a class definition. This is essentially the body of the class. The `__mro__` attribute is the method resolution order. This is the sequence of the superclasses of this class. Since Python uses multiple inheritance, there can be many superclasses, and the order of these superclasses determines the precedence for resolving names.

The following is an example of a concrete class:

```
class Simple_Broken(AbstractBettingStrategy):
    def bet( self, hand ):
        return 1
```

The preceding code can't be built because it doesn't provide necessary implementations for all three methods.

The following is what happens when we try to build it:

```
>>> simple= Simple_Broken()
Traceback (most recent call last):
  File "<stdin>", line 1, in <module>
TypeError: Can't instantiate abstract class Simple_Broken with
abstract methods record_loss, record_win
```

The error message indicates that the concrete class is incomplete. The following is a better concrete class that passes the completeness test:

```
class Simple(AbstractBettingStrategy):
    def bet( self, hand ):
        return 1
    def record_win(self, hand):
        pass
    def record_loss(self, hand):
        pass
```

We can build an instance of this class and use it as part of our simulation.

As we noted earlier, the `bet()` method should probably be the only *required* method. The other two methods should be allowed to default to the single statement `pass`.

Summary, design considerations, and trade-offs

In this chapter, we looked at the essential ingredients of abstract base classes. We saw a few features of each kind of abstraction.

We also learned that one rule for good class design is to inherit as much as possible. We saw two broad patterns here. We also saw common exceptions to this rule.

Some application classes don't have behaviors that overlap with internal features of Python. From our Blackjack examples, a `Card` isn't much like a number, a container, an iterator, or a context. It's just a playing card. In this case, we can generally invent a new class because there isn't any built-in features to inherit fro.

When we look at `Hand`, however, we see that a hand is clearly a container. As we noted when looking at hand classes in *Chapters 1, The __init__() Method*, and *Chapter 2, Integrating Seamlessly with Python – Basic Special Methods*, the following are three fundamental design strategies:

- Wrapping an existing container
- Extending an existing container
- Inventing a wholly new kind of container

Most of the time, we'll be wrapping or extending an existing container. This fits with our rule of inheriting as much as possible.

When we extend an existing class, our application class will fit into the class hierarchy neatly. An extension to the built-in `list` is already an instance of `collections.abc.MutableSequence`.

When we wrap an existing class, however, we have to consider carefully what parts of the original interface we want to support and what parts we don't want to support. In our examples in the previous chapters, we only wanted to expose the `pop()` method from the list object we were wrapping.

Because a wrapper class is not a complete mutable sequence implementation, there are many things it can't do. On the other hand, an extension class participates in a number of use cases that just might turn out to be useful. For example, a hand that extends `list` will turn out to be iterable.

If we find that extending a class doesn't meet our requirements, we can resort to building an entirely new collection. The ABC definitions provide a great deal of guidance on what methods are required in order to create a collection that can integrate seamlessly with the rest of the Python universe. We'll look at a detailed example of inventing a collection in *Chapter 6, Creating Containers and Collections*.

Looking forward

In the coming chapters, we'll make extensive use of these abstract base classes discussed in this chapter. In *Chapter 5, Using Callables and Contexts*, we'll look at the relatively simple features of callables and containers. In *Chapter 6, Creating Containers and Collections*, we'll look at the available containers and collections. We'll also look at building a unique, new kind of container in this chapter. Lastly, in *Chapter 7, Creating Numbers*, we'll look at various numeric types and how we can create our own kind of number.

5

Using Callables and Contexts

We can exploit the `collections.abc.Callable` ABC and employ a technique called **memoization** to create objects that behave like functions but perform very quickly because they are able to cache previous results. In some cases, memoization is essential for creating an algorithm that finishes within a reasonable amount of time.

The **context** concept allows us to create elegant, reliable resource management. The `with` statement defines a context and creates a context manager to control the resources used in that context. Python files are generally context managers; when used in a `with` statement, they are properly closed.

We'll look at several ways to create context managers using the tools in the `contextlib` module.

In Python 3.2, the abstract base classes were in the `collections` module.

In Python 3.3, the abstract base classes are in a separate submodule called `collections.abc`. In this chapter, we'll focus on Python Version 3.3. The basic definitions will also be true for Python 3.2, but the `import` statement will change.

We'll show a number of variant designs for callable objects. This will show us why a stateful callable object is sometimes more useful than a simple function. We'll also look at how to use some of the existing Python context managers before we dive in and write our own context manager.

Designing with ABC callables

There are two easy ways to create callable objects in Python, as follows:

- Using the `def` statement to create a function
- By creating an instance of a class that uses `collections.abc.Callable` as its base class

We can also assign a **lambda** form to a variable. A lambda is a small, anonymous function that consists of exactly one expression. We'd rather not emphasize saving lambdas in a variable as it leads to the confusing situation where we have a function-like callable that's not defined with a `def` statement. The following is a simple callable object that has been created from a class:

```
import collections.abc
class Power1( collections.abc.Callable ):
    def __call__( self, x, n ):
        p= 1
        for i in range(n):
            p *= x
        return p
pow1= Power1()
```

There are three parts to the preceding callable object, as follows:

- We defined the class as a subclass of `abc.Callable`
- We defined the `__call__()` method
- We created an instance of the class, `pow1()`

Yes, the algorithm seems inefficient. We'll address that.

Clearly, this is so simple that a full class definition isn't really necessary. In order to show the various optimizations, it's slightly simpler to start with a callable object rather than mutate a function into a callable object.

We can now use the `pow1()` function just as we'd use any other function. Here's how to use the `pow1()` function in a Python command line:

```
>>> pow1( 2, 0 )
1
>>> pow1( 2, 1 )
2
>>> pow1( 2, 2 )
4
>>> pow1( 2, 10 )
1024
```

We've evaluated the callable object with various kinds of argument values. It's not *required* to make a callable object a subclass of `abc.Callable`. However, it does help with debugging.

Consider this flawed definition:

```
class Power2( collections.abc.Callable ):
    def __call_( self, x, n ):
        p= 1
        for i in range(n):
            p *= x
        return p
```

The preceding class definition has an error and doesn't meet the definition of the callable abstraction.

Found the error yet? If not, it's at the end of the chapter.

The following is what happens when we try to create an instance of this class:

```
>>> pow2= Power2()
Traceback (most recent call last):
  File "<stdin>", line 1, in <module>
TypeError: Can't instantiate abstract class Power2 with abstract
methods __call__
```

It may not be obvious exactly what went wrong, but we have a fighting chance to debug this. If we hadn't subclassed `collections.abc.Callable`, we'd have a somewhat more mysterious problem to debug.

Here's what the more mysterious problem would look like. We'll skip the actual code for `Power3`. It's the same as `Power2`, except it doesn't subclass `collections.abc.Callable`. It starts `class Power3`; otherwise, it's identical.

The following is what happens when we try to use `Power3` as a class that doesn't meet the expectations of callables and isn't a subclass of the `abc.Callable` either:

```
>>> pow3= Power3()
>>> pow3( 2, 5 )
Traceback (most recent call last):
  File "<stdin>", line 1, in <module>
TypeError: 'Power3' object is not callable
```

This error provides less guidance as to why the `Power3` class definition is flawed. The `Power2` error is much more explicit about the nature of the problem.

Improving performance

We'll look at two performance tweaks for the `Power3` class.

First, a better algorithm. Then, a better algorithm combined with memoization, which involves a cache; therefore, the function becomes stateful. This is where callable objects shine.

The first modification is to use a **Divide and Conquer** design strategy. The previous version chopped x^n into n steps; the loop carried out n individual multiplication operations. If we can find a way to split the problem into two equal portions, the problem decomposes into $\log_2 n$ steps. Given `pow1(2,1024)`, the `Power1` callable performs the calculation 1024 multiplications by 2. We can optimize this down to 10 multiplications, a significant speedup.

Rather than simply multiplying by a fixed value, we'll use the "fast exponentiation" algorithm. It uses three essential rules for computing x^n, as follows:

- If $n = 0 : x^0 = 1$, the result is simply 1.
- If n is odd and $n \bmod 2 = 1$, the result is $x^{n-1} \times x$. This involves a recursive computation of x^{n-1}. This still does a multiplication but not a real optimization.
- If n is even and $n \bmod 2 = 0$, the result is $x^{n/2} \times x^{n/2}$. This involves a recursive computation of $x^{n/2}$. This chops the number of multiplications in half.

The following is the recursive callable object:

```
class Power4( abc.Callable ):
    def __call__( self, x, n ):
        if n == 0: return 1
        elif n % 2 == 1:
            return self.__call__(x, n-1)*x
        else: # n % 2 == 0:
            t= self.__call__(x, n//2)
            return t*t

pow4= Power4()
```

We applied the three rules to the input value. If n is zero, we'll return 1. If n is odd, we'll make a recursive call and return $x^{n-1} \times x$. If n is even, we'll make a recursive call and return $x^{n/2} \times x^{n/2}$.

The execution time is dramatically faster. We can use the `timeit` module to see the difference in performance. See *Some Preliminaries*, for information on using `timeit`. When we compare running `pow1(2,1024)` and `pow4(2,1024)` 10,000 times, we'll see something like 183 seconds for the previous version versus 8 seconds for this version. We can do better, however, with memoization.

The following is how we can gather performance data using `timeit`:

```
import timeit
iterative= timeit.timeit( "pow1(2,1024)","""
import collections.abc
class Power1( collections.abc.Callable ):
    def __call__( self, x, n ):
        p= 1
        for i in range(n):
            p *= x
        return p

pow1= Power1()
""", number=100000 ) # otherwise it takes 3 minutes
print( "Iterative", iterative )
```

We imported the `timeit` module. The `timeit.timeit()` function will evaluate a given statement in the defined context. In this case, our expression is the simple `pow1(2,1024)` expression. The context for this statement is the definition of the `pow1()` function; it includes the import, class definition, and creation of the instance.

Note that we provided `number=100000` to speed things up. If we had used the default value for the number of iterations, it could have taken almost 2 minutes.

Using memoization or caching

The idea behind memoization is to cache previous results to avoid recomputing them. We'll use considerably more memory, but we can also dramatically speed up performance by avoiding computation.

An ordinary function doesn't have a place to cache previous results. A function is not expected to be stateful. A callable object, however, can be stateful. It can include a cache of previous results.

The following is a memoized version of our `Power` callable object:

```
class Power5( collections.abc.Callable ):
    def __init__( self ):
        self.memo = {}
```

```
    def __call__( self, x, n ):
        if (x,n) not in self.memo:
            if n == 0:
                self.memo[x,n]= 1
            elif n % 2 == 1:
                self.memo[x,n]= self.__call__(x, n-1) * x
            elif n % 2 == 0:
                t= self.__call__(x, n//2)
                self.memo[x,n]= t*t
            else:
                raise Exception("Logic Error")
        return self.memo[x,n]
pow5= Power5()
```

We revised our algorithm to work with the `self.memo` cache.

If the value of x^n has been requested previously, that result is returned and no computation is performed. This is the big speedup that we spoke of earlier.

Otherwise, the value of x^n must be computed and saved in the memoization cache. The three rules to compute the fast exponent are used to get and put values in the cache. This assures us that future calculations will be able to exploit the cached values.

The importance of memoization can't be stressed enough. The reduction in computation can be dramatic. It is commonly done by replacing a slow, expensive function with a callable object.

Using functools for memoization

The Python library includes a memoization decorator in the `functools` module. We can use this module instead of creating our own callable object.

We can use it as follows:

```
from functools import lru_cache
@lru_cache(None)
def pow6( x, n ):
    if n == 0: return 1
    elif n % 2 == 1:
        return pow6(x, n-1)*x
    else: # n % 2 == 0:
        t= pow6(x, n//2)
        return t*t
```

This defined a function, `pow6()`, which is decorated with a **Least Recently Used** (**LRU**) cache. Previous requests are stored in a memoization cache. The requests are tracked in the cache, and the size is limited. The idea behind an LRU cache is that the most recently made requests are kept and the least recently made requests are quietly purged.

Using `timeit`, we can see that 10,000 iterations of `pow5()` run in about 1 second, while the iterations for `pow6()` run in about 8 seconds.

What this also shows is that a trivial use of `timeit` can misstate the performance of the memoization algorithms. The requests of the `timeit` module should be made more sophisticated to reflect more realistic use cases, to properly mix cache hits and cache misses. Simple random numbers aren't always appropriate for all problem domains.

Aiming for simplicity using the callable API

The idea behind a callable object is that we have an API that's focused on a single method.

Some objects have multiple relevant methods. A Blackjack `Hand`, for example, has to add cards and produce a total. A blackjack `Player` has to place bets, accept hands, and make play decisions (for example, hit, stand, split, insure, double down, and so on). These are more complex interfaces that are not suitable to be callables.

The betting strategy, however, is a candidate for being a callable.

The betting strategy can either be implemented as several methods (some setters and a getter method) or it can be a callable interface with a few public attributes.

The following is the straight betting strategy. It is always the same:

```
class BettingStrategy:
    def __init__( self ):
       self.win= 0
       self.loss= 0
    def __call__( self ):
        return 1
bet=  BettingStrategy()
```

The idea of this API is that a `Player` object will inform the betting strategy of win amounts and loss amounts. The `Player` object might have methods such as the following to inform the betting strategy about the outcome:

```
    def win( self, amount ):
        self.bet.win += 1
        self.stake += amount
```

```
    def loss( self, amount ):
         self.bet.loss += 1
         self.stake -= amount
```

These methods inform a betting strategy object (the `self.bet` object) whether the hand was a win or a loss. When it's time to place a bet, the `Player` will perform something like the following operation to get the current betting level:

```
    def initial_bet( self ):
        return self.bet()
```

This is a pleasantly short API. After all, the betting strategy doesn't do much other than encapsulate a few, relatively simple rules.

The shortness of this interface is one of the elegant features of a callable object. We don't have many method names, and we don't have a complex set of syntaxes for a simple thing.

Complexities and the callable API

Let's see how well this API holds up as our processing becomes more complex. The following is the double-up on each loss strategy (also known as the **Martingale** betting system):

```
class BettingMartingale( BettingStrategy ):
    def __init__( self ):
        self._win= 0
        self._loss= 0
        self.stage= 1
    @property
    def win(self): return self._win
    @win.setter
    def win(self, value):
        self._win = value
        self.stage= 1
    @property
    def loss(self): return self._loss
    @loss.setter
    def loss(self, value):
        self._loss = value
        self.stage *= 2
    def __call__( self ):
       return self.stage
```

Each loss doubles the betting by multiplying the stage by two. This goes on until we win and recoup our losses, reach the table limit, or go broke and can no longer place any bets. Casinos prevent this by imposing table limits.

Whenever we win, the betting is reset to the base bet. The stage is reset to have a value of one.

In order to keep the attribute interface—code such as `bet.win += 1`—we need to create properties to make the state changes correctly based on the wins and losses. We only really care about the setter properties, but we must define getter properties in order to clearly create setter properties.

We can see this class in action as follows:

```
>>> bet= BettingMartingale()
>>> bet()
1
>>> bet.win += 1
>>> bet()
1
>>> bet.loss += 1
>>> bet()
2
```

The API is still quite simple. We can either count the wins and reset the bet to the base, or we can count the losses, and the bets will double.

The use of properties made the class definition long and hideous. We're really only interested in the setters and not the getters, so we can use `__setattr__()` to streamline the class definition somewhat, as shown in the following code:

```
class BettingMartingale2( BettingStrategy ):
    def __init__( self ):
        self.win= 0
        self.loss= 0
        self.stage= 1
    def __setattr__( self, name, value ):
        if name == 'win':
            self.stage = 1
        elif name == 'loss':
            self.stage *= 2
        super().__setattr__( name, value )
    def __call__( self ):
        return self.stage
```

We used `__setattr__()` to monitor the updates to `win` and `loss`. In addition to setting the instance variables using `super().__setattr__()`, we also updated the internal state for the betting amount.

This is a nicer looking class definition, and it retains the simple API as a callable object with two attributes.

Managing contexts and the with statement

Contexts and context managers are used in several places in Python. We'll look at a few examples to establish the basic terminology.

A context is defined by the `with` statement. The following program is a small example that parses a logfile to create a useful CSV summary of that log. Since there are two open files, we expect to see nested `with` contexts. The example uses a complex regular expression, `format_1_pat`. We'll define this shortly.

We might see something like the following in an application program:

```
import gzip
import csv
with open("subset.csv", "w") as target:
    wtr= csv.writer( target )
    with gzip.open(path) as source:
        line_iter= (b.decode() for b in source)
        match_iter = (format_1_pat.match( line ) for line in
          line_iter)
        wtr.writerows( (m.groups() for m in match_iter if m is not
          None) )
```

Two contexts with two context managers were emphasized in this example.

The outermost context starts with `with open("subset.csv", "w") as target`. The built-in `open()` function opens a file that is also a context manager and assigns it to the `target` variable for further use.

The inner context starts with `with gzip.open(path, "r") as source`. This `gzip.open()` function behaves much like the `open()` function in that it opens a file that is also a context manager.

When the `with` statements end, the contexts exit and the files are properly closed. Even if there's an exception in the body of the `with` context, the context manager's exit will be processed correctly and the file will be closed.

Always use a with around a file()

Since files involve OS resources, it's important to be sure that the entanglements between our applications and the OS are released as soon as they're no longer needed. The `with` statement ensures that resources are used properly.

Just to complete the example, the following is the regular expression used to parse Apache HTTP server logfiles in **Common Log Format**:

```
import re
format_1_pat= re.compile(
    r"([\d\.]+)\s+" # digits and .'s: host
    r"(\S+)\s+"     # non-space: logname
    r"(\S+)\s+"     # non-space: user
    r"\[(.+?)\]\s+" # Everything in []: time
    r'"(.+?)"\s+'   # Everything in "": request
    r"(\d+)\s+"     # digits: status
    r"(\S+)\s+"     # non-space: bytes
    r'"(.*?)"\s+'   # Everything in "": referrer
    r'"(.*?)"\s*'   # Everything in "": user agent
)
```

The preceding expression located the various log format fields used in the previous example.

Using the decimal context

Another context that is used frequently is the decimal context. This context defines a number of properties of `decimal.Decimal` calculation, including the quantization rules used to round or truncate values.

We might see application programming that looks like the following:

```
import decimal
PENNY=decimal.Decimal("0.00")

price= decimal.Decimal('15.99')
rate= decimal.Decimal('0.0075')
print( "Tax=", (price*rate).quantize(PENNY), "Fully=", price*rate
)

with decimal.localcontext() as ctx:
    ctx.rounding= decimal.ROUND_DOWN
    tax= (price*rate).quantize(PENNY)
    print( "Tax=", tax )
```

The preceding example shows the default context as well as a local context. The default context has the default rounding rule. The localized context, however, shows how we can assure consistent operations by setting the decimal rounding for a particular calculation.

The `with` statement is used to assure that the original context is restored after the localized change. Outside this context, the default rounding applies. Inside this context, a specific rounding applies.

Other contexts

There are a few other common contexts. Almost all of them are associated with basic input/output operations. Most modules that open a file create a context along with the file-like object.

Contexts are also associated with locking and database transactions. We may acquire and release an external lock, like a semaphore, or we may want a database transaction to properly commit when it's successful or roll back when it fails. These are all the things that have defined contexts in Python.

The PEP 343 document provides a number of other examples of how the `with` statement and context managers might be used. There are other places where we might like to use a context manager.

We may need to create classes that are simply context managers, or we may need to create classes that can have multiple purposes, one of which is to be a context manager. The `file()` object is similar. We'll look at a number of design strategies for contexts.

We'll return to this again in *Chapter 8, Decorators and Mixins – Cross-cutting Aspects*, where we can cover a few more ways to create classes that have context manager features.

Defining the __enter__() and __exit__() methods

The defining feature of a context manager is that it has two special methods: `__enter__()` and `__exit__()`. These are used by the `with` statement to enter and exit the context. We'll use a simple context so that we can see how they work.

We'll often use context managers to make transient global changes. This might be a change to the database transaction status or a change to the locking status, something that we want to do and then undo when the transaction is complete.

For this example, we'll make a global change to the random number generator. We'll create a context in which the random number generator uses a fixed and known seed, providing a fixed sequence of values.

The following is the context manager class definition:

```
import random
class KnownSequence:
    def __init__(self, seed=0):
        self.seed= 0
    def __enter__(self):
        self.was= random.getstate()
        random.seed(self.seed, version=1)
        return self
    def __exit__(self, exc_type, exc_value, traceback):
        random.setstate(self.was)
```

We defined the required `__enter__()` and `__exit__()` methods. The `__enter__()` method will save the previous state of the random module and then reset the seed to a given value. The `__exit__()` method will restore the original state of the random number generator.

Note that `__enter__()` returns `self`. This is common for **mixin** context managers that have been added into other class definitions. We'll look at the concept of a mixin in *Chapter 8, Decorators And Mixins – Cross-cutting Aspects*.

The `__exit__()` method's parameters will have the value of `None` under normal circumstances. Unless we have specific exception-handling needs, we generally ignore the argument values. We'll look at exception-handling in the following code.

Here's an example of using the context:

```
print( tuple(random.randint(-1,36) for i in range(5)) )
with KnownSequence():
    print( tuple(random.randint(-1,36) for i in range(5)) )
print( tuple(random.randint(-1,36) for i in range(5)) )
with KnownSequence():
    print( tuple(random.randint(-1,36) for i in range(5)) )
print( tuple(random.randint(-1,36) for i in range(5)) )
```

Each time we create an instance of `KnownSequence`, we're modifying the way the `random` module works. During the context of the `with` statement, we'll get a fixed sequence of values. Outside the context, the random seed is restored, and we get random values.

The output will look like the following (in most cases):

```
(12, 0, 8, 21, 6)
(23, 25, 1, 15, 31)
(6, 36, 1, 34, 8)
(23, 25, 1, 15, 31)
(9, 7, 13, 22, 29)
```

Some of this output is machine-dependent. While the exact values may vary, the second and fourth lines will match because the seed was fixed by the context. The other lines will not necessarily match because they rely on the `random` module's own randomization features.

Handling exceptions

Exceptions that arise in a block will be passed to the `__exit__()` method of the context manager. The standard bits of an exception—the class, arguments, and the traceback stack—will all be provided as argument values.

The `__exit__()` method can do one of the following two things with the exception information:

- Silence the exception by returning some `True` value.
- Allow the exception to rise normally by returning any other `False` value. Returning nothing is the same as returning `None`, which is a `False` value; this allows the exception to propagate.

An exception might also be used to alter what the context manager does on exit. We might, for example, have to do special processing for certain types of OS errors that might arise.

Context manager as a factory

We can create a context manager class, which is a factory for an application object. This gives us a pleasant separation of design considerations without cluttering up an application class with context management features.

Let's say we want a deterministic `Deck` for dealing in blackjack. This isn't as useful as it might sound. For unit testing, we'll need a completely mock deck with specific sequences of cards. This has the advantage that the context manager works with the classes we already saw.

We'll extend the simple context manager shown earlier to create a `Deck` that can be used within the `with` statement context.

The following is a class that is a factory for `Deck` and also tweaks the `random` module:

```
class Deterministic_Deck:
    def __init__( self, *args, **kw ):
        self.args= args
        self.kw= kw
    def __enter__( self ):
        self.was= random.getstate()
        random.seed( 0, version=1 )
        return Deck( *self.args, **self.kw )
    def __exit__( self, exc_type, exc_value, traceback ):
        random.setstate( self.was )
```

The preceding context manager class preserves the argument values so that it can create a `Deck` with the given arguments.

The `__enter__()` method preserves the old random number state and then sets the `random` module in a mode that provides a fixed sequence of values. This is used to build and shuffle the deck.

Note that the `__enter__()` method returns a newly minted `Deck` object to be used in the `with` statement context. This is assigned via the `as` clause in the `with` statement.

We could have provided similar functionality in another way. We could create an instance of `random.Random(x=seed)` within the `Deck` class. While that also works well, it tends to clutter the `Deck` class with code that's only used for demonstrations.

The following is a way to use this factory context manager:

```
with Deterministic_Deck( size=6 ) as deck:
    h = Hand( deck.pop(), deck.pop(), deck.pop() )
```

The preceding example of code guarantees a specific sequence of cards that we can use for demonstration purposes.

Cleaning up in a context manager

In this section, we'll discuss a more complex context manager that attempts some cleanup when there are problems.

This addresses the common issue where we want to save a backup copy of a file that our application is rewriting. We want to be able to do something like the following:

```
with Updating( "some_file" ):
    with open( "some_file", "w" ) as target:
        process( target )
```

The intent is to have the original file renamed to `some_file copy`. If the context works normally—no exceptions—then the backup copy can be deleted or renamed to `some_file old`.

If the context doesn't work normally—there's an exception—we want to rename the new file to `some_file error` and rename the old file to `some_file`, putting the original file back the way it was before the exception.

We will need a context manager like the following:

```
import os
class Updating:
    def __init__( self, filename ):
        self.filename= filename
    def __enter__( self ):
        try:
            self.previous= self.filename+" copy"
            os.rename( self.filename, self.previous )
        except FileNotFoundError:
            # Never existed, no previous copy
            self.previous= None
    def __exit__( self, exc_type, exc_value, traceback ):
        if exc_type is not None:
            try:
                os.rename( self.filename, self.filename+ " error" )
            except FileNotFoundError:
                pass # Never even got created?
            if self.previous:
                os.rename( self.previous, self.filename )
```

This context manager's `__enter__()` method will attempt to preserve a previous copy of the named file if it already exists. If it didn't exist, there's nothing to preserve.

The `__exit__()` method be given information about any exception that occurred in the context. If there is no exception, it will simply return any previous file that exists was preserved the file created within the context will also exist. If there is an exception, then the `__exit__()` method will try to preserve the output (with a suffix of "error") for debugging purposes it will also put any previous version of file back in place.

This is functionally equivalent to a `try-except-finally` block. However, it has the advantage that it separates the relevant application processing from the context management. The application processing is written in the `with` statement. The context issues are set aside into a separate class.

Summary

We looked at three of the special methods for class definition. The `__call__()` method is used when creating a callable. The callable is used to create functions that are stateful. Our primary example is a function that memoizes previous results.

The `__enter__()` and `__exit__()` methods are used to create a context manager. The context is used to handle processing that is localized to the body of a with statement. Most of our examples include input-output processing. However, Python presents a number of other situations where a localized context can come handy. will focus on creating containers and collections.

Callable design considerations and trade-offs

When designing a callable object, we need to consider the following:

- The first is the API of the object. If there's a reason for the object to have a function-like interface, then a callable object is a sensible design approach. Using `collections.abc.Callable` assures that the callable API is built correctly, and it informs anyone reading the code what the intent of the class is.
- The second is the statefulness of the function. Ordinary functions in Python have no hysteresis—there's no saved state. A callable object, however, can easily save a state. The memoization design pattern makes good use of stateful callable objects.

The only disadvantage of a callable object is the amount of syntax that is required. An ordinary function definition is shorter and therefore less error prone and easier to read.

It's easy to migrate a defined function to a callable object, as follows:

```
def x(args):
    body
```

The preceding function can be converted into the following callable object:

```
class X(collections.abc.callable):
    def __call__(self, args):
        body
x= X()
```

This is the minimal set of changes required to get the function to pass unit tests in the new form. The existing body will work in the new context unmodified.

Once the change has been made, features can be added to the callable object's version of the function.

Context manager design considerations and trade-offs

A context is generally used to acquire/release, open/close, and lock/unlock types of operation pairs. Most of the examples are file I/O related, and most of the file-like objects in Python are already proper context managers.

A context manager is almost always required for anything that has steps which bracket the essential processing. In particular, anything that requires a final `close()` method should be wrapped by a context manager.

Some Python libraries have open/close operations, but the objects aren't proper contexts. The `shelve` module, for example, doesn't create a proper context.

We can (and should) use the `contextllib.closing()` context on a `shelve` file. We'll show this in *Chapter 9, Serializing and Saving – JSON, YAML, Pickle, CSV, and XML*.

For our own classes that require a `close()` method, we can use the `closing()` function. When confronted with a class that has any kind of acquire/release life cycle, we want to acquire resources in `__init__()` or a class-level `open()` method and release them in `close()`. That way, our class can integrate well with this `closing()` function.

The following is an example of some class being wrapped that requires a `close()` function:

```
with contextlib.closing( MyClass() ) as my_object:
    process( my_object )
```

The `contextllib.closing()` function will invoke the `close()` method of the object that is given as an argument. We can guarantee that `my_object` will have its `close()` method evaluated.

Looking forward

In the next two chapters, we'll look at the special methods used to create containers and numbers. In *Chapter 6, Creating Containers and Collections*, we'll look at the containers and collections in the standard library. We'll also look at building a unique, new kind of container. In *Chapter 7, Creating Numbers*, we'll look at the various numeric types and how we can create our own kind of number.

6
Creating Containers and Collections

We can extend a number of ABCs to create new kinds of collections. The ABCs provide us with design guidelines to extend the built-in containers. These allow us to fine-tune the features or radically define new data structures that fit our problem domain more precisely.

We'll look at the basics of ABC for container classes. There are a fairly large number of abstractions that are used to assemble the Python built-in types, such as `list`, `tuple`, `dict`, `set`, and `frozenset`.

We'll review the variety of special methods that are involved in being a container and offering the various features of containers. We'll split these into the core container methods, separate from more specialized sequence, map, and set methods.

We'll address extending built-in containers to add features. We'll also look at wrapping built-in containers and delegating methods through the wrapper to the underlying container.

Finally, we'll look at building entirely new containers. This is a challenging territory, because there's a huge variety of interesting and useful collection algorithms already present in the Python Standard Library. In order to avoid deep computer science research, we'll build a pretty lame collection. Before starting on a real application, a careful study of *Introduction to Algorithms* by Cormen, Leiserson, Rivest, and Stein is essential.

We'll finish by summarizing some of the design considerations that go into extending or creating new collections.

ABCs of collections

The `collections.abc` module provides a wealth of abstract base classes that decompose collections into a number of discrete feature sets.

We can successfully use the `list` class without thinking too deeply about the various features and how they relate to the `set` class or the `dict` class. Once we start looking at the ABCs, however, we can see that there's a bit of subtlety to these classes. By decomposing the aspects of each collection, we can see areas of overlapping that manifest themselves as an elegant polymorphism even among different data structures.

At the bottom of the base classes are some "one-trick pony" definitions. These are the base classes that require a single special method:

- The `Container` base class requires the concrete class to implement the `__contains__()` method. This special method implements the `in` operator.
- The `Iterable` base class requires `__iter__()`. This special method is used by the `for` statement and the generator expressions as well as the `iter()` function.
- The `Sized` base class requires `__len__()`. This method is used by the `len()` function. It's also prudent to implement `__bool__()`, but it's not required by this abstract base class.
- The `Hashable` base class requires `__hash__()`. This is used by the `hash()` function. If this is implemented, it means that the object is immutable.

Each of these abstract classes is used to build the higher-level, composite definitions of structures we can use in our applications. These composite constructs include the lower-level base classes of `Sized`, `Iterable`, and `Container`. Here are some composite base classes that we might use in an application:

- The `Sequence` and `MutableSequence` classes build on the basics and fold in methods such as `index()`, `count()`, `reverse()`, `extend()`, and `remove()`.
- The `Mapping` and `MutableMapping` classes fold in methods such as `keys()`, `items()`, `values()`, and `get()`, among others.
- The `Set` and `MutableSet` classes fold in comparison and arithmetic operators to perform set operations.

If we look more deeply into the built-in collections, we can see how the ABC class definitions serve to organize the special methods that we need to write or modify.

Examples of special methods

When looking at a blackjack `Hand` object, we have an interesting special case for containment. We often want to know if there's an ace in the hand. If we define `Hand` as an extension to `list`, then we can't ask for a generic ace. We can only ask for specific cards. We hate to write something like this:

```
any( card(1,suit) for suit in Suits )
```

That seems a long-winded way to look for an ace in a hand.

Here's a better example, but it still is less-than-ideal, perhaps:

```
any( c.rank == 'A' for c in hand.cards )
```

So, we'd like something like this:

```
'A' in hand.cards
```

This means that we're modifying the meaning of "contains" for a `Hand` object that extends `list`. We're not looking for a `Card` instance, we're merely looking for the rank property of a `Card` object. We can override the `__contains__()` method to do this:

```
def __contains__( self, rank ):
    return any( c.rank==rank for rank in hand.cards )
```

This allows us to use a simpler `in` test for a given rank in a hand.

Similar design considerations can be applied to `__iter__()` and `__len__()` special methods. Be cautious, however. Changing the semantics of `len()` or how a collection interacts with the `for` statement might be disastrous.

Using the standard library extensions

We'll look at some extensions to built-in classes that are already part of the standard library. These are the collections that extend or modify the built-in collections. Most of these are covered in one form or another in books such as *Python 3 Object Oriented Programming*.

We'll look at the following six library collections:

- The `namedtuple()` function creates subclasses of tuple subclasses with named attributes. We can use this instead of defining a complete class, which merely assigns names to the attribute values.

- `deque` (note the atypical spelling) is a double-ended queue, a list-like collection that can perform fast appends and pops on either end. A subset of the features of this class will create single-ended stacks or queues.
- In some cases, we can use `ChainMap` instead of merging mappings together. This is a view of multiple mappings.
- An `OrderedDict` collection is a mapping in which the original key entry order is maintained.
- `defaultdict` (note the atypical spelling) is a `dict` subclass that uses a factory function to provide values for missing keys.
- The `Counter` is a `dict` subclass that can be used for counting objects to create frequency tables. However, it's actually a more sophisticated data structure called a **multiset** or **bag**.

We'll see examples of each one of the preceding collections. There are two important lessons to be learned from studying the library collections:

- What's already present and doesn't need to be reinvented
- How to extend the ABCs to add interesting and useful structures to the language

Also, it's important to read the source for the libraries. The source will show us numerous Python object-oriented programming techniques. Beyond these basics are even more modules. They are as follows:

- The `heapq` module is a set of functions that impose a heap queue structure on an existing `list` object. The heap queue invariant is the set of those items in the heap that are maintained in order to allow rapid retrieval in an ascending order. If we use the `heapq` methods on a `list` structure, we will never have to explicitly sort the list. This can have significant performance improvements.
- The `array` module is a kind of sequence that optimizes storage for certain kinds of values. This provides list-like features over potentially large collections of simple values.

In addition, of course, there's the deeper computer science that supports these various data structure definitions.

The namedtuple() function

The `namedtuple()` function creates a new class definition from the supplied arguments. This will have a class name, field names, and a pair of optional keywords that define the behavior of the created class.

Using `namedtuple()` will condense a class definition into a very short definition of a simple immutable object. It saves us from having to write longer and more complex class definitions for the common case where we want to name a fixed set of attributes.

For something like a playing card, we might want to insert the following code in a class definition:

```
from collections import namedtuple
BlackjackCard = namedtuple('BlackjackCard','rank,suit,hard,soft')
```

We defined a new class and provided precisely four named attributes: `rank`, `suit`, `hard`, and `soft`. Since each of these objects is immutable, we don't need to worry about a badly behaved application attempting to change the rank of a `BlackjackCard` instance.

We can use a factory function to create instances of this class, as shown in the following code:

```
def card( rank, suit ):
    if rank == 1:
        return BlackjackCard( 'A', suit, 1, 11 )
    elif 2 <= rank < 11:
        return BlackjackCard( str(rank), suit, rank, rank )
    elif rank == 11:
        return BlackjackCard( 'J', suit, 10, 10 )
    elif rank == 12:
        return BlackjackCard( 'Q', suit, 10, 10 )
    elif rank == 13:
        return BlackjackCard( 'K', suit, 10, 10 )
```

This will build an instance of `BlackjackCard` with the hard and soft totals set properly for various card ranks. A new class called `namedtuple` is created by filling in a template for a subclass of `tuple` with the various parameters. Essentially, the template starts out with this kind of code:

```
class TheNamedTuple(tuple):
    __slots__ = ()
    _fields = {field_names!r}
    def __new__(_cls, {arg_list}):
        return _tuple.__new__(_cls, ({arg_list}))
```

The template code extends the built-in `tuple` class. Nothing surprising there.

It sets `__slots__` to an empty tuple. There are two ways to manage instance variables: `__slots__` and `__dict__`. By setting `__slots__`, the `__dict__` alternative is disabled, removing the ability to add new instance variables to an object of this class. Also, the resulting object is kept to the absolute minimum size.

The template creates a class-level variable named `_fields`, which names the fields. The `{field_names!r}` construct is where the template text is filled with the list of field names.

The template defines a `__new__()` method that is used to initialize the immutable object. The `{arg_list}` construct is where the template is filled with the list of arguments used to build each instance.

There are several other method functions, but this provides some hints as to how the `namedtuple` function works under the hood.

We can, of course, subclass a `namedtuple` class to add features. We have to be cautious about trying to add attributes to a `namedtuple` class, though. The list of attributes is encoded in `_fields`, as well as the arguments to `__new__()`.

Here's an example of subclassing a `namedtuple` class:

```
BlackjackCard = namedtuple('BlackjackCard','rank,suit,hard,soft')
class AceCard( BlackjackCard ):
    __slots__ = ()
    def __new__( self, rank, suit ):
        return super().__new__( AceCard, 'A', suit, 1, 11 )
```

We used `__slots__` to ensure that the subclass has no `__dict__`; we can't add any new attributes. We've overridden `__new__()` so that we can construct instances with only two values (`rank` and `suit`), yet populate all four values.

The deque class

A `list` object is designed to provide uniform performance for any element within the container. Some operations have performance penalties. Most notably, any operation at the front of the list (`list.insert(0, item)` or `list.pop(0)`) will incur some overheads because the list size is changed and the position of each element has changed.

A `deque`—a double-ended queue—is designed to provide uniform performance for the first and last elements of a list. The idea is that appending and popping will be faster than the built-in `list` object.

Spelling irregularity

Class names are usually in title case. However, the deque class isn't.

Our design for a deck of cards avoids the potential performance pitfall of a `list` object by always popping from the end, never from the beginning.

However, as we're using so few features of a `list` object, perhaps a structure like that of a deque is a better fit for our problem. We're only storing cards so that they can be shuffled and popped from the collection. Other than shuffling, our applications never reference elements within the list by their indexed positions.

While the `deque.pop()` method might be very fast, shuffling may suffer. A shuffle will make random access to the container, something for which a deque is not designed.

In order to confirm the potential costs, we can use `timeit` to compare `list` and `deque` shuffling performance as follows:

```
>>> timeit.timeit('random.shuffle(x)',"""
... import random
... x=list(range(6*52))""")
597.951664149994
>>>
>>> timeit.timeit('random.shuffle(d)',"""
... from collections import deque
... import random
... d=deque(range(6*52))""")
609.9636979339994
```

We invoked `timeit` using `random.shuffle()`. One works on a `list` object, the other works on a deque.

These results indicate that shuffling a deque is only a trifle slower than shuffling a `list` object—about 2 percent slower. This distinction is a hair not worth splitting. We can confidently try a `deque` object in place of `list`.

The change amounts to this:

```
from collections import dequeue
class Deck(dequeue):
    def __init__( self, size=1 ):
        super().__init__()
        for d in range(size):
           cards = [ card(r,s) for r in range(13) for s in Suits ]
```

```
            super().extend( cards )
        random.shuffle( self )
```

We replaced `list` with `deque` in the definition of `Deck`. Otherwise, the class is identical.

What is the actual performance difference? Let's create decks of 100,000 cards and deal them:

```
>>> timeit.timeit('x.pop()', "x=list(range(100000))",
number=100000)
0.032304395994287916
>>> timeit.timeit('x.pop()', "from collections import deque;
x=deque(range(100000))", number=100000)
0.013504189992090687
```

We invoked `timeit` using `x.pop()`. One works on a `list`, the other works on a deque.

The dealing time is cut almost by half (42 percent, actually). We had big savings from a tiny change in the data structure.

In general, it's important to pick the optimal data structure for the application. Trying several variations can show us what's more efficient.

The ChainMap use case

The use case for chaining maps together fits nicely with Python's concept of local versus global definitions. When we use a variable in Python, first the local namespaces, and then the global namespaces are searched, in that order. In addition to searching both namespaces for a variable, setting a variable works in the local namespace without disturbing the global namespace. This default behavior (without the `global` or `nonlocal` statements) is also how a `ChainMap` works.

When our applications start running, we often have properties that come from command-line parameters, configuration files, OS environment variables, and possibly, installation-wide settings. We'd like to merge this into a single dictionary-like structure so that we can easily locate a setting.

We might have an application startup that combines several sources of configuration options like this:

```
import argparse
import json
import os
```

```
parser = argparse.ArgumentParser(description='Process some
integers.')
parser.add_argument( "-c", "--configuration", type=open,
nargs='?')
parser.add_argument( "-p", "--playerclass", type=str, nargs='?',
default="Simple" )
cmdline= parser.parse_args('-p Aggressive'.split())

if cmdline.configuration:
    config_file= json.load( options.configuration )
    options.configuration.close()
else:
    config_file= {}

with open("defaults.json") as installation:
    defaults= json.load( installation )
# Might want to check ~/defaults.json and
/etc/thisapp/defaults.json, also.

from collections import ChainMap
options = ChainMap(vars(cmdline), config_file, os.environ,
defaults)
```

The preceding code shows us the configuration from several sources, such as the following:

- The command-line arguments. We saw one token argument called `playerclass`, but there are often many, many others.
- One of the arguments, `configuration`, is the name of a configuration file with additional parameters. This is expected to be in the JSON format, and the file's contents are read.
- Additionally, there's a `defaults.json` file with yet another place to look for the configuration values.

From the preceding sources, we can build a single `ChainMap` object use case that allows looking for a parameter in each of the listed locations. The `ChainMap` instance use case will search through each mapping, in an order, looking for the given value. This gives us a tidy, easy-to-use source for runtime options and parameters.

We'll look at this again in *Chapter 13, Configuration Files and Persistence*, as well as *Chapter 16, Coping with the Command Line*.

The OrderedDict collection

The `OrderedDict` collection class makes clever use of two storage structures. There's an underlying `dict` object type that maps keys to values. Plus, there's an additional doubly-linked list of keys that maintains the insertion order.

One common use for `OrderedDict` is when processing HTML or XML files, where the order of objects must be retained, but objects might have cross-references via ID and IDREF attributes. We can optimize the connections among objects by using the ID as a dictionary key. We can retain the source document's ordering with the `OrderedDict` structure.

We don't want to digress too far into the XML parsing here. That's a subject for *Chapter 9, Serializing and Saving – JSON, YAML, Pickle, CSV, and XML.*

Consider this short example of an XML document that has a rather complex network of references between several indexes. We'll imagine a simple microblog document with ordered entries that have IDs and indices that have IDREFs to the original entries.

We'll break the XML into two parts:

```
<blog>
    <topics> … </topics> <indices> … </indices>
</blog>
```

There will be a section on topics and another section on indices. Here's the topics' portion of the blog:

```
        <topics>
            <entry ID="UUID98766"><title>first</title><body>more
              words</body></entry>
            <entry
        ID="UUID86543"><title>second</title><body>words</body></entry>
            <entry
    ID="UUID64319"><title>third</title><body>text</body></entry>
        </topics>
```

Each topic has a sequence of entries. Each entry has a unique ID. We're hinting that they might belong to **Universally Unique ID** (**UUID**), but we didn't produce actual examples.

Here's one of the indices for the blog:

```
        <indices>
            <bytag>
                <tag text="#sometag">
```

```
                <entry IDREF="UUID98766"/>
                <entry IDREF="UUID86543"/>
            </tag>
            <tag text="#anothertag">
                <entry IDREF="UUID98766"/>
                <entry IDREF="UUID64319/>

            </tag>
        </bytag>
    </indices>
```

One index presents the blog entries by the tag. We can see that each tag has a list of entries. Each entry has a reference to the original microblog entry.

When we parse this XML document, we need to keep the topics in the original order. But, we also have to track the IDs as keys for each entry.

Here's a technical spike that will parse the document and build an `OrderedDict` collection:

```
from collections import OrderedDict
import xml.etree.ElementTree as etree

doc= etree.XML( source ) # Parse

topics= OrderedDict() # Gather
for topic in doc.findall( "topics/entry" ):
    topics[topic.attrib['ID']] = topic

for topic in topics: # Display
    print( topic, topics[topic].find("title").text )
```

The first part, `# Parse`, will parse the XML source document, creating an `ElementTree` object.

The second part, `# Gather`, will traverse the entries in the topics section of the XML document. Each topic is loaded into a topic's `OrderedDict` collection by ID. The original order is retained so that the material can be rendered in the correct order.

The final part, `# Display`, shows us the entries in their original order and their ID.

The defaultdict subclass

An ordinary `dict` type throws an exception when a key is not found. A `defaultdict` collection class evaluates a given function and inserts the value of that function into the dictionary.

Note the spelling irregularity

Class names are usually in TitleCase. However, the `defaultdict` class isn't.

A common use case for a `defaultdict` class is to create indices for objects. When several objects have a common key, we can create a list of objects that share this key.

Here's a part of a technical spike that shows us how we might accumulate a list of outcomes indexed by the dealer's upcard:

```
outcomes = defaultdict(list)
self.play_hand( table, hand )
outcome= self.get_payout()
outcomes[hand.dealer_card.rank].append(outcome)
```

Each value of `outcomes[rank]` will be a list of simulated payouts. We can average or total these to summarize the payouts. We can count wins versus losses or perform other quantitative analysis to determine a strategy for play that minimizes losses and maximizes wins.

In some cases, we might want to use a `defaultdict` collection class to provide a constant value. Instead of writing `container.get(key,"N/A")`, we'd like to write `container[key]` and have the string constant provided the value `"N/A"` if the key was not found. The difficulty with doing this is that a `defaultdict` class is created with a zero-argument function to create the default values. We can't use a constant trivially.

We can create a zero-argument `lambda` object. This works very nicely. Here's an example:

```
>>> from collections import defaultdict
>>> messages = defaultdict( lambda: "N/A" )
>>> messages['error1']= 'Full Error Text'
>>> messages['other']
'N/A'
```

The default value is returned, and the key (in this example, `'other'`) is added to the dictionary. We can determine how many new values were entered by looking for all the keys that have a value of `"N/A"`:

```
>>> [k for k in messages if messages[k] == "N/A"]
['other']
```

As you see in the preceding output, we found the key that was assigned the default value of `"N/A"`. This is often a helpful summary of the data that is being accumulated. It shows us all of the keys associated with the default value.

The counter collection

One of the most common use cases for a `defaultdict` class is when accumulating counts of events. We might write code that looks like this:

```
frequency = defaultdict(int)
for k in some_iterator():
    frequency[k] += 1
```

We're counting the number of times each key value, `k`, appears in the sequence of values from `some_iterator()`.

This use case is so common that there's a variation on the `defaultdict` theme that performs the same operation shown in the preceding code—it's called `Counter`. A `Counter` collection, however, is considerably more sophisticated than a simple `defaultdict` class. Consider the additional use case of determining the most common value, known to statisticians as the **mode**.

We need to restructure the values in the `defaultdict` object to find the mode. It's not difficult, but it can be irksome because it's a boilerplate code. It looks like this:

```
by_value = defaultdict(list)
for k in frequency:
    by_value[ frequency[k] ].append(k)
```

We created a second dictionary. The keys for this new `by_value` dictionary are the frequency values. Each key is associated with all of the original `some_iterator()` values that occurred with this frequency.

We can then use the following processing to locate and display the most common values in the order of frequency of the occurrence:

```
for freq in sorted(by_value, reverse=True):
    print( by_value[freq], freq )
```

This will create a kind of frequency histogram that shows us the list of key values with a given frequency and the frequency count shared by all those key values.

All of these features are already a part of the `Counter` collection. Here's an example to create a frequency histogram from some source of data:

```
from collections import Counter
frequency = Counter(some_iterator())
for k,freq in frequency.most_common():
    print( k, freq )
```

This example shows us how we can easily gather statistical data by providing any iterable item to `Counter`. It will gather frequency data on the values in that iterable item. In this case, we provided an iterable function named `some_iterator()`. We might have provided a sequence or some other collection.

We can then display the results in the descending order of popularity. But wait! That's *not* all.

The `Counter` collection is not merely a simplistic variation of the `defaultdict` collection. The name is misleading. A `Counter` object is actually a "multiset", sometimes called a "bag".

It's a collection that is set-like, but allows for repeats of values in the bag. It is not a sequence with items identified by an index or position; order doesn't matter. It is not a mapping with keys and values. It is like a set in which items stand for themselves and order doesn't matter. But it is unlike a set because, in this case, elements can repeat.

As elements can repeat, the `Counter` object represents multiple occurrences with an integer count. Hence, it's used as a frequency table. However, it does more than this. As a bag is like a set, we can compare the elements of two bags to create a union or an intersection.

Let's create two bags:

```
>>> bag1= Counter("aardwolves")
>>> bag2= Counter("zymologies")
>>> bag1
Counter({'a': 2, 'o': 1, 'l': 1, 'w': 1, 'v': 1, 'e': 1, 'd': 1,
's': 1, 'r': 1})
>>> bag2
Counter({'o': 2, 'm': 1, 'l': 1, 'z': 1, 'y': 1, 'g': 1, 'i': 1,
'e': 1, 's': 1})
```

We built each bag by examining a sequence of letters. For characters that occur more than once, there's a count that is more than one.

We can easily compute the union of the two bags:

```
>>> bag1+bag2
Counter({'o': 3, 's': 2, 'l': 2, 'e': 2, 'a': 2, 'z': 1, 'y': 1,
'w': 1, 'v': 1, 'r': 1, 'm': 1, 'i': 1, 'g': 1, 'd': 1})
```

This shows us the entire suite of letters between the two strings. There were three instances of `o`. Not surprisingly, other letters were less popular.

We can just as easily compute the difference between the bags:

```
>>> bag1-bag2
Counter({'a': 2, 'w': 1, 'v': 1, 'd': 1, 'r': 1})
>>> bag2-bag1
Counter({'o': 1, 'm': 1, 'z': 1, 'y': 1, 'g': 1, 'i': 1})
```

The first expression shows us characters in `bag1` that were not in `bag2`.

The second expression shows us characters in `bag2` that were not in `bag1`. Note that the letter `o` occurred twice in `bag2` and once in `bag1`. The difference only removed one of the `o` characters from `bag1`.

Creating new kinds of collections

We'll look at some extensions we might make to Python's built-in container classes. Although, we won't show an example of extending each container. If we did, the book would become out of control in size.

We'll pick an example of extending a specific container and see how the process works:

1. Define the requirements. This may include research on Wikipedia, generally starting here: `http://en.wikipedia.org/wiki/Data_structure`. Designs of data structures can be complex because there are often complex edge cases.
2. If necessary, look at the `collections.abc` module to see what methods must be implemented to create the new functionality.
3. Create some test cases. This also requires careful study of the algorithms to ensure that the edge cases are properly covered.
4. Code.

We need to emphasize the importance of researching the fundamentals before trying to invent a new kind of data structure. In addition to searching the Web for overviews and summaries, details will be necessary. See *Introduction to Algorithms* by Cormen, Leiserson, Rivest, and Stein or *Data Structures and Algorithms* by Aho, Ullman, and Hopcroft, or *The Algorithm Design Manual* by Steven Skiena.

As we saw earlier, the ABCs define three broad kinds of collections: sequences, mappings, and sets. We have three design strategies that we can use to create new kinds of collections of our own:

- **Extend**: This is an existing sequence.
- **Wrap**: This is an existing sequence.
- **Invent**: This is a new sequence from scratch.

In principle, we could give as many as nine examples—each basic flavor of collection with each basic design strategy. We won't beat this subject to death like that. We'll dig deep to create new kinds of sequences, learning how to extend and wrap existing sequences.

As there are so many extended mappings (such as `ChainMap`, `OrderedDict`, `defaultdict`, and `Counter`), we'll only touch lightly on creating new kinds of mappings. We'll also dig deep to create a new kind of ordered multiset or bag.

Defining a new kind of sequence

A common requirement that we have when performing statistical analysis is to compute basic means, modes, and standard deviations on a collection of data. Our blackjack simulation will produce outcomes that must be analyzed statistically to see if we have actually invented a better strategy.

When we simulate a playing strategy, we should wind up with some outcome data that will be a sequence of numbers that show us the final result of playing a sequence of hands with a given strategy. The rate of play varies from about 50 hands per hour at a crowded table to 200 hands per hour if one is alone with the dealer. We'll assume 200 hands as two hours of blackjack before having to take a biology break.

We could accumulate the outcomes into a built-in `list` class. We can compute the mean via $\frac{\sum x}{N}$, where N is the number of elements in x:

```
def mean( outcomes ):
    return sum(outcomes)/len(outcomes)
```

Standard deviation can be computed via $\frac{\sqrt{N(\sum x^2)-(\sum x)^2}}{N}$:

```
def stdev( outcomes ):
    n= len(outcomes)
    return math.sqrt( n*sum(x**2 for x in outcomes)-
sum(outcomes)**2 )/n
```

Both of these are relatively simple calculation functions that are easy to use. As things get more complex, however, loose functions like these become less helpful. One of the benefits of object-oriented programming is to bind the functionality with the data.

Our first example will not involve rewriting any of the special methods of `list`. We'll simply subclass `list` to add methods that will compute the statistics. This is a very common kind of extension.

We'll revisit this in the second example so that we can revise and extend the special methods. This will require some study of the ABC special methods to see what we need to add or modify so that our new list subclass properly inherits all the features of the built-in `list` class.

Because we're looking at sequences, we also have to wrestle with the Python `slice` notation. We'll look at what a slice is and how it works internally in the Working with `__getitem__`, `__setitem__`, `__delitem__`, and slices section.

The second important design strategy is wrapping. We'll create a wrapper around a list and see how we might delegate methods to the wrapped list. Wrapping has some advantages when it comes to object persistence, which is the subject of *Chapter 9, Serializing and Saving – JSON, YAML, Pickle, CSV, and XML.*

We can also look at the kind of things that need to be done to invent a new kind of sequence from scratch.

A statistical list

It makes good sense to incorporate mean and standard deviation features directly into a subclass of `list`. We can extend `list` like this:

```
class Statslist(list):
    @property
    def mean(self):
        return sum(self)/len(self)
    @property
    def stdev(self):
        n= len(self)
```

```
        return math.sqrt( n*sum(x**2 for x in self)-sum(self)**2
)/n
```

With this simple extension to the built-in `list` class, we can accumulate data and report statistics with relative ease.

We can imagine an overall simulation script that looks like this.

```
for s in SomePlayStrategy, SomeOtherStrategy:
    sim = Simulator( s, SimpleBet() )
    data = sim.run( hands=200 )
    print( s.__class__.__name__, data.mean, data.stdev )
```

Choosing eager versus lazy calculation

Note that our calculations are lazy; they are only done when requested. This also means that they're performed each and every time they're requested. This can be a considerable overhead, depending on the context in which objects of these classes are used.

It's actually sensible to transform these statistical summaries into eager calculations, as we know when elements are added and removed from a list. Although there's a hair more programming to create eager versions of these functions, it has a net impact of improving performance when there's a lot of data being accumulated.

The point of eager statistical calculations is to avoid the loops that compute sums. If we compute the sums eagerly, as the list is being created, we avoid extra looping through the data.

When we look at the special methods for a `Sequence` class, we can see all of the places where data is added to, removed from, and modified in the sequence. We can use this information to recompute the two sums that are involved. We start with the `collections.abc` section of the *Python Standard Library* documentation, section 8.4.1 at `http://docs.python.org/3.4/library/collections.abc.html#collections-abstract-base-classes`.

Here are the required methods for a `MutableSequence` class: `__getitem__`, `__setitem__`, `__delitem__`, `__len__`, `insert`, `append`, `reverse`, `extend`, `pop`, `remove`, and `__iadd__`. The documentation also mentions the **Inherited Sequence methods**. However, as those are for immutable sequences, we can certainly ignore them.

Here are the details of what must be done for each method:

- `__getitem__`: Nothing, as there's no change in the state.
- `__setitem__`: This changes an item. We need to take the old item out of each sum and fold the new item into each sum.

- `__delitem__`: This removes an item. We need to take the old item out of each sum.
- `__len__`: Nothing here either, as there's no change in the state.
- `insert`: As this adds a new item, we need to fold it into each sum.
- `append`: As this also adds a new item, we need to fold it into each sum.
- `reverse`: Nothing here either, as there's no change in the state of the mean or standard deviation.
- `extend`: This adds many new items such as `__init__`, for which we'll need to process each item before extending the list.
- `pop`: This removes an item. We need to take the old item out of each sum.
- `remove`: This also removes an item. We need to take the old item out of each sum.
- `__iadd__`: This is the `+=` augmented assignment statement, the in-place addition. It's effectively the same as the `extend` keyword.

We won't look at each method in detail, because there are really only two use cases:

- Fold in one new value
- Remove one old value

The replacement case is a combination of the remove and fold in operations.

Here are the elements of an eager `StatsList` class. We're going to see just `insert` and `pop`:

```
class StatsList2(list):
    """Eager Stats."""
    def __init__( self, *args, **kw ):
        self.sum0 = 0 # len(self)
        self.sum1 = 0 # sum(self)
        self.sum2 = 0 # sum(x**2 for x in self)
        super().__init__( *args, **kw )
        for x in self:
            self._new(x)
    def _new( self, value ):
        self.sum0 += 1
        self.sum1 += value
        self.sum2 += value*value
    def _rmv( self, value ):
        self.sum0 -= 1
        self.sum1 -= value
```

```
            self.sum2 -= value*value
        def insert( self, index, value ):
            super().insert( index, value )
            self._new(value)
        def pop( self, index=0 ):
            value= super().pop( index )
            self._rmv(value)
            return value
```

We provided three internal variables with quick comments to show the invariants that this class will maintain them. We'll call these the "sum invariants" because each of them contains a particular kind of sum that is maintained as invariant (always true) after each kind of state change. The essence of this eager calculation are the `_rmv()` and `_new()` methods, which update our three internal sums based on changes to the list, so that the relationships really remain invariant.

When we remove an item, that is, after a successful `pop()` operation, we have to adjust our sums. When we add an item (either initially, or via the `insert()` method), we also have to adjust our sums. The other methods we need to implement will make use of these two methods to ensure that the three sum invariants hold. We assure that L.sum0 is always $\sum_{x \in L} x^0 = \sum_{x \in L} 1 = len(L)$, sum1 is always $\sum_{x \in L} x$, and sum2 is always $\sum_{x \in L} x^2$.

Other methods such as `append()`, `extend()`, and `remove()`, are similar in many ways to these methods. We didn't show them because they're similar.

There's an important bit missing: individual item replacement via `list[index]= value`. We'll delve into it in the following paragraph.

We can see how this list works by playing with some data:

```
>>> sl2 = StatsList2( [2, 4, 3, 4, 5, 5, 7, 9, 10] )
>>> sl2.sum0, sl2.sum1, sl2.sum2
(9, 49, 325)
>>> sl2[2]= 4
>>> sl2.sum0, sl2.sum1, sl2.sum2
(9, 50, 332)
>>> del sl2[-1]
>>> sl2.sum0, sl2.sum1, sl2.sum2
(8, 40, 232)
>>> sl2.insert( 0, -1 )
>>> sl2.pop()
-1
```

```
>>> sl2.sum0, sl2.sum1, sl2.sum2
(8, 40, 232)
```

We can create a list and the sums are computed initially. Each subsequent change eagerly updates the various sums. We can change, remove, insert, and pop an item; each change results in a new set of sums.

All that's left is to add our mean and standard deviation calculations, which we can do as follows:

```
        @property
        def mean(self):
            return self.sum1/self.sum0
        @property
        def stdev(self):
            return math.sqrt( self.sum0*self.sum2-self.sum1*self.sum1 
)/self.sum0
```

These make use of the sums already computed. There's no additional looping over the data to compute these two statistics.

Working with __getitem__(), __setitem__(), __delitem__(), and slices

The `StatsList2` example didn't show us the implementation of `__setitem__()` or `__delitem__()` because they involve slices. We'll need to look at the implementation of a slice before we can implement these methods properly.

Sequences have two different kinds of indexes:

- `a[i]`: This is a simple Integer index.
- `a[i:j]` or `a[i:j:k]`: These are `slice` expressions with `start:stop:step` values. Slice expressions can be quite complex with seven different variations for different kinds of defaults.

This basic syntax works in three contexts:

- In an expression, relying on `__getitem__()` to get a value
- On the left-hand side of assignment, relying on `__setitem__()` to set a value
- On a `del` statement, relying on `__delitem__()` to delete a value

When we do something like `seq[:-1]`, we write a `slice` expression. The underlying `__getitem__()` method will be given a `slice` object instead of a simple integer.

The reference manual tells us a few things about slices. A `slice` object will have three attributes: `start`, `stop`, and `step`. It will also have a method function called `indices()`, which will properly compute any omitted attribute values for a slice.

We can explore the `slice` objects with a trivial class that extends `list`:

```
class Explore(list):
    def __getitem__( self, index ):
        print( index, index.indices(len(self)) )
        return super().__getitem__( index )
```

This class will dump the `slice` object and the value of the `indices()` function result. Then, use the superclass implementation so that the list behaves normally otherwise.

Given this class, we can try different `slice` expressions to see what we get:

```
>>> x= Explore('abcdefg')
>>> x[:]
slice(None, None, None) (0, 7, 1)
['a', 'b', 'c', 'd', 'e', 'f', 'g']
>>> x[:-1]
slice(None, -1, None) (0, 6, 1)
['a', 'b', 'c', 'd', 'e', 'f']
>>> x[1:]
slice(1, None, None) (1, 7, 1)
['b', 'c', 'd', 'e', 'f', 'g']
>>> x[::2]
slice(None, None, 2) (0, 7, 2)
['a', 'c', 'e', 'g']
```

In the preceding `slice` expressions, we can see that a `slice` object has three attributes, and the values for those attributes come directly from the Python syntax. When we provide the proper length to the `indices()` function, it returns a three-tuple value with start, stop, and step values.

Implementing __getitem__(), __setitem__(), and __delitem__()

When we implement the methods `__getitem__()`, `__setitem__()` and `__delitem__()`, we must work with two kinds of argument values: `int` and `slice`.

When we overload the various sequence methods, we must handle the slice situation appropriately.

Here is a `__setitem__()` method that works with slices:

```
def __setitem__( self, index, value ):
    if isinstance(index, slice):
        start, stop, step = index.indices(len(self))
        olds = [ self[i] for i in range(start,stop,step) ]
        super().__setitem__( index, value )
        for x in olds:
            self._rmv(x)
        for x in value:
            self._new(x)
    else:
        old= self[index]
        super().__setitem__( index, value )
        self._rmv(old)
        self._new(value)
```

The preceding method has two processing paths:

- If the index is a `slice` object, we'll compute the `start`, `stop`, and `step` values. Then, locate all the old values that will be removed. We can then invoke the superclass operation and fold in the new values that replaced the old values.
- If the index is a simple `int` object, the old value is a single item, and the new value is a single item, similarly.

Here's the `__delitem__()` method that works with slices:

```
def __delitem__( self, index ):
    # Index may be a single integer, or a slice
    if isinstance(index, slice):
        start, stop, step = index.indices(len(self))
        olds = [ self[i] for i in range(start,stop,step) ]
        super().__delitem__( index )
        for x in olds:
            self._rmv(x)
    else:
        old= self[index]
        super().__delitem__( index )
        self._rmv(old)
```

The preceding code, too, expands the slice to determine what values could be removed. If the index is a simple integer, then just one value is removed.

When we introduce proper slice processing to our `StatsList2` class, we can create lists that do everything the base `list` class does and also (rapidly) returns mean and standard deviation for the values that are currently in the list.

> Note that these method functions will each create a temporary list object, `olds`; this involves some overhead that can be removed. As an exercise for the reader, it's helpful to move the `_rmv()` functions forward in these methods to eliminate the use of the `olds` variable.

Wrapping a list and delegating

We'll look at how we might wrap one of Python's built-in container classes. Wrapping an existing class means that some methods will have to be delegated to the underlying container.

As there are a large number of methods in any of the built-in collections, wrapping a collection may require a fair amount of code. When it comes to creating persistent classes, wrapping has advantages over extending. That's the subject of *Chapter 9, Serializing and Saving – JSON, YAML, Pickle, CSV, and XML*. In some cases, we'll want to expose the internal collection to save writing a large number of sequence methods that delegate to an internal list.

A common restriction that applies to statistics data classes is that they need to be "insert only." We'll be disabling a number of method functions. This is the kind of dramatic change that requires a wrapper.

We can design a class that supports only `append` and `__getitem__`, for example. It would wrap a `list` class. The following code can be used to accumulate data from simulations:

```
class StatsList3:
    def __init__( self ):
        self._list= list()
        self.sum0 = 0 # len(self), sometimes called "N"
        self.sum1 = 0 # sum(self)
        self.sum2 = 0 # sum(x**2 for x in self)
    def append( self, value ):
        self._list.append(value)
        self.sum0 += 1
        self.sum1 += value
        self.sum2 += value*value
    def __getitem__( self, index ):
        return self._list.__getitem__( index )
```

```
    @property
    def mean(self):
        return self.sum1/self.sum0
    @property
    def stdev(self):
        return math.sqrt( self.sum0*self.sum2-self.sum1*self.sum1
          )/self.sum0
```

This class has an internal `_list` object that is the underlying list. The list is always initially empty. As we've only defined `append()` as a way to update the list, we can maintain the various sums easily. We need to be careful to delegate the work to the superclass to be sure that the list is actually updated before our subclass processes the argument value.

We can directly delegate `__getitem__()` to the internal list object without examining the arguments or the results.

We can use this class as follows:

```
>>> sl3= StatsList3()
>>> for data in 2, 4, 4, 4, 5, 5, 7, 9:
...     sl3.append(data)
...
>>> sl3.mean
5.0
>>> sl3.stdev
2.0
```

We created an empty list and appended items to the list. As we maintain the sums as items are appended, we can compute the mean and standard deviation extremely quickly.

We didn't intentionally make our class iterable. We didn't define `__iter__()`.

Because we've defined `__getitem__()`, several things now work. Not only can we get items, but it also turns out that there will be a default implementation that allows us to iterate through the sequence of values.

Here's an example:

```
>>> sl3[0]
2
>>> for x in sl3:
...     print(x)
...
2
4
```

```
4
4
5
5
7
9
```

The preceding output shows us that a minimal wrapper around a collection is often enough to satisfy many use cases.

Note that we didn't, for example, make the list sizeable. If we attempt to get the size, it will raise an exception, as shown in the following:

```
>>> len(sl3)
Traceback (most recent call last):
  File "<stdin>", line 1, in <module>
TypeError: object of type 'StatsList3' has no len()
```

We might want to add a `__len__()` method that delegates the real work to the internal `_list` object. We might also want to set `__hash__` to `None`, which would be prudent as this is a mutable object.

We might want to define `__contains__()` and delegate this feature to the internal `_list` too. This will create a minimalist container that offers the low-level feature set of a container.

Creating iterators with __iter__()

When our design involves wrapping an existing class, we'll need to be sure our class is iterable. When we look at the documentation for `collections.abc.Iterable`, we see that we only need to define `__iter__()` to make an object iterable. The `__iter__()` method can either return a proper `Iterator` object, or it can be a generator function.

Creating an `Iterator` object, while not terribly complex, is rarely necessary. It's so much simpler to create generator functions. For a wrapped collection, we should always simply delegate the `__iter__()` method to the underlying collection.

For our `StatsList3` class, it would look like this:

```
    def __iter__(self):
        return iter(self._list)
```

This method function would delegate the iteration to the underlying list's `Iterator`.

Creating a new kind of mapping

Python has a built-in mapping called `dict`, and numerous library mappings. In addition to the `collections` module extensions to `dict` (`defaultdict`, `Counter`, `OrderedDict`, and `ChainMap`), there are several other library modules that contain mapping-like structures.

The `shelve` module is an important example of another mapping. We'll look at this in *Chapter 10, Storing and Retrieving Objects via Shelve*. The `dbm` module is similar to `shelve`, in that it also maps a key to a value.

The `mailbox` module and `email.message` modules both have classes that provide an interface that is similar to `dict` for the mailbox structure used to manage local e-mails.

As far as design strategies go, we can extend or wrap one of the existing mappings to add even more features.

We could upgrade `Counter` to add mean and standard deviation to data stored as a frequency distribution. Indeed, we can also calculate median and mode very easily from this class.

Here's a `StatsCounter` extension to `Counter` that adds some statistical functions:

```
from collections import Counter
class StatsCounter(Counter):
    @property
    def mean( self ):
        sum0= sum( v for k,v in self.items() )
        sum1= sum( k*v for k,v in self.items() )
        return sum1/sum0
    @property
    def stdev( self ):
        sum0= sum( v for k,v in self.items() )
        sum1= sum( k*v for k,v in self.items() )
        sum2= sum( k*k*v for k,v in self.items() )
        return math.sqrt( sum0*sum2-sum1*sum1 )/sum0
```

We extended the `Counter` class with two new methods to compute the mean and standard deviation from the frequency distributions. The formulae are similar to the examples shown earlier for the eager calculations on a `list` object, even though they're lazy calculations on a `Counter` object.

We used `sum0= sum( v for k,v in self.items() )` to compute a sum of the values, `v`, ignoring the `k` keys. We could use an underscore (_) instead of `k` to emphasize that we're ignoring the keys. We could also use `sum( v for v in self.values() )` to emphasize that we're not using the keys. We prefer obvious parallel structures for `sum0` and `sum1`.

We can use this class to efficiently gather statistics and to perform quantitative analysis on the raw data. We might run a number of simulations, using a `Counter` object to gather the results.

Here's an interaction with a list of sample data that stands in for real results:

```
>>> sc = StatsCounter( [2, 4, 4, 4, 5, 5, 7, 9] )
>>> sc.mean
5.0
>>> sc.stdev
2.0
>>> sc.most_common(1)
[(4, 3)]
>>> list(sorted(sc.elements()))
[2, 4, 4, 4, 5, 5, 7, 9]
```

The results of `most_common()` are reported as a sequence of two-tuples with the mode value (4) and the number of times the value occurred (3). We might want to get the top three values to bracket the mode with the next two less-popular items. We get several popular values with an evaluation such as `sc.most_common(3)`.

The `elements()` method reconstructs a `list` that's like the original data with the items repeated properly.

From the sorted elements, we can extract the median, the middle-most item:

```
    @property
    def median( self ):
        all= list(sorted(sc.elements()))
        return all[len(all)//2]
```

This method is not only lazy, it's rather extravagant with memory; it creates an entire sequence of the available values merely to find the middle-most item.

While it is simple, this is often an expensive way to use Python.

A smarter approach would be to compute the effective length and mid-point via `sum(self.values())//2`. Once this is known, the keys can be visited in that order, using the counts to compute the range of positions for a given key. Eventually, a key will be found with a range that includes the midpoint.

The code would look something like the following:

```
@property
def median( self ):
    mid = sum(self.values())//2
    low= 0
    for k,v in sorted(self.items()):
        if low <= mid < low+v: return k
        low += v
```

We stepped through the keys and the number of times they occur to locate the key that is midmost. Note that this uses the internal `sorted()` function, which is not without its own cost.

Via `timeit`, we can learn that the extravagant version takes 9.5 seconds; the smarter version takes 5.2 seconds.

Creating a new kind of set

Creating a whole new collection requires some preliminary work. We need to have new algorithms or new internal data structures that offer significant improvements over the built-in collections. It's important to do thorough "Big-O" complexity calculations before designing a new collection. It's also important to use `timeit` after an implementation to be sure that the new collection really is an improvement on the built-in class.

We might, for example, want to create a binary search tree structure that will keep the elements in a proper order. As we want this to be a mutable structure, we'll have to perform the following kinds of design activities:

- Design the essential binary tree structure
- Decide which structure is the basis: `MutableSequence`, `MutableMapping`, or `MutableSet`
- Look at the special methods for the collection in the `collections.abc` section of the *Python Standard Library* documentation, section 8.4.1.

A binary search tree has nodes with two branches: a "less than" branch for all keys less than this node, and a "greater than or equal to" branch for keys greater than or equal to this node.

We need to examine the fit between our collection and the Python ABCs:

- It's not a great sequence because we don't usually use an index with a binary tree. We most often refer to elements in a search tree by their key. However, we can force an Integer index without too much difficulty.
- It could be used for the keys of a mapping; this would keep the keys in a sorted order. That's a common use for a binary search tree.
- It is a good alternative to a `set` or a `Counter` class because it trivially tolerates multiple items, making it easily bag-like.

We'll look at creating a sorted multiset or a bag. This can contain multiple copies of an object. It will rely on relatively simple comparison tests among objects.

This is a rather complex design. There are a great many details. To create a background, it's important to read articles such as `http://en.wikipedia.org/wiki/Binary_search_tree`. At the end of the previous Wikipedia page are a number of external links that will provide further information. It's essential to study the essential algorithms in books such as *Introduction to Algorithms* by Cormen, Leiserson, Rivest, and Stein or *Data Structures and Algorithms* by Aho, Ullman, and Hopcroft, or *The Algorithm Design Manual* by Steven Skiena.

Some design rationale

We're going to split the collection into two classes: `TreeNode` and `Tree`.

The `TreeNode` class will contains the item as well as the `more`, `less`, and `parent` references. We'll also delegate some functionality to this class.

For example, searching for a particular item in order to use `__contains__()` or `discard()` will be delegated to the node itself using a simple recursion. The algorithm's outline looks like this.

- If the target item is equal to the self item, then return `self`
- If the target item is less than `self.item`, then recursively use `less.find(target item)`
- If the target item is greater than `self.item`, then recursively use `more.find(target.item)`

We'll use similar delegation to the TreeNode class for more of the real work of maintaining the tree structure.

The second class will be a **Facade**, which defines the `Tree` itself. A Facade design can also be called a **Wrapper**; the idea is to add features required for a particular interface. We'll provide the external interface required by a `MutableSet` abstract base class.

The algorithms can be somewhat simpler if there's a root node that's empty and always compares as less than all other key values. This can be challenging in Python because we don't know—in advance—what types of data the nodes might have; we can't easily define a bottom value for the root node. Instead, we'll use a special case value of `None`, and endure the overheads of `if` statements checking for the root node.

Defining the Tree class

Here's the core of an extension to `MutableSet` class that provides the minimal method functions:

```
class Tree(collections.abc.MutableSet):
    def __init__( self, iterable=None ):
        self.root= TreeNode(None)
        self.size= 0
        if iterable:
            for item in iterable:
                self.root.add( item )
    def add( self, item ):
        self.root.add( item )
        self.size += 1
    def discard( self, item ):
        try:
            self.root.more.remove( item )
            self.size -= 1
        except KeyError:
            pass
    def __contains__( self, item ):
        try:
            self.root.more.find( item )
            return True
        except KeyError:
            return False
    def __iter__( self ):
        for item in iter(self.root.more):
            yield item
    def __len__( self ):
        return self.size
```

The initialization is similar to that of a `Counter` object; this class will accept an iterable and load the elements into the structure.

The add() and discard() methods keep track of the overall size. That saves counting nodes via a recursive traversal of the tree. These methods also delegate their work to the TreeNode object at the root of the tree.

The __contains__() special method performs a recursive find. It transforms a KeyError exception into a False return value.

The __iter__() special method is a generator function. It also delegates the real work to recursive iterators within the TreeNode class.

We defined discard(); mutable sets require this to be silent when attempting to discard the missing keys. The abstract superclass provides a default implementation of remove(), which raises an exception if a key is not found. Both method functions must be present; we defined discard() based on remove() by silencing the exception. In some cases, it might be easier to define remove() based on discard() by raising an exception if a problem is found.

Defining the TreeNode class

The overall Tree class relies on the TreeNode class to handle the detailed work of adding, removing, and iterating through the various items in the bag. This class is rather large, so we'll present it in three sections.

Here's the first part that includes finding and iterating through the nodes:

```
import weakref
class TreeNode:
    def __init__( self, item, less=None, more=None, parent=None ):
        self.item= item
        self.less= less
        self.more= more
        if parent != None:
            self.parent = parent
    @property
    def parent( self ):
        return self.parent_ref()
    @parent.setter
    def parent( self, value ):
        self.parent_ref= weakref.ref(value)
    def __repr__( self ):
        return( "TreeNode({item!r},{less!r},{more!r})".format(
          **self.__dict__ ) )
    def find( self, item ):
        if self.item is None: # Root
            if self.more: return self.more.find(item)
```

```
        elif self.item == item: return self
        elif self.item > item and self.less: return
          self.less.find(item)
        elif self.item < item and self.more: return
          self.more.find(item)
        raise KeyError
    def __iter__( self ):
        if self.less:
            for item in iter(self.less):
                yield item
        yield self.item
        if self.more:
            for item in iter(self.more):
                yield item
```

We defined the essential initialization for a node with two variants. We can provide as little as just the item; we can provide as much as the item, the two subtrees, and the parent link.

The properties are used to ensure that the parent attribute is actually a `weakref` attribute that appears like a strong reference. For more information on weak references, see *Chapter 2, Integrating Seamlessly with Python – Basic Special Methods*. We have mutual references between a `TreeNode` parent object and its children objects; this circularity could make it difficult to remove `TreeNode` objects. Using a `weakref` breaks the circularity.

We saw the `find()` method, which performs a recursive search from a tree through the appropriate subtree looking for the target item.

The `__iter__()` method does what's called an inorder traversal of this node and its subtrees. As is typical, this is a generator function that yields the values from iterators over each collection of subtrees. Although we could create a separate iterator class that's tied to our `Tree` class, there's little benefit when a generator function does everything we need.

Here's the next part of this class to add a new node to a tree:

```
    def add( self, item ):
        if self.item is None: # Root Special Case
            if self.more:
                self.more.add( item )
            else:
                self.more= TreeNode( item, parent=self )
        elif self.item >= item:
            if self.less:
                self.less.add( item )
```

```
            else:
                self.less= TreeNode( item, parent=self )
        elif self.item < item:
            if self.more:
                self.more.add( item )
            else:
                self.more= TreeNode( item, parent=self )
```

This is the recursive search for the proper place to add a new node. The structure parallels the `find()` method.

Finally, we have the (more complex) processing to remove a node from the tree. This requires some care to relink the tree around the missing node:

```
    def remove( self, item ):
        # Recursive search for node
        if self.item is None or item > self.item:
            if self.more:
                self.more.remove(item)
            else:
                raise KeyError
        elif item < self.item:
            if self.less:
                self.less.remove(item)
            else:
                raise KeyError
        else: # self.item == item
            if self.less and self.more: # Two children are present
                successor = self.more._least()
                self.item = successor.item
                successor.remove(successor.item)
            elif self.less:   # One child on less
                self._replace(self.less)
            elif self.more:  # On child on more
                self._replace(self.more)
            else: # Zero children
                self._replace(None)
    def _least(self):
        if self.less is None: return self
        return self.less._least()
    def _replace(self,new=None):
        if self.parent:
            if self == self.parent.less:
                self.parent.less = new
```

```
            else:
                self.parent.more = new
        if new is not None:
            new.parent = self.parent
```

The `remove()` method has two sections. The first part is the recursive search for the target node.

Once the node is found, there are three cases to consider:

- When we delete a node with no children, we simply delete it and update the parent to replace the link with `None`.
- When we delete a node with one child, we can push the single child up to replace this node under the parent.
- When there are two children, we need to restructure the tree. We locate the successor node (the least item in the `more` subtree). We can replace the to-be-removed node with the content of this successor. Then, we can remove the duplicative former successor node.

We rely on two private methods. The `_least()` method performs a recursive search for the least-valued node in a given tree. The `_replace()` method examines a parent to see whether it should touch the `less` or `more` attribute.

Demonstrating the binary tree set

We built a complete new collection. The ABC definitions included a number of methods automatically. These inherited methods might not be particularly efficient, but they're defined, they work, and we didn't write the code for them.

```
>>> s1 = Tree( ["Item 1", "Another", "Middle"] )
>>> list(s1)
['Another', 'Item 1', 'Middle']
>>> len(s1)
3
>>> s2 = Tree( ["Another", "More", "Yet More"] )
>>>
>>> union= s1|s2
>>> list(union)
['Another', 'Another', 'Item 1', 'Middle', 'More', 'Yet More']
>>> len(union)
6
>>> union.remove('Another')
>>> list(union)
['Another', 'Item 1', 'Middle', 'More', 'Yet More']
```

This example shows us that the set `union` operator for set objects works properly, even though we didn't provide code for it specifically. As this is a bag, items are duplicated properly, too.

Summary

In this chapter, we looked at a number of built-in class definitions. The built-in collections are the starting place for most design work. We'll often start with `tuple`, `list`, `dict`, or `set`. We can leverage the extension to `tuple`, created by `namedtuple()`, for an application's immutable objects.

Beyond these classes, we have other standard library classes in the `collections` mode that we can use:

- `deque`
- `ChainMap`
- `OrderedDict`
- `defaultdict`
- `Counter`

We have three standard design strategies, too. We can wrap any of these existing classes, or we can extend a class.

Finally, we can also invent an entirely new kind of collection. This requires defining a number of method names and special methods.

Design considerations and Trade-offs

When working with containers and collections, we have a multistep design strategy:

1. Consider the built-in versions of sequence, mapping, and set.
2. Consider the library extensions in the collection module as well as extras such as `heapq`, `bisect`, and `array`.
3. Consider a composition of existing class definitions. In many cases, a list of `tuple` objects or a `dict` of lists provides the needed features.
4. Consider extending one of the earlier mentioned classes to provide additional methods or attributes.
5. Consider wrapping an existing structure as another way to provide additional methods or attributes.

6. Finally, consider a novel data structure. Generally, there is a lot of careful analysis available. Start with Wikipedia articles like this:

   `http://en.wikipedia.org/wiki/List_of_data_structures`

Once the design alternatives have been identified, there are two parts of the evaluation left:

- How well the interface fits with the problem domain. This is a relatively subjective determination.
- How well the data structure performs as measured with `timeit`. This is an entirely objective result.

It's important to avoid the paralysis of analysis. We need to *effectively* find the proper collection.

In most cases, it is best to profile a working application to see which data structure is the performance bottleneck. In some cases, consideration of the complexity factors for a data structure will reveal its suitability for a particular kind of problem before starting the implementation.

Perhaps the most important consideration is this: "For highest performance, avoid search".

This is the reason sets and mappings require hashable objects. A hashable object can be located in a set or mapping with almost no processing. Locating an item by value (not by index) in a list can take a great deal of time.

Here's a comparison of a bad set-like use of a list and proper use of a set:

```
>>> import timeit
>>> timeit.timeit( 'l.remove(10); l.append(10)', 'l = 
list(range(20))' )
0.8182099789992208
>>> timeit.timeit( 'l.remove(10); l.add(10)', 'l = set(range(20))'
)
0.30278149300283985
```

We removed and added an item from a list as well as a set.

Clearly, abusing a list to get it to perform set-like operations makes the collection run 2.7 times as long.

As a second example, we'll abuse a list to make it mapping-like. This is based on a real-world example where the original code had two parallel lists to mimic the keys and values of a mapping.

We'll compare a proper mapping with two parallel lists, as follows:

```
>>> timeit.timeit( 'i= k.index(10); v[i]= 0', 'k=list(range(20));
v=list(range(20))' )
0.6549435159977293
>>> timeit.timeit( 'm[10]= 0', 'm=dict(zip(list(range(20)),list(ran
ge(20))))' )
0.0764331009995658
```

We used one list to look up a value and then set the value in a second, parallel list. In the other case, we simply updated a mapping.

Clearly, performing an index and update on two parallel lists is a horrifying mistake. It takes 8.6 times as long to locate something via `list.index()` as it does to locate it via a mapping and the hash value.

Looking forward

In the next chapter, we'll closely look at the built-in numbers and how to create new kinds of numbers. As with containers, Python offers a rich variety of built-in numbers. When creating a new kind of number, we'll have to define numerous special methods.

After looking at numbers, we can look at some more sophisticated design techniques. We'll look at how we can create our own decorators and use those to simplify the class definition. We'll also look at using mixin class definitions, which are similar to the ABC definitions.

7
Creating Numbers

We can extend the ABC abstractions in the `numbers` module to create new kinds of numbers. We might need to do this to create numeric types that fit our problem domain more precisely than the built-in numeric types.

The abstractions in the `numbers` module need to be looked at first, since they define the existing built-in classes. Before working with new kinds of numbers, it's essential to see how the existing numbers work.

We'll digress to look at Python's operator-to-method mapping algorithm. The idea is that a binary operator has two operands; either operand can define the class that implements the operator. Python's rules for locating the relevant class are essential to decide what special methods to implement.

The essential arithmetic operators such as `+`, `-`, `*`, `/`, `//`, `%`, and `**` form the backbone of numeric operations. There are additional operators that include `^`, `|`, and `&`. These are used for the bit-wise processing of integers. They're also used as operators among sets. There are some more operators in this class, including `<<`, `>>`. The comparison operators were covered in *Chapter 2, Integrating Seamlessly with Python - Basic Special Methods*. These include `<`, `>`, `<=`, `>=`, `==`, and `!=`. We'll review and extend our study of the comparison operators in this chapter.

There are a number of additional special methods for numbers. These include the various conversions to other built-in types. Python also defines "in-place" combinations of an assignment with an operator. These include `+=`, `-=`, `*=`, `/=`, `//=`, `%=`, `**=`, `&=`, `|=`, `^=`, `>>=`, and `<<=`. These are more appropriate for mutable objects than numbers. We'll finish by summarizing some of the design considerations that go into extending or creating new numbers.

ABCs of numbers

The `numbers` package provides a tower of numeric types that are all implementations of `numbers.Number`. Additionally, the `fractions` and `decimal` modules provide extension numeric types: `fractions.Fraction` and `decimal.Decimal`.

These definitions roughly parallel the mathematical thought on the various classes of numbers. An article available at `http://en.wikipedia.org/wiki/Number_theory` covers the basics of different kinds of numbers.

What's important is the question of how well computers implement mathematical abstractions. To be more specific, we want to be sure that anything that is computable in the abstract world of mathematics can be computed using a concrete computer. This is why the question of computability is so important. The idea behind a "Turing Complete" programming language is that it can compute anything that's computable by an abstract Turing Machine. A helpful article can be found at `http://en.wikipedia.org/wiki/Computability_theory`.

Python defines the following abstractions and their associated implementation classes. Further, these classes form an inheritance hierarchy where each abstract class inherits from the class above it. As we move down the list, the classes have more features. Since there are very few classes, it forms a *tower* rather than a tree.

- `numbers.Complex` implemented by `complex`
- `numbers.Real` implemented by `float`
- `numbers.Rational` implemented by `fractions.Fraction`
- `numbers.Integral` implemented by `int`

Additionally, we have `decimal.Decimal`, which is a bit like a float; it isn't a proper subclass of `numbers.Real`, but is somewhat like it.

While it may be obvious, it's still essential to repeat that the `float` value is merely an approximation. It's not exact.

Don't be surprised by this sort of thing. The following is an example of using the $\left(\frac{A}{B}\right) \times B \neq A$ approximations:

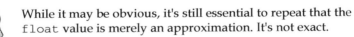

```
>>> (3*5*7*11)/(11*13*17*23*29)
0.0007123135264946712
>>> _*13*17*23*29
105.00000000000001
```

In principle, the further down the number tower we go, the smaller the order of infinity. This can be a confusing subject. While the various abstract definitions of numbers are each infinite, it's possible to prove that there are different orders of infinity. This leads to the idea that floats represent more numbers than integers in principle. Pragmatically, a 64-bit float and 64-bit integer have the same number of distinct values.

In addition to the numeric class definitions, there are also a number of conversions among the various classes. It's not possible to convert from every type to every other type, so we must work out a matrix that shows the conversions that work and conversions that can't work. The following is a summary:

- `complex`: This can't be converted to any other type. A `complex` value can be decomposed into the `real` and `imag` portions, both of which are `float`.
- `float`: This can be converted explicitly to any type including `decimal.Decimal`. Arithmetic operators won't implicitly coerce a `float` value to `Decimal`.
- `Fractions.Fraction`: This can be converted to any of the other types, except `decimal.Decimal`. To get to `decimal` requires a two-part operation: (1) to `float` (2) to `decimal.Decimal`. This leads to an approximation.
- `int`: This can be converted to any of the other types.
- `Decimal`: This can be converted to any other type. It is not implicitly coerced to other types via arithmetic operations.

The up and down conversions come from the tower of numeric abstractions shown previously.

Deciding which types to use

Because of the conversions, we see the following four general domains of numerical processing:

- **Complex**: Once we get involved in complex math, we'll be using `complex`, `float`, plus the `cmath` module. We probably aren't going to use `Fraction` or `Decimal` at all. However, there's no reason to impose restrictions on the numeric types; most numbers will be converted to complex.
- **Currency**: For currency-related operations, we absolutely must use `Decimal`. Generally, when doing currency calculations, there's no good reason to mix the decimal values with non-decimal values. Sometimes, we'll use the `int` values, but there's no good reason to work with `float` or `complex` along with `Decimal`. Remember, floats are approximations, and that's unacceptable when working with currency.

- **Bit kicking**: For operations that involve bit and byte processing, we'll generally use `int`, only `int`, and nothing but `int`.
- **Conventional**: The broad, vague "everything else" category. For most conventional mathematical operations `int`, `float`, and `Fraction` are all interchangeable. Indeed, a well-written function can often be properly polymorphic; it will work perfectly well with any numeric type. Python types, particularly `float` and `int`, will participate in a variety of implicit conversions. This makes the selection of a specific numeric type for these kinds of problems somewhat moot.

These are generally obvious aspects of a problem domain. It's usually easy to distinguish applications that might involve science or engineering and complex numbers from applications that involve financial calculations, currency, and decimal numbers. It's important to be as permissive as possible in the numeric types that are used in an application. Needlessly narrowing the domain of types via the `isinstance()` test is often a waste of time and code.

The method resolution and the reflected operator concept

The arithmetic operators (`+`, `-`, `*`, `/`, `//`, `%`, `**`, and so on) all map to special method names. When we provide an expression such as `355+113`, the generic `+` operator will be mapped to a concrete `__add__()` method of a specific numeric class. This example will turn out to be evaluated as though we had written `355.__add__(113)`. The simplest rule is that the left-most operand determines the class of the operator being used.

But wait, there's more! When we have an expression with mixed types, Python may end up with two implementations of the special methods, one in each class. Consider `7-0.14` as an expression. Using the left-side `int` class, this expression will be attempted as `7.__sub__(0.14)`. This involves an unpleasant complexity, since the argument to an `int` operator is a `float` value `0.14` and converting `float` to `int` could potentially lose precision. Converting up the tower of types (from `int` toward `complex`) won't lose precision. Converting down the tower of types implies a potential loss of precision.

Using the right-side `float` version, however, this expression will be attempted as: `0.14.__rsub__(7)`. In this case, the argument to a `float` operator is an `int` value `7`; converting `int` up the tower to `float` doesn't (generally) lose precision. (A truly giant `int` value can lose precision; however, that's a technical quibble, not a general principle.)

The `__rsub__()` operation is "reflected subtraction". The `X.__sub__(Y)` operation is the expected `X-Y`. The `A.__rsub__(B)` operation is the reflection `B-A`; the implementation method comes from the right-hand side operand's class. We've seen the following two rules:

- Try the left-hand side operand's class first. If that works, good. If the operand returns `NotImplemented` as a value, then use rule 2.
- Try the right-hand side operand with the reflected operator. If that works, good. If it returns `NotImplemented`, then it really is not implemented, so an exception must be raised.

The notable exception is when the two operands happen to have a subclass relationship. This additional rule applies before the first pair rules as a special case:

- If the right operand is a subclass of the left and the subclass defines the reflected special method name for the operator, then the subclass reflected operator will be tried. This allows a subclass override to be used, even if the subclass operand is on the right-hand side of the operator.
- Otherwise, use rule 1 and try the left side.

Imagine we wrote a subclass of float, `MyFloat`. In an expression like `2.0-MyFloat(1)`, the right operand is of a subclass of the left operand's class. Because of this subclass relationship, `MyFloat(1).__rsub__(2.0)` will be tried first. The point of this rule is to give precedence to the subclass.

This means that a class that will do implicit coercion from other types must implement the forward, as well as the reflected operators. When we implement or extend a numeric type, we must work out the conversions that our type is able to do.

The arithmetic operator's special methods

There are a total of 13 binary operators and their associated special methods. We'll focus on the obvious arithmetic operators first. The special method names match the operators (and functions), as shown in the following table:

Method	Operator
`object.__add__(self, other)`	`+`
`object.__sub__(self, other)`	`-`
`object.__mul__(self, other)`	`*`
`object.__truediv__(self, other)`	`/`

Method	Operator
`object.__floordiv__(self, other)`	`//`
`object.__mod__(self, other)`	`%`
`object.__divmod__(self, other)`	`divmod()`
`object.__pow__(self, other[, modulo])`	`pow()` as well as `**`

And yes, interestingly, two functions are included with the various symbolic operators. There are a number of unary operators and functions which have special method names, shown in the following table:

Method	Operator
`object.__neg__(self)`	`-`
`object.__pos__(self)`	`+`
`object.__abs__(self)`	`abs()`
`object.__complex__(self)`	`complex()`
`object.__int__(self)`	`int()`
`object.__float__(self)`	`float()`
`object.__round__(self[, n])`	`round()`
`object.__trunc__(self[, n])`	`math.trunc()`
`object.__ceil__(self[, n])`	`math.ceil()`
`object.__floor__(self[, n])`	`math.floor()`

And yes, there are a lot of functions in this list too. We can tinker with Python's internal trace to see what's going on under the hood. We'll define a simplistic trace function that will provide us with a little bit of visibility into what's going on:

```
def trace( frame, event, arg ):
    if frame.f_code.co_name.startswith("__"):
        print( frame.f_code.co_name, frame.f_code.co_filename, event )
```

This function will dump special method names when the code associated with the traced frame has a name that starts with `"__"`. We can install this trace function into Python using the following code:

```
import sys
sys.settrace(trace)
```

Once installed, everything passes through our `trace()` function. We're filtering the trace events for special method names. We'll define a subclass of a built-in class so that we can explore the method resolution rules:

```
class noisyfloat( float ):
    def __add__( self, other ):
```

```
            print( self, "+", other )
            return super().__add__( other )
        def __radd__( self, other ):
            print( self, "r+", other )
            return super().__radd__( other )
```

This class overrides just two of the operator's special method names. When we add `noisyfloat` values, we'll see a printed summary of the operation. Plus, the trace will tell us what's going on. The following is the interaction that shows Python's choice of class to implement a given operation:

```
>>> x = noisyfloat(2)
>>> x+3
__add__ <stdin> call
2.0 + 3
5.0
>>> 2+x
__radd__ <stdin> call
2.0 r+ 2
4.0
>>> x+2.3
__add__ <stdin> call
2.0 + 2.3
4.3
>>> 2.3+x
__radd__ <stdin> call
2.0 r+ 2.3
4.3
```

From `x+3`, we see how `noisyfloat+int` provided the `int` object, `3`, to the `__add__()` method. This value was passed to the superclass, `float`, which handled the coercion of 3 to a `float` and did the addition, too. `2+x` shows how the right side `noisyfloat` version of the operation was used. Again, `int` was passed to the superclass that handled the coercion to `float`. From `x+2.3`, we come to know that `noisyfloat+float` used the subclass that was on the left-hand side. On the other hand, `2.3+x` shows how `float+noisyfloat` used the subclass on the right-hand side and the reflected `__radd__()` operator.

Creating a numeric class

We'll try to design a new kind of number. This is no easy task when Python already offers integers of indefinite precision, rational fractions, standard floats, and decimal numbers for currency calculations. We'll define a class of "scaled" numbers. These are numbers that include an integer value coupled with a scaling factor. We can use these for currency calculations. For many currencies of the world, we can use a scale of 100 and do all our calculations to the nearest cent.

The advantage of scaled arithmetic is that it can be done very simply by using low-level hardware instructions. We could rewrite this module to be a C-language module and exploit hardware speed operations. The disadvantage of inventing new scaled arithmetic is that the `decimal` package already does a very neat job of exact decimal arithmetic.

We'll call this `FixedPoint` class because it will implement a kind of fixed decimal point number. The scale factor will be a simple integer, usually a power of 10. In principle, a scaling factor that's a power of 2 could be considerably faster, but wouldn't be ideally suited for currency.

The reason a scaling factor that's a power of 2 can be faster is that we can replace `value*(2**scale)` with `value << scale` and replace `value/(2**scale)` with `value >> scale`. The left and right shift operations are often hardware instructions that are much faster than multiplication or division.

Ideally, the scaling factor is a power of 10, but we don't explicitly enforce this. It's a relatively simple extension to track both a scaling power and the scale factor that goes with the power. We might store 2 as the power and $10^2 - 100$ as the factor. We've simplified this class definition to just track the factor.

Defining FixedPoint initialization

We'll start with initialization, which includes conversions of various types to the `FixedPoint` values as follows:

```
import numbers
import math

class FixedPoint( numbers.Rational ):
    __slots__ = ( "value", "scale", "default_format" )
    def __new__( cls, value, scale=100 ):
        self = super().__new__(cls)
        if isinstance(value,FixedPoint):
            self.value= value.value
            self.scale= value.scale
```

```
        elif isinstance(value,int):
            self.value= value
            self.scale= scale
        elif isinstance(value,float):
            self.value= int(scale*value+.5) # Round half up
            self.scale= scale
        else:
            raise TypeError
        digits= int( math.log10( scale ) )
        self.default_format= "{{0:.{digits}f}}".format(digits=digits)
        return self
    def __str__( self ):
        return self.__format__( self.default_format )
    def __repr__( self ):
        return "{__class__.__name__:s}({value:d},scale={scale:d})".
format( __class__=self.__class__, value=self.value, scale=self.scale )
    def __format__( self, specification ):
        if specification == "": specification= self.default_format
        return specification.format( self.value/self.scale ) # no
rounding
    def numerator( self ):
        return self.value
    def denominator( self ):
        return self.scale
```

Our `FixedPoint` class is defined as a `numbers.Rational` subclass. We're going to wrap two integer values, `scale` and `value`, and follow the general definitions for fractions. This requires a large number of special method definitions. The initialization is for an immutable object, so it overrides `__new__()` instead of `__init__()`. It defines a limited number of slots to prevent the adding of any additional attributes. The initialization includes several kinds of conversions as follows:

- If we're given another `FixedPoint` object, we'll copy the internal attributes to create a new `FixedPoint` object that's a kind of clone of the original. It will have a unique ID, but we can be sure it has the same hash value and compares as equal, making the clone largely indistinguishable.
- When given integral or rational values (concrete classes of `int` or `float`), these are used to set the `value` and `scale` attributes.
- We can add cases to handle `decimal.Decimal` and `fractions.Fraction`, as well as parsing input string values.

We've defined three special methods to produce string results: `__str__()`, `__repr__()`, and `__format__()`. For the format operation, we've decided to leverage the existing floating-point features of the format specification language. Because this is a rational number, we need to provide numerator and denominator methods.

Note that we could have also started with wrapping the existing `fractions.Fraction` class. Also, note that we're playing fast and loose with the rounding rules. This should also be defined with reasonable care before applying this class to a specific problem domain.

Defining FixedPoint binary arithmetic operators

The whole reason for defining a new class of numbers is to overload the arithmetic operators. Each `FixedPoint` object has two parts: `value` and `scale`. We can say this: $A = \frac{A_v}{A_s}$.

Note that we've worked out the algebra in the example below using correct but inefficient floating point expressions. We'll discuss the slightly more efficient, pure integer operations.

The general form for addition (and subtraction) is this: $A + B = \frac{A_v}{A_s} + \frac{B_v}{B_s} \frac{A_v B_s + B_v A_s}{A_s B_s}$. But it creates a result with a lot of useless precision.

Imagine adding 9.95 and 12.95. We'd have (in principle) 229000/10000. This can be properly reduced to 2290/100. The problem is that it also reduces to 229/10, which is no longer in cents. We'd like to avoid reducing fractions in a general way and instead stick with cents or mils to the extent possible.

We can identify two cases for $A + B = \frac{A_v}{A_s} + \frac{B_v}{B_s}$:

- **The scale factors match**: In this case, the sum is $A + B = \frac{A_v}{A_s} + \frac{B_v}{B_s} = \frac{A_v + B_v}{A_s}$. When adding `FixedPoint` and the plain old integer, this will also work, since we can force the plain old integer to have the required scale factor.
- **The scale factors don't match**: The right thing to do is to produce a result that has the maximum scale factor of the two input values, $R_s = max(A_s, B_s)$. From this, we can compute two scale factors, $\frac{R_s}{A_s}$ and $\frac{R_s}{B_s}$. One of those scale factors will be 1, the other will be less than 1. We can now add with a common value in the denominator. Algebraically, it's $\frac{A_v \frac{R_s}{A_s}}{A_s \frac{R_s}{A_s}} + \frac{B_v \frac{R_s}{B_s}}{B_s \frac{R_s}{B_s}} = \frac{A_v \frac{R_s}{A_s} + B_v \frac{R_s}{B_s}}{R_s}$. This can be further optimized into two cases, since one of the factors is 1 and the other is a power of 10.

We can't really optimize multiplication. It's essentially $A \times B = \frac{A_v}{A_s} \times \frac{B_v}{B_s} = \frac{A_v B_v}{A_s B_s}$. The precision really does increase when we multiply the `FixedPoint` values.

Division is multiplication by an inverse, $A \div B = \frac{A_v}{A_s} \times \frac{B_s}{B_v} = \frac{A_v B_s}{A_s B_v}$. If A and B have the same scale, these values will cancel so that we do have a handy optimization available. However, this changes the scale from cents to wholes, which might not be appropriate. The following is what the forward operators, built around a similar boilerplate, look like:

```
def __add__( self, other ):
    if not isinstance(other,FixedPoint):
        new_scale= self.scale
        new_value= self.value + other*self.scale
    else:
        new_scale= max(self.scale, other.scale)
        new_value= (self.value*(new_scale//self.scale)
        + other.value*(new_scale//other.scale))
    return FixedPoint( int(new_value), scale=new_scale )
def __sub__( self, other ):
    if not isinstance(other,FixedPoint):
        new_scale= self.scale
        new_value= self.value - other*self.scale
    else:
        new_scale= max(self.scale, other.scale)
        new_value= (self.value*(new_scale//self.scale)
        - other.value*(new_scale//other.scale))
    return FixedPoint( int(new_value), scale=new_scale )
def __mul__( self, other ):
    if not isinstance(other,FixedPoint):
        new_scale= self.scale
        new_value= self.value * other
    else:
        new_scale= self.scale * other.scale
        new_value= self.value * other.value
    return FixedPoint( int(new_value), scale=new_scale )
def __truediv__( self, other ):
    if not isinstance(other,FixedPoint):
        new_value= int(self.value / other)
    else:
        new_value= int(self.value / (other.value/other.scale))
    return FixedPoint( new_value, scale=self.scale )
def __floordiv__( self, other ):
    if not isinstance(other,FixedPoint):
        new_value= int(self.value // other)
    else:
```

```
            new_value= int(self.value // (other.value/other.scale))
        return FixedPoint( new_value, scale=self.scale )
    def __mod__( self, other ):
        if not isinstance(other,FixedPoint):
            new_value= (self.value/self.scale) % other
        else:
            new_value= self.value % (other.value/other.scale)
        return FixedPoint( new_value, scale=self.scale )
    def __pow__( self, other ):
        if not isinstance(other,FixedPoint):
            new_value= (self.value/self.scale) ** other
        else:
            new_value= (self.value/self.scale) ** (other.value/other.
scale)
        return FixedPoint( int(new_value)*self.scale, scale=self.scale
)
```

For the simple addition, subtraction, and multiplication cases, we've provided versions that can be optimized to eliminate some of the relatively slow floating point intermediate results.

For the two divisions, the `__mod__()` and `__pow__()` methods, we haven't done any optimization to try and eliminate noise being introduced via floating-point division. Instead, we've provided a working Python implementation that can be used with a suite of unit tests as a basis for optimization and refactoring.

It's important to note that the division operations can properly reduce the scale factors. However, that may be undesirable. When doing currency work, we might divide the currency rate (dollars) by a non-currency value (hours) to get the dollars-per-hour result. The proper answer might have zero relevant decimal places, this would be a scale of 1, but we might want to force the value to have a cents-oriented scale of 100. This implementation assures that the left-hand side operand dictates the desired number of decimal places.

Defining FixedPoint unary arithmetic operators

The following are the unary operators method functions:

```
    def __abs__( self ):
        return FixedPoint( abs(self.value), self.scale )
    def __float__( self ):
        return self.value/self.scale
    def __int__( self ):
        return int(self.value/self.scale)
    def __trunc__( self ):
```

```
        return FixedPoint( math.trunc(self.value/self.scale), self.
scale )
    def __ceil__( self ):
        return FixedPoint( math.ceil(self.value/self.scale), self.
scale )
    def __floor__( self ):
        return FixedPoint( math.floor(self.value/self.scale), self.
scale )
    def __round__( self, ndigits ):
        return FixedPoint( round(self.value/self.scale, ndigits=0),
self.scale )
    def __neg__( self ):
        return FixedPoint( -self.value, self.scale )
    def __pos__( self ):
        return self
```

For the `__round__()`, `__trunc__()`, `__ceil__()`, and `__floor__()` operators, we've delegated the work to a Python library function. There are some potential optimizations, but we've taken the lazy route of creating a float approximation and using that to create the desired result. This suite of methods assures that our `FixedPoint` objects will work with a number of arithmetic functions. Yes, there are a lot of operators in Python. This isn't the entire suite. We haven't covered comparison or bit-kicking operators.

Implementing FixedPoint reflected operators

The reflected operators are used in the following two cases:

- The right-hand operand is a subclass of the left-hand operand. In this case, the reflected operator is tried first to assure that the subclass overrides the parent class.
- The left-hand operand's class doesn't implement the needed special method. In this case, the right-hand operand's reflected special method is used.

The following table shows the mapping between reflected special methods and operators.

Method	Operator
`object.__radd__(self, other)`	`+`
`object.__rsub__(self, other)`	`-`
`object.__rmul__(self, other)`	`*`
`object.__rtruediv__(self, other)`	`/`
`object.__rfloordiv__(self, other)`	`//`

Method	Operator
`object.__rmod__(self, other)`	`%`
`object.__rdivmod__(self, other)`	`divmod()`
`object.__rpow__(self, other[, modulo])`	`pow()` as well as `**`

These reflected operation special methods are also built around a common boilerplate. Since these are reflected, the order of the operands in subtraction, division, modulus, and power is important. For commutative operations such as addition and multiplication, the order doesn't matter. The following are the reflected operators:

```
def __radd__( self, other ):
    if not isinstance(other,FixedPoint):
        new_scale= self.scale
        new_value= other*self.scale + self.value
    else:
        new_scale= max(self.scale, other.scale)
        new_value= (other.value*(new_scale//other.scale)
        + self.value*(new_scale//self.scale))
    return FixedPoint( int(new_value), scale=new_scale )
def __rsub__( self, other ):
    if not isinstance(other,FixedPoint):
        new_scale= self.scale
        new_value= other*self.scale - self.value
    else:
        new_scale= max(self.scale, other.scale)
        new_value= (other.value*(new_scale//other.scale)
        - self.value*(new_scale//self.scale))
    return FixedPoint( int(new_value), scale=new_scale )
def __rmul__( self, other ):
    if not isinstance(other,FixedPoint):
        new_scale= self.scale
        new_value= other*self.value
    else:
        new_scale= self.scale*other.scale
        new_value= other.value*self.value
    return FixedPoint( int(new_value), scale=new_scale )
def __rtruediv__( self, other ):
    if not isinstance(other,FixedPoint):
```

```
            new_value= self.scale*int(other / (self.value/self.scale))
        else:
            new_value= int((other.value/other.scale) / self.value)
        return FixedPoint( new_value, scale=self.scale )
    def __rfloordiv__( self, other ):
        if not isinstance(other,FixedPoint):
            new_value= self.scale*int(other // (self.value/self.
scale))
        else:
            new_value= int((other.value/other.scale) // self.value)
        return FixedPoint( new_value, scale=self.scale )
    def __rmod__( self, other ):
        if not isinstance(other,FixedPoint):
            new_value= other % (self.value/self.scale)
        else:
            new_value= (other.value/other.scale) % (self.value/self.
scale)
        return FixedPoint( new_value, scale=self.scale )
    def __rpow__( self, other ):
        if not isinstance(other,FixedPoint):
            new_value= other ** (self.value/self.scale)
        else:
            new_value= (other.value/other.scale) ** self.value/self.
scale
        return FixedPoint( int(new_value)*self.scale, scale=self.scale
)
```

We've tried to use math that is identical to the forward operators. The idea is to switch the operands in a simple way. This is the most common situation. Having the text of the forward and reverse methods match each other simplifies code inspections.

As with the forward operators, we've kept the division, modulus, and power operators simple to avoid optimizations. The versions shown here can introduce noise from the conversion to a floating-point approximation and back to a `FixedPoint` value.

Implementing FixedPoint comparison operators

The following are the six comparison operators and the special methods which implement them:

Method	Operator
`object.__lt__(self, other)`	`<`
`object.__le__(self, other)`	`<=`
`object.__eq__(self, other)`	`==`
`object.__ne__(self, other)`	`!=`
`object.__gt__(self, other)`	`>`
`object.__ge__(self, other)`	`>=`

The `is` operator compares object IDs. We can't meaningfully override this, since it's independent of any specific class. The `in` comparison operator is implemented by `object.__contains__( self, value )`. This isn't meaningful for numeric values.

Note that equality testing is a subtle business. Since floats are approximations, we have to be very careful to avoid direct equality testing with float values. We really need to compare to see if the values are within a small range, that is, epsilon. It should never be written as `a == b`. The general approach to compare floating-point approximations should be `abs(a-b) <= eps`. Or, more correctly, `abs(a-b)/a <= eps`.

In our `FixedPoint` class, the scale indicates how close two values need to be for a `float` value to be considered equal. For a scale of 100, the epsilon could be 0.01. We'll actually be more conservative than that and use 0.005 as the basis for comparison when the scale is 100.

Additionally, we have to decide whether `FixedPoint(123, 100)` should be equal to `FixedPoint(1230, 1000)` or not. While they're mathematically equal, one value is in cents and one is in mils. This can be taken as a claim about the different accuracies of the two numbers; the presence of an additional significant digit may indicate that they're not supposed to simply appear equal. If we follow this approach, then we need to be sure the hash values are different too.

We think the distinguishing scale is not appropriate for our application. We want `FixedPoint(123, 100)` to be equal to `FixedPoint(1230, 1000)`. This is the assumption behind the recommended `__hash__()` implementation too. The following are the implementations for our `FixedPoint` class comparisons:

```
def __eq__( self, other ):
    if isinstance(other, FixedPoint):
```

```
            if self.scale == other.scale:
                return self.value == other.value
            else:
                return self.value*other.scale//self.scale == other.
value
        else:
            return abs(self.value/self.scale - float(other)) < .5/
self.scale
    def __ne__( self, other ):
        return not (self == other)
    def __le__( self, other ):
        return self.value/self.scale <= float(other)
    def __lt__( self, other ):
        return self.value/self.scale <  float(other)
    def __ge__( self, other ):
        return self.value/self.scale >= float(other)
    def __gt__( self, other ):
        return self.value/self.scale >  float(other)
```

Each of the comparison functions tolerates a value that is not a `FixedPoint` value. The only requirement is that the other value must have a floating-point representation. We've defined a `__float__()` method for the `FixedPoint` objects, so the comparison operations will work perfectly well when comparing the two `FixedPoint` values.

We don't need to write all six comparisons. The `@functools.total_ordering` decorator can generate the missing methods from just two `FixedPoint` values. We'll look at this in *Chapter 8, Decorators and Mixins – Cross-cutting Aspects*.

Computing a numeric hash

We do need to define the `__hash__()` method properly. See section 4.4.4 of the *Python Standard Library* for information on computing hash values for numeric types. That section defines a `hash_fraction()` function, which is the recommended solution for what we're doing here. Our method looks like the following:

```
    def __hash__( self ):
        P = sys.hash_info.modulus
        m, n = self.value, self.scale
        # Remove common factors of P.  (Unnecessary if m and n already
coprime.)
        while m % P == n % P == 0:
            m, n = m // P, n // P
        if n % P == 0:
```

```
            hash_ = sys.hash_info.inf
        else:
            # Fermat's Little Theorem: pow(n, P-1, P) is 1, so
            # pow(n, P-2, P) gives the inverse of n modulo P.
            hash_ = (abs(m) % P) * pow(n, P - 2, P) % P
        if m < 0:
            hash_ = -hash_
        if hash_ == -1:
            hash_ = -2
        return hash_
```

This reduces a two-part rational fraction value to a single, standardized hash. This code is copied with a few modifications from the reference manual. The core of the calculation, which is highlighted, multiplies the numerator by the inverse of the denominator. In effect, it carries out the division of the numerator by the denominator, `mod P`. We can optimize this to make it more specific to our problem domain.

First, we can (and should) modify our `__new__()` method to assure that the scale is nonzero, eliminating any need for `sys.hash_info.inf`. Second, we should explicitly limit the range of the scale factor to be less than `sys.hash_info.modulus` (generally $2^{61}-1$ for 64-bit computers). We can eliminate the need to remove common factors of `P`. That would boil the hash down to `hash_ = (abs(m) % P) * pow(n, P - 2, P) % P`, the sign handling and the special case that -1 is mapped to -2.

Finally, we might want to memorize the result of any hash calculation. This requires an additional slot that's only populated once the first time a hash is requested. The `pow(n, P - 2, P)` expression is relatively expensive to evaluate and we don't want to compute it more often than necessary.

Designing more useful rounding

We truncated the presentation on rounding. We defined the required functions for `round()` and `trunc()` without further explanation. These definitions are the minimum requirements of the abstract superclass. However, these definitions are not quite enough for our purposes.

To process currency, we'll often have code that looks like the following:

```
>>> price= FixedPoint( 1299, 100 )
>>> tax_rate= FixedPoint( 725, 1000 )
>>> price * tax_rate
FixedPoint(941775,scale=100000)
```

Then, we need to round this value off to a scale of `100` to get a value of `942`. We need methods that will round (as well as truncate) a number to a new scale factor. The following is a method to round to a specific scale:

```
def round_to( self, new_scale ):
    f = new_scale/self.scale
    return FixedPoint( int(self.value*f+.5), scale=new_scale )
```

The following code allows us to properly rescale the value:

```
>>> price= FixedPoint( 1299, 100 )
>>> tax_rate= FixedPoint( 725, 1000 )
>>> tax= price * tax_rate
>>> tax.round_to(100)
FixedPoint(942,scale=100)
```

This shows that we have a minimal set of functions to calculate currency.

Implementing other special methods

In addition to the core arithmetic and comparison operators, we have a group of additional operators that (generally) we only define for the `numbers.Integral` values. Since we're not defining integral values, we can avoid these special methods:

Method	Operator
`object.__lshift__(self, other)`	`<<`
`object.__rshift__(self, other)`	`>>`
`object.__and__(self, other)`	`&`
`object.__xor__(self, other)`	`^`
`object.__or__(self, other)`	`|`

Also, there are reflected versions of these operators:

Method	Operator
`object.__rlshift__(self, other)`	`<<`
`object.__rrshift__(self, other)`	`>>`
`object.__rand__(self, other)`	`&`
`object.__rxor__(self, other)`	`^`
`object.__ror__(self, other)`	`|`

Additionally, there's a unary operator for a bit-wise inverse of the value:

Method	Operator
`object.__invert__(self)`	~

Interestingly, some of these operators are defined for the set collection, as well as integral numbers. They don't apply to our rational value. The principles to define these operators are the same as the other arithmetic operators.

Optimization with the in-place operators

Generally, numbers are immutable. However, the numeric operators are also used for mutable objects. Lists and sets, for example, respond to a few of the defined augmented assignment operators. As an optimization, a class can include an in-place version of a selected operator. These methods implement the augmented assignment statements for mutable objects. Note that these methods are expected to end with `return self` to be compatible with ordinary assignment.

Method	Operator
`object.__iadd__(self, other)`	+=
`object.__isub__(self, other)`	-=
`object.__imul__(self, other)`	*=
`object.__itruediv__(self, other)`	/=
`object.__ifloordiv__(self, other)`	//=
`object.__imod__(self, other)`	%=
`object.__ipow__(self, other[, modulo])`	**=
`object.__ilshift__(self, other)`	<<=
`object.__irshift__(self, other)`	>>=
`object.__iand__(self, other)`	&=
`object.__ixor__(self, other)`	^=
`object.__ior__(self, other)`	|=

Since our `FixedPoint` objects are immutable, we should not define any of these. Stepping outside this example, for a moment, we can see a more typical use for in-place operators. We could easily define some in-place operators for our Blackjack `Hand` objects. We might want to add this definition to `Hand` as follows:

```
def __iadd__( self, aCard ):
    self._cards.append( aCard )
    return self
```

This allows us to deal into `hand` with the following code:

```
player_hand += deck.pop()
```

This seems to be an elegant way to indicate that `hand` is updated with another card.

Summary

We've looked at the built-in numeric types. We've also looked at the vast number of special methods required to invent a new numeric type. Specialized numeric types that integrate seamlessly with the rest of Python is one of the core strengths of the language. That doesn't make the job easy. It merely makes it elegant and useful when done properly.

Design considerations and trade-offs

When working with numbers, we have a multistep design strategy:

1. Consider the built-in versions of `complex`, `float`, and `int`.
2. Consider the library extensions such as `decimal` and `fractions`. For financial calculations, `decimal` must be used; there is no alternative.
3. Consider extending one of the above classes with additional methods or attributes.
4. Finally, consider a novel number. This is particularly challenging, since Python's variety of available numbers is very rich.

Defining new numbers involves several considerations:

- **Completeness and consistency**: The new number must perform a complete set of operations and behave consistently in all kinds of expressions. This is really a question of properly implementing the formal mathematical definitions of this new kind of computable number.
- **Fit with the problem domain**: Is this number truly suitable? Does it help clarify the solution?
- **Performance**: As with other design questions, we must be sure that our implementation is efficient enough to warrant writing all that code. Our example in this chapter, for example, uses some inefficient floating-point operations that could be optimized by doing a little more math and a little less coding.

Looking forward

The next chapter is about using decorators and mixins to simplify and normalize class design. We can use decorators to define features that should be present in a number of classes, which are not in a simple inheritance hierarchy. Similarly, we can use mixin class definitions to create a complete application class from component class definitions. One of the decorators that is helpful to define comparison operators is the `@functools.total_ordering` decorator.

8 Decorators and Mixins – Cross-cutting Aspects

A software design often has aspects that apply across several classes, functions, or methods. We might have a technical aspect, examples include logging, auditing, or security, that must be implemented consistently. The general method for reuse of functionality in object-oriented programming is inheritance through a class hierarchy. However, inheritance doesn't always work out well. Some aspects of a software design are orthogonal to the class hierarchy. These are sometimes called "cross-cutting concerns". They cut across the classes, making design more complex.

A decorator provides a way to define functionality that's not bound to the inheritance hierarchy. We can use decorators to design an aspect of our application and then apply the decorators across classes, methods, or functions.

Additionally, we can use multiple inheritance in a disciplined way to create cross-cutting aspects. We'll consider a base class plus mixin class definitions to introduce features. Often, we'll use the mixin classes to build cross-cutting aspects.

It's important to note that cross-cutting concerns are rarely specific to the application at hand. They're often generic considerations. The common examples of logging, auditing, and security could be considered as infrastructure separate from the application's details.

Python comes with many decorators, and we can expand this standard set of decorators. There are several different use cases. We'll look at simple function decorators, function decorators with arguments, class decorators, and method decorators.

Class and meaning

One essential feature of objects is that they can be classified. Each object belongs to a class. This is a straightforward relationship between an object and class with a simple, single-inheritance design.

With multiple inheritance, the classification problem can become complex. When we look at real-world objects, such as coffee cups, we can classify them as containers without too much difficulty. That is, after all, their primary use case. The problem they solve is that of holding coffee. However, in another context, we may be interested in other use cases. In a decorative collection of ceramic mugs, we might be more interested in size, shape, and glaze than we are in the coffee-carrying aspect of a cup.

Most objects have a straightforward *is-a* relationship with a class. In our coffee-holding problem domain, the mug sitting on the desk is a coffee cup as well as a container. Objects may also have several *acts-as* relationships with other classes. A mug acts as a piece of ceramic art with size, shape, and glaze properties. A mug acts as a paper weight with mass and friction properties. Generally, these other features can be seen as mixin classes, and they define the additional interfaces or behaviors for an object.

When doing object-oriented design, it's common to identify the *is-a* class and the essential aspects defined by that class. Other classes can mix in interfaces or behaviors that an object will also have. We'll take a look at how classes are constructed and decorated. We'll start with function definition and decoration since it's somewhat simpler than class construction.

Constructing the functions

We construct functions in two stages. The first stage is the `def` statement with an original definition.

It's technically possible to build a function using a lambda and assignment; we'll avoid that.

A `def` statement provides a name, parameters, defaults, a `docstring`, a code object, and a number of other details. A function is a collection of 11 attributes, defined in section 3.2 of the *Python Language Reference* which is the standard type hierarchy. See `http://docs.python.org/3.3/reference/datamodel.html#the-standard-type-hierarchy`.

The second stage is applying a decorator to the original definition. When we apply a decorator (`@d`) to a function (`F`), the effect is as if we have created a new function, $F' = @d(F)$. The name is the same, but the functionality can be different depending on the kind of features that have been added, removed, or modified. Then, we will write the following code:

```
@decorate
def function():
    pass
```

The decorator is written immediately in front of the function definition. What happens is this:

```
def function():
    pass
function= decorate( function )
```

The decorator modifies the function definition to create a new function. Here is the list of attributes of a function:

Attribute	Contents
`__doc__`	The docstring, or `None`.
`__name__`	The original name of the function.
`__module__`	The name of the module the function was defined in, or `None`.
`__qualname__`	The function's fully qualified name, `__module__.__name__`.
`__defaults__`	The default argument values, or none if there are no defaults.
`__kwdefaults__`	The default values for keyword-only parameters.
`__code__`	The code object representing the compiled function body.
`__dict__`	A namespace for the function's attributes.
`__annotations__`	The annotations of parameters, including `'return'` for the return annotation.
`__globals__`	The global namespace of the module that the function was defined in; this is used to resolve global variables and is read only.
`__closure__`	Bindings for the function's free variables or none. It is read-only.

Except for `__globals__` and `__closure__`, a decorator can change any of these attributes. However, we'll see later that it's impractical to tinker with these too deeply.

Pragmatically, decoration usually involves defining a new function that *wraps* the existing function. A few of the previous attributes may need to be copied or updated. This defines a practical limit to what decorators can and should do.

Constructing the class

Class construction is a nested set of two-stage processes. Making class construction more complex is the way references are made to class methods that involve a multistep lookup. An object's class will define a **Method Resolution Order** (**MRO**). This defines how base classes are searched to locate an attribute or method name. The MRO works its way up the inheritance hierarchy; this means that subclass names override superclass names. This implementation method search meets our expectation for what inheritance means.

The first stage in class construction is the `class` statement with the original definition. This stage involves the evaluation of the metaclass followed by the execution of the sequence of assignment and `def` statements within a `class`. Each `def` statement within the class expands to a nested two-stage function construction, as described previously. Decorators can be applied to each method function as part of the process of building the class.

The second stage in class construction is to apply an overall class decorator to a class definition. Generally, a `decorator` function can add features. It's somewhat more common to add attributes rather than adding methods. However, we will see decorators that can also add method functions.

The features inherited from superclasses clearly cannot be modified through decorators since they are resolved lazily by method resolution lookup. This leads to some important design considerations. We generally introduce methods through classes and mixin classes. We're limited to introducing attributes either via decorators or mixin class definitions. Here's a list of some of the attributes that are built for a class. A number of additional attributes are part of the metaclass; they are described in the following table:

Attribute	Contents
`__doc__`	The class's documentation string, or `None` if undefined
`__name__`	The class name
`__module__`	The module name that the class was defined in
`__dict__`	The dictionary containing the class's namespace
`__bases__`	A tuple (possibly empty or a singleton) containing the base classes, in the order of their occurrence in the base class list; it is used to work out method resolution order
`__class__`	The superclass of this class, often the `type` class

Some additional method functions that are part of a class include `__subclasshook__`, `__reduce__`, and `__reduce_ex__`, which are part of the interface for `pickle`.

Some class design principles

When defining a class, we have the following three sources of attributes and methods:

- The class statement
- The decorators applied to the class definition
- The mixin classes with the base class that is given last

We need to be cognizant of the level of visibility for each of these. The `class` statement is the most obvious source for attributes and methods. The mixins and the base class are somewhat less obvious than the class body. It's helpful to make sure that the base class name clarifies its role as essential. We've tried to name our base classes after real-world objects.

The mixin classes will generally define additional interfaces or behaviors of a class. It's important to be clear how the mixin classes are used to build the final class definitions. While a `docstring` class is an important part of this, the overall module `docstring` is also important to show how a proper class can be assembled from the various parts.

When writing the `class` statement, the essential superclass is listed last and the mixins are listed before that. This is not merely convention. The last listed class is the essential *is-a* class. The application of the decorator to the class will lead to somewhat more obscure features. Typically, a decorator will do relatively little. A strong focus on one or a few features helps to clarify what the decorator does.

Aspect-oriented programming

Parts of **aspect-oriented programming** (**AOP**) are relevant to decorators. Our purpose here is to leverage a few aspect-oriented concepts to help show the purpose of decorators and mixins in Python. The idea of a **cross-cutting concern** is central to AOP. Here's some additional background: `http://en.wikipedia.org/wiki/Cross-cutting_concern`. There are several common examples of cross-cutting concerns, as follows:

- **Logging**: We often need to have logging features implemented consistently in many classes. We want to be sure the loggers are named consistently and logging events follow the class structure in a consistent manner.

- **Auditability**: A variation of the logging theme is to provide an audit trail that shows each transformation of a mutable object. In many commerce-oriented applications, the transactions are business records that represent bills or payments. Each step in the processing of a business record needs to be auditable to show that no errors have been introduced by the processing.
- **Security**: Our applications will often have security aspects that pervade each HTTP request and each piece of content downloaded by the website. The idea is to confirm that each request involves an authenticated user who is authorized to make the request. Cookies, secure sockets, and other cryptographic techniques must be used consistently to assure that an entire web application is secured.

Some languages and tools have deep, formal support for AOP. Python borrows a few of the concepts. The Pythonic approach to AOP involves the following language features:

- **Decorators**: With a decorator, we can establish a consistent aspect implementation at one of two simple join points in a function. We can perform the aspect's processing before or after the existing function. We can't easily locate join points inside the code of a function. It's easiest for decorators to transform a function or method by wrapping it with additional functionality.
- **Mixins**: With a mixin, we can define a class that exists outside a single class hierarchy. The mixin class can be used with other classes to provide a consistent implementation of a cross-cutting aspect. For this to work, the mixin API must be used by the classes that it is mixed into. Generally, mixin classes are considered abstract since they can't be meaningfully instantiated.

Using built-in decorators

Python has several built-in decorators that are part of the language. The `@property`, `@classmethod`, and `@staticmethod` decorators are used to annotate methods of a class. The `@property` decorator transforms a method function into a descriptor. We use this to give a method function the syntax of a simple attribute. The property decorator, when applied to a method, also creates an additional pair of properties that can be used to create a `setter` and `deleter` property. We looked at this in *Chapter 3, Attribute Access, Properties, and Descriptors*.

The @classmethod and @staticmethod decorators transform a method function into a class-level function. The decorated method can now be called from a class, not an object. In the case of a static method, there's no explicit reference to the class. With a class method, on the other hand, the class is the first argument of the method function. The following is an example of a class that includes @staticmethod and some @property definitions:

```
class Angle( float ):
    __slots__ = ( "_degrees", )
    @staticmethod
    def from_radians( value ):
        return Angle(180*value/math.pi)
    def __new__( cls, value ):
        self = super().__new__(cls)
        self._degrees= value
        return self
    @property
    def radians( self ):
        return math.pi*self._degrees/180
    @property
    def degrees( self ):
        return self._degrees
```

This class defines an Angle that can be represented in degrees or radians. The constructor expects degrees. However, we've also defined a from_radians() method function that emits an instance of the class. This function does not work with an instance variable; it works with the class itself and returns an instance of the class. The __new__() method is implicitly a class method. A decorator is not used.

Additionally, we provide the degrees() and radians() method functions that have been decorated so that they are properties. Under the hood, these decorators create a descriptor so that accessing the attribute name degrees or radians will invoke the named method function. We can use the static method to create an instance and then use a property method to access a method function:

```
>>> b=Angle.from_radians(.227)
>>> b.degrees
13.006141949469686
```

The static method is effectively a function because it's not tied to the self instance variable. It has the advantage that it is syntactically bound to the class; using Angle.from_radians can be microscopically more helpful than using a function named angle_from_radians. The use of these decorators assures that the implementation is done correctly and consistently.

Using standard library decorators

The standard library has a number of decorators. Modules such as `contextlib`, `functools`, `unittest`, `atexit`, `importlib`, and `reprlib` contain decorators that are excellent examples of cross-cutting aspects of a software design. For example, the `functools` library offers the `total_ordering` decorator that defines comparison operators. It leverages `__eq__()` and either `__lt__()`, `__le__()`, `__gt__()`, or `__ge__()` to create a complete suite of comparisons. The following is a variation on the `Card` class that defines just two comparisons:

```
import functools
@functools.total_ordering
class Card:
    __slots__ = ( "rank", "suit" )
    def __new__( cls, rank, suit ):
        self = super().__new__(cls)
        self.rank= rank
        self.suit= suit
        return self
    def __eq__( self, other ):
        return self.rank == other.rank
    def __lt__( self, other ):
        return self.rank < other.rank
```

Our class is wrapped by a class-level decorator, `@functools.total_ordering`. This decorator creates the missing method functions. We can use this class to create objects that can be compared using all of the comparison operators, even though only two were defined. Here's an example of comparisons we've defined as well as comparisons we have not defined:

```
>>> c1= Card( 3, '♠' )
>>> c2= Card( 3, '♥' )
>>> c1 == c2
True
>>> c1 < c2
False
>>> c1 <= c2
True
>>> c1 >= c2
True
```

This interaction shows that we are able to make comparisons that are not defined in the original class. The decorator added method functions to the original class definition.

Using standard library mixin classes

The standard library makes use of mixin class definitions. There are several modules that contain examples, including `io`, `socketserver`, `urllib.request`, `contextlib`, and `collections.abc`.

When we define our own collection based on the `collections.abc` abstract base classes, we're making use of mixins to assure that cross-cutting aspects of the containers are defined consistently. The top-level collections (`Set`, `Sequence`, and `Mapping`) are all built from multiple mixins. It's very important to look at section 8.4 of the *Python Standard Library* to see how the mixins contribute features, as the overall structure is built up from pieces.

Looking at just one line, the summary of `Sequence`, we see that it inherits from `Sized`, `Iterable`, and `Container`. These mixin classes lead to methods of `__contains__()`, `__iter__()`, `__reversed__()`, `index()`, and `count()`.

Using the context manager mixin class

When we looked at context managers in *Chapter 5, Using Callables and Contexts*, we ignored the `ContextDecorator` mixin and focused on the special methods themselves. Using the mixin can make the definition clearer.

> In the previous version of the example, we created a context manager that altered a global state; it reset the random number seed. We'll rework that design to make a deck that can be its own context manager. When used as a context manager, it can generate a fixed sequence of cards. This isn't really the best way to unit test a deck of cards. However, it's a simple use of a context manager.

Defining context management as a mixin of an application class requires some care. We may have to redesign the initialization method to remove some assumptions. Our application classes may be used in the following two distinct ways:

- When used outside a `with` statement, the `__enter__()` and `__exit__()` methods will not be evaluated
- When used inside a `with` statement, the `__enter__()` and `__exit__()` methods will be evaluated

In our case, we can't assume that it's valid to evaluate the `shuffle()` method during `__init__()` processing because we don't know whether or not the context manager methods will be used. We can't defer shuffling to `__enter__()` because it may not be used. This complexity may indicate that we're offering too much flexibility. Either we have to shuffle lazily, just before the first `pop()`, or we have to provide a method function that can be turned off by a subclass. The following is a simple `Deck` definition that extends `list`:

```
class Deck( list ):
    def __init__( self, size=1 ):
        super().__init__()
        self.rng= random.Random()
        for d in range(size):
            cards = [ card(r,s) for r in range(13) for s in Suits ]
            super().extend( cards )
        self._init_shuffle()
    def _init_shuffle( self ):
        self.rng.shuffle( self )
```

We've defined this deck to have a removable `_init_shuffle()` method. A subclass can override this method to change when the shuffling is complete. A subclass of `Deck` can seed the random number generator before shuffling. This version of the class can avoid shuffling during creation. The following is a subclass of `Deck` that includes the `contextlib.ContextDecorator` mixin:

```
class TestDeck( ContextDecorator, Deck ):
    def __init__( self, size= 1, seed= 0 ):
        super().__init__( size=size )
        self.seed= seed
    def _init_shuffle( self ):
        """Don't shuffle during __init__."""
        pass
    def __enter__( self ):
        self.rng.seed( self.seed, version=1 )
        self.rng.shuffle( self )
        return self
    def __exit__( self, exc_type, exc_value, traceback ):
        pass
```

This subclass prevents shuffling during initialization by overriding the `_init_shuffle()` method. Because this mixes in `ContextDecorator`, it must also define `__enter__()` and `__exit__()`. This subclass of `Deck` can work in a `with` context. When used in a `with` statement, the random number seed is set, and the shuffling will use a known sequence. If it's used outside a `with` statement, then the shuffling will use the current random number settings and there will be no `__enter__()` evaluation.

The purpose of this style of programming is to separate the truly essential features of a class from other aspects of the Deck implementation. We have separated some of the random seed processing from other aspects of Deck. Clearly, we can simplify things a great deal if we simply insist that a context manager is required. This is not typical of the way the open() function works. However, it can be helpful simplification. We can use examples like the following to see the differences in behavior:

```
for i in range(3):
    d1= Deck(5)
    print( d1.pop(), d1.pop(), d1.pop() )
```

This example shows how Deck can be used by itself to generate randomized shuffles. This is the simple use of having Deck produce shuffled cards. The next example shows TestDeck with a given seed:

```
for i in range(3):
    with TestDeck(5, seed=0) as d2:
        print( d2.pop(), d2.pop(), d2.pop() )
```

This shows TestDeck, the subclass of Deck, which is used as a context manager to produce a known sequence of cards. Each time we invoke it, we get the same sequence of cards.

Turning off a class feature

We've turned off the shuffle-during-initialization feature by redefining a method function to have a body of pass. This process may seem a bit long winded to remove a feature from a subclass. There's an alternative to remove functionality in a subclass: to set the method name to be None. We can do this inside TestDeck to remove the initial shuffle:

```
_init_shuffle= None
```

The preceding code requires a little more programming in the superclass to tolerate the missing method, which is shown in the following snippet:

```
try:
    self._init_shuffle()
except AttributeError, TypeError:
    pass
```

This can be a somewhat more explicit way to remove a feature in a subclass definition. This shows that the method could be missing or has intentionally been set to `None`. Yet another alternative design is to move the call to `_init_shuffle()` from `__init__()` to the `__enter__()` method. This will require the use of a context manager that will make the object behave properly. That's not too odious a burden if it's documented clearly.

Writing a simple function decorator

A `decorator` function is a function (or a callable object) that returns a new function. The simplest case involves a single argument: the function that is to be decorated. The result of a decorator is a function that has been wrapped. Essentially, the additional features are put either before or after the original functionality. These are the two readily available join points in a function.

When we define a decorator, we want to be sure that the decorated function has the original function's name and `docstring`. These attributes should be set by a decorator, which we will use to write the decorated functions. Using `functools.wraps` to write new decorators simplifies the work we need to do because this bit of bookkeeping is handled for us.

To illustrate the two places where functionality can be inserted, we can create a debug trace decorator that will log parameters and return values from a function. This puts functionality both before and after the called function. The following is some defined function, `some_function`, that we want to wrap:

```
logging.debug( "function(", args, kw, ")" )
result= some_function( *args, **kw )
logging.debug( "result = ", result )
return result
```

This snippet shows how we'll have new processing to wrap the original function.

It's difficult to insert processing into a defined function by poking at the underlying `__code__` object. In the rare case where it seems necessary to inject an aspect in the middle of a function, it's much easier to rewrite the function as a callable object, by breaking the functionality down into multiple method functions. Then, we can use mixin and subclass definitions rather than complex code rewriting. The following is a debug decorator that inserts logging before and after function evaluation:

```
def debug( function ):
    @functools.wraps( function )
    def logged_function( *args, **kw ):
        logging.debug( "%s( %r, %r )", function.__name__, args, kw, )
        result= function( *args, **kw )
```

```
        logging.debug( "%s = %r", function.__name__, result )
        return result
    return logged_function
```

We've used the `functools.wraps` decorator to assure that the original function name and `docstring` are preserved in the result function. Now, we can use our decorator to produce noisy, detailed debugging. For example, we can do this to apply the decorator to some function, `ackermann()`, as follows:

```
@debug
def ackermann( m, n ):
    if m == 0: return n+1
    elif m > 0 and n == 0: return ackermann( m-1, 1 )
    elif m > 0 and n > 0: return ackermann( m-1, ackermann( m, n-1 ) )
```

This definition wraps the `ackermann()` function with debugging information written via the logging module to the `root` logger. We configure the logger to produce the following debugging output:

```
logging.basicConfig(stream=sys.stderr, level=logging.DEBUG)
```

We'll revisit logging in detail in *Chapter 14, The Logging and Warning Modules*. We'll see this kind of result when we evaluate `ackermann(2,4)`:

```
DEBUG:root:ackermann( (2, 4), {} )
DEBUG:root:ackermann( (2, 3), {} )
DEBUG:root:ackermann( (2, 2), {} )
.
.
.
DEBUG:root:ackermann( (0, 10), {} )
DEBUG:root:ackermann = 11
DEBUG:root:ackermann = 11
DEBUG:root:ackermann = 11
```

Creating separate loggers

As a logging optimization, we might want to use a specific logger for each wrapped function and not overuse the root logger for this kind of debugging output. We'll return to the logger in *Chapter 14, The Logging and Warning Modules*. The following is a version of our decorator that creates a separate logger for each individual function:

```
def debug2( function ):
    @functools.wraps( function )
    def logged_function( *args, **kw ):
        log= logging.getLogger( function.__name__ )
```

```
        log.debug( "call( %r, %r )", args, kw, )
        result= function( *args, **kw )
        log.debug( "result %r", result )
        return result
    return logged_function
```

This version modifies the output to look like the following:

```
DEBUG:ackermann:call( (2, 4), {} )
DEBUG:ackermann:call( (2, 3), {} )
DEBUG:ackermann:call( (2, 2), {} )
.
.
.
DEBUG:ackermann:call( (0, 10), {} )
DEBUG:ackermann:result 11
DEBUG:ackermann:result 11
DEBUG:ackermann:result 11
```

The function name is now the logger name. This can be used to fine-tune the debugging output. We can now enable logging for individual functions. We can't trivially change the decorator and expect the decorated function to also change.

We need to apply the revised decorator to the function. This means that debugging and experimenting with decorators can't be done *trivially* from the `>>>` interactive prompt. We have to reload the function definitions after we tweak the decorator definition. This can involve a bunch of copy and paste, or it can involve rerunning a script that defines the decorator, the functions, and then runs tests or a demonstration script to show that everything works as expected.

Parameterizing a decorator

Sometimes we want to provide more elaborate parameters to a decorator. The idea is that we are going to customize the wrapping function. When we do this, decoration becomes a two-step process.

When we write the following code, we provide a parameterized decorator to a function definition:

```
@decorator(arg)
def func( ):
    pass
```

The use of the decorator is a shorthand for the following code:

```
def func( ):
    pass
func= decorator(arg)(func)
```

Both examples do the following three things:

- Defined a function, `func`
- Applied the abstract decorator to its arguments to create a concrete decorator, `decorator(arg)`
- Applied the concrete decorator to the defined function to create the decorated version of the function, `decorator(arg)(func)`

This means that a decorator with arguments will require indirect construction of the final function. Let's tweak our debugging decorator yet again. We'd like to do the following:

```
@debug("log_name")
def some_function( args ):
    pass
```

This kind of code allows us to specifically name the log that the debugging output will go to. We don't use the root logger nor default to a distinct logger for each function. The outline of a parameterized decorator is something like the following:

```
def decorator(config):
    def concrete_decorator(function):
        @functools.wraps( function )
        def wrapped( *args, **kw ):
            return function( *args, ** kw )
        return wrapped
    return concrete_decorator
```

Let's peel back the layers of this onion before looking at the example. The decorator definition (`def decorator(config)`) shows the parameters we will provide to the decorator when we use it. The body of this is the concrete decorator, which is returned. The concrete decorator (`def concrete_decorator(function)`) is the decorator that will be applied to the target function. This, then, is just like the simple function decorator shown in the previous section. It builds the wrapped function (`def wrapped(*args, **kw)`), which it returns. The following is our named logger version of debug:

```
def debug_named(log_name):
    def concrete_decorator(function):
        @functools.wraps( function )
```

```
        def wrapped( *args, **kw ):
            log= logging.getLogger( log_name )
            log.debug( "%s( %r, %r )", function.__name__, args, kw, )
            result= function( *args, **kw )
            log.debug( "%s = %r", function.__name__, result )
            return result
        return wrapped
    return concrete_decorator
```

This `decorator` function accepts an argument that is the name of the log to use. It creates and returns a concrete decorator function. When this is applied to a function, the concrete decorator returns the wrapped version of the given function. When the function is used in the following manner, the decorator adds noisy debug lines. They direct the output to a log named `recursion` as follows:

```
@debug_named("recursion")
def ackermann( m, n ):
    if m == 0: return n+1
    elif m > 0 and n == 0: return ackermann( m-1, 1 )
    elif m > 0 and n > 0: return ackermann( m-1, ackermann( m, n-1 ) )
```

Creating a method function decorator

A decorator for a method function of a class definition is identical to a decorator for a standalone function. It's simply used in a different context. One small consequence of this different context is that we often must explicitly name the `self` variable.

One application for method function decoration is to produce an audit trail for object state change. Business applications often create stateful records; commonly, these are represented as rows in a relational database. We'll look at object representation in *Chapter 9, Serializing and Saving – JSON, YAML, Pickle, CSV, and XML, Chapter10, Storing and Retrieving Objects via Shelve*, and *Chapter 11, Storing and Retrieving Objects via SQLite*.

> When we have stateful records, the state changes need to be auditable. An audit can confirm that appropriate changes have been made to the records. In order to do the audit, the before and after version of each record must be available somewhere. Stateful database records are a long-standing tradition but are not in any way required. Immutable database records are a viable design alternative.

When we design a stateful class, any setter method we write will cause a state change. These setter methods often use the `@property` decorator so that they appear to be simple attributes. If we do this, we can fold in an `@audit` decorator that can track changes to the object, so that we have a proper trail of changes. We'll create an audit log via the `logging` module. We'll use the `__repr__()` method function to produce a complete text representation that can be used to examine changes. The following is an audit decorator:

```
def audit( method ):
    @functools.wraps(method)
    def wrapper( self, *args, **kw ):
        audit_log= logging.getLogger( 'audit' )
        before= repr(self)
        try:
            result= method( self, *args, **kw )
            after= repr(self)
        except Exception as e:
           audit_log.exception(
               '%s before %s\n after %s', method.__qualname__, before,
after )
           raise
        audit_log.info(
               '%s before %s\n after %s', method.__qualname__, before,
after )
        return result
    return wrapper
```

We've created a text memento of the *before* version of the object. Then, we've applied the original method function. If there was an exception, we would produce an audit log that includes the exception details. Otherwise, we'll produce an `INFO` entry in the log that has the qualified name of the method, the before memento, and the after memento of the object being changed. The following is a modification of the `Hand` class that shows how we'd use this decorator:

```
class Hand:
    def __init__( self, *cards ):
        self._cards = list(cards)
    @audit
    def __iadd__( self, card ):
        self._cards.append( card )
        return self
    def __repr__( self ):
        cards= ", ".join( map(str,self._cards) )
        return "{__class__.__name__}({cards})".format(__
class__=self.__class__, cards=cards)
```

This definition modifies the `__iadd__()` method function, so that adding a card becomes an auditable event. This decorator will perform the audit operation, saving text mementos of `Hand` before and after the operation.

This use of a method decorator makes a formal declaration that a particular method function has made a significant state change. We can easily use code reviews to be sure that all of the appropriate method functions are marked for audit like this. An open issue is auditing object creation. It's not perfectly clear that object creation requires an audit record. It can be argued that object creation is not a state change.

In the event that we want to audit creation, we can't use this `audit` decorator on the `__init__()` method function. That's because there's no before image prior to the execution of `__init__()`. There are two things we can do as a remedy to this, as follows:

- We can add a `__new__()` method that assures that an empty `_cards` attribute is seeded into the class as an empty collection
- We can tweak the `audit()` decorator to tolerate `AttributeError` that will arise when `__init__()` is being processed

The second option is considerably more flexible. We can do the following:

```
try:
    before= repr(self)
except AttributeError as e:
    before= repr(e)
```

This would record a message such as `AttributeError: 'Hand' object has no attribute '_cards'` for the before status during initialization.

Creating a class decorator

Analogous to decorating a function, we can write a class decorator to add features to a class definition. The essential rules are the same. The decorator is a function (or callable object). It receives a class object as an argument and returns a class object as a result.

We have a limited number of join points inside a class definition as a whole. For the most part, a class decorator will fold additional attributes into a class definition. It's technically possible to create a new class that wraps an original class definition. This is challenging, since the wrapping class must be very generalized. It's also possible to create a new class that is a subclass of the decorated class definition. This may be baffling to users of the decorator. It's also possible to delete features from a class definition, which seems perfectly awful.

One sophisticated class decorator was shown previously. The `functools.Total_Ordering` decorator injects a number of new method functions into the class definition. The technique used in this implementation is to create lambda objects and assign them to attributes of the class.

We'll look at a somewhat simpler decorator. During debugging and logging, we could have a small problem creating loggers that are focused on our classes. Often, we'd like to have a unique logger for each class. We're often forced to do something like the following:

```
class UglyClass1:
    def __init__( self ):
        self.logger= logging.getLogger(self.__class__.__qualname__)
        self.logger.info( "New thing" )
    def method( self, *args ):
        self.logger.info( "method %r", args )
```

This class has the disadvantage that it creates a `logger` instance variable that's really not part of the class's operation, but is a separate aspect of the class. We'd like to avoid polluting the class with this additional aspect. That's not all. Even though `logging.getLogger()` is very efficient, the cost's nonzero. We'd like to avoid this additional overhead every time we create an instance of `UglyClass1`.

Here's a slightly better version. The logger is promoted to be a class-level instance variable and is separate from each individual object of the class:

```
class UglyClass2:
    logger= logging.getLogger("UglyClass2")
    def __init__( self ):
        self.logger.info( "New thing" )
    def method( self, *args ):
        self.logger.info( "method %r", args )
```

This has the advantage that it implements `logging.getLogger()` just once. However, it suffers from a profound DRY problem. We can't automatically set the class name within the class definition. The class hasn't been created yet, so we're forced to repeat the name. The DRY problem is solved by a small decorator as follows:

```
def logged( class_ ):
    class_.logger= logging.getLogger( class_.__qualname__ )
    return class_
```

This decorator tweaks the class definition to add the `logger` reference as a class-level attribute. Now, each method can use `self.logger` to produce audit or debug information. When we want to use this feature, we can use the `@logged` decorator on the class as a whole. The following is an example of a logged class, `SomeClass`:

```
@logged
class SomeClass:
    def __init__( self ):
        self.logger.info( "New thing" )
    def method( self, *args ):
        self.logger.info( "method %r", args )
```

Now, our class has a `logger` attribute that can be used by any method. The logger value is not a feature of the object, which keeps this aspect separated from the rest of the class aspects. This attribute has the added benefit that it creates the logger instances during module import, reducing the overhead of logging slightly. Let's compare this with `UglyClass1`, where `logging.getLogger()` was evaluated for each instance creation.

Adding method functions to a class

A class decorator creates new method functions using a two-step process: by creating the method function and then inserting it into the class definition. This is often better done via a mixin class than a decorator. The obvious and expected use of a mixin is to insert methods. Inserting methods another way is less obvious and can be astonishing.

In the example of the `Total_Ordering` decorator, the exact method functions inserted were flexible and depended on what was already provided. This was a kind of special case that was typical but also very clever.

We might want to define a standardized `memento()` method. We'd like to include this standard method function in a variety of classes. We'll look at the decorator and mixin versions of this design. The following is the decorator version of adding a standard method:

```
def memento( class_ ):
    def memento( self ):
        return "{0.__class__.__qualname__}({0!r})".format(self)
    class_.memento= memento
    return class_
```

This decorator includes a method function definition that is inserted into the class. The following is how we use this `@memento` decorator to add a method function to a class:

```
@memento
class SomeClass:
    def __init__( self, value ):
        self.value= value
    def __repr__( self ):
        return "{0.value}".format(self)
```

The decorator incorporates a new method, `memento()`, into the decorated class. However, this has the following disadvantages:

- We can't override the implementation of the `memento()` method function to handle special cases. It's built into the class *after* the definition.
- We can't extend the decorator function easily. We'd have to upgrade to a callable object to provide extensions or specializations. If we're going to upgrade to a callable object, we should discard this whole approach and use a mixin to add the method.

The following is the mixin class that adds a standard method:

```
class Memento:
    def memento( self ):
        return "{0.__class__.__qualname__}({0!r})".format(self)
```

The following is how we use this `Memento` mixin class to define an application class:

```
class SomeClass2( Memento ):
    def __init__( self, value ):
        self.value= value
    def __repr__( self ):
        return "{0.value}".format(self)
```

The mixin provides a new method, `memento()`; this is the expected, typical purpose of a mixin. We can more easily extend the `Memento` mixin class to add features. In addition, we can override the `memento()` method function to handle special cases.

Using decorators for security

Software is filled with cross-cutting concerns, aspects that need to be implemented consistently even if they're in separate class hierarchies. It's often a mistake to try and impose a class hierarchy around a cross-cutting concern. We've looked at a few examples, such as logging and auditing.

We can't reasonably demand that every class that might need to write to the log also be a subclass of some `loggable` superclass. We can design a `loggable` mixin or a `loggable` decorator. These don't interfere with the proper inheritance hierarchy that we need to design to make polymorphism work correctly.

Some important cross-cutting concerns revolve around security. Within a web application, there are two sides to the security question as follows:

- **Authentication**: Do we know who's making the request?
- **Authorization**: Is the authenticated user allowed to make the request?

Some web frameworks allow us to decorate our request handlers with security requirements. The Django framework, for example, has a number of decorators that allow us to specify security requirements for a view function or a view class. Some of these decorators are as follows:

- `user_passes_test`: This is a low-level decorator that's very generalized and is used to build the other two decorators. It requires a test function; the logged-in `User` object associated with the request must pass the given function. If the `User` instance is not able to pass the given test, they're redirected to a login page so that the person can provide the credentials required to make the request.
- `login_required`: This decorator is based on `user_passes_test`. It confirms that the logged-in user is authenticated. This kind of decorator is used on web requests that apply to all people accessing the site. Requests such as changing a password or logging out, for example, shouldn't require any more specific permissions.
- `permission_required`: This decorator works with Django's internally defined database permission scheme. It confirms that the logged-in user (or the user's group) is associated with the given permission. This kind of decorator is used on web requests where specific administrative permissions are required to make the request.

Other packages and frameworks also have ways to express this cross-cutting aspect of web applications. In many cases, a web application may have even more stringent security considerations. We might have a web application where user features are selectively unlocked based on contract terms and conditions. Perhaps, additional fees will unlock a feature. We might have to design a test like the following:

```
def user_has_feature( feature_name ):
    def has_feature( user ):
        return feature_name in (f.name for f in user.feature_set())
    return user_passes_test( has_feature )
```

We've defined a function that checks the logged-in User feature_set collection to see if the named feature is associated with User. We've used our has_feature() function with Django's user_passes_test decorator to create a new decorator that can be applied to the relevant view functions. We can then create a view function as follows:

```
@user_has_feature( 'special_bonus' )
def bonus_view( request ):
    pass
```

This assures that the security concerns will be applied consistently across a number of view functions.

Summary

We've looked at using decorators to modify function and class definitions. We've also looked at mixins that allow us to decompose a larger class into components that are knitted together.

The idea of both of these techniques is to separate application-specific features from generic features such as security, audit, or logging. We're going to distinguish between the inherent features of a class and aspects that aren't inherent but are additional concerns. The inherent features are part of the explicit design. They're part of the inheritance hierarchy; they define what an object is. The other aspects can be mixins or decorations; they define how an object might also act.

Design considerations and trade-offs

In most cases, this division between *is-a* and *acts-as* is quite clear. Inherent features are a part of the overall problem domain. When talking about simulating Blackjack play, things such as cards, hands, betting, hitting, and standing are clearly part of the problem domain. Similarly, the data collection and statistical analysis of outcomes is part of the solution. Other things, such as logging, debugging, and auditing are not part of the problem domain but associated with solution technology.

While most cases are quite clear, the dividing line between inherent and decoration aspects can be fine. In some cases, it may devolve to an aesthetic judgment. Generally, the decision becomes difficult when writing framework and infrastructure classes that aren't focused on a specific problem. The general strategy is as follows:

- First, aspects that are central to the problem will lead directly to class definitions. Many classes are inherent to the problem and form proper class hierarchies so that polymorphism works as expected.

- Second, some aspects will lead to mixin class definitions. This often happens when there are aspects that are multidimensional. We might have independent axes or dimensions to a design. Each dimension can contribute polymorphic alternatives. When we look at Blackjack play, there are two kinds of strategies: play strategies and betting strategies. These are independent and might be considered the mixin elements of an overall player design.

When we define separate mixins, we can have separate inheritance hierarchies for the mixins. For Blackjack betting strategies, we can define a polymorphic hierarchy that's unrelated to the polymorphic hierarchy for play strategies. We can then define players that have mixin elements from both hierarchies.

Methods are generally created from class definitions. They're either part of the primary class or a mixin class. As noted above, we have three design strategies: Wrap, Extend, and Invent. We can introduce functionality through "wrapping" a class with another class. In some cases, we find that we're forced to expose a large number of methods that are simply delegated to the underlying class. There's a hazy boundary where we have too much delegation; a decorator or mixin would have been a better idea. In other cases, wrapping a class may be clearer than introducing a mixin class definition.

Aspects that are orthogonal to the problem can often be handled by decorator definitions. The decorators can be used to introduce features that are not part of the *is-a* relationship that an object has with its class.

Looking forward

The coming chapters will change direction. We've seen almost all of Python's special method names. The next five chapters are going to focus on object persistence and serialization. We'll start out with serializing and saving objects in various external notations, including JSON, YAML, Pickle, CSV, and XML.

Serialization and persistence introduce yet more object-oriented design considerations for our classes. We'll have a look at object relationships and how they're represented. We'll also have a look at the cost complexity of serializing and deserializing objects, and at the security issues related to the de-serialization of objects from untrustworthy sources.

Part 2

Persistence and Serialization

Serializing and Saving – JSON, YAML, Pickle, CSV, and XML

Storing and Retrieving Objects via Shelve

Storing and Retrieving objects via SQLite

Transmitting and Sharing Objects

Configuration Files and Persistence

Persistence and Serialization

A persistent object is one that has been written to some storage medium. The object can be retrieved from storage and used in a Python application. Perhaps the object was represented in JSON and written to the filesystem. Perhaps an **object-relational mapping (ORM)** layer has represented the object as rows in SQL tables to store the object in a database.

Serializing objects has two purposes. We serialize objects in order to make them persistent in the local filesystem. We also serialize objects in order to exchange objects between processes or applications. While the focus is different, persistence generally includes serialization; so, a good persistence technique will also work for data interchange. We'll look at several ways in which Python handles serialization and persistence. The chapters in this part are organized as follows:

- *Chapter 9, Serializing and Saving – JSON, YAML, Pickle, CSV, and XML*, covers simple persistence using libraries focused on various data representations: JSON, YAML, pickle, XML, and CSV. These are common, widely used formats for Python data. They're suitable for persistence as well as data exchange. They tend to focus more on a single object rather than a large domain of objects.
- *Chapter 10, Storing and Retrieving Objects via Shelve*, covers basic database operations with Python modules such as Shelve (and dBm) in. These provide simple storage of Python objects and are focused on the persistence of multiple objects.
- *Chapter 11, Storing and Retrieving objects via SQLite*, moves to the more complex world of SQL and the relational database. Because SQL features don't match object-oriented programming features well, we have an impedance mismatch problem. A common solution is to use Object-Relational Mapping to allow us to persist a large domain of objects.

- For web applications, we'll often work with **Representation State Transfer (REST)**. *Chapter 12, Transmitting and Sharing Objects*, will look at the HTTP protocol, JSON, YAML, and XML representation for transmitting an object.
- Finally, *Chapter 13, Configuration Files and Persistence*, will cover various ways in which a Python application can work with a configuration file. There are a number of formats and a number of advantages and disadvantages to each. A configuration file is simply a collection of persistent objects that can be easily modified by a human user.

Important topics that arise throughout this part are the design patterns that are used at a higher level of abstraction. We'll call these architectural patterns because they describe the overall architecture of an application, separating it into layers or tiers. We are forced to break an application into pieces so that we can practice the principle that is often articulated as **Separation of Concerns**. We'll need to separate persistence from other features such as the core processing of our application and the presentation of data to users. Mastering object-oriented design means looking at higher-level, architectural design patterns.

9
Serializing and Saving – JSON, YAML, Pickle, CSV, and XML

To make a Python object persistent, we must convert it to bytes and write the bytes to a file. We'll call this **serialization**; it is also called marshaling, deflating or encoding. We'll look at several ways to convert a Python object to a string or a stream of bytes.

Each of these serialization schemes can also be called a **physical data format**. Each format offers some advantages and disadvantages. There's no *best* format to represent the objects. We must distinguish a **logical data format**, which may be a simple reordering or change in the use of whitespace that doesn't change the value of the object but changes the sequence of bytes.

It's important to note that (except for CSV) these representations are biased towards representing a single Python object. While that single object can be the list of objects, it's still list of a fixed size. In order to process one of the objects, the entire list must be de-serialized. There are ways to perform incremental serialization, but they involve extra work. Rather than fiddling with these formats to handle multiple objects, there are better approaches to process many distinct objects in *Chapters 10, Storing and Retrieving Objects via Shelve, Chapter 11, Storing and Retrieving objects via SQLite*, and *Chapter 12, Transmitting and Sharing Objects.*

As each of these schemes is focused on a single object, we're limited to objects that fit in the memory. When we need to process a large number of distinct items, not all of which can be in memory at once, we can't use these techniques directly; we'll need to move to a larger database, server, or message queue. We'll look at the following serialization representations:

- **JavaScript Object Notation (JSON)**: This is a widely used representation. For more information, see `http://www.json.org`. The `json` module provides the classes and functions necessary to load and dump data in this format. In *Python Standard Library*, look at section 19, *Internet Data Handling*, not section 12, *Persistence*. The `json` module is focused narrowly on the JSON representation more than the more general problem of Python object persistence.
- **YAML Ain't Markup Language (YAML)**: This is an extension to JSON and can lead to some simplification of the serialized output. For more information, see `http://yaml.org`. This is not a standard part of the Python library; we must add a module to handle this. The `PyYaml` package, specifically, has numerous Python persistence features.
- **pickle**: The `pickle` module has its own Python-specific representation for data. As this is a first-class part of the Python library, we'll closely look at how to serialize an object this way. This has the disadvantage of being a poor format for the interchange of data with non-Python programs. It's the basis for the `shelve` module in *Chapter 10, Storing and Retrieving Objects via Shelve*, as well as message queues in *Chapter 12, Transmitting and Sharing Objects*.
- **The Comma-Separated Values (CSV) module**: This can be inconvenient for representing complex Python objects. As it's so widely used, we'll need to work out ways to serialize Python objects in the CSV notation. For references, look at section 14, *File Formats*, of *Python Standard Library*, not section 12, *Persistence*, because it's simply a file format and little more. CSV allows us to perform an incremental representation of the Python object collections that cannot fit into memory.
- **XML**: In spite of some disadvantages, this is very widely used, so it's important to be able to convert objects into an XML notation and recover objects from an XML document. XML parsing is a huge subject. The reference material is in section 20, *Structured Markup Processing Tools*, of *Python Standard Library*. There are many modules to parse XML, each with different advantages and disadvantages. We'll focus on `ElementTree`.

Beyond these simple categories, we can also have hybrid problems. One example is a spreadsheet encoded in XML. This means that we have a row-and-column data representation problem wrapped in the XML parsing problem. This leads to more complex software to disentangle the various kinds of data that were flattened to CSV-like rows so that we can recover useful Python objects. In *Chapter 12, Transmitting and Sharing Objects*, and *Chapter 13, Configuration Files and Persistence*, we'll revisit a number of these topics as we use RESTful web services with serialized objects as well as editable serialized objects for configuration files.

Understanding persistence, class, state, and representation

Primarily, our Python objects exist in volatile computer memory. They can only live as long as the Python process is running. They may not even live that long; they may only live as long as they have references in a namespace. If we want an object that outlives the Python process or namespace, we need to make it persistent.

Most operating systems offer persistent storage in the form of a filesystem. This usually includes disk drives, flash drives, or other forms of non-volatile storage. It seems like it's simply a matter of transferring bytes from the memory to a disk file.

The complexity arises because our in-memory Python objects have references to other objects. An object refers to its class. The class refers to its metaclass and any base classes. The object might be a container and refer to other objects. The in-memory version of an object is a web of references and relationships. As the memory locations are not fixed, the relationships would be broken by trying simply to dump and restore memory bytes without rewriting addresses into some kind of location-independent key.

Many of the objects in the web of references are largely static—class definitions, for example, change very slowly compared to variables. Ideally, a class definition doesn't change at all. However, we may have class-level instance variables. More importantly, we need to upgrade our application software, changing class definitions, which changes object features. We'll call this the **Schema Migration Problem**, managing change to the schema (or class) of our data.

Python gives us a formal distinction between the instance variables of an object and other attributes that are part of the class. Our design decisions leverage this distinction. We define an object's instance variables to properly show the dynamic state of the object. We use class-level attributes for information that objects of that class will share. If we can persist only the dynamic state of an object—separated from the class and the web of references that are part of the class definition—that would be a workable solution to serialization and persistence.

We don't actually have to do anything to persist our class definitions; we already have an entirely separate and very simple method for that. Class definitions exist primarily as source code. The class definition in the volatile memory is rebuilt from the source (or the byte-code version of the source) every time it's needed. If we need to exchange class definition, we exchange Python modules or packages.

Common Python terminologies

Python terminology tends to focus on the words *dump* and *load*. Most of the various classes we're going to work will define methods such as the following:

- `dump(object, file)`: This will dump the given object to the given file
- `dumps(object)`: This will dump an object, returning a string representation
- `load(file)`: This will load an object from the given file, returning the constructed object
- `loads(string)`: This will load an object from a string representation, returning the constructed object

There's no standard; the method names aren't *guaranteed* by any formal ABC inheritance or the mixin class definition. However, they're widely used. Generally, the file used for the dump or load can be any *file-like* object. A short list of methods such as `read()` and `readline()` are required for the load, but we need little more than this. We can, therefore, use the `io.StringIO` objects as well as the `urllib.request` objects as sources for the load. Similarly, dump places few requirements on the data source. We'll dig into these file object considerations next.

Filesystem and network considerations

As the OS filesystem (and network) works in bytes, we need to represent the values of an object's instance variables as a serialized stream of bytes. Often, we'll use a two-step transformation to bytes; we'll represent the state of an object as a string and rely on the Python string to provide bytes in a standard encoding. Python's built-in features for encoding a string into bytes neatly solves this part of the problem.

When we look at our OS filesystems, we see two broad classes of devices: block-mode devices and character-mode devices. Block-mode devices can also be called *seekable* because the OS supports a seek operation that can access any byte in the file in an arbitrary order. Character-mode devices are not seekable; they are interfaces where bytes are transmitted serially. Seeking would involve travelling backwards in time.

This distinction between `character` and block mode can have an impact on how we represent the state of a complex object or a collection of objects. The serializations we'll look at in this chapter focus on the simplest common feature set: an ordered stream of bytes; these formats make no use of seekable devices; they will save the stream of bytes into either character-mode or block-mode block-mode file.

The formats we'll look at in *Chapter 10, Storing and Retrieving Objects via Shelve*, and *Chapter 11, Storing and Retrieving Objects via SQLite*, however, will require block-mode storage in order to encode more objects than could possibly fit into memory. The `shelve` module and the `SQLite` database make extensive use of seekable files.

A minor confounding factor is the way that the OS unifies block- and character-mode devices into a single filesystem metaphor. Some parts of the Python Standard Library implement the lowest-common feature set between the block and character devices. When we use Python's `urllib.request`, we can access the network resources, as well as local files for the data. When we open a local file, this module must impose the limited character-mode interface on an otherwise seekable kind of file.

Defining classes to support persistence

Before we can work with persistence, we need some objects that we want to save. There are several design considerations related to persistence, so we'll start with some simple class definitions. We'll look at a simple microblog and the posts on that blog. Here's a class definition for `Post`:

```
import datetime
class Post:
    def __init__( self, date, title, rst_text, tags ):
        self.date= date
        self.title= title
```

```
        self.rst_text= rst_text
        self.tags= tags
    def as_dict( self ):
        return dict(
            date= str(self.date),
            title= self.title,
            underline= "-"*len(self.title),
            rst_text= self.rst_text,
            tag_text= " ".join(self.tags),
        )
```

The instance variables are the attributes of each microblog post: a date, a title, some text, and some tags. Our attribute name provides us a hint that the text should be in RST markup, even though that's largely irrelevant to the rest of the data model.

To support simple substitution into templates, the `as_dict()` method returns a dictionary of values that have been converted into string format. We'll look at the template processing using `string.Template` later.

Additionally, we've added a few values to help with creating the RST output. The `tag_text` attribute is a flattened text version of the tuple of tag values. The `underline` attribute produces an underline string with a length that matches the title string; this helps the RST formatting work out nicely. We'll also create a blog as a collection of posts. We'll make this collection more than a simple list by including an additional attribute of a title. We have three choices for the collection design: wrap, extend, or invent a new class. We'll head off some confusion by providing this warning: don't extend a `list` if you intend to make it persistent.

> **Extending an iterable object can be confusing**
>
> When we extend a sequence, we might confuse some of the built-in serialization algorithms. The built-in algorithms may wind up bypassing the extended features we put in a subclass of a sequence. Wrapping a sequence is usually a better idea than extending one.

This forces us to look at wrapping or inventing. It's a simple sequence, so why invent something new? Wrapping is what we'll emphasize on as a design strategy. Here's a collection of microblog posts. We've wrapped a list, as extending a list won't always work well:

```
from collections import defaultdict
class Blog:
    def __init__( self, title, posts=None ):
        self.title= title
```

```
        self.entries= posts if posts is not None else []
    def append( self, post ):
        self.entries.append(post)
    def by_tag(self):
        tag_index= defaultdict(list)
        for post in self.entries:
            for tag in post.tags:
                tag_index[tag].append( post.as_dict() )
        return tag_index
    def as_dict( self ):
        return dict(
            title= self.title,
            underline= "="*len(self.title),
            entries= [p.as_dict() for p in self.entries],
        )
```

In addition to wrapping the list, we've also included an attribute that is the title of the microblog. The initializer uses a common technique to avoid providing a mutable object as a default value. We've provided `None` as the default value for `posts`. If `posts` is `None`, we use a freshly-minted empty list, `[]`. Otherwise, we use the given value for posts.

Additionally, we've defined a method that indexes the posts by their tags. In the resulting `defaultdict`, each key is a tag's text. Each value is a list of posts that share the given tag.

To simplify the use of `string.Template`, we've added another `as_dict()` method that boils the entire blog down to a simple dictionary of strings and dictionaries. The idea here is to produce only built-in types that have simple string representations. We'll show you the template rendering process next. Here's some sample data:

```
travel = Blog( "Travel" )
travel.append(
    Post( date=datetime.datetime(2013,11,14,17,25),
        title="Hard Aground",
        rst_text="""Some embarrassing revelation.
          Including ☹ and ⚓""",
        tags=("#RedRanger", "#Whitby42", "#ICW"),
        )
)
travel.append(
    Post( date=datetime.datetime(2013,11,18,15,30),
        title="Anchor Follies",
```

```
        rst_text="""Some witty epigram. Including < & >
characters.""",,
        tags=("#RedRanger", "#Whitby42", "#Mistakes"),
        )
)
```

We've serialized the `Blog` and `Post` as the Python code. This isn't really all bad as a way to represent the blog. There are some use cases where Python code is a perfectly fine representation for an object. In *Chapter 13, Configuration Files and Persistence*, we'll look more closely at simply using Python to encode data.

Rendering a blog and posts

Just to be complete, here's a way to render the blog into RST. From this output file, the docutils `rst2html.py` tool can transform the RST output into the final HTML file. This saves us from having to digress into HTML and CSS. Also, we're going to use RST to write the documentation in *Chapter 18, Quality and Documentation* For more information on docutils, see *Some Preliminaries*.

We can use the `string.Template` class to do this. However, it's clunky and complex. There are a number of add-on template tools that can perform a more sophisticated substitution, including loops and conditional processing within the template itself. Here's a list of alternatives: `https://wiki.python.org/moin/Templating`. We're going to show you an example using the Jinja2 template tool. See `https://pypi.python.org/pypi/Jinja2`. Here's a script to render this data in RST using a template:

```
from jinja2 import Template
blog_template= Template( """
{{title}}
{{underline}}

{% for e in entries %}
{{e.title}}
{{e.underline}}

{{e.rst_text}}

:date: {{e.date}}

:tags: {{e.tag_text}}
{% endfor %}
```

```
Tag Index
=========
{% for t in tags %}

*   {{t}}
    {% for post in tags[t] %}

    -   `{{post.title}}`_
    {% endfor %}
{% endfor %}
""")
print( blog_template.render( tags=travel.by_tag(), **travel.as_dict()
) )
```

The `{{title}}` and `{{underline}}` elements (and all similar elements) show us how values are substituted into the text of the template. The `render()` method is called with `**travel.as_dict()` to ensure that attributes such as `title` and `underline` will be keyword arguments.

The `{%for%}` and `{%endfor%}` constructs show us how Jinja can iterate through the sequence of `Post` entries in `Blog`. Within the body of this loop, the variable `e` will be the dictionary created from each `Post`. We've picked specific keys out of the dictionary for each post: `{{e.title}}`, `{{e.rst_text}}`, and so on.

We also iterated through a `tags` collection for the `Blog`. This is a dictionary with the keys of each tag and the posts for the tag. The loop will visit each key, assigned to `t`. The body of the loop will iterate through the posts in the dictionary value, `tags[t]`.

The `` `{{post.title}}`_ `` construct is an RST markup that generates a link to the section that has that title within the document. This kind of very simple markup is one of the strengths of RST. We've used the blog titles as sections and links within the index. This means that the titles *must* be unique or we'll get RST rendering errors.

Because this template iterates through a given blog, it will render all of the posts in one smooth motion. The `string.Template`, which is built-in to Python, can't iterate. This makes it a bit more complex to render all of the `Posts` of a `Blog`.

Dumping and loading with JSON

What is JSON? A section from the `www.json.org` web page states that:

> *JSON (JavaScript Object Notation) is a lightweight data-interchange format. It is easy for humans to read and write. It is easy for machines to parse and generate. It is based on a subset of the JavaScript Programming Language, Standard ECMA-262 3rd Edition - December 1999. JSON is a text format that is completely language independent but uses conventions that are familiar to programmers of the C-family of languages, including C, C++, C#, Java, JavaScript, Perl, Python, and many others. These properties make JSON an ideal data-interchange language.*

This format is used by a broad spectrum of languages and frameworks. Databases such as CouchDB represent their data as JSON objects, simplifying the transmission of data between applications. JSON documents have the advantage of looking vague like Python `list` and `dict` literal values. They're easy to read and easy to edit manually.

The `json` module works with the built-in Python types. It does not work with classes defined by us until we take some additional steps. We'll look at these extension techniques next. For the following Python types, there's a mapping to JavaScript types that JSON uses:

Python type	JSON
`dict`	`object`
`list, tuple`	`array`
`str`	`string`
`int, float`	`number`
`True`	`true`
`False`	`false`
`None`	`null`

Other types are not supported and must be coerced to one of these via the extension functions that we can plug into the dump and load functions. We can explore these built-in types by transforming our microblog objects into simpler Python `lists` and `dicts`. When we look at our `Post` and `Blog` class definitions, we have already defined the `as_dict()` methods that reduce our custom class objects to built-in Python objects. Here's the code required to produce a JSON version of our blog data:

```
import json
print( json.dumps(travel.as_dict(), indent=4) )
```

Here's the output:

```
{
    "entries": [
        {
            "title": "Hard Aground",
            "underline": "------------",
            "tag_text": "#RedRanger #Whitby42 #ICW",
            "rst_text": "Some embarrassing revelation. Including \
u2639 and \u2693",
            "date": "2013-11-14 17:25:00"
        },
        {
            "title": "Anchor Follies",
            "underline": "--------------",
            "tag_text": "#RedRanger #Whitby42 #Mistakes",
            "rst_text": "Some witty epigram. Including < & >
characters.",
            "date": "2013-11-18 15:30:00"
        }
    ],
    "title": "Travel"
}
```

The preceding output shows us how each of the various objects are translated from Python to the JSON notation. What's elegant about this is that our Python objects have been written into a standardized notation. We can share them with other applications. We can write them to disk files and preserve them. There are several unpleasant features of the JSON representation:

- We had to rewrite our Python objects into dictionaries. It would be much nicer to transform Python objects more simply, without explicitly creating additional dictionaries.
- We can't rebuild our original `Blog` and `Post` objects easily when we load this JSON representation. When we use `json.load()`, we won't get `Blog` or `Post` objects; we'll just get `dict` and list objects. We need to provide some additional hints to rebuild the `Blog` and `Post` objects.
- There are some values in the object's `__dict__` that we'd rather not persist, such as the underlined text for a `Post`.

We need something more sophisticated than the built-in JSON encoding.

Supporting JSON in our classes

In order to properly support JSON, we need to inform the JSON encoders and decoders about our classes. For encoding our objects into JSON, we need to provide a function that will reduce our objects to Python primitive types. This is called a *default* function; it provides a default encoding for an object of an unknown class.

To decode our objects from JSON, we need to provide a function that will transform a dictionary of Python primitive types back into an object of the proper class. This is called the *object hook* function; it's used to transform `dict` to an object of a customized class.

The `json` module documentation suggests that we might want to make use of class hinting. The Python documentation includes a reference to the JSON-RPC version 1 specification. See `http://json-rpc.org/wiki/specification`. This suggestion is to encode an instance of a customized class as a dictionary like the following:

```
{"__jsonclass__": ["class name", [param1,...]] }
```

The suggested value associated with the `"__jsonclass__"` key is a list of two items: the class name and a list of arguments required to create an instance of that class. The specification allows for more features, but they're not relevant to Python.

To decode an object from a JSON dictionary, we can look for the `"__jsonclass__"` key as a hint that one of our classes needs to be built, not a built-in Python object. The class name can be mapped to a class object and the argument sequence can be used to build the instance.

When we look at other sophisticated JSON encoders (such as the one that comes with the Django Web framework), we can see that they provide a bit more complex encoding of a custom class. They include the class, a database primary key, and the attribute values. We'll look at how we implement customized encoding and decoding. The rules are represented as simple functions that are plugged into the JSON encoding and decoding functions.

Customizing JSON encoding

For class hinting, we'll provide three pieces of information. We'll include a `__class__` key that names the target class. The `__args__` key will provide a sequence of positional argument values. A `__kw__` key will provide a dictionary of keyword argument values. This will cover all the options of `__init__()`. Here's an encoder that follows this design:

```
def blog_encode( object ):
    if isinstance(object, datetime.datetime):
        return dict(
            __class__= "datetime.datetime",
            __args__= [],
            __kw__= dict(
                year= object.year,
                month= object.month,
                day= object.day,
                hour= object.hour,
                minute= object.minute,
                second= object.second,
            )
        )
    elif isinstance(object, Post):
        return dict(
            __class__= "Post",
            __args__= [],
            __kw__= dict(
                date= object.date,
                title= object.title,
                rst_text= object.rst_text,
                tags= object.tags,
            )
        )
    elif isinstance(object, Blog):
        return dict(
            __class__= "Blog",
            __args__= [
                object.title,
                object.entries,
            ],
            __kw__= {}
        )
    else:
        return json.JSONEncoder.default(o)
```

This function shows us two different flavors of object encodings for the three classes:

- We encoded a `datetime.datetime` object as a dictionary of individual fields
- We also encoded a `Post` instance as a dictionary of individual fields
- We encoded a `Blog` instance as a sequence of title and post entries

If we can't process the class, we invoke the existing encoder's default encoding. This will handle the built-in classes. We can use this function to encode as follows:

```
text= json.dumps(travel, indent=4, default=blog_encode)
```

We provided our function, `blog_encode()`, as the `default=` keyword parameter to the `json.dumps()` function. This function is used by the JSON encoder to determine the encoding for an object. This encoder leads to JSON objects that look like the following code:

```
{
    "__args__": [
        "Travel",
        [
            {
                "__args__": [],
                "__kw__": {
                    "tags": [
                        "#RedRanger",
                        "#Whitby42",
                        "#ICW"
                    ],
                    "rst_text": "Some embarrassing revelation.
Including \u2639 and \u2693",
                    "date": {
                        "__args__": [],
                        "__kw__": {
                            "minute": 25,
                            "hour": 17,
                            "day": 14,
                            "month": 11,
                            "year": 2013,
                            "second": 0
                        },
                        "__class__": "datetime.datetime"
                    },
                    "title": "Hard Aground"
                },
```

```
                "__class__": "Post"
            },
    .
    .
    .
    "__kw__": {},
    "__class__": "Blog"
}
```

We've taken out the second blog entry because the output was rather long. A `Blog` object is now wrapped with a `dict` that provides the class and two positional argument values. The `Post` and `datetime` objects, similarly, are wrapped with the class name and the keyword argument values.

Customizing JSON decoding

In order to decode a JSON object, we need to work within the structure of a JSON parsing. Objects of our customized class definitions were encoded as simple `dicts`. This means that each `dict` decoded by the JSON decoder *could* be one of our customized classes. Or, `dict` could just be a `dict`.

The JSON decoder "object hook" is a function that's invoked for each `dict` to see if it represents a customized object. If `dict` isn't recognized by the `hook` function, then it's just a dictionary and should be returned without modification. Here's our object hook function:

```
def blog_decode( some_dict ):
    if set(some_dict.keys()) == set( ["__class__", "__args__", "__
kw__"] ):
        class_= eval(some_dict['__class__'])
        return class_( *some_dict['__args__'], **some_dict['__kw__'] )
    else:
        return some_dict
```

Each time this function is invoked, it checks for the keys that define an encoding of our objects. If the three keys are present, then the given function is called with the arguments and keywords. We can use this object hook to parse a JSON object as follows:

```
blog_data= json.loads(text, object_hook= blog_decode)
```

This will decode a block of text, encoded in a JSON notation, using our `blog_decode()` function to transform `dict` into proper `Blog` and `Post` objects.

The security and the eval() issue

Some programmers will object to the use of the `eval()` function in our `blog_decode()` function, claiming that it is a pervasive security problem. What's silly is the claim that `eval()` is a pervasive problem. It's a *potential* security problem if malicious code is written into the JSON representation of an object by some **Evil Genius Programmer (EGP)**. A local EGP has access to the Python source. Why mess with subtle tweaking JSON files? Why not just edit the Python source?

As a pragmatic issue, we have to look at transmission of the JSON documents through the Internet; this is an actual security problem. However, it does not indict `eval()` in general.

Some provision must be made for a situation where an untrustworthy document has been tweaked by a **Man In The Middle** attack. In this case, a JSON document is doctored while passing through a web interface that includes an untrustworthy server acting as a proxy. SSL is usually the preferred method to prevent this problem.

If necessary, we can replace `eval()` with a dictionary that maps from name to class. We can change `eval(some_dict['__class__'])` to `{"Post":Post, "Blog":Blog, "datetime.datetime":datetime.datetime`:

```
}[some_dict['__class__']]
```

This will prevent problems in the event that a JSON document is passed through a non-SSL-encoded connection. It also leads to a maintenance requirement to tweak this mapping each time the application design changes.

Refactoring the encode function

Ideally, we'd like to refactor our encoding function to focus on the responsibility for proper encoding on each defining class. We'd rather not pile all of the encoding rules into a separate function.

To do this with library classes such as `datetime`, we would need to extend `datetime.datetime` for our application. If we did that, we would need to be sure that our application used our extended `datetime` instead of the `datetime` library. This can become a bit of a headache to avoid using the built-in `datetime` classes. Often, we have to strike a balance between our customized classes and library classes. Here are two class extensions that will create JSON-encodable class definitions. We can add a property to `Blog`:

```
@property
def _json( self ):
    return dict( __class__= self.__class__.__name__,
```

```
            __kw__= {},
            __args__= [ self.title, self.entries ]
        )
```

This property will provide initialization arguments that are usable by our decoding function. We can add these two properties to `Post`:

```
    @property
    def _json( self ):
        return dict(
            __class__= self.__class__.__name__,
            __kw__= dict(
                date= self.date,
                title= self.title,
                rst_text= self.rst_text,
                tags= self.tags,
            ),
            __args__= []
        )
```

As with `Blog`, this property will provide initialization arguments that are usable by our decoding function. We can modify the encoder to make it somewhat simpler. Here's a revised version:

```
def blog_encode_2( object ):
    if isinstance(object, datetime.datetime):
        return dict(
            __class__= "datetime.datetime",
            __args__= [],
            __kw__= dict(
                year= object.year,
                month= object.month,
                day= object.day,
                hour= object.hour,
                minute= object.minute,
                second= object.second,
            )
        )
    else:
        try:
            encoding= object._json()
        except AttributeError:
            encoding= json.JSONEncoder.default(o)
        return encoding
```

We're still constrained by our choice to use the library `datetime` module. In this example, we elected not to introduce subclasses but handle the encoding as a special case, rather.

Standardizing the date string

Our formatting of dates doesn't make use of the widely-used ISO standard text format for dates. To be more compatible with other languages, we should properly encode the `datetime` object in a standard string and parse a standard string.

As we're already treating dates as a special case, this seems to be a sensible extension of that special case treatment. It can be done without too much change to our encoding and decoding. Consider this small change to the encoding:

```
if isinstance(object, datetime.datetime):
    fmt= "%Y-%m-%dT%H:%M:%S"
    return dict(
        __class__= "datetime.datetime.strptime",
        __args__= [ object.strftime(fmt), fmt ],
        __kw__= {}
    )
```

The encoded output names the static method `datetime.datetime.strptime()` and provides the argument encoded `datetime` as well as the format to be used to decode it. The output for a post now looks like the following snippet:

```
{
    "__args__": [],
    "__class__": "Post_J",
    "__kw__": {
        "title": "Anchor Follies",
        "tags": [
            "#RedRanger",
            "#Whitby42",
            "#Mistakes"
        ],
        "rst_text": "Some witty epigram.",
        "date": {
            "__args__": [
                "2013-11-18T15:30:00",
                "%Y-%m-%dT%H:%M:%S"
            ],
```

```
                    "__class__": "datetime.datetime.strptime",
                    "__kw__": {}
                }
            }
        }
```

This shows us that we now have an ISO-formatted date instead of individual fields. We've also moved away from the object creation using a class name. The `__class__` value is expanded to be a class name or a static method name.

Writing JSON to a file

When we write JSON files, we generally do something like this:

```
with open("temp.json", "w", encoding="UTF-8") as target:
    json.dump( travel3, target, separators=(',', ':'), default=blog_
j2_encode )
```

We open the file with the required encoding. We provide the file object to the `json.dump()` method. When we read JSON files, we will use a similar technique:

```
with open("some_source.json", "r", encoding="UTF-8") as source:
    objects= json.load( source, object_hook= blog_decode)
```

The idea is to segregate the JSON representation as text from any conversion to bytes on the resulting file. There are a few formatting options that are available in JSON. We've shown you an indent of four spaces because that seems to produce nice-looking JSON. As an alternative, we can make the output more compact by leaving the indent option. We can compact it even further by making the separators more terse. The following is the output created in `temp.json`:


```
{"__class__":"Blog_J","__args__":["Travel",[{"__class__":"Post_J","__
args__":[],"__kw__":{"rst_text":"Some embarrassing revelati
on.","tags":["#RedRanger","#Whitby42","#ICW"],"title":"Hard
Aground","date":{"__class__":"datetime.datetime.strptime","__
args__":["2013-11-14T17:25:00","%Y-%m-%dT%H:%M:%S"],"__
kw__":{}}}},{"__class__":"Post_J","__args__":[],"__kw__":{"rst_
text":"Some witty epigram.","tags":["#RedRanger","#Whitby42","#Mistak
es"],"title":"Anchor Follies","date":{"__class__":"datetime.datetime.
strptime","__args__":["2013-11-18T15:30:00","%Y-%m-%dT%H:%M:%S"],"__
kw__":{}}}}]],"__kw__":{}}
```

Dumping and loading with YAML

The `yaml.org` web page states that:

> *YAML™ (rhymes with "camel") is a human-friendly, cross language, Unicode-based data serialization language designed around the common native data types of agile programming languages.*

The Python Standard Library documentation for the `json` module states that:

> *JSON is a subset of YAML 1.2. The JSON produced by this module's default settings (in particular, the default separators value) is also a subset of YAML 1.0 and 1.1. This module can thus also be used as a YAML serializer.*

Technically, then, we can prepare YAML data using the `json` module. However, the `json` module cannot be used to de-serialize more sophisticated YAML data. There are two benefits of YAML. First, it's a more sophisticated notation, allowing us to encode additional details about our objects. Second, the PyYAML implementation has a deep level of integration with Python that allows us to very simply create YAML encodings of Python objects. The drawback of YAML is that it is not as widely used as JSON. We'll need to download and install a YAML module. A good one can be found at `http://pyyaml.org/wiki/PyYAML`. Once we've installed the package, we can dump our objects in the YAML notation:

```
import yaml
text= yaml.dump(travel2)
print( text )
```

Here's what the YAML encoding for our microblog looks like:


```
!!python/object:__main__.Blog
entries:
- !!python/object:__main__.Post
  date: 2013-11-14 17:25:00
  rst_text: Some embarrassing revelation. Including ☹ and □
  tags: !!python/tuple ['#RedRanger', '#Whitby42', '#ICW']
  title: Hard Aground
- !!python/object:__main__.Post
  date: 2013-11-18 15:30:00
  rst_text: Some witty epigram. Including < & > characters.
  tags: !!python/tuple ['#RedRanger', '#Whitby42', '#Mistakes']
  title: Anchor Follies
```

The output is relatively terse but also delightfully complete. Also, we can easily edit the YAML file to make updates. The class names are encoded with a YAML `!!` tag. YAML contains 11 standard tags. The `yaml` module includes a dozen Python-specific tags, plus five *complex* Python tags.

The Python class names are qualified by the defining module. In our case, the module happened to be a simple script, so the class names are `__main__.Blog` and `__main__.Post`. If we had imported these from another module, the class names would reflect the module that defined the classes.

Items in a list are shown in a block sequence form. Each item starts with a `-` sequence; the rest of the items are indented with two spaces. When `list` or `tuple` is small enough, it can flow onto a single line. If it gets longer, it will wrap onto multiple lines. To load Python objects from a YAML document, we can use the following code:

```
copy= yaml.load(text)
```

This will use the tag information to locate the class definitions and provide the values found in the YAML document to the class constructors. Our microblog objects will be fully reconstructed.

Formatting YAML data on a file

When we write YAML files, we generally do something like this:

```
with open("some_destination.yaml", "w", encoding="UTF-8") as target:
    yaml.dump( some_collection, target )
```

We open the file with the required encoding. We provide the file object to the `yaml.dump()` method; the output is written there. When we read YAML files, we will use a similar technique:

```
with open("some_source.yaml", "r", encoding="UTF-8") as source:
    objects= yaml.load( source )
```

The idea is to segregate the YAML representation as text from any conversion to bytes on the resulting file. We have several formatting options to create prettier YAML representation of our data. Some of the options are shown in the following table:

`explicit_start`	If `true`, writes a `---` marker before each object.
`explicit_end`	If `true`, writes a `...` marker after each object. We might use this or `explicit_start` if we're dumping a sequence of YAML documents to a single file and need to know when one ends and the next begins.
`version`	Given a pair of integers (x,y), writes a `%YAML x.y` directive at the beginning. This should be `version=(1,2)`.
`tags`	Given a mapping, it emits a YAML `%TAG` directive with different tag abbreviations.
`canonical`	If `true`, includes a tag on every piece of data. If false, a number of tags are assumed.
`indent`	If set to a number, changes the indentation used for blocks.
`width`	If set to a number, changes the width at which long items are wrapped to multiple, indented lines.
`allow_unicode`	If set to `true`, permits full Unicode without escapes. Otherwise, characters outside the ASCII subset will have escapes applied.
`line_break`	Uses a different line-ending character; the default is a newline.

Of these options, `explicit_end` and `allow_unicode` are perhaps the most useful.

Extending the YAML representation

Sometimes, one of our classes has a tidy representation that is nicer than the default YAML dump of attribute values. For example, the default YAML for our Blackjack `Card` class definitions will include several derived values that we don't really need to preserve.

The `yaml` module includes a provision for adding a **representer** and a **constructor** to a class definition. The representer is used to create a YAML representation, including a tag and value. The constructor is used to build a Python object from the given value. Here's yet another `Card` class hierarchy:

```
class Card:
    def __init__( self, rank, suit, hard=None, soft=None ):
        self.rank= rank
        self.suit= suit
        self.hard= hard or int(rank)
        self.soft= soft or int(rank)
    def __str__( self ):
        return "{0.rank!s}{0.suit!s}".format(self)
```

```
class AceCard( Card ):
    def __init__( self, rank, suit ):
        super().__init__( rank, suit, 1, 11 )

class FaceCard( Card ):
    def __init__( self, rank, suit ):
        super().__init__( rank, suit, 10, 10 )
```

We've used the superclass for number cards and defined two subclasses for aces and face cards. In previous examples, we made extensive use of a factory function to simplify the construction. The factory handled mapping from a rank of 1 to a class of `AceCar` and from ranks of 11, 12, and 13 to class of `FaceCard`. This was essential so that we could easily build a deck using a simple `range(1,14)` for the rank values.

When loading from YAML, the class will be fully spelled out via the YAML `!!` tags. The only missing information would be the hard and soft values associated with each subclass of the card. The hard and soft points have three relatively simple cases that can be handled through optional initialization parameters. Here's how it looks when we dump these objects into the YAML format using default serialization:

```
- !!python/object:__main__.AceCard {hard: 1, rank: A, soft: 11, suit:
♣}
- !!python/object:__main__.Card {hard: 2, rank: '2', soft: 2, suit: ♥}
- !!python/object:__main__.FaceCard {hard: 10, rank: K, soft: 10,
suit: ♦}
```

These are correct, but perhaps a bit wordy for something as simple as a playing card. We can extend the `yaml` module to produce smaller and more focused output for these simple objects. What we'll do is define representers and constructors for our `Card` subclasses. Here are the three functions and registrations:

```
def card_representer(dumper, card):
    return dumper.represent_scalar('!Card',
    "{0.rank!s}{0.suit!s}".format(card) )
def acecard_representer(dumper, card):
    return dumper.represent_scalar('!AceCard',
    "{0.rank!s}{0.suit!s}".format(card) )
def facecard_representer(dumper, card):
    return dumper.represent_scalar('!FaceCard',
    "{0.rank!s}{0.suit!s}".format(card) )

yaml.add_representer(Card, card_representer)
yaml.add_representer(AceCard, acecard_representer)
yaml.add_representer(FaceCard, facecard_representer)
```

We've represented each `Card` instance as a short string. YAML includes a tag to show which class should be built from the string. All three classes use the same format string. This happens to match the `__str__()` method, leading to a potential optimization.

The other problem we need to solve is constructing `Card` instances from the parsed YAML document. For that, we need constructors. Here are three constructors and the registrations:

```
def card_constructor(loader, node):
    value = loader.construct_scalar(node)
    rank, suit= value[:-1], value[-1]
    return Card( rank, suit )

def acecard_constructor(loader, node):
    value = loader.construct_scalar(node)
    rank, suit= value[:-1], value[-1]
    return AceCard( rank, suit )

def facecard_constructor(loader, node):
    value = loader.construct_scalar(node)
    rank, suit= value[:-1], value[-1]
    return FaceCard( rank, suit )

yaml.add_constructor('!Card', card_constructor)
yaml.add_constructor('!AceCard', acecard_constructor)
yaml.add_constructor('!FaceCard', facecard_constructor)
```

As a scalar value is parsed, the tag will be used to locate a specific constructor. The constructor can then decompose the string and build the proper subclass of a `Card` instance. Here's a quick demo that dumps one card of each class:

```
deck = [ AceCard('A','♣',1,11), Card('2','♥',2,2),
FaceCard('K','♦',10,10) ]
text= yaml.dump( deck, allow_unicode=True )
```

The following is the output:

```
[!AceCard 'A♣', !Card '2♥', !FaceCard 'K♦']
```

This gives us short, elegant YAML representations of cards that can be used to reconstruct Python objects.

We can rebuild our 3-card deck using the following simple statement:

```
cards= yaml.load( text )
```

This will parse the representation, use the constructor functions, and build the expected objects. Because the constructor function ensures that proper initialization gets done, the internal attributes for the hard and soft values are properly rebuilt.

Security and safe loading

In principle, YAML can build objects of any type. This allows an attack on an application that transmits YAML files through the Internet without proper SSL controls in place.

The YAML module offers a `safe_load()` method that refuses to execute arbitrary Python code as part of building an object. This severely limits what can be loaded. For insecure data exchanges, we can use `yaml.safe_load()` to create Python `dict` and `list` objects that contain only built-in types. We can then build our application classes from the `dict` and `list` instances. This is vaguely similar to the way we use JSON or CSV to exchange `dict` that must be used to create a proper object.

A better approach is to use the `yaml.YAMLObject` mixin class for our own objects. We use this to set some class-level attributes that provide hints to `yaml` and ensure the safe construction of objects. Here's how we define a superclass for safe transmission:

```
class Card2( yaml.YAMLObject ):
    yaml_tag = '!Card2'
    yaml_loader= yaml.SafeLoader
```

The two attributes will alert `yaml` that these objects can be safely loaded without executing arbitrary and unexpected Python code. Each subclass of `Card2` only has to set the unique YAML tag that will be used:

```
class AceCard2( Card2 ):
    yaml_tag = '!AceCard2'
```

We've added an attribute that alerts `yaml` that these objects use only this class definition. The objects can be safely loaded; they don't execute arbitrary untrustworthy code.

With these modifications to the class definitions, we can now use `yaml.safe_load()` on the YAML stream without worrying about the document having malicious code inserted over an unsecured Internet connection. The explicit use of the `yaml.YAMLObject` mixin class for our own objects coupled with setting the `yaml_tag` attribute has several advantages. It leads to slightly more compact files. It also leads to a better-looking YAML files—the long, generic `!!python/object:__main__.AceCard` tags are replaced with shorter `!AceCard2` tags.

Dumping and loading with pickle

The `pickle` module is Python's native format to make objects persistent.

The Python Standard Library says this about `pickle`:

> *The pickle module can transform a complex object into a byte stream and it can transform the byte stream into an object with the same internal structure. Perhaps the most obvious thing to do with these byte streams is to write them onto a file, but it is also conceivable to send them across a network or store them in a database.*

The focus of `pickle` is Python and only Python. This is not a data interchange format such as JSON, YAML, CSV, or XML that can be used with applications written in other languages.

The `pickle` module is tightly integrated with Python in a variety of ways. For example, the `__reduce__()` and `__reduce_ex__()` methods of a class exist to support the `pickle` processing.

We can easily pickle our microblog in the following manner:

```
import pickle
with open("travel_blog.p","wb") as target:
    pickle.dump( travel, target )
```

This exports the entire `travel` object to the given file. The file is written as raw bytes, so the `open()` function uses the `"wb"` mode.

We can easily recover a picked object in the following manner:

```
with open("travel_blog.p","rb") as source:
    copy= pickle.load( source )
```

As pickled data is written as bytes, the file must be opened in the `"rb"` mode. The pickled objects will be correctly bound to the proper class definitions. The underlying stream of bytes is not intended for human consumption. It is readable after a fashion, but it is not designed for readability like YAML.

Designing a class for reliable pickle processing

The `__init__()` method of a class is not actually used to unpickle an object. The `__init__()` method is bypassed by using `__new__()` and setting the pickled values into the object's `__dict__` directly. This distinction matters when our class definition includes some processing in `__init__()`. For example, if `__init__()` opens external files, creates some part of a GUI interface, or performs some external update to a database, then this will not be performed during unpickling.

If we compute a new instance variable during the `__init__()` processing, there is no real problem. For example, consider a Blackjack `Hand` object that computes the total of the `Card` instances when the `Hand` is created. The ordinary `pickle` processing will preserve this computed instance variable. It won't be recomputed when the object is unpickled. The previously computed value will simply be unpickled.

A class that relies on processing during `__init__()` has to make special arrangements to be sure that this initial processing will happen properly. There are two things we can do:

- Avoid eager startup processing in `__init__()`. Instead, do one-time initialization processing. For example, if there are external file operations, these must be deferred until required.
- Define the `__getstate__()` and `__setstate__()` methods that can be used by pickle to preserve the state and restore the state. The `__setstate__()` method can then invoke the same method that `__init__()` invokes to perform a one-time initialization processing in ordinary Python code.

We'll look at an example where the initial `Card` instances loaded into a `Hand` are logged for audit purposes by the `__init__()` method. Here's a version of `Hand` that doesn't work properly when unpickling:

```
class Hand_x:
    def __init__( self, dealer_card, *cards ):
        self.dealer_card= dealer_card
        self.cards= list(cards)
        for c in self.cards:
            audit_log.info( "Initial %s", c )
    def append( self, card ):
        self.cards.append( card )
        audit_log.info( "Hit %s", card )
    def __str__( self ):
```

```
        cards= ", ".join( map(str,self.cards) )
        return "{self.dealer_card} | {cards}".format( self=self,
cards=cards )
```

This has two logging locations: during `__init__()` and `append()`. The `__init__()` processing doesn't work consistently between initial object creation and unpickling to recreate an object. Here's the logging setup to see this problem:

```
import logging,sys
audit_log= logging.getLogger( "audit" )
logging.basicConfig(stream=sys.stderr, level=logging.INFO)
```

This setup creates the log and ensures that the logging level is appropriate for seeing the audit information. Here's a quick script that builds, pickles, and unpickles `Hand`:

```
h = Hand_x( FaceCard('K','♦'), AceCard('A','♣'), Card('9','♥') )
data = pickle.dumps( h )
h2 = pickle.loads( data )
```

When we execute this, we see that the log entries that are written during `__init__()` processing are not written when unpickling `Hand`. In order to properly write an audit log for unpickling, we could put lazy logging tests throughout this class. For example, we could extend `__getattribute__()` to write the initial log entries whenever any attribute is requested from this class. This leads to stateful logging and an `if` statement that is executed every time a hand object does something. A better solution is to tap into the way state is saved and recovered by `pickle`.

```
class Hand2:
    def __init__( self, dealer_card, *cards ):
        self.dealer_card= dealer_card
        self.cards= list(cards)
        for c in self.cards:
            audit_log.info( "Initial %s", c )
    def append( self, card ):
        self.cards.append( card )
        audit_log.info( "Hit %s", card )
    def __str__( self ):
        cards= ", ".join( map(str,self.cards) )
        return "{self.dealer_card} | {cards}".format( self=self,
cards=cards )
    def __getstate__( self ):
        return self.__dict__
    def __setstate__( self, state ):
        self.__dict__.update(state)
```

```
        for c in self.cards:
            audit_log.info( "Initial (unpickle) %s", c )
```

The `__getstate__()` method is used while picking to gather the current state of the object. This method can return anything. In the case of objects that have internal memoization caches, for example, the cache might not be pickled in order to save time and space. This implementation uses the internal `__dict__` without any modification.

The `__setstate__()` method is used while unpickling to reset the value of the object. This version merges the state into the internal `__dict__` and then writes the appropriate logging entries.

Security and the global issue

During unpickling, a global name in the pickle stream can lead to the evaluation of arbitrary code. Generally, the global names are class names or a function name. However, it's possible to include a global name that is a function in a module such as `os` or `subprocess`. This allows an attack on an application that attempts to transmit pickled objects through the Internet without strong SSL controls in place. This is no concern for completely local files.

In order to prevent the execution of arbitrary code, we must extend the `pickle.Unpickler` class. We'll override the `find_class()` method to replace it with something more secure. We have to account for several unpickling issues, such as the following:

- We have to prevent the use of the built-in `exec()` and `eval()` functions.
- We have to prevent the use of modules and packages that might be considered unsafe. For example, `sys` and `os` should be prohibited.
- We have to permit the use of our application modules.

Here's an example that imposes some restrictions:

```
import builtins
class RestrictedUnpickler(pickle.Unpickler):
    def find_class(self, module, name):
        if module == "builtins":
            if name not in ("exec", "eval"):
                return getattr(builtins, name)
        elif module == "__main__":
            return globals()[name]
        # elif module in any of our application modules...
        raise pickle.UnpicklingError(
        "global '{module}.{name}' is forbidden".format(module=module,
name=name))
```

This version of the `Unpickler` class will help us avoid a large number of potential problems that could stem from a pickle stream that was doctored. It permits the use of any built-in function except `exec()` and `eval()`. It permits the use of classes defined only in `__main__`. In all other cases, it raises an exception.

Dumping and loading with CSV

The `csv` module encodes and decodes simple `list` or `dict` instances into the CSV notation. As with the `json` module, discussed previously, this is not a very complete persistence solution. The wide adoption of CSV files, however, means that it often becomes necessary to convert between Python objects and CSV.

Working with CSV files involves a manual mapping between our objects and CSV structures. We need to design the mapping carefully, remaining cognizant of the limitations of the CSV notation. This can be difficult because of the mismatch between the expressive powers of objects and the tabular structure of a CSV file.

The content of each column of a CSV file is—by definition—pure text. When loading data from a CSV file, we'll need to convert these values to more useful types inside our applications. This conversion can be complicated by the way spreadsheets perform unexpected type coercion. We might, for example, have a spreadsheet where US ZIP codes have been changed into floating-point numbers by the spreadsheet application. When the spreadsheet saves to CSV, the ZIP codes could become odd-looking numeric values.

Consequently, we might need to use a conversion such as `('00000'+row['zip'])[-5:]` to restore the leading zeroes. Another scenario is having to use something such as `"{0:05.0f}".format(float(row['zip']))` to restore the leading zeroes. Also, don't forget that a file might have a mixture of ZIP and ZIP+4 postal codes, making this even more challenging.

To further complicate working with CSV files, we have to be aware that they're often touched manually and are often subtly incompatible because of human tweaks. It's important for software to be flexible in the face of real-world irregularities that arise.

When we have relatively simple class definitions, we can often transform each instance into a simple, flat row of data values. Often, `namedtuple` is a good match between a CSV source file and Python objects. Going the other way, we might need to design our Python classes around `namedtuples` if our application will save data in the CSV notation.

When we have classes that are containers, we often have a difficult time determining how to represent structured containers in flat CSV rows. This is an **impedance mismatch** between object models and flat normalized tabular structure used for CSV files or relational databases. There's no good solution for the impedance mismatch; it requires careful design. We'll start with simple, flat objects to show you some CSV mappings.

Dumping simple sequences to CSV

An ideal mapping is between the `namedtuple` instances and rows in a CSV file. Each row represents a different `namedtuple`. Consider the following Python class:

```
from collections import namedtuple
GameStat = namedtuple( "GameStat", "player,bet,rounds,final" )
```

We've defined the objects to be a simple, flat sequence of attributes. The database architects call this **First Normal Form**. There are no repeating groups and each item is an atomic piece of data. We might produce these objects from a simulation that looks like the following code:

```
def gamestat_iter( player, betting, limit=100 ):
    for sample in range(30):
        b = Blackjack( player(), betting() )
        b.until_broke_or_rounds(limit)
        yield GameStat( player.__name__, betting.__name__, b.rounds,
b.betting.stake )
```

This iterator will create Blackjack simulations with a given player and betting strategy. It will execute the game until the player is broke or has sat at the table for 100 individual rounds of play. At the end of each session, it will yield a `GameStat` object with the player strategy, betting strategy, the number of rounds, and the final stake. This will allow us to compute statistics for each play or betting strategy or combination. Here's how we can write this to a file for later analysis:

```
import csv
with open("blackjack.stats","w",newline="") as target:
    writer= csv.DictWriter( target, GameStat._fields )
    writer.writeheader()
    for gamestat in gamestat_iter( Player_Strategy_1, Martingale_Bet
):
        writer.writerow( gamestat._asdict() )
```

There are three steps to create a CSV writer:

1. Open a file with the newline option set to `""`. This will support the (possibly) nonstandard line ending for CSV files.
2. Create a CSV `writer` object. In this example, we created the `DictWriter` instance because it allows us to easily create rows from dictionary objects.
3. Put a header in the first line of the file. This makes data exchange slightly simpler by providing some hint as to what's in the CSV file.

Once `writer` object has been prepared, we can use the writer's `writerow()` method to write each dictionary to the CSV file. We can, to an extent, simplify this slightly by using the `writerows()` method. This method expects an iterator instead of an individual row. Here's how we can use `writerows()` with an iterator:

```
data = gamestat_iter( Player_Strategy_1, Martingale_Bet )
with open("blackjack.stats","w",newline="") as target:
    writer= csv.DictWriter( target, GameStat._fields )
    writer.writeheader()
    writer.writerows( g._asdict() for g in data )
```

We've assigned the iterator to a variable, `data`. For the `writerows()` method, we get a dictionary from each row produced by the iterator.

Loading simple sequences from CSV

We can load simple sequential objects from a CSV file with a loop that looks like the following code:

```
with open("blackjack.stats","r",newline="") as source:
    reader= csv.DictReader( source )
    for gs in ( GameStat(**r) for r in reader ):
        print( gs )
```

We've defined a `reader` object for our file. As we know that our file has a proper heading, we can use `DictReader`. This will use the first row to define the attribute names. We can now construct the `GameStat` objects from the rows in the CSV file. We've used a generator expression to build rows.

In this case, we've assumed that the column names match the attribute names of our `GameStat` class definition. We can, if necessary, confirm that the file matches the expected format by comparing `reader.fieldnames` with `GameStat._fields`. As the order doesn't have to match, we need to transform each list of field names into a set. Here's how we can check the column names:

```
assert set(reader.fieldnames) == set(GameStat._fields)
```

We've ignored the data types of the values that were read from the file. The two numeric columns will wind up being string values when we read from the CSV file. Because of this, we need a more sophisticated row-by-row transformation to create proper data values. Here's a typical factory function that performs the required conversions:

```
def gamestat_iter(iterator):
    for row in iterator:
        yield GameStat( row['player'], row['bet'], int(row['rounds']),
int(row['final']) )
```

We've applied the `int` function to the columns that are supposed to have numeric values. In the rare event where the file has the proper headers but improper data, we'll get an ordinary `ValueError` from a failed `int()` function. We can use this generator function as follows:

```
with open("blackjack.stats","r",newline="") as source:
    reader= csv.DictReader( source )
    assert set(reader.fieldnames) == set(GameStat._fields)
    for gs in gamestat_iter(reader):
        print( gs )
```

This version of the reader has properly reconstructed the `GameStat` objects by performing conversions on the numeric values.

Handling containers and complex classes

When we look back at our microblog example, we have a `Blog` object that contains many `Post` instances. We designed `Blog` as a wrapper around `list`, so that the `Blog` would contain a collection. When working with a CSV representation, we have to design a mapping from a complex structure to a tabular representation. We have three common solutions:

- We can create two files: a blog file and a posting file. The blog file has only the `Blog` instances. Each `Blog` has a title in our example. Each `Post` row can then have a reference to the `Blog` row to which the posting belongs. We need to add a key for each `Blog`. Each `Post` would then have a foreign key reference to the `Blog` key.

- We can create two kinds of rows in a single file. We will have the `Blog` rows and `Post` rows. Our writers entangle the various types of data; our readers must disentangle the types of data.
- We can perform a relational database join between the various kinds of rows, repeating the `Blog` parent information on each `Post` child.

There's no *best* solution among these choices. We have to design a solution to the impedance mismatch between flat CSV rows and more structured Python objects. The use cases for the data will define some of the advantages and disadvantages.

Creating two files requires that we create some kind of unique identifier for each `Blog` so that a `Post` can properly refer to the `Blog`. We can't easily use the Python internal ID, as these are not guaranteed to be consistent each time Python runs.

A common assumption is that the `Blog` title is a unique key; as this is an attribute of `Blog`, it is called a natural primary key. This rarely works out well; we cannot change a `Blog` title without also updating all of the `Posts` that refer to the `Blog`. A better plan is to invent a unique identifier and update the class design to include that identifier. This is called a **surrogate key**. The Python `uuid` module can provide unique identifiers for this purpose.

The code to use multiple files is nearly identical to the previous examples. The only change is to add a proper primary key to the `Blog` class. Once we have the keys defined, we can create writers and readers as shown previously to process the `Blog` and `Post` instances into their separate files.

Dumping and loading multiple row types in a CSV file

Creating multiple kinds of rows in a single file makes the format a bit more complex. The column titles must become a union of all the available column titles. Because of the possibility of name clashes between the various row types, we can either access rows by position—preventing us from simply using `csv.DictReader`—or we must invent a more sophisticated column title that combines class and attribute names.

The process is simpler if we provide each row with an extra column that acts as a class discriminator. This extra column shows us what type of object the row represents. The object's class name would work out well for this. Here's how we might write blogs and posts to a single CSV file using two different row formats:

```
with open("blog.csv","w",newline="") as target:
    wtr.writerow(['__class__','title','date','title','rst_
text','tags'])
```

```
        wtr= csv.writer( target )
        for b in blogs:
            wtr.writerow(['Blog',b.title,None,None,None,None])
            for p in b.entries:
                wtr.writerow(['Post',None,p.date,p.title,p.rst_text,p.
tags])
```

We created two varieties of rows in the file. Some rows have `'Blog'` in the first column and contain just the attributes of a `Blog` object. Other rows have `'Post'` in the first column and contain just the attributes of a `Post` object.

We did not make the titles unique, so we can't use a dictionary reader. When allocating columns by position like this, each row allocates unused columns based on the other types of rows with which it must coexist. These additional columns are filled with `None`. As the number of distinct row types grows, keeping track of the various positional column assignments can become challenging.

Also, the individual data type conversions can be somewhat baffling. In particular, we've ignored the data type of the timestamp and tags. We can try to reassemble our `Blogs` and `Posts` by examining the row discriminators:

```
with open("blog.csv","r",newline="") as source:
    rdr= csv.reader( source )
    header= next(rdr)
    assert header == ['__class__','title','date','title','rst_
text','tags']
    blogs = []
    for r in rdr:
        if r[0] == 'Blog':
            blog= Blog( *r[1:2] )
            blogs.append( blog )
        if r[0] == 'Post':
            post= post_builder( r )
            blogs[-1].append( post )
```

This snippet will construct a list of `Blog` objects. Each `'Blog'` row uses columns in `slice(1,2)` to define the `Blog` object. Each `'Post'` row uses columns in `slice(2,6)` to define a `Post` object. This requires that each `Blog` be followed by the relevant `Post` instances. A foreign key is not used to tie the two objects together.

We've used two assumptions about the columns in the CSV file that has the same order and type as the parameters of the class constructors. For `Blog` objects, we used `blog= Blog( *r[1:2] )` because the one-and-only column is text, which matches the class constructor. When working with externally supplied data, this assumption might prove to be invalid.

To build the `Post` instances, we've used a separate function to map from columns to class constructor. Here's the mapping function:

```
import ast
def builder( row ):
    return Post(
        date=datetime.datetime.strptime(row[2], "%Y-%m-%d %H:%M:%S"),
        title=row[3],
        rst_text=row[4],
        tags=ast.literal_eval(row[5]) )
```

This will properly build a `Post` instance from a row of text. It converts the text for `datetime` and the text for the tags to their proper Python types. This has the advantage of making the mapping explicit.

In this example, we're using `ast.literal_eval()` to decode more complex Python literal values. This allows the CSV data to include a tuple of string values: `"('#RedRanger', '#Whitby42', '#ICW')"`.

Filtering CSV rows with an iterator

We can refactor the previous load example to iterate through the `Blog` objects rather than constructing a list of the `Blog` objects. This allows us to skim through a large CSV file and locate just the relevant `Blog` and `Post` rows. This function is a generator that yields each individual `Blog` instance separately:

```
def blog_iter(source):
    rdr= csv.reader( source )
    header= next(rdr)
    assert header == ['__class__','title','date','title','rst_
text','tags']
    blog= None
    for r in rdr:
        if r[0] == 'Blog':
            if blog:
                yield blog
            blog= Blog( *r[1:2] )
        if r[0] == 'Post':
            post= post_builder( r )
            blog.append( post )
    if blog:
        yield blog
```

This `blog_iter()` function creates the `Blog` object and appends the `Post` objects. Each time a `Blog` header appears, the previous `Blog` is complete and can be yielded. At the end, the final `Blog` object must also be yielded. If we want the large list of `Blog` instances, we can use the following code:

```
with open("blog.csv","r",newline="") as source:
    blogs= list( blog_iter(source) )
```

This will use the iterator to build a list of `Blogs` in the rare cases that we actually want the entire sequence in memory. We can use the following to process each `Blog` individually, rendering it to create RST files:

```
with open("blog.csv","r",newline="") as source:
    for b in blog_iter(source):
        with open(blog.title+'.rst','w') as rst_file:
            render( blog, rst_file )
```

We used the `blog_iter()` function to read each blog. After being read, it can be rendered to an RST-format file. A separate process can run `rst2html.py` to convert each blog to HTML.

We can easily add a filter to process only selected `Blog` instances. Rather than simply rendering all the `Blog` instances, we can add an `if` statement to decide which `Blogs` should be rendered.

Dumping and loading joined rows in a CSV file

Joining the objects together means that each row is a child object, joined with all of the parent objects that child. This leads to repetition of the parent object's attributes for each child object. When there are multiple levels of containers, this can lead to large amounts of repeated data.

The advantage of this repetition is that each row stands alone and doesn't belong to a context defined by the rows above it. We don't need a class discriminator as parent values are repeated for each child object.

This works well for data that forms a simple hierarchy; each child has some parent attributes added to it. When the data involves more complex relationships, the simplistic parent-child pattern breaks down. In these examples, we've lumped the `Post` tags into a single column of text. If we tried to break the tags into separate columns, they would become children of each `Post`, meaning that the text of `Post` might be repeated for each tag. Clearly, this isn't a good idea!

The column titles must become a union of all the available column titles. Because of the possibility of name clashes between the various row types, we'll qualify each column name with the class name. This will lead to column titles such as `'Blog.title'` and `'Post.title'`, which prevents name clashes. This allows for the use of `DictReader` and `DictWriter` rather than the positional assignment of the columns. However, these qualified names don't trivially match the attribute names of the class definitions; this leads to somewhat more text processing to parse the column titles. Here's how we can write a joined row that contains parent as well as child attributes:

```
with open("blog.csv","w",newline="") as target:
    wtr= csv.writer( target )
    wtr.writerow(['Blog.title','Post.date','Post.title', 'Post.
tags','Post.rst_text'])
    for b in blogs:
        for p in b.entries:
            wtr.writerow([b.title,p.date,p.title,p.tags,p.rst_text])
```

We saw qualified column titles. In this format, each row now contains a union of the `Blog` attribute and the `Post` attributes. This is somewhat easier to prepare, as there's no need to fill unused columns with `None`. As each column name is unique, we could easily switch to a `DictWriter` too. Here's a way to reconstruct the original container from the CSV rows:

```
def blog_iter2( source ):
    rdr= csv.DictReader( source )
    assert set(rdr.fieldnames) == set(['Blog.title','Post.date','Post.
title', 'Post.tags','Post.rst_text'])
    row= next(rdr)
    blog= Blog(row['Blog.title'])
    post= post_builder5( row )
    blog.append( post )
    for row in rdr:
        if row['Blog.title'] != blog.title:
            yield blog
            blog= Blog( row['Blog.title'] )
        post= post_builder5( row )
        blog.append( post )
    yield blog
```

The first row of data is used to build a `Blog` instance and the first `Post` in that `Blog`. The invariant condition for the loop that follows assumes that there's a proper `Blog` object. Having a valid `Blog` instance makes the processing logic much simpler. The `Post` instances are built with the following function:

```
import ast
def post_builder5( row ):
    return Post(
        date=datetime.datetime.strptime(
            row['Post.date'], "%Y-%m-%d %H:%M:%S"),
        title=row['Post.title'],
        rst_text=row['Post.rst_text'],
        tags=ast.literal_eval(row['Post.tags']) )
```

We mapped the individual columns in each row through a conversion to the parameters of the class constructor. This makes all of the conversions explicit. It properly handles all of the type conversions from the CSV text to Python objects.

We might want to refactor the `Blog` builder to a separate function. However, it's so small that adherence to the DRY principle seems a bit fussy. Because the column titles match the parameter names, we might try to use something like the following code to build each object:

```
    def make_obj( row, class_=Post, prefix="Post" ):
        column_split = ( (k,)+tuple(k.split('.')) for k in row )
        kw_args = dict( (attr,row[key])
            for key,classname,attr in column_split if
classname==prefix )
        return class( **kw_args )
```

We used two generator expressions here. The first generator expression splits the column names into the class and attribute and builds a 3-tuple with the full key, the class name, and the attribute name. The second generator expression filters the class for the desired target class; it builds a sequence of 2-tuples with the attribute and value pairs that can be used to build a dictionary.

This doesn't handle the data conversion for `Posts`. The individual column mappings simply don't generalize well. Adding lots of processing logic to this isn't very helpful when we compare it to the `post_builder5()` function.

In the unlikely event that we have an empty file—one with a header row but zero `Blog` entries—the initial `row=next(rdr)` function will raise a `StopIteration` exception. As this generator function doesn't handle the exception, it will propagate to the loop that evaluated `blog_iter2()`; this loop will be terminated properly.

Dumping and loading with XML

Python's `xml` package includes numerous modules that parse XML files. There is also a **Document Object Model** (**DOM**) implementation that can produce an XML document. As with the previous `json` module, this is not a very complete persistence solution for Python objects. Because of the wide adoption of the XML files, however, it often becomes necessary to convert between Python objects and XML documents.

Working with XML files involves a manual mapping between our objects and XML structures. We need to design the mapping carefully, remaining cognizant of the constraints of XML's notation. This can be difficult because of the mismatch between the expressive powers of objects and the strictly hierarchical nature of an XML document.

The content of an XML attribute or tag is pure text. When loading an XML document, we'll need to convert these values to more useful types inside our applications. In some cases, the XML document might include attributes or tags to indicate the expected type.

If we are willing to put up with some limitations, we can use the `plistlib` module to emit some built-in Python structures as XML documents. We'll examine this module in *Chapter 13, Configuration Files and Persistence*, where we'll use it to load the configuration files.

The `json` module offers ways to extend the JSON encoding to include our customized classes; the `plistlib` module doesn't offer this additional hook.

When we look at dumping a Python object to create an XML document, there are three common ways to build the text:

- Include XML output methods in our class design. In this case, our classes emit strings that can be assembled into an XML document.
- Use `xml.etree.ElementTree` to build the `ElementTree` nodes and return this structure. This can be rendered as text.
- Use an external template and fill attributes into that template. Unless we have a sophisticated template tool, this doesn't work out well. The `string.Template` class in the standard library is only suitable for very simple objects.

There are some examples of generic Python XML serializers. The problem with trying to create a generic serializer is that XML is extremely flexible; each application of XML seems to have unique **XML Schema Definition** (**XSD**) or **Document Type Definition** (**DTD**) requirements.

One open design question is how to encode an atomic value. There are a large number of choices. We could use a type-specific tag with an attribute name in the tag's attributes: `<int name="the_answer">42</int>`. Another possibility is to use an attribute-specific tag with the type in the tag's attributes: `<the_answer type="int">42</the_answer>`. We can also use nested tags: `<the_answer><int>42</int></the_answer>`. Or, we could rely on a separate schema definition to suggest that `the_answer` should be an integer and merely encode the value as text: `<the_answer>42</the_answer>`. We can also use adjacent tags: `<key>the_answer</key><int>42</int>`. This is not an exhaustive list; XML offers us a lot of choices.

When it comes to recovering Python objects from an XML document, we are constrained by the APIs of our parsers. Generally, we have to parse the document and then examine the XML tag structure, assembling Python objects from the available data.

Some Web frameworks, such as Django, include XML serialization of Django-defined classes. This isn't general serialization of arbitrary Python objects. The serialization is narrowly defined by Django's data modeling components. Additionally, there are packages such as `dexml`, `lxml`, and `pyxser` as alternative bindings between Python objects and XML. See `http://pythonhosted.org/dexml/api/dexml.html`, `http://lxml.de`, and `http://coder.cl/products/pyxser/`. Here's a longer list of candidate packages: `https://wiki.python.org/moin/PythonXml`.

Dumping objects using string templates

One way to serialize a Python object into XML is by creating the XML text. This is a kind of manual mapping that's often implemented as a method function that emits a snippet of XML that corresponds to the Python object. In the case of a complex object, the container must get the XML for each item inside the container. Here are two simple extensions to our microblog class structure that add the XML output capability as text:

```
class Blog_X( Blog ):
    def xml( self ):
        children= "\n".join( c.xml() for c in self.entries )
        return """\
<blog><title>{0.title}</title>
<entries>
{1}
<entries></blog>""".format(self,children)
```

```
class Post_X( Post ):
    def xml( self ):
        tags= "".join( "<tag>{0}</tag>".format(t) for t in self.tags )
        return """\
<entry>
    <title>{0.title}</title>
    <date>{0.date}</date>
    <tags>{1}</tags>
    <text>{0.rst_text}</text>
</entry>""".format(self,tags)
```

We've written some highly class-specific XML output methods. These will emit the relevant attributes wrapped in XML syntax. This approach doesn't generalize well. The `Blog_X.xml()` method emits a `<blog>` tag with a title and entries. The `Post_X.xml()` method emits a `<post>` tag with the various attributes. In both of these methods, subsidiary objects were created using `"".join()` or `"\n".join()` to build a longer string from shorter string elements. When we convert a `Blog` object to XML, the results look like this:

```
<blog><title>Travel</title>
<entries>
<entry>
    <title>Hard Aground</title>
    <date>2013-11-14 17:25:00</date>
    <tags><tag>#RedRanger</tag><tag>#Whitby42</tag><tag>#ICW</tag></
tags>
    <text>Some embarrassing revelation. Including ⊠ and ⊠</text>
</entry>
<entry>
    <title>Anchor Follies</title>
    <date>2013-11-18 15:30:00</date>
    <tags><tag>#RedRanger</tag><tag>#Whitby42</tag><tag>#Mistakes</
tag></tags>
    <text>Some witty epigram.</text>
</entry>
<entries></blog>
```

This approach has two disadvantages:

- We've ignored the XML namespaces. That's a small change to the literal text for emitting the tags.
- Each class would also need to properly escape the `<`, `&`, `>`, and `"` characters into the XML entities `<`, `>`, `&`, and `"`. The `html` module includes the `html.escape()` function that does this.

This does emit proper XML; it can be relied upon to work; it isn't very elegant and doesn't generalize well.

Dumping objects with xml.etree.ElementTree

We can use the `xml.etree.ElementTree` module to build `Element` structures that can be emitted as XML. It's challenging to use `xml.dom` and `xml.minidom` for this. The DOM API requires a top-level document that then builds individual elements. The presence of this necessary context object creates clutter when trying to serialize a simple class with several attributes. We have to create the document first and then serialize all the elements of the document, providing the document context as an argument.

Generally, we'd like each class in our design to build a top-level element and return that. Most top-level elements will have a sequence of subelements. We can assign text as well as attributes to each element that we build. We can also assign a *tail* that is the extraneous text that follows a closed tag. In some content models, this is just whitespace. Because of the long name, it might be helpful to import `ElementTree` in the following manner:

```
import xml.etree.ElementTree as XML
```

Here are two extensions to our microblog class structure that add the XML output capability as the `Element` instances. We add the following method to the `Blog` class:

```
def xml( self ):
    blog= XML.Element( "blog" )
    title= XML.SubElement( blog, "title" )
    title.text= self.title
    title.tail= "\n"
    entities= XML.SubElement( blog, "entities" )
    entities.extend( c.xml() for c in self.entries )
    blog.tail= "\n"
    return blog
```

We add the following method to the `Post` class:

```
def xml( self ):
    post= XML.Element( "entry" )
    title= XML.SubElement( post, "title" )
    title.text= self.title
    date= XML.SubElement( post, "date" )
    date.text= str(self.date)
```

```
        tags= XML.SubElement( post, "tags" )
        for t in self.tags:
            tag= XML.SubElement( tags, "tag" )
            tag.text= t
        text= XML.SubElement( post, "rst_text" )
        text.text= self.rst_text
        post.tail= "\n"
        return post
```

We've written highly class-specific XML output methods. These will build the `Element` objects that have the proper text values.

There's no fluent shortcut for building the subelements. We have to insert each text item individually.

In the `blog` method, we were able to perform `Element.extend()` to put all of the individual post entries inside the `<entry>` element. This allows us to build the XML structure flexibly and simply. This approach can deal gracefully with the XML namespaces. We can use the `QName` class to build qualified names for XML namespaces. The `ElementTree` module correctly applies the namespace qualifiers to the XML tags. This approach also properly escapes the `<`, `&`, `>`, and `"` characters into the XML entities `<`, `>`, `&`, and `"`. The XML output from these methods will mostly match the previous section. The whitespace will be different.

Loading XML documents

Loading Python objects from an XML document is a two-step process. First, we need to parse the XML text to create the document objects. Then, we need to examine the document objects to produce Python objects. As noted previously, the tremendous flexibility of XML notation means that there isn't a single XML-to-Python serialization.

One approach to walk through an XML document involves making XPath-like queries to locate the various elements that were parsed. Here's a function to walk an XML document, emitting the `Blog` and `Post` objects from the available XML:

```
import ast
doc= XML.parse( io.StringIO(text.decode('utf-8')) )
xml_blog= doc.getroot()
blog= Blog( xml_blog.findtext('title') )
for xml_post in xml_blog.findall('entries/entry'):
    tags= [t.text for t in xml_post.findall( 'tags/tag' )]
    post= Post(
```

```
            date= datetime.datetime.strptime(
                xml_post.findtext('date'), "%Y-%m-%d %H:%M:%S"),
            title=xml_post.findtext('title'),
            tags=tags,
            rst_text= xml_post.findtext('rst_text')
        )
        blog.append( post )
    render( blog )
```

This snippet traverses a `<blog>` XML document. It locates the `<title>` tag and gathers all of the text within that element to create the top-level `Blog` instance. It then locates all the `<entry>` subelements found within the `<entries>` element. These are used to build each `Post` object. The various attributes of the `Post` object are converted individually. The text of each individual `<tag>` element within the `<tags>` element is turned into a list of text values. The date is parsed from its text representation. The `Post` objects are each appended to the overall `Blog` object. This *manual* mapping from XML text to Python objects is an essential feature of parsing XML documents.

Summary

We've looked at a number of ways to serialize Python objects. We can encode our class definitions in notations, including JSON, YAML, pickle, XML, and CSV. Each of these notations has a variety of advantages and disadvantages.

These various library modules generally work around the idea of loading objects from an external file or dumping objects to a file. These modules aren't completely consistent with each other, but they're very similar, allowing us to apply some common design patterns.

Using CSV and XML tends to expose the most difficult design problems. Our class definitions in Python can include object references that don't have a good representation in the CSV or XML notation.

Design considerations and trade-offs

There are many ways to serialize and persist Python objects. We haven't seen all of them yet. The formats in this section are focused on two essential use cases:

- **Data interchange with other applications**: We might be publishing data for other applications or accepting data from other applications. In this case, we're often constrained by the other applications' interfaces. Often, JSON and XML are used by other applications and frameworks as their preferred form of data interchange. In some cases, we'll use CSV to exchange data.

- **Persistent data for our own applications**: In this case, we're often going to choose `pickle` because it's complete and is already part of the Python Standard Library. However, one of the important advantages of YAML is its readability; we can view, edit and even modify the file.

When working with each of these formats, we have a number of design considerations. First and foremost, these formats are biased towards serializing a single Python object. It might be a list of other objects, but it is essentially a single object. JSON and XML, for example, have ending delimiters that are written after the serialized object. For persisting individual objects from a larger domain, we can look at `shelve` and `sqlite3` in *Chapter 10, Storing and Retrieving Objects via Shelve* and *Chapter 11, Storing and Retrieving Objects via SQLite.*

JSON is a widely-used standard. It's inconvenient for representing complex Python classes. When using JSON, we need to be cognizant of how our objects can be reduced to a JSON-compatible representation. JSON documents are human-readable. JSON's limitations make it potentially secure for the transmission of objects through the Internet.

YAML is not as widely used as JSON, but it solves numerous problems in serialization and persistence. YAML documents are human-readable. For editable configuration files, YAML is ideal. We can make YAML secure using the safe-load options.

Pickle is ideal for the simple, fast local persistence of Python objects. It is a compact notation for the transmission from Python-to-Python. CSV is a widely-used standard. Working out representations for Python objects in CSV notation is challenging. When sharing data in the CSV notation, we often end up using `namedtuples` in our applications. We have to design a mapping from Python to CSV and CSV to Python.

XML is another widely-used notation for serializing data. XML is extremely flexible, leading to a wide variety of ways to encode Python objects in XML notation. Because of the XML use cases, we often have external specifications in the form of an XSD or DTD. The process for parsing XML to create Python objects is always rather complex.

Because each CSV row is largely independent of the others, CSV allows us to encode or decode extremely large collections of objects. For this reason, CSV is often handy for encoding and decoding gargantuan collections that can't fit into the memory.

In some cases, we have a hybrid design problem. When reading most modern spreadsheet files, we have the CSV row-and-column problem wrapped in the XML parsing problem. For example, `OpenOffice.org`. ODS files are zipped archives. One of the files in the archive is the `content.xml` file. Using an XPath search for `body/spreadsheet/table` elements will locate the individual tabs of the spreadsheet document. Within each table, we'll find the `table-row` elements that (usually) map to Python objects. Within each row, we'll find the `table-cell` elements that contain the individual values that build up the attributes of an object.

Schema evolution

When working with persistent objects, we have to address the problem of schema evolution. Our objects have a dynamic state and a static class definition. We can easily persist the dynamic state. Our class definitions are the schema for the persistent data. The class, however, is not *absolutely* static. When a class changes, we need to make a provision to load data that was dumped by the previous release of our application.

It's best to think of external file compatibility to distinguish between major and minor release numbers. A major release should mean that a file is no longer compatible and a conversion must be done. A minor release should mean that the file formats are compatible and no data conversion will be involved in the upgrade.

One common approach is to include the major version number in the file extension. We might have filenames that end in `.json2` or `.json3` to indicate which format of data is involved. Supporting multiple versions of a persistent file format often becomes rather complex. To provide a seamless upgrade path, an application should be able to decode previous file formats. Often, it's best to persist data in the latest and greatest file format, even if the other formats are supported for input.

In the next chapters, we'll address serialization that's not focused on a single object. The `shelve` and `sqlite3` modules give us ways to serialize a universe of distinct objects. After that, we'll return to using these techniques for **Representational State Transfer** (**REST**) to transmit objects from process to process. Also, we'll use these techniques yet again to process the configuration files.

Looking forward

In *Chapter 10, Storing and Retrieving Objects via Shelve* and *Chapter 11, Storing and Retrieving Objects via SQLite*, we'll look at two common approaches to make larger collections of persistent objects. These two chapters show us different approaches to create a database of Python objects.

In *Chapter 12, Transmitting and Sharing Objects*, we'll apply these serialization techniques to the problem of making an object available in another process. We'll focus on RESTful web services as a simple and popular way to transmit an object among processes.

In *Chapter 13, Configuration Files and Persistence*, we'll apply these serialization techniques yet again. In this case, we'll use representations such as JSON and YAML to encode the configuration information for an application.

10
Storing and Retrieving Objects via Shelve

There are many applications where we need to persist objects individually. The techniques we looked at in *Chapter 9, Serializing and Saving – JSON, YAML, Pickle, CSV, and XML,* were biased towards handling a single object. Sometimes, we need to persist separate, individual objects from a larger domain.

Applications with persistent objects may demonstrate four use cases, summarized as the **CRUD Operations**: Create, Retrieve, Update, and Delete. In the general case, any of these operations may be applied to any object in the domain; this leads to the need for a more sophisticated persistence mechanism than a monolithic load or dump to a file. In addition to squandering memory, simple loads and dumps are often less efficient than fine-grained, object-by-object storage.

Using more sophisticated storage will lead us to look more closely at the allocation of responsibility. The various concerns give us overall design patterns for the architecture of the application software. One example of these higher-level design patterns is the **Three-Tier Architecture**:

- **Presentation tier**: This may be a web browser or mobile app, sometimes both.
- **Application tier**: This is often deployed on an application server. The application tier should be subdivided into an application layer and a data model layer. The processing layer involves the classes that embody an application's behavior. The data model layer defines the problem domain's object model.
- **Data tier**: This includes an access layer and a persistence layer. The access layer provides uniform access to persistent objects. The persistence layer serializes objects and writes them to the persistent storage.

This model can be applied to a single GUI application. The presentation tier is the GUI; the application tier is the relevant processor and the data model; the access tier is the persistence modules. It even applies to a command-line application where the presentation tier is merely an options parser as well as the `print()` functions.

The `shelve` module defines a mapping-like container in which we can store objects. Each stored object is pickled and written to a file. We can also unpickle and retrieve any object from the file. The `shelve` module relies on the `dbm` module to save and retrieve objects.

This section will focus on the data model taken from the application tier and the access and persistence taken from the data tier. The interface between these tiers can simply be a class interface within a single application. Or, it can be a more elaborate networked interface. We'll focus on the simple class-to-class interface in this chapter. We'll look at a network-based interface in *Chapter 12, Transmitting and Sharing Objects*, using REST.

Analyzing persistent object use cases

The persistence mechanisms we looked at in *Chapter 9, Serializing and Saving – JSON, YAML, Pickle, CSV, and XML*, focused on reading and writing a compact file with a serialized object. If we wanted to update any part of the file, we were forced to replace the entire file. This is a consequence of using a compact notation for the data; it's difficult to reach the position of an object within a file, and it's difficult to replace an object if the size changes. Rather than addressing these difficulties with clever, complex algorithms, the object was simply serialized and written. When we have a larger domain of many persistent, mutable objects, we introduce some additional depth to the use cases. Here are some additional considerations:

- We may not want to load all the objects into the memory at one time. For many *Big Data* applications, it might be impossible to load all the objects into the memory at one time.
- We may be updating only small subsets—or individual instances—from our domain of objects. Loading and then dumping all the objects to update one object is relatively inefficient processing.
- We may not be dumping all the objects at one time; we may be accumulating objects incrementally. Some formats such as YAML and CSV allow us to append themselves to a file with little complexity. Other formats such as JSON and XML have terminators that make it difficult to simply append to a file.

There are still more features we might want. It's common to conflate serialization, persistence, as well as concurrent update or write access into a single umbrella concept of *database*. The `shelve` module is not a comprehensive database solution by itself. The underlying `dbm` module used by `shelve` does not directly handle concurrent writes. It doesn't handle multioperation transactions either. It's possible to use low-level OS locking on the files to tolerate concurrent updating, but this tends to be highly OS-specific. For concurrent write access, it's better to either use a proper database or a RESTful data server. See *Chapter 11, Storing and Retrieving objects via SQLite*, and *Chapter 12, Transmitting and Sharing Objects*.

The ACID properties

Our design must consider how the **ACID properties** apply to our `shelve` database. Our application will often make changes in bundles of related operations that should change the database from one consistent state to the next consistent state. The collection of operations to change a database can be called a transaction.

An example of multiple-operation transactions could involve updating two objects so that a total is kept invariant. We might be deducting from one financial account and depositing into another. The overall balance must be held constant for the database to be in a consistent, valid state. The ACID properties characterize how we want the database transactions to behave as a whole. There are four rules that define our expectations:

- **Atomicity**: A transaction must be atomic. If there are multiple operations in a transaction, either all the operations should be completed or none of them should be completed. It should never be possible to view a shelf with a partially-completed transaction.
- **Consistency**: A transaction must assure consistency. It will change the database from one valid state to another. A transaction should not corrupt the database or create inconsistent views among concurrent users. All users see the same net effect of completed transactions.
- **Isolation**: Each transaction should operate properly as if in complete isolation. We can't have two concurrent users interfering with each other's attempted updates. We must be able to transform concurrent access into (possibly slower) serial access and the database updates will produce the same results.
- **Durability**: The changes to the database are **durable**; they persist properly in the filesystem.

When we work with in-memory Python objects, clearly, we get **ACI** but don't get **D**. In-memory objects are not durable by definition. If we attempt to use the `shelve` module from several concurrent processes without locking or versioning, we may get only D but lose the ACI properties.

The `shelve` module doesn't provide direct support for atomicity; it doesn't have a way to handle transactions that consists of multiple operations. If we have multiple-operation transactions and we need atomicity, we must ensure they all work or all fail as a unit. This can involve the rather complex `try:` statements that must restore the previous state of the database in the event of a failure.

The `shelve` module doesn't guarantee durability for all kinds of changes. If we place a mutable object onto the shelf and then change the object in memory, the persistent version on the shelf file will not change *automatically*. If we're going to mutate shelved objects, our application must be explicit about updating the shelf. We can ask a shelf object to track changes via the *writeback mode*, but using this feature can lead to poor performance.

Creating a shelf

The first part of creating a shelf is done using a module-level function, `shelve.open()`, to create a persistent shelf structure. The second part is closing the file properly so that all changes are written to the underlying filesystem. We'll look at this in a more complete example later.

Under the hood, the `shelve` module is using the `dbm` module to do the real work of opening a file and mapping from key to value. The `dbm` module itself is a wrapper around an underlying DBM-compatible library. Consequently, there are a number of potential implementations for the `shelve` features. The good news is that the differences among the `dbm` implementations are largely irrelevant.

The `shelve.open()` module function requires two parameters: the filename and the file access mode. Often, we want the default mode of `'c'` to open an existing shelf or create one if it doesn't exist. The alternatives are for specialized situations:

- `'r'` is a read-only shelf
- `'w'` is a read-write shelf that *must* exist or an exception will be raised
- `'n'` is a new, empty shelf; any previous version will be overwritten

It's absolutely essential to close a shelf to be sure that it is properly persisted to disk. The shelf is not a context manager itself, but the `contextlib.closing()` function can be used to make sure the shelf is closed. For more information on context managers, see *Chapter 5, Using Callables and Contexts*.

Under some circumstances, we might also want to explicitly synchronize a shelf to a disk without closing the file. The `shelve.sync()` method will persist changes prior to a close. The ideal lifecycle looks something like the following code:

```
import shelve
from contextlib import closing
with closing( shelve.open('some_file') ) as shelf:
    process( shelf )
```

We've opened a shelf and provided that open shelf to some function that does the real work of our application. When this process is finished, the context will ensure that the shelf is closed. If the `process()` function raises an exception, the shelf will still be properly closed.

Designing shelvable objects

If our objects are relatively simple, then putting them on a shelf will be trivial. For objects that are not complex containers or large collections, we only have to work out a key to value mapping. For objects that are more complex—typically objects that contain other objects—we have to make some additional design decisions regarding the granularity of access and references among objects.

We'll look at the simple case first, where all we have to design is the key that is used to access our objects. Then, we'll look at the more complex cases, where granularity and object references come into play.

Designing keys for our objects

The important feature of `shelve` (and `dbm`) is immediate access to any object in an arbitrarily huge universe of objects. The `shelve` module works with a mapping that is much like a dictionary. The shelf mapping exists on the persistent storage, so any object we put onto the shelf will be serialized and saved. The `pickle` module is used to do the actual serialization.

We must identify our shelved objects with some kind of key that will map to the object. As with a dictionary, the keys are hashed, which is a very quick calculation. It's fast because the key is limited to being a byte string; the hash is a modulus summation of those bytes. Since Python strings are trivially encoded into bytes, it means that string values are a common choice for keys. This is unlike a built-in `dict`, where any immutable object can be used as a key.

Since the key locates the value, it means the key must be unique. This imposes some design considerations on our classes to provide an appropriate unique key. In some cases, the problem domain will have an attribute that is an obvious unique key. In that case, we can simply use that attribute to construct this key: `shelf[object.key_attribute]= object`. This is the simplest case but doesn't generalize well.

In other cases, our application problem doesn't offer us an appropriate unique key. This problem arises frequently when every attribute of an object is potentially mutable or potentially non-unique. It arises when working with U.S. citizens, for example, because social security numbers are not unique; they can be reused by the Social Security Administration. Additionally, a person can misreport a SSN and the application might need to change it; as it can change, there's a second reason it's not acceptable as a primary key.

Our application may have non-string values that are candidate or primary keys. For example, we might have a `datetime` object, a number, or even a tuple as a unique identifier. In all of these cases, we might want to encode the value as bytes or a string.

In the cases where there is no obvious primary key, we can try to locate a combination of values that create a unique **composite key**. This isn't always a terribly good idea, because now the key is not atomic, and a change to any of the parts of the key creates data update problems.

It's often simplest to follow a design pattern called a **surrogate key**. This key doesn't depend on data within an object; it's a surrogate for the object. This means any of the attributes of the object can be changed without leading to complications or restrictions. Python's internal object IDs are an example of a kind of surrogate key. The string representation of a shelf key can follow this pattern: `class:oid`.

The key string includes the class of the object paired with the unique identifier for an instance of the class. We can easily store diverse classes of objects in a single shelf using keys of this form. Even when we think there will be only one type of object in the shelf, this format is still helpful to save a namespace for indexes, administrative metadata, and future expansion.

When we have a suitable natural key, we might do something like this to persist objects in the shelf: `self[object.__class__.__name__+":"+object.key_attribute]= object`

This provides us with a distinct class name along with the unique key value as a simple identifier for each object. For surrogate keys, we'll need to define some kind of generator for the key.

Generating surrogate keys for objects

We'll generate unique surrogate keys with an integer counter. To be sure that we keep this counter properly updated, we will store it in the shelf along with the rest of our data. Even though Python has an internal object ID, we should not use Python's internal identifier for a surrogate key. Python's internal ID numbers have no guarantees of any kind.

As we're going to add some administrative objects to our shelf, we must give these objects unique keys with a distinctive prefix. We'll use `_DB`. This will be a fake class of the objects in our shelf. The design decisions for these administrative objects are similar to the design of the application objects. We need to choose the granularity of storage. We have two choices:

- **Coarse-Grained**: We can create a single `dict` object with all the administrative overheads for surrogate key generations. A single key such as `_DB:max` can identify this object. Within this `dict`, we could map class names to maximum identifier values used. Every time we create a new object, we assign the ID from this mapping and then also replace the mapping in the shelf. We'll show the coarse-grained solution in the next section.
- **Fine-Grained**: We can add many items to the database, each of which has the maximum key value for a different class of objects. Each of these additional key items has the form `_DB:max:class`. The value for each of these keys is just an integer, the largest sequential identifier assigned so far for a given class.

An important consideration here is that we've separated the key design from the class design for our application's classes. We can (and should) design our application objects as simply as possible. We should add just enough overhead to make `shelve` work properly, but no more.

Designing a class with a simple key

It is helpful to store the `shelve` key as an attribute of a shelved object. Keeping the key in the object makes the object easier to delete or replace. Clearly, when creating an object, we'll start with a keyless version of the object until it's stored in the shelf. Once stored, the Python object needs to have a key attribute set so that each object in the memory contains a correct key.

When retrieving objects, there are two use cases. We might want a specific object that is known by the key. In this case, the shelf will map the key to the object. We might also want a collection of related objects, not known by their keys but perhaps known by the values of some other attributes. In this case, we'll discover the keys of objects through some kind of search or query. We'll look at the search algorithms in the next section.

To support saving the shelf keys in objects, we'll add an `_id` attribute to each object. It will keep the shelve key in each object that has been put onto the shelf or retrieved from the shelf. This will simplify managing objects that need to be replaced in or removed from the shelf. We have the following choices for adding this to the class:

- **No**: It's not essential to the class; it's just an overhead for the persistence mechanism
- **Yes**: It's important data, and we should initialize it properly in `__init__()`

We suggest not defining surrogate keys in the `__init__()` method; they're not essential, and are just part of a persistence implementation. A surrogate key won't have any method functions, for example, and it is never part of the processing layer of the application tier or the presentation tier. Here's a definition for an overall `Blog`:

```
class Blog:
    def __init__( self, title, *posts ):
        self.title= title
    def as_dict( self ):
        return dict(
            title= self.title,
            underline= "="*len(self.title),
        )
```

We've provided just a `title` attribute and a little more. The `Blog.as_dict()` method can be used with a template to provide string values in the RST notation. We'll leave the consideration of individual posts within the blog for the next section.

We can create a `Blog` object in the following manner:

```
>>> b1= Blog( title="Travel Blog" )
```

When we store this simple object in the shelf, we can do things like this:

```
>>> import shelve
>>> shelf= shelve.open("blog")
>>> b1._id= 'Blog:1'
>>> shelf[b1._id]= b1
```

We started by opening a new shelf. The file was called "`blog`". We put a key, '`Blog:1`', into our `Blog` instance, `b1`. We stored that `Blog` instance in the shelf using the key given in an `_id` attribute.

We can fetch the item back from the shelf like this:

```
>>> shelf['Blog:1']
<__main__.Blog object at 0x1007bccd0>
>>> shelf['Blog:1'].title
'Travel Blog'
>>> shelf['Blog:1']._id
'Blog:1'
>>> list(shelf.keys())
['Blog:1']
>>> shelf.close()
```

When we refer to `shelf['Blog:1']`, it will fetch our original `Blog` instance from the shelf. We've put only one object on the shelf, as we can see from the list of keys. Because we closed the shelf, the object is persistent. We can quit Python, start back up again, open the shelf, and see that the object remains on the shelf, using the assigned key. Previously, we mentioned a second use case for retrieval: locating an item without knowing the key. Here's a search that locates all blogs with a given title:

```
>>> shelf= shelve.open('blog')
>>> results = ( shelf[k] for k in shelf.keys() if
k.startswith('Blog:') and shelf[k].title == 'Travel Blog' )
>>> list(results)
[<__main__.Blog object at 0x1007bcc50>]
>>> r0= _[0]
>>> r0.title
'Travel Blog'
>>> r0._id
'Blog:1'
```

We opened the shelf to get access to the objects. The `results` generator expression examines each item in the shelf to locate those items where the key starts with `'Blog:'`, and the object's title attribute is the string `'Travel Blog'`.

What's important is that the key, `'Blog:1'`, is stored within the object itself. The `_id` attribute ensures that we have the proper key for any item that our application is working with. We can now mutate the object and replace it in the shelf using its original key.

Designing classes for containers or collections

When we have more complex containers or collections, we have more complex design decisions to make. The first question is about the scope of the containment. We must decide on the **granularity** of our shelved objects.

When we have a container, we can persist the entire container as a single, complex object on our shelf. To an extent, this might defeat the purpose of having multiple objects on a shelf in the first place. Storing one large container gives us coarse-grained storage. If we change one contained object, the entire container must be serialized and stored. If we wind up effectively pickling the entire universe of objects in a single container, why use `shelve`? We must strike a balance that is appropriate to the application's requirements.

The alternative is to decompose the collection into separate, individual items. In this case, our top-level `Blog` object won't be a proper Python container anymore. The parent might refer to each child with a collection of keys. Each child object could refer to the parent by the key. This use of keys is unusual in object-oriented design. Normally, objects simply contain references to other objects. When using `shelve` (or other databases), we must use indirect references by the key.

Each child will now have two keys: its own primary key, plus a **foreign key** that is the primary key of the parent object. This leads to a second design question about representing the key strings for the parents and their children.

Referring to objects via foreign keys

The key that we use to uniquely identify an object is its **primary key**. When child objects refer to a parent object, we have additional design decisions to make. How do we structure the children's primary keys? There are two common design strategies for child keys, based on the kind of dependence that exists between the classes of objects:

- `"Child:cid"`: We'll use this when we have children that can exist independently of an owning parent. For example, an item on an invoice refers to a product; the product can exist even if there's no invoice item for the product.
- `"Parent:pid:Child:cid"`: We'll use this when the child cannot exist without a parent. A customer address doesn't exist without a customer to contain the address in the first place. When the children are entirely dependent on the parent, the child's key can contain the owning parent's ID to reflect this dependency.

As with the parent class design, it's easiest if we keep the primary key and all foreign keys associated with each child object. We suggest not initializing them in the `__init__()` method, as they're just features of persistence. Here's the general definition for `Post` within `Blog`:

```
import datetime
class Post:
    def __init__( self, date, title, rst_text, tags ):
        self.date= date
        self.title= title
        self.rst_text= rst_text
        self.tags= tags
    def as_dict( self ):
        return dict(
            date= str(self.date),
            title= self.title,
            underline= "-"*len(self.title),
            rst_text= self.rst_text,
            tag_text= " ".join(self.tags),
        )
```

We've provided several attributes for each microblog post. The `Post.as_dict()` method can be used with a template to provide string values in the RST notation. We've avoided mentioning the primary key or any foreign keys for `Post`. Here are two examples of the `Post` instances:

```
p2= Post( date=datetime.datetime(2013,11,14,17,25),
        title="Hard Aground",
        rst_text="""Some embarrassing revelation.
          Including ☹ and □""",
        tags=("#RedRanger", "#Whitby42", "#ICW"),
        )

p3= Post( date=datetime.datetime(2013,11,18,15,30),
        title="Anchor Follies",
        rst_text="""Some witty epigram. Including < & >
characters.""",
        tags=("#RedRanger", "#Whitby42", "#Mistakes"),
        )
```

We can now associate these with their owning blog, both by setting attributes and by assigning keys that will define the relationships. We'll do this through several steps:

1. We'll open the shelf and retrieve a parent `Blog` object. We'll call it `owner`:

    ```
    >>> import shelve
    >>> shelf= shelve.open("blog")
    >>> owner= shelf['Blog:1']
    ```

    We've used the primary key to locate the owner item. An actual application might have used a search to locate this item by title. We might also have created an index to optimize the search. We'll look at the index and search below.

2. Now, we can assign this owner's key to each `Post` object and persist the objects:

    ```
    >>> p2._parent= owner._id
    >>> p2._id= p2._parent + ':Post:2'
    >>> shelf[p2._id]= p2

    >>> p3._parent= owner._id
    >>> p3._id= p3._parent + ':Post:3'
    >>> shelf[p3._id]= p3
    ```

    We put the parent information into each `Post`. We used the parent information to build the primary key. For this dependent kind of key, the `_parent` attribute value is redundant; it can be deduced from the key. If we used an independent key design for `Posts`, however, `_parent` would not be duplicated in the key. When we look at the keys, we can see the `Blog` plus both `Post` instances:

    ```
    >>> list(shelf.keys())
    ['Blog:1:Post:3', 'Blog:1', 'Blog:1:Post:2']
    ```

    When we fetch any child `Post`, we'll know the proper parent `Blog` for the individual posting:

    ```
    >>> p2._parent
    'Blog:1'
    >>> p2._id
    'Blog:1:Post:2'
    ```

Following the keys the other way—from parent `Blog` down to child `Post`—is a bit more complex. We'll address this separately because we often want to optimize the path from parent to children with an index.

Designing CRUD operations for complex objects

When we decompose a larger collection into a number of separate fine-grained objects, we will have multiple classes of objects on the shelf. Because they are independent objects, they will lead to separate sets of CRUD operations for each class. In some cases, the objects are independent, and operations on an object of one class have no impact outside that individual object.

In our example, however, the `Blog` and `Post` objects have a dependency relationship. The `Post` objects are children of a parent `Blog`; the child can't exist without the parent. When we have these dependent relationships, we have a more entangled collection of operations to design. Here are some of the considerations:

- CRUD operations on independent (or parent) objects:
    - We may create a new, empty parent, assigning a new primary key to this object. We can later assign children to this parent. Code such as `shelf['parent:'+object._id]= object` will create parent objects.
    - We may update or retrieve this parent without any effect on the children. We can perform `shelf['parent:'+some_id]` on the right-hand side of the assignment to retrieve a parent. Once we have the object, we can perform `shelf['parent:'+object._id]= object` to persist a change.
    - Deleting the parent can lead to one of two behaviors. One choice is to cascade the deletion to include all the children that refer to the parent. Alternatively, we may write code to prohibit the deletion of parents that still have child references. Both are sensible, and the choice is driven by the requirements imposed by the problem domain.
- CRUD operations on dependent (or child) objects:
    - We can create a new child that refers to an existing parent. We must tackle the key design issue to decide what kind of keys we want to use for children.
    - We can update, retrieve, or delete the child outside the parent. This can even include assigning the child to a different parent.

As the code to replace an object is the same as the code to update an object, half of the CRUD processing is handled through the simple assignment statement. Deletion is done with the `del` statement. The issue of deleting children associated with a parent might involve a retrieval to locate the children. What's left, then, is an examination of retrieve processing, which can be a bit more complex.

Searching, scanning, and querying

Don't panic; these are all just synonyms. We'll use the words interchangeably.

We have two design choices when looking at database searches. We can either return a sequence of keys or we can return a sequence of objects. As our design emphasizes storing the keys in each object, getting a sequence of objects from the database is sufficient, so we'll focus on that kind of design.

A search is inherently inefficient. We'd prefer to have more focused indices. We'll look at how we can create more useful indices in the following section. The fallback plan of brute-force scans, however, always works.

When a child class has an independent-style key, we can easily scan a shelf for all instances of some `Child` class using a simple iterator over the keys. Here's a generator expression that locates all the children:

```
children = ( shelf[k] for k in shelf.keys() if key.
startswith("Child:") )
```

This looks at every single key in the shelf to pick the subset that begins with `"Child:"`. We can build on this to apply more criteria by using a more complex generator expression:

```
children_by_title = ( c for c in children if c.title == "some title" )
```

We've used a nested generator expression to expand on the initial `children` query, adding criteria. Nested generator expressions like this are remarkably efficient in Python. This does not make two scans of the database. It's a single scan with two conditions. Each result from the inner generator feeds the outer generator to build the result.

When a child class has a dependent-style key, we can search the shelf for children of a specific parent using an iterator with a more complex matching rule. Here's a generator expression that locates all children of a given parent:

```
children_of = ( shelf[k] for k in shelf.keys() if key.
startswith(parent+":Child:") )
```

This dependent-style key structure makes it particularly easy to remove a parent and all children in a simple loop:

```
for obj in (shelf[k] for k in shelf.keys() if key.startswith(parent)):
    del obj
```

When using hierarchical "`Parent:`*pid*`:Child:`*cid*" keys, we do have to be careful when separating parents from their children. With this multi-part key, we'll see lots of object keys that start with "Parent:*pid*". One of these keys will be the proper parent, simply "`Parent:`*pid*". The other keys will be children with "`Parent:`*pid*`:Child:`*cid*". We have three kinds of conditions that we'll often use for these brute-force searches:

- `key.startswith("Parent:pid")` finds a union of parents and children; this isn't a common requirement.
- `key.startswith("Parent:pid:Child:")` finds just children of the given parent. We might use a regular expression such as `r"^(Parent:\d+):(Child:\d+)$"` to match the keys.
- `key.startswith("Parent:pid")` and `":Child:"` key finds just parents, excluding children. We might use a regular expression such as `r"^Parent:\d+$"` to match the keys.

All of these queries can be optimized by building indices.

Designing an access layer for shelve

Here's how `shelve` might be used by an application. We'll look at parts of an application that edits and saves microblog posts. We'll break the application into two tiers: the application tier and the data tier. Within an application tier, we'll distinguish between two layers:

- **Application processing**: These objects are not persistent. These classes will embody the behavior of the application as a whole. These classes respond to the user selection of commands, menu items, buttons, and other processing elements.
- **Problem domain data model**: These are the objects that will get written to a shelf. These objects embody the state of the application as a whole.

The definitions of blog and post shown previously have no formal association between blog and its collection of posts. The classes are independent so that we can process them separately on the shelf. We don't want to create a single, large container object by turning `Blog` into a collection class.

Within the data tier, there might be a number of features, depending on the complexity of the data storage. We'll focus on just two features:

- **Access**: These components provide uniform access to the problem domain objects. We'll define an `Access` class that provides access to the `Blog` and `Post` instances. It will also manage the keys to locate `Blog` and `Post` objects in the shelf.
- **Persistence**: The components serialize and write problem domain objects to persistent storage. This is the `shelve` module.

We'll break the `Access` class into three separate pieces. Here's the first part with various parts of file open and close:

```
import shelve
class Access:
    def new( self, filename ):
        self.database= shelve.open(filename,'n')
        self.max= { 'Post': 0, 'Blog': 0 }
        self.sync()
    def open( self, filename ):
        self.database= shelve.open(filename,'w')
        self.max= self.database['_DB:max']
    def close( self ):
        if self.database:
            self.database['_DB:max']= self.max
            self.database.close()
        self.database= None
    def sync( self ):
        self.database['_DB:max']= self.max
        self.database.sync()
    def quit( self ):
        self.close()
```

For `Access.new()`, we'll create a new, empty shelf. For `Access.open()`, we'll open an existing shelf. For closing and synchronizing, we've made sure to post a small dictionary of the current maximum key values into the shelf.

We haven't addressed things such as implementing a `Save As...` method to make a copy of the file. Nor have we addressed a quit-without-saving option to revert to the previous version of a database file. These additional features involve the use of the `os` module to manage the file copies. We've provided you with both `close()` and `quit()` methods. This can make it slightly simpler to design a GUI application. Here are the various methods to update the shelf with `Blog` and `Post` objects:

```
    def add_blog( self, blog ):
        self.max['Blog'] += 1
```

```
        key= "Blog:{id}".format(id=self.max['Blog'])
        blog._id= key
        self.database[blog._id]= blog
        return blog
    def get_blog( self, id ):
        return self.database[id]
    def add_post( self, blog, post ):
        self.max['Post'] += 1
        try:
            key= "{blog}:Post:{id}".format(blog=blog._id,id=self.
max['Post'])
        except AttributeError:
            raise OperationError( "Blog not added" )
        post._id= key
        post._blog= blog._id
        self.database[post._id]= post
        return post
    def get_post( self, id ):
        return self.database[id]
    def replace_post( self, post ):
        self.database[post._id]= post
        return post
    def delete_post( self, post ):
        del self.database[post._id]
```

We've provided a minimal set of methods to put `Blog` in the shelf with its associated `Post` instances. When we add `Blog`, the `add_blog()` method first computes a new key, then updates the `Blog` object with the key, and finally, it persists the `Blog` object in the shelf. We've highlighted the lines that change the shelf contents. Simply setting an item in the shelf, similar to setting an item in a dictionary, will make the object persistent.

When we add a post, we must provide the parent `Blog` so that the two are properly associated on the shelf. In this case, we get the `Blog` key, create a new `Post` key, and then update the `Post` with the key values. This updated `Post` can be persisted on the shelf. The highlighted line in `add_post()` makes the object persistent in the shelf.

In the unlikely event that we try to add a `Post` without having previously added the parent `Blog`, we'll have attribute errors because the `Blog._id` attribute will not be available.

We've provided representative methods to replace `Post` and delete `Post`. There are several other possible operations; we didn't include methods to replace `Blog` or delete `Blog`. When we write the method to delete `Blog`, we have to address the question of preventing the deletion when there are still `Posts` or cascading the deletion to include `Posts`. Finally, there are some search methods that act as iterators to query `Blog` and `Post` instances:

```
    def __iter__( self ):
        for k in self.database:
            if k[0] == "_": continue
            yield self.database[k]
    def blog_iter( self ):
        for k in self.database:
            if not k.startswith("Blog:"): continue
            if ":Post:" in k: continue # Skip children
            yield self.database[k]
    def post_iter( self, blog ):
        key= "{blog}:Post:".format(blog=blog._id)
        for k in self.database:
            if not k.startswith(key): continue
            yield self.database[k]
    def title_iter( self, blog, title ):
        return ( p for p in self.post_iter(blog) if p.title == title )
```

We've defined the default iterator, `__iter__()`, that filters out the internal objects that have keys beginning with `_`. So far, we've only defined one such key, `_DB:max`, but this design leaves us with room to invent others.

The `blog_iter()` method iterates through the `Blog` entries. As both `Blog` and `Post` entries have keys that begin with `"Blog:"`, we must explicitly discard the `Post` entries that are children of `Blog`. A purpose-built index object is often a better approach. We'll look at that in the following section.

The `post_iter()` method iterates through posts that are a part of a specific blog. The `title_iter()` method examines posts that match a particular title. This examines each key in the shelf—a potentially inefficient operation.

We've also defined an iterator that locates posts that have the requested title in a given blog. This is a simple generator function that uses the `post_iter()` method function and returns only matching titles.

Writing a demonstration script

We'll use a technology spike to show you how an application might use this `Access` class to process the microblog objects. The spike script will save some `Blog` and `Post` objects to a database to show a sequence of operations that an application might use. This demonstration script can be expanded into unit test cases. More complete unit tests would show us that all the features are present and work correctly. This small spike script shows us how `Access` works:

```
from contextlib import closing
with closing( Access() ) as access:
    access.new( 'blog' )
    access.add_blog( b1 )
    # b1._id is set.
    for post in p2, p3:
        access.add_post( b1, post )
        # post._id is set
    b = access.get_blog( b1._id )
    print( b._id, b )
    for p in access.post_iter( b ):
        print( p._id, p )
    access.quit()
```

We've created the `Access` class on the access layer so that it's wrapped in a context manager. The objective is to be sure that the access layer is closed properly, irrespective of any exceptions that might get raised.

With `Access.new()`, we've created a new shelf named `'blog'`. This might be done by a GUI by navigating to **File | New**. We added the new blog, `b1`, to the shelf. The `Access.add_blog()` method will update the `Blog` object with its shelf key. Perhaps someone filled in the blanks on a page and clicked on **New Blog** on their GUI application.

Once we've added `Blog`, we can add two posts to it. The key from the parent `Blog` entry will be used to build the keys for each of the child `Post` entries. Again, the idea is that a user filled in some fields and clicked on **New Post** on a GUI.

There's a final set of queries that dumps the keys and objects from the shelf. This shows us the final outcome of this script. We can perform `Access.get_blog()` to retrieve a blog entry that was created. We can iterate through the posts that are part of that blog using `Access.post_iter()`. The final `Access.quit()` assures that the maxima used to generate unique keys are recorded and the shelf is closed properly.

Creating indexes to improve efficiency

One of the rules of efficiency is to avoid search. Our previous example of using an iterator over the keys in a shelf is inefficient. To state that more strongly, search *defines* inefficiency. We'll emphasize this.

> Brute-force search is perhaps the worst possible way to work with data. We must always design indexes that are based on subsets or mappings to improve performance.

To avoid searching, we need to create indexes that list the items we want. This saves reading through the entire shelf to find an item or subset of items. A shelf index can't reference Python objects, as that would change the granularity at which the objects are stored. A shelf index must only list key values. This makes navigation among objects indirect but still much faster than a brute-force search of all items in the shelf.

As an example of an index, we can keep a list of the `Post` keys associated with each `Blog` in the shelf. We can easily change the `add_blog()`, `add_post()`, and `delete_post()` methods to update the associated `Blog` entry too. Here are the revised versions of these blog update methods:

```
class Access2( Access ):
    def add_blog( self, blog ):
        self.max['Blog'] += 1
        key= "Blog:{id}".format(id=self.max['Blog'])
        blog._id= key
        blog._post_list= []
        self.database[blog._id]= blog
        return blog

    def add_post( self, blog, post ):
        self.max['Post'] += 1
        try:
            key= "{blog}:Post:{id}".format(blog=blog._id,id=self.
max['Post'])
        except AttributeError:
            raise OperationError( "Blog not added" )
        post._id= key
        post._blog= blog._id
        self.database[post._id]= post
        blog._post_list.append( post._id )
        self.database[blog._id]= blog
        return post
```

```
    def delete_post( self, post ):
        del self.database[post._id]
        blog= self.database[blog._id]
        blog._post_list.remove( post._id )
        self.database[blog._id]= blog
```

The add_blog() method ensures that each Blog has an extra attribute, _post_list. This will be updated by other methods to maintain a list of keys for each Post that belongs to Blog. Note that we're not adding Posts themselves. If we do this, we collapse an entire Blog into a single entry into the shelf. By adding just the key information, we keep the Blog and Post objects separated.

The add_post() method adds Post to the shelf. It also appends Post._id to a list of keys maintained at the Blog level. This means any Blog object will have _post_list that provides a sequence of keys for the child posts.

This method makes two updates to the shelf. The first is simply saving the Post object. The second update is important. We do not attempt to simply mutate the Blog object that exists in the shelf. We intentionally store the object to the shelf to be sure that the object is persisted in its updated form.

Similarly, the delete_post() method keeps the index up-to-date by removing an unused post from _post_list of the owning blog. As with add_post(), two updates are done to the shelf: a del statement removes Post and then the Blog object is updated to reflect the change in the index.

This change alters our queries for the Post objects in profound ways. Here is the revised version of the search methods:

```
    def __iter__( self ):
        for k in self.database:
            if k[0] == "_": continue
            yield self.database[k]
    def blog_iter( self ):
        for k in self.database:
            if not k.startswith("Blog:"): continue
            if ":Post:" in k: continue # Skip children
            yield self.database[k]
    def post_iter( self, blog ):
        for k in blog._post_list:
            yield self.database[k]
    def title_iter( self, blog, title ):
        return ( p for p in self.post_iter(blog) if p.title == title )
```

We're able to replace the scan in `post_iter()` with a much more efficient operation. This loop will rapidly yield the `Post` objects based on the keys saved in the `_post_list` attribute of `Blog`. We could consider replacing this `for` statement with a generator expression:

```
return (self.database[k] for k in blog._post_list)
```

The point of this optimization to the `post_iter()` method is to eliminate the search of *all* the keys for the matching keys. We've replaced searching all keys with simple iteration over an appropriate sequence of relevant keys. A simple timing test, which alternates between updating `Blog` and `Post` and rendering the `Blog` to RST, shows us the following results:

```
Access2: 14.9
Access: 19.3
```

As expected, eliminating the search reduced the time required to process `Blog` and its individual `Posts`. The change is profound; almost 25 percent of the processing time is wasted in the search.

Creating top-level indices

We added an index to each `Blog` that locates `Posts` which belong to that `Blog`. We can also add a top-level index to the shelf that locates all `Blog` instances. The essential design is similar to what's been shown previously. For each blog to be added or deleted, we must update an index structure. We must also update the iterators to properly use the index. Here's another class design for mediating the access to our objects:

```
class Access3( Access2 ):
    def new( self, *args, **kw ):
        super().new( *args, **kw )
        self.database['_DB:Blog']= list()

    def add_blog( self, blog ):
        self.max['Blog'] += 1
        key= "Blog:{id}".format(id=self.max['Blog'])
        blog._id= key
        blog._post_list= []
        self.database[blog._id]= blog
        self.database['_DB:Blog'].append( blog._id )
        return blog

    def blog_iter( self ):
        return ( self.database[k] for k in self.database['_DB:Blog'] )
```

When creating a new database, we add an administrative object and an index, with a key of `"_DB:Blog"`. This index will be a list where we'll store the keys to each `Blog` entry. When we add a new `Blog` object, we also update this `"_DB:Blog"` object with the revised list of keys. We didn't show the delete implementation. It should be self-evident.

When we iterate through `Blog` postings, we use the index list instead of a brute-force search of keys in the database. Here are the performance results:

```
Access3: 4.0
Access2: 15.1
Access: 19.4
```

We can conclude from this that *most* of the processing time is wasted in a brute-force search of keys in the database. This should reinforce the notion that everything we can possibly do to avoid the search will dramatically improve the performance of our programs.

Adding yet more index maintenance

Clearly, the index maintenance aspect of a shelf can grow. With our simple data model, we could easily add more top-level indexes for tags, dates, and titles of `Posts`. Here's another access layer implementation that defines two indices for `Blogs`. One index simply lists the keys for `Blog` entries. The other index provides keys based on the `Blog` title. We'll assume the titles are not unique. We'll present this access layer in three parts. Here's the *Create* part of the CRUD processing:

```
class Access4( Access2 ):
    def new( self, *args, **kw ):
        super().new( *args, **kw )
        self.database['_DB:Blog']= list()
        self.database['_DB:Blog_Title']= defaultdict(list)

    def add_blog( self, blog ):
        self.max['Blog'] += 1
        key= "Blog:{id}".format(id=self.max['Blog'])
        blog._id= key
        blog._post_list= []
        self.database[blog._id]= blog
        self.database['_DB:Blog'].append( blog._id )
        blog_title= self.database['_DB:Blog_Title']
        blog_title[blog.title].append( blog._id )
        self.database['_DB:Blog_Title']= blog_title
        return blog
```

We've added two indices: a simple list of the `Blog` keys plus `defaultdict` that provides us with a list of keys for a given title string. If each title is unique, the lists will all be singletons. If the titles are not unique, then each title will have a list of the `Blog` keys.

When we add a `Blog` instance, we also update the two indices. The simple list of keys is updated by appending the new key and saving it to the shelf. The title index requires us to get the existing `defaultdict` from the shelf, append to the list of keys mapped to the `Blog's` title, and then put the `defaultdict` back onto the shelf. The next section shows us the *Update* part of the CRUD processing:

```
def update_blog( self, blog ):
    """Replace this Blog; update index."""
    self.database[blog._id]= blog
    blog_title= self.database['_DB:Blog_Title']
    # Remove key from index in old spot.
    empties= []
    for k in blog_title:
        if blog._id in blog_title[k]:
            blog_title[k].remove( blog._id )
            if len(blog_title[k]) == 0: empties.append( k )
    # Cleanup zero-length lists from defaultdict.
    for k in empties:
        del blog_title[k]
    # Put key into index in new spot.
    blog_title[blog.title].append( blog._id )
    self.database['_DB:Blog_Title']= blog_title
```

When we update a `Blog` object, we might be changing the title of the `Blog` attribute. If our model had more attributes and more indices, we might want to compare the revised value with the value in the shelf to see which attributes changed. For this simple model—with only one attribute—no comparison is required to determine which attributes have changed.

The first part of the operation is to remove the key of the `Blog` from the index. As we haven't cached the previous value of the `Blog.title` attribute, we can't simply remove the key based on the old title. Instead, we're forced to search the index for the key of `Blog` and remove the key from whatever title it's associated with.

`Blog` with a unique title will leave the title's list of keys empty. We should clean up an unused title too.

Once the key associated with the old title has been removed from the index, we can append the key to the index using the new title. These final two lines are identical to the code used when creating `Blog` in the first place. Here are some retrieve processing examples:

```
    def blog_iter( self ):
        return ( self.database[k] for k in self.database['_DB:Blog'] )

    def blog_title_iter( self, title ):
        blog_title= self.database['_DB:Blog_Title']
        return ( self.database[k] for k in blog_title[title] )
```

The `blog_iter()` method function iterates through all the blogs by fetching the index object from the shelf. The `blog_title_iter()` method function uses the index to fetch all the blogs with a given title. When there are many individual blogs, this should find a blog by title very quickly.

The writeback alternative to index updates

We can request that a shelf be opened with `writeback=True`. This will track changes to mutable objects by keeping a cached version of each object. Rather than burdening the `shelve` module with tracking all accessed objects to detect and preserve changes, the designs shown here will update a mutable object and specifically force the shelf to update the persistent version of the object.

This is a small shift in the runtime performance. An `add_post()` operation, for example, becomes slightly more costly because it also involves updating a `Blog` entry. If multiple `Posts` are added, these additional `Blog` updates become a kind of an overhead. However, this cost may be balanced by the improved performance of rendering `Blog` by avoiding a lengthy search of the shelf keys to track down the posts for a given blog. The designs shown here avoid creating a `writeback` cache that could grow unbounded during the running of an application.

Schema evolution

When working with `shelve`, we have to address the problem of schema evolution. Our objects have a dynamic state and a static class definition. We can easily persist the dynamic state. Our class definitions are the schema for the persistent data. The class, however, is not *absolutely* static. If we change a class definition, how will we fetch objects from the shelf? A good design often involves some combination of the following techniques.

Changes to method functions and properties don't change the persisted object state. We can classify these as minor changes, as the shelved data is still compatible with the changed class definition. A new software release can have a new minor version number and users should be confident that it will work without problems.

Changes to attributes will change the persisted objects. We can call these major changes, and the shelved data will no longer be compatible with the new class definition. These kinds of changes should not be made by *modifying* a class definition. These kinds of changes should be made by defining a new subclass and providing an updated factory function to create instances of any version of the class.

We can be flexible about supporting multiple versions, or we can use one-time conversions. To be flexible, we must rely on factory functions to create instances of objects. A flexible application will avoid creating objects directly. By using a factory function, we're assured that all parts of an application can work consistently. We might do something like this to support flexible schema changes:

```
def make_blog( *args, **kw ):
    version= kw.pop('_version',1)
    if version == 1: return Blog( *args, **kw )
    elif version == 2: return Blog2( *args, **kw )
    else: raise Exception( "Unknown Version {0}".format(version) )
```

This kind of factory function requires a `_version` keyword argument to specify which `Blog` class definition to use. This allows us to upgrade a schema to use different classes without breaking our application. The `Access` layer can rely on this kind of function to instantiate correct versions of objects. We can also make a fluent factory that looks like this:

```
class Blog:
    @staticmethod
    def version( self, version ):
        self.version= version
    @staticmethod
    def blog( self, *args, **kw ):
        if self.version == 1: return Blog1( *args, **kw )
        elif self.version == 2: return Blog2( *args, **kw )
        else: raise Exception( "Unknown Version {0}".format(self.
version) )
```

We can use this factory as follows:

```
blog= Blog.version(2).blog( title=this, other_attribute=that )
```

A shelf should include the schema version information, perhaps as a special `__version__` key. This will provide information for an access layer to determine what version of a class should be used. Applications should fetch this object first after opening the shelf and fail quickly when the schema version is wrong.

An alternative to this level of flexibility is a one-time conversion. This feature of the application will fetch all shelved objects using their old class definition, convert to the new class definition, and store them back to the shelf in the new format. For a GUI application, this may be part of an open file or a saved file. For a web server, this may be a script that is run by an administrator as part of an application release.

Summary

We've seen the basics of how to use the `shelve` module. This includes creating a shelf and designing keys to access the objects we've placed in the shelf. We've also seen the need for an access layer to perform the lower-level CRUD operations on the shelf. The idea is that we need to distinguish between the class definitions that are focused on our application and other administrative details that support persistence.

Design considerations and trade-offs

One of the strengths of the `shelve` module is allowing us to persist distinct items. This imposes a design burden to identify the proper granularity of the items. Too fine a granularity and we waste time assembling containers from their pieces. Too coarse a granularity and we waste time fetching and storing items that aren't relevant.

Since a shelf requires a key, we must design appropriate keys for our objects. We must also manage the keys for our various objects. This means using additional attributes to store keys and possibly creating additional collections of keys to act as indices for items on the shelf.

A key used to access an item in a `shelve` database is like a `weakref`; it's an indirect reference. This means that extra processing is required to track and access the items from the reference. For more information on `weakref`, see *Chapter 2, Integrating Seamlessly with Python – Basic Special Methods*.

One choice for a key is to locate an attribute or combination of attributes that are proper primary keys and cannot be changed. Another choice is to generate surrogate keys that cannot be changed; this allows all other attributes to be changed. As `shelve` relies on `pickle` to represent the items on the shelf, we have a high-performance native representation of the Python objects. This reduces the complexity of designing classes that will be placed onto a shelf. Any Python object can be persisted.

Application software layers

Because of the relative sophistication available when using `shelve`, our application software must become more properly layered. Generally, we'll look at software architectures with layers such as the following:

- **Presentation layer**: The top-level user interface, either a web presentation or a desktop GUI.
- **Application layer**: The internal services or controllers that make the application work. This could be called the processing model, different from the logical data model.
- **Business layer or problem domain model layer**: The objects that define the business domain or problem space. This is sometimes called the logical data model. We've looked at how we might model these objects, using a microblog `Blog` and `Post` example.
- **Infrastructure**: It often includes several layers as well as other cross-cutting concerns such as logging, security, and network access.
- **Data access layer**. These are protocols or methods to access data objects. We've looked at designing classes to access our application objects from the `shelve` storage.
- **Persistence layer**. This is the physical data model as seen in file storage. The `shelve` module implements persistence.

When looking at this chapter and *Chapter 11, Storing and Retrieving Objects via SQLite,* it becomes clear that mastering object-oriented programming involves some higher-level design patterns. We can't simply design classes in isolation, but we need to look at how classes are going to be organized into larger structures. Finally, and most importantly, brute-force search is a terrible thing. It simply must be avoided.

Looking forward

The next chapter will roughly parallel this chapter. We'll look at using SQLite instead of shelve for the persistence of our objects. The complexity is that a SQL database doesn't provide a way to store complex Python objects, leading to the impedance mismatch problem. We'll look at two ways to solve this problem when using a relational database such as SQLite.

Chapter 12, Transmitting and Sharing Objects, will shift the focus from simple persistence to transmitting and sharing objects. This will rely on the persistence we've seen in this part; it will add network protocols to the mix.

11
Storing and Retrieving Objects via SQLite

There are many applications where we need to persist objects individually. The techniques we looked at in *Chapter 9, Serializing and Saving - JSON, YAML, Pickle, CSV, and XML*, were biased towards handling a single, monolithic object. Sometimes, we need to persist separate, individual objects from a larger domain. We might be saving blog entries, blog posts, authors, and advertising in a single file structure.

In *Chapter 10, Storing and Retrieving Objects via Shelve*, we looked at storing distinct Python objects in a `shelve` data store. This allowed us to implement the CRUD processing on a large domain of objects. Any individual object can be created, retrieved, updated, or deleted without having to load and dump the entire file.

In this chapter, we'll look at mapping Python objects to a relational database; specifically, the `sqlite3` database that is bundled with Python. This will be another example of the **Three-Tier Architecture** design pattern.

In this case, the SQLite data tier is a more sophisticated database than Shelve. SQLite can allow concurrent updates via locking. SQLite offers an access layer based on the SQL language. It offers persistence by saving SQL tables to the filesystem. Web applications are one example where a database is used instead of simple file persistence to handle concurrent updates to a single pool of data. RESTful data servers, too, frequently use a relational database to provide access to persistent objects.

For scalability, a standalone database server process can be used to isolate all the database transactions. This means that they can be allocated to one relatively secure host computer, separate from the Web application servers and behind appropriate firewalls. MySQL, for example, can be implemented as a standalone server process. SQLite is not a standalone database server; it must exist as part of a host application; for our purposes, Python is the host.

SQL databases, persistence, and objects

When using SQLite, we will use a relational database with an access layer based on the SQL language. The SQL language is a legacy from an era when object-oriented programming was a rarity. The SQL language is heavily biased towards procedural programming, creating what's termed an impedance mismatch between the relational model of data and the object model of data. Within SQL databases, we generally focus on three tiers of data modeling, which are shown here:

- **Conceptual model**: These are the entities and relationships implied by the SQL model. In most cases, these can map to Python objects and should correspond with the data model layer of the application tier. This is the place where an **Object-Relational Mapping** layer is useful.
- **Logical model**: These are the tables, rows, and columns that appear to be in the SQL database. We'll address these entities in our SQL data manipulation statements. We say that these appear to exist because they're implemented by a physical model that may be somewhat different from the tables, rows, and columns in the database schema. The results of a SQL query, for example, look table-like, but may not involve storage that parallels the storage of any defined table.
- **Physical model**: These are the files, blocks, pages, bits, and bytes of persistent physical storage. These entities are defined by the administrative SQL statements. In some more complex database products, we can exercise some control over the physical model of the data to further tweak the performance. In SQLite, however, we have almost no control over this.

We are confronted with a number of design decisions when using SQL databases. Perhaps the most important one is deciding how to cover the impedance mismatch. How do we handle the mapping between SQL's legacy data model to a Python object model? There are three common strategies:

- **No mapping to Python**: This means that we don't fetch complex Python objects from the database but work entirely within the SQL framework of independent atomic data elements and processing functions. This approach will avoid a deep emphasis on object-oriented programming with persistent database objects. This limits us to the four essential SQLite types of NULL, INTEGER, REAL, and TEXT, plus the Python additions of `datetime.date` and `datetime.datetime`.
- **Manual mapping**: We define an access layer to map between our class definitions and the SQL logical model of tables, columns, rows, and keys.
- **ORM layer**: We download and install an ORM layer to handle the mapping between classes and the SQL logical model.

We'll look at all the three choices in the following examples. Before we can look at the mappings from SQL to objects, we'll look at the SQL logical model in some detail and cover the no-mapping option in the process.

The SQL data model – rows and tables

The SQL data model is based on named tables with named columns. The table contains multiple rows of data. Each row is vaguely like a mutable `namedtuple`. The overall table is like `list`.

When we define a SQL database, we define the tables and their columns. When we use a SQL database, we manipulate the rows of data in the tables. In the case of SQLite, we have a narrow domain of data types that SQL will process. SQLite handles `NULL`, `INTEGER`, `REAL`, `TEXT`, and `BLOB` data. Python types `None`, `int`, `float`, `str`, and `bytes` are mapped to these SQL types. Similarly, when data of these types is fetched from a SQLite database, the items are converted into Python objects.

We can mediate this conversion by adding even more conversion functions to SQLite. The `sqlite3` module adds the `datetime.date` and `datetime.datetime` extensions this way. We'll address this under manual mapping, which follows in the next section.

The SQL language can be partitioned into three sublanguages: a **data definition language (DDL)**, a **data manipulation language (DML)**, and a **data control language (DCL)**. The DDL is used to define tables, their columns, and indices. For an example of DDL, we might have some tables defined the following way:

```
CREATE TABLE BLOG(
    ID INTEGER PRIMARY KEY AUTOINCREMENT,
    TITLE TEXT );
CREATE TABLE POST(
    ID INTEGER PRIMARY KEY AUTOINCREMENT,
    DATE TIMESTAMP,
    TITLE TEXT,
    RST_TEXT TEXT,
    BLOG_ID INTEGER REFERENCES BLOG(ID)  );
CREATE TABLE TAG(
    ID INTEGER PRIMARY KEY AUTOINCREMENT,
    PHRASE TEXT UNIQUE ON CONFLICT FAIL );
CREATE TABLE ASSOC_POST_TAG(
  POST_ID INTEGER REFERENCES POST(ID),
  TAG_ID INTEGER REFERENCES TAG(ID) );
```

We've created four tables to represent the `Blog` and `Post` objects for a microblogging application. For more information on the SQL language processed by SQLite, see `http://www.sqlite.org/lang.html`. For a broader background in SQL, books such as *Creating your MySQL Database: Practical Design Tips and Techniques* will introduce the SQL language in the context of the MySQL database. The SQL language is case insensitive. For no good reason, we prefer to see SQL in all uppercase to distinguish it from the surrounding Python code.

The `BLOG` table defines a primary key with the `AUTOINCREMENT` option; this will allow SQLite to assign the key values, saving us from having to generate the keys in our code. The `TITLE` column is the title for a blog. We've defined it to be `TEXT`. In some database products, we must provide a maximum size; this is not required in SQLite, so we'll avoid the clutter.

The `POST` table defines a primary key as well as date, title, and RST text for the body of the post. Note that we did not reference the tags in this table definition. We'll return to the design patterns required for the following SQL tables. The `POST` table does, however, include a formal `REFERENCES` clause to show us that this is a foreign key reference to the owning `BLOG`. The `TAG` table defines the individual tag text items, and nothing more.

Finally, we have an association table between `POST` and `TAG`. This table has only two foreign keys. It associates tags and posts, allowing an unlimited number of tags per post as well as an unlimited number of posts to share a common tag. This association table is a common SQL design pattern to handle this kind of a relationship. We'll look at some other SQL design patterns in the following section. We can execute the preceding definitions to create our database:

```
import sqlite3
database = sqlite3.connect('p2_c11_blog.db')
database.executescript( sql_ddl )
```

All database access requires a connection, created with the module function, `sqlite3.connect()`. We provided the name of the file to assign to our database. We'll look at the additional parameters for this function in separate sections.

The DB-API presumes that there is a separate database server process on which our application process is connecting. In the case of SQLite, there isn't really a separate process. A `connect()` function is used, however, to comply with the standard.

The `sql_ddl` variable is simply a long string variable with the four `CREATE TABLE` statements. If there are no error messages, then it means that the table structures have been defined.

The `Connection.executescript()` method is described in the Python Standard Library as a *nonstandard shortcut*. Technically, database operations involve `cursor`. The following is a standardized approach:

```
crsr = database.cursor()
for stmt in sql_ddl.split(";"):
    crsr.execute(stmt)
```

As we're focused on SQLite, we'll use the nonstandard shortcuts heavily. If we were concerned about portability to other databases, we'd shift focus to a more strict compliance with DB-API. We'll return to the nature of a cursor object in the following section, when looking at queries.

CRUD processing via SQL DML statements

The following four canonical CRUD operations map directly to SQL language statements:

- The creation is done via the `INSERT` statement
- The Retrieval is done via the `SELECT` statement
- The Updates is done via the `UPDATE` statement as well as the `REPLACE` statement, when it's supported
- The deletion is done via the `DELETE` statement

We have to note that there's a literal SQL syntax, and syntax with binding variable placeholders instead of literal values. The literal SQL syntax is acceptable for scripts; however, because the values are always literal, it is perfectly awful for application programming. Building literal SQL statements in an application involves endless string manipulation and famous security problems. See `http://xkcd.com/327/` for a specific security issue with assembling literal SQL. We'll focus exclusively on SQL with binding variables.

Literal SQL is widely used, which is a mistake.

> Never build literal SQL DML statements with string manipulation.

The Python DB-API interface, **Python Enhancement Proposal (PEP)** 249, `http://www.python.org/dev/peps/pep-0249/`, defines several ways to bind application variables into SQL statements. SQLite can use positional bindings with `?` or named bindings with `:name`. We'll show you both styles of binding variables.

We use an `INSERT` statement to create a new `BLOG` row as shown in the following code snippet:

```
create_blog= """
INSERT INTO BLOG(TITLE) VALUES(?)
"""
database.execute(create_blog, ("Travel Blog",))
```

We created a SQL statement with a positional bind variable, `?`, for the `TITLE` column of the `BLOG` table. We then execute that statement after binding a tuple of values to the bind variables. There's only one bind variable, so there's only one value in the tuple. Once the statement has been executed, we have a row in the database.

We show the SQL statements clearly separated from the surrounding Python code in triple-quoted long string literals. In some applications, the SQL is stored as a separate configuration item. Keeping SQL separate is best handled as a mapping from a statement name to the SQL text. We could, for example, keep the SQL in a JSON file. This means we can use `SQL=json.load("sql_config.json")` to fetch all SQL statements. We can then use `SQL["some statement name"]` to refer to the text of a particular SQL statement. This can simplify application maintenance by keeping the SQL out of the Python programming.

The `DELETE` and `UPDATE` statements require a `WHERE` clause to specify which rows will be changed or removed. To change a blog's title, we might do something as follows:

```
update_blog="""
UPDATE BLOG SET TITLE=:new_title WHERE TITLE=:old_title
"""
database.execute( "BEGIN" )
database.execute( update_blog,
    dict(new_title="2013-2014 Travel", old_title="Travel Blog") )
database.commit()
```

The `UPDATE` statement has two named bind variables: `:new_title` and `:old_title`. This transaction will update all the rows in the `BLOG` table that have the given old title, setting the title to the new title. Ideally, the title is unique, and only a single row is touched. SQL operations are defined to work on sets of rows. It's a matter of database design to ensure that a desired row is the content of a set. Hence, the suggestion is to have a unique primary key for every table.

When implementing a delete operation, we always have two choices. We can either prohibit deletes of a parent when children still exist, or we can cascade the deletion of a parent to also delete the relevant children. We'll look at a cascading delete of `Blog`, `Post`, and tag associations. Here's a `DELETE` sequence of statements:

```
delete_post_tag_by_blog_title= """
DELETE FROM ASSOC_POST_TAG
```

```
WHERE POST_ID IN (
    SELECT DISTINCT POST_ID
    FROM BLOG JOIN POST ON BLOG.ID = POST.BLOG_ID
    WHERE BLOG.TITLE=:old_title)
"""
delete_post_by_blog_title= """
DELETE FROM POST WHERE BLOG_ID IN (
    SELECT ID FROM BLOG WHERE TITLE=:old_title)
"""
delete_blog_by_title="""
DELETE FROM BLOG WHERE TITLE=:old_title
"""
try:
    with database:
        title= dict(old_title="2013-2014 Travel")
        database.execute( delete_post_tag_by_blog_title, title )
        database.execute( delete_post_by_blog_title, title )
        database.execute( delete_blog_by_title, title )
    print( "Delete finished normally." )
except Exception as e:
    print( "Rolled Back due to {0}".format(e) )
```

We've done a three-step delete operation. First, we deleted all the rows from `ASSOC_POST_TAG` for a given `Blog` based on the title. Note the nested query; we'll look at queries in the next section. Navigation among tables is a common issue with SQL construction. In this case, we have to query the `BLOG-POST` relationship to locate the `POST` IDs that will be removed; then, we can remove rows from `ASSOC_POST_TAG` for the posts associated with a blog that will be removed. Next, we deleted all the posts belonging to a particular blog. This too involves a nested query to locate the IDs of the blog based on the title. Finally, we can delete the blog itself.

This is an example of an explicit cascade delete design, where we have to cascade the operation from the `BLOG` table to two other tables. We wrapped the entire suite of deletes in a `with` context so that it would all commit as a single transaction. In the event of failure, it would roll back the partial changes, leaving the database as it was.

Querying rows with the SQL SELECT statement

It's possible to write a substantial book on the `SELECT` statement alone. We'll skip all but the most fundamental features of `SELECT`. Our purpose is to cover just enough SQL to store and retrieve objects from a database.

Previously, we mentioned that, technically, we're supposed to use a cursor when executing SQL statements. For DDL and other DML statements, the presence or absence of a cursor doesn't matter very much. We'll use the explicit creation of the cursor because it greatly simplifies SQL programming.

For a query, however, the cursor is essential for retrieving the rows from the database. To locate a blog by title, we can start with something as simple as the following code:

```
"SELECT * FROM BLOG WHERE TITLE=?"
```

We need to fetch the resulting collection of row objects. Even when we're expecting one row as a response, in the SQL world, everything is a collection. Generally, every result set from a `SELECT` query looks like a table with rows and columns defined by the `SELECT` statement instead of any `CREATE TABLE` DDL.

In this case, using `SELECT *` means we've avoided enumerating the expected result columns. This might lead to a large number of columns being retrieved. Here's a common optimization for doing this using the SQLite shortcuts:

```
query_blog_by_title= """
SELECT * FROM BLOG WHERE TITLE=?
"""
for blog in database.execute( query_blog_by_title, ("2013-2014
Travel",) ):
    print( blog[0], blog[1] )
```

In the `SELECT` statement, the `*` is shorthand for all the available columns. It's only really useful for simple queries that involve a single table.

We've bound the requested blog title to the "`?`" parameter in the `SELECT` statement. The result of the `execute()` function is a cursor object. A cursor is iterable; it will yield all the rows in the result set and all the rows that match the selection criteria in the `WHERE` clause.

To be fully compliant with the Python DB-API standard, we could break it down into the following steps:

```
crsr= database.cursor()
crsr.execute( query_blog_by_title, ("2013-2014 Travel",) )
for blog in crsr.fetchall():
    print( blog[0], blog[1] )
```

This shows us how we use the connection to create a cursor object. We can then execute a query statement using the cursor object. Once we've executed the query, we can fetch all the rows in the result set. Each row will be a tuple of the values from the `SELECT` clause. In this case, as the `SELECT` clause is `*`, it means that all the columns from the original `CREATE TABLE` statement will be used.

SQL transactions and the ACID properties

As we've seen, the SQL DML statements map to the CRUD operations. When discussing the features of the SQL transactions, we'll be looking at the sequences of the `INSERT`, `SELECT`, `UPDATE`, and `DELETE` statements.

The SQL DML statements all work within the context of a SQL transaction. The SQL statements executed within a transaction are a logical unit of work. The entire transaction can be committed as a whole or rolled back as a whole. This supports the Atomicity property.

SQL DDL statements (that is, `CREATE`, `DROP`) do not work within a transaction. They implicitly end any previous in-process transaction. After all, they're changing the structure of the database; they're a different kind of statement, and the transaction concept doesn't apply.

The ACID properties are Atomic, Consistent, Isolated, and Durable. These are essential features of a transaction that consists of multiple database operations. For more information, see *Chapter 10, Storing and Retrieving Objects via Shelve*.

Unless working in a special **read uncommitted** mode, each connection to the database sees a consistent version of the data containing only the results of the committed transactions. Uncommitted transactions are generally invisible to other database client processes, supporting the Consistency property.

A SQL transaction also supports the Isolation property. SQLite supports several different **isolation level** settings. The isolation level defines how the SQL DML statements interact among multiple, concurrent processes. This is based on how locks are used and how a processes' SQL requests are delayed waiting for locks. From Python, the isolation level is set when the connection is made to the database.

Each SQL database product takes a different approach to the isolation level and locking. There's no single model.

In the case of SQLite, there are four isolation levels that define the locking and the nature of transactions. For details, see `http://www.sqlite.org/isolation.html`. Here are the isolation levels:

- `isolation_level=None`: This is the default, otherwise known as the **autocommit** mode. In this mode, each individual SQL statement is committed to the database as it's executed. This breaks Atomicity unless, by some weird quirk, all of the transactions happen to involve only a single SQL statement.
- `isolation_level='DEFERRED'`: In this mode, locks are acquired as late as possible in the transaction. The `BEGIN` statement, for example, does not immediately acquire any locks. Other read operations (that is, the `SELECT` statements) will acquire shared locks. Write operations will acquire reserved locks. While this can maximize the concurrency, it can also lead to deadlocks among competing processes.
- `isolation_level='IMMEDIATE'`: In this mode, the transaction `BEGIN` statement acquires a lock that prevents all writes. Reads, however, will continue normally.
- `isolation_level='EXCLUSIVE'`: In this mode, the transaction `BEGIN` statement acquires a lock that prevents almost all access. There's an exception for connections in a special read uncommitted mode that ignores locking.

The Durability property is guaranteed for all committed transactions. The data is written to the database file.

The SQL rules require us to execute `BEGIN TRANSACTION` and `COMMIT TRANSACTION` statements to bracket a sequence of steps. In the event of an error, a `ROLLBACK TRANSACTION` statement is required to unwind the potential changes. The Python interface simplifies this. We can execute a `BEGIN` statement. The other statements are provided as functions of the `sqlite3.Connection` object; we don't execute SQL statements to end a transaction. We might write things such as the following code to be explicit:

```
database = sqlite3.connect('p2_c11_blog.db', isolation_
level='DEFERRED')
try:
    database.execute( 'BEGIN' )
    database.execute( "some statement" )
    database.execute( "another statement" )
    database.commit()
except Exception as e:
    database.rollback()
    raise e
```

We selected an isolation level of DEFERRED when we made the database connection. This leads to a requirement that we explicitly begin and end each transaction. One typical scenario is to wrap the relevant DML in a try block and commit the transaction if things worked, or roll back the transaction in the case of a problem. We can simplify this by using the sqlite3.Connection object as a context manager:

```
database = sqlite3.connect('p2_c11_blog.db', isolation_
level='DEFERRED')
with database:
    database.execute( "some statement" )
    database.execute( "another statement" )
```

This is similar to the previous example. We opened the database in the same way. Rather than executing an explicit BEGIN statement, we entered a context; the context handles Begin for us.

At the end of the with context, database.commit() will be done automatically. In the event of an exception, a database.rollback() will be done, and the exception will be raised by the with statement.

Designing primary and foreign database keys

SQL tables don't specifically require a primary key. However, it's a rather poor design that omits primary keys for the rows of a given table. As we noted in *Chapter 10, Storing and Retrieving Objects via Shelve*, there might be an attribute (or a combination of attributes) that makes a proper primary key. It's also entirely possible that no attribute is suitable as a primary key and we must define surrogate keys.

The previous examples use surrogate keys created by SQLite. This is perhaps the simplest kind of design because it imposes the fewest constraints on the data. One kind of constraint is that a primary key cannot be updated; this becomes a rule that the application programming must enforce. In some cases—for example, when correcting an error in the primary key value—we need to somehow update the primary key. One way to do this is to drop and recreate the constraints. Another way to do this is to delete the faulty row and reinsert the row with the corrected key. When there are cascading deletes, then the transaction required to correct a primary key can become very complex. Using a surrogate key prevents these kinds of problems.

All relationships among tables are done via the primary keys and foreign key references. There are two extremely common design patterns for relationships. The preceding tables show us these two principle design patterns. There are three design patterns for relationships, shown in the following bullet list:

- **One-to-many**: This relationship is between one parent blog and many child posts. The `REFERENCES` clause shows us that many rows in the `POST` table will reference one row from the `BLOG` table. If viewed from the direction of child to parent, it would be called a **Many-to-One** relationship.
- **Many-to-many**: This relationship is between many posts and many tags. This requires an intermediate association table between the `POST` and `TAG` tables; the intermediate table has two (or more) foreign keys. The many-to-many association table can also have attributes of its own.
- **One-to-one**: This relationship is a less common design pattern. There's no technical difference from a one-to-many relationship; the cardinality of either zero rows or one row is a constraint that the application program must manage.

In a database design, there might be constraints on the relationships: the relationship might be described as optional or mandatory; there might be cardinality limits on the relationship. Sometimes, these optionality and cardinality constraints are summarized with short descriptions such as "0:m" meaning "zero to many" or "optional one to many". The optionality and cardinality constraints are part of the application programming logic; there are no formal ways to state these constraints in the SQLite database. The essential table relationships can be implemented in the database in either or both of the following ways:

- **Explicit**: We could call these declared, as they're part of the DDL declaration for a database. Ideally, they're enforced by the database server, and failure to comply with the relationship's constraints can lead to an error of some kind. These relationships will also be repeated in queries.
- **Implicit**: These are relationships that are stated only in queries; they are not a formal part of the DDL.

Note that our table definitions implemented a one-to-many relationship between a blog and the various entries within that blog. We've made use of these relationships in the various queries that we wrote.

Processing application data with SQL

The examples in the previous sections show us what we can call **procedural** SQL processing. We've eschewed any object-oriented design from our problem domain objects. Rather than working with the `Blog` and `Post` objects, we're working with the data elements that SQLite can process: string, date, float, and integer values. We've used mostly procedural-style programming.

We can see that a series of queries can be done to locate a blog, all posts that are part of the blog, and all tags that are associated with a post associated with a blog. The processing would look like the following code:

```
query_blog_by_title= """
SELECT * FROM BLOG WHERE TITLE=?
"""
query_post_by_blog_id= """
SELECT * FROM POST WHERE BLOG_ID=?
"""
query_tag_by_post_id= """
SELECT TAG.*
FROM TAG JOIN ASSOC_POST_TAG ON TAG.ID = ASSOC_POST_TAG.TAG_ID
WHERE ASSOC_POST_TAG.POST_ID=?
"""
for blog in database.execute( query_blog_by_title, ("2013-2014 
Travel",) ):
    print( "Blog", blog )
    for post in database.execute( query_post_by_blog_id, (blog[0],) ):
        print( "Post", post )
        for tag in database.execute( query_tag_by_post_id, (post[0],) 
):
            print( "Tag", tag )
```

We defined three SQL queries. The first will fetch the blogs by the title. For each blog, we fetched all the posts that belong to this blog. Finally, we fetched all tags that are associated with a given post.

The second query implicitly repeats the `REFERENCES` definition between the `POST` table and the `BLOG` table. We're finding child posts of a specific blog parent; we need to repeat some of the table definitions during the query.

The third query involves a relational join between rows of the `ASSOC_POST_TAG` table and the `TAG` table. The `JOIN` clause recapitulates the foreign key reference in the table definitions. The `WHERE` clause also repeats a `REFERENCES` clause in the table definitions.

Because multiple tables were joined in the third query, using `SELECT *` will produce columns from all of the tables. We're really only interested in attributes of the `TAG` table, so we use `SELECT TAG.*` to produce only the desired columns.

These queries provide us with all of the individual bits and pieces of the data. However, these queries don't reconstruct Python objects for us. If we have more complex class definitions, we have to build objects from the individual pieces of data that we retrieved. In particular, if our Python class definitions have important method functions, we'll need a better SQL to Python mapping to make use of more complete Python class definitions.

Implementing class-like processing in pure SQL

Let's look at a somewhat more complex definition of a `Blog` class. This definition is repeated from *Chapter 9, Serializing and Saving – JSON, YAML, Pickle, CSV, and XML*; we've highlighted a method function that's of interest:

```
from collections import defaultdict
class Blog:
    def __init__( self, title, *posts ):
        self.title= title
        self.entries= list(posts)
    def append( self, post ):
        self.entries.append(post)
    def by_tag(self):
        tag_index= defaultdict(list)
        for post in self.entries:
            for tag in post.tags:
                tag_index[tag].append( post )
        return tag_index
    def as_dict( self ):
        return dict(
            title= self.title,
            underline= "="*len(self.title),
            entries= [p.as_dict() for p in self.entries],
        )
```

The `Blog.by_tag()` feature of a blog will become a rather complex SQL query. As object-oriented programming, it simply iterates through a collection of `Post` instances, creating `defaultdict`, which maps each tag to a sequence of `Posts` that share that tag. Here's a SQL query that produces similar results:

```
query_by_tag="""
SELECT TAG.PHRASE, POST.TITLE, POST.ID
FROM TAG JOIN ASSOC_POST_TAG ON TAG.ID = ASSOC_POST_TAG.TAG_ID
JOIN POST ON POST.ID = ASSOC_POST_TAG.POST_ID
JOIN BLOG ON POST.BLOG_ID = BLOG.ID
WHERE BLOG.TITLE=?
"""
```

This query's result set is a table-like sequence of rows with three attributes: `TAG.PHRASE`, `POST.TITLE`, and `POST.ID`. Each `POST` title and the `POST` ID will be repeated with all of the associated `TAG` phrases. To turn this into a simple-looking, HTML-friendly index, we need to group all the rows with the same `TAG.PHRASE` into a subsidiary list, as shown in the following code:

```
tag_index= defaultdict(list)
for tag, post_title, post_id in database.execute( query_by_tag,
("2013-2014 Travel",) ):
    tag_index[tag].append( (post_title, post_id) )
print( tag_index )
```

This additional processing would group two-tuples of the `POST` title and the `POST` ID into a useful structure that can be used to produce the RST and HTML output. The SQL query plus associated Python processing is quite long—longer than the native object-oriented Python.

More importantly, the SQL query is dissociated from the table definition. SQL is not an object-oriented programming language. There's no tidy class to bundle data and processing together. Using procedural programming with SQL like this has effectively turned off object-oriented programming. From a strictly object-oriented programming perspective, we can label this "EPIC FAIL".

There is a school of thought that suggests that this kind of SQL-heavy, object-free programming is more appropriate for certain kinds of problems than Python. Often, these kinds of problems involve the SQL `GROUP BY` clause. While it is convenient in SQL, it is also implemented very effectively by Python's `defaultdict` and `Counter`. The Python version is often so effective that a small program that queries lots of rows using a `defaultdict` might be faster than a database server doing SQL with `GROUP BY`. When in doubt, measure. When exhorted by database administrators that SQL is magically faster, measure.

Mapping Python objects to SQLite BLOB columns

We can map SQL columns to class definitions so that we can create proper Python object instances from data in a database. SQLite includes a **Binary Large Object** (**BLOB**) data type. We can pickle our Python objects and store them in the BLOB columns. We can work out a string representation of our Python objects (for example, using the JSON or YAML notation) and use SQLite text columns too.

This technique must be used cautiously because it effectively defeats SQL processing. A BLOB column cannot be used for SQL DML operations. We can't index it or use it in the search criteria of DML statements.

SQLite BLOB mapping should be reserved for objects where it's acceptable to be opaque to the surrounding SQL processing. The most common examples are media objects such as videos, still images, or sound clips. SQL is biased towards text and numeric fields. It doesn't generally handle more complex objects.

If we're working with financial data, our application should use the `decimal.Decimal` values. We might want to query or calculate in SQL using this kind of data. As `decimal.Decimal` is not directly supported by SQLite, we need to extend SQLite to handle values of this type.

There are two directions to this: conversion and adaptation. We need to **adapt** Python data to SQLite, and we need to **convert** SQLite data back to Python. Here are two functions and the requests to register them:

```
import decimal

def adapt_currency(value):
    return str(value)
sqlite3.register_adapter(decimal.Decimal, adapt_currency)

def convert_currency(bytes):
    return decimal.Decimal(bytes.decode())
sqlite3.register_converter("DECIMAL", convert_currency)
```

We've written an `adapt_currency()` function that will adapt `decimal.Decimal` objects into a suitable form for the database. In this case, we've done nothing more than a simple conversion to a string. We've registered the adapter function so that SQLite's interface can convert objects of class `decimal.Decimal` using the registered adapter function.

We've also written a `convert_currency()` function that will convert SQLite bytes objects into the Python `decimal.Decimal` objects. We've registered the `converter` function so that columns of the `DECIMAL` type will be properly converted to Python objects.

Once we've defined the adapters and converters, we can use `DECIMAL` as a fully supported column type. For this to work properly, we must inform SQLite by setting `detect_types=sqlite3.PARSE_DECLTYPES` when making the database connection. Here's a table definition that uses our new column data type:

```
CREATE TABLE BUDGET(
    year INTEGER,
    month INTEGER,
    category TEXT,
    amount DECIMAL
)
```

We can use our new column definition like this:

```
database= sqlite3.connect( 'p2_c11_blog.db', detect_types=sqlite3.
PARSE_DECLTYPES )
database.execute( decimal_ddl )

insert_budget= """
INSERT INTO BUDGET(year, month, category, amount) VALUES(:year,
:month, :category, :amount)
"""
database.execute( insert_budget,
    dict(year=2013, month=1, category="fuel", amount=decimal.
Decimal('256.78')) )
database.execute( insert_budget,
    dict(year=2013, month=2, category="fuel", amount=decimal.
Decimal('287.65')) )

query_budget= """
SELECT * FROM BUDGET
"""
for row in database.execute( query_budget ):
    print( row )
```

We created a database connection that requires declared types to be mapped via a converter function. Once we have the connection, we can create our table using a new `DECIMAL` column type.

When we insert rows into the table, we use proper `decimal.Decimal` objects. When we fetch rows from the table, we'll see that we get proper `decimal.Decimal` objects back from the database. The following is the output:

```
(2013, 1, 'fuel', Decimal('256.78'))
(2013, 2, 'fuel', Decimal('287.65'))
```

This shows us that our `decimal.Decimal` objects were properly stored and recovered from the database. We can write adapters and converters for any Python class. We need to invent a proper byte representation. As a string is so easily transformed into bytes, creating a string is often the simplest way to proceed.

Mapping Python objects to database rows manually

We can map SQL rows to class definitions so that we can create proper Python object instances from the data in a database. If we're careful with our database and class definitions, this isn't impossibly complex. If, however, we're careless, we can create Python objects where the SQL representation is quite complex. One consequence of the complexity is that numerous queries are involved in mapping between object and database rows. The challenge is to strike a balance between object-oriented design and the constraints imposed by the SQL database.

We will have to modify our class definitions to be more aware of the SQL implementation. We'll make several modifications to the `Blog` and `Post` class designs shown in *Chapter 10, Storing and Retrieving Objects via Shelve*.

Here's a `Blog` class definition:

```
from collections import defaultdict
class Blog:
    def __init__( self, **kw ):
        """Requires title"""
        self.id= kw.pop('id', None)
        self.title= kw.pop('title', None)
        if kw: raise TooManyValues( kw )
        self.entries= list() # ???
    def append( self, post ):
        self.entries.append(post)
    def by_tag(self):
        tag_index= defaultdict(list)
        for post in self.entries: # ???
            for tag in post.tags:
```

```
                tag_index[tag].append( post )
        return tag_index
    def as_dict( self ):
        return dict(
            title= self.title,
            underline= "="*len(self.title),
            entries= [p.as_dict() for p in self.entries],
        )
```

We allowed for a database ID as a first-class part of the object. Further, we've modified the initialization to be entirely based on keywords. Each keyword value is popped from the `kw` parameter. Any extra values will raise a `TooManyValues` exception.

We have two previously unanswered questions. How do we handle the list of posts associated with a blog? We'll modify the following class to add this feature. Here's a `Post` class definition:

```
import datetime
class Post:
    def __init__( self, **kw ):
        """Requires date, title, rst_text."""
        self.id= kw.pop('id', None)
        self.date= kw.pop('date', None)
        self.title= kw.pop('title', None)
        self.rst_text= kw.pop('rst_text', None)
        self.tags= list()
        if kw: raise TooManyValues( kw )
    def append( self, tag ):
        self.tags.append( tag )
    def as_dict( self ):
        return dict(
            date= str(self.date),
            title= self.title,
            underline= "-"*len(self.title),
            rst_text= self.rst_text,
            tag_text= " ".join(self.tags),
        )
```

As with `Blog`, we've allowed for a database ID as a first-class part of the object. Further, we've modified the initialization to be entirely based on keywords. Here's the exception class definition:

```
class TooManyValues( Exception ):
    pass
```

Once we have these class definitions, we can write an access layer that moves data between objects of these classes and the database. The access layer implements a more complex version of converting and adapting Python classes to rows of a table in the database.

Designing an access layer for SQLite

For this small object model, we can implement the entire access layer in a single class. This class will include methods to perform CRUD operations on each of our persistent classes. In larger applications, we may have to decompose the access layer into an individual **Strategy** class for each persistent class. We'd then unify all of these under a single access layer **Facade** or **Wrapper**.

This example won't painstakingly include all of the methods for a complete access layer. We'll show you the important ones. We'll break this down into several sections to deal with `Blogs`, `Posts`, and iterators. Here's the first part of our access layer:

```
class Access:
    get_last_id= """
    SELECT last_insert_rowid()
    """
    def open( self, filename ):
        self.database= sqlite3.connect( filename )
        self.database.row_factory = sqlite3.Row
    def get_blog( self, id ):
        query_blog= """
        SELECT * FROM BLOG WHERE ID=?
        """
        row= self.database.execute( query_blog, (id,) ).fetchone()
        blog= Blog( id= row['ID'], title= row['TITLE'] )
        return blog
    def add_blog( self, blog ):
        insert_blog= """
        INSERT INTO BLOG(TITLE) VALUES(:title)
        """
        self.database.execute( insert_blog, dict(title=blog.title) )
        row = self.database.execute( get_last_id ).fetchone()
        blog.id= row[0]
        return blog
```

This class sets `Connection.row_factory` to use the `sqlite3.Row` class instead of a simple tuple. The `Row` class allows access via the numeric index as well as the column name.

The `get_blog()` method constructs a `Blog` object from the database row that is fetched. Because we're using the `sqlite3.Row` object, we can refer to columns by name. This clarifies the mapping between SQL and Python class.

The `add_blog()` method inserts a row into the `BLOG` table based on a `Blog` object. This is a two-step operation. First, we create the new row. Then, we perform a SQL query to get the row ID that was assigned to the row.

Note that our table definitions use `INTEGER PRIMARY KEY AUTOINCREMENT`. Because of this, the table's primary key will match the row ID and the assigned row ID will be available through the `last_insert_rowid()` function. This allows us to retrieve the row ID that was allocated; we can then put this into the Python object for future reference. Here's how we can retrieve an individual `Post` object from the database:

```
def get_post( self, id ):
    query_post= """
    SELECT * FROM POST WHERE ID=?
    """
    row= self.database.execute( query_post, (id,) ).fetchone()
    post= Post( id= row['ID'], title= row['TITLE'],
        date= row['DATE'], rst_text= row['RST_TEXT'] )


    query_tags= """
    SELECT TAG.*
    FROM TAG JOIN ASSOC_POST_TAG ON TAG.ID = ASSOC_POST_TAG.TAG_ID
    WHERE ASSOC_POST_TAG.POST_ID=?
    """
    results= self.database.execute( query_tags, (id,) )
    for id, tag in results:
        post.append( tag )
    return post
```

To build `Post`, we have two queries: first, we fetch a row from the `POST` table to build part of the `Post` object. Then, we fetch the association rows joined with the rows from the `TAG` table. This is used to build the tag list for the `Post` object.

When we save a `Post` object, it will have several parts. A row must be added to the `POST` table. Additionally, rows need to be added to the `ASSOC_POST_TAG` table. If a tag is new, then a row might need to be added to the `TAG` table. If the tag exists, then we're simply associating the post with an existing tag's ID. Here's the `add_post()` method function:

```
def add_post( self, blog, post ):
    insert_post="""
    INSERT INTO POST(TITLE, DATE, RST_TEXT, BLOG_ID)
```

```
            VALUES(:title, :date, :rst_text, :blog_id)
        """
        query_tag="""
        SELECT * FROM TAG WHERE PHRASE=?
        """
        insert_tag= """
        INSERT INTO TAG(PHRASE) VALUES(?)
        """
        insert_association= """
        INSERT INTO ASSOC_POST_TAG(POST_ID, TAG_ID) VALUES(:post_id,
:tag_id)
        """
        with self.database:
            self.database.execute( insert_post,
                dict(title=post.title, date=post.date,
                    rst_text=post.rst_text, blog_id=blog.id) )
            row = self.database.execute( get_last_id ).fetchone()
            post.id= row[0]
            for tag in post.tags:
                tag_row= self.database.execute( query_tag, (tag,)
).fetchone()
                if tag_row is not None:
                    tag_id= tag_row['ID']
                else:
                    self.database.execute(insert_tag, (tag,))
                    row = self.database.execute( get_last_id
).fetchone()
                    tag_id= row[0]
                self.database.execute(insert_association,
                    dict(tag_id=tag_id,post_id=post.id))
        return post
```

The process of creating a complete post in the database involves several SQL steps. We've used the `insert_post` statement to create the row in the `POST` table. We'll also use the generic `get_last_id` query to return the assigned primary key for the new `POST` row.

The `query_tag` statement is used to determine whether the tag exists in the database or not. If the result of the query is not `None`, it means that a `TAG` row was found, and we have the ID for that row. Otherwise, the `insert_tag` statement must be used to create a row; the `get_last_id` query must be used to determine the assigned ID.

Each POST is associated with the relevant tags by inserting rows into the ASSOC_POST_TAG table. The insert_association statement creates the necessary row. Here are two iterator-style queries to locate Blogs and Posts:

```
    def blog_iter( self ):
        query= """
        SELECT * FROM BLOG
        """
        results= self.database.execute( query )
        for row in results:
            blog= Blog( id= row['ID'], title= row['TITLE'] )
            yield blog
    def post_iter( self, blog ):
        query= """
        SELECT ID FROM POST WHERE BLOG_ID=?
        """
        results= self.database.execute( query, (blog.id,) )
        for row in results:
            yield self.get_post( row['ID'] )
```

The blog_iter() method function locates all the BLOG rows and builds Blog instances from the rows.

The post_iter() method function locates POST IDs that are associated with a BLOG ID. The POST IDs are used with the get_post() method to build the Post instances. As get_post() will perform another query against the POST table, there's an optimization possible between these two methods.

Implementing container relationships

Our definition of the Blog class included two features that required access to all the posts contained within that blog. The Blog.entries attribute and Blog.by_tag() method functions both assume that a blog contains the complete collection of the Post instances.

For this to work, the Blog class must be made aware of the Access object so that it can use the Access.post_iter() method to implement Blog.entries. We have two overall design patterns for this:

- A global Access object is simple and works nicely. We have to be sure that the global database connection is opened appropriately, something that can be challenging with a global Access object.
- Inject the Access object into each Blog object that we're going to persist. This is a bit more complex because we have to tweak each object associated with the database.

As each database-related object should be created by the `Access` class, the Access class would fit the **Factory** pattern. We can make three kinds of changes to this factory. These will ensure that a blog or post is made aware of the active `Access` object:

- Each `return blog` needs to be expanded to `blog._access= self; return blog`. This happens in `get_blog()`, `add_blog()`, and `blog_iter()`.
- Each `return post` needs to be expanded to `post._access= self; return post`. This happens in `get_post()`, `add_post()` and `post_iter()`.
- Revise the `add_blog()` method to accept arguments to build the `Blog` object rather than accepting a `Blog` or `Post` object that is built outside the `Access` factory. The definition would look something like the following: `def add_blog( self, title ):`
- Revise the `add_post()` method to accept a blog and the arguments to build a `Post` object. The definition would look something like: `def add_post( self, blog, title, date, rst_text, tags ):`

Once we have the `_access` attribute injected into each `Blog` instance, we can do this:

```
@property
def entries( self ):
  return self._access.post_iter( self )
```

This will return the sequence of Post objects that belong to a Blog object. This allows us to define the methods in our class definitions that will process children or parents as if they were contained within the object.

Improving performance with indices

One of the ways to improve the performance of a relational database such as SQLite is to make join operations faster. The ideal way to do this is to include enough index information so that slow search operations aren't done to find matching rows. Without an index, an entire table must be read to find referenced rows. With an index, just a relevant subset of rows can be read.

When we define a column that might be used in a query, we should consider building an index for that column. This means adding yet more SQL DDL statements to our table definitions.

An index is a separate storage but is tied to a specific table and column. The SQL looks like the following code:

```
CREATE INDEX IX_BLOG_TITLE ON BLOG( TITLE );
```

This will create an index on the `title` column of the `Blog` table. Nothing else needs to be done. The SQL database will use the index when performing queries based on the indexed column. When data is created, updated, or deleted, the index will be adjusted automatically.

Indexes involve storage and computational overheads. An index that's rarely used might be so costly to create and maintain that it becomes a performance hindrance rather than a help. On the other hand, some indexes are so important that they can have spectacular performance improvements. In all cases, we don't have direct control over the database algorithms being used; the best we can do is create the index and measure the performance's impact.

In some cases, defining a column to be a key might automatically include having an index added. The rules for this are usually stated quite clearly in the database's DDL section. SQLite, for example, says this:

> *In most cases, UNIQUE and PRIMARY KEY constraints are implemented by creating a unique index in the database.*

It goes on to list two exceptions. One of these, the integer primary key exception, is the design pattern we've been using to force the database to create surrogate keys for us. Therefore, our integer primary key design will not create any additional indices.

Adding an ORM layer

There are a fairly large number of Python ORM projects. A list of these can be found here: `https://wiki.python.org/moin/HigherLevelDatabaseProgramming`.

We're going to pick just one of these as an example. We'll use SQLAlchemy because it offers us a number of features and is reasonably popular. As with many things, there's no *best*; other ORM layers have different advantages and disadvantages.

Because of the popularity of using a relational database to support Web development, Web frameworks often include ORM layers. Django has its own ORM layer, as does web.py. In some cases, we can tease the ORMs out of the larger framework. However, it seems simpler to work with a standalone ORM.

The documentation, installation guide, and code for SQLAlchemy is available at `http://www.sqlalchemy.org`. When installing, using `--without-cextensions` can simplify the process if the high-performance optimizations aren't required.

It's important to note that SQLAlchemy can completely replace all of an application's SQL statements with first-class Python constructs. This has the profound advantage of allowing us to write applications in a single language, Python, even though a second language (SQL) is used under the hood as part of the data access layer. This can save some complexity in the development and debugging.

This does not, however, remove the obligation to understand the underlying SQL database constraints and how our design must fit within these constraints. An ORM layer doesn't magically obviate the design considerations. It merely changes the implementation language from SQL to Python.

Designing ORM-friendly classes

When using an ORM, we will fundamentally change the way we design and implement our persistent classes. We're going to expand the semantics of our class definitions to have three distinct levels of meaning:

- The class will be a Python class and can be used to create Python objects. The method functions are used by these objects.
- The class will also describe a SQL table and can be used by the ORM to create the SQL DDL that builds and maintains the database structure.
- The class will also define the mappings between the SQL table and Python class. It will be the vehicle to turn Python operations into SQL DML and build Python objects from SQL queries.

Most ORMs are designed so that we will use descriptors to formally define the attributes of our class. We do not simply define attributes in the `__init__()` method. For more information on descriptors, see *Chapter 3, Attribute Access, Properties, and Descriptors*.

SQLAlchemy requires us to build a **declarative base class**. This base class provides a metaclass for our application's class definitions. It also serves as a repository for the metadata that we're defining for our database. If we follow the defaults, it's easy to call this class `Base`.

Here's the list of imports that might be helpful:

```
from sqlalchemy.ext.declarative import declarative_base
from sqlalchemy import Column, Table
from sqlalchemy import BigInteger, Boolean, Date, DateTime, Enum, \
    Float, Integer, Interval, LargeBinary, Numeric, PickleType, \
    SmallInteger, String, Text, Time, Unicode, UnicodeText ForeignKey
from sqlalchemy.orm import relationship, backref
```

We imported some essential definitions to create a column of a table, column, and to create the rare table that doesn't specifically map to a Python class, `Table`. We imported all of the generic column type definitions. We'll only use a few of these column types. Not only does SQLAlchemy define these generic types, it defines the SQL standard types, and it also defines vendor-specific types for the various supported SQL dialects. It seems easy to stick to the generic types and allow SQLAlchemy to map between generic, standard, and vendor types.

We also imported two helpers to define the relationships among tables, `relationship`, and `backref`. SQLAlchemy's metaclass is built by the `declarative_base()` function:

```
Base = declarative_base()
```

The `Base` object that was created must be the metaclass for any persistent class that we're going to define. We'll define three tables that are mapped to Python classes. We'll also define a fourth table that's simply required by SQL to implement a many-to-many relationship.

Here's the `Blog` class:

```
class Blog(Base):
    __tablename__ = "BLOG"
    id = Column(Integer, primary_key=True)
    title = Column(String)
    def as_dict( self ):
        return dict(
            title= self.title,
            underline= '='*len(self.title),
            entries= [ e.as_dict() for e in self.entries ]
        )
```

Our `Blog` class is mapped to a table named `"BLOG"`. We've included two descriptors for the two columns we want in this table. The `id` column is defined as an `Integer` primary key. Implicitly, this will be an autoincrement field so that surrogate keys are generated for us.

The title column is defined as a generic string. We could have used `Text`, `Unicode`, or even `UnicodeText` for this. The underlying engine might have different implementations for these various types. In our case, SQLite will treat all of these nearly identically. Also note that SQLite doesn't need an upper limit on the length of a column; other database engines might require an upper limit on the size of `String`.

The `as_dict()` method function refers to an `entries` collection that is clearly not defined in this class. When we look at the definition of the `Post` class, we'll see how this `entries` attribute is built. Here's the definition of the `Post` class:

```
class Post(Base):
    __tablename__ = "POST"
    id = Column(Integer, primary_key=True)
    title = Column(String)
    date = Column(DateTime)
    rst_text = Column(UnicodeText)
    blog_id = Column(Integer, ForeignKey('BLOG.id'))
    blog = relationship( 'Blog', backref='entries' )
    tags = relationship('Tag', secondary=assoc_post_tag,
backref='posts')
    def as_dict( self ):
        return dict(
            title= self.title,
            underline= '-'*len(self.title),
            date= self.date,
            rst_text= self.rst_text,
            tags= [ t.phrase for t in self.tags],
        )
```

This class has five attributes, two relationships, and a method function. The `id` attribute is an integer primary key; this will be an autoincrement value by default. The `title` attribute is a simple string. The `date` attribute will be a `DateTime` column; `rst_text` is defined as `UnicodeText` to emphasize our expectation of any Unicode character in this field.

The `blog_id` is a foreign key reference to the parent blog that contains this post. In addition to the foreign key column definition, we also included an explicit `relationship` definition between post and the parent blog. This `relationship` definition becomes an attribute that we can use for navigation from the post to the parent blog.

The `backref` option includes a backwards reference that will be added to the `Blog` class. This reference in the `Blog` class will be the collection of `Posts` that are contained within the `Blog`. The `backref` option names the new attribute in the `Blog` class to reference the child `Posts`.

The `tags` attribute uses a `relationship` definition; this attribute will navigate via an association table to locate all the `Tag` instances associated with the post. We'll look at the following association table. This, too, uses `backref` to include an attribute in the `Tag` class that references the related collection of the `Post` instances.

The `as_dict()` method makes use of the `tags` attribute to locate all of `Tags` associated with this `Post`. Here's a definition for the `Tag` class:

```
class Tag(Base):
    __tablename__ = "TAG"
    id = Column(Integer, primary_key=True)
    phrase = Column(String, unique=True)
```

We defined a primary key and a `String` attribute. We included a constraint to ensure that each tag is explicitly unique. An attempt to insert a duplicate will lead to a database exception. The relationship in the `Post` class definition means that additional attributes will be created in this class.

As required by SQL, we need an association table for the many-to-many relationship between tags and posts. This table is purely a technical requirement in SQL and need not be mapped to a Python class:

```
assoc_post_tag = Table('ASSOC_POST_TAG', Base.metadata,
    Column('POST_ID', Integer, ForeignKey('POST.id') ),
    Column('TAG_ID', Integer, ForeignKey('TAG.id') )
)
```

We have to explicitly bind this to the `Base.metadata` collection. This binding is automatically a part of the classes that use `Base` as the metaclass. We defined a table that contains two `Column` instances. Each column is a foreign key to one of the other tables in our model.

Building the schema with the ORM layer

In order to connect to a database, we'll need to create an engine. One use for the engine is to build the database instance with our table declarations. The other use for the engine is to manage the data from a session, which we'll look at later. Here's a script that we can use to build a database:

```
from sqlalchemy import create_engine
engine = create_engine('sqlite:///./p2_c11_blog2.db', echo=True)
Base.metadata.create_all(engine)
```

When we create an `Engine` instance, we use a URL-like string that names the vendor product and provides all the additional parameters required to create the connection to that database. In the case of SQLite, the connection is a filename. In the case of other database products, there might be server host names and authentication credentials.

Once we have the engine, we've done some fundamental metadata operations. We've done the `create_all()`, which builds all of the tables. We might also perform a `drop_all()` that will drop all of the tables, losing all the data. We can, of course, create or drop an individual schema item, too.

If we change a table definition during software development, it will not automagically mutate the SQL table definition. We need to explicitly drop and rebuild the table. In some cases, we might want to preserve some operational data, leading to potentially complex surgery to create and populate new table(s) from old table(s).

The `echo=True` option writes log entries with the generated SQL statements. This can be helpful to determine whether the declarations are complete and create the expected database design. Here's a snippet of the output that is produced:

```
CREATE TABLE "BLOG" (
  id INTEGER NOT NULL,
  title VARCHAR,
  PRIMARY KEY (id)
)


CREATE TABLE "TAG" (
  id INTEGER NOT NULL,
  phrase VARCHAR,
  PRIMARY KEY (id),
  UNIQUE (phrase)
)

CREATE TABLE "POST" (
  id INTEGER NOT NULL,
  title VARCHAR,
  date DATETIME,
  rst_text TEXT,
  blog_id INTEGER,
  PRIMARY KEY (id),
  FOREIGN KEY(blog_id) REFERENCES "BLOG" (id)
)

CREATE TABLE "ASSOC_POST_TAG" (
  "POST_ID" INTEGER,
  "TAG_ID" INTEGER,
  FOREIGN KEY("POST_ID") REFERENCES "POST" (id),
  FOREIGN KEY("TAG_ID") REFERENCES "TAG" (id)
)
```

This shows SQL us the `CREATE TABLE` statements that were created based on our class definitions.

Once the database has been built, we can create, retrieve, update, and delete objects. In order to work with database objects, we need to create a session that acts as a cache for the ORM-managed objects.

Manipulating objects with the ORM layer

In order to work with objects, we'll need a session cache. This is bound to an engine. We'll add new objects to the session cache. We'll also use the session cache to query objects in the database. This assures us that all objects that need to be persistent are in the cache. Here is a way to create a working session:

```
from sqlalchemy.orm import sessionmaker
Session= sessionmaker(bind=engine)
session= Session()
```

We used the SQLAlchemy `sessionmaker()` function to create a `Session` class. This is bound to the database engine that we created previously. We then used the `Session` class to build a `session` object that we can use to perform data manipulation. A session is required to work with the objects in general.

Generally, we build one `sessionmaker` class along with the engine. We can then use that one `sessionmaker` class to build multiple sessions for our application processing.

For simple objects, we create them and load them into the session as in the following code:

```
blog= Blog( title="Travel 2013" )
session.add( blog )
```

This puts a new `Blog` object into the session named `session`. The `Blog` object is not *necessarily* written to the database. We need to commit the session before the database writes are performed. In order to meet the Atomicity requirements, we'll finish building a post before committing the session.

First, we'll look up the `Tag` instances in the database. If they don't exist, we'll create them. If they do exist, we'll use the tag found in the database:

```
tags = [ ]
for phrase in "#RedRanger", "#Whitby42", "#ICW":
    try:
        tag= session.query(Tag).filter(Tag.phrase == phrase).one()
    except sqlalchemy.orm.exc.NoResultFound:
        tag= Tag(phrase=phrase)
```

```
            session.add(tag)
        tags.append(tag)
```

We use the `session.query()` function to examine instances of the given class. Each `filter()` function appends a criterion to the query. The `one()` function ensures that we've found a single row. If an exception is raised, then it means that `Tag` doesn't exist. We need to build a new `Tag` and add it to the session.

Once we've found or created the `Tag` instance, we can append it to a local list named `tags`; we'll use this list of `Tag` instances to create the `Post` object. Here's how we build a `Post`:

```
p2= Post( date=datetime.datetime(2013,11,14,17,25),
    title="Hard Aground",
    rst_text="""Some embarrassing revelation. Including ⊠ and ⊠""",
    blog=blog,
    tags=tags
    )
session.add(p2)
blog.posts= [ p2 ]
```

This includes a reference to the parent blog. It also includes the list of `Tag` instances that we built (or found in the database).

The `Post.blog` attribute was defined as a relationship in the class definitions. When we assign an object, SQLAlchemy plucks out the proper ID values to create the foreign key reference that the SQL database uses to implement the relationship.

The `Post.tags` attribute was also defined as a relationship. The `Tag` objects are referenced via the association table. SQLAlchemy tracks the ID values properly to build the necessary rows in the SQL association table for us.

In order to associate the `Post` with the `Blog`, we'll make use of the `Blog.posts` attribute. This, too, was defined as a relationship. When we assign a list of `Post` objects to this relationship attribute, the ORM will build the proper foreign key reference in each `Post` object. This works because we provided the `backref` attribute when defining the relationship. Finally, we commit the session:

```
session.commit()
```

The database inserts are all handled in a flurry of automatically generated SQL. The objects remained cached in the session. If our application continues using this session instance, then the pool of objects remains available without necessarily performing any actual queries against the database.

If, on the other hand, we would like to be absolutely sure that any updates written by other concurrent processes are included in a query, we can create a new, empty session for that query. When we discard a session and use an empty session, objects must be fetched from the database to refresh the session.

We can write a simple query to examine and print all of the `Blog` objects:

```
session= Session()
for blog in session.query(Blog):
    print( "{title}\n{underline}\n".format(**blog.as_dict()) )
    for p in blog.entries:
        print( p.as_dict() )
```

This will retrieve all the `Blog` instances. The `Blog.as_dict()` method will retrieve all of the posts within a blog. The `Post.as_dict()` method will retrieve all of the tags. The SQL queries will be generated and executed automatically by SQLAlchemy.

We didn't include the rest of the template-based formatting from *Chapter 9, Serializing and Saving - JSON, YAML, Pickle, CSV, and XML*. It doesn't change. We are able to navigate from the `Blog` object via the `entries` list to the `Post` objects without writing elaborate SQL queries. Translating navigation into queries is the job of SQLAlchemy. Using a Python iterator is sufficient for SQLAlchemy to generate the right queries to refresh the cache and return the expected objects.

If we have `echo=True` defined for the `Engine` instance, then we'll be able to see the sequence of SQL queries performed to retrieve the `Blog`, `Post`, and `Tag` instances. This information can help us understand the workload that our application places on the database server process.

Querying post objects given a tag string

An important benefit of a relational database is our ability to follow the relationships among the objects. Using SQLAlchemy's query capability, we can follow the relationship from `Tag` to `Post` and locate all `Posts` that share a given `Tag` string.

A query is a feature of a session. This means that objects already in the session don't need to be fetched from the database, a potential time-saver. Objects not in the session are cached in the session so that updates or deletes can be handled at the time of the commit.

To gather all of the posts that have a given tag, we need to use the intermediate association table as well as the `Post` and `Tag` tables. We'll use the query method of the session to specify what kinds of objects we expect to get back. We'll use the fluent interface to join in the various intermediate tables and the final table that we want with the selection criteria. Here's how it looks:

```
for post in session.query(Post).join(assoc_post_tag).join(Tag).filter(
    Tag.phrase == "#Whitby42" ):
    print( post.blog.title, post.date, post.title, [t.phrase for t in
post.tags] )
```

The `session.query()` method specifies the table that we want to see. If we left it at that, we'd see every row. The `join()` methods identify the additional tables that must be matched. Because we provided the relationship information in the class definitions, SQLAlchemy can work out the SQL details required to use primary keys and foreign keys to match rows. The final `filter()` method provides the selection criteria for the desired subset of rows. Here's the SQL that was generated:

```
SELECT "POST".id AS "POST_id", "POST".title AS "POST_title", "POST".
date AS "POST_date", "POST".rst_text AS "POST_rst_text", "POST".blog_
id AS "POST_blog_id"
FROM "POST" JOIN "ASSOC_POST_TAG" ON "POST".id = "ASSOC_POST_
TAG"."POST_ID"
JOIN "TAG" ON "TAG".id = "ASSOC_POST_TAG"."TAG_ID"
WHERE "TAG".phrase = ?
```

The Python version is a bit easier to understand, as the details of the key matching can be elided. The `print()` function uses `post.blog.title` to navigate from the `Post` instance to the associated blog and show the `title` attribute. If the blog was in the session cache, this navigation is done quickly. If the blog was not in the session cache, it will be fetched from the database.

This navigation behavior applies to `[t.phrase for t in post.tags]`, too. If the object is in the session cache, it's simply used. In this case, the collection of the `Tag` objects associated with a post might lead to a complex SQL query:

```
SELECT "TAG".id AS "TAG_id", "TAG".phrase AS "TAG_phrase"
FROM "TAG", "ASSOC_POST_TAG"
WHERE ? = "ASSOC_POST_TAG"."POST_ID"
AND "TAG".id = "ASSOC_POST_TAG"."TAG_ID"
```

In Python, we simply navigated via `post.tags`. SQLAlchemy generated and executed the SQL for us.

Improving performance with indices

One of the ways to improve the performance of a relational database such as SQLite is to make join operations faster. We don't want SQLite to read an entire table to find matching rows. By building an index on a particular column, SQLite can examine the index and read just the relevant rows from the table.

When we define a column that might be used in a query, we should consider building an index for that column. This is a simple process that uses SQLAlchemy. We simply annotate the attribute of the class with `index=True`.

We can make fairly minor changes to our `Post` table, for example. We can do this to add indexes:

```
class Post(Base):
    __tablename__ = "POST"
    id = Column(Integer, primary_key=True)
    title = Column(String, index=True)
    date = Column(DateTime, index=True)
    blog_id = Column(Integer, ForeignKey('BLOG.id'), index=True)
```

Adding two indices for the title and date will usually speed up queries for the posts by the title or by the date. There's no guarantee that there must be an improvement in the performance. Relational database performance involves a number of factors. It's important to measure the performance of a realistic workload both with the index and without it.

Adding an index by `blog_id`, similarly, might speed up the join operation between rows in the `Blog` and `Post` tables. It's also possible that the database engine uses an algorithm that doesn't benefit from having this index available.

Indexes involve storage and computational overheads. An index that's rarely used might be so costly to create and maintain that it becomes a problem, not a solution. On the other hand, some indexes are so important that they can have spectacular performance improvements. In all cases, we don't have direct control over the database algorithms being used; the best we can do is create the index and measure the performance impact.

Schema evolution

When working with a SQL database, we have to address the problem of schema evolution. Our objects have a dynamic state and a static class definition. We can easily persist the dynamic state. Our class definitions are part of the schema for the persistent data; we also have mappings to the formal SQL schema. Neither class nor SQL schema is *absolutely* static.

If we change a class definition, how will we fetch objects from the database? If the database must change, how do we upgrade the Python mappings and still map the data? A good design often involves some combination of several techniques.

The changes to the method functions and properties of the Python classes don't change the mapping to the SQL rows. These can be termed minor changes, as the tables in the database are still compatible with the changed class definition. A new software release can have a new minor version number.

The changes to Python class attributes will not necessarily change the persisted object state. SQL can be somewhat flexible when converting the data types from the database to the Python objects. An ORM layer can add flexibility. In some cases, we can make some class or database changes and call it a minor version update because the existing SQL schema will still work with new class definitions. We can, for example, alter a SQL table from an integer to a string without significant breakage because of SQL and ORM conversions.

Changes to the SQL table definitions will clearly modify the persisted objects. These can be called major changes when the existing database rows will no longer be compatible with the new class definition. These kinds of changes should not be made by *modifying* the Python class definitions. These kinds of changes should be made by defining a new subclass and providing an updated factory function to create instances of either the old or new class.

When working with persistent SQL data, a schema change can be accomplished by one of the following two ways:

- Using SQL `ALTER` statements on the existing schema. Some kinds of changes can be done incrementally to a SQL schema. There are a number of constraints and restrictions on what changes are permitted. This doesn't generalize well; it should be seen as an exceptional situation that might work for minor changes.
- Creating new tables and dropping old tables. In general, a SQL schema change will be significant enough for us to require to create a new version of table(s) from old table(s), making profound changes to the data's structure.

SQL database schema changes typically involve running a one-time conversion script. This script will use the old schema to query the existing data, transform it to new data, and use the new schema to insert new data into the database. Of course, this must be tested on a backup database before being run on the user's preferred, live, operational database. Once the schema change has been accomplished, the old schema can be safely ignored and later dropped to free up storage.

This kind of transformation can be done in a single database using different table names or different schema names (for databases that support named schema.) If we keep old data and new data side-by-side, we have a flexible upgrade path from old applications to the new applications. This is particularly important with websites that try to offer 24 x 7 availability.

In some situations, it becomes necessary to add tables to the schema with purely administrative details such as the identification of schema version. Applications can then query this table first after establishing a database connection and fail quickly when the schema version is wrong.

Summary

We looked at the basics of using SQLite in three ways: directly, via an access layer, and via the SQLAlchemy ORM. We have to create SQL DDL statements; we can do this directly in our applications or in an access layer. We can also have DDL built by the SQLAlchemy class definitions. To manipulate data, we'll use SQL DML statements; we can do this directly in a procedural style, or we can use our own access layer or SQLAlchemy to create the SQL.

Design considerations and trade-offs

One of the strengths of the `sqlite3` module is that it allows us to persist distinct items. As we're using a database that supports concurrent writes, we can have multiple processes updating the data, relying on SQLite to handle concurrency via its own internal locking.

Using a relational database imposes numerous restrictions. We must consider how to map our objects to rows of tables in the database:

- We can use SQL directly, using only the supported SQL column types and largely eschewing object-oriented classes
- We can use a manual mapping that extends SQLite to handle our objects as SQLite BLOB columns
- We can write our own access layer to adapt and convert between our objects and SQL rows
- We can use an ORM layer to implement a row-to-object mapping

Mapping alternatives

The problem with mixing Python and SQL is that there can be an impetus towards something that we might call the "All Singing, All Dancing, All SQL" solution. The idea here is that the relational database is somehow the ideal platform and Python corrupts this by injecting needless object-oriented features.

The all-SQL, object-free design strategy is sometimes justified as being more appropriate for certain kinds of problems. Specifically, proponents will point out summarizing large sets of data using the SQL `GROUP BY` clause as an ideal use for SQL.

This is implemented very effectively by Python's `defaultdict` and `Counter`. The Python version is often so effective that a small Python program querying lots of rows and accumulating summaries using `defaultdict` might be faster than a database server performing SQL with `GROUP BY`.

When in doubt, measure. Some nonsense is spouted by SQL database proponents. When confronted with claims that SQL should magically be faster that Python, gather evidence. This data gathering is not confined to one-time initial technical spike situations either. As usage grows and changes, the relative merit of SQL database versus Python will shift too.

A home-brewed access layer will tend to be highly specific to a problem domain. This might have the advantage of high performance and relatively transparent mapping from row to object. It might have the disadvantage of being annoying to maintain every time a class changes or the database implementation changes.

A well-established ORM project might involve some initial effort to learn the features of the ORM, but the long-term simplifications are important benefits. Learning the features of an ORM layer can involve both initial work and rework as lessons are learned. The first attempts at a design that has good object features and still fits within the SQL framework will have to be redone as the application trade-offs and considerations become clearer.

Keys and key designs

Because SQL depends on keys, we must take care to design and manage keys for our various objects. We must design a mapping from an object to the key that will be used to identify that object. One choice is to locate an attribute (or combination of attributes) that are proper primary keys and cannot be changed. Another choice is to generate surrogate keys that cannot be changed; this allows all other attributes to be changed.

Most relational databases can generate surrogate keys for us. This is usually the best approach. For other unique attributes or candidate key attributes, we can define SQL indexes to improve the processing performance.

We must also consider the foreign key relationships among objects. There are several common design patterns: One-to-Many, Many-to-One, Many-to-Many, and Optional One-to-One. We need to be cognizant of how SQL uses keys to implement these relationships and how SQL queries will be used to fill in the Python collections.

Application software layers

Because of the relative sophistication available when using `sqlite3`, our application software must become more properly layered. Generally, we'll look at software architectures with layers resembling the following ones:

- The presentation layer: This is a top-level user interface, either a web presentation or a desktop GUI.
- The application layer: This is the internal service or controllers that make the application work. This could be called the processing model, different from the logical data model.
- The business layer or the problem domain model layer: These are the objects that define the business domain or the problem space. This is sometimes called the logical data model. We looked at how we might model these objects using a microblog blog and post example.
- Infrastructure: This often includes several layers as well as other cross-cutting concerns such as logging, security, and network access:
    - The data access layer: These are protocols or methods to access the data objects. It is often an ORM layer. We've looked at SQLAlchemy. There are numerous other choices for this.
    - The persistence layer: This is the physical data model as seen in file storage. The `sqlite3` module implements persistence. When using an ORM layer such as SQLAlchemy, we only reference SQLite when creating an Engine.

When looking at `sqlite3` in this chapter and `shelve` in *Chapter 10, Storing and Retrieving Objects via Shelve*, it becomes clear that mastering object-oriented programming involves some higher-level design patterns. We can't simply design classes in isolation, but we need to look at how classes are going to be organized into larger structures.

Looking forward

In the next chapter, we'll look at transmitting and sharing objects using REST. This design pattern shows us how to manage the representation of the state and how to transfer the object state from process to process. We'll leverage a number of persistence modules to represent the state of an object that is being transmitted.

In *Chapter 13, Configuration Files and Persistence*, we'll look at configuration files. We'll look at several ways to make use of persistent representations of data that controls an application.

12
Transmitting and Sharing Objects

We'll expand on our serialization techniques for the object representation shown in *Chapter 9, Serializing and Saving – JSON, YAML, Pickle, CSV, and XML*. When we need to transmit an object, we're performing some kind of **Representational State Transfer** (**REST**). When we serialize an object, we're creating a representation of the state of an object. This representation can be transferred to another process (usually on another host computer); the other process can then build a version of the original object from the representation of the state and a local definition of the class.

We can perform REST processing in a number of ways. One aspect of it is the state representation that we can use. Another aspect is the protocol to control the transfer. We won't cover all of the combinations of these aspects. Instead, we'll focus on two combinations.

For internet transfers, we'll leverage the HTTP protocol to implement **Create-Retrieve-Update-Delete** (**CRUD**) processing operations. This is commonly called a REST web server. We'll look at providing RESTful web services as well. This will be based on Python's **Web Service Gateway Interface** (**WSGI**) reference implementation, the `wsgiref` package.

For local transfers among processes on the same host, we'll look at the local message queues provided by the `multiprocessing` module. There are numerous sophisticated queue management products. We'll focus on the standard library offerings.

This kind of processing builds on using JSON or XML to represent an object. For WSGI, we're adding the HTTP protocol and a set of design patterns to define transactions in a web server. For multiprocessing, we're adding a processing pool.

There is an additional consideration when working with REST transfers: the source or the data might not be trustworthy. We must implement some security. When it comes to the commonly used representations, JSON and XML, there are few security considerations. YAML introduces a security concern and supports a safe load operation; see *Chapter 9, Serializing and Saving – JSON, YAML, Pickle, CSV, and XML* for more information on this. Because of the security issue, the `pickle` module also offers a restricted unpickler that can be trusted to not import unusual modules and execute damaging code.

Class, state, and representation

In some cases, we might be creating a server that will provide data to remote clients. In other cases, we might want to consume data from remote computers. We may have a hybrid situation where our application is both a client of remote computers and servers to mobile applications. There are many situations where our application works with objects that are persisted remotely.

We need a way to transmit objects from process to process. We can decompose the larger problem into two smaller problems. The inter-networking protocols can help us transmit bytes from a process on one host to a process on another host. Serialization can transform our objects into bytes.

Unlike the object state, we transmit class definitions through an entirely separate and very simple method. We exchange class definitions via the source code. If we need to supply a class definition to a remote host, we send the Python source code to that host. The code must be properly installed to be useful; this is often a manual operation performed by an administrator.

Our networks transmit bytes. Therefore, we need to represent the values of an object's instance variables as a stream of bytes. Often, we'll use a two-step transformation to bytes; we'll represent the state of an object as a string and rely on the string to provide bytes in one of the standard encodings.

Using HTTP and REST to transmit objects

Hypertext Transfer Protocol (**HTTP**) is defined through a series of **Request for Comments** (**RFC**) documents. We won't review all of the particulars, but we will touch on three high points.

The HTTP protocol includes requests and replies. A request includes a method, a **Uniform Resource Identifier** (**URI**), some headers, and optional attachments. A number of available methods are defined in the standards. Most browsers focus on making the `GET` and `POST` requests. The standard browsers include the `GET`, `POST`, `PUT`, and `DELETE` requests, which are the ones that we'll leverage because they correspond to the CRUD operations. We'll ignore most of the headers and focus on the path portion of the URI.

A reply includes a status code number and reason, headers, and some data. There are a variety of status code numbers. Of them, we're interested in just a few. The `200` status code is the generic `OK` response from a server. A `201` status code is the `Created` response, which might be appropriate to show us that a post worked and data was posted. A `204` status code is the `No Content` response, which might be appropriate for `DELETE`. The `400` status code is `Bad Request`, the `401` status code is `Unauthorized`, the `404` status code is `Not Found`. These status code are commonly used to reflect operations that cannot be performed, or are not valid.

Most `2xx` successful replies will include an encoded object or sequence of objects. A `4xx` error reply may include a more detailed error message.

HTTP is defined to be stateless. The server is not expected to have any recollection of previous interactions with a client. We have a number of candidate workarounds to this limitation. For interactive websites, cookies are used to track the transaction state and improve the application behavior. For web services, however, the client will not be a person; each request can include the authentication credentials. This imposes the further obligation to secure the connection. For our purposes, we'll assume that the server will use **Secure Sockets Layer** (**SSL**) and use an HTTPS connection on port 443 instead of HTTP on port 80.

Implementing CRUD operations via REST

We'll look at three fundamental ideas behind the REST protocol. The first idea is to use any handy text serialization of an object's state. Second, we can use the HTTP request URI to name an object; a URI can include any level of detail, including a schema, module, class, and object identity in a uniform format. Finally, we can use the HTTP method to map to CRUD rules to define the action to be performed on the named object.

The use of HTTP for RESTful services pushes the envelope on the original definitions of HTTP requests and replies. This means that some of the request and reply semantics are open to active, ongoing discussion. Rather than presenting all of the alternatives, each of which has unique merits, we'll suggest a single approach. Our focus is on the Python language, not the more general problem of designing RESTful web services. A REST server will often support CRUD operations via the following five essential use cases:

- **Create**: We'll use an `HTTP POST` request to create a new object and a URI that provides class information only. A path such as `//host/app/blog/` might name the class. The response could be a 201 message that includes a copy of the object as it was finally saved. The returned object information may include the URI assigned by the RESTful server for the newly created object or the relevant keys to construct the URI. A `POST` request is expected to change the RESTful resources by creating something new.
- **Retrieve – Search**: This is a request that can retrieve multiple objects. We'll use an `HTTP GET` request and a URI that provides search criteria, usually in the form of a query string after the `?` character. The URI might be `//host/app/blog/?title="Travel 2012-2013"`. Note that `GET` never makes a change to the state of any RESTful resources.
- **Retrieve – Instance**: This is a request for a single object. We'll use an `HTTP GET` request and a URI that names a specific object in the URI path. The URI might be `//host/app/blog/id/`. While the response is expected to be a single object, it might still be wrapped in a list to make it compatible with a search response. As this response is `GET`, there's no change in the state.
- **Update**: We'll use an `HTTP PUT` request and a URI that identifies the object to be replaced. The URI might be `//host/app/blog/id/`. The response could be a 200 message that includes a copy of the revised object. Clearly, this is expected to make a change to the RESTful resources. There are good reasons to use other status responses than 200. We'll stick to 200 for our examples here.
- **Delete**: We'll use an `HTTP DELETE` request and a URI that looks like `//host/app/blog/id/`. The response could be a simple `204 NO CONTENT` without providing any object details in the response.

As the HTTP protocol is stateless, there's no provision for logon and logoff. Each request must be separately authenticated. We will often make use of the HTTP `Authorization` header to provide the username and password credentials. When doing this, we absolutely must also use SSL to provide security for the content of the `Authorization` header. There are more sophisticated alternatives that leverage separate identity management servers to provide authentication tokens rather than credentials.

Implementing non-CRUD operations

Some applications will have operations that can't be easily characterized as CRUD. We might, for example, have a **Remote Procedure Call** (**RPC**) style application that performs a complex calculation. The calculation's arguments are provided via the URI, so there's no change RESTful in the server state.

Most of the time, these calculation-focused operations can be implemented as the `GET` requests as there's no change in the state. However, we might consider making them `POST` requests if we are going to preserve a log of the request and reply as part of a non-repudiation scheme. This is particularly important in websites where a fee is charged for the services.

The REST protocol and ACID

The ACID properties are defined in *Chapter 10, Storing and Retrieving Objects via Shelve*. These properties are Atomic, Consistent, Isolated, and Durable. These are essential features of a transaction that consists of multiple database operations. These properties don't automatically become part of the REST protocol. We must consider how HTTP works when we ensure that the ACID properties are met.

Each HTTP request is atomic; therefore, we should avoid designing an application that makes a series of related `POST` requests that we hope become atomic. Instead, we should look for a way to bundle all of the information into a single request. Additionally, we have to be aware that requests will often be interleaved from a variety of clients; therefore, we don't have a tidy way to handle isolation among interleaved sequences of requests. If we have a properly multilayered design, we should delegate the durability to a separate persistence module.

In order to achieve the ACID properties, a common technique is to define the `POST`, `PUT`, or `DELETE` requests that contain *all* the relevant information. By providing a single composite object, the application can perform all of the operations in a single REST request. These larger objects become *documents* that might contain several items that are part of the more complex transaction.

When looking at our blog and post relationships, we see that we might want to handle two kinds of `HTTP POST` requests to create a new `Blog` instance. The two requests are as follows:

- **A blog with only a title and no additional post entries**: We can easily implement ACID properties for this, as it's only a single object.

- **A composite object that is a blog plus a collection of post entries**: We need to serialize the blog and all of the relevant `Post` instances. This needs to be sent as a single `POST` request. We can then implement the ACID properties by creating the blog, the related posts, and returning a single `201 Created` status when the entire collection of objects has been made durable. This may involve a complex multistatement transaction in the database that supports the RESTful web server.

Choosing a representation – JSON, XML, or YAML

There's no good reason to pick a single representation; it's relatively easy to support a number of representations. The client should be permitted to demand a representation. There are several places where a client can specify the representation:

- We can use a part of a query string, `https://host/app/class/id/?form=XML`.
- We can use a part of the URI: `https://host/app;XML/class/id/`. In this example, we've used a sub-delimiter for the application to identify the required representation. The `app;XML` syntax names the application, `app`, and the format, `XML`.
- We can use the fragment identifier, `https://host/app/class/id/#XML`.
- We can provide it in a header. The `Accept` header, for example, can be used to specify the representation.

None of these is *clearly* superior. Compatibility with existing RESTful web services may suggest a particular format. The relative ease with which a framework parses a URI pattern may suggest a format.

JSON is preferred by many JavaScript presentation layers. Other representations such as XML or YAML can be helpful for other presentation layers or other kinds of clients. In some cases, there may be yet another representation. For example, MXML or XAML might be required by a particular client application.

Implementing a REST server – WSGI and mod_wsgi

As REST is built on HTTP, a REST sever is an extension to an HTTP server. For robust, high-performance, secure operations, common practice is to build on a server such as **Apache httpd** or the **nginx**. These servers don't support Python by default; they require an extension module to interface with a Python application.

One widely used interface between web servers and Python is the WSGI. For more information, see `http://www.wsgi.org`. The Python Standard Library includes a WSGI reference implementation. See PEP 3333, `http://www.python.org/dev/peps/pep-3333/`, for the ways this reference implementation works in Python 3.

The idea behind WSGI is to standardize the HTTP request-reply processing around a relatively simple and extensible Python API. This allows us to architect complex Python solutions out of relatively independent components. The goal is to create a nested series of applications that perform incremental processing on the request. This creates a kind of pipeline where each stage adds information to the request environment.

Each WSGI application must have this API:

```
result = application(environ, start_response)
```

The `environ` variable must be `dict` with environmental information. The `start_response` function must be used to start preparing a response to the client; this is how the response status code and headers are sent. The return value must be an iterable over strings; that is, the body of the response.

The term *application* is used flexibly in the WSGI standard. A single server might have many WSGI applications. It's not the intent of WSGI to encourage or require programming at a low level of WSGI-compliant applications. The intent is to use larger, more sophisticated web frameworks. The web frameworks would all use the WSGI API definition to ensure compatibility.

The WSGI reference implementation is not intended to be a public-facing web server. This server doesn't handle SSL directly; some work needs to be done to wrap the sockets with proper SSL encryption. In order to access port 80 (or port 443), the process must execute in the `setuid` mode with a privileged user ID. One common practice is to install the WSGI extension module in a web server or use a web server that supports a WSGI API. This means that web requests are routed to Python from the web server using the standard WSGI interface. This allows the web server to provide static content. The Python applications available through the WSGI interface will provide the dynamic content.

Here's a list of web servers that are either written in Python or have Python plugins, `https://wiki.python.org/moin/WebServers`. These servers (or plugins) are intended to provide robust, secure, public-facing web servers.

An alternative is to build a standalone Python server and use redirection to shunt requests from the public-facing server to the separate Python daemon. When working with Apache httpd, a separate Python daemon can be created via the `mod_wsgi` module. As our focus is Python, we'll avoid nginx or Apache httpd details.

Creating a simple REST application and server

We'll write a very simple REST server that provides spins of a Roulette wheel. This is an example of a service that makes a response to a simple request. We'll focus on the RESTful web server programming in Python. There are additional details required to plug this software into a larger web server such as Apache httpd or nginx.

First, we'll define a simplified Roulette wheel:

```
class Wheel:
    """Abstract, zero bins omitted."""
    def __init__( self ):
        self.rng= random.Random()
        self.bins= [
            {str(n): (35,1),
            self.redblack(n): (1,1),
            self.hilo(n): (1,1),
            self.evenodd(n): (1,1),
            } for n in range(1,37)
        ]
    @staticmethod
    def redblack(n):
        return "Red" if n in (1, 3, 5, 7, 9,  12, 14, 16, 18,
            19, 21, 23, 25, 27,  30, 32, 34, 36) else "Black"
    @staticmethod
    def hilo(n):
        return "Hi" if n >= 19 else "Lo"
    @staticmethod
    def evenodd(n):
        return "Even" if n % 2 == 0 else "Odd"
    def spin( self ):
        return self.rng.choice( self.bins )
```

The `Wheel` class is a list of bins. Each bin is `dict`; the keys are bets that will be winners if the ball lands in that bin. The values in a bin are the payout ratios. We've only shown you a short list of bets. The complete list of available Roulette bets is quite large.

Also, we've omitted the zero or double zero bins. There are two different kinds of commonly used wheels. Here are two mixin classes that define the different kinds of commonly used wheels:

```
class Zero:
    def __init__( self ):
        super().__init__()
```

```
        self.bins += [ {'0': (35,1)} ]

class DoubleZero:
    def __init__( self ):
        super().__init__()
        self.bins += [ {'00': (35,1)} ]
```

The `Zero` mixin includes an initialization for a single zero. The `DoubleZero` mixin includes the double zero. These are relatively simple bins; they only payoff if a bet is made on the number itself.

We've used mixins here because we're going to tweak the definition of `Wheel` in some of the following examples. By using mixins, we can ensure that each extension to the base class, `Wheel`, will work consistently. For more information on the mixin-style design, see *Chapter 8, Decorators and Mixins – Cross-cutting Aspects*.

Here are the two subclasses that define the different kinds of commonly used wheels:

```
class American( Zero, DoubleZero, Wheel ):
    pass

class European( Zero, Wheel ):
    pass
```

These two definitions extend the basic `Wheel` class with mixins that will initialize the bins properly for each kind of wheel. These concrete subclasses of `Wheel` can be used as follows:

```
american = American()
european = European()
print( "SPIN", american.spin() )
```

Each evaluation of `spin()` produces a simple dictionary like the following one:

```
{'Even': (1, 1), 'Lo': (1, 1), 'Red': (1,   1), '12': (35, 1)}
```

The keys in this `dict` are the bet names. The value is a two-tuple with the payout ratio. The previous example shows us the Red 12 as a winner; it's also low and even. If we had placed a bet on 12, our winnings would be 35 times our bet, a payout of 35 to 1. The other propositions have payout of 1 to 1: we'd double our money.

We'll define a WSGI application that uses a simple path to determine which type of wheel to use. A URI such as `http://localhost:8080/european/` will use the European wheel. Any other path will use the American wheel.

Here's a WSGI application that uses a `Wheel` instance:

```
import sys
import wsgiref.util
import json
def wheel(environ, start_response):
    request= wsgiref.util.shift_path_info(environ) # 1. Parse.
    print( "wheel", request, file=sys.stderr ) # 2. Logging.
    if request.lower().startswith('eu'): # 3. Evaluate.
        winner= european.spin()
    else:
        winner= american.spin()
    status = '200 OK' # 4. Respond.
    headers = [('Content-type', 'application/json; charset=utf-8')]
    start_response(status, headers)
    return [ json.dumps(winner).encode('UTF-8') ]
```

This shows us some of the essential ingredients in a WSGI application.

First, we used the `wsgiref.util.shift_path_info()` function to examine the `environ['PATH_INFO']` value. This will parse one level of the path information in the request; it will either return the string value that was found, or return `None` in the case of a path not being provided at all.

Second, the logging line shows us that we *must* write to `sys.stderr` if we want to produce a log. Anything written to `sys.stdout` will be used as part of the response from the WSGI application. Anything that we attempt to print before the call to `start_response()` will lead to exceptions because the status and headers were not sent.

Third, we evaluated the request to compute the response. We used two globals, `european` and `american`, to provide a consistently randomized sequence of responses. If we attempt to create a unique `Wheel` instance for each request, we make inappropriate use of the random number generator.

Fourth, we formulated a response with a proper status code and HTTP headers. The body of the response is a JSON document that we've encoded using UTF-8 to make a proper byte stream as required by HTTP.

We can start a demonstration version of this server with a function such as the following:

```
from wsgiref.simple_server import make_server
def roulette_server(count=1):
    httpd = make_server('', 8080, wheel)
    if count is None:
```

```
        httpd.serve_forever()
    else:
        for c in range(count):
            httpd.handle_request()
```

The `wsgiref.simple_server.make_server()` function creates the server object. The object will invoke the callable `wheel()` to process each request. We've used the local hostname `''` and a non-privileged port, `8080`. Using the privileged port `80` requires `setuid` privileges and is better handled by the **Apache httpd** server.

Once the server is built, it can be left to run by itself; this is the `httpd.serve_forever()` method. For unit testing, however, it often works out much better to handle a finite number of requests and then stop the server.

We can run this function from the command line in a terminal window. Once we are running the function, we can use a browser to see the responses when we make requests to `http://localhost:8080/`. This can be helpful when creating a technical spike or debugging.

Implementing a REST client

Before looking at a smarter REST server application, we'll look at writing a REST client. Here's a function that will make a simple `GET` request to a REST server:

```
import http.client
import json
def json_get(path="/"):
    rest= http.client.HTTPConnection('localhost', 8080)
    rest.request("GET", path)
    response= rest.getresponse()
    print( response.status, response.reason )
    print( response.getheaders() )
    raw= response.read().decode("utf-8")
    if response.status == 200:
        document= json.loads(raw)
        print( document )
    else:
        print( raw )
```

This shows us the essence of working with a RESTful API. The `http.client` module has a four-step process:

- To establish a connection via `HTTPConnection()`
- To send a request with a command and a path

- To get a response
- To read the data in the response

The request can include an attached document (used for POST) as well as additional headers. In this function, we printed several parts of the response. In this example, we read the status code number and the reason text. Most of the time, we expect a status of 200 and a reason of `OK`. We also read and printed all of the headers.

Finally, we read the entire response into a temporary string, named `raw`. If the status code was 200, we used the `json` module to load objects from the response string. This recovered whatever JSON-encoded objects were serialized and sent from the server.

If the status code is not 200, we just print the available text. It might be an error message or other information that is useful for debugging.

Demonstrating and unit testing the RESTful services

It's relatively easy to perform a spike demonstration of a RESTful server. We can import the server class and function definitions and run the server function from a terminal window. We can connect with `http://localhost:8080` to see the responses.

For proper unit testing, we want a more formal exchange between a client and a server. For a controlled unit test, we'll want to start and then stop a server process. We can then exercise the server and examine the responses to the client.

We can use the `concurrent.futures` module to create a separate subprocess to run the server. Here's a snippet that shows us the kind of processing that can become part of a unit test case:

```
import concurrent.futures
import time
with concurrent.futures.ProcessPoolExecutor() as executor:
    executor.submit( roulette_server, 4 )
    time.sleep(2) # Wait for the server to start
    json_get()
    json_get()
    json_get("/european/")
    json_get("/european/")
```

We created a separate process by creating an instance of `concurrent.futures.ProcessPoolExecutor`. We can then submit a function to this server, with appropriate argument values.

In this case, we executed our `json_get()` client function to read the default path, /, twice. Then we performed the `GET` operation on the "`/european/`" path two times.

The `executor.submit()` function makes the process pool evaluate the `roulette_server(4)` function. This will handle four requests and then terminate. Because `ProcessPoolExecutor` is a context manager, we're assured that all of the resources will be properly cleaned up. The output log from the unit test includes groups of lines in the following way:

```
wheel 'european'
127.0.0.1 - - [08/Dec/2013 09:32:08] "GET /european/ HTTP/1.1" 200 62
200 OK
[('Date', 'Sun, 08 Dec 2013 14:32:08 GMT'), ('Server', 'WSGIServer/0.2
CPython/3.3.3'), ('Content-type', 'application/json; charset=utf-8'),
('Content-Length', '62')]
{'20': [35, 1], 'Even': [1, 1], 'Black': [1, 1], 'Hi': [1, 1]}
```

The `wheel 'european'` line is the log output from our `wheel()` WSGI application. The `127.0.0.1 - - [08/Dec/2013 09:32:08] "GET /european/ HTTP/1.1" 200 62` log line is written by default from the WSGI server, which shows us that the request was processed completely without an error.

The next three lines are written by the client `json_get()` function. The `200 OK` line is the first `print()` function. These lines are the headers that were sent as part of the server response. Finally, we show you the decoded dictionary object that was sent from the server to the client. In this case, the winner was 20 Black.

Also, note that our original tuples were transformed into lists by the JSON encoding and decoding process. Our original dict had `'20': (35, 1)`. The result here after encoding and decoding is `'20': [35, 1]`.

Note that the module being tested will be imported by the `ProcessPool` server. This import will locate the named function, `roulette_server()`. Because the server will import the module under test, the module under test must properly use `__name__ == "__main__"` guards to be sure that it won't perform any additional processing during the import; it must only provide definitions. We must be sure to use this kind of construct in the script that defines a server:

```
if __name__ == "__main__":
    roulette_server()
```

Using Callable classes for WSGI applications

We can implement WSGI applications as `Callable` objects instead of standalone functions. This allows us to have stateful processing in our WSGI server without the potential confusion of global variables. In our previous example, the `get_spin()` WSGI application relied on two global variables, `american` and `european`. The binding between the application and global can be mysterious.

The point of defining a class is to encapsulate the processing and data into a single package. We can use `Callable` objects to encapsulate our applications in a better manner. This can make the binding between stateful `Wheel` and WSGI applications clearer. Here is an extension to the `Wheel` class that makes it into a callable WSGI application:

```
from collections.abc import Callable
class Wheel2( Wheel, Callable ):
    def __call__(self, environ, start_response):
        winner= self.spin() # 3. Evaluate.
        status = '200 OK' # 4. Respond.
        headers = [('Content-type', 'application/json;
charset=utf-8')]
        start_response(status, headers)
        return [ json.dumps(winner).encode('UTF-8') ]
```

We extended the base `Wheel` class to include the WSGI interface. This doesn't do any parsing of the request; the WSGI processing has been pared down to just two steps: evaluation and response. We'll handle parsing and logging in a higher-level, wrapper application. This `Wheel2` application simply picks a result and encodes it as the result.

Note that we've added a distinct design feature to the `Wheel2` class. This is an example of a concern that is not part of the *is-a* definition of `Wheel`. This is more of an *acts-as* feature. This should, perhaps, be defined as a mixin or a decorator rather than a first-class feature of the class definition.

Here are two subclasses that implement American and European variations on Roulette:

```
class American2( Zero, DoubleZero, Wheel2 ):
    pass

class European2( Zero, Wheel2 ):
    pass
```

These two subclasses rely on the `__call__()` method function in the superclass. As with the preceding examples, we're using the mixins to add appropriate zero bins to the wheel.

We've changed the wheel from being a simple object to being a WSGI application. This means that our higher-level wrapper application can be somewhat simpler. Rather than evaluating some other object, the higher-level application simply delegates the request to the object. Here's a revised wrapper application that selects the wheel to be spun and delegates the request:

```
class Wheel3( Callable ):
    def __init__( self ):
        self.am = American2()
        self.eu = European2()
    def __call__(self, environ, start_response):
        request= wsgiref.util.shift_path_info(environ) # 1. Parse
        print( "Wheel3", request, file=sys.stderr ) # 2. Logging
        if request.lower().startswith('eu'): # 3. Evaluate
            response= self.eu(environ,start_response)
        else:
            response= self.am(environ,start_response)
        return response # 4. Respond
```

When we create an instance of this `Wheel3` class, it will create the two wheels. Each wheel is a WSGI application.

When a request is handled, the `Wheel3` WSGI application will parse the request. It will then hand the two arguments (`environ` and the `start_response` function) over to another application to perform the actual evaluation and compute a response. In many cases, this delegation will also include updating the `environ` variable with arguments and parameters parsed from the request path or headers. Finally, this `Wheel3.__call__()` function will return the response from the other application that was invoked.

This style of delegation is characteristic of WSGI applications. It's the reason that WSGI applications nest together so elegantly. Note that a wrapper application has two places to inject the processing:

- Before invoking another application, it will tweak the environment to add information
- After invoking another application, it can tweak the response document

Generally, we like to focus on tweaking the environment in a wrapping application. In this case, however, there was no real need to update the environment with any additional information, as the request was so trivial.

Designing RESTful object identifiers

Object serialization involves defining some kind of identifier for each object. For `shelve` or `sqlite`, we need to define a string key for each object. A RESTful web server makes the same demands to define a workable key that can be used to unambiguously track down objects.

A simple, surrogate key can work out for a RESTful web service identifier as well. It can easily parallel the key used for `shelve` or `sqlite`.

What's important is the idea that *cool URIs don't change*. See `http://www.w3.org/Provider/Style/URI.html`.

It is important for us to define a URI that isn't going to change, ever. It's essential that stateful aspects of an object are never used as part of the URI. For example, a microblogging application may support multiple authors. If we organize blog posts into folders by the author, we create problems for shared authorship and we create larger problems when one author takes over another author's content. We don't want the URI to switch when a purely administrative feature such as *ownership* changes.

A RESTful application may offer a number of indices or search criteria. However, the essential identification of a resource or object should never change as the indices are changed or reorganized.

For relatively simple objects, we can often find some sort of identifier—often, a database surrogate key. In the case of blog posts, it's common to use a publication date (as that can't change) and a version of the title with punctuation and spaces replaced by _ characters. The idea is to create an identifier that will not change no matter how the site gets reorganized. Adding or changing indexes can't change the essential identification of a microblog post.

For more complex objects that are containers, we have to decide on the granularity with which we can refer to these more complex objects. Continuing the microblog example, we have blogs as a whole, which contain a number of individual posts.

The URI for a blog can be something simple like this:

```
/microblog/blog/bid/
```

The top-most name (`microblog`) is the overall application. Then, we have the type of resource (`blog`) and finally, an ID for a specific instance.

URI names for a post, however, have several choices:

```
/microblog/post/title_string/
/microblog/post/bid/title_string/
/microblog/blog/bid/post/title_string/
```

The first URI doesn't work well when different blogs have posts with the same title. In this case, an author may see their title made unique with an extra `_2` or some other decoration that forces the title to be unique. This is often undesirable.

The second URI uses the blog ID (`bid`) as a context or namespace to ensure that the `Post` titles are treated as unique within the context of a blog. This kind of technique is often extended to include additional subdivisions such as a date to further shrink the search space.

The third example uses an explicit class/object naming at two levels: `blog/bid` and the `post/title_string`. This has the disadvantage of longer paths, but it has the advantage of allowing a complex container to have multiple items in distinct internal collections.

Note that REST services have the effect of defining an API for persistent storage. In effect, the URIs are similar to names of the interface methods. They must be chosen with an eye toward clarity, meaning, and durability.

Multiple layers of REST services

Here's a smarter, multilayered REST server application. We'll show you this in pieces. First, we need to supplement our `Wheel` class with a Roulette table:

```
from collections import defaultdict
class Table:
    def __init__( self, stake=100 ):
        self.bets= defaultdict(int)
        self.stake= stake
    def place_bet( self, name, amount ):
        self.bets[name] += amount
    def clear_bets( self, name ):
        self.bets= defaultdict(int)
    def resolve( self, spin ):
        """spin is a dict with bet:(x:y)."""
        details= []
        while self.bets:
            bet, amount= self.bets.popitem()
            if bet in spin:
                x, y = spin[bet]
```

```
                self.stake += amount*x/y
                details.append( (bet, amount, 'win') )
            else:
                self.stake -= amount
                details.append( (bet, amount, 'lose') )
        return details
```

The `Table` class tracks bets from a single, anonymous player. Each bet is a string name for a space on the Roulette table and an integer amount. When resolving the bets, a single spin from the `Wheel` class is provided to the `resolve()` method. The bets that are placed are compared to the winning bets from the spin and the player's stake is adjusted as bets are won or lost.

We'll define a RESTful Roulette server that shows us a stateful transaction that is implemented via an `HTTP POST` method. We'll break the game of Roulette into three URIs:

- `/player/`
    - `GET` to this URI will retrieve a JSON-encoded `dict` with facts about the player, including their stake and the number of rounds played so far. A future expansion would be to define a proper `Player` object and return a serialized instance.
    - A future expansion would be to handle `POST` to create additional players who place bets.
- `/bet/`
    - `POST` to this URI will include a JSON-encoded `dict` or a list of dicts that will create bets. Each bet dictionary will have two keys: `bet` and `amount`.
    - `GET` will return a JSON-encoded `dict` that shows us the bets and amounts placed so far.
- `/wheel/`
    - `POST`—with no data—to this URI will spin and compute the payout. This is implemented as `POST` to reinforce the sense that it is making a stateful change to the available bets and the player.
    - `GET` could, perhaps, repeat the previous results, showing us the last spin, last payout, and player's stake. This might be part of a non-repudiation scheme; it returns an additional copy of a spin receipt.

Here are two helpful class definitions for our family of WSGI applications:

```
class WSGI( Callable ):
    def __call__( self, environ, start_response ):
        raise NotImplementedError

class RESTException( Exception ):
    pass
```

We made a simple extension to `Callable` to make it clear that we're going to define a WSGI application class. We also defined an exception that we can use within our WSGI applications to send back error status codes that are different from the generic 500 error that the `wsgiref` implementation provides for Python errors. Here's the top level of the Roulette server:

```
class Roulette( WSGI ):
    def __init__( self, wheel ):
        self.table= Table(100)
        self.rounds= 0
        self.wheel= wheel
    def __call__( self, environ, start_response ):
        #print( environ, file=sys.stderr )
        app= wsgiref.util.shift_path_info(environ)
        try:
            if app.lower() == "player":
                return self.player_app( environ, start_response )
            elif app.lower() == "bet":
                return self.bet_app( environ, start_response )
            elif app.lower() == "wheel":
                return self.wheel_app( environ, start_response )
            else:
                raise RESTException("404 NOT_FOUND",
                    "Unknown app in {SCRIPT_NAME}/{PATH_INFO}".format_
map(environ))
        except RESTException as e:
            status= e.args[0]
            headers = [('Content-type', 'text/plain; charset=utf-8')]
            start_response( status, headers, sys.exc_info() )
            return [ repr(e.args).encode("UTF-8") ]
```

We defined a WSGI application that wraps the other applications. The `wsgiref.util.shift_path_info()` function will parse the path, breaking on / to get the first word. Based on this, we'll invoke one of three other WSGI applications. In this case, each application is going to be a method function within this class definition.

We provided an overall exception handler that will turn any of the `RESTException` instances into a proper RESTful response. Exceptions that we did not catch will turn into generic status code 500 errors from `wsgiref`. Here's the `player_app` method function:

```
    def player_app( self, environ, start_response ):
        if environ['REQUEST_METHOD'] == 'GET':
            details= dict( stake= self.table.stake, rounds= self.
rounds )
            status = '200 OK'
            headers = [('Content-type', 'application/json;
charset=utf-8')]
            start_response(status, headers)
            return [ json.dumps( details ).encode('UTF-8') ]
        else:
            raise RESTException("405 METHOD_NOT_ALLOWED",
                "Method '{REQUEST_METHOD}' not allowed".format_
map(environ))
```

We created a response object, `details`. We then serialized this object into a JSON string and further encoded that string into bytes using UTF-8.

In the unlikely event of an attempt to Post (or Put or Delete) to the `/player/` path, an exception will be raised. This will be caught in the top-level `__call__()` method and transformed into an error response.

Here's the `bet_app()` function:

```
    def bet_app( self, environ, start_response ):
        if environ['REQUEST_METHOD'] == 'GET':
            details = dict( self.table.bets )
        elif environ['REQUEST_METHOD'] == 'POST':
            size= int(environ['CONTENT_LENGTH'])
            raw= environ['wsgi.input'].read(size).decode("UTF-8")
            try:
                data = json.loads( raw )
                if isinstance(data,dict): data= [data]
                for detail in data:
                    self.table.place_bet( detail['bet'],
int(detail['amount']) )
            except Exception as e:
                raise RESTException("403 FORBIDDEN",
                 Bet {raw!r}".format(raw=raw))
            details = dict( self.table.bets )
        else:
```

```
            raise RESTException("405 METHOD_NOT_ALLOWED",
                "Method '{REQUEST_METHOD}' not allowed".format_
map(environ))
        status = '200 OK'
        headers = [('Content-type', 'application/json;
charset=utf-8')]
        start_response(status, headers)
        return [ json.dumps(details).encode('UTF-8') ]
```

This does two things, depending on the request method. When a `GET` request is used, the result is a dictionary of current bets. When a `POST` request is used, there must be some data to define the bets. When any other method is attempted, an error is returned.

In the `POST` case, information on the bet is provided as the data stream attached to the request. We have to perform several steps to read and process this data. The first step is to use the value of `environ['CONTENT_LENGTH']` to determine how many bytes to read. The second step is to decode the bytes to get the string value that was sent.

We used the JSON encoding of the request. This, emphatically, is not the way a browser or web application server handles the `POST` data from an HTML form. When using a browser to post data from an HTML form, the encoding is a simple set of escapes, implemented by the `urllib.parse` module. The `urllib.parse.parse_qs()` module function will parse the encoded query string with HTML data.

For RESTful web services, `POST` compatible data is sometimes used so that form-based processing is very similar to RESTful processing. In other cases, a separate encoding such as JSON is used to create data structures that are easier to work with than the quoted data produced by a web form.

Once we have the string, `raw`, we use `json.loads()` to get the object represented by that string. We expect one of the two classes of objects. A simple `dict` object will define a single bet. A sequence of `dict` objects will define multiple bets. As a simple generalization, we make the single `dict` into a singleton sequence. We can then use the general sequence of `dict` instances to place the required bets.

Note that our exception handling will leave some bets in place but will send an overall `403 Forbidden` message. A better design is to follow the **Memento** design pattern. When placing bets, we would also create a memento object that can be used to undo any bets. One implementation of the Memento is to use the **Before Image** design pattern. The Memento could include a copy of all the bets prior to applying a change. In the event of an exception, we can delete the damaged version and restore the previous one. When working with nested containers of mutable objects, this can be complex, because we have to be sure to make a copy of any mutable objects. As this application uses only immutable strings and integers, a shallow copy of `table.bets` will work nicely.

For both `POST` and `GET` methods, the response is the same. We'll serialize the `table.bets` dictionary into JSON and send it back to the REST client. This will confirm that the expected bets were placed.

The final part of this class is the `wheel_app()` method:

```
    def wheel_app( self, environ, start_response ):
        if environ['REQUEST_METHOD'] == 'POST':
            size= environ['CONTENT_LENGTH']
            if size != '':
                raw= environ['wsgi.input'].read(int(size))
                raise RESTException("403 FORBIDDEN",
                    "Data '{raw!r}' not allowed".format(raw=raw))
            spin= self.wheel.spin()
            payout = self.table.resolve( spin )
            self.rounds += 1
            details = dict( spin=spin, payout=payout,
                stake= self.table.stake, rounds= self.rounds )
            status = '200 OK'
            headers = [('Content-type', 'application/json;
charset=utf-8')]
            start_response(status, headers)
            return [ json.dumps( details ).encode('UTF-8') ]
        else:
            raise RESTException("405 METHOD_NOT_ALLOWED",
                "Method '{REQUEST_METHOD}' not allowed".format_
map(environ))
```

This method first checks that it is invoked with a post that supplies no data. Just to be sure that the socket is properly closed, all the data is read and ignored. This can prevent a poorly written client from crashing when the socket is closed with unread data.

Once that bit of housekeeping is out of the way, the remaining processing is performed to develop a new spin from the wheel, resolve the various bets, and produce a response that includes the spin, the payout, the player's stake, and the number of rounds. This report is built as a `dict` object. It's then serialized into JSON, encoded into UTF-8, and sent back to the client.

Note that we've avoided handling multiple players. This would add a class and another `POST` method under the `/player/` path. It would add a bit of definition and bookkeeping. The `POST` processing to create a new player would be similar to the processing for placing a bet. This is an interesting exercise, but it doesn't introduce any new programming techniques.

Creating the roulette server

Once we have a callable `Roulette` class, we can create a WSGI server in the following manner:

```
def roulette_server_3(count=1):
    from wsgiref.simple_server import make_server
    from wsgiref.validate import validator
    wheel= American()
    roulette= Roulette(wheel)
    debug= validator(roulette)
    httpd = make_server('', 8080, debug)
    if count is None:
        httpd.serve_forever()
    else:
        for c in range(count):
            httpd.handle_request()
```

This function creates our Roulette WSGI application, `roulette`. It uses `wsgiref.simple_server.make_server()` to create a server that will use the `roulette` callable for each request.

In this case, we've also included the `wsgiref.validate.validator()` WSGI application. This application validates the interface used by the roulette application; it decorates the various APIs with assert statements to provide some diagnostic information. It also produces slightly easier-to-read error messages in the event of a more serious programming problem in a WSGI application.

Creating the roulette client

It's common practice to define a module with a RESTful client API. Often, the client API will have functions that are specifically tailored to the requested services.

Instead of defining a specialized client, we'll define a generic client function that works with a variety of RESTful servers. This might serve as the foundation for a Roulette-specific client. Here's a generic client function that will work with our `Roulette` server:

```
def roulette_client(method="GET", path="/", data=None):
    rest= http.client.HTTPConnection('localhost', 8080)
    if data:
        header= {"Content-type": "application/json; charset=utf-8'"}
        params= json.dumps( data ).encode('UTF-8')
        rest.request(method, path, params, header)
    else:
        rest.request(method, path)
    response= rest.getresponse()
    raw= response.read().decode("utf-8")
    if 200 <= response.status < 300:
        document= json.loads(raw)
        return document
    else:
        print( response.status, response.reason )
        print( response.getheaders() )
        print( raw )
```

This client makes the `GET` or `POST` requests, and it will encode the data for a `POST` request as a JSON document. Note that the JSON encoding of the request data is emphatically not the way a browser handles an HTML form's `POST` data. Browsers use the encoding implemented by the `urllib.parse.urlencode()` module function.

Our client function decodes the JSON document and returns it when the status code is in the half-open range, $[200, 300)$. These are the success status codes. We can exercise our client and server as follows:

```
    with concurrent.futures.ProcessPoolExecutor() as executor:
        executor.submit( roulette_server_3, 4 )
        time.sleep(3) # Wait for the server to start
        print( roulette_client("GET", "/player/" ) )
        print( roulette_client("POST", "/bet/", {'bet':'Black',
'amount':2}) )
        print( roulette_client("GET", "/bet/" ) )
        print( roulette_client("POST", "/wheel/" ) )
```

First, we create `ProcessPool` as the context for the exercise. We submit a request to this server; in effect, the request is `roulette_server_3(4)`. Once the server has started, we can exercise that server.

In this case, we made four requests. We check the player's status. We place a bet and then we check the bet. Finally, we spin the wheel. At each step, we print the JSON response documents.

The log looks like this:

```
127.0.0.1 - - [09/Dec/2013 08:21:34] "GET /player/ HTTP/1.1" 200 27
{'stake': 100, 'rounds': 0}
127.0.0.1 - - [09/Dec/2013 08:21:34] "POST /bet/ HTTP/1.1" 200 12
{'Black': 2}
127.0.0.1 - - [09/Dec/2013 08:21:34] "GET /bet/ HTTP/1.1" 200 12
{'Black': 2}
127.0.0.1 - - [09/Dec/2013 08:21:34] "POST /wheel/ HTTP/1.1" 200 129
{'stake': 98, 'payout': [['Black', 2, 'lose']], 'rounds': 1, 'spin':
{'27': [35, 1], 'Odd': [1, 1], 'Red': [1, 1], 'Hi': [1, 1]}}
```

This shows us that our server responds to requests, creates bets on the table, creates random spins of the wheel, and properly updates the player with the outcomes.

Creating a secure REST service

We can break application security down into two considerations: authentication and authorization. We need to know who the user is and we need to be sure that the user is authorized to execute the particular WSGI application. This is handled relatively simply using both the HTTP `Authorization` header for credentials to ensure an encrypted transmission of these credentials.

If we use SSL, we can simply use the HTTP Basic Authorization mode. This version of the `Authorization` header can include a username and password in each request. For more elaborate measures, we can use HTTP Digest Authorization, which requires an exchange with the server to get a piece of data called a **nonce** that's used to create the digest in a more secure fashion.

Generally, we'll handle authentication as early in the process as possible. This means a frontend WSGI application that checks for the `Authorization` header and updates the environment or returns an error. Ideally, we'll be using a sophisticated web framework that offers us this feature. See the next section for more information on these web framework considerations.

Perhaps the most important advice that can possibly be offered on the subject of security is the following:

> **Never Store Passwords**
>
> The only thing that can be stored is a repeated cryptographic hash of password plus salt. The password itself must be unrecoverable; research fully on *Salted Password Hashing* or download a trusted library for this. Do not ever store a plaintext password or an encrypted password.

Here's an example class that shows us how salted password hashing works:

```
from hashlib import sha256
import os
class Authentication:
    iterations= 1000
    def __init__( self, username, password ):
        """Works with bytes. Not Unicode strings."""
        self.username= username
        self.salt= os.urandom(24)
        self.hash= self._iter_hash( self.iterations, self.salt,
username, password )
    @staticmethod
    def _iter_hash( iterations, salt, username, password ):
        seed= salt+b":"+username+b":"+password
        for i in range(iterations):
            seed= sha256( seed ).digest()
        return seed
    def __eq__( self, other ):
        return self.username == other.username and self.hash == other.
hash
    def __hash__( self, other ):
        return hash(self.hash)
    def __repr__( self ):
        salt_x= "".join( "{0:x}".format(b) for b in self.salt )
        hash_x= "".join( "{0:x}".format(b) for b in self.hash )
        return "{username} {iterations:d}:{salt}:{hash}".format(
            username=self.username, iterations=self.iterations,
            salt=salt_x, hash=hash_x)
    def match( self, password ):
        test= self._iter_hash( self.iterations, self.salt, self.
username, password )
        return self.hash == test # Constant Time is Best
```

This class defines an `Authentication` object for a given username. The object contains the username, a unique random salt created each time the password is set or reset, and the final hash of the salt plus the password. This class also defines a `match()` method that will determine whether a given password will produce the same hash as the original password.

Note that the passwords are not stored. Only hashes of passwords are retained. We provided a comment ("`# Constant Time is Best`") on the comparison function. An algorithm that runs in constant time—and isn't particularly fast—is ideal for this comparison. We haven't implemented it.

We also included an equality test and a hash test to emphasize that this object is immutable. We can't tweak any of the values. We can only discard and rebuild the entire `Authentication` object when users changes their password. An additional design feature would be to use `__slots__` to save storage.

Note that these algorithms work with byte strings, not Unicode strings. We either need to work with bytes or we need to work with the ASCII encoding of a Unicode username or password. Here's how we might create a collection of users:

```
class Users( dict ):
    def __init__( self, *args, **kw ):
        super().__init__( *args, **kw )
        # Can never match -- keys are the same.
        self[""]= Authentication( b"__dummy__", b"Doesn't Matter" )
    def add( self, authentication ):
        if authentication.username == "":
            raise KeyError( "Invalid Authentication" )
        self[authentication.username]= authentication
    def match( self, username, password ):
        if username in self and username != "":
            return self[username].match(password)
        else:
            return self[""].match(b"Something which doesn't match")
```

We created an extension to `dict` that introduces an `add()` method to save an `Authentication` instance and a match method that determines whether the users are in this dictionary and whether their credentials match.

Note that our match needs to be a constant time comparison. We created an additional dummy user for a situation where an unknown username is supplied. By performing the match against a dummy user—which will always fail—the execution timing doesn't provide many hints as to what's wrong with the credentials. If we simply returned `False`, a mismatched username would respond faster than a mismatched password.

We specifically disallowed setting the authentication for a username of `""` or matching a username of `""`. This will ensure that the dummy username is never changed to a valid entry that might possibly match, and any attempt to match it will always fail. Here's a sample user that we built:

```
users = Users()
users.add( Authentication(b"Aladdin", b"open sesame") )
```

Just to see what's going on inside this class, we can manually create a user:

```
>>> al= Authentication(b"Aladdin", b"open sesame")
>>> al
b'Aladdin' 1000:16f56285edd9326282da8c6aff8d602a682bbf83619c7f:9b86a2a
d1ae0345029ae11de402ba661ade577df876d89b8a3e182d887a9f7
```

The salt is a string of 24 bytes that's reset when the user's password is created or changed. The hash is a repeated hash of username, password, and salt.

The WSGI Authentication application

Once we have a way to store the users and credentials, we can examine the `Authentication` header in a request. Here's a WSGI application that checks the header and updates the environment for validated users:

```
import base64
class Authenticate( WSGI ):
    def __init__( self, users, target_app ):
        self.users= users
        self.target_app= target_app
    def __call__( self, environ, start_response ):
        if 'HTTP_AUTHORIZATION' in environ:
            scheme, credentials = environ['HTTP_AUTHORIZATION'].
split()
            if scheme == "Basic":
                username, password= base64.b64decode( credentials
).split(b":")
                if self.users.match(username, password):
                    environ['Authenticate.username']= username
                    return self.target_app(environ, start_response)
        status = '401 UNAUTHORIZED'
        headers = [('Content-type', 'text/plain; charset=utf-8'),
            ('WWW-Authenticate', 'Basic realm="roulette@localhost"')]
        start_response(status, headers)
        return [ "Not authorized".encode('utf-8') ]
```

This WSGI application contains a pool of users in addition to a a target application. When we create an instance of this `Authenticate` class, we'll provide another WSGI application as `target_app`; this wrapped application will only see requests from authenticated users. When the `Authenticate` application is invoked, it performs several tests to be sure that the request is from an authenticated user:

- There must be an HTTP `Authorization` header. This header is saved with the `HTTP_AUTHORIZATION` key in the `environ` dict
- The header must have `Basic` as the authentication scheme
- The credentials in the Basic scheme must be base 64 encoding of `username+b":"+password`; this must match the credentials of one of the defined users

If all of these tests are passed, we can update the `environ` dict with the authenticated username. Then, the target application can be invoked.

The wrapped application can then handle the authorization details knowing that the user is authenticated. This separation of concerns is one elegant feature of WSGI applications. We have put the authentication in exactly one place.

Implementing REST with a web application framework

As a REST web server is a web application, we can leverage any of the popular Python web application frameworks. Writing a RESTful server from scratch is a step that can be taken after demonstrating that a framework provides unacceptable problems. In many cases, a technical spike using a framework can help clarify any issues and allow a detailed comparison against a REST application written without a framework.

Some of the Python web frameworks include one or more REST components. In some cases, the RESTful features are almost entirely built-in. In other cases, an add-on project can help define RESTful web services with minimal programming.

Here's a list of Python web frameworks: `https://wiki.python.org/moin/WebFrameworks`. The point of these projects is to provide a reasonably complete environment to build web applications.

Here's a list of Python web component packages: `https://wiki.python.org/moin/WebComponents`. These are bits and pieces that can be used to support web application development.

Searching PyPI, `https://pypi.python.org`, for REST will turn up a large number of packages. Clearly, there are numerous solutions that are already available.

Taking time to search, download, and learn a number of existing frameworks can reduce some of the development effort. Security, in particular, is challenging. Home-brewed security algorithms are often filled with serious deficiencies. Using someone else's proven security tools can have some advantages.

Using a message queue to transmit objects

The `multiprocessing` module uses serialization and transmission of objects, too. We can use queues and pipes to serialize objects that are then transmitted to other processes. There are numerous external projects to provide sophisticated message queue processing. We'll focus on the `multiprocessing` queue because it's built-in to Python and works nicely.

For high-performance applications, a faster message queue may be necessary. It may also be necessary to use a faster serialization technique than pickling. For this chapter, we'll focus only on the Python design issues. The multiprocessing module relies on `pickle` to encode objects. See *Chapter 9, Serializing and Saving – JSON, YAML, Pickle, CSV, and XML*, for more information. We can't provide a restricted unpickler easily; therefore, this module offers us some relatively simple security measures put into place to prevent unpickle problems.

There is one important design consideration when using `multiprocessing`: it's generally best to avoid having multiple processes (or multiple threads) attempting to update shared objects. The synchronization and locking issues are so profound (and easy to get wrong) that the standard joke is,

> *When confronted with a problem, the programmer thinks,*
> *"I'll use multiple threads."*

Using process-level synchronization via RESTful web services or `multiprocessing` can prevent synchronization issues because there are no shared objects. The essential design principle is to look at the processing as a pipeline of discrete steps. Each processing step will have an input queue and an output queue; the step will fetch an object, perform some processing, and write the object.

The `multiprocessing` philosophy matches the POSIX concept of a shell pipeline written as `process1 | process2 | process3`. This kind of shell pipeline involves three concurrent processes interconnected with pipes. The important difference is that we don't need to use STDIN, STDOUT, and explicit serialization of the objects. We can trust the `multiprocessing` module to handle the OS-level infrastructure.

The POSIX shell pipelines are limited, in that each pipe has a single producer and a single consumer. The Python `multiprocessing` module allows us to create message queues that include multiple consumers. This allows us to have a pipeline that fans out from one source process to multiple sink processes. A queue can also have multiple consumers that allow us to build a pipeline where the results of multiple source processes can be combined by a single sink process.

To maximize throughput on a given computer system, we need to have enough work pending so that no processor or core is ever left with nothing useful to do. When any given OS process is waiting for a resource, at least one other process should be ready to run.

When looking at our casino game simulations, for example, we need to gather statistically significant simulation data by exercising a player strategy or betting strategy (or both) a number of times. The idea is to create a queue of processing requests so that our computer's processors (and cores) are fully engaged in processing our simulations.

Each processing request can be a Python object. The `multiprocessing` module will pickle that object so that it is transmitted via the queue to another process.

We'll revisit this in *Chapter 14, The Logging and Warning Modules*, when we look at how the `logging` module can use `multiprocessing` queues to provide a single, centralized log for separate producer processes. In these examples, the objects transmitted from process to process will be the `logging.LogRecord` instances.

Defining processes

We must design each processing step as a simple loop that gets a request from a queue, processes that request, and places the results into another queue. This decomposes the larger problem into a number of stages that form a pipeline. As each of these stages will run concurrently, the system resource use will be maximized. Furthermore, as the stages involve simple gets and puts into independent queues, there's no issue with complex locking or shared resources. A process can be a simple function or a callable object. We'll focus on defining processes as subclasses of `multiprocessing.Process`. This gives us the most flexibility.

For the simulation of our casino game, we can break the simulation down into a three-step pipeline:

1. An overall driver puts simulation requests into a processing queue.
2. A pool of simulators will get a request from the processing queue, perform the simulation, and put the statistics into a results queue.
3. A summarizer will get the results from the results queue and create a final tabulation of the results.

Using a process pool allows us to have as many simulations running concurrently as our CPU can handle. The pool of simulators can be configured to ensure that simulations run as quickly as possible.

Here's a definition of the simulator process:

```
import multiprocessing
class Simulation( multiprocessing.Process ):
    def __init__( self, setup_queue, result_queue ):
        self.setup_queue= setup_queue
        self.result_queue= result_queue
        super().__init__()
    def run( self ):
        """Waits for a termination"""
        print( self.__class__.__name__, "start" )
        item= self.setup_queue.get()
        while item != (None,None):
            table, player = item
            self.sim= Simulate( table, player, samples=1 )
            results= list( self.sim )
            self.result_queue.put( (table, player, results[0]) )
            item= self.setup_queue.get()
        print( self.__class__.__name__, "finish" )
```

We've extended `multiprocessing.Process`. This means that we must do two things to work properly with multiprocessing: we must assure that `super().__init__()` is executed, and we must override `run()`.

Within the body of `run()`, we're using two queues. The `setup_queue` queue instance will contain two-tuples of the `Table` and `Player` objects. The process will use these two objects to run a simulation. It will put the resulting three-tuple into `result_queue` queue instance. The API for the `Simulate` class is this:

```
class Simulate:
    def __init__( self, table, player, samples ):
    def __iter__( self ): yields summaries
```

The iterator will yield the requested number, `samples`, of statistical summaries. We've included a provision for a **sentinel object** to arrive via `setup_queue`. This object will be used to gracefully close down the processing. If we don't use a sentinel object, we're forced to terminate the processes, which can disrupt locks and other system resources. Here's the summarization process:

```
class Summarize( multiprocessing.Process ):
    def __init__( self, queue ):
        self.queue= queue
        super().__init__()
    def run( self ):
        """Waits for a termination"""
        print( self.__class__.__name__, "start" )
        count= 0
        item= self.queue.get()
        while item != (None, None, None):
            print( item )
            count += 1
            item= self.queue.get()
        print( self.__class__.__name__, "finish", count )
```

This also extends `multiprocessing.Process`. In this case, we're fetching items from a queue and simply counting them. A more useful process might use several `collection.Counter` objects to accumulate more interesting statistics.

As with the `Simulation` class, we're also going to detect a sentinel and gracefully close down the processing. The use of a sentinel object allows us to close down processing as soon as the work is completed by the process. In some applications, the child process can be left running indefinitely.

Building queues and supplying data

Building queues involves creating instances of `multiprocessing.Queue` or one of its subclasses. For this example, we can use the following:

```
setup_q= multiprocessing.SimpleQueue()
results_q= multiprocessing.SimpleQueue()
```

We created two queues that define the processing pipeline. When we put a simulation request into `setup_q`, we expect that a `Simulation` process will pick up the request pair and run the simulation. This should generate a results three-tuple of table, player and results in the `results_q` Queue. in `results_q`. The results triple should, in turn, lead to work being done by the `Summarize` process. Here's how we can start a single `Summarize` process:

```
result= Summarize( results_q )
result.start()
```

Here's how we can create four concurrent simulation processes:

```
simulators= []
for i in range(4):
    sim= Simulation( setup_q, results_q )
    sim.start()
    simulators.append( sim )
```

The four concurrent simulators will be competing for work. Each one will be attempting to grab the next request from the queue of pending requests. Once all four simulators are busy working, the queue will start to get filled with unprocessed requests. Once the queues and processes are waiting, the driver function can start putting requests into the `setup_q` queue. Here's a loop that will generate a flood of requests:

```
table= Table( decks= 6, limit= 50, dealer=Hit17(),
    split= ReSplit(), payout=(3,2) )
for bet in Flat, Martingale, OneThreeTwoSix:
    player= Player( SomeStrategy, bet(), 100, 25 )
    for sample in range(5):
        setup_q.put( (table, player) )
```

We created a `Table` object. For each of the three betting strategies, we created a `Player` object, and then queued up a simulation request. The pickled two-tuple will be fetched from the queue by the `Simulation` object and then it will be processed. In order to have an orderly termination, we'll need to queue sentinel objects for each simulator:

```
for sim in simulators:
    setup_q.put( (None,None) )

for sim in simulators:
    sim.join()
```

We put a sentinel object into the queue for each simulator to consume. Once all the simulators have consumed the sentinels, we can wait for the processes to finish execution and join back into the parent process.

Once the `Process.join()` operation is finished, no more simulation data will be created. We can enqueue a sentinel object into the simulation results queue as well:

```
results_q.put( (None,None,None) )
result.join()
```

Once the results sentinel object is processed, the `Summarize` process will stop accepting input and we can `join()` it as well.

We used multiprocessing to transmit objects from one process to another. This gives us a relatively simple way to create high-performance, multi-processing data pipelines. The `multiprocessing` module uses `pickle`, so there are few limitations on the nature of objects that can be pushed through the pipelines.

Summary

We looked at transmitting and sharing objects using RESTful web services and the `wsgiref` module, as well as the `multiprocessing` module. Both of these architectures provide for communicating a representation of an object's state. In the case of `multiprocessing`, pickle is used to represent the state. In the case of building RESTful web services, we have to choose the representation(s) used. In the examples used here, we focused on JSON because it's widely used and has a simple implementation. Many frameworks will offer simple implementations of XML as well.

Performing RESTful web services using a WSGI application framework formalizes the process of receiving HTTP requests, deserializing any objects, performing the requested processing, serializing any results, and providing a response. Because WSGI applications have a simple, standardized API, we can easily create composite applications and write wrapper applications. We can often leverage wrapper applications to handle the authentication elements of security in a simple, consistent manner.

We also looked at using `multiprocessing` to enqueue and dequeue messages from shared queues. The beauty of using message queues is that we can avoid the locking problems associated with concurrent updates to shared objects.

Design considerations and trade-offs

We must also decide what grain of objects to make available and how to identify those objects with sensible URIs. With larger objects, we can easily achieve ACID properties. However, we may also be uploading and downloading too much data for our application's use cases. In some cases, we'll need to provide alternative levels of access: large objects to support ACID properties, small objects to allow rapid response when a client application wants a subset of the data.

To implement more localized processing, we can leverage the `multiprocessing` module. This is focused more on building high-performance processing pipelines within a trusted host or network of hosts.

In some cases, the two design patterns are combined so that a RESTful request is handled by a multiprocessing pipeline. A conventional web server (such as Apache HTTPD) working through the `mod_wsgi` extension can use multiprocessing techniques to pass a request through a named pipe from the Apache frontend to the WSGI application backend.

Schema evolution

When working with a public-facing API for RESTful services, we have to address the schema evolution problem. If we change a class definition, how will we change the response messages? If the external RESTful API must change for compatibility with other programs, how do we upgrade the Python web services to support a changing API?

Often, we'll have to provide a major release version number as part of our API. This might be provided explicitly as part of the path, or implicitly via data fields included in the `POST`, `PUT`, and `DELETE` requests.

We need to distinguish between changes that don't alter the URI paths or responses and changes that will alter a URI or response. Minor changes to functionality will not change a URI or the structure of a response.

Changes to the URIs or the structure of a response may break an existing application. These are major changes. One way to make an application work gracefully through schema upgrades is to include version numbers in the URI paths. For example, `/roulette_2/wheel/` specifically names the second release of the roulette server.

Application software layers

Because of the relative sophistication available when using `sqlite3`, our application software must become more properly layered. For a REST client, we might look at a software architecture with layers.

When we are building a RESTful server, the presentation layer becomes greatly simplified. It is pared down to the essential request-response processing. It parses URIs and responds with documents in JSON or XML (or some other representation.) This layer should be reduced to a thin RESTful facade over the lower level features.

In some complex cases, the front-most application—as viewed by human users—involves data from several distinct sources. One easy way to integrate data from diverse sources is to wrap each source in a RESTful API. This provides us with a uniform interface over distinct sources of data. It allows us to write applications that gather these diverse kinds of data in a uniform way.

Looking forward

In the next chapter, we'll use persistence techniques to handle configuration files. A file that's editable by humans is the primary requirement for the configuration data. If we use a well-known persistence module, then our application can parse and validate the configuration data with less programming on our part.

13
Configuration Files and Persistence

A configuration file is a form of object persistence. It contains a serialized, editable representation of some default state for an application program or server. We'll expand on our serialization techniques for the object representation shown in *Chapter 9, Serializing and Saving – JSON, YAML, Pickle, CSV, and XML* to create configuration files.

In addition to having a plain-text editable configuration file, we must also design our application to be configurable. Further, we must define some kind of configuration object (or collection) that our application can use. In many cases, we'll have a series of default values that include system-wide defaults and user-specific overrides to those defaults. We'll look at six representations for the configuration data:

- INI files use a format that was pioneered as part of Windows. It's popular in part because it is an incumbent format, and many other configuration files might use this notation.
- PY files are plain-old Python code. This has numerous advantages because of the familiarity and simplicity of working with it.
- JSON or YAML are both designed to be human-friendly and easy to edit.
- Property files are often used in a Java environment. They're relatively easy to work and are also designed to be human-friendly.
- XML files are popular but are wordy and are sometimes difficult to edit properly. The Mac OS uses an XML-based format called a property list or the `.plist` file.

Each of these forms offers us some advantages and some disadvantages. There's no single technique that's the best. In many cases, the choice is based on compatibility with other software or familiarity with another format in the user community.

Configuration file use cases

There are two configuration file use cases. Sometimes, we can stretch the definition a bit to add a third use case. The first two should be pretty clear:

- A person needs to edit a configuration file
- A piece of software will read a configuration file and make use of the options and arguments to tailor its behavior

Configuration files are rarely the *primary* input to an application program. The big exception is a simulation where the configuration might be the primary input. In most other cases, the configuration isn't primary. For example, a web server's configuration file might tailor the behavior of the server, but the web requests are one primary input, and a database or filesystem is the other primary input. In the case of a GUI application, the user's interactive events are one input, and files or database may be another input; a configuration file may fine-tune the application.

There's a blurry edge to this distinction between primary and configuration input. Ideally, an application has one behavior irrespective of the configuration details. Pragmatically, however, the configuration might introduce additional strategies or states to an existing application, changing its behavior. In this case, the configuration can straddle the line and become part of the code, not merely a configuration to a fixed code base.

A possible third use case is to save a configuration back to a file after an application has updated it. This use of persistent stateful objects is atypical because the configuration file has morphed into a primary input in which the program is saving its operating state. This use case may indicate that two things have been conflated into a single file: configuration parameters and the persistent operating state. It's better to design this as a persistent state that uses a human-readable format.

A configuration file can provide a number of kinds of arguments and parameter values to an application. We need to look a little more deeply at some of these various kinds of data to decide how to represent them best:

- Default values
- Device names, which may overlap with the filesystem's location
- Filesystem locations and search paths
- Limits and boundaries
- Message templates and data format specifications
- Message text, possibly translated for internationalization
- Network names, addresses, and port numbers

- Optional behaviors
- Security keys, tokens, usernames, passwords
- Value domains:

  These values are values of relatively common types: strings, integers, and floating-point numbers. All of those values have a tidy textual representation that's relatively easy for a person to edit. They're also straightforward for our Python applications to parse the human input.

  In some cases, we may have lists of values. For example, a domain of values or a path might be a collection of simpler types. Often, this is a simple sequence or a sequence of tuples. A dict-like mapping is often used for message texts so that an application's software key can be mapped to customized natural language wording.

There is one additional configuration value that isn't a simple type with a tidy text representation. We could add this bullet to the preceding list:

- Additional features, plugins, and extensions that are code:

  This is challenging because we're not necessarily providing a simple string value to the application. The configuration provides an object that the application will use. When the plugin has more of Python code, we can provide the path to an installed Python module as it would be used in an `import` statement using this dotted name: '`package.module.object`'. An application can then perform the expected '`from package.module import object`' code and use the given class or function.

For non-Python code, we have two other techniques to import the code in a way it can be used:

- For binaries that aren't proper executable programs, we can try to use the `ctypes` module to call defined API methods
- For binaries that are executable programs, the `subprocess` module gives us ways to execute them

Both of these techniques aren't about Python specifically and push the edge of the envelope for this chapter. We'll focus on the core issue of getting the arguments or the parameter values. How these values are used is a very large topic.

Representation, persistence, state, and usability

When looking at a configuration file, we're looking at a human-friendly version of the state of one or more objects. When we edit a configuration file, we're changing the persistent state of an object that will get reloaded when the application is started (or restarted.) We have two common ways to look at a configuration file:

- A mapping or a group of mappings from parameter names to values
- A serialized object that's more than a simple mapping

When we try to reduce a configuration file to a mapping, we might be limiting the scope of relationships that may exist within the configuration. In a simple mapping, everything must be referred to by a name, and we have to work through the same key design issues that we looked at in *Chapter 10, Storing and Retrieving Objects via Shelve*, and *Chapter 11, Storing and Retrieving Objects via SQLite*, when talking about the keys for `shelve` and `sqlite`. We provide a unique name in one part of a configuration so that other parts can refer to it properly.

It's helpful to look at the `logging` configuration for examples of how it can be very challenging to configure a complex system. The relationships among Python logging objects—loggers, formatters, filters, and handlers—must all be bound together to create usable loggers. Section 16.8 of *Standard Library Reference* shows us two different syntaxes for the logging configuration files. We'll look at logging in *Chapter 14, The Logging and Warning Modules.*

In some cases, it may be simpler to serialize complex Python objects or resort to using Python code directly as the configuration file. If a configuration file adds too much complexity, then it may not be of any real value.

Application configuration design patterns

There are two core design patterns for the application configuration:

- **Global property map**: A global object will contain all of the configuration parameters. This can be either a map of `name:value` pairs, or a big namespace object of attribute values. This may follow a **Singleton** design pattern to ensure that only one instance exists.
- **Object Construction**: Instead of a single object, we'll define a kind of **Factory** or collection of **Factories** that use the configuration data to build the objects of the application. In this case, the configuration information is used once when a program is started and never again. The configuration information isn't kept around as a global object.

The global property map design is very popular because it is simple and extensible. We might have an object as simple as the following code:

```
class Configuration:
    some_attribute= "default_value"
```

We can use the preceding class definition as a global container of attributes. During the initialization, we might have something like this as part of parsing a configuration file:

```
Configuration.some_attribute= "user-supplied value"
```

Everywhere else in the program, we can use the value of `Configuration.some_attribute`. A variation on this theme is to make a more formal **Singleton** object design pattern. This is often done with a global module, as that can be easily imported in a way that provides us with an accessible global definition.

We might have a module named `configuration.py`. In that file, we can have a definition like the following:

```
settings= dict()
```

Now, the application can use `configuration.settings` as a global repository for all of the application's settings. A function or class can parse the configuration file, loading this dictionary with the configuration values that the application will then use.

In a Blackjack simulation, we might see code like the following:

```
shoe= Deck( configuration.settings['decks'] )
```

Or, we might possibly see code like the following one:

```
If bet > configuration.settings['limit']: raise InvalidBet()
```

Often, we'll try to avoid having a global variable. Because a global variable is implicitly present everywhere, it can be overlooked. Instead of a global variable, we can often handle the configuration slightly more neatly through object construction.

Configuring via object construction

When configuring an application via object construction, the objective is to build the required objects. In effect, the configuration file defines the various initialization parameters for the objects that will be built.

We can often centralize much of this kind of initial object construction in a single, overall the `main()` function. This will create the objects that do the real work of the application. We'll revisit and expand on these design issues in *Chapter 16, Coping with the Command Line*.

Consider a simulation of Blackjack playing and betting strategies. When we run a simulation, we want to gather the performance of a particular combination of independent variables. These variables might include some casino policies including the number of decks, table limits, and dealer rules. The variables might include the player's game strategies for when to hit, stand, split, and double down. It would also include the player's betting strategies of flat betting, Martingale betting, or some more Byzantine betting system. Our baseline code starts out something like the following code:

```
import csv
def simulate_blackjack():
    dealer_rule= Hit17()
    split_rule= NoReSplitAces()
    table= Table( decks=6, limit=50, dealer=dealer_rule,
        split=split_rule, payout=(3,2) )
    player_rule= SomeStrategy()
    betting_rule= Flat()
    player= Player( play=player_rule, betting=betting_rule,
rounds=100, stake=50 )

    simulator= Simulate( table, player, 100 )
    with open("p2_c13_simulation.dat","w",newline="") as results:
        wtr= csv.writer( results )
        for gamestats in simulator:
            wtr.writerow( gamestats )
```

This is a kind of technology spike that has hardcoded all of the object classes and initial values. We'll need to add configuration parameters to determine the classes of objects and their initial values.

The `Simulate` class has an API that looks like the following code:

```
class Simulate:
    def __init__( self, table, player, samples ):
        """Define table, player and number of samples."""
        self.table= table
        self.player= player
        self.samples= samples
    def __iter__( self ):
        """Yield statistical samples."""
```

This allows us to build the `Simulate()` object with some appropriate initialization parameters. Once we've built an instance of `Simulate()`, we can iterate through that object to get a series of statistical summary objects.

The interesting part is using the configuration parameters instead of class names. For example, some parameter should be used to decide whether to create an instance of `Hit17` or `Stand17` for the `dealer_rule` value. Similarly, the `split_rule` value should be a choice among several classes that embody several different split rules used in casinos.

In other cases, parameters should be used to provide arguments to the class `__init__()` method. For example, the number of decks, the house betting limit, and the Blackjack payout values are configuration values used to create the `Table` instance.

Once the objects are built, they interact normally via the `Simulate.run()` method to produce statistical output. No further need of a global pool of parameters is required: the parameter values are bound into the objects via their instance variables.

The object construction design is not as simple as a global property map. It has the advantage of avoiding a global variable, and it also has the advantage of making the parameter processing central and obvious in some main factory function.

Adding new parameters when using object construction may lead to refactoring the application to expose a parameter or a relationship. This can make it seem more complex than a global mapping from name to value.

One significant advantage of this technique is the removal of the complex `if` statements deep within the application. Using the `Strategy` design patterns tends to push decision making forward into object construction. In addition to simplifying the processing, the elimination of the `if` statements can be a performance boost.

Implementing a configuration hierarchy

We often have several choices on where a configuration file should be placed. There are five common choices, and we can use all five to create a kind of inheritance hierarchy for the parameters:

- **The application's installation directory**: In effect, these are analogous to base class definitions. There are two subchoices here. Smaller applications can be installed in Python's library structure; an initialization file too can be installed there. Larger applications will often have their own username that owns one or more installation directory trees.

- **Python installation directory**: We can find the installed location for a module using the `__file__` attribute of the module. From here, we can use `os.path.split()` to locate a configuration file:

```
>>> import this
>>> this.__file__
'/Library/Frameworks/Python.framework/Versions/3.3/lib/
  python3.3/this.py'
```

- **Application installation directory**: This will be based on an owning username, so we can use `~theapp/` and `os.path.expanduser()` to track down the configuration defaults.

- **A system-wide configuration directory**: This is often present in `/etc`. This can be transformed into `C:\etc` on Windows. Alternatives include the value of `os.environ['WINDIR']` or `os.environ['ALLUSERSPROFILE']`.
- **The current user's home directory**: We can generally use `os.path.expanduser()` to translate `~/` into the user's home directory. For Windows, Python will properly use the `%HOMEDRIVE%` and `%HOMEPATH%` environment variables.
- **The current working directory**: The directory is usually known as `./`, although `os.path.curdir` is more portable.
- **A file named in the command-line parameters**: This is an explicitly named file and no further processing should be done to the name.

An application can integrate configuration options from all of these sources from the base class (listed first) to the command-line options. In this way, the installation default values are the most generic and least user-specific; these values can be overridden by more specific and less-generic values.

This means that we'll often have a list of files like the following code:

```
import os
config_name= "someapp.config"
config_locations = (
  os.path.expanduser("~thisapp/"), # or thisapp.__file__,
  "/etc",
  os.path.expanduser("~/"),
  os.path.curdir,
)
candidates = ( os.path.join(dir,config_name)
    for dir in config_locations )
config_names = [ name for name in candidates if os.path.exists(name) ]
```

We've taken a tuple of alternative file directories and created a list of candidate filenames by joining the directory with the configuration filename.

Once we have this list of configuration filenames, we can append any filename supplied via the command-line arguments to the end of the list with the following code:

```
config_names.append(command_line_option)
```

This gives us a list of locations that we can examine to locate a configuration file or configuration defaults.

Storing the configuration in the INI files

The INI file format has historical origins from early Windows OS. The module to parse these files is `configparser`.

For additional details on the INI file, see this Wikipedia article: `http://en.wikipedia.org/wiki/INI_file`.

An INI file has sections and properties within each section. Our sample main program has three sections: the table configuration, player configuration, and overall simulation data gathering.

We can imagine an INI file that looks like the following code:

```
; Default casino rules
[table]
    dealer= Hit17
    split= NoResplitAces
    decks= 6
    limit= 50
    payout= (3,2)

; Player with SomeStrategy
; Need to compare with OtherStrategy
[player]
    play= SomeStrategy
    betting= Flat
    rounds= 100
    stake= 50

[simulator]
    samples= 100
    outputfile= p2_c13_simulation.dat
```

We've broken the parameters into three sections. Within each section, we've provided some named parameters that correspond to the class names and initialization values shown in our preceding model application initialization.

A single file can be parsed very simply:

```
import configparser
config = configparser.ConfigParser()
config.read('blackjack.ini')
```

We've created an instance of the parser and provided the target configuration filename to that parser. The parser will read the file, locate the sections, and locate the individual properties within each section.

If we want to support multiple locations for files, we can use `config.read(config_names)`. When we provide the list of filenames to `ConfigParser.read()`, it will read the files in an order. We want to provide the files from the most generic first to the most specific last. The generic configuration files that are part of the software installation will be parsed first to provide defaults. The user-specific configuration will be parsed later to override these defaults.

Once we've parsed the file, we need to make use of the various parameters and settings. Here's a function that constructs our objects based on a given configuration object created by parsing the configuration files. We'll break this into three parts. Here's the part that builds the `Table` instance:

```
def main_ini( config ):
    dealer_nm= config.get('table','dealer', fallback='Hit17')
    dealer_rule= {'Hit17': Hit17(),
        'Stand17': Stand17()}.get(dealer_nm, Hit17())
    split_nm= config.get('table','split', fallback='ReSplit')
    split_rule= {'ReSplit': ReSplit(),
        'NoReSplit': NoReSplit(),
        'NoReSplitAces': NoReSplitAces()}.get(split_nm, ReSplit())
    decks= config.getint('table','decks', fallback=6)
    limit= config.getint('table','limit', fallback=100)
    payout= eval( config.get('table','payout', fallback='(3,2)') )
    table= Table( decks=decks, limit=limit, dealer=dealer_rule,
        split=split_rule, payout=payout )
```

We've used properties from the `[table]` section of the INI file to select class names and provide initialization values. There are three broad kinds of cases here:

- **Mapping string to a class name**: We've used a mapping to look up an object based on a string class name. This was done to create `dealer_rule` and `split_rule`. If this was subject to considerable change, we might be able to extract this mapping into a separate factory function.
- **Getting a value that ConfigParser can parse for us**: The class can directly handle `str`, `int`, `float`, and `bool`. The class has a sophisticated mapping from string to Boolean, using a wide variety of common code and synonyms for `True` and `False`.
- **Evaluating something that's not built-in**: In the case of `payout`, we had a string value, `'(3,2)'`, that is not a directly supported data type for `ConfigParser`. We have two choices to handle this. We can try and parse it ourselves, or we can insist that the value be a valid Python expression and make Python do this. In this case, we've used `eval()`. Some programmers call this a *security problem*. The next section deals with this.

Here's the second section of this example, which uses properties from the `[player]` section of the INI file to select classes and argument values:

```
    player_nm= config.get('player','play', fallback='SomeStrategy')
    player_rule= {'SomeStrategy': SomeStrategy(),
        'AnotherStrategy': AnotherStrategy()}.get(player_
nm,SomeStrategy())
    bet_nm= config.get('player','betting', fallback='Flat')
    betting_rule= {'Flat': Flat(),
        'Martingale': Martingale(),
        'OneThreeTwoSix': OneThreeTwoSix()}.get(bet_nm,Flat())
    rounds= config.getint('player','rounds', fallback=100)
    stake= config.getint('player','stake', fallback=50)
    player= Player( play=player_rule, betting=betting_rule,
        rounds=rounds, stake=stake )
```

This uses string-to-class mapping as well as built-in data types. It initializes two strategy objects and then creates `Player` from those two strategies plus two integer configuration values.

Here's the final section; this creates the overall simulator:

```
    outputfile= config.get('simulator', 'outputfile',
fallback='blackjack.csv')
    samples= config.getint('simulator', 'samples', fallback=100)
    simulator= Simulate( table, player, samples )
    with open(outputfile,"w",newline="") as results:
        wtr= csv.writer( results )
        for gamestats in simulator:
            wtr.writerow( gamestats )
```

We've used two parameters from the `[simulator]` section that are outside the narrow confines of object creation. The `outputfile` property is used to name a file; the `samples` property is provided as an argument to a method function.

Handling more literals via the eval() variants

A configuration file may have values of types that don't have simple string representations. For example, a collection might be provided as a `tuple` or `list` literal; a mapping might be provided as a `dict` literal. We have several choices to handle these more complex values.

The choices resolve around an issue of how much Python syntax the conversion is able to tolerate. For some types (`int`, `float`, `bool`, `complex`, `decimal.Decimal`, `fractions.Fraction`), we can safely convert the string to a literal value because the object `__init__()` for these types handle string values without tolerating any additional Python syntax.

For other types, however, we can't simply do the string conversion. We have several choices on how to proceed:

- Forbid these data types and rely on the configuration file syntax plus processing rules to assemble complex Python values from very simple parts. This is tedious but can be made to work.
- Use `ast.literal_eval()` as it handles many cases of Python literal values. This is often the ideal solution.
- Use `eval()` to simply evaluate the string and create the expected Python object. This will parse more kinds of objects than `ast.literal_eval()`. Is this level of generality really needed?

Use the `ast` module to compile and vet the resulting code object. This vetting process can check for the `import` statements as well as use some small set of permitted modules. This is quite complex; if we're effectively allowing code, perhaps we should be designing a framework instead of an application with a configuration file.

In the case where we are performing RESTful transfers of Python objects through the network, `eval()` of the resulting text absolutely cannot be trusted. See *Chapter 9 - Serializing and Saving - JSON, YAML, Pickle, CSV and XML.*

In the case of reading a local configuration file, however, `eval()` may be usable. In some cases, the Python code is as easily modified as the configuration file. Worrying about `eval()` may not be helpful when the base code can be tweaked.

Here's how we use `ast.literal_eval()` instead of `eval()`:

```
>>> import ast
>>> ast.literal_eval('(3,2)')
(3, 2)
```

This broadens the domain of possible values in a configuration file. It doesn't allow arbitrary objects, but it allows a broad spectrum of literal values.

Storing the configuration in PY files

The PY file format means using Python code as the configuration file as well as the language to implement the application. We will have a configuration file that's simply a module; the configuration is written in the Python syntax. This removes the need to parse the module.

Using Python gives us a number of design considerations. We have two overall strategies to use Python as the configuration file:

- **A top-level script**: In this case, the configuration file is simply the top-most main program
- **An exec() import**: In this case, our configuration file provides parameter values that are collected into module global variables

We can design a top-level script file that looks like the following code:

```
from simulator import *
def simulate_SomeStrategy_Flat():
    dealer_rule= Hit17()
    split_rule= NoReSplitAces()
    table= Table( decks=6, limit=50, dealer=dealer_rule,
        split=split_rule, payout=(3,2) )
    player_rule= SomeStrategy()
    betting_rule= Flat()
    player= Player( play=player_rule, betting=betting_rule,
rounds=100, stake=50 )
    simulate( table, player, "p2_c13_simulation3.dat", 100 )

if __name__ == "__main__":
    simulate_SomeStrategy_Flat()
```

This shows us our various configuration parameters that are used to create and initialize objects. We've simply written the configuration parameters directly into the code. We've factored out the processing into a separate function, `simulate()`.

One potential disadvantage of using Python as the configuration language is the potential complexity of the Python syntax. This is usually an irrelevant problem for two reasons. First, with some careful design, the syntax of the configuration should be simple assignment statements with a few `()` and `,`. Second, and more important, other configuration files have their own complex syntax, distinct from the Python syntax. Using a single language with a single syntax is a reduction in the complexity.

The `simulate()` function is imported from the overall `simulator` application. This `simulate()` function might look like the following code:

```
import csv
def simulate( table, player, outputfile, samples ):
    simulator= Simulate( table, player, samples )
    with open(outputfile,"w",newline="") as results:
        wtr= csv.writer( results )
        for gamestats in simulator:
            wtr.writerow( gamestats )
```

This function is generic with respect to the table, player, filename, and number of samples.

The difficulty with this kind of configuration technique is the lack of handy default values. The top-level script must be complete: *all* of the configuration parameters must be present. It can be tiresome to provide all of the values; why provide default values that are rarely changed?

In some cases, this is not a limitation. In the cases where default values are important, we'll look at two ways around this limitation.

Configuration via class definitions

The difficulty that we sometimes have with top-level script configuration is the lack of handy default values. To provide defaults, we can use ordinary class inheritance. Here's how we can use the class definition to build an object with the configuration values:

```
import simulation
class Example4( simulation.Default_App ):
    dealer_rule= Hit17()
    split_rule= NoReSplitAces()
    table= Table( decks=6, limit=50, dealer=dealer_rule,
        split=split_rule, payout=(3,2) )
    player_rule= SomeStrategy()
    betting_rule= Flat()
```

```
    player= Player( play=player_rule, betting=betting_rule,
rounds=100, stake=50 )
    outputfile= "p2_c13_simulation4.dat"
    samples= 100
```

This allows us to define `Default_App` with a default configuration. The class that we've defined here can be reduced to providing only override values from the `Default_App` version.

We can also use mixins to break the definition down into reusable pieces. We might break our classes down into the table, player, and simulation components and combine them via mixins. For more information on the mixin class design, see *Chapter 8, Decorators and Mixins – Cross-cutting Aspects.*

In two small ways, this use of a class definition pushes the envelope. There are no method definitions; we're only going to use this class to define one instance. However, it is a very tidy way to pack up a small block of code so that the assignment statements fill in a small namespace.

We can modify our `simulate()` function to accept this class definition as an argument:

```
def simulate_c( config ):
    simulator= Simulate( config.table, config.player, config.samples )
    with open(config.outputfile,"w",newline="") as results:
        wtr= csv.writer( results )
        for gamestats in simulator:
            wtr.writerow( gamestats )
```

This function has picked out the relevant values from the overall configuration object and used them to build a `Simulate` instance and execute that instance. The results are the same as the previous `simulate()` function, but the argument structure is different. Here's how we provide the single instance of the class to this function:

```
if __name__ == "__main__":
    simulation.simulate_c(Example4())
```

One small disadvantage of this approach is that it is not compatible with `argparse` to gather command-line arguments. We can solve this by using a `types.SimpleNamespace` object.

Configuration via SimpleNamespace

Using a `types.SimpleNamespace` object allows us to simply add attributes as needed. This will be similar to using a class definition. When defining a class, all of the assignment statements are localized to the class. When creating a `SimpleNamespace` object, we'll need to explicitly qualify every name with the `NameSpace` object that we're populating. Ideally, we can create `SimpleNamespace` like the following code:

```
>>> import types
>>> config= types.SimpleNamespace(
...     param1= "some value",
...     param2= 3.14,
... )
>>> config
namespace(param1='some value', param2=3.14)
```

This works delightfully well if all of the configuration values are independent of each other. In our case, however, we have some complex dependencies among configuration values. We can handle this in one of the following two ways:

- We can provide only the independent values and leave it to the application to build the dependent values
- We can build the values in the namespace incrementally

To create only the independent values, we might do something like this:

```
import types
config5a= types.SimpleNamespace(
  dealer_rule= Hit17(),
  split_rule= NoReSplitAces(),
  player_rule= SomeStrategy(),
  betting_rule= Flat(),
  outputfile= "p2_c13_simulation5a.dat",
  samples= 100,
  )

config5a.table= Table( decks=6, limit=50, dealer=config5a.dealer_rule,
        split=config5a.split_rule, payout=(3,2) )
config5a.player= Player( play=config5a.player_rule, betting=config5a.
betting_rule,
        rounds=100, stake=50 )
```

Here, we created SimpleNamespace with the six independent values for the configuration. Then, we updated the configuration to add two more values that are dependent on four of the independent values.

The config5a object is nearly identical to the object that was created by evaluating Example4() in the preceding example . The base class is different, but the set of attributes and their values are identical. Here's the alternative, where we build the configuration incrementally in a top-level script:

```
import types
config5= types.SimpleNamespace()
config5.dealer_rule= Hit17()
config5.split_rule= NoReSplitAces()
config5.table= Table( decks=6, limit=50, dealer=config5.dealer_rule,
        split=config5.split_rule, payout=(3,2) )
config5.player_rule= SomeStrategy()
config5.betting_rule= Flat()
config5.player= Player( play=config5.player_rule, betting=config5.
betting_rule,
        rounds=100, stake=50 )
config5.outputfile= "p2_c13_simulation5.dat"
config5.samples= 100
```

The same simulate_c() function shown previously can be used for this kind of configuration.

Sadly, this suffers from the same problem as configuration via a top-level script. There's no handy way to provide default values to a configuration object. We might want to have a factory function that we can import, which creates SimpleNamespace with the appropriate default values:

```
From simulation import  make_config
config5= make_config()
```

If we used something like the preceding code, then we could have the default values assigned by the factory function, make_config(). Each user-supplied configuration could then provide only the necessary overrides to the default values.

Our default-supplying make_config() function would have the following kind of code:

```
def make_config( ):
    config= types.SimpleNamespace()
    # set the default values
    config.some_option = default_value
    return config
```

The `make_config()` function would build a default configuration through a sequence of assignment statements. An application can then set only the interesting *override* values:

```
config= make_config()
config.some_option = another_value
simulate_c( config )
```

This allows the application to build the configuration and then use it in a relatively simple way. The main script is quite short and to the point. If we use keyword arguments, we can easily make this more flexible:

```
 def make_config( **kw ):
    config= types.SimpleNamespace()
    # set the default values
    config.some_option = kw.get("some_option", default_value)
    return config
```

This allows us to create a configuration including the overrides like this:

```
config= make_config( some_option= another_value )
simulate_c( config )
```

This is slightly shorter and seems to retain the clarity of the previous example.

All of the techniques from *Chapter 1, The __init__() Method*, apply to the definition of this kind of configuration factory function. We can build in a great deal of flexibility if we need to. This has the advantage of fitting nicely with the way that the `argparse` module parses command-line arguments. We'll expand on this in *Chapter 16, Coping with the Command Line*

Using Python with exec() for the configuration

When we decide to use Python as the notation for a configuration, we can use the `exec()` function to evaluate a block of code in a constrained namespace. We can imagine writing configuration files that look like the following code:

```
# SomeStrategy setup

# Table
dealer_rule= Hit17()
split_rule= NoReSplitAces()
table= Table( decks=6, limit=50, dealer=dealer_rule,
        split=split_rule, payout=(3,2) )

# Player
```

```
player_rule= SomeStrategy()
betting_rule= Flat()
player= Player( play=player_rule, betting=betting_rule,
        rounds=100, stake=50 )

# Simulation
outputfile= "p2_c13_simulation6.dat"
samples= 100
```

This is a pleasant, easy-to-read set of configuration parameters. It's similar to an INI file and a property file that we'll look at in the following section. We can evaluate this file, creating a kind of namespace, with the `exec()` function:

```
with open("config.py") as py_file:
    code= compile(py_file.read(), 'config.py', 'exec')
config= {}
exec( code, globals(), config  )
simulate( config['table'], config['player'],
    config['outputfile'], config['samples'])
```

In this example, we decided to explicitly build a code object with the `compile()` function. This isn't required; we can simply provide the text of the file to the `exec()` function and it will compile the code.

The call to `exec()` provides three arguments: the code, a dictionary that should be used to resolve any global names, and a dictionary that will be used for any locals that get created. When the code block is finished, the assignment statements will have been used to build values in the local dictionary; in this case, the `config` variable. The keys will be the variable names.

We can then use this to build objects during the program's initialization. We pass the necessary objects to the `simulate()` function to perform the simulation. The `config` variable will get all the local assignments and will have a value like the following code:

```
{'betting_rule': <__main__.Flat object at 0x101828510>,
 'dealer_rule': <__main__.Hit17 object at 0x101828410>,
 'outputfile': 'p2_c13_simulation6.dat',
 'player': <__main__.Player object at 0x101828550>,
 'player_rule': <__main__.SomeStrategy object at 0x1018284d0>,
 'samples': 100,
 'split_rule': <__main__.NoReSplitAces object at 0x101828450>,
 'table': <__main__.Table object at 0x101828490>}
```

However, the initialization must be a written dictionary notation: `config['table']`, `config['player']`.

As the dictionary notation is inconvenient, we'll use a design pattern based on ideas from *Chapter 3, Attribute Access, Properties, and Descriptors*. This is a class that provides named attributes based on the keys of a dictionary:

```
class AttrDict( dict ):
    def __getattr__( self, name ):
        return self.get(name,None)
    def __setattr__( self, name, value ):
        self[name]= value
    def __dir__( self ):
        return list(self.keys())
```

This class can only work if the keys are proper Python variable names. Interestingly, this is all that can be created by the `exec()` function if we initialize the `config` variable this way:

```
config= AttrDict()
```

Then, we can use a simpler attribute notation, `config.table`, `config.player`, for doing the initial object construction and initialization. This little bit of syntactic sugar can be helpful in a complex application. An alternative is to define this class:

```
class Configuration:
    def __init__( self, **kw ):
        self.__dict__.update(kw)
```

We can then do this to convert a simple `dict` to an object with pleasant, named attributes:

```
config= Configuration( **config )
```

This will convert `dict` to an object with easy-to-use attribute names. This only works, of course, if the dictionary keys are already Python variable names. It's also limited to structures that are flat. This won't work for nested dictionary-of-dictionary structures that we see with other formats.

Why is exec() a nonproblem?

The previous section has a discussion on `eval()`. The same considerations apply to `exec()`.

Generally, the set of available `globals()` is tightly controlled. Access to the `os` module or the `__import__()` function can be eliminated by removing them from the globals provided to `exec()`.

If you have an evil programmer who will cleverly corrupt the configuration files, recall that they have complete access to all Python source. Why would they waste time cleverly tweaking configuration files when they can just change the application code itself?

One common question is this: "What if someone thinks they can monkey patch a broken application by forcing new code in via the configuration file?" This person is just as likely to break the application into a number of other equally clever/deranged ways. Avoiding Python configuration files won't stop the unscrupulous programmer from breaking things by doing something that's ill-advised. There are a myriad of potential weaknesses; needless worrying about `exec()` may not be beneficial.

In some cases, it may be necessary to change the overall philosophy. An application that's highly customizable might actually be a general framework, not a tidy, finished application.

Using ChainMap for defaults and overrides

We'll often have a configuration file hierarchy. Previously, we listed several locations where configuration files can be installed. The `configparser` module, for example, is designed to read a number of files in an order and integrate the settings by having later files override values from earlier files.

We can implement an elegant default-value processing using the `collections.ChainMap` class. See *Chapter 6, Creating Containers and Collections*, for some background on this class. We'll need to keep the configuration parameters as `dict` instances, which is something that works out well using `exec()` to evaluate Python-language initialization files.

Using this will require us to design our configuration parameters as a flat dictionary of values. This may be a bit of a burden for applications with a large number of complex configuration values that are integrated from several sources. We'll show you a sensible way to flatten names.

First, we'll build a list of files based on the standard locations:

```
from collections import ChainMap
import os
config_name= "config.py"
config_locations = (
  os.path.expanduser("~thisapp/"), # or thisapp.__file__,
  "/etc",
```

```
        os.path.expanduser("~/"),
        os.path.curdir,
    )
    candidates = ( os.path.join(dir,config_name)
        for dir in config_locations )
    config_names = ( name for name in candidates if os.path.exists(name) )
```

We started with a list of directories: the installation directory, a system global directory, a user's home directory, and the current working directory. We put the configuration filename into each directory and then confirmed that the file actually exists.

Once we have the names of the candidate files, we can build `ChainMap` by folding each file in:

```
config = ChainMap()
for name in config_names:
    config= config.new_child()
    exec(name, globals(), config)
simulate( config.table, config.player, config.outputfile, config.
samples)
```

Each file involves creating a new, empty map that can be updated with local variables. The `exec()` function will add the file's local variables to the empty map created by `new_child()`. Each new child is more localized, overriding previously loaded configurations.

In `ChainMap`, every name is resolved by searching through the sequence of maps looking for a value. When we've loaded two configuration files into `ChainMap`, we have a structure like the following code:

```
ChainMap(
    {'player': <__main__.Player object at 0x10101a710>, 'outputfile':
'p2_c13_simulation7a.dat', 'player_rule': <__main__.AnotherStrategy
object at 0x10101aa90>},
    {'dealer_rule': <__main__.Hit17 object at 0x10102a9d0>, 'betting_
rule': <__main__.Flat object at 0x10101a090>, 'split_rule': <__main__.
NoReSplitAces object at 0x10102a910>, 'samples': 100, 'player_rule':
<__main__.SomeStrategy object at 0x10102a8d0>, 'table': <__main__.
Table object at 0x10102a890>, 'outputfile': 'p2_c13_simulation7.dat',
'player': <__main__.Player object at 0x10101a210>},
    {})
```

We have a sequence of maps; the first map is the most local variables, defined last. These are overrides. The second map has application defaults. There's a third, empty map because `ChainMap` always has at least one map; when we build the initial value for `config`, an empty map has to be created.

The only downside of this is that the initialization will be using dictionary notation, `config['table']`, `config['player']`. We can extend `ChainMap()` to implement the attribute access in addition to the dictionary item access.

Here's a subclass of `ChainMap` that we can use if we find the `getitem()` dictionary notation too cumbersome:

```
class AttrChainMap( ChainMap ):
    def __getattr__( self, name ):
        if name == "maps":
            return self.__dict__['maps']
        return super().get(name,None)
    def __setattr__( self, name, value ):
        if name == "maps":
            self.__dict__['maps']= value
            return
        self[name]= value
```

We can now say `config.table` instead of `config['table']`. This reveals an important restriction on our extension to `ChainMap`: we can't use `maps` as an attribute. The `maps` key is a first-class attribute of the parent `ChainMap` class.

Storing the configuration in JSON or YAML files

We can store configuration values in JSON or YAML files with relative ease. The syntax is designed to be user friendly. We can represent a wide variety of things in YAML. We're somewhat restricted to a narrower variety of object classes in JSON. We can use a JSON configuration file that looks like the following code:

```
{
    "table":{
        "dealer":"Hit17",
        "split":"NoResplitAces",
        "decks":6,
        "limit":50,
        "payout":[3,2]
    },
    "player":{
        "play":"SomeStrategy",
        "betting":"Flat",
        "rounds":100,
        "stake":50
```

```
        },
        "simulator":{
            "samples":100,
            "outputfile":"p2_c13_simulation.dat"
        }
    }
```

The JSON document looks like a dictionary of dictionaries. This is precisely the object that will be built when we load this file. We can load a single configuration file with the following code:

```
import json
config= json.load( "config.json" )
```

This allows us to use `config['table']['dealer']` to look up the specific class to be used for the dealer's rules. We can use `config['player']['betting']` to locate the player's particular betting strategy class name.

Unlike INI files, we can easily encode `tuple` like a sequence of values. So, the `config['table']['payout']` value will be a proper two-element sequence. It won't—strictly speaking—be `tuple`, but it will be close enough for us to use it without having to use `ast.literal_eval()`.

Here's how we'd use this nested structure. We'll only show you the first part of the `main_nested_dict()` function:

```
def main_nested_dict( config ):
    dealer_nm= config.get('table',{}).get('dealer', 'Hit17')
    dealer_rule= {'Hit17':Hit17(),
        'Stand17':Stand17()}.get(dealer_nm, Hit17())
    split_nm= config.get('table',{}).get('split', 'ReSplit')
    split_rule= {'ReSplit':ReSplit(),
        'NoReSplit':NoReSplit(),
        'NoReSplitAces':NoReSplitAces()}.get(split_nm, ReSplit())
    decks= config.get('table',{}).get('decks', 6)
    limit= config.get('table',{}).get('limit', 100)
    payout= config.get('table',{}).get('payout', (3,2))
    table= Table( decks=decks, limit=limit, dealer=dealer_rule,
        split=split_rule, payout=payout )
```

This is very similar to the `main_ini()` function shown previously. When we compare this with the preceding version, using `configparser`, it's clear that the complexity is almost the same. The naming is slightly simpler. We use `config.get('table',{}).get('decks')` instead of `config.getint('table','decks')`.

The largest difference is shown in the highlighted line. The JSON format provides us properly decoded integer values and proper sequences of values. We don't need to use `eval()` or `ast.literal_eval()` to decode the tuple. The other parts, to build `Player` and configure the `Simulate` object, are similar to the `main_ini()` version.

Using flattened JSON configurations

If we want to provide for default values by integrating multiple configuration files, we can't use both `ChainMap` and a nested dictionary-of-dictionaries like this. We have to either flatten out our program's parameters or look at an alternative to merging the parameters from different sources.

We can easily flatten the names by using simple `.` separators between names. Our JSON file might then look like the following code:

```
{
"player.betting": "Flat",
"player.play": "SomeStrategy",
"player.rounds": 100,
"player.stake": 50,
"table.dealer": "Hit17",
"table.decks": 6,
"table.limit": 50,
"table.payout": [3, 2],
"table.split": "NoResplitAces",
"simulator.outputfile": "p2_c13_simulation.dat",
"simulator.samples": 100
}
```

This has the advantage of allowing us to use `ChainMap` to accumulate the configuration values from various sources. It also slightly simplifies the syntax to locate a particular parameter value. Given a list of configuration filenames, `config_names`, we might do something like this:

```
config = ChainMap( *[json.load(file) for file in reversed(config_
names)] )
```

This builds a proper `ChainMap` from a *reversed* list of configuration file names. Why reversed? We must reverse the list because we want the list to be ordered from the most specific first to the most general last. This is the reverse of how the list is used by `configparser` and the reverse of how we incrementally built `ChainMap` by adding children to the front of the list of mappings. Here, we're simply loading a list of `dict` into `ChainMap`, and the first `dict` will be the first one searched for by the key.

We can use a method like this to exploit `ChainMap`. We'll only show you the first part, which builds the `Table` instance:

```
def main_cm( config ):
    dealer_nm= config.get('table.dealer', 'Hit17')
    dealer_rule= {'Hit17':Hit17(),
        'Stand17':Stand17()}.get(dealer_nm, Hit17())
    split_nm= config.get('table.split', 'ReSplit')
    split_rule= {'ReSplit':ReSplit(),
        'NoReSplit':NoReSplit(),
        'NoReSplitAces':NoReSplitAces()}.get(split_nm, ReSplit())
    decks= int(config.get('table.decks', 6))
    limit= int(config.get('table.limit', 100))
    payout= config.get('table.payout', (3,2))
    table= Table( decks=decks, limit=limit, dealer=dealer_rule,
        split=split_rule, payout=payout )
```

The other parts, to build `Player` and configure the `Simulate` object, are similar to the `main_ini()` version.

When we compare this to the previous version, using `configparser`, it's clear that the complexity is almost the same. The naming is slightly simpler. Here, we use `int(config.get('table.decks'))` instead of `config.getint('table','decks')`.

Loading a YAML configuration

As YAML syntax contains JSON syntax, the previous examples can be loaded with YAML as well as JSON. Here's a version of the nested dictionary-of-dictionaries technique from the JSON file:

```
player:
  betting: Flat
  play: SomeStrategy
  rounds: 100
  stake: 50
table:
  dealer: Hit17
  decks: 6
  limit: 50
  payout: [3, 2]
  split: NoResplitAces
simulator: {outputfile: p2_c13_simulation.dat, samples: 100}
```

This is a better file syntax than pure JSON; it's easier to edit. For applications where the configuration is dominated by strings and integers, this has a number of advantages. The process to load this file is the same as the process to load the JSON file:

```
import yaml
config= yaml.load( "config.yaml" )
```

This has the same limitations as the nested dictionaries. We don't have an easy way to handle default values unless we flatten the names.

When we move beyond simple strings and integers, however, we can try to leverage YAML's ability to encode class names and create instances of our customized classes. Here's a YAML file that will directly build the configuration objects that we need for our simulation:

```
# Complete Simulation Settings
table: !!python/object:__main__.Table
  dealer: !!python/object:__main__.Hit17 {}
  decks: 6
  limit: 50
  payout: !!python/tuple [3, 2]
  split: !!python/object:__main__.NoReSplitAces {}
player: !!python/object:__main__.Player
  betting:  !!python/object:__main__.Flat {}
  init_stake: 50
  max_rounds: 100
  play: !!python/object:__main__.SomeStrategy {}
  rounds: 0
  stake: 63.0
samples: 100
outputfile: p2_c13_simulation9.dat
```

We have encoded class names and instance construction in YAML, allowing us to define the complete initialization for `Table` and `Player`. We can use this initialization file as follows:

```
import yaml
if __name__ == "__main__":
    config= yaml.load( yaml1_file )
    simulate( config['table'], config['player'],
        config['outputfile'], config['samples'] )
```

This shows us that a YAML configuration file can be used for human editing. YAML provides us with the same capabilities as Python, but with a different syntax. For this type of example, a Python configuration script might be better than YAML.

Storing the configuration in property files

The property files are often used with Java programs. There's no reason we can't use them with Python. They're relatively easy to parse and allow us to encode the configuration parameters in a handy, easy-to-use format. For more information on the format, see this: `http://en.wikipedia.org/wiki/.properties`. Here's what a properties file might look like:

```
# Example Simulation Setup

player.betting: Flat
player.play: SomeStrategy
player.rounds: 100
player.stake: 50

table.dealer: Hit17
table.decks: 6
table.limit: 50
table.payout: (3,2)
table.split: NoResplitAces

simulator.outputfile = p2_c13_simulation8.dat
simulator.samples = 100
```

This has some advantages in terms of simplicity. The `section.property` qualified names are commonly used. These can become long in a very complex configuration file.

Parsing a properties file

There's no built-in properties parser in the Python Standard Library. We can download a property file parser from the Python Package Index (`https://pypi.python.org/pypi`). However, it's not a complex class, and it's a good exercise in advanced object-oriented programming.

We'll break the class down into the top-level API functions and the lower-level parsing functions. Here are some of the overall API methods:

```
import re
class PropertyParser:
```

```
    def read_string( self, data ):
        return self._parse(data)
    def read_file( self, file ):
        data= file.read()
        return self.read_string( data )
    def read( self, filename ):
        with open(filename) as file:
            return self.read_file( file )
```

The essential feature here is that it will parse a filename, a file, or a block of text. This follows the design pattern from `configparser`. A common alternative is to have fewer methods and use `isinstance()` to determine the type of the argument, and also determine what processing to perform on it.

File names are strings. Files themselves are generally instances of `io.TextIOBase`. A block of text is also a string. For this reason, many libraries use `load()` to work with files or filenames and `loads()` to work with a simple string. Something like this would echo the design pattern of `json`:

```
    def load( self, file_or_name ):
        if isinstance(file_or_name, io.TextIOBase):
            self.loads(file_or_name.read())
        else:
            with open(filename) as file:
                self.loads(file.read())
    def loads( self, string ):
        return self._parse(data)
```

These methods will also handle a file, filename, or block of text. These extra method names give us an alternative API that might be easier to work. The deciding factor is achieving a coherent design among the various libraries, packages, and modules. Here's the `_parse()` method:

```
    key_element_pat= re.compile(r"(.*?)\s*(?<!\\)[:=\s]\s*(.*)")
    def _parse( self, data ):
        logical_lines = (line.strip()
            for line in re.sub(r"\\\n\s*", "", data).splitlines())
        non_empty= (line for line in logical_lines
            if len(line) != 0)
        non_comment= (line for line in non_empty
            if not( line.startswith("#") or line.startswith("!") ) )
        for line in non_comment:
            ke_match= self.key_element_pat.match(line)
            if ke_match:
```

```
        key, element = ke_match.group(1), ke_match.group(2)
    else:
        key, element = line, ""
    key= self._escape(key)
    element= self._escape(element)
    yield key, element
```

This method starts with three generator expressions to handle some overall features of the physical lines and logical lines within a properties file. The generator expressions separate three syntax rules. Generator expressions have the advantage of being executed lazily; no intermediate results are created from these expressions until they're evaluated by the `for line in non_comment` statement.

The first expression, assigned to `logical_lines`, merges physical lines that end with \ to create longer logical lines. The leading (and trailing) spaces are stripped away, leaving just the line content. **Regular Expression (RE)** `r"\\\n\s*"` is intended to match \ at the end of a line and all of the leading spaces from the next line.

The second expression, assigned to `non_empty`, will only iterate over lines with a nonzero length. Blank lines will be rejected by this filter.

Third, the `non_comment` expression will only iterate over lines that do not start with `#` or `!`. Lines that start with `#` or `!` will be rejected by this filter.

Because of these three generator expressions, the `for line in non_comment` loop only iterates through noncomment, nonblank, logical lines that are properly merged with spaces stripped. The body of the loop picks apart each remaining line to separate the key and element and then apply the `self._escape()` function to expand any escape sequences.

The key-element pattern, `key_element_pat`, looks for explicit separators of non-escaped `:`, `=` or a space surrounded by whitespace. This pattern uses the negative look behind an assertion, an RE of `(?<!\\)`, to indicate that the following RE must be non-escaped; the following pattern must not be preceded by \. This means that `(?<!\\)[:=\s]` is non-escaped `:`, or `=`, or space.

If the key-element pattern can't be found, there's no separator. We interpret this lack of a matching pattern to indicate that the line is a degenerate case of only a key; no value was provided.

As the keys and elements form a sequence of 2-tuples, the sequence can be easily turned into a dictionary, providing a configuration map much like other configuration representation schemes that we've seen. They can also be left as a sequence to show the original content of the file in an order. The final part is a small method function to transform the escapes to their final character:

```
    def _escape( self, data ):
        d1= re.sub( r"\\([:#!=\s])", lambda x:x.group(1), data )
        d2= re.sub( r"\\u([0-9A-Fa-f]+)", lambda x:chr(int(x.
group(1),16)), d1 )
        return d2
```

This _escape() method function performs two substitution passes. The first pass replaces the escaped punctuation marks with their plain-text versions: \:, \#, \!, \=, and \ all have \ removed. For the Unicode escapes, the string of digits is used to create a proper Unicode character that replaces the \uxxxx sequence. The hex digits are turned into an integer, which is turned into a character for the replacement.

The two substitutions can be combined into a single operation to save creating an intermediate string that will only get discarded. This will improve the performance. It might look like the following code:

```
        d2= re.sub( r"\\([:#!=\s])|\\u([0-9A-Fa-f]+)",
            lambda x:x.group(1) if x.group(1) else chr(int(x.
group(2),16)), data )
```

The benefit of better performance might be outweighed by the complexity of the RE and the replacement function.

Using a properties file

We have two choices for how we use a properties file. We could follow the design pattern of configparser and parse multiple files to create a single mapping from the union of the various values. Or, we could follow the ChainMap pattern and create a sequence of properties mappings for each configuration file.

The ChainMap processing is reasonably simple and provides us with all the required features:

```
config= ChainMap(
    *[dict( pp.read(file) )
        for file in reversed(candidate_list)] )
```

We've taken the list in a reverse order: the most specific settings will be first in the internal list; the most general settings will be the last. Once ChainMap has been loaded, we can use the properties to initialize and build our Player, Table, and Simulate instances.

This seems simpler than updating a single mapping from several sources. Also, this follows the pattern used to process JSON or YAML configuration files.

We can use a method like this to exploit `ChainMap`. This is very similar to the `main_cm()` function shown previously. We'll only show you the first part, which builds the `Table` instance:

```
import ast
def main_cm_str( config ):
    dealer_nm= config.get('table.dealer', 'Hit17')
    dealer_rule= {'Hit17':Hit17(),
        'Stand17':Stand17()}.get(dealer_nm, Hit17())
    split_nm= config.get('table.split', 'ReSplit')
    split_rule= {'ReSplit':ReSplit(),
        'NoReSplit':NoReSplit(),
        'NoReSplitAces':NoReSplitAces()}.get(split_nm, ReSplit())
    decks= int(config.get('table.decks', 6))
    limit= int(config.get('table.limit', 100))
    payout= ast.literal_eval(config.get('table.payout', '(3,2)'))
    table= Table( decks=decks, limit=limit, dealer=dealer_rule,
        split=split_rule, payout=payout )
```

The difference between this version and the `main_cm()` function is the handling of the payout tuple. In the previous version, JSON (and YAML) could parse the tuple. When using the properties files, all values are simple strings. We must use `eval()` or `ast.literal_eval()` to evaluate the given value. The other portions of this `main_cm_str()` function are identical to `main_cm()`.

Storing the configuration in XML files – PLIST and others

As we noted in *Chapter 9, Serializing and Saving – JSON, YAML, Pickle, CSV, and XML*, Python's `xml` package includes numerous modules that parse the XML files. Because of the wide adoption of the XML files, it often becomes necessary to convert between XML documents and Python objects. Unlike JSON or YAML, the mapping from XML is not simple.

One common way to represent the configuration data in XML is the `.plist` file. For more information on the `.plist` format, see this: `http://developer.apple.com/documentation/Darwin/Reference/ManPages/man5/plist.5.html`

Macintosh users can perform `man plist` to see this man page. The advantages of the `.plist` format are that it uses a few, very general tags. This makes it easy to create `.plist` files and parse them. Here's the sample `.plist` file from with our configuration parameters.

```
<?xml version="1.0" encoding="UTF-8"?>
<!DOCTYPE plist PUBLIC "-//Apple//DTD PLIST 1.0//EN" "http://www.
apple.com/DTDs/PropertyList-1.0.dtd">
<plist version="1.0">
<dict>
  <key>player</key>
  <dict>
    <key>betting</key>
    <string>Flat</string>
    <key>play</key>
    <string>SomeStrategy</string>
    <key>rounds</key>
    <integer>100</integer>
    <key>stake</key>
    <integer>50</integer>
  </dict>
  <key>simulator</key>
  <dict>
    <key>outputfile</key>
    <string>p2_c13_simulation8.dat</string>
    <key>samples</key>
    <integer>100</integer>
  </dict>
  <key>table</key>
  <dict>
    <key>dealer</key>
    <string>Hit17</string>
    <key>decks</key>
    <integer>6</integer>
    <key>limit</key>
    <integer>50</integer>
    <key>payout</key>
    <array>
      <integer>3</integer>
      <integer>2</integer>
    </array>
    <key>split</key>
    <string>NoResplitAces</string>
  </dict>
</dict>
</plist>
```

We're showing you the nested dictionary-of-dictionary structure in this example. There are a number of Python-compatible types encoded with XML tags.

Python type	Plist tag
`str`	`<string>`
`float`	`<real>`
`int`	`<integer>`
`datetime`	`<date>`
`boolean`	`<true/>` or `<false/>`
`bytes`	`<data>`
`list`	`<array>`
`dict`	`<dict>`

As shown in the preceding example, the dict `<key>` values are strings. This makes the plist a very pleasant encoding of our parameters for our simulation application. We can load a `.plist` with relative ease:

```
import plistlib
print( plistlib.readPlist(plist_file) )
```

This will reconstruct our configuration parameters. We can then use this nested dictionary-of-dictionaries structure with the `main_nested_dict()` function shown in the preceding section on JSON configuration files.

Using a single module function to parse the file makes the `.plist` format very appealing. The lack of support for any customized Python class definitions makes this equivalent to JSON or a properties file.

Customized XML configuration files

For a more complex XML configuration file, see `http://wiki.metawerx.net/wiki/Web.xml`. These files contain a mixture of special-purpose tags and general-purpose tags. These documents can be challenging to parse. There are two general approaches:

- Write a document processing class that uses XPath queries to locate the tags in a document that contain interesting data. In this case, we'll write properties (or methods) that will locate the requested information in the XML document structure.
- Unwind the XML document into a Python data structure. This is the approach followed by the `plist` module, shown previously.

Based on examples of the `web.xml` files, we'll design our own customized XML document to configure our simulation application:

```
<?xml version="1.0" encoding="UTF-8"?>
<simulation>
    <table>
        <dealer>Hit17</dealer>
        <split>NoResplitAces</split>
        <decks>6</decks>
        <limit>50</limit>
        <payout>(3,2)</payout>
    </table>
    <player>
        <betting>Flat</betting>
        <play>SomeStrategy</play>
        <rounds>100</rounds>
        <stake>50</stake>
    </player>
    <simulator>
        <outputfile>p2_c13_simulation11.dat</outputfile>
        <samples>100</samples>
    </simulator>
</simulation>
```

This is a specialized XML file. We didn't provide a DTD or an XSD, so there's no formal way to validate the XML against a schema. However, this file is small, easily debugged, and parallels other example initialization files. Here's a `Configuration` class that can use XPath queries to retrieve information from this file:

```
import xml.etree.ElementTree as XML
class Configuration:
    def read_file( self, file ):
        self.config= XML.parse( file )
    def read( self, filename ):
        self.config= XML.parse( filename )
    def read_string( self, text ):
        self.config= XML.fromstring( text )
    def get( self, qual_name, default ):
        section, _, item = qual_name.partition(".")
        query= "./{0}/{1}".format( section, item )
        node= self.config.find(query)
        if node is None: return default
        return node.text
    def __getitem__( self, section ):
```

```
        query= "./{0}".format(section)
        parent= self.config.find(query)
        return dict( (item.tag, item.text) for item in parent )
```

We've implemented three methods to load the XML document: `read()`, `read_file()`, and `read_string()`. Each of these simply delegates itself to an existing method function of the `xml.etree.ElementTree` class. This parallels the `configparser` API. We could use `load()` and `loads()` too, as they would delegate themselves to `parse()` and `fromstring()`, respectively.

For access to the configuration data, we implemented two methods: `get()` and `__getitem__()`. The `get()` method allows us to use code like this: `stake= int(config.get('player.stake', 50))`. The `__getitem__()` method allows us to use code like this: `stake= config['player']['stake']`.

The parsing is a trifle more complex than a `.plist` file. However, the XML document is much simpler than an equivalent `.plist` document.

We can use the `main_cm_str()` function shown in the previous section on the property files to process this configuration.

Summary

We looked at a number of ways to represent the configuration parameters. Most of these are based on more general serialization techniques that we saw in *Chapter 9, Serializing and Saving – JSON, YAML, Pickle, CSV, and XML*. The `configparser` module provides an additional format that's comfortable for some users.

The key feature of a configuration file is that the content can be easily edited by a human. For this reason, pickle files aren't suggested as a good representation.

Design considerations and trade-offs

Configuration files can simplify running application programs or starting servers. This can put all the relevant parameters in one easy-to-read and easy-to-modify file. We can put these files under the configuration control, track change history, and generally use them to improve the software's quality.

We have several alternative formats for these files, all of which are reasonably human friendly to edit. They vary in how easy they are to parse and any limitations on the Python data that can be encoded:

- **INI files**: These files are easy to parse and are limited to strings and numbers.
    - **Python code (PY files)**: These files use the main script for the configuration. No parsing, no limitations. They use an `exec()` file. It is easy to parse and has no limitations.
- **JSON or YAML files**: These files are easy to parse. They support strings, numbers, dicts, and lists. YAML can encode Python, but why not just use Python?
- **Property Files**: These files require a special parser. They are limited to strings.
- **XML files**:
    - `.plist` **files**: These files are easy to parse. They supports strings, numbers, dicts, and lists.
    - **Customized XML**: These files require a special parser. They are limited to strings.

Coexistence with other applications or servers will often determine a preferred format for the configuration files. If we have other applications that use the `.plist` or INI files, then our Python applications should make choices that are more comfortable for users to use.

Viewed from the breadth of objects that can be represented, we have four broad categories of configuration files:

- **Simple files with only strings**: Custom XML, properties files.
- **Simple files with simple Python literals**: INI files.
- **More complex files with Python literals, lists, and dicts**: JSON, YAML, `.plist`, and XML.
- **Anything. Python**: We can use YAML for this, but it seems silly when Python has a clearer syntax.

Creating a shared configuration

When we look at module design considerations in *Chapter 17*, The *Module and Package Design*, we'll see how a module conforms to the **Singleton** design pattern. This means that we can import a module only once, and the single instance is shared.

Because of this, it's often necessary to define a configuration in a distinct module and import it. This allows separate modules to share a common configuration. Each module will import the shared configuration module; the configuration module will locate the configuration file(s) and create the actual configuration objects.

Schema evolution

The configuration file is part of the public-facing API. As application designers, we have to address the problem of schema evolution. If we change a class definition, how will we change the configuration?

Because configuration files often have useful defaults, they are often very flexible. In principle, the content is entirely optional.

As a piece of software undergoes major version changes— changes that alter the APIs or the database schema—the configuration files too might undergo major changes. The configuration file's version number may have to be included in order to disambiguate legacy configuration parameters from current release parameters.

For minor version changes, the configuration files, such as database, input and output files, and APIs should remain compatible. Any configuration parameter handling should have appropriate defaults to cope with minor version changes.

A configuration file is a first-class input to an application. It's not an after-thought or a workaround. It must be as carefully designed as the other inputs and outputs. When we look at larger application architecture design in *Chapter 14, The Logging and Warning Modules* and *Chapter 16, Coping with the Command Line*, we'll expand on the basics of parsing a configuration file.

Looking Forward

In the next chapters, we'll look at larger-scale design considerations. *Chapter 14, The Logging and Warning Modules*, will look at using the `logging` and `warnings` modules to create audit information as well as to debug. We'll look at designing for testability and how we use `unittest` and `doctest` in *Chapter 15, Designing for Testability*. *Chapter 16, Coping with the Command Line*, will look at using the `argparse` module to parse options and arguments. We'll take this a step further and use the **Command** design pattern to create program components that can be combined and expanded without resorting to writing shell scripts. In *Chapter 17, The Module and Package Design*, we'll look at module and package design. In *Chapter 18, Quality and Documentation*, we'll look at how we can document our design to create the trust that our software is correct and is properly implemented.

Part 3

Testing, Debugging, Deploying, and Maintaining

Testing, Debugging, Deploying, and Maintaining

Application development involves a number of skills beyond object-oriented designing and programming in Python. We'll take a look at some additional topics that help us move from merely programming towards solving the user's problems:

- *Chapter 14, The Logging and Warning Modules*, will look at using the `logging` and `warnings` modules to create audit information as well as debugging. We'll take a significant step beyond using the `print()` function. The `logging` module provides us with a number of features that allow us to produce audit, debug, and informational messages in a simple and uniform way. Because this is so highly configurable, we can provide useful debugging as well as verbose processing options.
- We'll look at designing for testability and how we use `unittest` and `doctest` in *Chapter 15, Designing for Testability*. Automated testing should be considered absolutely essential. No programming should be considered complete until there are automated unit tests that provide ample evidence to show us that the code works.
- The command-line interface to our programs provides us with options and arguments. This applies mostly to small, text-oriented programs as well as long-running application servers. However, even a GUI application may use command-line options for configuration. *Chapter 16, Coping with the Command Line*, will look at using the `argparse` module to parse options and arguments. We'll take this a step further and use the **Command** design pattern to create program components that can be combined and expanded without resorting to writing shell scripts.

- In *Chapter 17, The Module and Package Design*, we'll look at the module and package design. This is a higher-level set of considerations than the class design topics we've been looking at so far. Module and class design repeat strategies of Wrap, Extend, or Invent. Rather than looking at related data and operations, we're looking at related classes in a module and related modules in a package.
- In *Chapter 18, Quality and Documentation*, we'll look at how we can document our design to create the trust that our software is correct and is properly implemented.

This part emphasizes ways to improve the quality of our software using these additional modules. Unlike the topics of *Part 1, Pythonic Classes via Special Methods* and *Part 2, Persistence and Serialization* these tools and techniques aren't narrowly focused on solving a particular problem. These topics are more broadly applicable to mastering object-oriented Python.

14
The Logging and Warning Modules

There are some essential logging techniques that we can use both for debugging as well as operational support of an application. In particular, a good log can help demonstrate that an application meets its security and auditability requirements.

There are times when we'll have multiple logs with different kinds of information. We might separate security, audit, and debugging into separate logs. In some cases, we might want a unified log. We'll look at a few examples of doing this.

Our users may want verbose output to confirm that the program works correctly. This is different from the debugging output; end users are examining how the program solves their problem. They might, for example, want to change their inputs or process your program's outputs differently. Setting the verbosity level produces a log focused on the needs of users.

The `warnings` module can provide helpful information for developers as well as users. In the case of developers, we may use warnings to show you that an API has been deprecated. In the case of users, we might want to show you that the results are questionable but not—strictly speaking—erroneous. There might be questionable assumptions or possibly confusing default values that should be pointed out to users.

Software maintainers will need to enable logging to perform useful debugging. We rarely want *blanket* debugging output: the resulting log might be unreadably dense. We often need focused debugging to track down a specific problem so that we can revise the unit test cases and fix the software.

In the case of trying to solve problems with a program that crashes, we might want to create a small circular queue to capture the last few events. We may be able to use this to isolate problems without having to filter through giant logfiles.

Creating a basic log

There are two necessary steps to logging:

- Get a `logging.Logger` instance with the `logging.getLogger()` function.
- Create messages with that `Logger`. There are a number of methods with names such as `warn()`, `info()`, `debug()`, `error()`, and `fatal()` that create messages with different levels of importance.

These two steps are not sufficient to give us any output, however. There's a third step that we take only when we need to see the output. Some logging is for debugging purposes, and seeing a log isn't always required. The optional step is to configure the `logging` module's handlers, filters, and formatters. We can use the `logging.basicConfig()` function for this.

It's technically possibly to even skip the first step. We can use the default logger that's part of the `logging` module's top-level functions. We showed you this in *Chapter 8, Decorators and Mixins – Cross-cutting Aspects*, because the focus was on decoration, not logging. We advise you against using the default root logger. We'll need a little background to see why it's good to avoid using the root logger.

Instances of `Logger` are identified by name. The names are `.`-separated strings that form a hierarchy. There's a root logger with a name of `""` – the empty string. All other `Loggers` are children of this root `Logger`.

Because of this tree of named `Loggers`, we'll generally use the root `Logger` to configure the entire tree. We'll also use it when an appropriately named `Logger` can't be found. We'll only sow confusion if we also use the root `Logger` as the first class log for a particular module.

In addition to a name, `Logger` can be configured with a list of handlers that determines where the messages are written and a list of `Filters` to determine which kinds of messages are passed or rejected. A logger is the essential API for logging: we use a logger to create `LogRecords`. These records are then routed to `Filters` and `Handlers`, where the passed records are formatted and eventually wind up getting stored in a local file or transmitted over a network.

The best practice is to have a distinct logger for each of our classes or modules. As `Logger` names are `.`-separated strings, the `Logger` names can parallel class or module names; our application's hierarchy of component definitions will have a parallel hierarchy of loggers. We might have a class that starts like the following code:

```
import logging
class Player:
    def __init__( self, bet, strategy, stake ):
```

```
        self.logger= logging.getLogger( self.__class__.__qualname__ )
        self.logger.debug( "init bet {0}, strategy {1}, stake {2}".
format(
            bet, strategy, stake) )
```

This will ensure the `Logger` object used for this class will have a name that matches the qualified name of the class.

Creating a shared class-level logger

As we noted in *Chapter 8, Decorators and Mixins – Cross-cutting Aspects*, creating a class-level logger is made slightly cleaner by defining a decorator that creates the logger outside the class definition itself. Here's the decorator that we defined:

```
def logged( class_ ):
    class_.logger= logging.getLogger( class_.__qualname__ )
    return class_
```

This creates `logger` as a feature of the class, shared by all the instances. Now, we can define a class like the following code:

```
@logged
class Player:
    def __init__( self, bet, strategy, stake ):
        self.logger.debug( "init bet {0}, strategy {1}, stake {2}".
format(
            bet, strategy, stake) )
```

This will assure us that the class has the logger with the expected name. We can then use `self.logger` in the various methods with the confidence that it will be a valid instance of `logging.Logger`.

When we create an instance of `Player`, we're going to exercise the logger. By default, we won't see anything. The initial configuration for the `logging` module doesn't include a handler or a level that produces any output. We'll need to change the `logging` configuration to see anything.

The most important benefit of the way the `logging` module works is that we can include logging features in our classes and modules without worrying about the overall configuration. The default behavior will be silent and introduce very little overhead. For this reason, we can always include logging features in every class that we define.

Configuring the loggers

There are two configuration details that we need to provide to see the output in our logs:

- The logger we're using needs to be associated with a handler that produces conspicuous output
- The handler needs a logging level that will pass our logging messages

The `logging` package has a variety of configuration methods. We'll show you `logging.basicConfig()` here. We'll take a look at `logging.config.dictConfig()` separately.

The `logging.basicConfig()` method permits a few parameters to create a single `logging.handlers.StreamHandler` for logging the output. In many cases, this is all we need:

```
import logging
import sys
logging.basicConfig( stream=sys.stderr, level=logging.DEBUG )
```

This will configure a `StreamHandler` instance that will write to `sys.stderr`. It will pass messages that have a level that is greater than or equal to the given level. By using `logging.DEBUG`, we're assured of seeing all the messages. The default level is `logging.WARN`.

After performing this configuration, we'll see our debugging messages:

```
>>> p= Player( 1, 2, 3 )
DEBUG:Player:init bet 1, strategy 2, stake 3
```

The default format shows us the level (`DEBUG`), the name of the logger (`Player`), and the string that we produced. There are more attributes in `LogRecord` that can be shown. Often, this default format is acceptable.

Starting up and shutting down the logging system

The `logging` module is defined in a way that avoids manually managing the global state information. The global state is handled within the `logging` module. We can write applications in separate parts and be well assured that those components will cooperate properly through the `logging` interface. We can, for example, include `logging` in some modules and omit it entirely from other modules without worrying about the compatibility or configuration.

Most importantly, we can include logging requests throughout an application and never configure any handlers. The top-level main script can omit `import logging` entirely. In this case, there will be no errors or problems from the logging code.

Because of the decentralized nature of logging, it's easy to configure it just once at the top level of an application. We should only configure `logging` inside the `if __name__ == "__main__":` portion of an application. We'll look at this in more detail in *Chapter 16, Coping with the Command Line*.

Many of our logging handlers involve buffering. For the most part, the buffers will flush in the normal course of events. While we can ignore how logging shuts down, it's slightly more reliable to use `logging.shutdown()` to be sure that all the buffers are flushed to the devices.

When handling top-level errors and exceptions, we have two explicit techniques to ensure all buffers are written. One technique is to use a `finally` clause on a `try:` block:

```
import sys
if __name__ == "__main__":
    logging.config.dictConfig( yaml.load("log_config.yaml") )
    try:
        application= Main()
        status= application.run()
    except Exception as e:
        logging.exception( e )
        status= 2
    finally:
        logging.shutdown()
    sys.exit(status)
```

This example shows us how we configure `logging` as early as possible and shut down `logging` as late as possible. This ensures as much of the application as possible is properly bracketed by properly configured loggers. This includes an exception logger; in some applications, the `main()` function handles all exceptions, making the except clause here redundant.

Another approach is to include an `atexit` handler to shut down `logging`:

```
import atexit
import sys
if __name__ == "__main__":
    logging.config.dictConfig( yaml.load("log_config.yaml") )
    atexit.register(logging.shutdown)
    try:
        application= Main()
```

```
        status= application.run()
    except Exception as e:
        logging.exception( e )
        status= 2
    sys.exit(status)
```

This version shows us how to use the `atexit` handler to invoke `logging.shutdown()`. When the application exits, the given function will be called. If the exceptions are properly handled inside the `main()` function, the `try:` block can be replaced with much simpler `status= main(); sys.exit(status)`.

There's a third technique that uses a context manager to control logging. We'll look at that alternative in *Chapter 16, Coping with the Command Line*.

Naming the loggers

There are four common use cases for using `logging.getLogger()` to name our `Loggers`. We often pick names to parallel our application's architecture:

- **Module names**: We might have a module global `Logger` instance for modules that contain a large number of small functions or classes for which a large number of objects are created. When we extend `tuple`, for example, we don't want a reference to `Logger` in each instance. We'll often do this globally, and usually this logger creation is kept close to the front of the module. In this example, right after the imports:

  ```
  import logging
  logger= logging.getLogger( __name__ )
  ```

- **Object instances**: This is shown previously, when we created `Logger` in the `__init__()` method. This `Logger` will be unique to the instance; using only a qualified class name might be misleading, because there will be multiple instances of the class. A better design is to include a unique instance identifier in the logger's name:

  ```
  def __init__( self, player_name )
      self.name= player_name
      self.logger= logging.getLogger( "{0}.{1}".format(
          self.__class__.__qualname__, player_name ) )
  ```

- **Class names**: This is shown previously, when we defined a simple decorator. We can use `__class__.__qualname__` as the `Logger` name and assign `Logger` to the class as a whole. It will be shared by all instances of the class.

- **Function names**: For small functions that are used frequently, we'll often use a module-level log, shown previously. For larger functions that are rarely used, we might create a log within the function:

  ```
  def main():
      log= logging.getLogger("main")
  ```

The idea here is to be sure that our `Logger` names match our software architecture. This provides us with the most transparent logging, simplifying debugging.

In some cases, however, we might have a more complex collection of `Loggers`. We might have several distinct types of informational messages from a class. Two common examples are financial audit logs and security access logs. We might want several parallel hierarchies of `Loggers`: one with names that start with `audit.` and another with names that start with `security.`. A class might have the more specialized `Loggers` with names such as `audit.module.Class` or `security.module.Class`:

```
self.audit_log= logging.getLogger( "audit." + self.__class__.__
qualname__ )
```

Having multiple logger objects available in a class allows us to finely control the kinds of output. We can configure each `Logger` to have different `handlers`. We'll use the more advanced configurations in the following section to direct the output to different destinations.

Extending the logger levels

The `logging` module has five predefined levels of importance. Each level has a global variable (or two) with the level number. The level of importance represents a spectrum of optionality from debugging messages (rarely important enough to show) to critical or fatal errors (always important).

Logging module variable	Value
`DEBUG`	`10`
`INFO`	`20`
`WARNING or WARN`	`30`
`ERROR`	`40`
`CRITICAL or FATAL`	`50`

We can add additional levels for even more nuanced control over what messages are passed or rejected. For example, some applications support multiple levels of verbosity. Similarly, some applications include multiple levels of debugging details.

For ordinary silent output, we might set the logging level to `logging.WARNING` so that only warnings and errors are shown. For the first level of verbosity, we can set the level of `logging.INFO` to see informational messages. For the second level of verbosity, we might want to add a level with a value of 15 and set the root logger to include this new level.

We can use this to define our new level of verbose messages:

```
logging.addLevelName(15, "VERBOSE")
logging.VERBOSE= 15
```

We can use our new levels via the `Logger.log( )` method, which takes the level number as an argument:

```
self.logger.log( logging.VERBOSE, "Some Message" )
```

While there's little overhead to add levels such as this, they can be overused. The subtlety is that a level conflates multiple concepts—visibility and erroneous behavior—into a single numeric code. The levels should be confined to a simple visibility or error spectrum. Anything more complex must be done via the `Logger` names or the actual `Filter` objects.

Defining handlers for multiple destinations

We have several use cases to send the log output to multiple destinations, which are shown in the following bullet list:

- We might want duplicate logs to improve the reliability of operations.
- We might be using the sophisticated `Filter` objects to create distinct subsets of messages.
- We might have different levels for each destination. We can use this to separate debugging messages from informational messages.
- We might have different handlers based on the `Logger` names to represent different foci.

Of course, we can also combine these to create quite complex scenarios. In order to create multiple destinations, we must create multiple `Handlers`. Each `Handler` might contain a customized `Formatter`; it can contain an optional level, and an optional list of filters that can be applied.

Once we have multiple `Handlers`, we can bind `Loggers` to the desired `Handlers`. The `Loggers` form a proper hierarchy; this means we can bind `Loggers` to `Handlers` using high-level or low-level names. As `Handlers` have a level filter, we can have multiple handlers that will show us different groups of messages based on the level. Also, we can explicitly use the `Filter` objects if we need even more sophisticated filtering.

While we can configure this through the `logging` module API, it's often more clear to define most of the logging details in a configuration file. One elegant way to handle this is to use the YAML notation for a configuration dictionary. We can then load the dictionary with a relatively straightforward use of `logging.config.dictConfig(yaml.load(somefile))`.

The YAML notation is somewhat more compact than the notation accepted by `configparser`. The documentation for `logging.config` in *Python Standard Library* uses YAML examples because of their clarity. We'll follow this pattern.

Here's an example of a configuration file with two handlers and two families of loggers:

```
version: 1
handlers:
  console:
    class: logging.StreamHandler
    stream: ext://sys.stderr
    formatter: basic
  audit_file:
    class: logging.FileHandler
    filename: p3_c14_audit.log
    encoding: utf-8
    formatter: basic
formatters:
  basic:
    style: "{"
    format: "{levelname:s}:{name:s}:{message:s}"
loggers:
  verbose:
    handlers: [console]
    level: INFO
  audit:
    handlers: [audit_file]
    level: INFO
```

We defined two handlers: `console` and `audit_file`. The `console` is `StreamHandler` that is sent to `sys.stderr`. Note that we have to use a URI-style syntax of `ext://sys.stderr` to name an *external* Python resource. In this context, external means external to the configuration file. The default assumption is that the value is a simple string, not a reference to an object. The `audit_file` is `FileHandler` that will write to a given file. By default, files are opened with a mode of `a` to append.

We also defined the formatter, named `basic`, to produce the log format that we get from `basicConfig()`. If we don't use this, our messages will use a slightly different default format that only has the message text.

Finally, we defined two top-level loggers: `verbose` and `audit`. The `verbose` instance will be used by all the loggers that have a top-level name of `verbose`. We can then use a `Logger` name such as `verbose.example.SomeClass` to create an instance that is a child of `verbose`. Each logger has a list of handlers; in this case, there's just one element in each list. Additionally, we've specified the logging level for each logger.

Here's how we can load this configuration file:

```
import logging.config
import yaml
config_dict= yaml.load(config)
logging.config.dictConfig(config_dict)
```

We parsed the YAML text into `dict` and then used the `dictConfig()` function to configure the logging with the given dictionary. Here are some examples of getting loggers and writing messages:

```
verbose= logging.getLogger( "verbose.example.SomeClass" )
audit= logging.getLogger( "audit.example.SomeClass" )
verbose.info( "Verbose information" )
audit.info( "Audit record with before and after" )
```

We created two `Logger` objects, one under the `verbose` family tree and the other under the `audit` family tree. When we write to the `verbose` logger, we'll see the output on the console. When we write to the `audit` logger, however, we'll see nothing on the console; the record will go to the file that is named in the configuration.

When we look at the `logging.handlers` module, we see a large number of handlers that we can leverage. By default, the `logging` module uses older-looking `%` style formatting specifications. These are not like the format specifications for the `str.format()` method. When we defined our formatter parameters, we used the `{` style formatting, which is consistent with `str.format()`.

Managing the propagation rules

The default behavior for `Loggers` is for a logging record to propagate from the named `Logger` up through all parent-level `Loggers` to the root `Logger`. We may have lower-level `Loggers` that have special behaviors and a root `Logger` that defines the default behavior for all `Loggers`.

Because logging records propagate, a root-level logger will *also* handle any log records from the lower-level `Loggers` that we define. If child loggers produce output and allow propagation, this will lead to duplicated output: first from the child and then from the parent. If we want to avoid duplication when child loggers produce output, we must turn the propagation off for the lower-level logger.

Our previous example does not configure a root-level `Logger`. If some part of our application creates the logger with a name that doesn't start with `audit.` or `verbose.`, then that additional logger won't be associated with `Handler`. Either we need more top-level names or we need to configure a catch-all, root-level logger.

If we add a root-level logger to capture all these other names, then we have to be careful about the propagation rules. Here's a modification to the configuration file:

```
loggers:
  verbose:
    handlers: [console]
    level: INFO
    propagate: False # Added
  audit:
    handlers: [audit_file]
    level: INFO
    propagate: False # Added
root: # Added
  handlers: [console]
  level: INFO
```

We turned the propagation off for the two lower-level loggers: `verbose` and `audit`. We added a new root-level logger. As this logger has no name, this is done as a separate top-level dictionary named `root:` in parallel with the `loggers:` entry.

If we didn't turn the propagation off in the two lower-level loggers, each `verbose` or `audit` record would have been handled twice. In the case of an audit log, the double handling may actually be desirable. The audit data would go to the console as well as the audit file.

What's important about the `logging` module is that we don't have to make any application changes to refine and control the logging. We can do almost anything required through the configuration file. As YAML is a relatively elegant notation, we can encode a lot of capability very simply.

Configuration gotcha

The `basicConfig()` method of logging is careful about preserving any loggers created before the configuration is made. The `logging.config.dictConfig()` method, however, has the default behavior of disabling any loggers created prior to configuration.

When assembling a large and complex application, we may have module-level loggers that are created during the `import` process. The modules imported by the main script can potentially create loggers before `logging.config` is created. Also, any global objects or class definitions might have loggers created prior to the configuration.

We often have to add a line such as this to our configuration file:

```
disable_existing_loggers: False
```

This will ensure all the loggers created prior to the configuration will still propagate to the root logger created by the configuration.

Specializing logging for control, debug, audit, and security

There are many kinds of logging; we'll focus on these four varieties:

- **Errors and Control**: Basic error and control of an application leads to a main log that helps users confirm that the program really is doing what it's supposed to do. This would include enough error information with which the users can correct their problems and rerun the application. If a user enables verbose logging, it will amplify this main error and control the log with additional user-friendly details.
- **Debugging**: This is used by developers and maintainers; it can include rather complex implementation details. We'll rarely want to enable *blanket* debugging, but will often enable debugging for specific modules or classes.
- **Audit**: This is a formal confirmation that tracks the transformations applied to data so we can be sure that processing was done correctly.

- **Security**: This can be used to show us who has been authenticated; it can help confirm that the authorization rules are being followed. It can also be used to detect some kinds of attacks that involve repeated password failures.

We often have different formatting and handling requirements for each of these kinds of logs. Also, some of these are enabled and disabled dynamically. The main error and control log is often built from the non-DEBUG messages. We might have an application with a structure like the following code:

```
from collections import Counter
class Main:
    def __init__( self ):
        self.balance= Counter()
        self.log= logging.getLogger( self.__class__.__qualname__ )
    def run( self ):
        self.log.info( "Start" )

        # Some processing
        self.balance['count'] += 1
        self.balance['balance'] += 3.14

        self.log.info( "Counts {0}".format(self.balance) )

        for k in self.balance:
            self.log.info( "{0:.<16s} {1:n}".format(
                k, self.balance[k]) )
```

We created a logger with a name that matches the class qualified name (`Main`). We've written informational messages to this logger to show you that our application started normally and finished normally. In this case, we used `Counter` to accumulate some balance information that can be used to confirm that the right amount of data was processed.

In some cases, we'll have more formal balance information displayed at the end of the processing. We might do something like this to provide a slightly easier-to-read display:

```
    for k in balance:
        self.log.info( "{0:.<16s} {1:n}".format(k, balance[k]) )
```

This version will show us the keys and values on separate lines in the log. The errors and control log often uses the simplest formats; it might show us just the message text with little or no additional context. A logging `Formatter` object like this might be used:

```
formatters:
  control:
```

```
        style: "{"
        format: "{levelname:s}:{message:s}"
```

This configures `formatter` to show us the level name (`INFO`, `WARNING`, `ERROR`, `CRITICAL`) along with the message text. This eliminates a number of details, providing just the essential facts for the benefit of the users. We've called the formatter `control`.

In the following code, we have associated the control formatter with the console handler:

```
    handlers:
      console:
        class: logging.StreamHandler
        stream: ext://sys.stderr
        formatter: control
```

This will use `control formatter` with the `console handler`.

Creating a debugging log

A debugging log is usually enabled by a developer to monitor a program under development. It's often narrowly focused on specific features, modules, or classes. Consequently, we'll often enable and disable loggers by name. A configuration file might set the level of a few loggers to `DEBUG`, leaving others at `INFO`, or possibly even a `WARNING` level.

We'll often design debugging information into our classes. Indeed, we might use the debugging ability as a specific quality feature for a class design. This may mean introducing a rich set of logging requests. For example, we might have a complex calculation for which the class state is essential information:

```
@logged
class OneThreeTwoSix( BettingStrategy ):
    def __init__( self ):
        self.wins= 0
    def _state( self ):
        return dict( wins= self.wins )
    def bet( self ):
        bet= { 0: 1, 1: 3, 2: 2, 3: 6 }[self.wins%4]
        self.logger.debug( "Bet {1}; based on {0}".format(self._
state(), bet) )
    def record_win( self ):
        self.wins += 1
        self.logger.debug( "Win: {0}".format(self._state()) )
    def record_loss( self ):
```

```
        self.wins = 0
        self.logger.debug( "Loss: {0}".format(self._state()) )
```

In this class definition, we created a `_state()` method that exposes the relevant internal state. This method is only used to support debugging. We've avoided using `self.__dict__` because this often has too much information to be helpful. We can then audit the changes to this state information in several places in our method functions.

Debugging output is often selectively enabled by editing the configuration file to enable and disable debugging in certain places. We might make a change such as this to the logging configuration file:

```
loggers:
    betting.OneThreeTwoSix:
       handlers: [console]
       level: DEBUG
       propagate: False
```

We identified the logger for a particular class based on the qualified name for the class. This example assumes there's a handler named `console` already defined. Also, we've turned off the propagation to prevent the debugging messages from being duplicated into the root logger.

Implicit in this design is the idea that debugging is not something we want to simply enable from the command line via a simplistic `-D` option or a `--DEBUG` option. To perform effective debugging, we'll often want to enable selected loggers via a configuration file. We'll look at command-line issues in *Chapter 16, Coping with the Command Line*.

Creating audit and security logs

Audit and security logs are often duplicated between two handlers: the main control handler plus a file handler that is used for audit and security reviews. This means we'll do the following things:

- Define additional loggers for the audit and security
- Define multiple handlers for these loggers
- Optionally, define additional formats for the audit handler

As shown previously, we'll often create separate hierarchies of the `audit` or `security` logs. Creating separate hierarchies of loggers is considerably simpler than trying to introduce audit or security via a new logging level. Adding new levels is challenging because the messages are essentially `INFO` messages; they don't belong on the `WARNING` side of `INFO` because they're not errors, nor do they belong on the `DEBUG` side of `INFO` because they're not optional.

Here's a decorator that can be used to build a class that includes auditing:

```
def audited( class_ ):
    class_.logger= logging.getLogger( class_.__qualname__ )
    class_.audit= logging.getLogger( "audit." + class_.__qualname__ )
    return class_
```

This creates two loggers. One logger has a name simply based on the qualified name of the class. The other logger uses the qualified name, but with a prefix that puts it in the `audit` hierarchy. Here's how we can use this decorator:

```
@audited
class Table:
    def bet( self, bet, amount ):
        self.audit.info( "Bet {0} Amount {1}".format(bet, amount) )
```

We created a class that will produce records on a logger in the `audit` hierarchy. We can configure logging to handle this additional hierarchy of loggers. We'll look at the two handlers that we need:

```
handlers:
  console:
    class: logging.StreamHandler
    stream: ext://sys.stderr
    formatter: basic
  audit_file:
    class: logging.FileHandler
    filename: p3_c14_audit.log
    encoding: utf-8
    formatter: detailed
```

The `console` handler has the user-oriented log entries that use the `basic` format. The `audit_file` handler uses a more complex formatter named `detailed`. Here are the two `formatters` referenced by these `handlers`:

```
formatters:
  basic:
    style: "{"
    format: "{levelname:s}:{name:s}:{message:s}"
```

```
    detailed:
      style: "{"
      format: "{levelname:s}:{name:s}:{asctime:s}:{message:s}"
      datefmt: "%Y-%m-%d %H:%M:%S"
```

The `basic` format shows us just three attributes of the message. The `detailed` format rules are somewhat complex because the date formatting is done separate from the rest of the message formatting. The `datetime` module uses the `%` style formatting. We used the { style formatting for the overall message. Here are the two `Logger` definitions:

```
loggers:
  audit:
    handlers: [console,audit_file]
    level: INFO
    propagate: True
root:
  handlers: [console]
  level: INFO
```

We defined a logger for the `audit` hierarchy. All the children of `audit` will write their messages to both `console Handler` as well as `audit_file Handler`. The root logger will define all the other loggers to use the console only. We'll now see two forms of the audit messages.

The console might contain lines like this:

```
INFO:audit.Table:Bet One Amount 1
INFO:audit.Table:Bet Two Amount 2
```

The audit file might look like this:

```
INFO:audit.Table:2013-12-29 10:24:57:Bet One Amount 1
INFO:audit.Table:2013-12-29 10:24:57:Bet Two Amount 2
```

This duplication provides us with the audit information in the context of the main console log, plus a focused audit trail in a separate log that can be saved for later analysis.

Using the warnings module

Object-oriented development often involves performing a significant refactoring of a class or module. It's difficult to get the API exactly right the very first time we write an application. Indeed, the design time required to get the API exactly right might get wasted: Python's flexibility permits us great latitude in making changes as we learn more about the problem domain and the user's requirements.

One of the tools that we can use to support the design evolution is the `warnings` module. There are two clear use cases for `warnings` and one fuzzy use case:

- To alert developers of the API changes, usually features that are deprecated or pending deprecation. The deprecation and pending deprecation warnings are silent by default. These messages are not silent when running the `unittest` module; this helps us ensure that we're making proper use of upgraded library packages.
- To alert the users about a configuration problem. For example, there might be several alternative implementations of a module: when the preferred implementation is not available, we might want to provide a warning that an optimal implementation is not being used.
- We might push the edge of the envelope by alerting users that the results of the computation may have other problems. There's a blurry spectrum of ways in which our applications can behave.

For the first two use cases, we'll often use Python's `warnings` module to show you that there are correctable problems. For the third blurry use case, we might use the `logger.warn()` method to alert the user about the potential issues. We shouldn't rely on the `warnings` module for this, because the default behavior is to show a warning just once.

We may see any of the following behaviors in an application:

- Ideally, our application finishes normally and everything works. The results are unambiguously valid.
- An application produces warning messages but finishes normally; the warning messages mean that the results are not trustworthy. Any output files will be readable, but the quality or completeness may be questionable. This is potentially confusing to the users; we'll wander around in the morass of these specific kinds of ambiguities showing possible software problems with a warning section, in the following section.
- An application may produce error messages but still come to an orderly conclusion. It is clear that the results are unambiguously erroneous and shouldn't be used for anything other than debugging. The `logging` module allows us to further subdivide this world of errors. A program that produces an error may still come to an orderly conclusion. We often use the `CRITICAL` (or `FATAL`) error message to indicate that the Python program may not have terminated properly and any output files are probably damaged. We often reserve the `CRITICAL` message for a top-level `try:` block.
- An application might crash at the OS level. In this case, there may be no messages from Python's exception handling or logging. This, too, is very clear as there are no usable results.

This second sense of *questionable results* is not a good design. Using warnings—either via the `warnings` module or the `WARN` messages from `logging`—doesn't really help the users.

Showing API changes with a warning

When we change the API for one of our modules, packages, or classes, we can provide a handy marking via the `warnings` module. This will raise a warning in the method that is deprecated or is pending deprecation:

```
import warnings
class Player:
    __version__= "2.2"
    def bet( self ):
        warnings.warn( "bet is deprecated, use place_bet",
          DeprecationWarning, stacklevel=2 )
        etc.
```

When we do this, any part of the application that uses `Player.bet()` will receive `DeprecationWarning`. By default, this warning is silent. We can, however, adjust the `warnings` filter to see the message, as shown here:

```
>>> warnings.simplefilter("always", category=DeprecationWarning)
>>> p2= Player()
>>> p2.bet()
__main__:4: DeprecationWarning: bet is deprecated, use place_bet
```

This technique allows us to locate all of the places where our application must change because of an API change. If we have unit test cases with close to 100 percent code coverage, this simple technique is likely to reveal all the uses of deprecated methods.

Because this is so valuable for planning and managing software change, we have three ways to be sure that we see all of the warnings in our applications:

- The command-line `-Wd` option will set the action to `default` for all warnings. This will enable the normally silent deprecation warnings. When we run `python3.3 -Wd`, we'll see all the deprecation warnings.
- Using `unittest`, which always executes in the `warnings.simplefilter('default')` mode.
- Including `warnings.simplefilter('default')` in our application program. This will also apply the `default` action to all warnings; it's equivalent to the `-Wd` command-line option.

Showing configuration problems with a warning

We may have multiple implementations for a given class or module. We'll often use a configuration file parameter to decide which implementation is appropriate. See *Chapter 13, Configuration Files and Persistence*, for more information on this technique.

In some cases, however, an application may silently depend on whether or not other packages are part of the Python installation. One implementation may be optimal, and another implementation may be the fallback plan. A common technique is to try multiple `import` alternatives to locate a package that's installed. We can produce warnings that show us the possible configuration difficulties. Here's a way to manage this alternative implementation import:

```
import warnings
try:
    import simulation_model_1 as model
except ImportError as e:
    warnings.warn( e )
if 'model' not in globals():
    try:
        import simulation_model_2 as model
    except ImportError as e:
        warnings.warn( e )
if 'model' not in globals():
    raise ImportError( "Missing simulation_model_1 and simulation_
model_2" )
```

We tried one import for a module. If this fails, we'll try another import. We used an `if` statement to reduce the nesting of the exceptions. If there are more than two alternatives, nested exceptions can lead to a very complex-looking exception. By using extra `if` statements, we can flatten a long sequence of alternatives so that the exceptions aren't nested.

We can better manage this warning message by changing the class of the message. In the preceding code, this will be `UserWarning`. These are shown by default, providing the users with some evidence that the configuration is not optimal.

If we change the class to `ImportWarning`, it will be silent by default. This provides a normally silent operation in the cases where the choice of packages doesn't matter to the users. The typical developer's technique of running with the `-Wd` option will reveal the `ImportWarning` messages.

To change the class of the warning, we change the call to `warnings.warn()`:

```
warnings.warn( e, ImportWarning )
```

This changes the warning to a class that is silent by default. The message can still be visible to developers who should be using the `-Wd` option.

Showing possible software problems with a warning

The idea of warnings aimed at end users is a bit nebulous: did the application work or did it fail? What does a warning really mean? Is there something the user should do differently?

Because of this potential ambiguity, warnings in the user interface aren't a great idea. To be truly usable, a program should either work correctly or should not work at all. When there's an error, the error message should include advice for the user's response to the problem. We shouldn't impose a burden on the user to judge the quality of the output and determine its fitness for purpose. We'll emphasize on this point.

A program should either work correctly or should not work at all.

One potential unambiguous use for end user warnings is to alert the user that the output is incomplete. An application may have a problem completing a network connection, for example. The essential results are correct, but one of the data sources didn't work properly.

There are situations where the application is taking an action that is not what the user requested, and the output is valid and useful. In the case of a network problem, a default behavior was used instead of a behavior based on the network resources. Generally, replacing something faulty with something correct but not exactly what the user requested is a good candidate for a warning. This kind of warning is best done with `logging` at the WARN level, not with the `warnings` module. The warnings module produces one-time messages; we may want to provide more details to the user. Here's how we might use a simple `Logger.warn()` message to describe the problem in the log:

```
try:
    with urllib.request.urlopen("http://host/resource/", timeout= 30 )
as resource:
        content= json.load(resource)
```

```
    except socket.timeout as e:
        self.log.warn("Missing information from  http://host/resource")
        content= []
```

If a timeout occurs, a warning message is written to the log and the program keeps running. The content of the resource will be set to an empty list. The log message will be written every time. A `warnings` module warning is ordinarily shown only once from a given location in the program and is suppressed after that.

Advanced logging – the last few messages and network destinations

We'll look at two more advanced techniques that can help provide useful debugging information. The first of these is a *log tail*: this is a buffer of the last few log messages before some significant event. The idea is to have a small file that can be read to see the last few log messages before an application died. It's a bit like having the OS `tail` command automatically applied to the full log output.

The second technique uses a feature of the logging framework to send log messages through a network to a centralized log-handling service. This can be used to consolidate logs from a number of parallel web servers. We need to create both senders and receivers for the logs.

Building an automatic tail buffer

The log tail buffer is an extension to the `logging` framework. We're going to extend `MemoryHandler` to slightly alter its behavior. The built-in behavior for `MemoryHandler` includes three use cases for writing: it will write to another `handler` when the capacity is reached; it will write any buffered messages when `logging` shuts down; most importantly, it will write the entire buffer when a message of a given level is logged.

We'll change the first use case slightly. Instead of writing when the buffer is full, we'll remove just the oldest message, leaving the others in the buffer. The other two use cases will be left alone. This will have the effect of dumping the last few messages before the shutdown as well as dumping the last few messages before an error.

We'll often configure the memory handler to buffer messages until a message greater than or equal to the error level is logged. This will lead to dumping the buffer ending with the error.

To understand this example, it's important to locate your Python installation and review the logging.handlers module in detail.

This extension to MemoryHandler will keep the last few messages, based on the defined capacity when the TailHandler class is created:

```
class TailHandler(logging.handlers.MemoryHandler):
    def shouldFlush(self, record):
        """
        Check for buffer full or a record at the flushLevel or higher.
        """
        if record.levelno >= self.flushLevel: return True
        while len(self.buffer) >= self.capacity:
            self.acquire()
            try:
                del self.buffer[0]
            finally:
                self.release()
```

We extended MemoryHandler so that it will accumulate log messages up to the given capacity. When the capacity is reached, old messages will be removed as new messages are added. Note that we must lock the data structure to permit multithreaded logging.

If a message with an appropriate level is received, then the entire structure is emitted to the target handler. Usually, the target is FileHandler, which writes to a tail file for debugging and support purposes.

Additionally, when logging shuts down, the final few messages will also be written to the tail file. This should indicate a normal termination that doesn't require any debugging or support.

Generally, we'd send DEBUG level messages to this kind of handler so that we have a great deal of detail surrounding a crash situation. The configuration should specifically set the level to DEBUG rather than allowing the level to default.

Here's a configuration that uses this TailHandler:

```
version: 1
disable_existing_loggers: False
handlers:
  console:
    class: logging.StreamHandler
    stream: ext://sys.stderr
    formatter: basic
  tail:
```

```
      (): __main__.TailHandler
      target: cfg://handlers.console
      capacity: 5
formatters:
  basic:
    style: "{"
    format: "{levelname:s}:{name:s}:{message:s}"
loggers:
  test:
    handlers: [tail]
    level: DEBUG
    propagate: False
root:
  handlers: [console]
  level: INFO
```

The definition of `TailHandler` shows us several additional features of the `logging` configuration. It shows us class references as well as other elements of the configuration file.

We referred to a customized class definition in the configuration. A label of `()` specifies that the value should be interpreted as a module and class name. In this case, it is an instance of our `__main__.TailHandler` class. A label of `class` instead of `()` uses a module and class that are part of the `logging` package.

We referred to another logger that's defined within the configuration. The text `cgf://handlers.console` in the preceding configuration file refers to the `console` handler defined within the `handlers` section of this configuration file. For demonstration purposes, we've had the tail target `StreamHandler` that uses `sys.stderr`. As noted previously, an alternative design might be to use a `FileHandler` that targets a debugging file.

We created the `test` hierarchy of loggers that used our `tail` handler. The messages written to these loggers will be buffered and only shown on the error or shutdown.

Here's a demonstration script:

```
logging.config.dictConfig( yaml.load(config8) )
log= logging.getLogger( "test.demo8" )

print( "Last 5 before error" )
for i in range(20):
    log.debug( "Message {:d}".format(i) )
log.error( "Error causes dump of last 5" )

print( "Last 5 before shutdown" )
for i in range(20,40):
```

```
    log.debug( "Message {:d}".format(i) )
logging.shutdown()
```

We generated 20 messages prior to an error. Then, we generated 20 more messages before shutting down the logging and flushing the buffers. This will produce output like the following one:

```
Last 5 before error
DEBUG:test.demo8:Message 16
DEBUG:test.demo8:Message 17
DEBUG:test.demo8:Message 18
DEBUG:test.demo8:Message 19
ERROR:test.demo8:Error causes dump of last 5
Last 5 before shutdown
DEBUG:test.demo8:Message 36
DEBUG:test.demo8:Message 37
DEBUG:test.demo8:Message 38
DEBUG:test.demo8:Message 39
```

The intermediate messages were silently dropped by the `tail` handler. As the capacity was set to five, the last five messages prior to an error (or shutdown) are displayed.

Sending logging messages to a remote process

One high-performance design pattern is to have a cluster of processes that are being used to solve a single problem. We might have an application that is spread across multiple application servers or multiple database clients. For this kind of architecture, we often want a centralized log among all of the various processes.

One technique to create a unified log is to include accurate timestamps and then sort records from multiple logfiles into a single, unified log. This sorting and merging is extra processing that can be avoided by remotely logging from a number of concurrent producer processes to a single consumer process.

Our shared logging solution makes use of the shared queues from the `multiprocessing` module. For additional information on multiprocessing, see *Chapter 12, Transmitting and Sharing Objects*.

There's a three-step process to build a multiprocessing application:

- Firstly, we'll create the shared queue object so that the logging consumer can apply filters to the messages

- Secondly, we'll create the consumer process that gets the logging records from the queue
- Thirdly, we'll create the pool of source processes that do the real work of our application and produce logging records into the shared queue

The `ERROR` and `FATAL` messages could provide immediate notification via an SMS or e-mail to concerned users. The consumer can also handle the (relatively) slow processing associated with rotating logfiles.

The overall parent application that creates the producers and consumers is roughly analogous to the Linux `init` program that starts the various OS-level processes. If we follow the `init` design pattern, then the parent application can monitor the various producer children to see if they crash, and it can either log the associated errors or even attempt to restart them.

Here's the definition of a consumer process:

```
import collections
import logging
import multiprocessing
class Log_Consumer_1(multiprocessing.Process):
    """In effect, an instance of QueueListener."""
    def __init__( self, queue ):
        self.source= queue
        super().__init__()
        logging.config.dictConfig( yaml.load(consumer_config) )
        self.combined= logging.getLogger(
            "combined." + self.__class__.__qualname__ )
        self.log= logging.getLogger( self.__class__.__qualname__  )
        self.counts= collections.Counter()
    def run( self ):
        self.log.info( "Consumer Started" )
        while True:
            log_record= self.source.get()
            if log_record == None: break
            self.combined.handle( log_record )
            words= log_record.getMessage().split()
            self.counts[words[1]] += 1
        self.log.info( "Consumer Finished" )
        self.log.info( self.counts )
```

This process is a subclass of `multiprocessing.Process`. We will start it with the `start()` method; the superclass will fork a subprocess that executes the `run()` method.

While the process is running, it will get the log records from the queue and then route them to a logger instance. In this case, we're going to create a special logger named with a parent name of `combined.`; this will be given each record from a source process.

Additionally, we'll provide some counts based on the second word of each message. In this example, we've designed the applications so that the second word will be the process ID number from the message text. The counts will show us how many messages were processed correctly.

Here's a `logging` configuration file for this process:

```
version: 1
disable_existing_loggers: False
handlers:
  console:
    class: logging.StreamHandler
    stream: ext://sys.stderr
    formatter: basic
formatters:
  basic:
    style: "{"
    format: "{levelname:s}:{name:s}:{message:s}"
loggers:
  combined:
    handlers: [ console ]
    formatter: detail
    level: INFO
    propagate: False
root:
  handlers: [ console ]
  level: INFO
```

We defined a simple console `Logger` with a basic format. We also defined the top-level of a hierarchy of loggers with names that begin with `combined.`. These loggers will be used to display the combined output of the various producers.

Here's the logging producer:

```
class Log_Producer(multiprocessing.Process):
    handler_class= logging.handlers.QueueHandler
    def __init__( self, proc_id, queue ):
        self.proc_id= proc_id
        self.destination= queue
        super().__init__()
```

```
        self.log= logging.getLogger(
            "{0}.{1}".format(self.__class__.__qualname__, self.proc_
id) )
        self.log.handlers = [ self.handler_class( self.destination ) ]
        self.log.setLevel( logging.INFO )
    def run( self ):
        self.log.info( "Producer {0} Started".format(self.proc_id) )
        for i in range(100):
            self.log.info( "Producer {:d} Message {:d}".format(self.
proc_id, i) )
        self.log.info( "Producer {0} Finished".format(self.proc_id) )
```

The producer doesn't do much in the way of configuration. It simply gets a logger to use the qualified class name and an instance identifier (`self.proc_id`). It sets the list of handlers to be just `QueueHandler` wrapped around the destination a `Queue` instance. The level of this logger is set to `INFO`.

We made `handler_class` an attribute of the class definition because we plan to change it. For the first example, it will be `logging.handlers.QueueHandler`. For a later example, we'll change to another class.

The process to actually do this work uses the logger to create log messages. These messages will be enqueued for processing by the centralized consumer. In this case, the process simply floods the queue with 102 messages as quickly as possible.

Here's how we can start the consumer and producers. We'll show this in small groups of steps. First, we create the queue:

```
import multiprocessing
queue= multiprocessing.Queue(100)
```

This queue is way too small to handle 10 producers blasting 102 messages in a fraction of a second. The idea of a small queue is to see what happens when messages are lost. Here's how we start the consumer process:

```
consumer = Log_Consumer_1( queue )
consumer.start()
```

Here's how we start an array of producer processes:

```
producers = []
for i in range(10):
    proc= Log_Producer( i, queue )
    proc.start()
    producers.append( proc )
```

As expected, 10 concurrent producers will overflow the queue. Each producer will receive a number of queues full of exceptions to show us that the messages were lost.

Here's how we cleanly finish the processing:

```
for p in producers:
    p.join()
queue.put( None )
consumer.join()
```

First, we wait for each producer process to finish and then rejoin the parent process. Then, we put a sentinel object into the queue so that the consumer will terminate cleanly. Finally, we wait for the consumer process to finish and join the parent process.

Preventing queue overrun

The default behavior of the logging module puts messages into the queue with the `Queue.put_nowait()` method. The advantage of this is that it allows the producers to run without the delays associated with logging. The disadvantage of this is that messages will get lost if the queue is too small to handle the worst-case burst of logging messages.

We have two choices to gracefully handle this burst of messages:

- We can switch from `Queue` to `SimpleQueue`. `SimpleQueue` has an indefinite size. As it has a slightly different API, we'll need to extend `QueueHandler` to use `Queue.put()` instead of `Queue.put_nowait()`.
- We can slow down the producer in the rare case that the queue is full. This is a small change to `QueueHandler` to use `Queue.put()` instead of `Queue.put_nowait()`.

Interestingly, the same API change works for both `Queue` and `SimpleQueue`. Here's the change:

```
class WaitQueueHandler( logging.handlers.QueueHandler ):
    def enqueue(self, record):
        self.queue.put( record )
```

We replaced the body of the `enqueue()` method to use a different method of `Queue`. Now, we can use `SimpleQueue` or `Queue`. If we use `Queue`, it will wait when the queue is full, preventing the loss of logging messages. If we use `SimpleQueue`, the queue will silently expand to hold all the messages.

Here's the revised producer class:

```
class Log_Producer_2(Log_Producer):
    handler_class= WaitQueueHandler
```

This class uses our new `WaitQueueHandler`. Otherwise, the producer is identical to the previous version.

The rest of the script to create `Queue` and start the consumer is identical. The producers are instances of `Log_Producer_2`, but otherwise, the script to start and join remains identical to the first example.

This variation runs more slowly, but never loses a message. We can improve the performance by creating a larger queue capacity. If we create a queue with a capacity of 1,020 messages, the performance is maximized for this example. Finding an optimal queue capacity requires careful experimentation.

Summary

We saw how to use the logging module with more advanced object-oriented design techniques. We created logs associated with modules, classes, instances, and functions. We used decorators to create logging as a consistent cross-cutting aspect across multiple class definitions.

We saw how to use the `warnings` module to show you that there's a problem with the configuration or the deprecated methods. We can use warnings for other purposes, but we need to be cautious about the overuse of warnings and creating murky situations where it's not clear whether the application worked correctly or not.

Design considerations and trade-offs

The `logging` module supports auditability and debugging ability as well as some security requirements. We can use logging as a simple way to keep records of the processing steps. By selectively enabling and disabling logging, we can support developers who are trying to learn what the code is really doing when processing real-world data.

The `warnings` module supports debugging ability as well as maintainability features. We can use warnings to alert the developers about the API problems, configuration problems, and other potential sources of bugs.

When working with the `logging` module, we'll often be creating large numbers of distinct loggers that feed a few `handlers`. We can use the hierarchical nature of the `Logger` names to introduce new or specialized collections of logging messages. There's no reason why a class can't have two loggers: one for audit and one for more general-purpose debugging.

We can introduce new logging-level numbers, but this should be done reluctantly. The levels tend to conflate the developer focus (debug, info, warning) with user focus (info, error, fatal). There's a kind of spectrum of *optionality* from debug messages that are not required for fatal error messages, which should never be silenced. We might add a level for verbose information or possibly detailed debugging, but that's about all that should be done with levels.

The `logging` module allows us to provide a number of configuration files for different purposes. As developers, we may use a configuration file that sets the logging levels to `DEBUG` and enables specific loggers for modules under development. For final deployment, we can provide a configuration file that sets the logging levels to `INFO` and provides different handlers to support more formal audit or security review needs.

We'll include some thoughts from the *Zen of Python*:

> *Errors should never pass silently.*
> *Unless explicitly silenced.*

The `warnings` and `logging` module directly support this idea.

These modules are oriented more towards the overall quality than towards the specific solution of a problem. They allow us to provide consistency via fairly simple programming. As our object-oriented designs become larger and more complex, we can focus more on the problem being solved without wasting time on the infrastructure considerations. Further, these modules allow us to tailor the output to provide information needed by the developer or user.

Looking forward

In the following chapters, we take a look at designing for testability and how we use `unittest` and `doctest`. Automated testing is essential; no programming should be considered complete until there are automated unit tests that provide ample evidence to show us that the code works. We'll look at object-oriented design techniques that will make software easier to test.

15
Designing for Testability

High-quality programs have automated tests. We need to use everything at our disposal to be sure that our software works. The golden rule is this: *to be deliverable, the feature must have a unit test.*

Without an automated unit test, the feature cannot be trusted to work and should not be used. According to Kent Beck, in *Extreme Programming Explained*:

> "*Any program feature without an automated test simply doesn't exist.*"

There are two essential points regarding the automated testing of program features:

- **Automated**: This means that there's no human judgment involved. The testing involves a script that compares actual responses to expected responses.
- **Features**: These are tested in isolation to be sure that they work separately. This is unit testing, where each "unit" has enough software to implement a given feature. Ideally, it's a small unit such as a class. However, it can also be a larger unit such as a module or package.

Python has two built-in testing frameworks, making it easy to write automated unit tests. We'll look at using both `doctest` and `unittest` for automating testing. We'll look at some of the design considerations required to make testing practical.

For more ideas, read about *Ottinger and Langr's* **FIRST** properties of unit tests: **Fast, Isolated, Repeatable, Self-validating,** and **Timely**. For the most part, Repeatable and Self-validating require an automated test framework. Timely means that the test is written before the code under test. See `http://pragprog.com/magazines/2012-01/unit-tests-are-first`.

Defining and isolating units for testing

As testing is essential, testability is an important design consideration. Our designs must also support testing and debugging because a class that merely appears to work is of no value. A class that has evidence that it works is much more valuable.

Ideally, we'd like a hierarchy of testing. At the foundation is unit testing. Here, we test each class or function in isolation to be sure that it meets the contractual obligations of the API. Each class or function is a single unit under test. Above this comes integration testing. Once we know that each class and function works individually, we can test groups and clusters of classes. We can test whole modules and whole packages, too. After the integration tests work, we can look at the automated testing of the complete application.

This is not an exhaustive list of the types of tests. We can do performance testing or security vulnerability testing too. We'll focus, however, on automated unit testing because it is central to all applications. This hierarchy of testing reveals an important complexity. Test cases for an individual class or group of classes can be very narrowly defined. As we introduce more units into integration testing, the domain of inputs grows. When we attempt to test a whole application, the entire spectrum of human behavior becomes a candidate input; this includes shutting devices off mid-test, pulling out plugs, and pushing things off tables to see whether they still work after being dropped three feet onto a hardwood floor. The hugeness of the domain of behavior makes it difficult to *fully* automate application testing.

We'll focus on the things that are easiest to test automatically. Once the unit tests work, the larger, aggregate systems are more likely to work.

Minimizing the dependencies

When we design a class, we must also consider the network of dependencies around that class: classes on which it depends and classes that depend on it. In order to simplify testing a class definition, we need to isolate it from the surrounding classes.

An example of this is the `Deck` class that depends on the `Card` class. We can easily test `Card` in isolation but, when we want to test a `Deck` class, we need to tease it away from the definition of `Card`.

Here's one (of many) previous definitions of `Card` that we've looked at:

```
class Card:
    def __init__( self, rank, suit, hard=None, soft=None ):
        self.rank= rank
        self.suit= suit
        self.hard= hard or int(rank)
```

```
        self.soft= soft or int(rank)
    def __str__( self ):
        return "{0.rank!s}{0.suit!s}".format(self)

class AceCard( Card ):
    def __init__( self, rank, suit ):
        super().__init__( rank, suit, 1, 11 )

class FaceCard( Card ):
    def __init__( self, rank, suit ):
        super().__init__( rank, suit, 10, 10 )
```

We can see that each of these classes has a straightforward inheritance dependency. Each class can be tested in isolation because there are only two methods and four attributes.

We can (mis-)design a `Deck` class to have some problematic dependencies:

```
Suits = '♣', '♦', '♥', '♠'
class Deck1( list ):
    def __init__( self, size=1 ):
        super().__init__()
        self.rng= random.Random()
        for d in range(size):
            for s in Suits:
                cards = ([AceCard(1, s)]
                + [Card(r, s) for r in range(2, 12)]
                + [FaceCard(r, s) for r in range(12, 14)])
                super().extend( cards )
        self.rng.shuffle( self )
```

This design has two deficiencies. First, it's intimately bound to the three classes in the `Card` class hierarchy. We can't isolate `Deck` from `Card` for a standalone unit test. Second, it is dependent on the random number generator, making it difficult to create a repeatable test.

On the one hand, `Card` is a pretty simple class. We could test this version of `Deck` with `Card` left in place. On the other hand, we might want to reuse `Deck` with poker cards or pinochle cards that have different behaviors from Blackjack cards.

The ideal situation is to make `Deck` independent of any particular `Card` implementation. If we do this well, then we can not only test `Deck` independently of any `Card` implementation, but we can also use any combination of `Card` and `Deck` definitions.

Here's our preferred method to separate one of the dependencies. We can use a factory function:

```
def card( rank, suit ):
    if rank == 1: return AceCard( rank, suit )
    elif 2 <= rank < 11: return Card( rank, suit )
    elif 11 <= rank < 14: return FaceCard( rank, suit )
    else: raise Exception( "LogicError" )
```

The `card()` function will build proper subclasses of `Card` based on the requested rank. This allows the `Deck` class to use this function instead of directly building instances of the `Card` class. We separated the two class definitions by inserting an intermediate function.

We have other techniques to separate the `Card` class from the `Deck` class. We can refactor the factory function to be a method of `Deck`. We can also make the class names a separate binding via class-level attributes or even initialization method parameters.

Here's an example that avoids a factory function by using more complex bindings in the initialization method:

```
class Deck2( list ):
    def __init__( self, size=1,
        random=random.Random(),
        ace_class=AceCard, card_class=Card, face_class=FaceCard ):
        super().__init__()
        self.rng= random
        for d in range(size):
            for s in Suits:
                cards =  ([ace_class(1, s)]
                + [ card_class(r, s) for r in range(2, 12) ]
                + [ face_class(r, s) for r in range(12, 14) ] )
                super().extend( cards )
        self.rng.shuffle( self )
```

While this initialization is wordy, the `Deck` class isn't intimately bound to the `Card` class hierarchy or a specific, random number generator. For testing purposes, we can provide a random number generator that has a known seed. We can also replace the various `Card` class definitions with other classes (such as `tuple`) that can simplify our testing.

In the next section, we'll focus on another variation of the `Deck` class. This will use the `card()` factory function. That factory function encapsulates the `Card` hierarchy bindings and the rules for separating card classes by rank into a single, testable location.

Creating simple unit tests

We'll create some simple unit tests of the Card class hierarchy and the card() factory function.

As the Card classes are so simple, there's no reason for overly sophisticated testing. It's always possible to err on the side of needless complication. An *unthinking* slog through a test-driven development process can make it seem as though we need to write a fairly large number of not very interesting unit tests for a class that only has a few attributes and methods.

It's important to understand that test-driven development is *advice*, not a natural law such as the conservation of mass. Nor is it a ritual that must be followed without thinking.

There are several schools of thought on naming test methods. We'll emphasize a style of naming that includes describing a test condition and expected results. Here are three variations on this theme:

- We can use a two-part name separated by _should_ such as StateUnderTest_should_ExpectedBehavior. We summarize the state and the response. We'll focus on names of this form.
- We can use a two-part name with when_, and _should_ such as when_StateUnderTest_should_ExpectedBehavior. We still summarize the state and response, but we provide a little more syntax.
- We can use a three-part name, UnitOfWork_StateUnderTest_ExpectedBehavior. This incorporates the unit under test, which may be helpful for reading test output logs.

For more information, read http://osherove.com/blog/2005/4/3/naming-standards-for-unit-tests.html.

It's possible to configure the unittest module to use different patterns for discovering test methods. We could change it to look for when_. To keep things simple, we'll rely on the built-in pattern of having test method names begin with test.

This, for example, is a test of the Card class:

```
class TestCard( unittest.TestCase ):
    def setUp( self ):
        self.three_clubs= Card( 3, '♣' )
    def test_should_returnStr( self ):
        self.assertEqual( "3♣", str(self.three_clubs) )
    def test_should_getAttrValues( self ):
        self.assertEqual( 3, self.three_clubs.rank )
        self.assertEqual( "♣", self.three_clubs.suit )
```

```
        self.assertEqual( 3, self.three_clubs.hard )
        self.assertEqual( 3, self.three_clubs.soft )
```

We defined a test `setUp()` method that creates an object of the class that is under test. We also defined two tests on this object. As there's no real interaction here, there's no *state under test* in the test names: they're simple universal behaviors that should always work.

Some ask if this kind of test is excessive because there's more test than application code. The answer is *no*; this is not excessive. There's no law that says that there should be more application code than test code. Indeed, it doesn't make sense to compare the volumes of test with application code. Most importantly, even a tiny class definition can still have bugs.

Simply testing the values of attributes doesn't seem to test the processing in this class. There are two perspectives on testing attribute values, as shown in this example:

- The **black box** perspective means that we disregard the implementation. In this case, we need to test all of the attributes. The attributes could, for example, be properties, and they must be tested.
- The **white box** perspective means that we can examine the implementation details. When performing this style of testing, we can be a little more circumspect in deciding which attributes we test. The `suit` attribute, for example, doesn't deserve much testing. The `hard` and `soft` attributes, however, do require testing.

For more information, see `http://en.wikipedia.org/wiki/White-box_testing` and `http://en.wikipedia.org/wiki/Black-box_testing`.

Of course, we need to test the rest of the `Card` class hierarchy. We'll just show you the `AceCard` test case. The `FaceCard` test case should be clear after this example:

```
class TestAceCard( unittest.TestCase ):
    def setUp( self ):
        self.ace_spades= AceCard( 1, '♠' )
    def test_should_returnStr( self ):
        self.assertEqual( "A♠", str(self.ace_spades) )
    def test_should_getAttrValues( self ):
        self.assertEqual( 1, self.ace_spades.rank )
        self.assertEqual( "♠", self.ace_spades.suit )
        self.assertEqual( 1, self.ace_spades.hard )
        self.assertEqual( 11, self.ace_spades.soft )
```

This test case also sets up a particular `Card` instance so that we can test the string output. It checks the various attributes of this fixed card.

Creating a test suite

It is often helpful to formally define a test suite. The `unittest` package is capable of discovering tests by default. When aggregating tests from multiple test modules, it's sometimes better to create a test suite in every test module. If each module defines a `suite()` function, we can replace test discovery with importing the `suite()` functions from each module. Also, if we customize `TestRunner`, we must use a suite. We can execute our tests as follows:

```
def suite2():
    s= unittest.TestSuite()
    load_from= unittest.defaultTestLoader.loadTestsFromTestCase
    s.addTests( load_from(TestCard) )
    s.addTests( load_from(TestAceCard) )
    s.addTests( load_from(TestFaceCard) )
    return s
```

We built a suite from our three `TestCases` class definitions and then provided that suite to a `unittest.TextTestRunner()` instance. We used the default `TestLoader` in `unittest`. This `TestLoader` examines a `TestCase` class to locate all the test methods. The value of `TestLoader.testMethodPrefix` is `test`, which is how test methods are identified within a class. Each method name is used by the loader to create a separate test object.

Using `TestLoader` to build test instances from appropriately named methods of `TestCase` is one of the two ways to use `TestCases`. In a later section, we'll look at creating instances of `TestCase` manually; we won't rely on `TestLoader` for these examples. We can run this suite like the following code:

```
if __name__ == "__main__":
    t= unittest.TextTestRunner()
    t.run( suite2() )
```

We'll see output like the following code:

```
...F.F
======================================================================
FAIL: test_should_returnStr (__main__.TestAceCard)
----------------------------------------------------------------------
Traceback (most recent call last):
  File "p3_c15.py", line 80, in test_should_returnStr
    self.assertEqual( "A♠", str(self.ace_spades) )
AssertionError: 'A♠' != '1♠'
- A♠
+ 1♠
```

```
======================================================================
FAIL: test_should_returnStr (__main__.TestFaceCard)
----------------------------------------------------------------------
Traceback (most recent call last):
  File "p3_c15.py", line 91, in test_should_returnStr
    self.assertEqual( "Q♥", str(self.queen_hearts) )
AssertionError: 'Q♥' != '12♥'
- Q♥
+ 12♥


----------------------------------------------------------------------
Ran 6 tests in 0.001s

FAILED (failures=2)
```

The `TestLoader` class created two tests from each `TestCase` class. This gives us a total of six tests. The test names are the method names that begin with `test`.

Clearly, we have a problem. Our tests provide an expected result that our class definitions don't meet. We've got more development work to do for the `Card` classes in order to pass this simple suite of unit tests. The fix should be clear and we'll leave it as an exercise for the reader.

Including edge and corner cases

When we move to testing the `Deck` class as a whole, we'll need to have some things confirmed: that it produces all of the required `Cards` class, and that it actually shuffles properly. We don't really need to test that it deals properly because we're depending on the `list` and `list.pop()` method; as these are first-class parts of Python, they don't require additional testing.

We'd like to test the `Deck` class construction and shuffling, independently of any specific `Card` class hierarchy. As noted previously, we can use a factory function to make the two `Deck` and `Card` definitions independent. Introducing a factory function introduces yet more testing. Not a bad thing, considering the bugs previously revealed in the `Card` class hierarchy.

Here's a test of the factory function:

```
class TestCardFactory( unittest.TestCase ):
    def test_rank1_should_createAceCard( self ):
        c = card( 1, '♣' )
        self.assertIsInstance( c, AceCard )
    def test_rank2_should_createCard( self ):
```

```
        c = card( 2, '♦' )
        self.assertIsInstance( c, Card )
    def test_rank10_should_createCard( self ):
        c = card( 10, '♥' )
        self.assertIsInstance( c, Card )
    def test_rank10_should_createFaceCard( self ):
        c = card( 11, '♠' )
        self.assertIsInstance( c, Card )
    def test_rank13_should_createFaceCard( self ):
        c = card( 13, '♣' )
        self.assertIsInstance( c, Card )
    def test_otherRank_should_exception( self ):
        with self.assertRaises( LogicError ):
            c = card(14, '♦')
        with self.assertRaises( LogicError ):
            c = card(0, '♦')
```

We didn't test all 13 ranks, as 2 through 10 should all be identical. Instead, we followed this advice from *Boris Beizer*:

> "*Bugs lurk in corners and congregate at boundaries.*"

The test cases involve the edge values for each card range. Consequently, we have test cases for the values 1, 2, 10, 11, and 13, as well as illegal values of 0 and 14. We bracketed each range with the least value, the maximum value, one below the least value, and one above the maximum value.

When this is run, there will be problems reported by this test case too. One of the biggest problems will be an undefined exception, `LogicError`. This is simply a subclass of `Exception` that defines that the exception still isn't enough to get the test case to pass. The rest of the fix is left as an exercise for the reader.

Mocking dependencies for testing

In order to test `Deck`, we have two choices to handle the dependencies:

- **Mocking**: We can create a mock (or stand-in) class for the `Card` class and a mock `card()` factory function that produces the mock class. The advantage of using mock objects is that we create real confidence that the unit under test is free from workarounds in one class; this makes up for bugs in another class. A rare potential disadvantage is that we may have to debug the behavior of a super-complex mock class to be sure it's a valid stand-in for a real class.

- **Integrating**: If we have a degree of trust that the `Card` class hierarchy works, and the `card()` factory function works, we can leverage these to test `Deck`. This strays from the high road of pure unit testing, in which all dependencies are excised for test purposes. It can work out well in practice, however, as a class that passes all its unit tests can be as trustworthy as a mock class. In the cases of very complex, stateful APIs, an application class may be more trustworthy than a mock. The disadvantage of this is that a broken foundational class will cause a large number of testing failures in all the classes that depend on it. Also, it's difficult to make detailed tests of API conformance with non-mock classes. Mock classes can track the call history, making it possible to track the number of times it was called and the arguments used.

The `unittest` package includes the `unittest.mock` module that can be used to patch the existing classes for test purposes. It can also be used to provide complete mock class definitions.

When we design a class, we must consider the dependencies that must be mocked for unit testing. In the case of `Deck`, we have three dependencies to mock:

- **The Card class**: This class is so simple that we could create a mock for this class without basing it on an existing implementation. As the `Deck` class behavior doesn't depend on any specific feature of `Card`, our mock object can be simple.
- **The card() factory**: This function needs to be replaced with a mock that we can use to determine if `Deck` makes proper calls to this function.
- **The random.Random.shuffle() method**: To determine if the method was called with proper argument values, we can provide a mock that will track usage rather than actually doing any shuffling.

Here's a version of `Deck` that uses the `card()` factory function:

```
class Deck3( list ):
    def __init__( self, size=1,
        random=random.Random(),
        card_factory=card ):
        super().__init__()
        self.rng= random
        for d in range(size):
            super().extend(
                card_factory(r,s) for r in range(1,13) for s in Suits
)
        self.rng.shuffle( self )
    def deal( self ):
```

```
        try:
            return self.pop(0)
        except IndexError:
            raise DeckEmpty()
```

This definition has two dependencies that are specifically called out as arguments to the `__init__()` method. It requires a random number generator, `random`, and a card factory, `card_factory`. It has suitable default values so that it can be used in an application very simply. It can also be tested by providing mock objects instead of the default objects.

We've included a `deal()` method that makes a change to the object by popping a card. If the deck is empty, the `deal()` method will raise a `DeckEmpty` exception.

Here's a test case to show you that the deck is built properly:

```
import unittest
import unittest.mock

class TestDeckBuid( unittest.TestCase ):
    def setUp( self ):
        self.test_card= unittest.mock.Mock( return_value=unittest.
mock.sentinel )
        self.test_rng= random.Random()
        self.test_rng.shuffle= unittest.mock.Mock( return_value=None )
    def test_deck_1_should_build(self):
        d= Deck3( size=1, random=self.test_rng, card_factory= self.
test_card )
        self.assertEqual( 52*[unittest.mock.sentinel], d )
        self.test_rng.shuffle.assert_called_with( d )
        self.assertEqual( 52, len(self.test_card.call_args_list) )
        expected = [
            unittest.mock.call(r,s)
                for r in range(1,14)
                    for s in ('♣', '♦', '♥', '♠') ]
        self.assertEqual( expected, self.test_card.call_args_list )
```

We created two mocks in the `setUp()` method of this test case. The mock card factory function, `test_card`, is a `Mock` function. The defined return value is a `mock.sentinel` object instead of a `Card` instance. The sentinel is a unique object that allows us to confirm that the right number of instances was created. It's distinct from all other Python objects, so we can distinguish functions without proper `return` statements that return `None`.

We created an instance of the `random.Random()` generator, but we replaced the `shuffle()` method with a mock function that returns `None`. This provides us with an appropriate return value for the method and allows us to determine that the `shuffle()` method was called with the proper argument values.

Our test creates a `Deck` class with our two mock objects. We can then make a number of assertions about this `Deck` instance, `d`:

- 52 objects were created. These are expected to be 52 copies of `mock.sentinel`, showing us that only the factory function was used to create objects.
- The `shuffle()` method was called with the `Deck` instance as the argument. This shows us how a mock object tracks its calls. We can use `assert_called_with()` to confirm that the argument values were as required when `shuffle()` was called.
- The factory function was called 52 times.
- The factory function was called with a specific list of expected rank and suit values.

There is a small bug in the `Deck` class definition, so this test doesn't pass. The fix is left as an exercise for the reader.

Using more mocks to test more behaviors

The preceding mock objects were used to test how a `Deck` class was built. Having 52 identical sentinels makes it difficult to confirm that a `Deck` deals properly. We'll define a different mock to test the deal feature.

Here's a second test case to ensure that the `Deck` class deals properly:

```
class TestDeckDeal( unittest.TestCase ):
    def setUp( self ):
        self.test_card= unittest.mock.Mock( side_effect=range(52) )
        self.test_rng= random.Random()
        self.test_rng.shuffle= unittest.mock.Mock( return_value=None )
    def test_deck_1_should_deal( self ):
        d= Deck3( size=1, random=self.test_rng, card_factory= self.
test_card )
        dealt = []
        for c in range(52):
            c= d.deal()
            dealt.append(c)
        self.assertEqual( dealt, list(range(52)) )
```

```
    def test_empty_deck_should_exception( self ):
        d= Deck3( size=1, random=self.test_rng, card_factory= self.
test_card )
        for c in range(52):
            c= d.deal()
        self.assertRaises( DeckEmpty, d.deal )
```

This mock for the card factory function uses the `side_effect` argument to `Mock()`. When provided with an iterable, this returns another value of the iterable each time it's called.

We mocked the `shuffle()` method to be sure that the cards aren't actually rearranged. We want them to stay in their original order so that our tests have a predictable expected value.

The first test (`test_deck_1_should_deal`) accumulates the results of dealing 52 cards into a variable, `dealt`. It then asserts that this variable has the 52 expected values from the original mock card factory.

The second test (`test_empty_deck_should_exception`) deals all of the cards from a `Deck` instance. However, it makes one more API request. The assertion is that the `Deck.deal()` method will raise the proper exception after dealing all of the cards.

Because of the relative simplicity of the `Deck` class, it's possible to combine both `TestDeckBuild` and `TestDeckDeal` into a single, more sophisticated mock. While that's possible with this example, it's neither essential, nor necessarily desirable to refactor the test cases to make them simpler. Indeed, too much simplification of tests may miss out on API features.

Using doctest to define test cases

The `doctest` module provides us with a simpler form of testing than the `unittest` module. There are many cases where a simple interaction can be shown in the docstring and the test can be automated via `doctest`. This will combine the documentation and test cases into one tidy package.

The `doctest` cases are written into the docstring for a module, class, method, or function. A `doctest` case shows us the interactive Python prompt `>>>`, statements and responses. The `doctest` module contains an application that looks for these examples in docstrings. It runs the given examples and compares the expected results shown in the docstrings with the actual outputs.

For larger and more complex class definitions, this can be challenging. In some cases, we may find that simple, printable results are difficult to work with, and we need more sophisticated comparisons to be made available from `unittest`.

With careful design of an API, we can create a class that can be used interactively. If it can be used interactively, then a `doctest` example can be built from that interaction.

Indeed, two attributes of a well-designed class are that it can be used interactively and it has `doctest` examples in the documentation strings. Many built-in modules contain `doctest` examples of the API. Many other packages that we might choose to download will also include `doctest` examples.

With a simple function, we can provide documentation such as the following:

```
def ackermann( m, n ):
    """Ackermann's Function
    ackermann( m, n ) -> 2↑^{m-2}(n+3) - 3

    See http://en.wikipedia.org/wiki/Ackermann_function and
    http://en.wikipedia.org/wiki/Knuth%27s_up-arrow_notation.

    >>> from p3_c15 import ackermann
    >>> ackermann(2,4)
    11
    >>> ackermann(0,4)
    5
    >>> ackermann(1,0)
    2
    >>> ackermann(1,1)
    3

    """
    if m == 0: return n+1
    elif m > 0 and n == 0: return ackermann( m-1, 1 )
    elif m > 0 and n > 0: return ackermann( m-1, ackermann( m, n-1 ) )
```

We've defined a version of Ackermann's function that includes docstring comments that include five sample responses from interactive Python. The first sample output is the `import` statement, which should produce no output. The other four sample outputs show us the different values of the function.

In this case, the results are all correct. There's no hidden bug left as an exercise for the reader. We can run these tests with the `doctest` module. When run as a program, the command-line argument is the file that should be tested. The `doctest` program locates all docstrings and looks for interactive Python examples in those strings. It's important to note that the `doctest` documentation provides details on the regular expressions used to locate the strings. In our example, we added a hard-to-see blank line after the last `doctest` example to help the `doctest` parser.

We can run `doctest` from the command line:

```
python3.3 -m doctest p3_c15.py
```

If everything is correct, this is silent. We can make it show us some details by adding the `-v` option:

```
python3.3 -m doctest -v p3_c15.py
```

This will provide us with the details of each docstring parsed and each test case gleaned from the docstrings.

This will show us the various classes, functions, and methods without any tests as well as the components that have tests. This provides some confirmation that our tests were properly formatted in the docstrings.

In some cases, we have output that will not match interactive Python easily. In these cases, we may need to supplement the docstring with some annotations that modify how the test cases and expected results are parsed.

There's a special comment string that we can use for more complex outputs. We can append any one of the following two commands to enable (or disable) the various kinds of directives that are available. The following is the first command:

```
# doctest: +DIRECTIVE
```

The following is the second command:

```
# doctest: -DIRECTIVE
```

There are a dozen modifications that we can make to how the expected results are handled. Most of them are rare situations regarding spacing and how actual and expected values should be compared.

The `doctest` documentation emphasizes on the **Exact Match Principle**:

"doctest is serious about requiring exact matches in expected output."

If even a single character doesn't match, the test fails. You'll need to build flexibility into some of the expected outputs. If building in flexibility gets too complex, it's a hint that `unittest` might be a better choice.

Here are some specific situations where expected and actual values of `doctest` won't match easily:

- The dictionary key order is not guaranteed by Python. Use a construct such as `sorted(some_dict.items())` instead of `some_dict`.
- The method functions `id()` and `repr()` involve physical memory addresses; Python makes no guarantee that they will be consistent. If you show `id()` or `repr()`, use the `#doctest: +ELLIPSIS` directive and replace the ID or address with `...` in the sample output.
- Floating-point results may not be consistent across platforms. Always show floating-point numbers with formatting or rounding to reduce the number of digits to digits that are meaningful. Use `"{:.4f}".format(value)` or `round(value,4)` to ensure that insignificant digits are ignored.
- A set order is not guaranteed by Python. Use a construct such as `sorted(some_set)` instead of `some_set`.
- The current date or time, of course, cannot be used, as that won't be consistent. A test that involves time or date needs to force a specific date or time, generally by mocking `time` or `datetime`.
- Operating system details such as file sizes or timestamps are likely to vary and should not be used without ellipsis. Sometimes, it's possible to include a useful setup or teardown in the `doctest` script to manage OS resources. In other cases, mocking the `os` module is helpful.

These considerations mean that our `doctest` module may contain some additional processing that's not simply a part of the API. We may have done something such as this at the interactive Python prompt:

```
>>> sum(values)/len(values)
3.142857142857143
```

This shows us the full output from a particular implementation. We can't simply copy-and-paste this into a docstring; the floating-point results might differ. We'll need to do something resembling the following code:

```
>>> round(sum(values)/len(values),4)
3.1429
```

This is rounded to a value that should not vary between implementations.

Combining doctest and unittest

There's a hook in the `doctest` module that will create a proper `unittest.TestSuite` from docstring comments. This allows us to use both `doctest` and `unittest` in a large application.

What we'll do is create an instance of `doctest.DocTestSuite()`. This will build a suite from a module's docstrings. If we don't specify a module, the module that is currently running is used to build the suite. We can use a module such as the following one:

```
import doctest
suite5= doctest.DocTestSuite()
t= unittest.TextTestRunner(verbosity=2)
t.run( suite5 )
```

We built a suite, `suite5`, from the `doctest` strings in the current module. We used `unittest TextTestRunner` on this suite. As an alternative, we can combine the `doctest` suite with other `TestCases` to create a larger, more complete suite.

Creating a more complete test package

For larger applications, each application module can have a parallel module that includes `TestCases` for that module. This can form two parallel package structures: a `src` structure with the application module and a `test` structure with the test modules. Here are two parallel directory trees that show us the collections of modules:

```
src
    __init__.py
    __main__.py
    module1.py
    module2.py
    setup.py
test
    __init__.py
    module1.py
    module2.py
    all.py
```

Clearly, the parallelism isn't exact. We don't usually have an automated unit test for `setup.py`. A well-designed `__main__.py` may not require a separate unit test, as it shouldn't have much code in it. We'll look at some ways to design `__main__.py` in *Chapter 16, Coping with the Command Line*.

We can create a top-level `test/all.py` module with a body that builds all of the tests into a single suite:

```
import module1
import module2
import unittest
import doctest
all_tests= unittest.TestSuite()
for mod in module1, module2:
    all_tests.addTests( mod.suite() )
    all_tests.addTests( doctest.DocTestSuite(mod) )
t= unittest.TextTestRunner()
t.run( all_tests )
```

We built a single suite, `all_tests`, from the suites within the other test modules. This provides us with a handy script that will run all of the tests that are available as part of the distribution.

There are ways to use the test discovery features of the `unittest` module to do this as well. We perform package-wide testing from the command line, with something resembling the following code:

```
python3.3 -m unittest test/*.py
```

This will use the default test discovery features of `unittest` to locate `TestCases` in the given files. This has the disadvantage of relying on shell script features rather than pure Python features. The wild-card file specification can sometimes make development more complex because incomplete modules might get tested.

Using setup and teardown

There are three levels of setup and teardown available for the `unittest` modules. Here are the three different kinds of testing scopes: method, class, and module.

- **Test case setUp() and tearDown() methods**: These methods ensure that each individual test method within a `TestCase` class has had a proper setup and teardown. Often, we'll use the `setUp()` method to create the unit objects and any mock objects that are required. We don't want to do something costly such as creating whole databases, as these methods are used before and after each test method.

- **Test case setUpClass() and tearDownClass() methods**: These methods perform a one-time setup (and teardown) around all the tests in a `TestCase` class. These methods bracket the sequence of `setUp()-testMethod()-tearDown()` for each method. This can be a good place to create and destroy the test data or a test schema inside a database.
- **Module setUpModule() and tearDownModule() functions**: These standalone functions provide us with a one-time setup before all of the `TestCase` classes in a module. This is a good place to create and destroy a test database as a whole before running a series of `TestCase` classes.

We rarely need to define all of these `setUp()` and `tearDown()` methods. There are several testing scenarios that are going to be part of our design for testability. The essential difference between these scenarios is the degree of integration involved. As noted previously, we have three tiers in our testing hierarchy: isolated unit tests, integration tests, and overall application tests. There are several ways in which these tiers of testing work with the various setup and teardown features:

- **No integration – no dependencies**: Some classes or functions have no external dependencies; they don't rely on files, devices, other processes, or other hosts. Other classes have some external resources that can be mocked. When the cost and complexity of the `TestCase.setUp()` method are small, we can create the needed objects there. If the mock objects are particularly complex, a class-level `TestCase.setUpClass()` might be more appropriate to amortize the cost of recreating the mock objects over several test methods.
- **Internal Integration – some dependencies**: Automated integration testing among classes or modules often involves more complex setup situations. We may have a complex class-level `setUpClass()` or even a module-level `setUpModule()` to prepare an environment for integration testing. When working with the database access layers in *Chapter 10, Storing and Retrieving Objects via Shelve*, and *Chapter 11, Storing and Retrieving Objects via SQLite*, we often perform integration testing that includes our class definitions as well as our access layer. This may involve seeding a test database or shelf with appropriate data for the tests.
- **External Integration**: We may perform automated integration testing with larger and more complex pieces of an application. In these cases, we may need to spawn external processes or create databases and seed them with data. In this case, we may have `setUpModule()` to prepare an empty database for use by all of the `TestCase` classes in a module. When working with RESTful web services in *Chapter 12, Transmitting and Sharing Objects*, or testing **Programming In The Large (PITL)** in *Chapter 17, The Module and Package Design*, this approach could be helpful.

Note that the concept of unit testing does not define what the unit under test is. The *unit* can be a class, a module, a package, or even an integrated collection of software components. It merely needs to be isolated from its environment to be a unit under test.

When designing automated integration tests, it's important to be aware of the components to be tested. We don't need to test Python libraries; they have their own tests. Similarly, we don't need to test the OS. An integration test must focus on testing the code we wrote, not the code we downloaded and installed.

Using setup and teardown with OS resources

In many cases, a test case may require a particular OS environment. When working with external resources such as files, directories, or processes, we may need to create or initialize them before a test. We may also need to remove the resources before a test. We may need to tear down these resources at the end of the test.

Let's assume that we have a function, `rounds_final()` that is supposed to process a given file. We need to test the function's behavior in the rare case that the file doesn't exist. It's common to see `TestCases` with a structure such as the following one:

```
import os
class Test_Missing( unittest.TestCase ):
    def setUp( self ):
        try:
            os.remove( "p3_c15_sample.csv" )
        except OSError as e:
            pass
    def test_missingFile_should_returnDefault( self ):
        self.assertRaises( FileNotFoundError, rounds_final,  "p3_c15_
sample.csv", )
```

We have to handle the possible exception of trying to remove a file that doesn't exist in the first place. This test case has a `setUp()` method that ensures that the required file is missing. Once `setuUp()` ensures that the file is truly gone, we can execute the `rounds_final()` function with an argument of the missing file, "`p3_c15_sample.csv`". We expect this to raise a `FileNotFoundError` error.

Note that raising `FileNotFoundError` is a default behavior of Python's `open()` method. This may not require testing at all. This leads to an important question: *why test a built-in feature*? If we're performing black-box testing, we need to exercise all features of the external interface, including the expected default behaviors. If we're performing white-box testing, we may need to test the exception-handling `try:` statement within the body of the `rounds_final()` function.

The `p3_c15_sample.csv` filename is repeated within the body of the test. Some people feel that the DRY rule should apply even to the test code. There's a limit to how much of this kind of optimization is valuable while writing tests. Here's the suggestion:

> It's okay for test code to be brittle. If a small change to the application leads to test failures, this really is a good thing. Tests should value simplicity and clarity, not robustness, and reliability.

Using setup and teardown with databases

When working with a database and ORM layer, we often have to create test databases, files, directories, or server processes. We may need to tear down a test database after the tests pass, to be sure that the other tests can run. We may not want to tear down a database after failed tests; we may need to leave the database alone so that we can examine the resulting rows to diagnose the test failures.

It's important to manage the scope of testing in a complex, multilayered architecture. Looking back at *Chapter 11, Storing and Retrieving Objects via SQLite*, we don't need to specifically test the SQLAlchemy ORM layer or the SQLite database. These components have their own test procedures outside our application tests. However, because of the way the ORM layer creates database definitions, SQL statements, and Python objects from our code, we can't easily mock SQLAlchemy and hope that we've used it properly. We need to test the way our application uses the ORM layer without digressing into testing the ORM layer itself.

One of the more complex test case setup situations will involve creating a database and then populating it with appropriate sample data for the given test. When working with SQL, this can involve running a fairly complex script of SQL DDL to create the necessary tables and then another script of SQL DML to populate those tables. The associated teardown will be another complex SQL DDL script.

This kind of test case can become long-winded, so we'll break it into three sections: a useful function to create a database and schema, the `setUpClass()` method, and the rest of the unit test.

Here's the create-database function:

```
from p2_c11 import Base, Blog, Post, Tag, assoc_post_tag
import datetime

import sqlalchemy.exc
from sqlalchemy import create_engine

def build_test_db( name='sqlite:///./p3_c15_blog.db' ):
```

```
        engine = create_engine(name, echo=True)
        Base.metadata.drop_all(engine)
        Base.metadata.create_all(engine)
        return engine
```

This builds a fresh database by dropping all of the tables associated with the ORM classes and recreating the tables. The idea is to ensure a fresh, empty database that conforms to the current design, no matter how much that design has changed since the last time the unit tests were run.

In this example, we built a SQLite database using a file. We can use the *in-memory* SQLite database feature to make the test run somewhat more quickly. The downside of using an in-memory database is that we have no persistent database file that we can use to debug failed tests.

Here's how we use this in a `TestCase` subclass:

```
from sqlalchemy.orm import sessionmaker
class Test_Blog_Queries( unittest.TestCase ):
    @staticmethod
    def setUpClass():
        engine= build_test_db()
        Test_Blog_Queries.Session = sessionmaker(bind=engine)
        session= Test_Blog_Queries.Session()

        tag_rr= Tag( phrase="#RedRanger" )
        session.add( tag_rr )
        tag_w42= Tag( phrase="#Whitby42" )
        session.add( tag_w42 )
        tag_icw= Tag( phrase="#ICW" )
        session.add( tag_icw )
        tag_mis= Tag( phrase="#Mistakes" )
        session.add( tag_mis )

        blog1= Blog( title="Travel 2013" )
        session.add( blog1 )
        b1p1= Post( date=datetime.datetime(2013,11,14,17,25),
            title="Hard Aground",
            rst_text="""Some embarrassing revelation.
              Including ☹ and □""",
            blog=blog1,
            tags=[tag_rr, tag_w42, tag_icw],
            )
        session.add(b1p1)
        b1p2= Post( date=datetime.datetime(2013,11,18,15,30),
```

```
            title="Anchor Follies",
            rst_text="""Some witty epigram. Including ☺ and ☀""",
            blog=blog1,
            tags=[tag_rr, tag_w42, tag_mis],
            )
        session.add(b1p2)

        blog2= Blog( title="Travel 2014" )
        session.add( blog2 )
        session.commit()
```

We defined `setUpClass()` so that a database is created before the tests from this class are run. This allows us to define a number of test methods that will share a common database configuration. Once the database has been built, we can create a session and add data.

We've put the session maker object into the class as a class-level attribute, `Test_Blog_Queries.Session = sessionmaker(bind=engine)`. This class-level object can then be used in `setUp()` and individual test methods.

Here is `setUp()` and two of the individual test methods:

```
    def setUp( self ):
        self.session= Test_Blog_Queries.Session()

    def test_query_eqTitle_should_return1Blog( self ):
        results= self.session.query( Blog ).filter(
            Blog.title == "Travel 2013" ).all()
        self.assertEqual( 1, len(results) )
        self.assertEqual( 2, len(results[0].entries) )

    def test_query_likeTitle_should_return2Blog( self ):
        results= self.session.query( Blog ).filter(
            Blog.title.like("Travel %") ).all()
        self.assertEqual( 2, len(results) )
```

The `setUp()` method creates a new, empty session object. This will ensure that every query must generate SQL and fetch data from the database.

The `query_eqTitle_should_return1Blog()` test will find the requested `Blog` instance and navigate to the `Post` instances via the `entries` relationship. The `filter()` portion of the request doesn't really test our application definitions; it exercises SQLAlchemy and SQLite. The `results[0].entries` test in the final assertion is a meaningful test of our class definitions.

The `query_likeTitle_should_return2Blog()` test is almost entirely a test of SQLAlchemy and SQLite. It isn't really making a meaningful use of anything in our application except the presence of an attribute named `title` in `Blog`. These kinds of tests are often left over from creating initial technical spikes. They can help clarify an application API, even if they don't provide much value as a test case.

Here are two more test methods:

```
    def test_query_eqW42_tag_should_return2Post( self ):
        results= self.session.query(Post)\
        .join(assoc_post_tag).join(Tag).filter(
            Tag.phrase == "#Whitby42" ).all()
        self.assertEqual( 2, len(results) )
    def test_query_eqICW_tag_should_return1Post( self ):
        results= self.session.query(Post)\
        .join(assoc_post_tag).join(Tag).filter(
            Tag.phrase == "#ICW" ).all()
        self.assertEqual( 1, len(results) )
        self.assertEqual( "Hard Aground", results[0].title )
        self.assertEqual( "Travel 2013", results[0].blog.title )
        self.assertEqual( set(["#RedRanger", "#Whitby42", "#ICW"]),
set(t.phrase for t in results[0].tags) )
```

The `query_eqW42_tag_should_return2Post()` test performs a more complex query to locate the posts that have a given tag. This exercises a number of relationships defined in the classes.

The `query_eqICW_tag_should_return1Post()` test, similarly, exercises a complex query. It tests the navigation from `Post` to owning `Blog` via `results[0].blog.title`. It also tests navigation from `Post` to an associated collection of `Tags` via `set(t.phrase for t in results[0].tags)`. We must use an explicit `set()` because the order of results in SQL is not guaranteed.

What's important about this `Test_Blog_Queries` subclass of `TestCase` is that it creates a database schema and a specific set of defined rows via the `setUpClass()` method. This kind of test setup is helpful for database applications. It can become rather complex and is often supplemented by loading sample rows from files or JSON documents rather than coding the rows in Python.

The TestCase class hierarchy

Inheritance works among the `TestCase` classes. Ideally, each `TestCase` is unique. Pragmatically, there may be common features among cases. There are three common ways in which `TestCase` classes may overlap:

- **Common setUp()**: We may have some data that is used in multiple `TestCases`. There's no reason to repeat the data. A `TestCase` class that only defines `setUp()` or `tearDown()` with no test methods is legal, but it may lead to a confusing log because there are zero tests involved.
- **Common tearDown()**: It's common to have a common cleanup for tests that involve OS resources. We might need to remove files and directories or kill subprocesses.
- **Common results checking**: For algorithmically complex tests, we may have a results checking method that verifies some properties of a result.

Looking back at *Chapter 3, Attribute Access, Properties, and Descriptors*, for example, consider the `RateTimeDistance` class. This class fills in a missing value in a dictionary based on two other values:

```
class RateTimeDistance( dict ):
    def __init__( self, *args, **kw ):
        super().__init__( *args, **kw )
        self._solve()
    def __getattr__( self, name ):
        return self.get(name,None)
    def __setattr__( self, name, value ):
        self[name]= value
        self._solve()
    def __dir__( self ):
        return list(self.keys())
    def _solve(self):
        if self.rate is not None and self.time is not None:
            self['distance'] = self.rate*self.time
        elif self.rate is not None and self.distance is not None:
            self['time'] = self.distance / self.rate
        elif self.time is not None and self.distance is not None:
            self['rate'] = self.distance / self.time
```

Each unit test method for this can include the following code:

```
self.assertAlmostEqual( object.distance, object.rate * object.time )
```

If we use a number of `TestCase` subclasses, we can inherit this validity check as a separate method:

```
def validate( self, object ):
    self.assertAlmostEqual( object.distance, object.rate * object.time
)
```

This way, each test need only include `self.validate(object)` to be sure that all the tests provide a consistent definition of correctness.

An important feature of the definition of the `unittest` module is that the test cases are proper classes with proper inheritance. We can design the `TestCase` class hierarchy with the same care and attention to detail that we apply to the application classes.

Using externally defined expected results

For some applications, users can articulate processing rules that describe the software's behavior. In other cases, the job of an analyst or a designer transforms the user's desires into procedural descriptions of the software.

In many cases, it's easier for users to provide concrete examples of expected results. For some business-oriented applications, the users may be more comfortable creating a spreadsheet that shows us sample inputs and expected results. Working from user-supplied, concrete sample data can simplify the developing software.

Whenever possible, have real users produce concrete examples of correct results. Creating procedural descriptions or software specifications is remarkably difficult. Creating concrete examples and generalizing from the examples to a software specification is less fraught with complexity and confusion. Further, it plays into a style of development where the test cases drive the development effort. Given a suite of test cases, we have a concrete definition of *done*. Tracking the software development project status leads to asking how many test cases we have today and how many of them pass.

Given a spreadsheet of concrete examples, we need to turn each row into a `TestCase` instance. We can then build a suite from these objects.

For the previous examples in this chapter, we loaded the test cases from a `TestCase`-based class. We used `unittest.defaultTestLoader.loadTestsFromTestCase` to locate all the methods with a name that start with `test`. The loader creates a test object from each method and combines them into a test suite. In effect, each object built by the loader is a discrete object created by invoking the class constructor using the test case name: `SomeTestCase("test_method_name")`. The parameters to the `SomeTestCase__init__()` method will be the method names which were used to define the class. Each method is individually elaborated into a test case.

For this example, we're going to use the other approach to build test case instances. We're going to define a class with a single test and load multiple instances of this `TestCase` class into a suite. When we do this, the `TestCase` class must define only one test and, by default, that method's name should be `runTest()`. We won't be using the loader to create the test objects; we'll be creating them directly from rows of externally supplied data.

Let's take a look at a concrete function that we need to test. This is from *Chapter 3, Attribute Access, Properties, and Descriptors*:

```
from p1_c03 import RateTimeDistance
```

This is a class that eagerly computes a number of attributes when it is initialized. The users of this simple function provided us with some test cases as a spreadsheet, from which we extracted the CSV file. For more information on CSV files, see *Chapter 9, Serializing and Saving – JSON, YAML, Pickle, CSV, and XML*. We need to transform each row into `TestCase`:

```
rate_in,time_in,distance_in,rate_out,time_out,distance_out
2,3,,2,3,6
5,,7,5,1.4,7
,11,13,1.18,11,13
```

Here's the test case that we can use to create test instances from each row of the CSV file:

```
def float_or_none( text ):
    if len(text) == 0: return None
    return float(text)

class Test_RTD( unittest.TestCase ):
    def __init__( self, rate_in,time_in,distance_in,
        rate_out,time_out,distance_out ):
        super().__init__()
        self.args = dict( rate=float_or_none(rate_in),
            time=float_or_none(time_in),
            distance=float_or_none(distance_in) )
        self.result= dict( rate=float_or_none(rate_out),
            time=float_or_none(time_out),
            distance=float_or_none(distance_out) )
    def shortDescription( self ):
        return "{0} -> {1}".format(self.args, self.result)
    def setUp( self ):
        self.rtd= RateTimeDistance( **self.args )
    def runTest( self ):
```

```
        self.assertAlmostEqual( self.rtd.distance, self.rtd.rate*self.
rtd.time )
        self.assertAlmostEqual( self.rtd.rate, self.result['rate'] )
        self.assertAlmostEqual( self.rtd.time, self.result['time'] )
        self.assertAlmostEqual( self.rtd.distance, self.
result['distance'] )
```

The `float_or_none()` function is a common way to handle the CSV source data. It converts the text of a cell to a `float` value or `None`.

The `Test_RTD` class does three things:

- The `__init__()` method parses a row of a spreadsheet into two dictionaries: the input values, `self.args` and the expected output values, `self.result`
- The `setUp()` method creates a `RateTimeDistance` object and provides the input argument values
- The `runTest()` method can simply validate the output by checking the results against the user-supplied values

We also provided you with a `shortDescription()` method that returns a pithy summary of the test. This can help with any debugging. We can build a suite as follows:

```
import csv
def suite9():
    suite= unittest.TestSuite()
    with open("p3_c15_data.csv","r",newline="") as source:
        rdr= csv.DictReader( source )
        for row in rdr:
            suite.addTest( Test_RTD(**row) )
    return suite
```

We opened the CSV file and read each test case row of that file as a `dict` object. If the CSV column titles properly match the expectations of the `Test_RTD.__init__()` method, then each row becomes a test case object and can be added to the suite. If the CSV column titles don't match, we'll have a `KeyError` exception; we'll have to fix the spreadsheet to match the `Test_RTD` class. We run the tests as follows:

```
    t= unittest.TextTestRunner()
    t.run( suite9() )
```

The output looks like this:

```
..F
======================================================================
FAIL: runTest (__main__.Test_RTD)
```

```
{'rate': None, 'distance': 13.0, 'time': 11.0} -> {'rate': 1.18,
'distance': 13.0, 'time': 11.0}
----------------------------------------------------------------------
Traceback (most recent call last):
  File "p3_c15.py", line 504, in runTest
    self.assertAlmostEqual( self.rtd.rate, self.result['rate'] )
AssertionError: 1.1818181818181819 != 1.18 within 7 places

----------------------------------------------------------------------
Ran 3 tests in 0.000s

FAILED (failures=1)
```

The user-supplied data has a small problem; the users provided a value that has been rounded off to only two places. Either the sample data needs to provide more digits, or our test assertions need to cope with the rounding.

Getting users to supply precise example data may not work out well. If the users can't be more precise, then our test assertions need to include some rounding based on the user's input. This can be challenging because of the way spreadsheets display data as if it's a precise decimal value, when it's really a rounded and formatted floating-point approximation. In many cases, a blanket rounding assumption can be used rather than trying to parse the user's intent via reverse-engineering a spreadsheet.

Automated integration or performance testing

We can use the `unittest` package to perform testing that isn't focused on a single, isolated class definition. As noted previously, we can use the `unittest` automation to test a unit that is an integration of multiple components. This kind of testing can only be performed on software that has passed unit tests on isolated components. There's no point in trying to debug a failed integration test when a component's unit test didn't work correctly.

Performance testing can be done at several levels of integration. For a large application, performance testing with the entire build may not be completely helpful. One traditional view is that a program spends 90 percent of its time executing just 10 percent of the available code. Therefore, we don't often need to optimize an entire application; we only need to locate the small fraction of the program that represents the real performance bottleneck.

In some cases, it's clear that we have a data structure that involves a search. We know that removing the search will lead to a tremendous improvement in the performance. As we saw in *Chapter 5, Using Callables and Contexts*, implementing memoization can lead to dramatic performance improvements by avoiding recalculation.

In order to perform proper performance testing, we need to follow a three-step work cycle:

1. Use a combination of design reviews and code profiling to locate the parts of the application that are likely to be a performance problem. Python has two profiling modules in the standard library. Unless there are more complex requirements, `cProfile` will locate the part of the application that requires focus.
2. Create an automated test scenario with `unittest` to demonstrate any actual performance problem. Collect the performance data with `timeit` or `time.perf_counter()`.
3. Optimize the code for the selected test case until the performance is acceptable.

The point is to automate as much as possible and avoid vaguely tweaking things in the hope of an improvement in the performance. Most of the time, a central data structure or algorithm (or both) must be replaced, leading to extensive refactoring. Having automated unit tests makes wholesale refactoring practical.

An awkward situation can arise when a performance test lacks specific pass-fail criteria. It may be necessary to make something *faster* without a concrete definition of *fast enough*. It's always simpler when there are measurable performance objectives; formal, automated testing can be used to assert both that the results are correct and that the time taken to get those results is acceptable.

For performance testing, we might use something like the following code:

```
import unittest
import timeit
class Test_Performance( unittest.TestCase ):
    def test_simpleCalc_shouldbe_fastEnough( self ):
        t= timeit.timeit(
        stmt="""RateTimeDistance( rate=1, time=2 )""",
        setup="""from p1_c03 import RateTimeDistance"""
        )
        print( "Run time", t )
        self.assertLess( t, 10, "run time {0} >= 10".format(t) )
```

This use of `unittest` gives us an automated performance test. As the `timeit` module executes the given statement 1,000,000 times, this should minimize the variability in the measurement from the background work on the computer that does the testing.

In the preceding example, each execution of the RTD constructor is required to take less than 1/100,000 of a second. A million executions should take less than 10 seconds.

Summary

We looked at using `unittest` and `doctest` to create automated unit tests. We also looked at creating a test suite so that collections of tests can be packaged for reuse and aggregation into suites with larger scopes, without relying on the automated test discovery process.

We looked at how to create mock objects so that we can test software units in isolation. We also looked at the various kinds of setup and teardown features. These allow us to write tests with complex initial states or persistent results.

The **FIRST** properties of unit tests fit well with both `doctest` and `unittest`. The FIRST properties are as follows:

- **Fast**: Unless we write egregiously bad tests, the performance of `doctest` and `unitest` should be very fast.
- **Isolated**: The `unittest` package offers us a mock module that we can use to isolate our class definitions. In addition, we can exercise some care in our design to ensure that our components are isolated from each other.
- **Repeatable**: Using `doctest` and `unittest` for automated testing ensures repeatability.
- **Self-validating**: Both `doctest` and `unittest` bind the test results with the test case condition, ensuring that no subjective judgment is involved in testing.
- **Timely**: We can write and run the test cases as soon as we have the skeleton of a class, function, or module. A class whose body has simply `pass` is sufficient to run the test script.

For the purposes of project management, a count of written tests and passed tests is sometimes a very useful status report.

Design considerations and trade-offs

Test cases are a required to be deliverable when creating software. Any feature that is without an automated test might as well not exist. A feature certainly can't be trusted to be correct if there's no test. If it can't be trusted, it shouldn't be used.

The only real trade-off question is whether to use `doctest` or `unittest` or both. For simple programming, `doctest` may be perfectly suitable. For more complex situations, `unittest` will be necessary. For frameworks where the API documentation needs to include examples, a combination works out well.

In some cases, simply creating a module full of `TestCase` class definitions may be sufficient. The `TestLoader` class and test discovery features may be perfectly adequate to locate all of the tests.

More generally, `unittest` involves using `TestLoader` to extract multiple test methods from each `TestCase` subclass. We package the test methods into a single class based on who they can share class-level `setUp()`, and possibly with the `setUpClass()` methods.

We can also create the `TestCase` instances without `TestLoader`. In this case, the default method of `runTest()` is defined to have the test case assertions. We can create a suite from instances of this kind of class.

The most difficult part can be designing for testability. Removing dependencies so that units can be tested independently can sometimes feel like adding to the level of software design complexity. In most cases, the time expended to expose dependencies is time invested in creating more maintainable and more flexible software.

The general rule is this: *an implicit dependency among classes is bad design.*

A testable design has explicit dependencies; these can easily be replaced with mock objects.

Looking forward

The next chapter will look at writing complete applications that are started from the command line. We'll look at ways to handle startup options, environment variables, and configuration files in Python applications.

In *Chapter 17, The Module and Package Design*, we'll expand on application design. We'll add the ability to compose applications into larger applications as well as decompose applications into smaller pieces.

16
Coping With the Command Line

Command-line startup options, environment variables, and configuration files are important to many applications, particularly the implementation of servers. There are a number of ways of dealing with program startup and object creation. We'll look at two issues in this chapter: argument parsing and the overall architecture for an application.

This chapter will extend the configuration file handling from *Chapter 13, Configuration Files and Persistence*, with yet more techniques for command-line programs and the top-level of a server. It will also extend some logging design features from *Chapter 14, The Logging and Warning Modules*.

In the next chapter, we'll extend these principles to continue looking at a kind of architectural design that we'll call *programming in the Large*. We'll use the **Command** design pattern to define software components that can be aggregated without resorting to shell scripts. This is particularly helpful when writing the background processing components used by application servers.

The OS interface and the command line

Generally, the shell starts applications with several pieces of information that constitute the OS API:

- The shell provides each application its collection of environment variables. In Python, these are accessed through `os.environ`.
- The shell prepares three standard files. In Python, these are mapped to `sys.stdin`, `sys.stdout`, and `sys.stderr`. There are some other modules such as `fileinput` that can provide access to `sys.stdin`.

- The command line is parsed by the shell into words. Parts of the command line are available in `sys.argv`. Python will provide some of the original command line; we'll look at the details in the following sections. For POSIX operating systems, the shell may replace shell environment variables and glob wildcard filenames. In Windows, the simple `cmd.exe` shell will not glob filenames for us.
- The OS also maintains context settings such as the current working directory, user ID, and group. These are available through the `os` module. They aren't provided as arguments on the command line.

The OS expects an application to provide a numeric status code when terminating. If we want to return a specific numeric code, we can use `sys.exit()` in our applications. Python will return a zero if our program is terminated normally.

The shell's operation is an important part of this OS API. Given a line of input, the shell performs a number of substitutions, depending on the (rather complex) quoting rules and substitution options. It then parses the resulting line into space-delimited words. The first word must be either a built-in shell command (such as `cd` or `set`), or it must be the name of a file. The shell searches its defined `PATH` for this file.

The file named on the first word of a command must have `execute (x)` permission. The shell command, `chmod +x somefile.py`, marks a file as executable. A filename that matches but isn't executable gets an *OS Permission Denied error*.

The first bytes of an executable file have a magic number that is used by the shell to decide how to execute that file. Some magic numbers indicate that the file is a binary executable; the shell can fork a subshell and execute it. Other magic numbers, specifically `b'#!'`, indicate that the file is properly a text script and requires an interpreter. The rest of the first line of this kind of file is the name of the interpreter.

We often use a line like this:

```
#!/usr/bin/env python3.3
```

If a Python file has permission to execute, and has this as the first line, then the shell will run the `env` program. The `env` program's argument (`python3.3`) will cause it to set up an environment and run the Python3.3 program with the Python file as the first positional argument.

In effect, the conceptual sequence of steps from the OS shell via an executable script to Python looks like the following steps:

1. The shell parses the `ourapp.py -s someinput.csv` line. The first word is `ourapp.py`. This file is on the shell's `PATH` and has the `x` executable permission. The shell opens the file and finds the `#!` bytes. The shell reads the rest of this line and finds a new command: `/usr/bin/env python3.3`
2. The shell parses the new `/usr/bin/env` command, which is a binary executable. So, the shell starts this program. This program, in turn, starts `python3.3`. The sequence of words from the original command line is provided to Python as part of the OS API.
3. Python will parse this sequence of words from the original command line to extract any options that are prior to the first argument. These first options are used by Python. The first argument is the Python filename to be run. This filename argument and all of the remaining words on the line will be saved separately in `sys.argv`.
4. Python does its normal startup based on the options that have been found. Depending on the `-s` option, the `site` module may be used to setup the import path, `sys.path`. If we used the `-m` option, Python will use the `runpy` module to start our application. The given script files may be (re)compiled to byte code.
5. Our application can make use of `sys.argv` to parse options and arguments with the `argparse` module. Our application can use environment variables in `os.environ`. It can also parse configuration files; see *Chapter 13, Configuration Files and Persistence*, for more on this topic.

On lacking a filename, the Python interpreter will read from standard input. If the standard input is a console (called a TTY in Linux parlance), then Python will enter **Read-Execute-Print Loop (REPL)** and display the `>>>` prompt. While we use this mode as developers, we don't generally make use of this mode for a finished application.

Another possibility is that standard input is a redirected file; for example, `python <some_file` or `some_app | python`. Both are valid but potentially confusing.

Arguments and options

In order to run programs, the shell parses a command line into words. This sequence of words is made available to all programs that are started. Generally, the first word of this sequence is the shell's understanding of the command. The remaining words on the command line are understood to be options and arguments.

There are a number of guidelines to handle options and arguments. The essential rules are these:

- Options come first. They are preceded by `-` or `--`. There are two formats: `-letter` and `--word`. There are two species of options: options with no arguments and options with arguments. Examples of options without arguments are to use `-V` to show a version or use `--version` to show the version. An examples of options with arguments is `-m module`, where the `-m` option must be followed by a module name.
- Short format (single-letter) options with no option arguments can be grouped behind a single `-`. We might use `-bqv` to combine the `-b -q -v` options for convenience.
- Arguments come last. They don't have a leading `-` or `--`. There are two common kinds of arguments:
    - For positional arguments, the position is semantically significant. We might have two positional arguments: an input filename and an output filename. The order matters because the output file will be modified. When files will be overridden, simply distinguishing by position needs to be done carefully to prevent confusion.
    - A list of arguments, all of which are semantically equivalent. We might have arguments that are all the names of input files. This fits nicely with the way the shell performs filename globbing. When we say `process.py *.html`, the `*.html` command is expanded by the shell to filenames that become the positional parameters. (This doesn't work in Windows, so the `glob` module must be used.)

There are still more details. For more information on command-line options, see `http://pubs.opengroup.org/onlinepubs/9699919799/basedefs/V1_chap12.html#tag_12_02`. The Python command line has 12 or so options that can control some details of Python's behavior. See the *Python Setup and Usage* document for more information on what these options are. The positional argument to the Python command is the name of the script to be run; this will be our application's top-most file.

Parsing the command line with argparse

The general approach to using `argparse` involves four steps.

1. Create `ArgumentParser`. We can provide you with overall information about the command-line interface here. This might include a description, format changes for the displayed options and arguments, and whether or not `-h` is the "help" option. Generally, we only need to provide the description; the rest of the options have sensible defaults.

2. Define the command-line options and arguments. This is done by adding arguments with the `ArgumentParser.add_argument()` method function.
3. Parse the `sys.argv` command line to create a namespace object that details the options, option arguments and overall command-line arguments.
4. Use the resulting namespace object to configure the application and process the arguments. There are a number of alternative approaches to handle this gracefully. It may involve parsing configuration files, as well as command-line options. We'll look at several designs.

An important feature of `argparse` is that it provides us with a unified view of options and arguments. The principle difference between the two is the number of times they can occur. Options are—well—optional and can occur zero or one time. Arguments generally occur one or more times.

We can create a parser as easily as the following code:

```
parser = argparse.ArgumentParser( description="Simulate Blackjack" )
```

We provided the description, as there's no good default value for that. Here are some common patterns to define the command-line API for an application:

- **A simple on-off option**: We'll often see this as a `-v` or `--verbose` option
- **An option with an argument**: This might be a `-s ','` or `-separator '|'` option
- **A positional argument**: This might be used when we have an input file and an output file as command-line arguments
- **All other arguments**: We'd use these when we have a list of input files
- **--version**: This is a special option to display the version number and exit
- **--help**: This option will display the help and exit. This is a default, we don't need to do anything to make this happen

Once the arguments have been defined, we can parse them and use them. Here's how we parse them:

```
config= parser.parse_args()
```

The `config` object is an `argparse.Namespace` object; the class is similar to `types.SimpleNamespace`. It will have a number of attributes, and we can easily add more attributes to this object.

We'll look at each of these six common kinds of arguments individually. There are a lot of clever and sophisticated parsing options available in the `ArgumentParser` class. Most of them go beyond the simplistic guidelines commonly suggested for command-line argument processing. In general, we should avoid the kind of super-complex options that characterize programs such as `find`. When the options get terribly complex, we may have drifted into creating a domain-specific language on top of Python. Why not just use Python?

A simple on/off option

We'll define a simple on-off option with the one-letter short name, we can also provide a longer name; we should also provide an explicit action. We might want to provide a destination variable if we omit the longer name or the longer name is unpleasant as a Python variable:

```
parser.add_argument( '-v', '--verbose', action='store_true',
default=False )
```

This will define the long and short versions of the command-line option. If the option is present, it will set the `verbose` option to `True`. If the option is absent, the verbose option will default to `False`. Here are some common variations of this theme:

- We might change the action to `'store_false'` with a default of `True`.
- Sometimes, we'll have a default of `None` instead of `True` or `False`.
- Sometimes, we'll use an action of `'store_const'` with an additional `const=` argument. This allows us to move beyond simple Boolean values and store things such as logging levels or other objects.
- We might also have an action of `'count'`, which allows the option to get repeated, increasing the count. In this case, the default is often zero.

If we're using the logger, we might define a debugging option like the following code:

```
parser.add_argument( '--debug', action='store_const', const=logging.
DEBUG, default=logging.INFO, dest="logging_level" )
```

We changed the action to `store_const`, which stores a constant value and provides a specific constant value of `logging.DEBUG`. This means that the resulting options object will directly provide the value needed to configure the root logger. We can then simply configure the logger using `config.logging_level` without any further mapping or conditional processing.

An option with an argument

We'll define an option that has an argument with the long and optional short name. We'll provide an action that stores the value provided with the argument. We can also provide a type conversion, in case we want `float` or `int` values instead of a string:

```
parser.add_argument( "-b", "--bet", action="store", default="Flat",
choices=["Flat", "Martingale", "OneThreeTwoSix"], dest='betting_rule')
parser.add_argument( "-s", "--stake", action="store", default=50,
type=int )
```

The first example will define two versions of the command-line syntax, both long and short. When parsing the command-line argument values, a string value must follow the option, and it must be from the available choices. The destination name, `betting_rule`, will receive the option's argument string.

The second example also defines two versions of the command-line syntax; it includes a type conversion. When parsing argument values, this will store an integer value that follows the option. The long name, `stake`, will be the value in the options object created by the parser.

In some cases, there may be a list of values associated with the argument. In this case, we may provide a `nargs="+"` option to collect multiple values separated by spaces into a list.

Positional arguments

We define positional arguments using a name with no `"-"` decoration. In the case where we have a fixed number of positional arguments, we'll add them appropriately to the parser:

```
parser.add_argument( "input_filename", action="store" )
parser.add_argument( "output_filename", action="store" )
```

When parsing argument values, the two positional argument strings will be stored into the final namespace object. We can use `config.input_filename` and `config.output_filename` to work with these argument values.

All other arguments

We define argument lists with a name that has no - decoration and a piece of advice in the `nargs=` parameter. If the rule is one-or-more argument values, we specify `nargs="+"`. If the rule is zero-or-more argument values, we specify `nargs="*"`. If the rule is *optional*, we specify `nargs="?"`. This will collect all other argument values into a single sequence in the resulting namespace:

```
parser.add_argument( "filenames", action="store", nargs="*",
metavar="file..." )
```

When the list of filenames is optional, it generally means that `STDIN` or `STDOUT` will be used if no specific filenames are provided.

If we specify `nargs=`, then the result becomes a list. If we specify `nargs=1`, then the resulting object is a one-element list. If we omit `nargs`, then the result is just the single value that was provided.

Creating a list (even if it has only one element) is handy because we might want to process the arguments in this manner:

```
for filename in config.filenames:
    process( filename )
```

In some cases, we may want to provide a sequence of input files that includes `STDIN`. The common convention for this is a filename of - as an argument. We'll have to handle this within our application with something like the following code:

```
for filename in config.filenames:
    if filename == '-':
        process(sys.stdin)
    else:
        with open(filename) as input:
            process(input)
```

This shows us a loop that will attempt to handle a number of filenames, potentially including - to show when to process standard input among a list of files. A `try:` block should probably be used around the `with` statement.

--version display and exit

An option to display the version number is so common that there's a special shortcut to show us the version information:

```
parser.add_argument( "-V", "--version", action="version",
version=__version__ )
```

This example assumes that we have a global module `__version__= "3.3.2"` somewhere in the file. This special `action="version"` will have the side effect of exiting the program after displaying the version information.

--help display and exit

An option to display help is a default feature of `argparse`. Another special case allows us to change the `help` option from the default setting of `-h` or `--help`. This requires two things. First, we must create the parser with `add_help=False`. This will turn off the built-in `-h`, `--help` feature. After doing that, we will add the argument that we want to use (for example, `'-?'`) with `action="help"`. This will display the help text and exit.

Integrating command-line options and environment variables

The general policy for environment variables is that they are configuration inputs, similar to command-line options and arguments. For the most part, we use environment variables for settings that rarely change. We'll often set them via the `.bashrc` or `.bash_profile` files so that the values apply every time we log in. We may set the environment variables more globally in an `/etc/bashrc` file so that they apply to all users. We can also set environment variables on the command line, but these settings only last as long as the session is logged in.

In some cases, all of our configuration settings can be provided on the command line. In this case, the environment variables could be used as a kind of backup syntax for slowly changing variables.

In other cases, the configuration values we provide may be segregated into settings provided by environment variables different from settings provided by command-line options. We may need to get some values from the environment and merge in values that come from the command line.

We can leverage environment variables to set the default values in a configuration object. We want to gather these values prior to parsing the command-line arguments. This way, command-line arguments can override environment variables. There are two common approaches to this:

- **Explicitly setting the values when defining the command-line options**: This has the advantage of making the default value show up in the help message. It only works for environment variables that overlap with command-line options. We might do something like this to use the `SIM_SAMPLES` environment variable to provide a default value that can be overridden:

  ```
  parser.add_argument( "--samples", action="store",
      default=int(os.environ.get("SIM_SAMPLES",100)),
      type=int, help="Samples to generate" )
  ```

- **Implicitly setting the values as part of the parsing process**: This makes it simple to merge environment variables with command-line options into a single configuration. We can populate a namespace with default values and then overwrite it with the parsed values from the command line. This provides us with three levels of option values: the default defined in the parser, an override value seeded into the namespace, and finally, any override value provided on the command line.

  ```
  config4= argparse.Namespace()
  config4.samples= int(os.environ.get("SIM_SAMPLES",100))
  config4a= parser.parse_args( namespace=config4 )
  ```

The argument parser can perform type conversions for values that are not simple strings. Gathering environment variables, however, doesn't automatically involve a type conversion. For options that have non-string values, we must perform the type conversion in our application.

Providing more configurable defaults

We can incorporate configuration files along with environment variables and the command-line options. This gives us three ways to provide a configuration to an application program:

- A hierarchy of configuration files can provide defaults values. See *Chapter 13, Configuration Files and Persistence*, for examples on the ways to do this.
- Environment variables can provide overrides to the configuration files. This may mean translating from an environment variable namespace to the configuration namespace.
- The command-line options define the final overrides.

Using all three may be too much of a good thing. Tracking down a setting can become murky if there are too many places to search. The final decision on the configuration often rests on staying consistent with the overall collection of applications and frameworks. We should strive to make our programming fit seamlessly with other components.

We'll look at two minor variations on this theme. The first example shows us how we can have environment variables that override configuration file settings. The second example shows us configuration files that override global environment variable settings.

Overriding configuration file settings with environment variables

We'll use a three-stage process to incorporate environment variables and consider them more important than configuration file settings. First, we'll build some default settings from the environment variables:

```
env_values= [
    ("attribute_name", os.environ.get( "SOMEAPP_VARNAME", None )),
    ("another_name", os.environ.get( "SOMEAPP_OTHER", None )),
    etc.
]
```

Creating a mapping like this has the effect of rewriting the external environment variable names (`SOMEAPP_VARNAME`) into internal configuration names (`attribute_name`) that will match our application's configuration attributes. For environment variables that were not defined, we'll get `None` as the default value. We'll filter these out later.

Next, we'll parse a hierarchy of configuration files to gather the background configuration:

```
config_name= "someapp.yaml"
config_locations = (
        os.path.curdir,
        os.path.expanduser("~/"),
        "/etc",
        os.path.expanduser("~thisapp/"), # or thisapp.__file__,
)
candidates = ( os.path.join(dir,config_name)
   for dir in config_locations )
config_names = ( name for name in candidates if os.path.exists(name) )
files_values = [yaml.load(file) for file in config_names]
```

We built a list of locations, in priority order from the most important (owned by the user) to the least important (part of the installation.) For each file that actually exists, we parsed the content to create a mapping from names to values. We relied on the YAML notation, as it's flexible and easy for people to work with.

We can build instance of a `ChainMap` object from these sources:

```
defaults= ChainMap( dict( (k,v) for k,v in env_values if v is not None
), *files_values )
```

We combined the various mappings into a single `ChainMap`. The environment variables are searched first. When values are present there, the values are looked up from the user's configuration file first and then other configurations, if the user configuration file didn't provide a value.

We can use the following code to parse the command-line arguments and update these defaults:

```
config= parser.parse_args( namespace=argparse.Namespace( **defaults )
)
```

We transformed our `ChainMap` of configuration file settings into an `argparse.Namespace` object. Then, we parsed the command-line options to update that namespace object. As the environment variables are first in `ChainMap`, they override any configuration files.

Overriding environment variables with the configuration files

Some applications use environment variables as the foundational defaults that can be overridden by configuration files. In this case, we will change the order to build `ChainMap`. In the previous example, we put the environment variables first. We can put `env_config` in `defaults.maps` last to make it the final fallback:

```
defaults= ChainMap( *files_values )
defaults.maps.append( dict( (k,v) for k,v in env_values if v is not
None ) )
```

Finally, we can use the following code to parse the command-line arguments and update these defaults:

```
config= parser.parse_args( namespace=argparse.Namespace( **defaults )
)
```

We transform our `ChainMap` of configuration file settings into an `argparse.Namespace` object. Then, we parse the command-line options to update that namespace object. As the environment variables are last in `ChainMap`, they provide any values that are missing from the configuration files.

Making the configuration aware of the None values

This three-stage process to set the environment variables includes many common sources of parameters and configuration settings. We don't always need environment variables, configuration files, and command-line options. Some applications may only need a subset of these techniques.

We often need type conversions that will preserve the `None` values. Keeping the `None` values will ensure that we can tell when an environment variable was not set. Here's a more sophisticated type conversion that is `None-aware`:

```
def nint( x ):
    if x is None: return x
    return int(x)
```

We can use this `nint()` conversion in the following context to gather the environment variables:

```
env_values= [
    ('samples', nint(os.environ.get("SIM_SAMPLES", None)) ),
    ('stake', nint(os.environ.get( "SIM_STAKE", None )) ),
    ('rounds', nint(os.environ.get( "SIM_ROUNDS", None )) ),
]
```

If an environment variable is not set, a default of `None` will be used. If the environment variable is set, then the value will be converted to an integer. In later processing steps, we can depend on the `None` value to build a dictionary from only the proper values that are not `None`.

Customizing the help output

Here's some typical output that comes directly from the default `argparse.print_help()` code:

```
usage: p3_c16.py [-v] [--debug] [--dealerhit {Hit17,Stand17}]
                 [--resplit {ReSplit,NoReSplit,NoReSplitAces}]
[--decks DECKS]
                 [--limit LIMIT] [--payout PAYOUT]
```

```
                 [-p {SomeStrategy,AnotherStrategy}]
                 [-b {Flat,Martingale,OneThreeTwoSix}] [-r ROUNDS] [-s 
STAKE]
                 [--samples SAMPLES] [-V] [-?]
                 output

Simulate Blackjack

positional arguments:
  output

optional arguments:
  -v, --verbose
  --debug
  --dealerhit {Hit17,Stand17}
  --resplit {ReSplit,NoReSplit,NoReSplitAces}
  --decks DECKS
  --limit LIMIT
  --payout PAYOUT
  -p {SomeStrategy,AnotherStrategy}, --playerstrategy 
{SomeStrategy,AnotherStrategy}
  -b {Flat,Martingale,OneThreeTwoSix}, --bet {Flat,Martingale,OneThre
eTwoSix}
  -r ROUNDS, --rounds ROUNDS
  -s STAKE, --stake STAKE
  --samples SAMPLES
  -V, --version         show program's version number and exit
  -?, --help
```

The default help text is built from four things in our parser definition:

- The usage line is a summary of the options. We can replace the default calculation with our own usage text that omits the less commonly used details.
- This is followed by the description. By default, the text we provide is cleaned up a bit. In this example, we provided a shabby two-word description, so there's no obvious cleanup.
- Then, the arguments are shown. First the positional arguments and then the options, in the order that we defined them.
- After this, an optional epilog text is shown.

In some cases, this kind of terse reminder is adequate. In other cases, however, we may need to provide more details. We have three tiers of support for more detailed help:

- **Add help= to the argument definitions**: This is the place to start when customizing the help details
- **Use one of the other help formatter classes that create better-looking output**: This is done with the `formatter_class=` argument when building `ArgumentParser`. Note that `ArgumentDefaultsHelpFormatter` requires `help=` for an argument definition; it will add the default to the help text that we supply.
- **Extend the ArgumentParser class and override the print_usage() and print_help() methods**: We can always write a new help formatter as well. If we have options so complex that this is required, perhaps we've gone too far.

Our goal is to improve usability. Even if our programs work correctly, we can build trust by providing command-line support that makes our program easier to use.

Creating a top-level main() function

In *Chapter 13, Configuration Files and Persistence*, we suggested two application configuration design patterns:

- **The global property map**: In the previous examples, we implemented the global property map with a `Namespace` object created by `ArgumentParser`.
- **Object construction**: The idea behind object construction was to build the required object instances from the configuration parameters, effectively demoting the global property map to a local property map inside the `main()` function and not saving the properties.

What we showed you in the previous section was the use of a local `Namespace` object to collect all of the parameters. From this, we can build the necessary application objects that will do the real work of the application. The two design patterns aren't a dichotomy; they're complementary. We used `Namespace` to accumulate a consistent set of values and then built the various objects based on the values in that namespace.

This leads us to a design for a top-level function. Before looking at the implementation, we need to consider a proper name for this function; there are two ways to name the function:

- Name it `main()` because that's a common term for the starting point of the application as a whole
- Don't name it `main()` because `main()` is too vague to be meaningful in the long run

We think this is not a dichotomy either, and we should do two things. Define a top-level function with a name that's a `verb_noun()` phrase that describes the operation fairly. Add a line `main= verb_noun` to provide a `main()` function that helps other developers see how the application works.

This two-part implementation lets us change the definition of `main()` through extension. We can add functions and reassign the name `main`. Old function names are left in place as part of a stable, growing API.

Here's a top-level application script that builds objects from a configuration `Namespace` object:

```
import ast
import csv
def simulate_blackjack( config ):
    dealer_rule= {'Hit17': Hit17, 'Stand17': Stand17,
  }[config.dealer_rule]()
    split_rule= {'ReSplit': ReSplit,
  'NoReSplit': NoReSplit, 'NoReSplitAces':NoReSplitAces,
  }[config.split_rule]()
    try:
       payout= ast.literal_eval( config.payout )
       assert len(payout) == 2
    except Exception as e:
       raise Exception( "Invalid payout {0}".format(config.payout) )
from e
    table= Table( decks=config.decks, limit=config.limit,
dealer=dealer_rule,
         split=split_rule, payout=payout )
    player_rule= {'SomeStrategy': SomeStrategy,
  'AnotherStrategy': AnotherStrategy,
  }[config.player_rule]()
    betting_rule= {"Flat":Flat,
  "Martingale":Martingale, "OneThreeTwoSix":OneThreeTwoSix,
  }[config.betting_rule]()
```

```
    player= Player( play=player_rule, betting=betting_rule,
        rounds=config.rounds, stake=config.stake )
    simulate= Simulate( table, player, config.samples )
    with open(config.outputfile, "w", newline="") as target:
        wtr= csv.writer( target )
        wtr.writerows( simulate )
```

This function depends on an externally supplied `Namespace` object with the configuration attributes. It's not named `main()` so that we can make future changes that would change the meaning of `main`.

We built the various objects—`Table`, `Player`, `Simulate`—that are required. We configured these objects with the initial values based on the configuration parameters.

We've actually done the real work. After all of the object construction, the actual work is a single, highlighted line: `wtr.writerows( simulate )`. 90 percent of the program's time will be spent here, generating samples and writing them to the required file.

A similar pattern holds for GUI applications. They enter a main loop to process GUI events. The pattern also holds for servers that enter a main loop to process requests.

We've depended on having a configuration object passed in as an argument. This follows from our testing strategy of minimizing dependencies. This top-level `simulate_blackjack()` function doesn't depend on the details of how the configuration was created. We can then use this function in an application script:

```
if __name__ == "__main__":
        logging.config.dictConfig( yaml.load("logging.config") )
    config5= gather_configuration()
    simulate_blackjack( config5 )
    logging.shutdown()
```

This represents a separation of concerns. We've nested the work of the application into two levels of enclosure.

The outer level of enclosure is defined by logging. We configured logging outside of all other application components to ensure that there are no conflicts among various top-level modules, classes, or functions attempting to configure logging. If any particular portion of the application attempts to configure logging, then making changes can lead to conflicts. In particular, when we look at combining applications into larger composite processing, we need to be sure that the two applications being combined don't make conflicting logging configurations.

The inner level of enclosure is defined by the application's configuration. We don't want conflicts among separate application components. We'd like to allow our command-line API to evolve separately from our application. We'd like to be able to embed our application processing into separate environments, perhaps defined by `multiprocessing` or a RESTful web server.

Ensuring DRY for the configuration

We have a potential DRY issue between our construction of the argument parser and the use of the arguments to configure the application. We built the arguments using some keys that are repeated.

We can eliminate this repetition by creating some global internal configurations. For example, we might define this global as shown:

```
dealer_rule_map = { "Hit17": Hit17, "Stand17", Stand17 }
```

We can use it to create the argument parser:

```
parser.add_argument( "--dealerhit", action="store", default="Hit17",
choices=dealer_rule_map.keys(), dest='dealer_rule')
```

We can use it to create the working objects:

```
dealer_rule= dealer_rule_map[config.dealer_rule]()
```

This eliminates the repetition. It allows us to add new class definitions and parameter key mappings in one place as the application evolves. It also allows us to abbreviate or otherwise rewrite the external API as shown here:

```
dealer_rule_map = { "H17": Hit17, "S17": Stand17 }
```

There are four of these kinds of mappings from the command-line (or configuration file) string to application class. Using these internal mappings simplifies the `simulate_blackjack()` function.

Managing nested configuration contexts

In a way, the presence of nested contexts means that top level scripts ought to look like the following code:

```
if __name__ == "__main__":
    with Logging_Config():
        with Application_Config() as config:
            simulate_blackjack( config )
```

We add two context managers. For more information, see *Chapter 5, Using Callables and Contexts*. Here are two context managers:

```
class Logging_Config:
    def __enter__( self, filename="logging.config" ):
        logging.config.dictConfig( yaml.load(filename) )
    def __exit__( self, *exc ):
        logging.shutdown()

class Application_Config:
    def __enter__( self ):
        # Build os.environ defaults.
        # Load files.
        # Build ChainMap from environs and files.
        # Parse command-line arguments.
        return namespace
    def __exit__( self, *exc ):
        pass
```

The `Logging_Config` context manager configures the logging. It also ensures that logging is properly shut down when the application is finished.

The `Application_Config` context manager can gather configuration from a number of files as well as command-line arguments. The use of a context manager isn't essential in this case. However, it leaves room for ready extension.

This design pattern may clarify the various concerns that surround the application startup and shutdown. While it may be a bit much for most applications, this design fits with the philosophy of Python context managers seems like it could be helpful as an application grows and expands.

When we're confronted with an application that grows and expands, we often wind up doing larger-scale programming. For this, it's important to separate the changeable application processing from the less changeable processing context.

Programming In The Large

Let's add a feature to our Blackjack simulation: analysis of results. We have several paths to implement this added feature. There are two dimensions to our considerations, leading to a large number of combinations. One dimension of our consideration is how to design the new features:

- Add a function
- Use the Command design pattern

The other dimension is how to package the new features:

- Write a new top-level script file. We would have new commands based on files with names such as `simulate.py` and `analyze.py`.
- Add a parameter to an application that allows one script to perform the simulation or analysis. We would have commands that look like `app.py simulate` and `app.py analyze`.

All four combinations are sensible ways to implement this. We'll focus on using the **command** design pattern. First, we'll revise our existing application to use the command design pattern. Then, we'll extend our application by adding features.

Designing command classes

Many applications involve an implicit Command design pattern. After all, we're *processing* data. To do this, there must be at least one active-voice verb that defines how the application transforms, creates, or consumes data. A very simple application may have only a single verb, implemented as a function. Using the Command class design pattern may not be helpful.

More complex applications will have multiple, related verbs. One of the key features of GUIs and web servers is that they can do multiple things, leading to multiple commands. In many cases, the GUI menu options define the domain of the verbs for an application.

In some cases, an application's design stems from a decomposition of a larger, more complex verb. We may factor the overall processing into several smaller command steps that are combined into the final application.

When we look at the evolution of an application, we often see a pattern where new functionality is accreted. In these cases, each new feature can become a kind of separate command subclass that is added to the application class hierarchy.

Here's an abstract superclass for commands:

```
class Command:
    def set_config( self, config ):
        self.__dict__.update( config.__dict__ )
    config= property( fset=set_config )
    def run( self ):
        pass
```

We configure this `Command` class by setting the `config` property to a `types.SimpleNamespace` or `argparse.Namespace`, or even another `Command` instance. This will populate the instance variables from the `namespace` object.

Once the object is configured, we can set it to doing the work of the command by calling the `run()` method. This class implements a relatively simple use case:

```
main= SomeCommand()
main.config= config
main.run()
```

Here's a concrete subclass that implements a Blackjack simulation:

```
class Simulate_Command( Command ):
    dealer_rule_map = {"Hit17": Hit17, "Stand17": Stand17}
    split_rule_map = {'ReSplit': ReSplit,
        'NoReSplit': NoReSplit, 'NoReSplitAces': NoReSplitAces}
    player_rule_map = {'SomeStrategy': SomeStrategy,
        'AnotherStrategy': AnotherStrategy}
    betting_rule_map = {"Flat": Flat,
        "Martingale": Martingale, "OneThreeTwoSix": OneThreeTwoSix}

    def run( self ):
        dealer_rule= self.dealer_rule_map[self.dealer_rule]()
        split_rule= self.split_rule_map[self.split_rule]()
        try:
           payout= ast.literal_eval( self.payout )
           assert len(payout) == 2
        except Exception as e:
           raise Exception( "Invalid payout {0}".format(self.payout) )
from e
        table= Table( decks=self.decks, limit=self.limit,
dealer=dealer_rule,
            split=split_rule, payout=payout )
        player_rule= self.player_rule_map[self.player_rule]()
        betting_rule= self.betting_rule_map[self.betting_rule]()
        player= Player( play=player_rule, betting=betting_rule,
            rounds=self.rounds, stake=self.stake )
        simulate= Simulate( table, player, self.samples )
        with open(self.outputfile, "w", newline="") as target:
            wtr= csv.writer( target )
            wtr.writerows( simulate )
```

This class implements the essential top-level function that configures the various objects and then executes the simulation. We wrapped the `simulate_blackjack()` function shown previously to create a concrete extension of the `Command` class. This can be used in the main script like the following code:

```
if __name__ == "__main__":
    with Logging_Config():
```

```
        with Application_Config() as config:
            main= Simulate_Command()
            main.config= config
            main.run()
```

While we could make this command into `Callable` and use `main()` instead of `main.run()`, the use of a callable can be confusing. We're explicitly separating three design issues:

- **Construction**: We've specifically kept the initialization empty. In the later section, we'll show you some examples of PITL, where we'll build a larger composite command from smaller component commands.
- **Configuration**: We've put the configuration in via a `property` setter, isolated from the construction and control.
- **Control**: This is the real work of the command after it's been built and configured.

When we look at a callable or a function, the construction is part of the definition. The configuration and control are combined into the function call itself. We sacrifice a small bit of flexibility if we try to define a callable.

Adding the analysis command subclass

We'll extend our application by adding the analysis feature. As we're using the Command design pattern, we can add yet another subclass for analysis.

Here's our analysis feature:

```
class Analyze_Command( Command ):
    def run( self ):
        with open(self.outputfile, "r", newline="") as target:
            rdr= csv.reader( target )
            outcomes= ( float(row[10]) for row in rdr )
            first= next(outcomes)
            sum_0, sum_1 = 1, first
            value_min = value_max = first
            for value in outcomes:
                sum_0 += 1 # value**0
                sum_1 += value # value**1
                value_min= min( value_min, value )
                value_max= max( value_max, value )
            mean= sum_1/sum_0
            print(
```

```
        "{4}\nMean = {0:.1f}\nHouse Edge = {1:.1%}\nRange = {2:.1f}
{3:.1f}".format(
        mean, 1-mean/50, value_min, value_max, self.outputfile) )
```

This is not too statistically meaningful, true, but the point is to show you a second command that uses the configuration namespace to do work related to our simulation. We used the `outputfile` configuration parameter to name the file that is read to perform some statistical analysis.

Adding and packaging more features into an application

Previously, we noted one common approach to supporting multiple features. Some applications use multiple top-level main programs in separate `.py` script files.

When we want to combine commands that are in separate files, we're forced to write a shell script to create a higher-level, composite program. It doesn't seem optimal to introduce yet another tool and another language to do PITL.

A slightly more flexible alternative to creating separate script files is using a positional parameter to select a specific top-level `Command` object. For our example, we'd like to select either the simulation or the analysis command. To do this, we would add a parameter to the command-line argument parsing the following code:

```
parser.add_argument( "command", action="store", default='simulate',
choices=['simulate', 'analyze'] )
parser.add_argument( "outputfile", action="store", metavar="output" )
```

This would change the command-line API to add the top-level verb to the command line. We can easily map our argument values to class names:

```
{'simulate': Simulate_Command, 'analyze': Analyze_Command}[options.
command]
```

This allows us to create even higher-level composite features. For example, we might want to combine simulation and analysis into a single, overall program. Also, we'd like to do this without resorting to using the shell.

Designing a higher-level composite command

Here's how we can design a composite command that's built from other commands. We have two design strategies: object composition and class composition.

If we use object composition, then our composite command is based on the built-in `list` or `tuple`. We can extend or wrap one of the existing sequences. We'll create the composite `Command` object as a collection of instances of other `Command` objects. We might consider writing something like the following code:

```
simulate_and_analyze = [Simulate(), Analyze()]
```

This has the disadvantage that we haven't created a new class for our unique composite command. We created a generic composite and populated it with instances. If we want to create even higher-level compositions, we'll have to address this asymmetry between low-level `Command` classes and higher-level composite `Command` objects based on built-in sequence classes.

We'd prefer to have a composite command also be a subclass of command. If we use class composition, then we'll have a more consistent structure for our low-level commands and our higher-level composite commands.

Here's a class that implements a sequence of other commands:

```
class Command_Sequence(Command):
    sequence = []
    def __init__( self ):
        self._sequence = [ class_() for class_ in self.sequence ]
    def set_config( self, config ):
        for step in self._sequence:
            step.config= config
    config= property( fset=set_config )
    def run( self ):
        for step in self._sequence:
            step.run()
```

We defined a class-level variable, `sequence`, to contain a sequence of command classes. During the object initialization, `__init__()` will construct an internal instance variable, `_sequence`, with objects of the named classes in `self.sequence`.

When the configuration is set, it will be pushed into each constituent object. When the composite command is executed via `run()`, it is delegated to each component in the composite command.

Here's a `Command` subclass built from two other `Command` subclasses:

```
class Simulate_and_Analyze(Command_Sequence):
    sequence = [Simulate_Command, Analyze_Command]
```

We can now create a class that is a sequence of individual steps. As this is a subclass of the `Command` class itself, it has the necessary polymorphic API. We can now create compositions with this class because it's compatible with all other subclasses of `Command`.

We can now make a very small modification to argument parsing to add this feature to the application:

```
parser.add_argument( "command", action="store", default='simulate',
choices=['simulate', 'analyze', 'simulate_analyze'] )
```

We simply added another choice to the argument option values. We'll also need to tweak the mapping from the argument option string to the class:

```
{'simulate': Simulate_Command, 'analyze': Analyze_Command, 'simulate_
analyze': Simulate_and_Analyze}[options.command]
```

Note that we shouldn't use a vague name such as `both` to combine two commands. If we avoid vagueness, we create opportunities to expand or revise our application. Using the Command design pattern makes it pleasant to add features. We can define composite commands, or we can decompose a larger command into smaller subcommands.

Packaging and implementation may involve adding an option choice and mapping that choice to a class name. If we use a more sophisticated configuration file (see *Chapter 13, Configuration Files and Persistence*), we can provide the class name directly in the configuration file and save the mapping from an option string to a class.

Additional composite command design patterns

We can identify a number of composite design patterns. In the previous example, we designed a sequence composite. For inspiration, we can look at the bash shell composite operators: `;`, `&`, `|`, as well as `()` for grouping. Beyond these, we have `if`, `for`, and `while` loops within the shell.

We looked at the sequence operator (`;`) in the `Command_Sequence` class definition. This concept of *sequence* is so ubiquitous that many programming languages (such as the shell and Python) don't require an explicit operator; the syntax simply uses end-of-line as an implied sequence operator.

The shell's `&` operator creates two commands that run concurrently instead of sequentially. We can create a `Command_Concurrent` class definition with a `run()` method that uses `multiprocessing` to create two subprocesses and waits for both to finish.

The | operator in the shell creates a pipeline: one command's output buffer is another command's input buffer; the commands run concurrently. In Python, we'd need to create a queue as well as two processes to read and write that queue. This is a more complex situation; it involves populating the queue objects into the configurations of each of the various children. *Chapter 12, Transmitting and Sharing Objects*, has some examples of using `multiprocessing` with queues to pass objects among concurrent processes.

The `if` command in the shell has a number of use cases. However, there's no compelling reason to provide anything more than a native Python implementation via a method in a subclass of `Command`. Creating a complex `Command` class to mimic Python's `if-elif-else` processing isn't helpful. We can—and should—just use Python.

The `while` and `for` commands in the shell, similarly, aren't the sort of things we need to define in a higher-level `Command` subclass. We can simply write this in a method in Python.

Here's an example of a *for-all* class definition that applies an existing command to all the values in a collection:

```
class ForAllBets_Simulate( Command ):
    def run( self ):
        for bet_class in "Flat", "Martingale", "OneThreeTwoSix":
            self.betting_rule= bet_class
            self.outputfile= "p3_c16_simulation7_{0}.dat".format(bet_
class)
            sim= Simulate_Command()
            sim.config= self
            sim.run()
```

We enumerated the three classes of betting in our simulation. For each of these classes, we tweaked the configuration, created a simulation, and executed that simulation.

Note that this *for-all* class won't work with the `Analyze_Command` class defined previously. We can't simply create composites that reflect different scopes of work. The `Analyze_Command` class runs a single simulation, but the `ForAllBets_Simulate` class runs a collection of simulations. We have two choices to create compatible scopes of work: we could create an `Analyze_All` command or `ForAllBets_Sim_and_Analyze` command. The design decision depends on the needs of the users.

Integrating with other applications

There are several ways in which we can use Python when integrating with other applications. It's difficult to provide a comprehensive overview, as there are so many applications, each with unique, distinctive features. We can show you some broad design patterns:

- Python may be the application's scripting language. For many examples, here's a list of applications that simply include Python as the primary method to add features: `https://wiki.python.org/moin/AppsWithPythonScripting`
- A Python module can implement the application's API. There are numerous applications that include Python modules that provide a binding to the application's API. Application developers working in one language will often provide API libraries for other languages, including Python.
- We can use the `ctypes` module to implement another application's API directly in Python. This works out well in the case of an application library that is focused on C or C++.
- We can use `STDIN` and `STDOUT` to create a shell-level pipeline that connects us to another application. We might also want to look at the `fileinput` module when building shell-compatible applications.
- We can use the `subprocess` module to access an application's command-line interface. This may also involve connecting to an application's stdin and stdout to interact properly with it.
- We can also write our own Python-compatible module in C or C++. In this case, we can implement the foreign application's API in C, offering classes or functions that a Python application can leverage. This may be a better performance than using the `ctypes` API. As this requires compiling C or C++, it's also a bit more tool intensive.

This level of flexibility means that we often use Python as the integration framework or glue to create a larger, composite application from smaller applications. When using Python for integration, we'll often have Python classes and objects that mirror the definitions in another application.

There are some additional design considerations that we'll save for *Chapter 17, The Modules and Package Design*. These are higher-level architectural design considerations, above and beyond coping with the command line.

Summary

We looked at how to use `argparse` and `os.environ` to gather command-line argument and configuration parameters. This builds on the techniques shown in *Chapter 13, Configuration Files and Persistence*.

We can implement a number of common command-line features using `argparse`. This includes common features, such as showing the version number and exiting or showing the help text and exiting.

We looked at using the Command design pattern to create applications that can be expanded or refactored to offer new features. Our goal is to explicitly keep the body of the top-level main function as small as possible.

Design considerations and trade-offs

The command-line API is an important part of a finished application. While most of our design effort focuses on what the program does while it's running, we do need to address two boundary states: startup and shutdown. An application must be easy to configure when we start it up. Also, it must shut down gracefully, properly flushing all of the output buffers and releasing all of the OS resources.

When working with a public-facing API, we have to address a variation on the problem of schema evolution. As our application evolves—and as our knowledge of the users evolves—we will modify the command-line API. This may mean that we'll have legacy features or legacy syntax. It may also mean that we need to break the compatibility with the legacy command-line design.

In many cases, we'll need to be sure that the major version number is part of our application's name. We shouldn't write a top-level module named `someapp`. We should consider starting with `someapp1` so that the number is always part of the application name. We shouldn't change the command-line API by adding the version number as a new suffix; starting with `someapp1` anticipates a possible transition to `someapp2`.

Looking forward

In the next chapter, we'll expand some of these top-level design ideas and look at the module and package design. A small Python application can also be a module; it can be imported into a larger application. A complex Python application may be a package. It may include other application modules and it may be included into larger-scale applications.

17
The Module and Package Design

Python gives us several higher-level constructs to organize software. In *Part 1, Pythonic Classes via Special Methods* we looked at advanced techniques to use class definitions to properly bind the structure and behavior together. In this chapter, we'll look at modules to encapsulate classes, functions, and global objects. Above the module grouping, we also have packages as a design pattern to group related modules together.

Python makes it very easy to create simple modules. Any time we create a Python file, we're creating a module. As the scope of our designs gets larger and more sophisticated, the use of packages becomes more important to maintain a clear organization among the modules.

We have some specialized modules as well. For a larger application, we may implement a `__main__` module. This module must be designed to expose the OS command-line interface to the application. It must also be defined in such a way that it doesn't block the simple reuse of the application to create larger, composite applications.

We also have some flexibility in how we install the modules. We can use the default working directory, an environment variable setting, `.pth` files, as well as the Python `lib/site-packages` directory. Each of these has advantages and disadvantages.

We're going to avoid the more complex problem of distributing Python code. There are a number of techniques to create a source distribution for a Python project. The various distribution technologies move outside object-oriented design. *Chapter 30* of *Python Standard Library* addresses some of the physical file-packaging issues. The *Distributing Python Modules* document provides information on creating a code distribution.

Designing a module

A module is the unit of the Python implementation and reuse. All Python programming is provided at the module level. The class is the foundation of object-oriented design and programming. The module—a collection of classes—is a higher-level grouping and is the unit of reuse in Python. We can't easily reuse a single class in isolation. A properly designed module can be reused.

A Python module is a file. The filename extension must be `.py`. The filename in front of `.py` must be a valid Python name. Section 2.3 of *Python Language Reference* provides us with the complete definition of a name. One of the clauses in this definition is: *Within the ASCII range (U+0001..U+007F), the valid characters for identifiers are the uppercase and lowercase letters A through Z, the underscore _ and, except for the first character, the digits 0 through 9.*

OS filenames permit more characters from the ASCII range than Python names; this extra OS complexity must be ignored. The filename (without `.py`) is the module name.

Every time we create a `.py` file, we create a module. Often, we'll create a Python file without doing too much design work. In this chapter, we'll take a look at some of the design considerations to create a reusable module.

Python may also create `.pyc` and `.pyo` files for its own private purposes; it's best to simply ignore these files. Many brain calories have been wasted by programmers trying to exploit the `.pyc` file as a kind of compiled object-code that can be used instead of the `.py` file to somehow keep the source code a secret. We need to emphasize the *wasted* part of that. The `.pyc` files can be decompiled easily; they don't keep anything secret. If you need to prevent the reverse-engineering of your application, you might want to consider using a different language.

Some module design patterns

There are three commonly seen design patterns for Python modules:

- **Pure library modules**: These are meant to be imported. They contain definitions of classes, functions, and perhaps some assignment statements to create a few global variables. They do not do any real work so that they can be imported without any worry about the side effects of the import operation. There are two use cases that we'll look at:

    - **Whole module**: Some modules are designed to be imported as a whole, creating a module namespace that contains all of the items
    - **Item collection**: Some modules are designed to have individual items imported instead of creating a module object

- **Main script modules**: These are meant to be executed from the command line. They contain much more than class and function definitions. They will include statements that will do the real work; they may have side effects; they cannot be meaningfully imported because of an astonishing side effect. If a main script module import is attempted, it will actually execute—doing work, possibly updating files, or doing whatever the module is designed to do when run.
- **Conditional script modules**: These modules have two use cases: they can be imported and they can also be run from the command line. These modules will have the main-import switch as described in *Python Standard Library*, section 28.4, *__main__ – top-level script environment*.

Here's the simplified conditional script switch from the library documentation:

```
if __name__ == "__main__":
    main()
```

The `main()` function does the work of the script. This design supports two use cases: `run` and `import`. When the module is run from the command line, it evaluates `main()` and does the expected work. When the module is imported, the function will not be evaluated, and the import will simply provide definitions without doing any real work.

We suggest something a bit more sophisticated, as shown in *Chapter 16, Coping with the Command Line*:

```
if __name__ == "__main__":
    with Logging_Config():
        with Application_Config() as config:
            main= Simulate_Command()
            main.config= config
            main.run()
```

Our point is to echo the following essential design tip:

Importing a module should have few side effects.

Creating a few module-level variables is an acceptable side effect of an import. The real work—accessing network resources, printing output, updating files, and other kinds of side effects—should not happen when a module is getting imported.

A main script module without a `__name__ == "__main__"` section is often a bad idea because it can't be imported and reused. Beyond that, it's difficult for documentation tools to work with a main script module, and it's difficult to test. The documentation tools tend to import modules, causing work to be done unexpectedly. Similarly, testing requires care to avoid importing the module as part of a test setup.

Module versus class

There are numerous parallels between a module and a class definition:

- A module and a class each have a Python name. Modules usually have a leading lowercase letter; classes usually have a leading uppercase letter.
- A module and a class definition are namespaces that contain other objects.
- A module is a **singleton** object within a global namespace, `sys.modules`. A class definition is unique within a namespace, either the global namespace, `__main__` or some local namespace. A class isn't a proper **Singleton**; the definition can be replaced. Once imported, a module isn't imported again unless it's deleted.
- The definition of the class or module is evaluated as a sequence of statements within a namespace.
- A function defined in a module is analogous to a static method within a class definition.
- A class defined in a module is analogous to a class defined within another class.

There are two significant differences between a module and class:

- We can't create an instance of a module; it's always a singleton. We can create multiple instances of a class.
- An assignment statement in a module creates a variable that's global within the module's namespace; it can be used inside the module without a qualifier. An assignment statement within a class definition creates a variable that's part of the class namespace it requires a qualifier to distinguish it from the global variables.

A module is like a class. Modules, packages, and classes can be used to encapsulate data and processing—attributes and operations—into a tidy object.

The similarities between modules and classes mean that choosing between them is a design decision with trade-offs and alternatives. In most cases, the need for an *instance of* is the deciding factor. A module's singleton feature means that we'll use a module (or package) to contain class and function definitions that are expanded just once even if imported multiple times.

However, there are some modules that might be very class-like. The `logging` module, for example, is often imported in multiple other modules. The singleton feature means that the logging configuration can be done once and will apply to all other modules.

A configuration module, similarly, might be imported in several places. The singleton nature of a module ensures the configuration can be imported by any module but will be truly global.

When writing applications that work with a single connected database, a module with a number of functions will be similar to a singleton class. The database access layer can be imported throughout an application but will be a single, shared global object.

The expected content of a module

Python modules have a typical organization. To an extent, this is defined by PEP 8, `http://www.python.org/dev/peps/pep-0008/`.

The first line of a module can be a `#!` comment; a typical version looks like the following code:

```
#!/usr/bin/env python3.3
```

This is used to help OS tools such as `bash` locate the Python interpreter for an executable script file. For Windows, this line may be something like `#!C:\Python3\python.exe`.

Older Python modules may include a coding comment to specify the encoding for the rest of the text. This may look like the following code:

```
# -*- coding: utf-8 -*-
```

The coding comment is not generally needed for Python 3; the OS encoding information is adequate. Older Python implementations assumed the files were encoded in ASCII; a coding comment was required for files that were not in ASCII.

The next lines of a module should be a triple-quoted module docstring that defines the contents of the module file. As with other Python docstrings, the first paragraph of the text should be a summary. This should be followed by a more complete definition of the module's contents, purpose, and usage. This may include RST markup so that the documentation tools can produce elegant-looking results from the docstring. We'll address this in *Chapter 18, Quality and Documentation*.

After the docstring, we can include any version's control information. For example, we might have the following code:

```
__version__ = "2.7.18"
```

This is a global module that we might use elsewhere in our application to determine the version number of the module. This is after the docstring but before the body of the module. Below this comes the module's `import` statement. Conventionally, they're in a big block at the front of the module.

After the `import` statements come the various class and function definitions of the module. These are presented in whatever order is required to ensure that they work correctly and make sense to someone who is reading the code.

Java and C++ tend to focus on one class per file.

That's a silly limitation. It doesn't apply to Python, nor is it a natural law of the universe.

If the file has a lot of classes, we might find that the module is a bit hard to follow. If we find ourselves using big comment blocks to break a module into sections, this is a hint that what we're writing may be more complex than a single module. We certainly have multiple modules; we may have a package.

Another common feature of some modules is the creation of objects within the module's namespace. Stateful module variables, such as class-level attributes, are not a great idea. The lack of visibility of these variables is a potential area for confusion.

Sometimes, global modules are handy. The `logging` module makes heavy use of this. Another example is the way the `random` module creates a default instance of the `Random` class. This allows a number of module-level functions to provide a simple API for random numbers. We're not forced to create an instance of `random.Random`.

Whole module versus module items

There are two approaches to the contents of a library module. Some modules are an integrated whole, some are more like a collection of less-well-related items. When we've designed a module as a whole, it will often have a few classes or functions that are the public-facing API of the module. When we've designed a module as a collection of loosely related items, each individual class or function tends to stand alone.

We often see this distinction in the way we import and use a module. We'll look at three variations:

- Using the `import some_module` command

  The `some_module.py` module file is evaluated and the resulting objects are collected into a single namespace called `some_module`. This requires us to use qualified names for all of the objects in the module. We must use `some_module.this` and `some_module.that`. This use of qualified names makes the module an integrated whole.

- Using the `from some_module import this` command

  The `some_module.py` module file is evaluated and only the named objects are created in the current local namespace. Often, this is the global namespace. We can now use `this` or `that` without the qualification. This use of unqualified names claims that the module seems like a collection of disjointed objects.

- Using the `from math import sqrt, sin, cos` command

  This will provide us with a few math functions that we can use without qualification.

- Using the `from some_module import *` command

  The default behavior is to make all non-private names part of the namespace perform the import. A private name begins with _. We can explicitly limit the number of names imported by a module by providing an `__all__` list within the module. This is a list of string object names; these are the names that are elaborated by the `import *` statement.

We can use the `__all__` variable to conceal the utility functions that are part of building the module but not part of the API that's provided to clients of the module.

When we look back at our design for decks of cards, we could elect to keep the suits as an implementation detail that's not imported by default. If we had a `cards.py` module, we could include the following code:

```
__all__ = ["Deck", "Shoe"]
class Suit:
    etc.
suits = [ Suit("♣"), Suit("◇"), Suit("⊠"), Suit("♠") ]
class Card:
    etc.
def card( rank, suit ):
    etc.
class Deck:
    etc.
class Shoe( Deck ):
    etc.
```

The use of the `__all__` variable keeps the class definitions of the `Suit` and `Card` classes, the `card()` function, and the `suits` variable as implementation details that are not imported by default. For example, when we perform the following code:

```
from cards import *
```

This statement will only create `Deck` and `Shoe` in an application script, as those are the only explicitly given names in the `__all__` variable.

When we execute the following command, it will import the module without putting any names into the global namespace:

```
import cards
```

Even though it's not imported into the namespace, we can still access the qualified `cards.card()` method to create a `Card` class.

There are advantages and disadvantages of each technique. A whole module requires using the module name as a qualifier; this makes the origin of an object explicit. Importing items from a module shortens their names, which can make complex programming more compact and easier to understand.

Designing a package

One important consideration to design a package is *don't*. The *Zen of Python* poem (also known as `import this`) includes this line:

> "*Flat is better than nested*"

We can see this in the Python Standard Library. The structure of the library is relatively flat; there are few nested modules. Deeply nested packages can be overused. We should be skeptical of excessive nesting.

A package is essentially a directory with an extra file, `__init__.py`. The directory name must be a proper Python name. OS names include a lot of characters that are not allowed in Python names.

We often see three design patterns for packages:

- Simple packages are a directory with an empty `__init__.py` file. This package name becomes a qualifier for the internal module names. We'll use the following code:

  ```
  import package.module
  ```

- A module package can have an `__init__.py` file that is effectively a module definition. This can import other modules from the package directory. Or, it can stand as a part of a larger design that includes the top-level module and the qualified submodules. We'll use the following code:

  ```
  import package
  ```

- Directories are where the `__init__.py` file selects among alternative implementations. We'll use the following code:

  ```
  import package
  ```

The first kind of package is relatively simple. We add an `__init__.py` file and we're done creating a package. The other two are a bit more involved; we'll look at these in detail.

Designing a module-package hybrid

In some cases, a design evolves into a module that is very complex—so complex that a single file becomes a bad idea. We might need to refactor this complex module into a package with several smaller modules.

In this case, the package can be as simple as the following kind of structure. Here's the `__init__.py` file from a package directory named `blackjack`:

```
"""Blackjack package"""
from blackjack.cards import Shoe
from blackjack.player import Strategy_1, Strategy_2
from blackjack.casino import ReSplit, NoReSplit, NoReSplitAces,
Hit17, Stand17
from blackjack.simulator import Table, Player, Simulate
from betting import Flat, Martingale, OneThreeTwoSix
```

This shows us how we can build a module-like package that is actually an assembly of parts imported from other subsidiary modules. An overall application can then do this:

```
from blackjack import *
table= Table( decks=6, limit=500, dealer=Hit17(),
        split=NoReSplitAces(), payout=(3,2)  )
player= Player( play=Strategy_1(),  betting=Martingale(), rounds=100,
stake=100 )
simulate= Simulate( table, player, 100 )
for result in simulate:
    print( result )
```

This snippet shows us how we can use `from blackjack import *` to create a number of class definitions that originate in a number of other packages. Specifically, there's an overall `blackjack` package that has the following modules within it:

- The `blackjack.cards` package contains the `Card`, `Deck`, and `Shoe` definitions
- The `blackjack.player` package contains various strategies for play
- The `blackjack.casino` package contains a number of classes that customize how casino rules vary
- The `blackjack.simulator` package contains the top-level simulation tools
- The `betting` package is also used by the application to define various betting strategies that are not unique to Blackjack but apply to any casino game

The architecture of this package may simplify upgrading our design. If each module is smaller and more focused, it's more readable and more understandable. It may be simpler to update each module in isolation.

Designing a package with alternate implementations

In some cases, we'll have a top-level `__init__.py` file that chooses between some alternative implementations within the package directory. The decision might be based on the platform, CPU architecture, or the availability of OS libraries.

There are two common design patterns and one less common design pattern for packages with alternative implementations:

- Examine `platform` or `sys` to determine the details of the implementation and decide what to import with an `if` statement.

- Attempt `import` and use a `try` block exception handling to work out the configuration details.
- As a less common alternative, an application may examine a configuration parameter to determine what should be imported. This is a bit more complex. We have an ordering issue between importing an application configuration and importing other application modules based on the configuration. It's far simpler to import without this potentially complex sequence of steps.

Here's `__init__.py` for a `some_algorithm` package, which chooses an implementation based on the platform information:

```
import platform
bits, linkage = platform.architecture()
if bits == '64bit':
    from some_algorithm.long_version import *
else:
    from some_algorithm.short_version import *
```

This uses the `platform` module to determine the details of the platform's architecture. There is an ordering dependency here, but depending on a standard library module is superior to a more complex application configuration module.

We will provide two modules within the `some_algorithm` package the `long_version` module provides an implementation appropriate for a 64-bit architecture; the `short_version` module provides an alternate implementation. The design must have module isomorphism; this is similar to class isomorphism. Both the modules must contain classes and functions with the same names and same APIs.

If both the files define a class named `SomeClass`, then we can write the following code in an application:

```
import some_algorithm
process= some_algorithm.SomeClass()
```

We can import the `some_algorithm` package as if it were a module. The package locates an appropriate implementation and provides the needed class and function definitions.

The alternative to an `if` statement is to use a `try` statement to locate a candidate's implementation. This technique works well when there are different distributions. Often, a platform-specific distribution may include files that are unique to the platform.

In *Chapter 14, The Logging and Warning Modules*, we showed you this design pattern in the context of providing warnings in the event of a configuration error or problem. In some cases, tracking down variant configurations doesn't deserve a warning, because the variant configuration is a design feature.

Here's `__init__.py` for a `some_algorithm` package, which chooses an implementation based on the availability of the module files within the package:

```
try:
    from some_algorithm.long_version import *
except ImportError as e:
    from some_algorithm.short_version import *
```

This depends on having two distinct distributions that will include either the `some_algorithm/long_version.py` file or the `some_algorithm/short_version.py` file. If the `some_algorithm.long_version` module is not found, then `short_version` will be imported.

This doesn't scale to more than two or three alternative implementations. As the number of choices grows, the `except` blocks will become very deeply nested. The alternative is to wrap each `try` in `if` to create a flatter design.

Designing a main script and the __main__ module

A top-level main script will execute our application. In some cases, we may have multiple main scripts because our application does several things. We have three general approaches to writing the top-level main script:

- For very small applications, we can run the application with `python3.3 some_script.py`. This is the style that we've shown you in most examples.
- For some larger applications, we'll have one or more files that we mark as executable with the OS `chmod +x` command. We can put these executable files into Python's `scripts` directory with our `setup.py` installation. We run these applications with `some_script.py` at the command line.
- For complex applications, we might add a `__main__.py` module in the application's package. To provide a tidy interface, the standard library offers the `runpy` module and the `-m` command-line option that will use this specially named module. We can run this with `python3.3 -m some_app`.

We'll look at the last two options in detail.

Creating an executable script file

To use an executable script file, we have a two-step implementation: make it executable and include a `#!` ("shebang") line. We will take a look at the details.

We mark the script executable with `chmod +x some_script.py`. Then, we include a `#!` shebang line:

```
#!/usr/bin/env python3.3
```

This line will direct the OS to use the named program to execute the script file. In this case, we used the `/usr/bin/env` program to locate the `python3.3` program to run the script. The Python3.3 program will be given the script file as its input.

Once the script file is marked executable—and includes the `#!` line—we can use `some_script.py` at the command line to run the script.

For a more complex application, this top-level script may import other modules and packages. It's important that these top-level executable script files should be as simple as possible. We have emphasized the design of top-level executable script files.

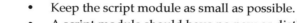

- Keep the script module as small as possible.
- A script module should have no new or distinctive code. It should always import existing code.
- No program stands alone.

Our design goals must always include the idea of composite, larger-scale programming. It's awkward to have some parts of our program in the proper Python library but other parts in the scripts directory. A main script file should be as short as possible. Here's our example:

```
import simulation
with simulation.Logging_Config():
   with simulation.Application_Config() as config:
       main= simulation.Simulate_Command()
       main.config= config
       main.run()
```

All of the relevant working code is imported from a module named `simulation`. There's no unique or distinctive new code introduced in this module.

Creating a __main__ module

To work with the runpy interface, we have a simple implementation. We add a small __main__.py module to our application's top-level package. We have emphasized the design of this top-level executable script file.

We should always permit refactoring an application to build a larger, more sophisticated composite application. If there's functionality buried in __main__.py, we need to pull this into a module with a clear, importable name so that it can be used by other applications.

A __main__.py module should be something small like the following code:

```
import simulation
with simulation.Logging_Config():
    with simulation.Application_Config() as config:
        main= simulation.Simulate_Command()
        main.config= config
        main.run()
```

We've done the minimum to create the working contexts for our application. All of the real processing is imported from the package. Also, we've assumed that this __main__.py module will never be imported.

This is about all that should be in a __main__ module. Our goal is to maximize the reuse potential of our application.

Programming in the large

Here's an example that shows us why we shouldn't put unique, working code into the __main__.py module. We'll show you a quick hypothetical example to extend existing packages.

Imagine that we have a generic statistical package, named stats, with a top-level __main__.py module. This implements a command-line interface that will compute descriptive statistics of a given CSV file. This application has a command-line API as follows:

```
python3.3 -m stats -c 10 some_file.csv
```

This command uses a -c option to specify which column to analyze. The input filename is provided as a positional argument on the command line.

Let's assume, further, that we have a terrible design problem. We've defined a high-level function, analyze(), in the stats/__main__.py module.

Our goal is to combine this with our Blackjack simulation. As we have a design error, this won't work out well. We might *think* we can do this:

```
import stats
import simulation
import types
def sim_and_analyze():
    with simulation.Application_Config() as config_sim:
        config_sim.outputfile= "some_file.csv"
        s = simulation.Simulate()
        s.run()
    config_stats= types.SimpleNamespace( column=10, input="some_file.
csv" )
    stats.analyze( config_stats )
```

We tried to use `stats.analyze()`, assuming that the useful, high-level interface is part of the package, not part of `__main__.py`. This kind of simple composition was made needlessly difficult by defining a function in `__main__`.

We want to avoid being forced to do this:

```
def analyze( column, filename ):
    import subprocess
    subprocess.check_call( "python3.3 -m stats -c {0} {1}".format(
        column, filename) )
```

We shouldn't need to create composite Python applications via the command-line API. In order to create a sensible composition of the existing applications, we might be forced to refactor `stats/__main__.py` to remove any definitions from this module and push them up into the package as a whole.

Designing long-running applications

A long-running application server will be reading requests from some kind of queue and formulating responses to those requests. In many cases, we leverage the HTTP protocol and build application servers into a web server framework. See *Chapter 12, Transmitting and Sharing Objects*, for details on how to implement RESTful web services following the WSGI design pattern.

A desktop GUI application has a lot of features in common with a server. It reads events from a queue that includes mouse and keyboard actions. It handles each event and gives some kind of GUI response. In some cases, the response may be a small update to a text widget. In other cases, a file might get opened or closed, and the state of menu items may change.

In both cases, the central feature of the application is a loop that runs forever, handling events or requests. Because these loops are simple, they're often part of the framework. For a GUI application, we might have a loop like the following code:

```
root= Tkinter.Tk()
app= Application(root)
root.mainloop()
```

For `Tkinter` applications, the top-level widget's `mainloop()` gets each GUI event and hands it to the appropriate framework component for handling. When the object handling events—the top-level widget, `root`, in the example—executes the `quit()` method, then the loop will be gracefully terminated.

For a WSGI-based web server framework, we might have a loop like the following code:

```
httpd = make_server('', 8080, debug)
httpd.serve_forever()
```

In this case, the server's `serve_forever()` method gets each request and hands it to the application—`debug` in this example—for handling. When the application executes the server's `shutdown()` method, the loop will be gracefully terminated.

We often have some additional requirements that distinguish long-running applications:

- **Robust**: In one sense, this requirement is needless; all software should work. However, when dealing with external OS or network resources, there are timeouts and other errors that must be confronted successfully. An application framework that allows for plugins and extensions enjoys the possibility of an extension component harboring an error that the overall framework must handle gracefully. Python's ordinary exception handling is perfectly adequate for writing robust servers.
- **Auditable**: A simple, centralized log is not always sufficient. In *Chapter 14, The Logging and Warning Modules*, we addressed techniques to create multiple logs to support the security or financial audit requirements.
- **Debuggable**: Ordinary unit testing and integration testing reduces the need for complex debugging tools. However, external resources and software plugins or extensions create complexities that may be difficult to handle without providing some debugging support. More sophisticated logging can be helpful.

- **Configurable**: Except for simple technology spikes, we want to be able to enable or disable the application features. Enabling or disabling debugging logs, for example, is a common configuration change. In some cases, we want to make these changes without completely stopping and restarting an application. In *Chapter 13, Configuration Files and Persistence*, we looked at some techniques to configure an application. In *Chapter 16, Coping with the Command Line*, we extended these techniques.
- **Controllable**: A simplistic long-running server can simply be killed to restart it with a different configuration. In order to ensure that buffers are flushed properly and OS resources are released properly, it's better to use a signal other than `SIGKILL` to force termination. Python has signal-handling capabilities available in the `signal` module.

These last two requirements—dynamic configuration and clean shutdown—lead us to separate the primary event or request input from a secondary control input. This control input can provide additional requests for configuration or shutdown.

We have a number of ways to provide asynchronous inputs through an additional channel:

- One of the simplest ways is to create a queue using the `multiprocessing` module. In this case, a simple administrative client can interact with this queue to control or interrogate the server or GUI. For more examples of `multiprocessing`, see *Chapter 12, Transmitting and Sharing Objects*. We can transmit the control or status objects between the administrative client and the server.
- Lower-level techniques are defined in *Chapter 18* of *Python Standard Library*. These modules can also be used to coordinate with a long-running server or GUI application. They're not as sophisticated as creating a queue or a pipe via `multiprocessing`.

Generally, we're going to be most successful using the higher-level APIs available through `multiprocessing`. The lower-level techniques (`socket`, `signal`, `mmap`, `asyncore`, and `asynchat`) are relatively primitive and provide few features. They should be viewed as the internal support for higher-level modules such as `multiprocessing`.

Organizing code into src, bin, and test

As we noted in the previous section, there's no essential need for a complex directory structure. Simple Python applications can be built in a simple, flat directory. We can include the application modules, test modules, as well as `setup.py` and `README`. This is pleasantly simple and easy to work with.

When the modules and packages get more complex, however, we'll often need to be a bit more structured. For complex applications, one common approach is to segregate Python code into three bundles. To make the examples concrete, let's assume that our application is called `my_app`. Here are the typical directories we might create:

- `my_app/my_app`: This directory has all of the working application code. All of the various modules and packages are here. A vaguely named `src` directory is uninformative. This `my_app` directory should include an empty `__init__.py` file so that the application also acts as a package.
- `my_app/bin` or `my_spp/scripts`: This directory can have any scripts that form an OS-level command-line API. These scripts can be copied to the Python `scripts` directory by `setup.py`. As noted previously, these should be like the `__main__.py` module; they should be very short, and they can be thought of as OS filename aliases for Python code.
- `my_app/test`: This directory can have the various `unittest` modules. This directory, too, should include an empty `__init__.py` file so that it acts as a package. It can also include `__main__.py` to run all of the tests in the entire package.

The top-level directory name, `my_app`, might be augmented with a version number to permit having versions without confusion. We might have `my_app-v1.1` as a top-level directory name. The application within that top-level directory must have a proper Python name, so we'd see `my_app-v1.1/my_app` as the path to the application.

The top-level directory should contain the `setup.py` file to install the application into Python's standard library structure. See *Distributing Python Modules* for more information. Additionally, of course, a `README` file would be placed in this directory.

When the application modules and test modules are in separate directories, we need to refer to the application as an installed module when running tests. We can use the `PYTHONPATH` environment variable for this. We can run the test suite like the following code:

```
PYTHONPATH=my_app python3.3 -m test
```

We set an environment variable on the same line where we execute a command. This may be surprising, but it's a first-class feature of the `bash` shell. This allows us to make a very localized override to the `PYTHONPATH` environment variable.

Installing Python modules

We have several techniques to install a Python module or package:

- We can write `setup.py` and use the distribution utilities module, `distutils`, to install the package into Python's `lib/site-packages` directory. See *Distributing Python Modules*.
- We can set the `PYTHONPATH` environment variable to include our packages and modules. We can set this temporarily in a shell, or we can set it more permanently by editing our `~/.bash_profile` or the system's `/etc/profile`. We'll take a look at this in a little more depth in the later section.
- We can include the `.pth` files to add directories to the import path. These files can be located in the local directory or `lib/site-packages` to provide an indirect reference to a module or package. See the `site` module documentation in *Python Standard Library* for more information.
- The local directory is a package as well. It's always first on the `sys.path` list. When working on a simple one-module Python application, this is very handy. When working on a more complex application, the current working directory may change as we edit different files, making it a poor choice.

Setting the environment variable can be done transiently or persistently. We can set it in an interactive session with a command like the following code:

```
export PYTHONPATH=~/my_app-v1.2/my_app
```

This sets `PYTHONPATH` to include the named directory when searching for a module. The module is effectively installed through this simple change to the environment. Nothing is written to Python's `lib/site-packages`.

This is a transient setting that may be lost when we end the terminal session. The alternative is to update our `~/.bash_profile` to include a more permanent change to the environment. We simply append that `export` line to `.bash_profile` so that the package is used every time we log in.

For users on a shared server, we might include the environment setting in `/etc/profile` so that they do not have to make changes to their `~/.bash_profile`. For users on individual workstations, offering `setup.py` based on `distutils` may be simpler than tweaking system settings.

For web applications, the Apache configuration may need to be updated to include access to the necessary Python modules. To support the rapid deployment of application changes, it's generally not necessary to use `setup.py` for a large, complex application. Instead, we often use a series of application directories and a simple `.pth` change or `PYTHONPATH` change to move to the new release.

We might have the following kind of directories owned by a fake user, `myapp`:

```
/Users/myapp/my_app-v1.2/my_app
/Users/myapp/my_app-v1.3/my_app
```

This allows us to build a new release in parallel with an existing release. We can switch from Version 1.2 to Version 1.3 by changing `PYTHONPATH` to refer to `/Users/myapp/my_app-v1.3/my_app`.

Summary

We looked at a number of considerations to design modules and packages. The parallels between a module and singleton class are deep. When we design a module, the essential questions of the encapsulation of the structure and processing are as relevant as they are for class design.

When we design a package, we need to be skeptical of the need for deeply nested structures. We'll need to use packages when there are variant implementations; we looked at a number of ways to handle this variability. We may also need to define a package to combine a number of modules into a single module-like package. We looked at how `__init__.py` can import from within the package.

Design considerations and trade-offs

We have a deep hierarchy of packaging techniques. We can simply organize the functionality into defined functions. We can combine the defined functions and their related data into a class. We can combine related classes into a module. We can combine related modules into a package.

When we think of software as a language to capture knowledge and representation, we have to consider what a class or module *means*. A module is the unit of the Python software construction, distribution, use, and reuse. With rare exceptions, modules must be designed around the possibility of reuse.

In most cases, we'll use a class because we expect to have multiple objects that are instances of the class. Often—but not universally—a class will have stateful instance variables.

When we look at classes with only a single instance, it's not perfectly clear if a class is truly necessary. Standalone functions may be as meaningful as a single-instance class. In some instances, a module of separate functions may be an appropriate design because modules are inherently singletons.

A stateful module—such as a stateful class—is the general expectation. A module is a namespace with local variables that can be modified.

While we can create immutable classes (using `__slots__`, extending `tuple`, or overriding the attribute setter methods), we can't easily create an immutable module. There doesn't seem to be a use case for an immutable module object.

A small application may be a single module. A larger application will often be a package. As with module design, packages should be designed for reuse. A larger application package should properly include a `__main__` module.

Looking forward

In the next chapter, we'll consolidate a number of our OO design techniques. We'll take a look at the overall quality of our design and implementation. One consideration is assuring others that our software is trustworthy. One aspect of trustworthy software is coherent, easy-to-use documentation.

18
Quality and Documentation

Good software doesn't just happen; it's crafted. A deliverable product includes readable, accurate documentation. We'll look at two tools to produce the documentation from the code: `pydoc` and Sphinx. The Sphinx tool is enhanced if we write the documentation using a lightweight markup language. We'll describe some features of **ReStructured Text** (**RST**) to help make our documentation more readable.

Documentation is an important quality aspect of software; it is one aspect of building trust. Test cases are another way to build trust. Using `doctest` to write test cases addresses both the quality aspects.

We'll also take a brief look at literate programming techniques. The idea is to write a pleasant, easy-to-understand document that contains the entire body of the source code along with explanatory notes and design details. Literate programming isn't simple, but it can produce good code coupled with a resulting document that is very clear and complete.

Writing docstrings for the help() function

Python provides numerous places to include the documentation. The definition of a package, module, class, or function has room for a string that includes a description of the object that is being defined. Throughout this book, we avoided showing you docstrings in each example because our focus is on the Python programming details, not the overall software product that is being delivered.

As we move beyond advanced OO design and look at the overall deliverable product, docstrings become an important part of the deliverable. Docstrings can provide us with several key pieces of information:

- The API: the parameters, return values, and exceptions raised.
- A description of what to expect.
- Optionally, the `doctest` test results. For more information, see *Chapter 15, Designing for Testability*.

We can, of course, write even more in a docstring. We can provide more details on the design, architecture, and requirements. At some point, these more abstract, higher-level considerations are not directly tied to the Python code. This higher-level design and the requirements don't properly belong to the code or the docstrings.

The `help()` function extracts and displays the docstrings. It performs some minimal formatting on the text. The `help()` function is installed into the interactive Python environment by the `site` package. The function is actually defined in the `pydoc` package. In principle, we can import and extend this package to customize the `help()` output.

Writing documentation that is suitable for `help()` is relatively simple. Here's a typical example of output from `help(round)`.

```
round(...)
    round(number[, ndigits]) -> number

    Round a number to a given precision in decimal digits (default 0
digits).
    This returns an int when called with one argument, otherwise the
    same type as the number. ndigits may be negative.
```

This shows us the required elements: the summary, the API, and the description. The API and the summary are the first line: `function( parameters ) -> results`.

The description text defines what the function does. More complex functions may describe exceptions or edge cases that might be important or unique to this function. The `round()` function, for example, doesn't detail things, such as `TypeError`, that might get raised.

A `help()` oriented docstring is expected to be pure text with no markup. We can add some RST markup but it isn't used by `help()`.

To make `help()` work, we simply provide docstrings. As it's so simple, there's no reason not to do it. Every function or class needs a docstring so that `help()` shows us something useful.

Using pydoc for documentation

We use the library module `pydoc` to produce HTML documentation from Python code. It turns out that we're using it when we evaluate the `help()` function in interactive Python. This function produces the *text mode* documentation with no markup.

When we use pydoc to produce the documentation, we'll use it in one of the following three ways:

- Prepare text-mode documentation files and view them with command-line tools such as more or less
- Prepare HTML documentation and save a file for browsing later
- Run an HTTP server and create the HTML files as needed for browsing immediately

We can run the following command-line tool to prepare the text-based documentation for a module:

```
pydoc somemodule
```

We can also use the following code:

```
python3.3 -m pydoc somemodule
```

Either command will create text documentation based on the Python code. The output will be displayed with programs such as less (on Linux or Mac OS X) or more (on Windows) that paginate the long stream of output.

Ordinarily, pydoc presumes that we're providing a module name to import. This means that the module must be on the Python path for ordinary import. As an alternative, we can specify a physical filename by including a path separator character / (on Linux or Mac OS X) or \ (on Windows) and the .py filename extension. Something such as pydoc ./mymodule.py will work to pick a file that's not on the import path.

To view the HTML documentation, we use the -w option. This will write an HTML file into the local directory:

```
python3.3 -m pydoc -w somemodule
```

We can then open somemodule.html in a browser to read the documentation for the given module. The third option is to start a special-purpose web server to browse a package or module's documentation. In addition to simply starting the server, we can combine starting the server and launching our default browser. Here's a way to simply start a server on port 8080:

```
python3.3 -m pydoc -p 8080
```

This will start an HTTP server that looks at the code in the current directory. If the current directory is a proper package (that is, it has a __init__.py file), then there will be a nice top-level module index.

Once we've started a server, we can point a browser at `http://localhost:8080` to view the documentation. We can also use a rewrite rule to point a local Apache server at this `pydoc` server so that a team can share the documentation on a web server.

We can also start both a local server and a browser at the same time:

```
python3.3 -m pydoc -b
```

This will locate an unused port, start a server, and then launch your default browser to point at the server. Note the use of the `python3.3` command; this doesn't work in the older releases of Python.

It's not easy to customize the output from `pydoc`. The various styles and colors are effectively hardcoded into the class definitions. Revising and expanding `pydoc` to use the external CSS styles would be an interesting exercise.

Better output via the RST markup

Our documentation can be much nicer if we use a more sophisticated toolset. There are several things that we'd like to be able to do, such as the following:

- Fine-tune the presentation to include emphasis such as bold, italic, or color.
- Provide the semantic markup for the parameters, return values, exceptions, and cross-references among Python objects.
- Provide a link to view the source code.
- Filter the code that's included or rejected. We can fine-tune this filtering to include or exclude a number of components and members: standard library modules, private members with a leading __, system members with a leading __, or superclass members.
- Adjust the CSS to provide a different style for the resulting HTML pages.

We can address the first two requirements through more sophisticated markup in our docstrings; we'll need to use the RST markup language. We'll need an additional tool to address the last three requirements.

Once we start using more sophisticated markup, we can branch out beyond HTML to include LaTeX for even better-looking documentation. This allows us to also produce PostScript or PDF output in addition to HTML from a single source.

RST is a simple, lightweight markup. There are plenty of good tutorials and summaries associated with the Python `docutils` project. See `http://docutils.sourceforge.net` for details.

A quick overview is available here: `http://docutils.sourceforge.net/docs/user/rst/quickstart.html`.

The point of the `docutils` toolset is that a very smart parser allows us to use very simple markup. HTML and XML rely on a relatively unsophisticated parser and put the burden on the human (or an editing tool) to create the complex markup. While XML and HTML allow for a wide variety of use cases, the `docutils` parser is more narrowly focused on the natural language text. Because of the narrow focus, `docutils` is able to deduce our intent based on the use of blank lines and some ASCII punctuation characters.

For our purposes, the `docutils` parser recognizes the following three fundamental things:

- Blocks of text: paragraphs, headings, lists, block quotes, code samples, and the `doctest` blocks. These are all separated by blank lines.
- Inline markup can appear inside the text blocks. This involves the use of simple punctuation to mark the characters within the text block. There are two kinds of inline markup; we'll look at the details in the later section.
- Directives are also blocks of text, but they begin with `..` as the first two characters of the line. Directives are open-ended and can be extended to add features to docutils.

Blocks of text

A block of text is simply a paragraph, set off from other paragraphs by a blank line. This is the fundamental unit of the RST markup. RST recognizes a number of kinds of paragraphs, based on the pattern that is followed. Here's an example of a heading:

```
This Is A Heading
=================
```

This is recognized as a heading because it's *underlined* with a repeated string of special characters.

The `docutils` parser deduces the hierarchy of title underlines based entirely on their usage. We must be consistent with our headings and their nesting. It helps to pick a standard and stick to it. It also helps to keep documents fairly *flat* without complex, nested headings. Three levels are often all that's needed; this means that we can use `====`, `----`, and `~~~~` for the three levels.

A bullet list item begins with a special character; the content must also be indented. As Python uses a 4-space indent, this is common in RST as well. However, almost any consistent indent will work:

```
Bullet Lists

-   Leading Special Character.

-   Consistent Indent.
```

Note the blank line between paragraphs. For some kinds of simple bullet lists, the blank lines aren't required. In general, blank lines are a good idea.

A numeric list begins with a digit or letter and a roman numeral. To have numbers generated automatically, # can be used as the list item:

```
Number Lists

1.  Leading digit or letter.

2.  Auto-numbering with #.

#.  Looks like this.
```

We can use the indent rules to create lists within lists. It can be complex, and the `docutils` RST parser will usually figure out what you meant.

A block quote is simply indented text:

```
Here's a paragraph with a cool quote.

    Cool quotes might include a tip.

Here's another paragraph.
```

Code samples are indicated with a `::` double colon; they are indented and they end with a blank line. While `::` can be at the end of a line or on a line by itself, putting `::` on a separate line makes it slightly easier to find code samples.

Here's a code sample:

```
::

    x = Deck()
    first_card= x.pop()

This shows two lines of code. It will be distinguished from
surrounding text.
```

The docutils parser will also locate the doctest material and set it aside for special formatting, similar to a code block. They begin with >>> and end with a blank line.

Here's some sample output from doctest:

```
>>> x= Unsorted_Deck()
>>> x.pop()
'A♣'
```

The blank line at the end of the test output is essential and is easily overlooked.

The RST inline markup

Within most blocks of text, we can include inline markup. We can't include inline markup in the code samples or doctest blocks. Note that we cannot nest inline markup, either.

The RST inline markup includes a variety of common ASCII treatments of text. For example, we have *emphasis* and **strong emphasis**, which will usually produce italic and bold respectively. We might want to emphasize code segments within a block of text; we use ``literal`` to force a monospaced font.

We can also include cross-references as the inline markup. A trailing _ indicates a reference, and it points away; a leading _ indicates a target, and it points toward. For example, we might have `some phrase`_ as a reference. We can then use _`some phrase` as the target for that reference. We don't need to provide explicit targets for section titles: we can reference `This Is A Heading`_ because all the section titles are already defined as targets. For the HTML output, this will generate the expected <a> tags. For the PDF output, in-text links will be generated.

We cannot nest inline markup. There's little need for nested inline markup; using too many typographic tricks devolves to visual clutter. If our writing is so sensitive to typography, we should probably use LaTeX directly.

Inline markup can also have explicit role indicators. This is :role: followed by `text`. Simple RST has relatively few roles. We might use :code:`some code` to be more explicit about the presence of a code sample in the text. When we look at Sphinx, there are numerous role indicators. The use of explicit roles can provide a great deal of semantic information.

When doing things that have more complex math, we might use the LaTeX math typesetting capabilities. This uses the `:math:` role; it looks like this: `:math:`a=\pi r^2``.

Roles are open-ended. We can provide a configuration to docutils that adds new roles.

RST directives

RST also includes directives. A directive is written in a block that starts with `..`; it may have content that's indented. It may also have parameters. RST has a large number of directives that we might use to create a more sophisticated document. For docstring preparation, we'll rarely use more than a few of the available directives. The directives are open-ended; tools such as Sphinx will add directives to produce more sophisticated documentation.

Three commonly used directives are `image`, `csv-table`, and `math`. If we have an image that should be part of our document, we might include it in the following way:

```
..  image:: media/some_file.png
    :width: 6in
```

We named the file `media/some_file.png`. We also provided it with a `width` parameter to ensure that our image fits our document page layout. There are a number of other parameters that we can use to adjust the presentation of an image.

- `:align`: We can provide keywords such as `top`, `middle`, `bottom`, `left`, `center`, or `right`. This value will be provided to the `align` attribute of the HTML `<img>` tag.
- `:alt`: This is the alternative text for the image. This value will be provided to the `alt` attribute of the HTML `<img>` tag.
- `:height`: This is the height of the image.
- `:scale`: This is a scale factor that can be provided instead of the height and width.
- `:width`: This is the width of the image.
- `:target`: This is a target hyperlink for the image. This can be a complete URI or an RST reference of the `` `name`_ `` form.

For the height and width, any of the length units available in CSS can be used. These include `em` (the height of the element's font), `ex` (the height of the letter "x"), `px` (pixels), as well as absolute sizes: `in`, `cm`, `mm`, `pt` (point), and `pc` (pica).

We can include a table in our document in the following manner:

```
..  csv-table:: Suits
    :header: symbol, name

    "'♣'", Clubs
    "'♦'", Diamonds
    "'♥'", Hearts
    "'♠'", Spades
```

This allows us to prepare data that will become a complex HTML table in a simple CSV notation. We can have a more complex formula using the `math` directive:

```
..  math::
    c = 2 \pi r
```

This allows us to write larger LaTeX math that will be a separate equation. These can be numbered and cross-referenced as well.

Learning RST

One way to build skills in RST is to install `docutils` and use the `rst2html.py` script to parse an RST document and convert it to HTML pages. A simple practice document can easily show us the various RST features.

All of a project's requirements, architecture, and documentation can be written using RST and transformed into HTML or LaTeX. It's relatively inexpensive to write user stories in RST and drop those files into a directory that can be organized and reorganized as stories are groomed, put into development, and implemented. More complex tools may not be any more valuable than `docutils`.

The advantage of using pure text files and the RST markup is that we can easily manage our documentation in parallel with our source code. We're not using a proprietary word processing file format. We're not using a wordy and long-winded HTML or XML markup that must be compressed to be practical. We're simply storing more text along with the source code.

If we're using RST to create the documentation, we can also use the `rst2latex.py` script to create a `.tex` file that we can run through a LaTeX toolset to create postscript or PDF documents. This requires a LaTeX toolset; usually, the **TeXLive** distribution is used for this. See `http://www.tug.org/texlive/` for a comprehensive set of tools to transform TeX into elegant, final documents. TeXLive includes the pdfTeX tool that can be used to convert the LaTeX output into a PDF file.

Writing effective docstrings

When writing docstrings, we need to focus on the essential information that our audience needs. When we look at using a library module, what do we need to know? Whatever questions we ask, other programmers will often have similar questions. There are two boundaries that we should stay inside when we write docstrings:

- It's best to avoid abstract overviews, high-level requirements, user stories, or background that is not tied directly to the code. We should focus the docstring on the code itself. We should provide the background in a separate document. A tool such as Sphinx can combine background material and code into a single document.
- It's best to also avoid overly detailed *how it works* implementation trivia. The code is readily available, so there's no point in recapitulating the code in the documentation. If the code is too obscure, perhaps it should be rewritten to make it clearer.

Perhaps the single most important thing that developers want is a working example of how to use the Python object. The RST `::` literal block is the backbone of these examples.

We'll often write code samples in the following manner:

```
Here's an example::

    d= Deck()
    c= d.pop()
```

The double colon, `::`, precedes an indented block. The indented block is recognized by the RST parser as code and will be literally passed through to the final document.

In addition to an example, the formal API is also important. We'll take a look at several API definition techniques in the later section. These rely on the RST *field list* syntax. It's very simple, which makes it very flexible.

Once we're past the example and the API, there are a number of other things that compete for third place. What else we need to write depends on the context. There appear to be three cases:

- **Files (including packages and modules)**: In these cases, we're providing an overview or introduction to a collection of modules, classes, or function definitions. We need to provide a simple roadmap or overview of the various elements in the file. In the case where the module is relatively small, we might provide the doctest and code samples at this level.

- **Classes (including method functions)**: This is where we often provide code samples and `doctest` blocks that explain the class API. Because a class may be stateful and may have a relatively complex API, we may need to provide rather lengthy documentation. Individual method functions will often have detailed documentation.
- **Functions**: We may provide code samples and `doctest` blocks that explain the function. Because a function is often stateless, we may have a relatively simple API. In some cases, we may avoid more sophisticated RST markup and focus on the `help()` function's documentation.

We'll take a look at each of these broad, vague documentation contexts in some detail.

Writing file-level docstrings, including modules and packages

A package or a module's purpose is to contain a number of elements. A package contains modules as well as classes, global variables, and functions. A module contains classes, global variables, and functions. The top-level docstrings on these containers can act as road-maps to explain the general features of the package or module. The details are delegated to the individual classes or functions.

We might have a module docstring that looks like the following code:

```
Blackjack Cards and Decks
=========================

This module contains a definition of ``Card``, ``Deck`` and ``Shoe``
suitable for Blackjack.

The ``Card`` class hierarchy
-----------------------------

The ``Card`` class hierarchy includes the following class definitions.

``Card`` is the superclass as well as being the class for number
cards.
``FaceCard`` defines face cards: J, Q and K.
``AceCard`` defines the Ace. This is special in Blackjack because it
creates a soft total for a hand.

We create cards using the ``card()`` factory function to create the
proper
``Card`` subclass instances from a rank and suit.

The ``suits`` global variable is a sequence of Suit instances.
```

```
>>> import cards
>>> ace_clubs= cards.card( 1, cards.suits[0] )
>>> ace_clubs
'A♣'
>>> ace_diamonds= cards.card( 1, cards.suits[1] )
>>> ace_clubs.rank ==  ace_diamonds.rank
True

The ``Deck`` and ``Shoe`` class hierarchy
-------------------------------------------

The basic ``Deck`` creates a single 52-card deck. The ``Shoe``
subclass creates a given number of decks. A ``Deck`` can be shuffled
before the cards can be extracted with the ``pop()`` method. A
``Shoe`` must be shuffled and *burned*. The burn operation sequesters
a random number of cards based on a mean and standard deviation. The
mean is a number of cards (52 is the default.) The standard deviation
for the burn is also given as a number of cards (2 is the default.)
```

Most of the text in this docstring provides a roadmap to the contents of this module. It describes the class hierarchies, making it slightly easier to locate a relevant class.

The docstring includes a simple example of the `card()` factory function based on `doctest`. This advertises this function as an important feature of the module as a whole. It might make sense to provide the `doctest` explanation of the `Shoe` class, as that's perhaps the most important part of this module.

This docstring includes some inline RST markup to put class names into a monospaced font. The section titles are *underlined* with `===` and `---` lines. The RST parser can determine that the heading underlined with `===` is the parent of the headings underlined with `---`.

We'll look at using Sphinx to produce the documentation, in the later section. Sphinx will leverage the RST markup to produce great-looking HTML documentation.

Writing API details in RST markup

One of the benefits of using the RST markup is that we can provide formal API documentation. The API parameters and return values are formatted using an RST *field list*. Generally, a field list has the following form:

```
:field1: some value
:field2: another value
```

A field list is a sequence of field labels (as `:label:`) and a value associated with that label. The label is generally short, and the value can be as long as needed. Field lists are also used to provide parameters to directives.

When the field list's text is present in an RST document, the docutils tools can create a nice-looking, table-like display. In PDF, it might look like the following code:

```
field1    some value
field2    another value
```

We'll use an extended form of the RST field list syntax to write the API documentation. We'll extend the field name to become a multipart item. We'll add prefixes with keywords such as `param` or `type`. The prefix will be followed by the parameter's name.

There are several field prefixes. We can use any of these: `param`, `parameter`, `arg`, `argument`, `key`, and `keyword`. For example, we might write the following code:

```
:param rank: Numeric rank of the card
:param suit: Suit of the card
```

We generally use `param` (or `parameter`) for the positional parameters and `key` (or `keyword`) for the keyword parameters. We advise you against using `arg` or `argument` to document Python code, as they don't fit the Python syntax categories. These prefixes could be used to document shell scripts or APIs in other languages.

These field list definitions will be collected into an indented section. The Sphinx tool will also compare the names in the documentation with the names in the function argument list to be sure that they match.

We can also define the type of a parameter using `type` as a prefix:

```
:type rank: integer in the range 1-13.
```

Because of Python's flexibility, this can be a needless detail. In many cases, the argument value need only be numeric, and simple `:param somearg:` can include generic type information as part of the description. We showed you this style in the earlier example: `Numeric rank of the card`.

For functions that return a value, we should describe the result. We can summarize the return value with the field label of `returns` or `return`. We can also formally specify the type of the return value with `rtype`. We might write the following code:

```
:returns: soft total for this card
:rtype: integer
```

Additionally, we should also include information about exceptions that are unique to this function. We have four aliases for this field: `raises`, `raise`, `except`, and `exception`. We would write the following code:

```
:raises TypeError: rank value not in range(1, 14).
```

We can also describe the attributes of a class. For this, we can use `var`, `ivar`, or `cvar`. We might write the following code:

```
:ivar soft: soft points for this card; usually hard points, except for aces.
:ivar hard: hard points for this card; usually the rank, except for face cards.
```

We should use `ivar` for instance variables and `cvar` for class variables. However, there's no visible difference in the final HTML output.

These field list constructs are used to prepare docstrings for classes, class methods, and standalone functions. We'll look at each case in the later section.

Writing class and method function docstrings

A class will often contain a number of elements, including attributes and method functions. A stateful class may also have a relatively complex API. Objects will be created, undergo changes in state, and possibly be garbage-collected at the end of their lives. We might want to describe some (or all) of these state changes in the class docstring or the method function docstrings.

We'll use the field list technique to document the class variables in the overall class docstring. This will generally focus on using the `:ivar variable:`, `:cvar variable:`, and `:var variable:` field list items.

Each individual method function will also use field lists to define the parameters and return the values and exceptions raised by each method function. Here's how we might start to write a class with docstrings for the class and method functions:

```
class Card:
    """Definition of a numeric rank playing card.
    Subclasses will define ``FaceCard`` and ``AceCard``.

    :ivar rank: Rank
    :ivar suit: Suit
    :ivar hard: Hard point total for a card
    :ivar soft: Soft total; same as hard for all cards except Aces.
    """
    def __init__( self, rank, suit, hard, soft=None ):
```

```
        """Define the values for this card.

        :param rank: Numeric rank in the range 1-13.
        :param suit: Suit object (often a character from '♣⊠◇♠')
        :param hard: Hard point total (or 10 for FaceCard or 1 for
AceCard)
        :param soft: The soft total for AceCard, otherwise defaults to
hard.
        """
        self.rank= rank
        self.suit= suit
        self.hard= hard
        self.soft= soft if soft is not None else hard
```

When we include this kind of RST markup in the docstring, then a tool such as Sphinx can format very nice-looking HTML output. We've provided you with both class-level documentation of the instance variables as well as method-level documentation of the parameters to one of the method functions.

When we look at this with `help()`, the RST is visible. It's not too objectionable, as it's semantically meaningful and not very confusing. This points out a balance that we may need to strike between the `help()` text and the Sphinx documents.

Writing function docstrings

A function docstring can be formatted using field lists to define the parameters and return the values and raised exceptions. Here's an example of a function that includes a docstring:

```
def card( rank, suit ):
    """Create a ``Card`` instance from rank and suit.

    :param rank: Numeric rank in the range 1-13.
    :param suit: Suit object (often a character from '♣♡◇♠')
    :returns: Card instance
    :raises TypeError: rank out of range.

    >>> import p3_c18
    >>> p3_c18.card( 3, '♡' )
    3♡
    """
    if rank == 1: return AceCard( rank, suit, 1, 11 )
    elif 2 <= rank < 11: return Card( rank, suit, rank )
    elif 11 <= rank < 14: return FaceCard( rank, suit, 10 )
```

```
    else:
        raise TypeError( 'rank out of range' )
```

This function docstring includes parameter definitions, return values, and the raised exceptions. There are four individual field list items that formalize the API. We've included a `doctest` sequence as well. When we document this module in Sphinx, we'll get very nice-looking HTML output. Additionally, we can use the `doctest` tool to confirm that the function matches the simple test case.

More sophisticated markup techniques

There are some additional markup techniques that can make a document easier to read. In particular, we often want useful cross-references between class definitions. We may also want cross-references between sections and topics within a document.

In *pure* RST (that is, without Sphinx), we need to provide proper URLs that reference different sections of our documents. We have three kinds of references:

- **Implicit references to section titles**: We can use ``` `Some Heading`_ ``` to refer to the `Some Heading` section. This will work for all the headings that docutils recognizes.
- **Explicit references to targets**: We can use `target_` to reference the location of `_target` in the document.
- **Inter-document references**: We have to create a full URL that explicitly references a section title. Docutils will translate section titles into all lowercase, replacing the punctuation with `-`. This allows us to create a reference to a section title in an external document like this: ``` `Design <file:build.py.html#design>`_ ```.

When we use Sphinx, we get even more inter-document, cross-reference capabilities. These capabilities allow us to avoid trying to write detailed URLs.

Using Sphinx to produce the documentation

The Sphinx tool produces very good-looking documentation in a variety of formats. It can easily combine documentation from source code as well as external files with additional design notes, requirements, or background.

The Sphinx tool can be found at `http://sphinx-doc.org`. The download can become complex because Sphinx depends on several other projects. It may be easier to first install `setuptools`, which includes the `easy_install` script, and then use this to install Sphinx. This can help us with the details of tracking down the additional projects that must be installed first.

See `https://pypi.python.org/pypi/setuptools` for help on `setuptools`.

Some developers prefer to use `pip` for this kind of installation. See `https://pypi.python.org/pypi/pip` for information on `pip`.

The Sphinx tutorial is outstanding. Start there and be sure that you can use `sphinx-quickstart` and `sphinx-build`. Often, running `sphinx-build` is handled via the `make` program, which slightly simplifies the command-line use of Sphinx.

Using the Sphinx quickstart

The handy feature of `sphinx-quickstart` is that it populates the rather complex `config.py` file via an interactive question-and-answer session.

Here's a part of one such session that shows how the dialog looks; we've highlighted a few responses where the defaults don't seem to be optimal.

For more complex projects, it's simpler in the long run to separate the documentation from the working code. It's often a good idea to create a `doc` directory within the overall project tree:

```
Enter the root path for documentation.
> Root path for the documentation [.]: doc
```

For very small documents, it's fine to interleave the source and HTML. For larger documents, particularly documents where there may be a need to produce LaTeX and PDF, it's handy to keep these files separate from the HTML version of the documentation:

```
You have two options for placing the build directory for Sphinx
output.
Either, you use a directory "_build" within the root path, or you
separate
"source" and "build" directories within the root path.
> Separate source and build directories (y/N) [n]: y
```

The next batch of questions identifies specific add-ons; it starts with the following note:

```
Please indicate if you want to use one of the following Sphinx
extensions:
```

We'll suggest a set of add-ons that seem most useful for general Python development. For first-time users of Sphinx, this will be enough to get started and produce excellent documentation. Clearly, specific project needs and objectives will override these generic suggestions.

We'll almost always want to include the `autodoc` feature to produce the documentation from the docstrings. If we're using Sphinx to produce the documentation outside the Python programming, perhaps we might turn `autodoc` off:

```
> autodoc: automatically insert docstrings from modules (y/N) [n]: y
```

If we have `doctest` examples, we can have Sphinx run the doctest for us. For small projects, where most of the testing is done via `doctest`, this can be very handy. For larger projects, we'll often have a unit test script that includes doctest. Performing the doctest via Sphinx as well as through the formal unit test is still a good idea:

```
> doctest: automatically test code snippets in doctest blocks (y/N)
[n]: y
```

A mature development effort may have many projects that are closely related; this might have multiple, related Sphinx documentation directories:

```
> intersphinx: link between Sphinx documentation of different projects
(y/N) [n]:
```

The `todo` extension allows us to include a `.. todo::` directive in our docstrings. We can then add a special `.. todolist::` directive to create an official to-do list in the documentation:

```
> todo: write "todo" entries that can be shown or hidden on build
(y/N) [n]:
```

The coverage report could be a handy quality assurance metric:

```
> coverage: checks for documentation coverage (y/N) [n]:
```

For projects that involve any math, having a LaTeX toolset allows us to have the math nicely typeset as graphic images and included into HTML. It also leaves the raw math in the LaTeX output. MathJax is a web-based JavaScript library that also works in the following manner:

```
> pngmath: include math, rendered as PNG images (y/N) [n]: y
> mathjax: include math, rendered in the browser by MathJax (y/N) [n]:
```

For very complex projects, we might need to produce the variant documentation:

```
> ifconfig: conditional inclusion of content based on config values
(y/N) [n]:
```

Most application documentations describe an API. We should include both the `autodoc` and `viewcode` features. The `viewcode` option allows the reader to view the source so they can understand the implementation in detail:

```
> viewcode: include links to the source code of documented Python
objects (y/N) [n]: y
```

The `autodoc` and `doctest` features mean that we can focus on writing docstrings within our code. We only need to write very small Sphinx documentation files to extract the docstring information. For some developers, the ability to focus on the code reduces the fear factor associated with writing the documentation.

Writing the Sphinx documentation

There are two common starting points for software development projects:

- Some inception documentation has been created, and this should be preserved
- Nothing; inception starts from a blank slate

In the cases where a project starts with some legacy documentation, this might include the requirements, user stories, or architectural notes. It may also include notes on organizational politics, out-of-date budgets and schedules, and other technically irrelevant material.

Ideally, these inception documents are already text files. If not, they may be in some word processor format that can be saved as text. When we have text-oriented inception documents, it's relatively easy to add enough RST markup to show us the outline structure and organize these text files into a simple directory structure.

There's little reason to preserve the content as a word-processing document. Once it's part of the technical content of a software development project, RST permits more flexible use of the inception information.

One of the difficult cases is a project where the inception documentation is a slideshow built using Keynote, PowerPoint, or a similar tool. These don't readily convert to text-centric RST, as the diagrams and images are first-class parts of the content. In these cases, it's sometimes best to export the presentation as an HTML document and put this into the Sphinx `doc/source/_static` directory. This will allow us to integrate the original material into Sphinx via simple RST links of the `` `Inception <_static/inception_doc/index.html>`_ `` form.

When an interactive, web-based tool is used to manage the project or user stories, the inception and background documentation needs to be handled via simple URL references of this form: `` `Background <http://someservice/path/to/page.html>`_ ``.

It's often easiest to start with an outline of placeholders for the documentation that will accumulate as the software development proceeds. One structure that might be helpful is based on the 4+1 views of an architecture. The inception documents are often part of the scenarios or user stories in the 4+1 views. Sometimes, the inception documents are part of the development or physical deployment.

For more information, see this:

`http://en.wikipedia.org/wiki/4%2B1_architectural_view_model`

We can create five top-level documents under our `index.html` root: `user_stories`, `logical`, `process`, `implementation`, and `physical`. Each of these must have an RST title but needs nothing more in the file.

We can then update the `.. toctree::` directive that's generated in the Sphinx `index.rst` file by default:

```
.. Mastering OO Python documentation master file, created by
   sphinx-quickstart on Fri Jan 31 09:21:55 2014.
   You can adapt this file completely to your liking, but it should at
least
   contain the root `toctree` directive.

Welcome to Mastering OO Python's documentation!
===============================================

Contents:

.. toctree::
   :maxdepth: 2

   user_stories
   logical
   process
   implementation
   physical

Indices and tables
==================
```

```
* :ref:`genindex`
* :ref:`modindex`
* :ref:`search`
```

Once we have a top-level structure, we can use the `make` command to build our documentation:

```
make doctest html
```

This will run our doctests; if all the tests pass, it will create the HTML documentation.

Filling in the 4+1 views for documentation

As the development proceeds, the 4+1 views can be used to organize the details that accumulate. This is used for the information that belongs outside the narrow focus of docstrings.

The `user_stories.rst` document is where we collect user stories, requirements, and other high-level background notes. This might evolve into a directory tree if the user stories become complex.

The `logical.rst` document will collect our initial OO designs for the class, module, and package. This should be the origin of our design thinking. It might contain alternatives, notes, mathematical backgrounds, proofs of correctness, and diagrams of the logical software design. For relatively simple projects—where the design is relatively clear—this may remain empty. For complex projects, this may describe some sophisticated analysis and design that serve as the background or justification for the implementation.

The final OO design will be the Python modules and classes that belong in the `implementation.rst` file. We'll take a look at this in a little more detail, as this will become our API documentation. This part will be based in a direct way on our Python code and the RST-markup docstrings.

The `process.rst` document can collect information about the dynamic, runtime behavior. This would include topics such as concurrency, distribution, and integration. It might also contain information on the performance and scalability. The network design and protocols used might be described here.

For smaller applications, the material that should go into the process document isn't perfectly clear. This document may overlap with the logical design and the overall architectural information. When in doubt, we have to strive for clarity based on the audience's need for information. For some users, many small documents are helpful. For other users, a single large document is preferred.

The `physical.rst` file is where the deployment details can be recorded. A description of the configuration details would go here: the environment variables, the configuration file format details, the available logger names, and other information required for the administration and support. This might also include configuration information such as server names, IP addresses, account names, directory paths, and related notes. In some organizations, an administrator might feel that some of these details are not appropriate for general software documentation.

Writing the implementation document

The `implementation.rst` document can be based on using `automodule` to create the documentation. Here's how an `implementation.rst` document might start.

```
Implementation
================

Here's a reference to the `inception document <_static/inception_doc/
index.html>`_

The p3_c18 module
-----------------------

..   automodule:: p3_c18
     :members:
     :undoc-members:
     :special-members:

The simulation_model module
--------------------------------

..   automodule:: simulation_model
     :members:
     :undoc-members:
     :special-members:
```

We used two kinds of RST headings: there's a single top-level heading and two subheadings. RST deduces the relationship between the parent and the children. In this example, we've used "`===`" underlines for the parent heading (also the title) and "`---`" for the subheadings.

We've provided you with an explicit reference to a document that was copied into the `_static` directory as `inception_doc`. We created a sophisticated RST link from the words *inception document* to the actual document's `index.html` file.

Within the two subheadings, we used the Sphinx `.. automodule::` directive to extract the docstrings from two modules. We've provided you with three parameters to the automodule directives:

- `:members::` This includes all the members of the module. We can list explicit member classes and functions instead of listing all the members.
- `:undoc-members::` This includes members who lack proper docstrings. This is handy when starting development; we'll still get some API information, but it will be minimal.
- `:undoc-members::` This includes special-method name members, not included in the Sphinx documentation by default.

This gives us a relatively complete view that is too complete sometimes. If we leave out all of these parameters, `:undoc-members:` and `:special-members:`, we'll get a smaller, more focused document.

Our `implementation.rst` file can evolve as our project evolves. We'll add the `automodule` references as the modules are completed.

The organization of the `.. automodule::` directives can provide us with a useful roadmap or overview of a complex collection of modules or packages. A little time spent organizing the presentation so that it shows us how the software components work together is more valuable than a great deal of verbiage. The point is not to create great narrative literature; the point is to provide guidance to the other developers.

Creating the Sphinx cross-references

Sphinx expands the cross-reference techniques available via RST. The most important set of cross-reference capabilities is the ability to directly refer to specific Python code features. These make use of the inline RST markup using the ``:role:`text` `` syntax. In this case, a large number of additional roles is part of Sphinx.

We have the following kinds of cross-reference roles available:

- The ``:py:mod:`some_module` `` syntax will generate a link to the definition of this module or package.
- The ``:py:func:`some_function` `` syntax will generate a link to the definition of the function. A qualified name with `module.function` or `package.module.function` can be used.
- The ``:py:data:`variable` `` and ``:py:const:`variable` `` syntax will generate a link to a module variable that's defined with a `.. py:data:: variable` directive. A *constant* is simply a variable that should not be changed.

- The :py:class:`some_class` syntax will link to the class definition. Qualified names such as module.class can be used.
- The :py:meth:`class.method` syntax will link to a method definition.
- The :py:attr:`class.attribute` syntax will link to an attribute that's defined with a .. py:attribute:: name directive.
- The :py:exc:`exception` syntax will link to a defined exception.
- The :py:obj:`some_object` syntax can create a generic link to an object.

If we use ``SomeClass`` in our docstring, we'll get the class name in a monospaced font. If we use :py:class:`SomeClass`, we get a proper link to the class definition, which is often far more helpful.

The :py: prefix on each role is there because Sphinx can be used to write the documentation about other languages in addition to Python. By using this :py: prefix on each role, Sphinx can provide proper syntax additions and highlighting.

Here's a docstring that includes explicit cross-references to other classes and exceptions:

```
def card( rank, suit ):
    """Create a :py:class:`Card` instance from rank and suit.

    :param rank: Numeric rank in the range 1-13.
    :param suit: Suit object (often a character from '♣⊠◇♠')
    :returns: :py:class:`Card` instance
    :raises :py:exc:`TypeError`: rank out of range.
    Etc.
    """
```

By using :py:class:`Card` instead of ``Card``, we're able to create explicit links between this comment block and the definition of the Card class. Similarly, we used :py:exc:`TypeError` to permit an explicit link to this exception's definition.

Additionally, we can define a link target via .._some-name:: and reference that label from any document in the Sphinx documentation tree with :ref:`some-name`. The name, some-name, must be globally unique. To ensure this, it's often good to define a kind of hierarchy so that the names are a kind of path from the document to the section to the topic.

Refactoring Sphinx files into directories

For larger projects, we'll need to use directories instead of simple files. In this case, we'll perform the following steps to refactor a file into a directory:

1. Add the directory: `implementation`, for example.
2. Move the original `implementation.rst` file to `implementation/index.rst`.
3. Change the original `index.rst` file. Switch the `.. toctree::` directive to reference `implementation/index` instead of `implementation`.

We can then work within the `implementation` directory using the `.. toctree::` directive in the `implementation/index.rst` file to include other files that are in this directory.

When our documentation is split into simple directories of simple text files, we can edit small, focused files. Individual developers can make significant contributions without encountering any file-sharing conflicts that arise when trying to edit a large word-processing document.

Writing the documentation

An important part of software quality comes from noting that the product is not simply *code* directed at a compiler or interpreter. As we noted in *Chapter 15, Designing for Testability*, code that cannot be trusted cannot be used. In that chapter, we suggested that testing was essential to establishing trust. We'd like to generalize that a bit. In addition to detailed testing, there are several other quality attributes that make the code usable, and trustworthiness is one of those attributes.

We trust code in the following scenarios:

- We understand the use cases
- We understand the data model and processing model
- We understand the test cases

When we look at more technical quality attributes, we see that these are really about understanding. For example, debugging seems to mean that we can confirm our understanding of how the application works. Auditability also seems to mean that we can confirm our understanding of processing by viewing specific examples to show that they work as expected.

Documentation creates trust. For more information on the software quality, start here: `http://en.wikipedia.org/wiki/Software_quality`. There is a lot to learn about software quality; it's a very large subject, and this is only one small aspect.

Literate programming

The idea of separating *documentation* from *code* can be viewed as an artificial distinction. Historically, we wrote documentation outside the code because the programming languages were relatively opaque and biased toward efficient compilation rather than clear exposition. Different techniques have been tried to reduce the distance between the working code and documentation about the code. Embedding more sophisticated comments, for example, is a long-standing tradition. Python takes this a step further by including a formal docstring in packages, modules, classes, and functions.

The literate programming approach to software development was pioneered by *Don Knuth*. The idea is that a single source document can produce efficient code as well as good-looking documentation. For machine-oriented assembler languages, and languages such as C, there's an additional benefit of moving away from the source language—a notation that emphasizes translation—toward a document that emphasizes clear exposition. Additionally, some literate programming languages act as a higher-level programming language; this might be appropriate for C or Pascal, but it is decidedly unhelpful for Python.

Literate programming is about promoting a deeper understanding of the code. In the case of Python, the source starts out very readable. Sophisticated literate programming isn't required to make a Python program understandable. Indeed, the main benefit of literate programming for Python is the idea of carrying deeper design and use case information in a form that is more readable than simple Unicode text.

For more information, see `http://www.literateprogramming.com` and `http://xml.coverpages.org/xmlLitProg.html`. The book *Literate Programming* by *Donald Knuth* is the seminal title on this topic.

Use cases for literate programming

There are two essential goals when creating a literate program:

- **A working program**: This is the code, extracted from the source document(s) and prepared for the compiler or interpreter.

- **Easy-to-read documentation**: This is the explanation plus the code plus any helpful markup prepared for the presentation. This document could be in HTML, ready to be viewed. Or it could be in RST, and we'd use docutils `rst2html.py` to convert it to HTML. Or, it could be in LaTeX and we run it through a LaTeX processor to create a PDF document.

The *working program* goal means that our literate programming document will cover the entire suite of the source code files. While this seems daunting, we have to remember that well-organized code snippets don't require a lot of complex hand-waving; in Python, code itself can be clear and meaningful.

The *easy-to-read documentation* goal means that we want to produce a document that uses something other than a single font. While most code is written in a monospaced font, it isn't the easiest on our eyes. The essential Unicode character set doesn't include helpful font variants such as bold or italic either. These additional display details (the font change, size change, and style change) have evolved over the centuries to make a document more readable.

In many cases, our Python IDE will color-code the Python source. This is helpful too. The history of written communication includes a lot of features that can enhance readability, none of which are available in simple Python source using a single font.

Additionally, a document should be organized around the problem and the solution. In many languages, the code itself *cannot* follow a clear organization because it's constrained by purely technical considerations of syntax and the order of the compilation.

Our two goals boil down to two technical use cases:

- Convert an original source text into the code
- Covert an original source text into the final documentation

We can—to an extent—refactor these two use cases in some profound ways. For example, we can extract the documentation from the code. This is what the `pydoc` module does, but it doesn't handle the markup very well.

Both versions, code and final document, can be made isomorphic. This is the approach taken by the PyLit project. The final documentation can be embedded entirely in Python code via docstrings as well as `#` comments. The code can be embedded entirely in RST documents using `::` literal blocks.

Working with a literate programming tool

Many **Literate Programming** (**LP**) tools are available. The essential ingredient — that varies from tool to tool—is the high-level markup language that separates the explanation from the code.

The source files that we write will contain the following three things:

- Text with markup that is the explanation and the description
- Code
- High-level markup to separate the text (with markup) from the code

Because of the flexibility of XML, this can be used as the high-level markup for literate programming. It's not easy to write, however. There are tools that work with a LaTeX-like markup based on the original Web (and later CWeb) tools. There are some tools that work with RST as the high-level markup.

The essential step in choosing a tool, then, is to take a look at the high-level markup that is used. If we find that the markup is easy to write, we can comfortably use it to produce the source document.

Python presents an interesting challenge. Because we have RST-based tools such as Sphinx, we can have very literate docstrings. This leads us to two tiers of documentation:

- Literate Programming explanations and the background that is outside the code. This should be the background material that's too general and not focused on the code itself.
- The reference and API documentation embedded inside the docstrings.

This leads to a pleasant, evolutionary approach to literate programming:

- Initially, we can start by embedding the RST markup in our docstrings so that a Sphinx-produced document looks good and provides a tidy explanation for the implementation choices.
- We can step beyond a narrow docstring focus to create the background documentation. This might include information on the design decisions, architecture, requirements, and user stories. In particular, descriptions of nonfunctional quality requirements belong outside the code.
- Once we've started to formalize this higher-level design documentation, we can more easily pick an LP tool. This tool will then dictate how we combine the documentation and code into a single, overall documentation structure. We can use an LP tool to extract the code and produce the documentation. Some LP tools can be used to run the test suite too.

Our goal is to create software that is not only well designed, but also trustworthy. As noted previously, we create trust in a number of ways, including providing a tidy, clear explanation of why our design is good.

If we use a tool such as PyLit, we might create RST files that look like the following code:

```
#############
Combinations
#############

..  contents::

Definition
==========

For some deeper statistical calculations,
we need the number of combinations of *n* things
taken *k* at a time, :math:`\binom{n}{k}`.

..  math::

    \binom{n}{k} = \dfrac{n!}{k!(n-k)!}

The function will use an internal ``fact()`` function because
we don't need factorial anywhere else in the application.

We'll rely on a simplistic factorial function without memoization.

Test Case
=========

Here are two simple unit tests for this function provided
as doctest examples.

>>> from combo import combinations
>>> combinations(4,2)
6
>>> combinations(8,4)
70

Implementation
===============
```

```
Here's the essential function definition, with docstring:
::

  def combinations( n, k ):
      """Compute :math:`\binom{n}{k}`, the number of
      combinations of *n* things taken *k* at a time.

      :param n: integer size of population
      :param k: groups within the population
      :returns: :math:`\binom{n}{k}`
      """

An important consideration here is that someone hasn't confused
the two argument values.
::

      assert k <= n

Here's the embedded factorial function. It's recursive. The Python
stack limit is a limitation on the size of numbers we can use.
::

      def fact(a):
          if a == 0: return 1
          return a*fact(a-1)

Here's the final calculation. Note that we're using integer division.
Otherwise, we'd get an unexpected conversion to float.
::

      return fact(n)//( fact(k)*fact(n-k) )
```

This is a file written entirely in an RST markup. It contains some explanatory text, some formal math, and even some test cases. These provide us with additional details to support the relevant code sections. Because of the way PyLit works, we named the file `combo.py.txt`. There are three things we can do with this file:

- We can use PyLit to extract the code from this text file in the following manner:

  ```
  python3.3 -m pylit combo.py.txt
  ```

  This creates `combo.py` from `combo.py.txt`. This is a Python module that is ready to be used.

- We can also use docutils to format this RST into an HTML page that provides the documentation and code in a form that we can read more easily than the original single-font text.

  ```
  rst2html.py combo.py.txt combo.py.html
  ```

  This creates `combo.py.html` ready for browsing. The `mathjax` package will be used by docutils to typeset the mathematical portions, leading to very nice-looking output.

- We can, additionally, use PyLit to run `doctest` and confirm that this program really works.

  ```
  python3.3 -m pylit --doctest combo.py.txt
  ```

  This will extract the `doctest` blocks from the code and run them through the `doctest` tool. We'll see that the three tests (the import and the two function evaluations) all produce the expected results.

The final web page produced by this would look something like the following screenshot:

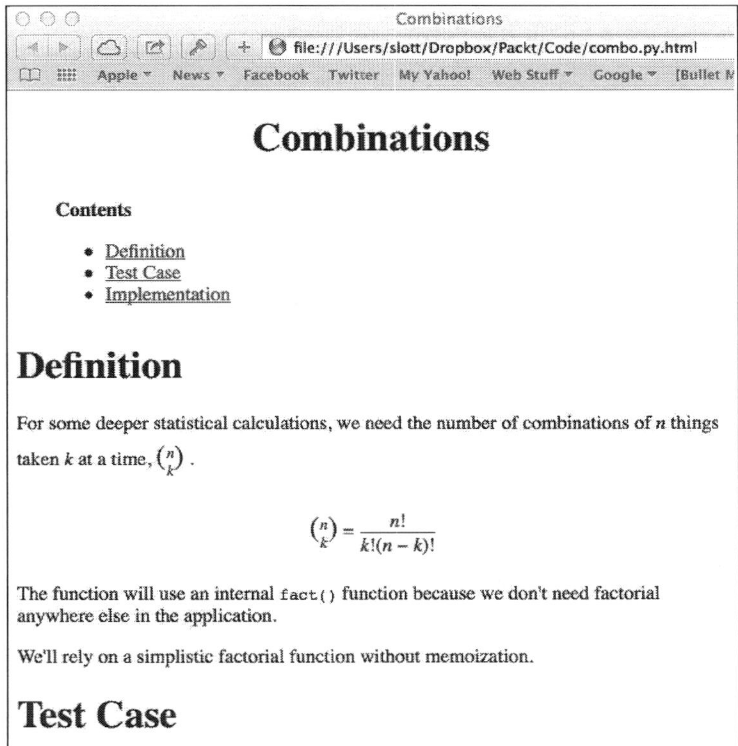

Our goal is to create software that is trustworthy. A tidy, clear explanation of why our design is good is an important part of this trust. By writing the software and the documentation side-by-side in a single source text, we can be sure that our documentation is complete and provides a sensible review of the design decisions and the overall quality of the software. A simple tool can extract working code and documentation from a single source, making it easy for us to create the software and the documentation.

Summary

We looked at the following four ways to create usable documentation:

- We can incorporate the information into the docstrings in our software
- We can use `pydoc` to extract the API reference information from our software.
- We can use Sphinx to create more sophisticated and elaborate documentation
- Also, we can use a literate programming tool to create even deeper and more meaningful documentation

Design considerations and trade-offs

The docstring should be considered as essential as any other part of the Python source. This ensures that the `help()` function and `pydoc` will work correctly. As with unit test cases, this should be viewed as a mandatory element of the software.

The documentation created by Sphinx can be very good looking; it will tend to parallel the Python documentation. Our objective all along has been seamless integration with the other features of Python. Using Sphinx tends to introduce an additional directory structure for the documentation source and build.

As we design our classes, the question of how to describe the design is almost as important as the resulting design itself. Software that can't be explained quickly and clearly will be viewed as untrustworthy.

Taking the time to write an explanation may identify hidden complexities or irregularities. In these cases, we might not refactor a design to correct a bug or to improve the performance, but rather to make it easier to explain. The ability to explain is a quality factor that has tremendous value.

Index

Symbols

A

B

C

D

E

F

K

L

M

N

Q

R

S

T

U

V

W

Thank you for buying
Mastering Object-oriented Python

About Packt Publishing

Packt, pronounced 'packed', published its first book "*Mastering phpMyAdmin for Effective MySQL Management*" in April 2004 and subsequently continued to specialize in publishing highly focused books on specific technologies and solutions.

Our books and publications share the experiences of your fellow IT professionals in adapting and customizing today's systems, applications, and frameworks. Our solution based books give you the knowledge and power to customize the software and technologies you're using to get the job done. Packt books are more specific and less general than the IT books you have seen in the past. Our unique business model allows us to bring you more focused information, giving you more of what you need to know, and less of what you don't.

Packt is a modern, yet unique publishing company, which focuses on producing quality, cutting-edge books for communities of developers, administrators, and newbies alike. For more information, please visit our website: `www.packtpub.com`.

About Packt Open Source

In 2010, Packt launched two new brands, Packt Open Source and Packt Enterprise, in order to continue its focus on specialization. This book is part of the Packt Open Source brand, home to books published on software built around Open Source licences, and offering information to anybody from advanced developers to budding web designers. The Open Source brand also runs Packt's Open Source Royalty Scheme, by which Packt gives a royalty to each Open Source project about whose software a book is sold.

Writing for Packt

We welcome all inquiries from people who are interested in authoring. Book proposals should be sent to `author@packtpub.com`. If your book idea is still at an early stage and you would like to discuss it first before writing a formal book proposal, contact us; one of our commissioning editors will get in touch with you.

We're not just looking for published authors; if you have strong technical skills but no writing experience, our experienced editors can help you develop a writing career, or simply get some additional reward for your expertise.

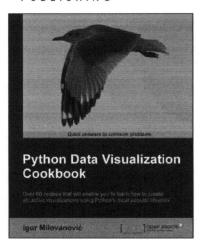

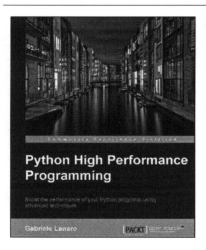

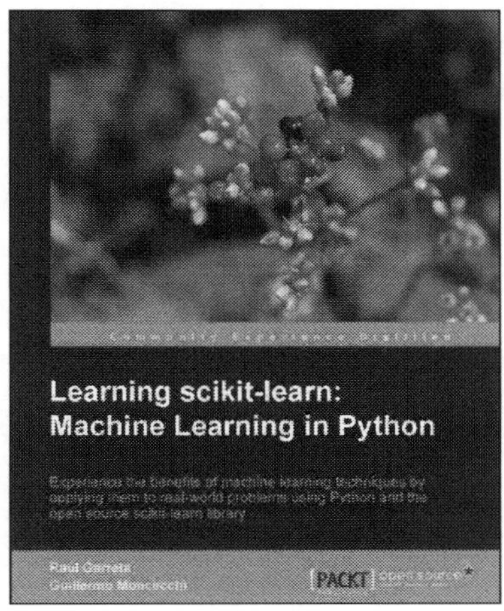

Learning scikit-learn: Machine Learning in Python

ISBN: 978-1-78328-193-0 Paperback: 118 pages

Experience the benefits of machine learning techniques by applying them to real-world problems using Python and the open source scikit-learn library

1. Use Python and scikit-learn to create intelligent applications.
2. Apply regression techniques to predict future behavior and learn to cluster items in groups by their similarities.
3. Make use of classification techniques to perform image recognition and document classification.

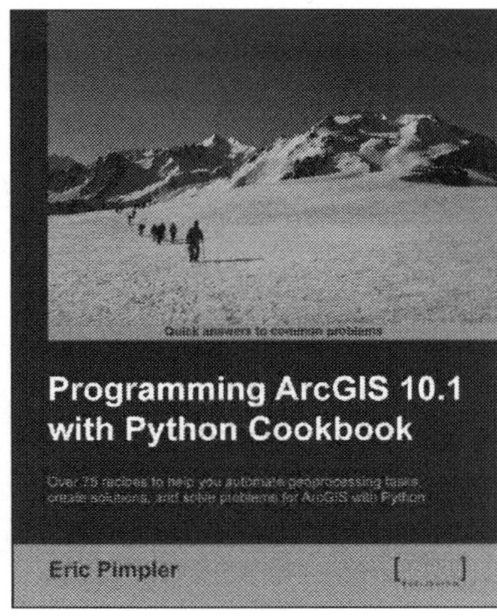

Programming ArcGIS 10.1 with Python Cookbook

ISBN: 978-1-84969-444-5 Paperback: 304 pages

Over 75 recipes to help you automate geoprocessing tasks, create solutions, and solve problems for ArcGIS with Python

1. Learn how to create geoprocessing scripts with ArcPy.
2. Customize and modify ArcGIS with Python.
3. Create time-saving tools and scripts for ArcGIS.

Made in the USA
Middletown, DE
25 February 2017